952
E360j
Eisenstadt, S.N.
Japanese civilization

DATE DUE

~~NEW BOOK~~	
JUN 0 5 2000	
JAN 0 8 2001	
FEB 0 8 2001	
MAR 1 3 2001	
2002	
APR 1 2 2002	
APR 2 3 2009	
MAY 2 2 2009	

BRODART, CO.   Cat. No. 23-221-003

JAPANESE CIVILIZATION

JAPANESE CIVILIZATION

A Comparative View

S. N. EISENSTADT

The University of Chicago Press
Chicago and London

S. N. Eisenstadt is the Rose Isaacs Professor Emeritus of
Sociology at the Hebrew University of Jerusalem. He also
teaches in the Committee on Social Thought at the University of
Chicago. Among his many works is *Power, Trust, and Meaning:
Essays in Sociological Theory and Analysis,* published by the
University of Chicago Press in 1995.

The University of Chicago Press gratefully acknowledges a
subvention from the Suntory Foundation in partial support of
the costs of production of this volume.

The costs have also been defrayed in part by the 1996 Hiromi
Arisawa Memorial Awards from the Books of Japan Fund with
repect to *Discourses of the Vanishing: Modernity, Phantasm.
Japan* and *Writing Ground Zero: Japanese Literature and the
Atomic Bomb,* published by University of Chicago Press. The
Awards are financed by The Japan Foundation from generous
donations contributed by Japanese individuals and companies.

The University of Chicago Press, Chicago 60637
The University of Chicago Press, Ltd., London
© 1996 by The University of Chicago
All rights reserved. Published 1996
Printed in the United States of America

05 04 03 02 01 00 99 98 97 96   1 2 3 4 5

ISBN: 0-226-19557-0 (cloth)
       0-226-19558-9 (paper)

Library of Congress Cataloging-in-Publication Data

Eisenstadt, S. N. (Shmuel Noah), 1923–
    Japanese civilization : a comparative view / S. N. Eisenstadt.
       p.   cm.
    Includes bibliographical references and index.
    1. Japan—Civilization.   I. Title.
    DS821.E49   1996
    952—dc20
                                            96-726
                                            CIP

⊗ The paper used in this publication meets the minimum
requirements of the American National Standard for Information
Sciences—Permanence of Paper for Printed Library Materials,
ANSI Z39.48-1984.

For Shulamit

*Toward half a century
of a journey together*

With love

C O N T E N T S

PART TWO
ASPECTS OF JAPANESE HISTORICAL EXPERIENCE

PART THREE
THE FRAMEWORK OF JAPANESE HISTORICAL EXPERIENCE

PREFACE

This book is the result of a very long-standing interest of mine in Japan, Japanese society, and civilization. I still have the rather detailed notes I took on Norman's *Japan's Emergence as a Modern State* in the late 1940s, and since then I have attempted to follow continually and systematically the literature on Japan in Western languages, as well as translations from Japanese into these languages. It was, however, only seven or eight years ago that the analysis of Japan in the framework of the comparative analysis of civilizations became a central focus of my research—for reasons spelled out in the first chapter of this book.

I started the research on which this book is based while a visiting fellow at the Hoover Institution and a visiting professor at Stanford University during the summers of 1987–90 and continued it while a visiting fellow at the Russell Sage Foundation in New York in the fall of 1988, during my stays as a visiting professor of the Committee on Social Thought at the University of Chicago in the springs of 1989–93, and as a fellow at the Swedish Collegium for Advanced Social Studies in Uppsala in the fall of 1992 and spring of 1994.

Above all, both research and writing were pursued at my home base in Jerusalem at the Department of Sociology and Anthropology and the Truman Research Institute of the Hebrew University, and at the Van Leer Jerusalem Institute. At all these institutions I received many types of support—library facilities, research assistance, secretarial services, and the like. At the various universities I greatly enjoyed the discussions with students who participated in seminars I conducted on subjects related to the study of Japanese society and civilization, and at both the universities and the research institutes I gained much from discussions with colleagues. This research has also been supported in its various phases by the Israel Academy of Sciences and Humanities, Jerusalem, the Israel Foundations Trustees, Jerusalem, the Chiang Ching-kuo Foundation for International Scholarly Exchange, Taiwan, and the Stiftung Weltgesellschaft, Zurich.

The book has also greatly benefited from the discussions at lectures and seminars I have given on related subjects at various institutions and academic gatherings—among them the University of Stockholm, the University of Hong Kong, J. Nehru University and the Nehru Memorial Foundation in New Delhi, Taipei University and the Institute of Ethnology of the Academia Sinica at Taipei, Ohio State University, the University of Washington in Seattle, the University of California at Los Angeles, Columbia University (at T. W. de Barry's seminar), George Mason University, the German Institute of Japanese Studies in Tokyo, the University of Kobe, the 1988 meeting of the Japanese Society for Comparative Civilizations, the Conference on Japanese Studies in Kyoto in the fall of 1994, the meeting on Max Weber and Japan convened by W. Mommsenn in Munich in March 1992, and the Breuningen Kolleg in June 1994. In 1989 I gave the Tanner lectures at the University of California at Berkeley and, especially at the seminar connected with these lectures, under the chairmanship of Robert Scalapino, I discussed some of the topics analyzed here.

In 1987 Ben Ami Shilloni, Eyal Ben Ari, and I conducted a seminar that culminated in a small international workshop at the Hebrew University. This collaboration resulted in a book on patterns of conflict resolution in Japan.[1]

During the preparation of this work—and before, in my more general interest in Japan—I have been helped by many friends. Above all I am indebted to the friends and colleagues with whom I have discussed various aspects of the study of Japan, especially those who took time to read parts of the drafts of this book. My oldest and most continuous conversations about Japan have been with Henry Rosovsky and Robert N. Bellah in the United States, Ishida Takeshi in Japan, and R. J. Z. Werblowsky in Jerusalem, R. P. Dore in England, and, in the last decade or so, Ben-Ami Shilloni in Jerusalem. R. J. Z. Werblowsky and Ben-Ami Shilloni have also been among the most faithful readers and critics of several drafts of the book. More intermittently through the years I have had discussions with Al Craig, Herbert Passin, and Irwin Scheiner, who also commented on earlier drafts of some of the chapters.

During the preparation of the book I discussed different aspects with

1. S. N. Eisenstadt and Eyal Ben Ari (eds.), *Japanese Models of Conflict Resolution* (London: Kegan Paul International, 1990).

J. C. Alexander, Masahiko Aoki, Jane Bachnik, Andrew Barshay, Bruce Bueno de Mosquita, Chang Hao, T. W. de Barry, Gianni Fodella, Carol Gluck, John Haley, Hamaguchi Eshen, Susan Hanley, Chou-yen Hsu, Alex Inkeles, Hide Ishiguru, M. B. Jansen, Ron Jepperson, Tomi Kashioka, John Kelly, Take Lebra, S. M. Lipset, Tom Metzger, John Meyer, Tu Wei Ming, the late Murakami Yasusuke, Nagai Michio, Chie Nakane, Peter Nosco, Kenneth Pyle, Ilana F. Silber, E. Tiryakian, Fred Wakeman, Joji Watanuki, Bjorn Wittrock, Kozo Yamamura, and the participants in the meetings and symposia on Japan mentioned earlier. I also had discussions with Dan Okimoto, James Raphael, and Tom Rohlen and the participants in the seminar on Japanese capitalism they organized at Stanford, and with Nadia Spang, who wrote a critical review of my analysis of the Meiji Restoration.

All these discussions were of great importance in crystallizing my approach to the study of Japanese civilization and to the continual revisions of this book.

My greatest debt is, of course, to those colleagues and friends who gave of their time both in conversation and in reading drafts of parts or even the entire manuscript.

In addition to those mentioned above I would like to thank Johann P. Arnason, Harumi Befu, Eyal Ben Ari, Carl Bielefeld, Mary Brinton, Peter Duus, Raymond Grew, H. Harootunian, Don Levine, Robert C. McAdams, Elizabeth McSweeney, Tetsuo Najita, Emiko Ohnuki-Tierney, Frank Reynolds, B. Silberman, Robert Smith, Ezra Vogel, and Kate Wildman-Nakai, all of whom gave me invaluable advice, help, and criticism of large parts of the manuscript, in some cases two times over. Yui Kumitso, during his stay in Jerusalem in the spring and summer of 1994, read through the manuscript, gave me highly valuable comments, and helped very much in its preparation. Eric Cohen and Yael Ben Tor commented in great detail on the chapter on the transformation of Confucianism and Buddhism in Japan.

The comments of all these friends—and of two anonymous readers for the University of Chicago Press—were of immense importance for me, both in pointing out problems in my analytical argument and in helping to overcome at least some—certainly not all—of the pitfalls of a study of Japan written by somebody who does not read Japanese and has not direct access to sources and scholarly works in the Japanese language. Whatever merits this book might have are very much due to them—and I wish I could follow all their advice; needless to say, I am solely responsible for the many remaining faults.

Many persons have helped me as research assistants and in providing secretarial and research support. My secretary Batia Slonim at her outpost at the Van Leer Jerusalem Institute has been the faithful coordinator of all the many stages of the preparation of the manuscript. Debby Mazo, David Kohan, Cynthia and Alberto Gluzman, and above all Mario Schejtman and Noemi Lerner have been extremely helpful as research assistants in chasing down the innumerable references and in the preparation of the endnotes. Doron Cohen has been very helpful in going over the manuscripts, paying special attention to Japanese spelling, and in the checking of the endnotes. I have been greatly helped by the libraries of the institutions mentioned above, as well as that of the International House of Japan in Tokyo and the manager of the House, Mr. M. Kato.

Morris Levy and, above all, Esther Rosenfeld in Jerusalem helped type and retype the innumerable drafts of this manuscript, as did Barbara Canon at Stanford, Camille Yezzi at the Russell Sage Foundation, Richard Kelso, Aso Linberg, and Lena Foster at SCASS in Uppsala, and Claude Gragnier in Chicago. Claude Gragnier has also assisted in the editing of many of the drafts, notably the crucial last stage of editing and shortening the manuscript.

Doug Mitchell of the University of Chicago Press has been a very supportive and faithful editor and friend, whose support has made the entire editorial process so enjoyable, as has also that of Matt Howard. Joel Score has done wonders in copyediting the manuscript and has helped me to avoid many pitfalls, as have Sandra Ward, a graduate student in Japanese History at the University of Chicago who assisted in correcting the proofs, and Margaret Mahan of the University of Chicago Press, who has supervised the editing and proofreading.

Whether all this effort and all the debts I have incurred to these friends has been worthwhile is not for me but for the readers of this book to judge.

S. N. Eisenstadt
Jerusalem, the Hebrew University
and the Van Leer Jerusalem Institute

Japanese names appear in Japanese order (family name first) except for those authors who customarily publish in English. Japanese words are transliterated according to the Kenkyūsha dictionary system.

O N E

Introduction
The Enigma of Japan

1 *The Enigma of Japanese Power* is the title of a recent influential—and controversial—book on Japan by the Dutch journalist Karel van Wolferen.[1] Japan has been an enigma to the West almost since their mutual encounter in the sixteenth century—but especially since the nineteenth century. Japan has intrigued Western scholars and the informed public. It has been a magnet of fascination, admiration, revulsion, or some combination thereof, and the quest to unravel this unique society and culture has constituted a continuous challenge.

In Europe and the United States, interest in Japan developed as part of the exploration of alien, "exotic" cultures—an exploration that gathered momentum with the great discoveries and the expansion of Europe and later culminated in ethnological and anthropological works—and in artistic styles. Almost from the beginning of such exploration, and certainly from the nineteenth century on, the fascination with Japan differed from that with other exotic or alien societies in two crucial respects. Japan's distinctiveness or peculiarity was very soon perceived to reside, not in its being totally different from Europe or the United States, but in its combining such great differences with far-reaching similarities to the West. The concern with Japan's uniqueness was also, in the West, continuously reactivated by the encounter between the West and Japan in the international arena, by the fact that Japan evolved into a major international power, first a military one and then, after the Second World War, an industrial one. These Japanese achievements called for a reexamination of some of the most basic assumptions of Western civilization.[2]

Soon after Japan was opened to Western exploration in the nineteenth

1

century, Western anthropologists, sociologists, historians, and journalists, and the wider public as well, discovered that Japan was not just another faraway, "primitive" or "esoteric" society that could be seen either as the proper setting for some utopian way of life or as one in which the elementary forms of human life could be found. Of course, various baffling aspects of Japanese society had been noted and reported with great relish by Western travelers and observers, at least from the second half of the nineteenth century.[3]

But very quickly these observers, and the more scholarly literature, emphasized another aspect of the Japanese scene—to a degree unprecedented in Western literature on Asian countries—namely, that Japan was, in some crucial aspects of social organization and structure, very similar to the West. Even before the great push to modernization under the Meiji, many Western missionaries who visited or stayed in Japan observed that it was in many ways a well-organized, civilized country.[4] In the first decades of the twentieth century it could compare very well with any Western country on indices of "modernization," urbanization, levels of education, communication, and the like. Comparisons of Japan with the West, stressing similarities as well as differences, became a constant part of the scholarly agenda and of public discourse.

E. H. Norman's classic work *Japan's Emergence as a Modern State*[5] focused on the analysis of the Tokugawa regime as a feudal system comparable to the European one, even if in some ways different from it. Japan's process of modernization was often compared with those of European nations, especially Germany, with which it shared the combination of rapid, state-sponsored industrialization and the development of a modern, autocratic, semiconstitutional regime.

Even Japan's failures or crises, for instance the breakdown of would-be democratic trends in the Taishō period and the development of military rule in the 1930s, were often seen as variants on the fascist movements of the same period. Its military expansion could be compared, as was done by Talcott Parsons, with that of Nazi Germany.[6] The Meiji Restoration was often compared with the great European revolutions. Similarities in institutional patterns between Japan and the industrially more successful countries of Europe—especially England—were identified in the late 1940s and early 1950s, by Marion J. Levy Jr.[7] and later by John Pelzel,[8] with respect to family and kinship organization, while the political pattern of modern Japan was often compared, as for instance by Reinhard Bendix, with that of Germany. They stressed the importance, in Japan as in England, of the nuclear family, of primogeniture or some of its functional substitutes like adoption, and of the looseness of wider kinship ties. All these characteristics were important because of the ways in which they enabled the mobilization and channeling of family resources to industrialization. In the mid-1950s R. N. Bellah published his very influential *Tokugawa Religion*, in which he looked for possible equivalents of the Protestant ethic in Japan.[9]

In the late 1940s and early 1950s Japan was examined as a possible case of democratization from above, and, from the 1950s on, Japan constituted a major focus in the burgeoning studies of modernization. Far-reaching researches and conferences studied both the specific characteristics of these processes in Japan and their indications of a distinct pattern of modernization.

Not only with respect to modern times have the institutional similarities and differences between Japanese and European societies been noted. Already at the beginning of this century, Durkheim had noted the marked similarity of the institutional history of Japan to a European one—from a tribal monarchy aiming at the establishment of an empire, through a prolonged feudal period, to an absolutist monarchy.[10] Marc Bloch, in his classic study of feudalism, singled out the Japanese case as the closest to the European.[11] Even earlier, the Japanese historian Asakawa Kanichi had presented a penetrating comparison of Japanese and European feudalism. This theme was taken up more recently by Jean Baechler, who attributed the successful development of capitalism in Japan to the existence, as in Europe, of a strong feudal system.[12] As will be documented later, many such comparisons have been made recently with respect to different aspects and periods of Japanese history—such as that of the Tokugawa regime with seventeenth-century absolutist states in Europe.[13] The Meiji Restoration was often, as mentioned above, compared with the great European revolutions.[14]

Relatively quickly, however, it was noted not only that Japan became the sole non-Western country to become fully and relatively successfully industrialized and modernized, but also that it appeared to organize its life in ways radically different from the West. Thus the uniqueness of Japan was more and more seen to lie in its combination of many institutional similarities with the West, especially with Europe, with very specific, almost mysterious patterns of culture that seemed not only to persist but also in some ways to shape the very patterns of its modernization and industrialization. Recognition of such combinations—similarities to the West along with far-reaching differences that seemed to influence many aspects of Japanese behavior and institutional contours—informed many of the books written or published in the 1930s and 1940s, such as E. Lederer's and E. Lederer-Seidler's "Japan in Transition";[15] Kurt Singer's *Mirror, Sword and Jewel*[16] (published only after the Second World War in the United States); Ruth Benedict's seminal *The Chrysanthemum and the Sword*,[17] written during the Second World War and published immediately thereafter, which was to dominate the discourse about Japan for many years; and George Sansom's lectures on the West and Japan.[18] This basic approach continued apace in later periods, as in Jean Stoetzel's postwar *Without the Chrysanthemum and the Sword.*[19]

It was only natural that scholarly attempts to explain Japan should begin to multiply with the first signs of its great economic success after the Second World War. Here the comparisons were made, especially from the 1970s on, more frequently with the United States than with Europe.[20] Probably the single most important illustration of Japan's unique mode of modernization and industrialization, which caught the eye of both Western and Japanese scholars, especially after the Second World War, was the pattern of industrial relations that developed in Japan. At least initially, this pattern was presented in somewhat glowing terms as a harmonious patriarchal relation.[21] Emphasis was given to the relatively low incidence of strikes; the prevalence, at least in the private sector, of company unions; the system of seniority and lifetime employment; and the generally high degree of identification of workers with their companies.

With Japan's successful economic development in the 1950s and 1960s, systematic studies flourished of those arenas in which Japan appeared closest to the West, such as in the structure of its political system, law and legal behavior, and the relationship between the police and the public. These studies consistently emphasized not only the similarities with the West but also the great differences from it.[22] The nature of the differences, however, became more important as Japan's success continued, especially when its great industrial success was measured against the experience in the West after the oil crisis in the 1970s. Thus the fascination with Japan's similarities to and differences from the West became closely related to the encounters of Japan with the West on the international scene.

II   Japan's success touched some nerves central to Western self-identity, giving rise to extensive heart-searching among many in the West. Large parts of this discourse went back to the awareness, already present in the second half of the nineteenth century, that Japan is a highly complex country—fully civilized, even if in a different way than is the West— almost an up-to-date, industrial version of China as seen, for example, by Leibniz.[23] The question which informed some of the earlier explorations of Japan—whether it is possible to find happiness and human fulfillment in a hierarchical, seemingly repressive, yet highly civilized society that emphasizes aesthetics and personal cultivation—became transformed into another question, about the possibility of combining these qualities with economic success. In all of these discussions the themes of strong group commitment, loyalty, harmony, and consensus, alluded to earlier,[24] become strongly emphasized, in Western and Japanese discourse alike, as the keys to an understanding of the uniqueness of Japanese society and of its processes of modernization. These themes were sharply contrasted with Western, highly principled, individualistic, and utilitarian attitudes and ideological confrontations.

Fosco Maraini, an acute Italian observer, scholar, and analyst of Japan, formulated this question very succinctly:

> Japan was a shock. It woke me up. Here was a highly civilized country which had reached maturity and splendor along other paths, owing practically nothing to the spiritual forces which had become such fetishes in the West: classical learning, Christianity, the Reformation (or the Counter-Reformation, according to longitudes and latitudes). Here were also, all around, examples of moral coherence, or righteousness, of spiritual maturity, often more numerous and more striking than anything I had seen before. I cannot deal in detail with what was a long spiritual process, but finally the question appeared simply and clearly: does Christianity include history, or does history include Christianity? The answer is obvious. Christianity, the West itself, are not absolutes, they are relative, historical steps in the story of man. Civilization may flourish on many stems. The gods may be called by many names. Only man and the mysteries surrounding him are something final. All religions, all philosophies are attempts to bridge the chasm between the world of conscience and the challenges of existence, time, death, evil. No one has the key. There are no chosen people. All men—from Neanderthalers chiseling their stones to Einstein distilling theories about the universe—are spiritually equal, all live through the same predicament.
>
> Perhaps I have reached a similar view through other contacts and experiences, but I wonder if the itinerary would have been so clear and direct without the impact of Japan. The very existence of Japan is a challenge to most familiar notions cherished as true. Its symbolic importance is far greater than its puny place in world history. If there were no Japan it would be expedient to invent one.[25]

Angela Carter, the British novelist, has painted a similar picture in a somewhat more concrete way:

> The experience of a young Japanese of my age is very much like mine. I'm not talking about the fact that he may be able to establish the same equilibrium that I have due to the acute cynicism, the fortunate decadence, my country has given me. But they will have read the same book, they will have read "The Catcher in the Rye" at the same impressionable age, they will have seen James Dean when they were fifteen, they will have heard early Elvis Presley at the same time that I was listening to him, they will have read Camus at the same time, when it changes your life—though it might not have changed theirs to quite the same extent because Japan's is a

less flexible society than my own. Their intellectual experience will have been very similar to mine. And then what you come up against is the jarring fact—for instance, I was standing somewhere once and I saw this young girl running down a flight of steps, and clear as anything, I thought, She never realized that Christ died for her sins. . . .

. . . Not only does she not know, she wouldn't care if you told her. Yes, because he never did. I mean, he didn't for mine either but for twenty years an awful lot of people told me he did. And although I think that in my heart I always thought there was something funny about this proposition, nevertheless it is part of the equipment I grew up with. What I mean is that the Judeo-Christian tradition was built into me at some point. I've consciously rejected it, but I've obviously retained some of it on an unconscious level. And it isn't in them! And I think this makes an immense difference. It makes them happier. And it gives them the potentiality for being very, very much nicer. And it does make a sense of a different destiny. Maybe that's it. But it means they don't have to work so hard, and I'm a great Puritan and I think people should work very hard at making themselves.[26]

III Concern with Japan as Western society's "other" was pronounced not only in literary and journalistic pronouncements. It also pervaded the development of Western scholarship about Japan—although different aspects of such "otherness" were often emphasized in different countries.[27]

Two opposing trends can be identified in the last three decades' discourse about Japan in the West. Probably the more prevalent and popular one stresses the importance for the United States of learning from the Japanese example. Ezra Vogel's *Japan as Number One*,[28] written in the 1970s in an attempt to explain Japan's successful weathering of the oil crisis, and Chalmer Johnson's analysis of MITI (the Ministry of International Trade and Industry) are representative of this trend.[29] Ronald Dore's *Flexible Rigidities* and *Taking Japan Seriously*, written later, carried a similar message.[30] Other scholars, such as Dutch journalist Karel van Wolferen, mentioned above,[31] and a group of French scholars who published an interesting collection about the presumed Japanese consensus,[32] see the Japanese as a frightening model of a highly controlled, depoliticized society based on a manipulated ideological consensus.

These developments seem to call for a reexamination of many of the basic premises and assumptions of Western civilization. Such a reexamination was hinted at in Roland Barthes's *Empire of Signs*[33] and became much more explicit in the debates in Japan and in the West, above all in the United States, about Japan's postmodernity. In these debates the possibility was raised that Japan may become the epitome of a postmodern civilization without ever having been a fully modern one.[34]

IV Fascination with Japan's unusual combination of similarities to and differences from the West naturally gave rise to a search for explanations, which were often found in characteristics presumed to be distinctive of Japanese people and culture—characteristics which thus emphasize the otherness of Japanese civilization.

Among the major explanations of this type was Ruth Benedict's designation of Japanese society as a "shame society," as against the West's being a "guilt society," and of Japanese morality as "situational" and not based on universal principles.[35] Benedict also noted the unusual combination of great aesthetic sensitivity, which permeates all areas of Japanese life, and such extreme expressions of cruelty and aggression as were observed, for instance, in the treatment of prisoners of war during the Second World War. Zbigniew Brzezinski would later wonder at the Protestant-like commitment to work combined with the very un-Protestant hedonistic attitude toward the pleasures of daily life.[36]

Another aspect of Japanese culture that puzzled some Western scholars was the strong commitment to groups, to family, to work and workplace, to feudal lords, and to the emperor. What intrigued Western observers was not just the more extreme manifestations of such commitment, like the pattern of patriotic suicide; the relation of this commitment to Japanese religion was also a puzzle.

Among many Westerners a monotheistic-centered view had been prevalent, which associated high levels of commitment with an orientation toward some transcendental realm, above all toward a God who is beyond the mundane world, and assumed such commitment would therefore be either very weak or entirely absent among so-called pagan religions. Japan appeared to contradict this picture. Its religions—above all Shinto, but also the mixture of Shinto, Buddhism, and Confucianism that characterized Japan—seemed to lack a strong transcendental dimension or orientation. Some Western scholars identified such religions as pagan, while others claimed that it was difficult to find any religion in the Western sense in Japan. This lack of any transcendental dimension in Japanese religion has been asserted both by some Japanese scholars, such as Maruyama Masao,[37] and by Western ones—Kurt Singer, who visited Japan in the thirties;[38] George Sansom, who emphasized in his Columbia lectures on the encounters between Japan and the West that, despite many structural similarities, Japanese civilization lacked those universalistic orientations which shaped many aspects of Western historical dynamics;[39] and later on Robert N. Bellah, John Pelzel,[40] and scholars of Japanese religion such as Joseph Kitagawa and William La Fleur.[41] The very strong sense of commitment found among the Japanese seemed to be oriented, as Bellah put it, to an "empty center"—itself a rather thought-provoking phenomenon.[42]

Closely connected with this puzzle of commitment was that of the strong drive to achievement among the Japanese—a puzzle which led to great interest in patterns of socialization and education in Japan. The theme of an "empty center" was further developed in a brilliant if controversial way by Roland Barthes in his *Empire of Signs,* in which he characterized Japanese culture as a system of empty signifiers without any relation to signified objects, and further elaborated by others.[43] In the 1930s Kurt Singer also made a series of tantalizing observations (unpublished until the 1950s) about the ways in which Japanese conceive of space, time, and nature, always comparing them explicitly or implicitly with possible conceptions in the West and often looking at the West through such Japanese mirrors.[44]

The close relation of this ambivalent, problematic attitude toward Japan with Western self-examination, in the intellectual discourse on the premises of Western civilization, has been manifest in a rather paradoxical way in some recent approaches to the problem of the Japanese uniqueness. While many social science and literary works have emphasized the importance of understanding the emic categories of thought of foreign societies, the emphasis on such categories in Japan has sometimes been criticized as the acceptance of an ideological format—often described as fascist or totalitarian—forced on the Japanese people by their oligarchic elites. This format has been seen as stifling the potential emancipatory orientations of wider sectors of Japanese society—orientations which have often been analyzed in terms of Western "critical" themes.[45]

V   The interest of Japanese scholars and intellectuals in the distinctiveness of Japan—spurred of course by much stronger ideological, personal, and national, even nationalistic, motivations—has been to some degree a mirror image of that of their Western counterparts. Their interest is rooted in the quest to assert their own cultural identity, their own collective consciousness, in the face of the Western impact on their civilization. This situation to some degree parallels the much earlier encounter of Japan with China; in many ways much of this modern literature goes back to the preoccupations of Japanese scholars with the distinctiveness of their culture vis-à-vis the Chinese.[46] Indeed, some scholars search for the roots of Japanese culture in the first articulation of Shinto ideology, in the eighth century—an approach already developed by the Kokugaku school, the school of "nativistic learning" in the Tokugawa period.[47]

A rather asymmetrical relation developed between the Western and the Japanese orientation toward the other. While concern with Japan constituted an important component of scholarly discourse in the West, until the late 1980s few Europeans or Americans (like the Chinese before them) were much interested in what the Japanese thought about them. But the Japanese were very much interested in how the West viewed them and in how to present themselves to the West.[48]

Even in late-nineteenth-century Japanese literature, but more so in modern studies, the most distinctive feature to emerge in descriptions of Japanese society was the emphasis on loyalty and commitment, group life, and a unique sense of nationhood, harmony, and consensus. These trends were usually presented in a holistic way, as always coming together and as encompassing all the arenas of life and culture in Japan. The epitome of these scholarly and popular approaches was Nakane Chie's *Japanese Society* (1970).[49] In this book, Nakane stressed strong group cohesion, the predominance of vertical as opposed to horizontal loyalties and networks, and the seemingly vibrant resulting consensus and harmony as the most distinctive cultural and institutional characteristics of Japanese society. This book, as well as Doi Takeo's *Anatomy of Dependence*, which presented an analysis of the distinctive psychodynamics of the Japanese in terms of their strong emotional dependence on their mothers,[50] were among the most forceful attempts, in Japan or the West, to analyze Japanese society in a scholarly but basically holistic fashion.

VI Numerous popularized versions of these major books have become, as it were, the symbol of the *Nihonjinron*, the literature on the question of the uniqueness of Japanese, and of the controversies—scholarly, ideological, and journalistic—that have developed around this thesis.[51] It would not be possible to analyze here all of these controversies, nor am I competent to do so. I would like instead to address briefly some of the major theoretical and analytical foci of these controversies, all of which touch directly on the central problem of the nature of the uniqueness of Japanese society and culture.

The major disputes were, first, over the identification of the presumably distinctive features of Japanese society and culture. Group harmony, loyalty, and commitment; the importance of vertical networks as the major organizing principle of social relations; and the supposed nonexistence or weakness of individualism were the features usually emphasized as singularly Japanese. The second of these disputes focused on whether such features were indeed peculiar to Japan, or if they were comparable with those of other societies—for instance, whether the Japanese language, often portrayed as the key to understanding Japanese culture, can be systematically compared to other languages. A third dispute focused on the extent to which these features are to be found in most sectors of Japanese society, and a fourth on whether to explain these features in terms of Japanese culture or tradition, which could be seen as almost

incomparable to other cultures, or in terms of specific historical configurations of social forces, seemingly much more amenable to comparable
analysis.

The controversies about the relative importance of cultural, as against
structural or organizational, modes of explanation of social phenomena
raged around the analysis of almost all central arenas of Japanese society.
These theoretical controversies were, of course, closely related to others
that developed from the 1960s on throughout the social sciences. Some
of the major lines of this debate developed first with respect to the explanation of specific characteristics of the Japanese system of industrial relations. A continuous stream of works appeared contradicting books such
as Abegglen's,[52] which painted a rosy picture of industrial relations in
Japanese factories, stressing lifelong employment and strong identification of the workers with the company and attributing them to such "traditional" cultural themes like feudal loyalty.[53]

Some of these works demonstrated that the seemingly optimistic, harmonious picture of the industrial scene in Japan is applicable, if at all, only
to the larger private companies—certainly not to the numerous middle
to small enterprises, nor to large parts of the public sector.[54]

Other works showed that many of the special characteristics of the Japanese industrial scene, for instance, the system of lifelong employment,
seniority payment, and the like, can be better explained in terms of the specific historical conditions in which the Japanese industrial system developed than in any cultural terms.[55] Similar controversies have developed
with respect to the analysis of many other arenas of Japanese society.[56]

VII These themes and controversies have also been taken up, explicitly
or implicitly, in the research on other aspects of Japanese society that has
proliferated since the mid-1960s. Some of this research has been biased
toward "structuralist" and some toward "culturalist" explanations. The
more structural studies have been concerned with the analysis of organizations and institutions,[57] while others emphasized cultural patterns of
behavior and personality traits which often came from anthropological
traditions.[58]

Most of the explanations provided in these studies were couched
in terms of various structural, organizational, or demographic factors.
Sometimes these explanations seemed to deny the existence of any
unique characteristics of the Japanese scene—except perhaps in terms of
contingent historical constellations of social forces. Anthropological, literary, and psychological studies, on the other hand, focused on specific
problems; cultural explanations predominated in these studies but were
attempted in more sophisticated terms than in earlier periods.

Most of these studies moved beyond the tendency to identify general "themes" and overall characteristics of Japanese society, into more differentiated and detailed studies of specific areas or problems, including some comparative dimensions or references. Moreover, they indicated the possibility of bridging the gap between the structural-historical approach on the one hand and the cultural on the other. Studies starting from cultural points of view inquired more and more about institutional and behavioral patterns—and in much more differentiated ways than before—while institutional and organizational studies, which stressed more structural, historical, and demographic variables, tended, when confronted with the necessity to explain specific characteristics of the Japanese scene, to point at cultural themes (for instance Vogel's examination of the specific characteristics of patterns of public and private organization in Japan,[59] Befu's critique of the possibility of analyzing Japanese bureaucracy in Weberian terms,[60] or some of the studies of agencies of social control—such as the police or the law).

Of special interest here is the very wide literature on conflict in Japanese society, which, as we have seen, developed to a large extent as a reaction against the harmonious-group model. Yet at the same time, these revisionist studies have shown in great detail that the modes of definition, management, and resolution of conflicts, and of different societal and political crises, differ greatly from those to be found either in Western societies, with which Japan shares many structural characteristics, or in China and other East Asian countries, with which it shares major cultural orientations.[61]

The word "modes," in the plural, is very important here. It is indeed quite clear that several modes of resolving conflicts or coping with crises have continuously existed in Japanese society; yet at the same time they are not limitless—and they greatly differ from the parallel modes of conflict resolution in other historical or modern societies.

VIII Whatever the theoretical starting point of any one of these studies, the overall conclusion emerging from them is the inadequacy of the dichotomy between "cultural" and "structural" (or historical) approaches and the necessity of analyzing both cultural and social structural dimensions of social interaction and organization, on different levels and in different sectors of social life.

Many of these studies have also combined analyses of micro and macro situations and have shown how some of the specificities of the Japanese historical or social experience can be best explored through the analysis of micro situations—festivals, shrines, modes of neighborhood, associations, and the like. While this is in principle true of any society, it seems that—for whatever reasons—it has become more fully visible in the studies of Japan and other Asian societies.

The very momentum of these studies, and their close relation to the major controversies in the social sciences, indicates a way in which the numerous studies of Japan can be brought within the framework of a systematic comparative sociological analysis—a framework within which the uniqueness of Japanese society is analyzed in basically the same way as the uniqueness of any other society. Such an approach can build on earlier leads. Already in the late 1940s and early 1950s, Marion Levy had contrasted Japan with China.[62] In the 1960s wide-ranging attempts by F. L. K. Hsu[63] and Nakane Chie[64] to compare Japan, India, China, and the United States from a psychological and anthropological point of view followed Nakane's original analysis of Japanese society, as did comparable analyses of the structure of interpersonal and group relations in Japan, India, and Tibet. At the same time Nakamura Hajime presented a powerful, if metahistorical, analysis of the "ways of thinking" of the Japanese in comparison with other "Eastern people" (Chinese, Indian, and Tibetan).[65] In the mid-1970s Barrington Moore's *Social Origins of Dictatorship and Democracy* presented an interesting and influential analysis of Japanese modern development in a comparative framework,[66] some aspects of which were taken up later by Kay Trimberger in her *Revolution from Above*.[67] More recently, Robert Smith analyzed Japanese society in a combination of cultural and structural terms that makes the analysis of Japanese society more amenable to systematic comparative analysis.[68]

Among the most ambitious attempts at such a systematic analysis of Japanese society within the framework of comparative studies of civilizations is the analysis of Japan as a *ie* type of civilization by Murakami Yasusuke, Kumon Shumpei, and Sato Seizaburo.[69] According to them, this civilization is characterized by the predominance of the *ie* type of organization, the major features of which are a combination of strong kinship (or, in their words, kin-tractship), strong collective goals, functional hierarchy, and a very high degree of autonomy of the organizational units. This attempt has sometimes been criticized as yet another version of Nihonjinron, as well as on various methodological points. Such criticisms are perhaps justified to some extent, because in these writers' scheme Japan constituted the *only* case of *ie* society; yet even this uniqueness was put in broad comparative terms, in which other civilizations could also be seen as unique. Hence there can be no doubt that this analysis contains some very important comparative indications.[70]

All these studies have highlighted important aspects of Japanese historical experience in a way that can be put in a comparative framework.

IX   The analysis presented in this book will indeed attempt to examine the Japanese historical experience and contemporary scene in such a comparative framework—above all in the framework of comparative studies of civilizations. From such a comparative point of view, the most important feature of the Japanese historical experience is that it is the only non-Axial civilization to have had a continuous, autonomous—and very turbulent—history up to and including modern times.

By Axial civilizations (to use Karl Jaspers' nomenclature)[71] I refer to those civilizations that crystallized during the period from 500 B.C. to the first century of the Christian era, or even to the rise of Islam, within which new types of ontological visions, conceptions of a basic tension between the transcendental and the mundane orders, emerged and were institutionalized. This occurred in many parts of the world: in ancient Israel and later second-Temple Judaism and Christianity; in ancient Greece; in Zoroastrian Iran; in early imperial China (although some scholars have expressed—to our mind, as we shall show in chapter 16, incorrectly—doubts as to whether China can be seen as an Axial civilization); in Hinduism and Buddhism; and, beyond the Axial Age proper, in Islam.

These ontological conceptions, which first developed among small groups of autonomous, relatively unattached "intellectuals"—such as prophets or visionaries—a new social element at the time, and particularly among the carriers of models of cultural and social order, were ultimately transformed into the basic "hegemonic" premises of their respective civilizations. That is, they became institutionalized as the dominant orientations of both the ruling and many secondary elites, fully embodied in their respective centers or subcenters, as was the case, for instance, in the institutionalization of the monotheistic vision attributed to Moses in ancient Israel, the Pauline vision in Christianity, and Confucian metaphysics in China.

The development and institutionalization of such conceptions of a basic tension, or chasm, between the transcendental and the mundane orders, gave rise in all these civilizations to attempts to reconstruct the mundane world—human personality and the sociopolitical and economic order—according to transcendental vision. The given, mundane order was perceived in these civilizations as incomplete, inferior, often bad or polluted—at least in some of its parts—and in need of being reconstructed according to the principles of a higher ontological or ethical order that bridged the chasm between the transcendental and the mundane orders. In all these civilizations, in other words, there developed an urge to implement in the mundane institutional arenas the precepts of the higher ethical or metaphysical order. That is, in Weberian terms, "salvation," basically a Christian concept, some equivalents of which are to be found in all the Axial civilizations.

The political order—as the central locus, or one of the central loci, of the mundane order—was usually conceived as lower than the transcendental one and accordingly had to be restructured according to the precepts of the latter, above all according to the perception of the proper mode of overcoming the tension between the transcendental and the mundane order, of attaining salvation or the implementation of the appropriate transcendental vision. It was the rulers who were usually held to be responsible for organizing the political order according to such precepts.

It is the expansion of these civilizations and their encounters with one another and with the great non-Axial civilizations—with, for instance, the Mongols—that have occupied the center stage of history as it was depicted by the historians of these civilizations. These histories depicted the ways in which the Axial civilizations succeeded in creating institutional frameworks which dominated over those of the non-Axial ones. These histories also pushed many of the non-Axial civilizations into the margins of history—as people without history or, to be more accurate, people with, from the point of view of the historiographies of the Axial civilizations, only local histories. It was also within one of these Axial civilizations that modernity developed and from which it later expanded throughout the world.

The distinctiveness of Japan lies in its being the only non-Axial civilization that maintained—throughout its history, up to the modern time—a history of its own, without becoming in some way marginalized by the Axial civilizations, China and Korea, Confucianism and Buddhism, with which it was in continuous contact.

But Japan should be compared not only with Axial civilizations, but also with other non-Axial civilizations (which usually were, however, also pre-Axial), those, for instance, of ancient Egypt or Mesopotamia, or Java before its Hindustanization. In contrast with other non-Axial civilizations, there developed in Japan not only an elaborate "wisdom" literature and discourse, but also a highly sophisticated philosophical and aesthetical discourse, the like of which can only be found in Axial civilizations.

These rather general characteristics, which distinguish Japan from Axial and other non-Axial civilizations, hence are closely related to some of the distinctive aspects of the Japanese historical experience—namely a tendency to continuous internal institutional change, and an openness to outside influences combined with a great ability to "Japanize" these influences on both the institutional and the ideological levels. Outside items—ideas, artifacts, technologies, styles of dress—have continuously been adopted, so much so that Japan has often been called a country of imitations and imitators. But the overall institutional dynamics, as well as the mode of institutional change and openness to external influences, have evinced in Japan some very distinct characteristics.

Japanization, as well as the mode of structuring internal changes and responding to the numerous movement protests that have developed in Japan throughout its history, has been characterized by a double-pronged tendency: On the one hand, a continuous creation of new social spaces, new types of social relations, cultural activities, and consciousness has taken place; on the other hand, a strong tendency has developed to restructure and reinforce the basic conceptions of the social order and the basic premises of the major institutional arenas, and the numerous new activities have not directly challenged or changed the hegemonic premises.

Last, and closely related to the processes of Japanization of foreign influences, has been the fact that Japanese civilization, unlike that of Western and Central Europe, with which it shares many structural similarities, and that of China, by which it was particularly influenced, did not see itself as a part of a broader civilization, as sharing basic premises and identity with other societies. Together these characteristics constitute the core of the Japanese historical experience and the major challenge for comparative analysis, which will constitute the major focus of our analysis.

Should these characteristics be explained in cultural or structural terms? Or should an explanation combine elements both of the cultural and of the structural research perspectives? Our major analytical approach is, as has already been suggested, that it is wrong even to pose this question in terms of such dichotomic categories. Instead one should ask about the modes of interweaving of cultural and structural dimensions of social organization and behavior in different situations, sectors, and levels of social life. We shall pursue this analytical line throughout our comparative analysis.

I shall start with what has obviously been, and continues to be, the major focus of discussion about the distinctiveness of modern Japanese society—its unusual position as a modern, industrial, capitalist, constitutional democratic society which at the same time evinces some distinct, seemingly "traditional" or "esoteric" features. The first step will therefore be the analysis of the crystallization of the modern Japanese state and society, starting from the Meiji period and moving to the contemporary scene. This analysis will naturally be couched in comparative terms and will look above all at the ways in which modern Japan differs from the modern Western nation-states and industrial societies. Such a problematic does not necessarily imply the imposition of a Western-centered view of Japan; it is, rather, a highly legitimate approach, in that the Japanese themselves, on the eve of the Meiji Ishin, or Restoration, and during the Restoration, looked to Western models in considering how to organize themselves into a modern state.

Such an exploration of the distinct characteristics of modern and contemporary Japanese society naturally calls for explanation in terms of some combination of cultural and structural elements and historical contingency. Before attempting such an explanation, however, I shall make a kind of semihistorical turnabout: I shall present an analysis of several institutional arenas and periods of Japanese history, which indeed show a close similarity to the Western ones, yet also evince some very important differences from them.

I shall concentrate on the analysis of selected aspects of Japanese history, such as feudalism, the Tokugawa state, patterns of rebellion and reform leading to the disintegration of this state, and patterns of urban development, all of which have evinced similarities to aspects of Western European history. This analysis will not of course pretend to be a comprehensive history of Japan. It will rather explore ways in which these institutional formations, despite many similarities, differ in some dimensions from those of Western Europe and how these differences are also evident in the processes of change that are taking place in Japanese history.

Thus the problem of Japan's unusual combination of similarities and differences with Western societies will come up again in all of these chapters. In cases predating the modern period, in which there was no contact between the West and Japan, this combination of similarities and differences is particularly surprising and baffling.

At the same time, however, Japan has been in close contact, almost from the beginning of its history, with China and Korea and, more recently, with India. From these countries came two of the most formative influences on Japan, Buddhism and Confucianism. There were also threats of invasion—possibly the first settlements in Japan came from Korea. And China has always been very much in the minds of the Japanese, at least up until the modern period. One interpretation of the Meiji Ishin, proposed by Ben-Ami Shilloni, is that it aimed, by creating a new imperial order, to establish Japanese hegemony against China.[72] But although the influences of China, of Confucianism, and of (Mahayana) Buddhism were paramount in shaping Japan, Japan never became part of these universalistic civilizations. Concomitantly, Confucianism and Buddhism were transformed in Japan in radical ways. These transformations, as well as the way in which Japan related to these civilizations, constitute a crucial dimension of the Japanese historical experience—yet another illustration of a combination of similarities with, and differences from, other civilizations. We shall accordingly analyze these problems in the last chapter of the historical part of our analysis.

In the last part of the book we shall first bring together some of the major results of the analysis of the first two parts, by analyzing some of the distinctive characteristics of the Japanese historical experience. We shall then analyze the central aspects of Japanese culture, attempt to determine their relation to the specific characteristics of the Japanese historical experience, and consider how such relations might be explained, that is, the nature of the social processes through which such relations are effected and the major features of Japanese institutional formations and dynamics produced, reproduced, and changed, Lastly, on the basis of these considerations we shall present a summary conclusion on the nature of the Japanese historical experience in a comparative perspective and shall analyze some specific characteristics of Japan as a modern society and a distinct modern civilization.

X Such a comparison with Western Europe—and with China—will, I hope, avoid the pitfalls of either Western- or Japanese-centeredness, of the excesses of the *Nihonjinron* literature, of "orientalism," and even of the "inverted orientalism" sometimes found among more critical Western and Japanese scholars of Japan. Inverted orientalism, which developed in reaction against *Nihonjinron* claims about the incomparable uniqueness of Japan, almost gave rise to a near denial of the validity of applying emic Japanese categories of thought—as opposed to *critical* Western categories—to the analysis of Japanese historical and contemporary experience. Such an approach appears paradoxical, as it goes against the emphasis critics of orientalism place on the exploration of such emic categories. The paradox may perhaps be explained by the fact that, given that Japan has become the only non-Western fully industrialized society, any emphasis on emic categories might lead (as was indeed the case with the *Nihonjinron* literature) to the abandonment of any critical stance toward the system. But at the same time such a stance may obviate the need to search for understanding in more emic critical attitudes or categories that developed within various sectors of Japanese society.[73]

One of the most vehement critics of *Nihonjinron*, Peter N. Dale, admitted as much when he reappraised his own earlier work:

> There is, therefore, an unresolved paradox in my approach, one complicated by a further order of contradiction. The methods I was ostensibly to use to dismantle the *nihonjinron* so that a truly empirical study of Japan might take place are, in large measure, in themselves "unempirical." The ideas of Marx and Freud appear to be used as curettes to cleanse the wombs of abortive thinking in order to allow for the possibility of proper conceptions; or, to change the metaphor somewhat, they serve as "unempirical" midwives for the birth of that empirical science of Japan concerning which I proclaim the Annunciation, and hail the imminent Immaculate Conception—one devoid of the besetting original sins of the older interpretative

Testament constituted by the *nihonjinron*. Am I not, therefore, using one ideological system to dispose of another, praying in the meantime for miraculous succour from a positivistic sociology to pull me out of those very meshes I cast to trap my erstwhile quarry?

Thirdly, reading between the lines it becomes clear that the tacit interpretation of at least parts of the Japanese world which sneaks around the periphery of what was originally intended as a purely negative critique of a mythological system posing as objective science, betrays strong traces of what some would identify as "bourgeois nostalgia." The *nihonjinron* are shown to orchestrate the kind of ideological world view that precipitates when late modernisers use every device in their power, social engineering and socio-ideological coercion, to obviate the challenges to internal order likely to arise from the emergence of bourgeois consciousness and institutional reform. I am using, as it were, the ideas of two great critics of bourgeois pretensions in order to expose the incoherencies of a way of thinking that defiantly attempts to bypass the bourgeois culture of the west and legitimise those barely post-feudal structures which the Japanese elite have managed to weld into the modern industrial system.

Thus, for instance, instead of inquiring whether the Japanese think in logical terms, one would have to ask what are the specific patterns of the logic according to which Japanese thought has been structured and crystallized—and concomitantly, according to what principle the Japanese concept of reality is structured and how it is related to the other, more emotional aspects of Japanese personality.

Even if we accept that many of these tenets are constructs created by manipulating elites, we face the central problem or puzzle—in this case, as probably in all others—of how to explain the success of those elites and influentials who attain, in every society and historical period, hegemony relative to any potentially "oppositionary" forces.

Be that as it may, the existence of debates around these problems does attest to some of the basic problems of the analysis of any—especially non-Western—society or civilization. The root of these problems lies not only in the fact that, at least until recently, most of the scholars who addressed themselves to these problems came from the West, but above all in the fact that such a mode of analysis, of social science or historical analysis in general and comparative analysis in particular, has developed almost entirely—Ibn Khaldun notwithstanding—as part of the Western modern discourse.

Taking up various critical stances toward the earlier orientalist literature, both in the West and in India, Japan, and other non-Western countries, has been part of the expansion of this discourse. Needless to say, such expansion, and the continuous reconstruction of these modes of discourse by intellectuals in non-Western countries, has transformed many of the modes of this discourse and of the *Problemstellungen* within it. But basically it did not go beyond such discourse. This applies also to the distinction between "emic" and "etic" modes of analysis. There is probably no way out of this dilemma—which means that in some way an analysis derived from this discourse *imposes* its categories on the subject analyzed. The only way to minimize the distorting effect of such an analysis is to be conscious of the problem, to search as far as possible for understanding (even, if necessary, in Western or Western-derived terms) of the emic categories of the civilizations under analysis, and to bear in mind the possibility of multiple *Problemstellungen*—hegemonic and "subaltern" alike.

In the following analysis I shall attempt to follow these guidelines—without any illusion that the problems mentioned above can be entirely resolved. The basic premise of the approach I shall follow is that the full implication of a comparison of, for instance, Western and Japanese feudalism or absolutism, or the Meiji Restoration and the great revolutions, is that neither of these cases is the "natural" one against which the other must be measured—even if sometimes an emphasis on one or the other cannot be avoided. Rather, each of these societies or civilizations has developed its own specific dynamics—its own distinct, fully legitimate historical experience—and such distinctiveness, such uniqueness, can be best understood in the framework of comparative analysis.

At the same time the very fact that these dynamics and experiences can be compared means that however unique each civilization may be, its uniqueness denotes a specific constellation of institutional and cultural elements or components which, at least to some extent, are common to many, possibly all, human societies.

Part One

MODERN AND CONTEMPORARY JAPAN

TWO

The Meiji State and
Modern Japanese Society

THE TRANSITION TO THE MODERN JAPANESE STATE

I The modern period in Japanese history was ushered in by the Meiji Ishin, the so-called Meiji Restoration, which pushed Japan into the modern world and shaped the major contours of the patterns of modernity that developed in Japan. The analysis of these patterns constitutes the major focus of this and the next four chapters. As indicated in the first chapter, we shall focus our analysis on some of the most salient aspects of Japanese modern experience and compare them with parallel developments in other modern, especially Western, societies, by which Japanese modernity was greatly influenced.

Such a comparison is of course especially appropriate with respect to the modern period, as in this period Japanese society and state modeled themselves on Western, especially European, states. At the same time, such comparison will bring out quite forcefully the specific characteristics of the modern Japanese historical experience.

We start with an analysis of the basic features of the transformation from Tokugawa to Meiji. Marius Jansen and Gilbert Rozman have aptly summarized the most important features of this transition. It was effected, as they have shown, relatively quickly, although certainly not without conflict. Building on the high levels of literacy, urbanization, and economic integration, the Meiji elites, who developed relatively homogeneous attitudes, transformed the basic principles and organization of the economy and of the government.[1] Several other characteristics of the Japanese premodern society—especially the pluralism of centers of power, which, though substantially suppressed under the Tokugawa, was never obliterated—have been singled out in the literature.[2]

Out of this transition there crystallized, in a period of about two decades, the major specific features of the Meiji state and society. This crystallization was greatly influenced by orientations toward the strengthening of the national community and the state through economic development and military strength, which would ensure Japan could find its place in the new international order.

II   The most visible aspect of the new Meiji state was the high level of political and administrative centralization, which was effected in a remarkably short period. "This administrative centralization came in stages and eventually took three main forms: 1) rule in the name of the emperor as the unifying central authority; 2) direct administration through a unified central bureaucracy and the establishment of a hierarchy of offices that linked the center to the localities without sharing power; and 3) equality of the population before the state through universal conscription, the abolition of samurai status, and the stipulation of uniform rights."[3] Closely related to the processes of administrative and political centralization was the promulgation, early in 1900, of the first fully unified legal code in the history of Japan. These policies of centralization quickly transformed Japan from a country of hundreds of daimyō to a unified state, with centralized authority permeating all sectors of society as the former semiautonomous local authorities and legal traditions gave way to a general, common legal framework.

These processes of centralization, economic development, social mobilization, and construction of a new political system with kernels of representative institutions were in their basic outlines similar to the processes of nation building in European nation-states—and in many ways were patterned after them. Yet very quickly there developed some distinctive characteristics of modern Japanese political, economic, and social systems. Among these, the most important was the role of the state in initiating changes and guiding the transformation of society. Such guidance was greatly influenced by the awareness of foreign experience and involved the deliberate borrowing of models from the West in an effort to catch up; this resulted in a very high degree of centralization in relation to the level of development, and in the compression into a relatively short period of changes in state building, organizational formations, and ways of life.[4]

But it was not only with respect to the tempo of modernization and the role of the state in it that Japan evinced distinctive characteristics. From the very beginning of the crystallization of the modern Japanese state and society, there developed major social, political, and economic features that were not found in such predominant forms elsewhere. These features of the Meiji state did not develop according to a clear, preconceived plan or vision; indeed, as we shall see in chapter 12, except for the general model of the Western nation-state, such a plan was lacking or at least weak. Rather, they developed out of a process of trial and error undertaken by the leading elite groups of the Restoration and crystallized through continuous struggles during the first two decades after the toppling of the Tokugawa regime.

During this period many sectors of Japanese society, their leaders, and numerous intellectuals were exposed to external influences and promulgated a great variety of new models of social and political order. Initially the leaders of the Restoration, guided by the goal of ensuring for Japan an independent standing in the international arena, explored many new options. Indeed, the first two decades after the Meiji Restoration were infused with a tendency to look outward, as epitomized by the slogan *bunmei kaika*—"civilization and enlightenment."[5]

At the same time, this period was characterized by many uprisings—those of Tokugawa loyalist peasants, local Buddhist priests, dislocated samurai groups, and more modern popular movements such as the Citizen Rights. Many sectors of society broke through the former hegemonic molds and spawned new forms and themes of popular culture.[6]

The relatively coherent policies that developed in this period of trial and error, toward the end of the 1890s, crystallized to a large extent in response to trends and movements seen by the Meiji elite—the so-called oligarchs and the slowly emerging bureaucracy—as threats to national unity and cohesion and, consequently, to international standing. These ruling groups perceived threats not only from the various uprisings and popular movements, but also from groups of younger intellectuals and would-be political leaders, who were very open to various Western liberal trends, from nativistic groups participating in the Restoration, and from the growing economic and administrative difficulties of the two decades of the Meiji state.[7]

These policies were characterized, first, by the abolition of almost all the ascriptive hierarchical social restrictions that had prevailed in Tokugawa society, a change that generated far-reaching processes of economic and social mobility (a new aristocracy, the peerage, was created, but it was a very limited and "ceremonial" one, with the House of Peers as a counterweight to the more "democratic" legislative chamber). Second, a strong guiding hand from the center channeled, even if it did not always directly control, these processes, aiming to minimize the development of autonomous social forces—be they regional, occupational, religious, or class ones—or, in a more general parlance, of an autonomous civil society.

Along with the push to economic development came the establishment of universal military conscription; a centralized police organization, which provided a very effective instrument of social control; and a centralized, modern educational system. These agencies—above all the educational system and the army—became both the channels through which the values and ideology of the regime, with its strong emphasis on nationhood and progress, were instilled into the population, and some of the main avenues of social and occupational mobility.[8]

It was the oligarchy and the bureaucracy that shaped these major initial features of Meiji society. They attempted, in a schoolmaster fashion, to use R. N. Bellah's felicitous expression (albeit, as Peter Duus put it, a schoolmaster with a rod as well as a lesson plan), to channel some of the traditional loyalties of the wider sectors of society into the new frameworks. This channeling was effected through a combination of administrative directives and repression, by drawing the various strata into the new central frameworks without really granting them, at least at first, full political rights or allowing them much autonomous social-political expression. It involved continuous consultations and coalitions between different echelons of the bureaucracy, the emerging political parties, and various, in the beginning rather limited, economic entrepreneurs.

The regulation by the newly emerging elites of this very intensive mobility, and the channeling of the motivations of large sectors of society into new institutional arenas, were to no small degree implemented by the promulgation of a new ethic. This ethic, the kernels of which were already present in the Tokugawa period, was based on the intensification of the conceptions of loyalty prevalent in many sectors of Japanese society, strongly reformulated in Confucian terms, and on the combination of these conceptions with modern civic virtues like patriotism, obedience to general laws, and the like. The leaders of the Meiji schoolmaster state intensively promulgated selected Confucian themes—especially those of discipline, education, and harmony.[9] Paradoxically it was in this period that the Confucian model—but not its concrete contents—of selecting the ruling classes through education was in some way achieved, blended, in Harumi Befu's coinage, with a strong tendency toward the "samurai-zation" of the new ruling classes, to their being imbued with the "bushido" ethos.[10]

III   Administrative and political centralization in the Meiji state gave rise to far-reaching changes in the economic structure, creating the basis for a system that was capitalist, yet, as we shall see in chapter 3, had some very distinctive characteristics.[11] The economic policies first focused on providing, through agricultural taxation, the basic financial and manpower resources necessary for economic development and urbanization, and on laying the foundations of national economic and military strengths.

The Meiji regime changed the legal bases of ownership of resources and of their uses, fully legalizing private property in general and private land ownership in particular, which were already prevalent under the Tokugawa. This made possible the development of a capitalist system and an urban proletariat. It also further weakened the cohesion of older, wider (especially village) solidary groups already undermined by internal developments in the Tokugawa period.

This new organizational complex was not legitimized, as in the beginning of modern capitalist development in parts of Europe, in terms of either a search for transcendental salvation through this-worldly activities or individual economic advancement, but rather in terms of its contribution to the well-being, strength, and expansion of the collectivity of the nation, and the various economic activities were often initiated and continuously supervised by the Meiji oligarchs and the bureaucracy. As Runciman has indicated, "the managers of the great plants were mostly ex-samurai and ex-chōnin, merchants, and the smaller plants organized on artisan lines and often dependent on part-time and family labor; employers and unionists alike conformed to the hierarchical, factional, leader-follower norm of social relations."[12]

By the late nineteenth century, economic activity and capitalism were also often internally legitimized in terms of classical economics, social Darwinism, and the like, giving rise to far-reaching laissez-faire policies. Such justifications were often used with respect both to ensuring Japan's standing in the world and to the new internal social divisions and dislocations created by the developing capitalist economy.

The processes of economic development were connected with far-reaching social mobility, the pattern of which was not, at least initially, egalitarian or fully open; on the whole differences between various sectors of the society were de facto perpetuated.[13] Nevertheless, there took place a rise in the scope of mobility—the army served as an important channel of mobility—and of new status configurations, with a very strong emphasis on achievement.

> This pattern of social mobility developed, with rather strong pushes from the center, so as to attract new blood into many new roles on an individual basis, thus preventing the development of a distinctive status or class consciousness of their own.
>
> . . . It was only the rural ex-smallholders whose collective consciousness found expression in the formation of a national Peasant Union in 1922, and it was weakened from the outset by both factional and doctrinal differences.[14]

But the most distinctive characteristic of this new status system was probably the fact that the ultimate legitimation of these new symbols and criteria of status was constructed neither in transcendental universalistic terms nor even mainly in terms of their functional contributions to particular institutional arenas or organizations. True enough, there developed, especially in the educational arena—but also, in principle at least, in the occupational one—an emphasis on achievement and on universal access to achievement, emphases ultimately legitimated in terms of their functional contribution to the collectivity, and not, as in the West, in terms of conceptions of principled individualism.[15] But in general the legitimation of achievement was vested in the center and in the various networks spawned by it, and was based on a combination of imperial symbolism with the new modes of "modern" knowledge espoused by the new leading groups, especially by the bureaucracy. At the same time, the various channels of mobility and advancement, like the schools and universities, tended to be organized in complicated vertical hierarchies and were connected through strong networks that developed among them.

IV   In line with these characteristics of the economic arena and with the structuring of status and status hierarchies, there developed some distinctive political features. The major innovations in the political arena were the process of centralization, to which we have referred above, the promulgation of a constitution, and the establishment of representative institutions. The last two were not just cosmetic changes made under foreign influence in order to catch up, as it were, with the Western powers.

Many of the Meiji leaders promoted the establishment of these institutions in order to enhance the social cohesion of the new state, to bring the broader classes into more direct relations with the emperor and the new state. These institutions were not seen as grounded in popular sovereignty, as representing the interests of different sectors of the population, but rather as organs of the new state and its symbol or pivot—the emperor. The constitution was indeed promulgated as a gift of the emperor.

To follow Peter Duus, "In sum, the drafters of the Meiji constitution saw representative democratic institutions as having an integrating rather than a cathartic function. . . . Representative institutions were a means of assuring the 'united rule of monarch and people'—*kunmin dōchi*—a slogan, ironically enough, later often flung in the face of the Meiji leaders by the political opposition. . . . *Kunmin dōchi* implied that the ruler would respond to the needs of the people, but it also meant that the people would be loyal to the ruler as the embodiment of their 'general will.' This view of democratic institutions was closer to Rousseau's than to J. S. Mill's . . . and the new political practices were ultimately justified in traditional terms."[16]

The prevalence of these conceptions influenced also the concrete contours of the political institutions that developed in the Meiji state. Among these the most important were the weakness of parliamentary control of ministers, highly restricted suffrage, the predominance of oligarchs and bureaucrats organized in complex, often not clearly visible networks, the concomitant highly dispersed system of authority and accountability, the vesting of ultimate authority in an emperor who was not able to exercise it, the concentration of coercive power in the hands of the army and the police, and the consequent dispersion of power and difficulty in rendering accountability.[17]

The processes of political innovation and decision making in Japan were, in the first periods of the Meiji regime, concentrated in the oligarchy and the emerging bureaucracy, with but minimal recourse to formal representative institutions or to public opinion. Only later, in the first decades of the twentieth century, did such groups as parliamentary cliques, parties and partylike organizations, newspapers, economic interest groups, and labor organizations become important in the political processes.

Orientation to the international scene constituted a major component of the Meiji state; the wish to avoid the fate of China and the colonized Asian countries, to attain the status of an independent, possibly major power, guided many of the political decisions.[18] This orientation gave rise to very strong military-expansionist policies. The first fruit of these policies was the victory over Russia in 1905. Later on military and colonial expansion—in Korea, the Chinese war, and World War I and in the expansionist policies of the 1930s—constituted a central component of the Japanese political scene. It was this orientation that provided the background for the special place of the army in the political area of the modern Japanese state—until the end of the Second World War.[19]

V The various policies through which these initial basic features of the Meiji state were shaped were implemented through a combination of coercive, often repressive means, with the regulation of the most important institutional arenas and the major markets—in land, capital, and labor. These centralizing, state-guiding policies were resisted, especially by local movements—for instance those opposing shrine reforms, or the rice revolts of the early twentieth century—which, despite the state's efforts to incorporate them, continued to provide buffers against state intrusion. They were not, however, able to change the general trend toward centralization.

However important the coercive means might have been, it was the mode of state guidance as it developed in Japan that was most distinctive. In the first two decades of this century, when the old oligarchies faced a new, largely urbanized and modernized country, a bureaucratized polity, and new interest groups, there crystallized a set of "creative conservative" policies.[20] The most distinctive characteristic of these policies was the fact that various sectors of society were granted some measure of autonomy in their own arenas of activity but no autonomous access to the centers of power and the political arena.

Within these various sectors, numerous new types of organization developed, similar in many ways to—and often seemingly copied from—what could be found in Western societies. The representatives of such sectors, of the various interest groups, were often co-opted in consultative roles into the different organs of the state; through such formal and informal networks the state organs, especially the bureaucracies, maintained continuous connections with representatives of other sectors. In the beginning, the range of such interest groups was quite limited and but few of their direct representatives were consulted. But their numbers continually increased and consultations with them became more routinized; in such exchanges the state officials usually remained the gatekeepers, not granting the groups any autonomous, independent political role, but they did listen to the problems or demands of the various sectors. Thus these organizations and their representatives were not able to challenge the basic guiding role of the oligarchs and the bureaucracy, even though they could greatly influence the details of their decisions.

THE IDEOLOGY AND CIVIC THEOLOGY OF THE MEIJI STATE

VI Although specific institutional features of the Meiji state and society often developed in an ad hoc way, their overall pattern did exhibit a distinctive logic. This logic was grounded in the overall cultural program that crystallized in the period and was promulgated above all by the new elites. This modern, restorationist ideology comprised, at least at the beginning, two central components—already visible in the late Tokugawa period—which Tetsuo Najita identifies as idealism and a pragmatic, utilitarian view of politics and national strategy. The idealist component initially had a strongly nativistic, semiutopian orientation but later developed a restorationist focus; this was closely combined with a distinctive cultural program emphasizing new knowledge, new learning, and a pragmatist orientation.

These two components of the ideology also provided, at least at the beginning of the Meiji period, the major compass according to which the elites and the bureaucracy guided the processes of social mobilization and economic development. The promulgation of this cultural program entailed, in line with parallel processes in the construction of a modern nation-state, the constitution of new conceptions of man, woman, the human body, the family, and gender relations[21]—of the political realm and of public space—all grounded in the distinctly modern legitimation of the State.

Tensions developed, however, between the core components of this ideology. While mythical or religious conceptions of the emperor and the national community based on social and primordial criteria were central to its agenda, it also presented the emperor's authority as being to some degree derived from the people, albeit not in the Lockean "liberal," contractual sense.[22] This ideology also stressed the importance of "modern" types of knowledge as a basis of the new regime and as a pragmatic guide in the shaping of the new society—usually without directly specifying the ways in which such new knowledge related to the restorationist vision.[23]

This cultural program or ideology with its internal tensions entailed a distinctive conception of legitimation of the political regime and of politics. To follow Peter Duus again:

> The new constitutional structure, promulgated as an "imperial gift" to the people, grounded its legitimacy in imperial benevolence. In modern legal language the constitution asserted that sovereignty was located in the emperor. As in traditional political culture, the emperor was neither an accountable nor a responsible figure; it was to him that others were accountable. In this sense the imperial institution was "above politics." But just what this might mean in practice provoked intense debate among constitutional theorists. . . .
>
> The "apolitical" character of the imperial institution was fortified by a distinction made in political discourse between *kokutai* (national structure) and *seitai* (political structure)—originally adumbrated in the writings of the Mito school in the 1820s. The *kokutai* was seen as absolute, unchanging, eternal, essential; the *seitai* as relative, transient, temporary, and contingent.[24]

This distinction compartmentalized political behavior into two distinct moral spheres. While the *kokutai* (represented by the imperial institution) was sacralized, the *seitai*, the realm of government or politics, remained profane and secular. The emperor, at once identified with and symbolic of the *kokutai*, remained detached from partisan struggles within the Diet or between the cabinet and the Diet. To the realm of representative democratic institutions was left the pursuit of mundane, profane, and quotidian concerns. The Imperial Diet was not a forum where ideals, or ultimate values, were debated or determined; rather it was a political marketplace where policy and interest were negotiated.[25]

Thus the place of the emperor in the Meiji, and later in the modern, Japanese system was ambiguous. He was, just as his predecessors, outside politics but, symbolizing the *kokutai*, he also delegated positions and constituted the pivot of political systems, to whom the major political agents were accountable. It was these ambiguous roles of the emperor that created a vacuum in the process of decision making and in accountability for decisions, thus enabling the bureaucracy and the army to play a special, crucial role in the political process.

VII   It is this mode of legitimation of the new regime, its civic ideology or civic theology to follow W. Davis's formulation, that distinguished the Meiji state from other modern regimes—even state-guided ones—and that provides the clue to many of its specific institutional patterns.

The construction of such a civil theology or ideology aimed, as did the parallel processes in postrevolutionary France and later in postrevolutionary Russia, to mold a new national consciousness, to make, in Eugene Weber's phrase, "peasants into Frenchmen"[26]—or in this case into Japanese. But here some specific characteristics of the construction of the modern Japanese nation clearly stand out.

Even if the conception of the national community was greatly influenced by Western notions of nationalism, it was formulated in the ideology of the Meiji regime in ways different from those of the Western nation-states. The crux of this difference was the fact that this new Japanese collective consciousness was constructed in primordial sacralnatural terms.[27] The primordial and national collective identity or consciousness promulgated by this ideology was closely bound to the figure of the emperor, who became a half-mythical figure epitomizing the new Japanese political system.[28]

Unlike most modern Western—and later also Asian—national or nationalist ideologies, the ideology of the Meiji regime did not formulate the distinctiveness of the Japanese collectivity in relation to some universal religion or civilization of which it was a part, or which it might, as in the case of extreme European national movements, sometimes negate. Building on the basic conceptions of the *kokutai* as developed by the nativistic schools of the Tokugawa period (which were rooted in even earlier, if quite weak, formulations), it defined the Japanese nation as a unique type of collectivity, defined in primordial sacral-natural terms. References to "other" civilizations—whether to Confucian and Buddhist civilizations, which were indeed frequently made in the Tokugawa period, or to the West in the Meiji period—did not denote full participation in a broader, universal civilization. Unlike in Europe, or later in India or China, where the construction of national ideologies usually entailed strong tensions between universalistic religious and primordial, particularistic orientations, no such tensions developed in the ideology of *kokutai*. At most this ideology—as attested to by some of the most interesting attempts by modern Japanese historians, following here some Tokugawa scholars, to place Japan in a scheme of universal but not Western progressivist history[29]—emphasized that the Japanese nation, by virtue of its primordial and sacral qualities, epitomized to a much higher degree than any other civilization the very virtues extolled by those other civilizations—the Chinese earlier on, and the West in the modern era. The construction of this ideology entailed also, as we shall see in greater detail later on, a distinctive mode of reconstruction of tradition.

This ideology did not emerge automatically as a sort of natural continuation of Japanese tradition, even if its crystallization was in many ways reminiscent of that of the Tokugawa ideology, especially in the ways both transformed the same components of neo-Confucianism. In both cases the crystallization and the institutionalization of the ideology was the result of a long struggle against challenges by intellectual and popular movements. The institutionalization of the Meiji ideology was effected through a series of measures of social control undertaken by the government, including some that aimed to suppress, or at least to weaken, popular movements and spontaneous public opinion and organizations.

But it was not only, perhaps not even mainly, these repressive measures that were crucial; a central aspect of the institutionalization of this civic religion was the conscious promulgation of its doctrine among wider sectors of the population. This was accomplished through civic and moral education in the schools, and through the establishment of multiple rituals, from those involving the imperial court to the many local ones in which the emperor was symbolically presented to the public—as was the case when thousands of national priests were sent out to present the new image of the emperor to large sectors of the population and to create in this way a new national consensus.

VIII   The pivot of this new ideology of national identity was the newly constructed image and symbolism of the emperor. While claiming to restore an ancient imperial system, the Meiji elites and bureaucracy in fact combined the different components of the emperor symbols in a new way. These components had developed in Japanese history from the ancient role of the emperor as the officiant in rituals for the soul and growth of rice; as Emiko Ohnuki-Tierney has put it:

> What remains constant through history is the emperor's identity as a deity (*kami*) in the Japanese sense. I think the way the Japanese view the *kami* is responsible for the way the imperial system has undergone such dramatic changes at the hand of historical actors and yet has survived.[30]

Building on these ancient foundations, the modern Meiji ideology transformed the emperor symbol, presenting the imperial institution as the symbolic center of the new nation and emphasizing the direct relations between the emperor and the nation.[31]

The promulgation of this imperial symbolism, and of the ethical pre-cepts of the Meiji schoolmaster state, constituted, as B. Silberman has shown, a highly modernistic project—a project not unlike those promul-gated in the West—at least partially rooted in the elites' perception of the disorganization of social solidarity and the fear of the upsurge of embedded individualistic, hedonistic behavior. The promulgation of the emperor's symbols and the civic theology of the Meiji state constituted the specific Japanese answer to such perception and fear.[32]

IX The promulgation of this imperial image and symbolism and the concomitant doctrine started in the very first years of the Meiji regime, with acts such as the Imperial Edict on the Promulgation of the Great Teaching Ordinance, but it was probably most fully crystallized in the Education Ordinance of 1879.

The conceptions of the Japanese modern state presented in this and many other rescripts and ordinances, were promulgated also by local opinion leaders, intellectuals, journalists, political leaders, and other elites and influential persons in a great variety of ways. In schools, for example, history courses played a very important role, emphasizing the reaction against materialistic Western civilization and aiming to strengthen social bonds to unify the country.[33] "They [these various groups] argued that this definition of the nation might then become the center of a national-ism (*kokuminshugi*) that would admit Western influence and at the same time preserve Japan's distinctive national character (*kokuminsei*)."[34]

Even later, in the Taishō period and after the Second World War when far-reaching changes had taken place in Japanese society and cultural dis-course, some of the basic premises of this ideology and collective con-ceptualization remained pervasive—albeit they were formulated in new ways. The ideology of *kokutai* proved to be the most persistent compo-nent of the new Japanese collective identity, even when its mythical com-ponents were shed away after the Second World War.

This ideology or civic religion did not emerge immediately or un-ambiguously, nor, as Carol Gluck has shown, did all sectors of the popu-lation fully identify with it or commit to it. It was also in many ways a relatively loose ideology. But notwithstanding, or possibly owing to, such looseness it became the dominant hegemonic ideology of the Meiji polity and society, and, as we shall see, even later, in Taishō Japan, most oppo-sitionary views were formulated in its terms and addressed to it.

X This distinct Meiji civic religion or ideology, in which the national community was constructed as encompassing all arenas of life, had im-portant—and rather paradoxical—repercussions in the structuring of the political arena and of the relations between state and civil society in

Japan. The most important of these was the conflation of state and civil society within the broader national community. This could be seen in the *Kokken* (constitution); the almost total elimination, institutionalized in the civil code, of the "social" as an autonomous arena; the almost total absence of an autonomous public arena independent from the state; a distrust of politics; and the concomitant development of a relatively weak conception of the state as a distinct ontological unit, and of an even weaker conception of civil society.

One of the most paradoxical aspects of this civil religion was the fact that no concept of the state—as distinct from the national community embodied in and symbolized by the figure of the emperor—fully developed; the concept of the national community encompassing political and administrative activities was predominant. As Germaine A. Hoston has put it:

> The emperor (*tennō* or *mikado*) occupied the central position in official Meiji political thought. It compressed the concepts of nation and state into one and demonstrated the extent to which traditionally the state—the political organization—absorbed the nation—the political community or society in general—in indigenous Japanese thought. The *tennō* was at the apex of both, as the patriarchal head of the uniquely Japanese *kokutai* (which can be translated only inadequately as "national polity" or "national body"), incorporating race, ethnicity, lineage, and spirituality into a single concept; and as the political ruler of a constitutional monarchic form of state (*seitai*). Within the context of the militaristic international system to which the Meiji Restoration itself was a response, the *tennō* was at once: (1) a constitutional monarch, the monarch of an authoritarian state as established by the Meiji Constitution granted by the emperor [not demanded by the people]; (2) the generalissimo (*daigensui*), the monarch as the summit of authority of supreme command over the armed forces, independent from the control of the cabinet; and (3) a monarch of divine right, a monarch representing religious or spiritual authority in place of that of the West's Christianity.[35]

This concept was closely related to the weakness of any autonomous public space and civil society. The processes of economic development, urbanization, and education gave rise of course to kernels of a new modern civil society—various associations, academic institutions, journalistic activities, and the like. But these kernels were not allowed to develop into a fully fledged civil society with a wide-ranging autonomous public space and autonomous access to the political center. Public space and discourse were monopolized by the government and the bureaucracy as representatives of the national community legitimized by the emperor.[36]

Closely related was the distrust of politics, the conflation of politics and morality and their symbolic vesting in the figure of the emperor. Indeed, such conflation of state and civil society was indicative of the great distrust of open politics, of *seitai*, as potentially subversive of the "general will" and gave rise to the appropriation of the political arena by the center, which put it seemingly beyond politics and legitimized it in terms of the new "objective" knowledge which it used to serve the community.[37]

These conceptions of politics, and basic distrust of politics, had their roots, as Harry Harootunian and Bernard Silberman have shown, in the ideologies of the Tokugawa period, especially in the nativistic school.[38] According to this view,

> to be political really meant, then, involvement in the Emperor's realm, and a political act in this sense carried with it the charge of lese majesty.
>
> The behavioral expectations of the ruled were guaranteed by reifying a traditional relationship between private and public. Underlying this construct was a conception of a public personality whose inner self corresponded to required outer behavior, and whose meaning was disclosed in the exercise of duties corresponding to his public role. Nothing was more important for this conception of personality than the ethical education of the whole person. But moral training promised inactivity and a reverent quietism toward the social order; the guidelines for actual behavior were marked out by accumulated precedent relating to a whole range of publicly accepted situations.[39]

Thus an attempt was made to create a modern political system capable of mobilizing the resources necessary to assert its place on the international scene, yet one that deemphasized politics and political participation and was not based on universal principles binding both rulers and subjects, which could in turn have given rise to the principle conception of accountability of rulers.

XI The mode of structuring public and private life that developed in Meiji Japan was closely related to this distrust of politics and to the construction of civil society in its relations to the state. Activity within the public space was almost entirely monopolized by the government and the bureaucracy, in conjunction with or oriented to the elites. This activity was seen, not only by the "interested" elites but by wide sectors of society, as defining the proper arenas of public discourse.

Other intellectual and journalistic activities were relegated to the private sphere and often designated as egotistical and subversive of the public order. The oligarchs and bureaucrats (and later the politicians) were on the whole successful in their attempt to control access to these arenas and to define the basic terms of public discourse which were ultimately accepted by a great majority of the intellectuals.[40] As Andrew Barshay has put it:

Who then stands as the "representative" public man? It seems that in terms of content, publicness in Japan continues to entail some attempt to mediate "universality" to the particular political and social nexus of Japan, but that the public sense has been weakened by its burden of bureaucratism and statism. I believe, following Ishida Takeshi, that the links of private individuals and groups to each other have grown tighter, but that this remains a "corporate privatism," exclusive rather than inclusive. The links of society to the public remain tenuous. I would argue that this is true to a surprising degree even among the academic (and literary) "counter-establishment."[41]

One interesting way in which this core theology affected the structuring of the relation between public and private spheres can be seen in the construction of gender and work roles as they developed in the context of urbanization and state formation. Women's roles in Meiji Japan were defined, not as in many Western countries with a strong emphasis on the private family sphere as against the public order, but as agents of the state. This was manifested in the strong orientations of women's movements to the state—yet another example of the conflation of state and civil society.[42]

XII The distinction between *kokutai* and *seitai*—along with the conflation of state and civil society with the national community and the distrust of politics it entailed—explains the special place of bureaucracy in the Japanese political scene, as well as its capacity to approach the ideal type of legal-rational bureaucracy. Given the distrust of politics the bureaucracy could relatively easily appropriate for itself, with the legitimization of the emperor, the representation of *kokutai*, "the general will"—unsullied by the consideration of *seitai*. The bureaucracy legitimized this appropriation, first, by portraying itself as exhibiting the combined samurai and Confucian virtues of the true rulers. As these could no longer be based on hereditary status, the bureaucracy cast its modern knowledge and education as a new basis. But such knowledge and education, distilled through the emerging elite universities, were also considered to be of dynamic moral quality, by virtue of the fact that they represented and served the general will.

The structure of the bureaucracy itself emerged out of the struggles between various leading groups in the beginning of the Meiji era. To quote B. Silberman:

> From the mid 1870's those who continued to hold offices sought to utilize the administrative role as the basis of the creation of a systematic structure of leadership. The central problem for them was how to transform the role from one that was characterized by domain and personal loyalty to one that

appeared to be dominated by transcendent public interest. They pursued, with extraordinary single-mindedness, strategies which would make the bureaucracy the primary structure of political leadership.

By imposing the qualifications of higher education, the Meiji leaders maintained exclusiveness, rejected the elective principle, while at the same time maintaining the ideal of equality before the emperor. Anyone who was qualified could enter the ranks of the emperor's servants. But to become qualified required, considerably before the end of the century, an early commitment to an expensive educational career. To provide incentives to maintain a flow of eligibles, the leadership had to create a systematic structure of rewards. Out of this emerged a bureaucratic structure that possessed all of the characteristics of Weber's legal-rational organizational structure.[43]

It was basically only the army which could—and did—compete with the different echelons of the bureaucracy in claims based on direct relation to the emperor—that is, to special, autonomous standing in the political arena.

RELIGIOUS POLICIES: SEPARATION OF STATE AND RELIGION AND THE SACRALIZATION OF THE STATE

XIII One of the most telling manifestations of the conflation of state, civil society, and public space could be seen in the policies in the religious arena. The crux of these religious policies, which effected a radical reconstruction of the religious arena, was the acceptance of Western assumptions about the dissociation between state and religion simultaneous with an emphasis on the conflation of sacrality and public space, as embodied by the emperor.

These attitudes toward religion led to the construction of a distinctive definition of religion that separated the religious arena from the state but subjected it to state regulation. Buddhist, Shinto, and Western Christian groups were declared in Western-like terms to be purely religious organizations. At the same time the authorities, aware of the subversive potential of religious activism, supervised the groups closely and instituted policies intended to limit their capacity for autonomous political action. The repressive policies of the Meiji state, directed especially against Buddhists, not only aimed to prevent rebellious or subversive activities and to confiscate the groups' wealth; they also had a more general aim: to prevent the possibility of these religious organizations' establishing bases of autonomous activity in the public arena, kernels of autonomous civil society with independent access to the central political arena. To what extent these various religious organizations would have been able to create such continuous autonomous frameworks is, of course, a moot question. Given the quick adjustment by most of them to the Meiji policies—especially the combination by Buddhist scholars of the construction of a transsectarian, universal Buddhism with the emphasis on "the universal" being tantamount to the Japanese spiritual essence—one may perhaps doubt that they would have. In any case, whatever potential existed in this regard was almost totally stifled by the religious policies of the Meiji regime.[44]

Closely related was a tendency to demarcate the various religions—Buddhism, Shinto, and needless to say Christianity—far more clearly than had been attempted in the Tokugawa period, when the blurring of boundaries between different religious practices was accepted, especially in daily life.

The tendencies toward the separation of religion and the state seemingly go against the strong tendency toward the sacralization of the natural community and the emperor, and it is here that some of the basic premises of the civil ideology of the Meiji state, as well as the contradictions between them, become most clearly visible. These contradictions could be most fully seen in the development of attitudes and policies with respect to Shinto. As Helen Hardacre has put it:

> The Meiji Constitution's provision for freedom of religion and the idea that Shinto was not a religion emerged in tandem in an atmosphere of considerable diplomatic pressure on Japan to satisfy foreign governments on the question of religious freedom and under the burden of peculiarly Protestant notions of religion at odds with Japan's own religious history. The result for Shinto was its alignment with civic duty and patriotism, while the consequences for recognized religious associations was a tight circumscription of the exercise of religious freedom. In effect, Japanese subjects were free to believe in a religion but not necessarily to practice it publicly. Members of unrecognized religious associations frequently fell victim to suppression and persecution.[45]

The state oscillated between defining Shinto as a religion and defining it as the repository of civic worship, its policies reflecting the basic ambivalence of the conception of *total* separation between state and religion. Shinto gradually acquired a general, rather ambiguous place, essentially not as a religion but as the repository of official state rites, with a strong emphasis on ancestor worship and civic worship as ways of sacralizing the state.[46] Hardacre notes that "as Shinto drew closer to the state, its alliance with the nationalistic, chauvinistic patriotism of the times and its assumption of a pseudo-obligatory character increasingly divided the priesthood from parishioners, whose attachment to shrines continued to be religious in character."[47]

Whatever the fortunes of Shinto priests or details of the oscillation between defining Shinto as a religion and as a state cult, and however much Western concepts were applied to the definition of religion, the basic conception of the conflation of the sacral-national and the civic arenas continued to predominate in Japan. One of the most interesting and paradoxical aspects of this definition of religion in specifically "Western" terms was that religion in this sense was effectively bracketed out of the realm of the sacral.

XIV   The conception of society, as symbolized by the emperor, having a strong sacral component—the separation between state and religion notwithstanding—can be seen to the present day in the combination of secular and religious, or rather sacral, Shinto ceremonies connected with the enthronement or death of emperors.[48] It was these ceremonies that celebrated the transformation of the emperor that took place in the Meiji era.

Peter Nosco has succinctly stated the contemporary problematic of this implicit sacralization of the state and the emperor in the following way:

> In November of this year . . . the new emperor will participate in a sequence of ceremonial activities that will officially confirm and complete his imperial accession in Japan as the emperor of the current Heisei period. The most religious and in that sense "mysterious" of these ceremonies are those known collectively as the *daijōsai,* and it is these which are generating considerable controversy in Japan and internationally.
>
> The key issue in this controversy is deceptively simple and embarrassingly obvious: Why, if the emperor is not and does not regard himself as a divine descendant of the Shinto deity Amaterasu, should he participate in ceremonies which at least some believe will transform him into a living deity?[49]

A rather similar issue has been exposed by many others—for instance in Felicia Bock's commentary on the contemporary enthronement ceremony: "Today, the postwar constitution purports to separate church and state, religion and government, but the distinction between the two areas, like other concepts introduced from an alien culture, is far from clear."[50]

This does not mean that wide sectors of the population believe in the partial divinity of the emperor or of the imperial position, or that the imperial symbolism plays a central part in their daily life and conduct. Indeed, it seems that the enthronement was not even viewed by large sectors of the population, and the element of sacral devotion was certainly rather weak, as was probably also true with respect to the burial ceremonies of Hirohito. Nevertheless, the emperor symbolism, however vague, retains some central charismatic qualities; however skeptical people may be of its "validity," yet no other symbol has so permeated the daily consciousness of large sectors of Japanese society as to displace it as the sign of the national community.[51] Even if much of this symbolism as well as that of *kokutai* has become, as Winston Davis puts it, "an empty shell," it is probably the only shell available.[52]

THE LOOSENESS AND HEGEMONY OF THE MEIJI IDEOLOGY

XV The Meiji ideology or civic religion did not crystallize all at once, nor was it all-pervasive; Carol Gluck has demonstrated that not all sectors of the population fully identified with it, were committed to it, or accepted it at face value.[53] It was also not free of internal contradictions and tensions, as, for instance, with respect to the construction of the emperor's legitimacy in the constitution.

The most important inherent contradictions concerned the grounding of the knowledge in terms of which the ideology was legitimized, whether, that is, it was rooted in nature or in some primordial myth; the closely related tension between the search for enlightenment and national aggrandizement; that between the national restorative vision and more pragmatic attitudes and policies; and perhaps especially that between the orientation toward collectivity and the emphasis on economic advancement and achievement with its potential individualistic, materialistic, and egoistical orientations.

It was also in many ways a relatively loose ideology, comprising many different elements.[54] But it was this ideology that became the dominant one in the Meiji polity and society and, as we shall see later, in Taishō Japan. For all its looseness and contradictions, however, it was this ideology that set the parameters of the discourses of various sectors of society, especially leading ones, with respect to newly emerging social problems. Even most of its opponents—whether intellectual groups or popular sectors—rarely transcended its basic premises and parameters.[55] The problems that this ideology faced, from at least the end of the Meiji era if not before that, were generated by the continuous economic development and changes, the social unrest they generated, and the growing distance between the older generation, for whom the establishment of a strong Japan was a great dream, and the younger one, which took the existence of such an order for granted and lacked any strong commitment to it.

The major oppositional responses to these problems were constructed around the evaluation of the newly emerging "modern" capitalistic bureaucratic reality—the growing urbanization and industrialization—in terms of some pristine vision. On the extreme right there developed the nationalistic response that negated the new mundane reality compromised by growing materialism and egoism. On the extreme left, especially among many Marxist intellectuals, there developed a total negation of the existing order—yet also a continuous intellectual struggle to understand it in Marxist terms. But neither of these two visions could—as we shall see in chapter 4—develop fully fledged political programs capable of competing with or undermining the Meiji ideology.[56]

Some individuals and groups, especially on the left and to some extent among Christians, challenged the ideology—often at great cost as the challengers were imprisoned and repressed. But however great their commitment to breaking through the confines of ideology, they had little impact on the wider public—even if their heroism was admired—or on the basic modes of political discourse in Meiji, Taishō, and early Shōwa Japan.[57]

The tensions between the more pragmatically oriented groups and the more extreme nationalistic visionaries, who denounced the pragmatic solution, however, were of great direct consequence in the playground of Meiji and Taishō politics. For instance, the various bearers of the pristine national *kokutai* vision—army groups, younger military officers, and right-wing intellectuals—played an important role in numerous military expeditions and in the attempts at a coup in the 1930s; they also exerted an important influence in creating the background for the Pacific War.[58] But even they could not break through the basic parameters of the Meiji ideology.

XVI The fact that none of the opponents of the dominant ideology was able to break through it effectively and create a viable, alternative political program acceptable to wider sectors of the population, can be illustrated with respect to the tension or contradiction between, on the one hand, the Meiji ideology's potential orientation toward individualistic achievement and, on the other, its collectivity-oriented framework.

Although an emphasis on achievement was promulgated early on by the Meiji ideologists, it was not until the last decade of the Meiji era and the early Taishō period that more utilitarian, achievement-oriented tendencies developed, giving rise to the image of the self-made man and contradicting the naive communal vision. It was then that the promulgators of the ideology attempted to encompass such potentially individualistic orientations within the basic framework set up by the national ideology of *kokutai* and to bind them to the overall collective goal of modernizing Japan and making it strong on the international scene. Thus Meiji educators stressed the importance of practicability as against either principled individualism or materialism, in order to offset the politically subversive effects of these orientations.[59]

This emphasis on practicability reinforced the strong tendency toward the depoliticization of the public arena. Most attempts in the direction of principled individualism were defined as egoistical. Thus while such individualistic attitudes could become very widespread, they did not become geared toward constructive social or political activity or the reconstruction of an autonomous civil society with access to the centers of political power. Rather, they tended to breed political apathy, cynicism, and withdrawal into the private realm.

These responses were also reinforced by another major contradiction that developed within the Meiji ideology—namely the growing awareness, in many sectors of society, that this ideology was something not natural, but basically arbitrary and potentially oppressive. This awareness became especially acute after the first decades of the Meiji era, with the passing away of the semiheroic figures of the Restoration, the growing confrontation between the original vision of the Restoration and the more diversified one that was developing, and the growing tensions that accompanied urbanization, industrialization, consumerism, and the emergence of a social and economic order that certainly went beyond the rustic imagery of the original Meiji ideology.[60]

The tendencies among many in intellectual circles to withdraw from politics were also reinforced by more general trends toward what has sometimes been designated hedonistic consumerism, which started to develop already in the Taishō era and gathered momentum thereafter.

While these contradictions had far-reaching implications for the structure of political life in Meiji and Taishō Japan, and gave rise to reformulations of many of its basic premises, they did not lead to a radical transformation of these premises, even when, as in the Taishō era, the awareness of their arbitrariness became highly intensified. Rather, as Harootunian has shown,

> it was this and the consciousness of the basic arbitrariness of the Meiji orthodoxy, I would suggest, that produced the search, common to all the ideologues described in the essays [in the volume edited by Silberman and Harootunian] for a universal source of moral behavior that could transform the public order, that would fulfill the need for and firmly establish the relationship between private moral impulse and society. For some, the arbitrary secularism of the administrative state was so oppressive that they sought to withdraw from the public into a private world that fed, often destructively, upon itself in the search for creative tension. For others, this awareness that society was an object of will led them to attempt to contest the Meiji bureaucrats' conception that administrative law alone encompassed the kokutai—the imperial will. Indeed, the ideologues of Taishō, viewing politics as an arena or marketplace in which men without moral

convictions sought to impose their will, came finally to reject all politics as corrupt.[61]

Yet another important illustration of the strength of this hegemony can be seen in the transformation of the attitude towards Buddhism and of the Buddhists' own self-definition. Starting from the persecution of Buddhism in the early stages of the Meiji era, and through the continuous regulation of Buddhism by the government, the orientation of Buddhist intellectuals and the image of Buddhism in the Japanese collective consciousness was slowly but significantly transformed. As James Ketelaar has shown, the image of Buddhists changed over time, from heretics to martyrs to the "true bearers" of Japanese (and hence Asian) culture. Such change was closely connected with the transformations of the Buddhist self-perception and image that developed out of attempts to purify Buddhism from sectarian canonical tendencies and to create a unified narrative "designed to produce a unity of spirit, society and civilization: very much in line with the basic premises of Meiji ideology."[62]

The same is true, as we shall see soon, of the more "romantic," traditionalist opposition to the Meiji state and its ideology. Thus, the various contradictions of the Meiji ideology gave rise to great skepticism regarding many of its tenets, even to the discarding of some of its concrete components, but not to its transformation—nothing, that is, transcended it. Needless to say, the concrete contours and contexts of this ideology have undergone many changes, especially after the Second World War. But even then, many of its basic tenets, especially the emphasis on the distinctiveness of the national collectivity, defined in primordial-natural (if perhaps less sacral) terms, were retained.

Yet at the same time, critical evaluations of the contradictions of the Meiji ideology, and of consumerism and the like, gave rise to numerous social and cultural spaces in which new forms of cultural creativity were tried out, and rapid economic changes created many spaces in which to try out new styles of life.[63] The discussions and popular cultural activities that developed in these spaces were often subversive of the hegemonic mold and skeptical about its ideological premises, but even they could not break through these premises. They did, however, become, as we shall see in chapters 4 and 6, important starting points for the widening of political discourse in Japan, giving rise to the broadening of the range of themes of such discourse.

XVII One of the most interesting derivatives of the ideology of the Meiji period—with its construction of the conception of the national community in traditional, semiarchaic and semimythological terms—lies in the way it reconstructed Japanese tradition.

The Meiji elites—and to a lesser degree those of the Taishō period, and the different periods of the Shōwa reign—continuously legitimized the new modes of life by reference to Japanese tradition. This tradition was a new construct, which built on existing, more dispersed and localized traditions, but organized them in more formalized, bureaucratic ways.

This was true, as we have seen, of the cult of the emperor itself. Such formalization and bureaucratization of tradition was also to be seen in the supervision of religious organizations and events, including, as W. Davis has shown, the great pilgrimage to the Ise shrine by the authorities.[64] It was also evident in the appropriation of many local traditions by the organs of the center, coupled with the denial of the validity of local autonomy, and in the suppression, or at least segregation, of attempts by various local or popular groups to maintain or construct distinct, autonomous local cultures.[65]

Many activities and organizations, old and new, were legitimized in the name of tradition and traditionalism. This general orientation—promulgated by the elites but accepted also to no small extent by broader sectors of the society as well as by many groups of intellectuals—constituted a central focus of social and political discourse, which the elites and the state attempted to monopolize by virtue of their representing the imperial symbols. While they were not always successful in doing so, the very fact that the Meiji regime was legitimated in such terms, and the concomitant bureaucratic reconstruction and appropriation of "tradition" and traditionalism, had some interesting implications for the cultural and political discourse that developed in modern and contemporary Japan. These included attempts to develop autonomous traditional spaces, not only in segregated local areas, but also in more central intellectual arenas.

The most important such repercussion was that in many arenas of discourse—for instance, in the attempts by Origuchi, Shinobu, and Karatani to construct a theory of national literature[66] as an integral criticism of political institutions—the orientation toward tradition gave rise to the construction of an ahistorical natural space that was, in a way, bracketed out of the social and political scene, providing no bases for distinct autonomous participation in this scene.[67] One of the most interesting such results can be seen the development of folklore studies in Japan, especially those connected with the name and work of Yanagita Kunio.

The school of folklore studies that Yanagita and his followers sponsored was indeed one of the most influential ones to develop in Japan in the first decades of this century. Its central concern was to search for the most authentic expressions of Japanese culture—in a way seemingly not dissimilar from that of many schools of folklore that developed in close relation to romantic and national movements in nineteenth-century Europe. Yet on both the intellectual and political level, it differed rather sharply from most of these European movements. The crucial intellectual difference was, as Harootunian has pointed out, in Yanagita's approach (and that of other scholars of the Taishō period) to history. Yanagita conceived of culture in such a way that "ethology sought to project a narrative while the folk constituted a 'primal given' natural and prior to the artificial system of society. Culture, now posing as nature, became the great antagonist of history . . . thereby setting the stage for a new national subjectivity."[68]

Politically this approach represented, as Victor Koschman has pointed out, a conservative counterutopia.[69] Precisely because it was oriented both against bourgeois liberalism and the bureaucratic state, the political effect of this counterutopia was rather limited.[70] This antiutopian stance, with all its inherent limitations, is indicative of the problems of "genuine" romantic, conservative protest in a society whose center has appropriated traditional symbols, or rather symbols of tradition, and tried to formalize them and imbue them with a "total," "legal" orientation and vision of history. Thus it attests yet again, from yet another vantage point, to the durability of the seemingly relatively loose hegemonic Meiji ideology.

THE MEIJI STATE IN A COMPARATIVE PERSPECTIVE

XVIII   The various specific characteristics of the Meiji state and society have given rise to a variety of attempts to put it in a comparative framework.[71] Some of the first such attempts were based on the explication of some implications of Herbert Norman's work by Perry Anderson and, more recently, by Johann Arnason, both of whom designate the Meiji state as an absolutist one.[72] But the Meiji state cannot really be so designated. Despite the fact that it exhibited strong absolutist tendencies, absolutism cannot be seen as its core character because its context was radically different from that of the early modern absolutist states in Europe. This is evidenced, among other places, in the relatively high level of social mobilization and of economic development it spawned, which are characteristic not of the absolutist era but of the modern nineteenth century.

Given these distinctive characteristics of the Meiji state, of the dominant ideology and its institutional corollaries, and of the measures—often repressive and manipulative—through which this ideology was promulgated, it is not surprising that the Meiji state and the later military regime of the 1930s have often been compared with modern authoritarian or totalitarian regimes. Yet the similarity is at most only part of the truth, and in many ways the comparison is misleading and does not contribute to an understanding of the specific dynamics of modern Japanese state and society.

The Meiji regime cannot be seen as just another semitraditional or modernizing authoritarian state aiming—as, for instance, in Franco's regime in Spain or Salazar's in Portugal—to minimize the political involvement and mobilization of the periphery. In contrast, the Meiji oligarchy and bureaucracy undertook a strong and active policy of permeation of the periphery.

From this point of view it might then be seen as very similar to modern postrevolutionary regimes, whether the French or the more totalitarian Russian or even Chinese versions. Yet the mobilization of the periphery by the Meiji center was not intended to restructure the periphery in terms of some universalistic or utopian vision. Nor was it effected by overall coercive measures, although repressive measures abounded in the activities of the center. Rather, the center emphasized a combination of the primordial sacral components of the Japanese collectivity as a whole—embodied in the semimythical figure of the emperor—and the alleged virtues of communal harmony at the periphery. It promoted the total identity of center and periphery in these terms, and not in terms of some new vision which would stand in contrast to that upheld by the preceding regime or by the periphery.

The emphasis of official Meiji ideology was on expanding the "old" ideology, even if this ideology was in fact a new construct. To quote Carol Gluck again:

> Injunctions to filiality, affection, harmony, modesty, and benevolence—whether labeled Confucian or not—were indeed part of the familiar code of customary social morality. And the exhortation to loyalty and the link to the imperial ancestors and *kokutai*, though not part of the ethos of "all the people," were common enough in elite opinion in most sectors and on most levels of society not to excite great comment.[73]

Indeed the civil religion promulgated by the Meiji ideology extolled and emphasized what it defined as the traditional virtues of the folk religion, the village community, and the common man, defined without reference to any social or cultural division—class, religion, or ethnicity.

The image of the village community promulgated in these ideologies was a new construct reflecting nonexistent entities. It imposed, in W. Davis's words, an ideological unity on an hitherto diversified world. But it found considerable resonance in many of the basic tenets of folk attitudes and created a strong bond between village and nation. This bond was based on the extension of primordial family and kinship themes—the tradition of the *ie* group—up to the emperor as the symbol of the nation.[74] "What began as an assertion of native values and social ethics became a civil morality: an index of loyalty and patriotism *(chūkun ai-koku)* not only for the schools, but for wherever allegiance to the state was an ideological issue."[75]

XIX Ideological differences between the Meiji regime and the post-revolutionary regimes of Europe and the United States are also evident in the most "material" aspects of the construction of symbols, especially of space and time in architectural works, and in the promulgation of festivities and the like. In the French Revolution, as analyzed by Mona Ozouf, Lynn Hunt, and others,[76] and the Russian Revolution, such constructions aimed at the destruction of the symbols of the old, hierarchical order and the assertion of a strong egalitarian ethos oriented to the future and rooted in universalistic premises.[77] This was also the case, even if in a different mode, in the far-reaching changes in the internal architecture of churches effected by Protestantism and especially by Puritan groups, which were so important in the English and American revolutions.

As against this, in Meiji Japan the symbols and symbolic constructs promulgated by the bearers of the official ideology, whether in the constitution, the civil code, or the rescript on education—and their appropriation and reconstruction of tradition, which included the use of existing religious settings, especially the Shinto shrines, for the promulgation of their ideology—continuously emphasized the sanctity of an ostensibly older primordial-sacral hierarchical order, even if these "traditional" themes were actually entirely new constructs. The Meiji ideology, which emphasized the familylike relation between the nation and the emperor and the continuity between family and imperial ancestor worship, in reality went far beyond what the emperor symbolism might have meant in the medieval and early modern periods.

Differences of no less importance developed between the processes in the Meiji state and in Western postrevolutionary democratic-constitutional or totalitarian regimes through which the center permeated the peripheries.

Common to all of these regimes was, as we have seen, the establishment of wide administrative, educational, local governmental, and military frameworks. In the Western postrevolutionary and totalitarian regimes these agencies—whatever their actual performance and achievement—purportedly aimed at the total reconstruction of society. In Japan, however, the center pretended to strengthen existing organizations and sectors of the periphery, although in fact many of them were created by the very processes of modernization generated by the center.[78]

Moreover, the center in Japan developed few special organizations, such as the mass parties of the totalitarian regimes, that aimed at the mobilization and restructuring of the periphery. Rather, it guided the various sectors of the society—most of which were almost entirely reconstructed by the Meiji policies—by means of suppression, manipulation, and other "schoolmaster" modes of regulation and by legitimizing them in traditional, often semiarchaic and semimythological, terms.

It was these characteristics of the first modern Meiji center that produced the initial institutional frameworks of modern Japan, as we shall see in the subsequent chapters, frameworks within which the specific course of modern Japanese society has developed.

Modern and Contemporary Japan
Institutional Formations

I The institutional and ideological characteristics of the Meiji "school-master" state analyzed above crystallized from about the late 1880s, the second decade of the Meiji reign, until the death of the Meiji emperor, Mutsuhito, in 1912. By that time—especially since the Russo-Japanese war—Japan was recognized as an international power with strong imperialist ambitions.

It was also in this period that there started to develop in Japan, if rather slowly, a more diversified, modernized, and urbanized economic and social structure, more like that of other modern industrial nations of the period.

By the second decade of the century the question of whether Japan's development would follow a course basically similar to that of other modern industrial countries or would go on a different road began to be of great interest both to the Japanese and to others, especially in the West. This question continues to loom large in public and academic discourse in and about Japan. It became especially acute in periods of great turmoil and social change: the early Meiji period; the Taishō, in which it seemed that a liberal democracy might be instituted in Japan; during the emergence of the military regime in the 1930s; and, perhaps even more forcefully, in the first decade after the Second World War, when a fully fledged constitutional democratic regime was crystallized. The developments in these periods could be, and were, both in Japan and in the West, compared with similar or parallel ones in other modern societies—at various times, with the establishment of liberal democratic, fascist totalitarian, and constitutional regimes in different European societies.

The changes that occurred in the modern period have in many ways been even more far-reaching than those that resulted from the impact of Buddhism and Confucianism, which we shall discuss later on. The Meiji Ishin ushered in, as we have seen, far-reaching processes of modernization.

While the changes in the Taishō period were less dramatic (they were basically the consequences of changes during the Meiji era) there developed in this period a growing social mobility, a plethora of new, active, seemingly autonomous political parties, great intellectual and political ferment, and many other changes that appeared to point to growing liberalism and democracy. The establishment of the military regime in the 1930s was in many ways a reaction to some of the political repercussions of these processes. It reversed many of these changes but not the processes of economic development or of social mobility.

Most dramatic and far reaching were the changes that took place after the Second World War: the promulgation of a democratic constitution, the abolition of the emperor system and official desacralization of the emperor, the restructuring of many arenas of life, the full legitimation of political parties, the institutionalization of freedom of the press, the granting of equal rights to women, far-reaching land reform, and, ultimately, the ushering in of economic development and industrialization and the growth of standards of living and of consumer orientations. Concomitantly there took place the intensive development of mass media and the unprecedented opening up of new arenas of public discussion.[1]

The changes that took place in these periods of transition were connected with the impingement of external political and cultural forces, an intensive and dramatic confrontation with other societies or civilizations (as, we shall see later, was also the case with the dissemination of Confucianism and Buddhism). Accordingly, many of these changes were patterned after conditions prevalent in other civilizations. Hence, in all these periods there arose the problem of the extent to which changes in Japan would be patterned according to the basic principles and orientations of other civilizations.

II The relation between change in Japan and change in other civilizations has not been just an academic question, of interest mainly from the point of view of comparative research. It pertained also to the basic principles guiding the crystallization of concrete institutional arrangements—of the political, industrial, and educational systems, for example. Throughout the Meiji, Taishō, and Shōwa periods this issue was the focus of intense internal debate. Debates coalesced around several basic themes, the common denominator of which was the applicability in Japan of the orientations inherent in the transcendental premises of the new, "external" ideologies and their possible institutional derivatives. In other words the specific modern and contemporary question was whether or to what extent the various universalistic, egalitarian, and both individualistic and communitarian premises presumed inherent in modernization were to predominate in shaping the major institutions of Japanese society (as had the universalistic premises inherent in Confucianism and Buddhism). Most of these debates—with the partial exception of that following the Second World War—focused on the problem of legitimating the new political system and the place of the emperor and imperial symbolism within it and on the major characteristics of Japanese collectivity and collective identity in relation to the broader civilizational frameworks and ideologies that impinged on it.

Many of these discussions followed on debates that developed—as we shall see later—in the Tokugawa period, in the discourse within and around neo-Confucianism, when questions concerning the possibility of the emperor's reigning under the Mandate of Heaven, the divinity of the emperor, and the relation of the Japanese collectivity to the overarching East Asian, especially Chinese-Confucian, civilization constituted the major foci of debate. During the Meiji and to a large extent also the Taishō period, it was the legitimation of the new, modern, political system in terms of the newly constructed emperor symbolism—as against some version of popular sovereignty—and the implications of such legitimation for constitutional arrangements, above all for the locus of accountability of authorities, that constituted one of the major foci of such debates.

In the Taishō period the focus of the debate was the possibility and extent of the liberalization and opening up of the oligarchic features of the Meiji system, and the scope of political participation. Special emphasis was put on the possibility of instituting a "real" party system, with the cabinet being responsible to a legislature constituted by the parties, and on the growing liberalization of many aspects of public life, of the press, of the scope of private associations, and the like. The debate on participation focused on the age for suffrage (twenty-one or twenty-five years), and on the exclusion of those who might harbor "dangerous" thoughts and of women. A seemingly obverse question emerged in the mid-1930s with the ascendance of the military regime—namely, to what extent this regime was a fascist or totalitarian one.

During and in the decade immediately after the American occupation the major issue in such debates was the kind of democratic regime to be instituted—whether it would be, as one scholar has put it, an institutional or a participatory democracy.[2]

In this period the concrete issues were, first, the nature and possible scope of the opposition in general, and of a socialist or labor opposition in particular; second, the impact of the political participation of different sectors of society and of various movements of protest; and third, the influence of public debate and protest movements on policy making, and the importance of principled as against pragmatic, very often informal, "pork barrel" politics.

In all these periods the problem of the basic characteristics of the Japanese collectivity in relation to the broader international settings served as yet another focus of debate. This debate has gone on since then under different guises, as has the debate about the validity of the transcendental and universalistic orientations promulgated by these foreign civilizations.

What then was the impact on the format of major Japanese institutions of the tremendous changes that transpired as a result of policies initiated by the Meiji government? Did these changes give rise to institutional formations that were similar overall to Western ones, with only local variations, or were they shaped in distinctly Japanese modes? The answer to these questions was shaped by the continual interaction between the numerous processes of intensive change within modern Japanese society, and by the basic policy orientations and ideological premises of the Meiji state. It is this interaction and its outcome that constitutes, as it were, the stuff of contemporary Japanese history.

Thus, in all these periods there arose, in one way or another, the problem which is central to the understanding and self-understanding of modern and contemporary Japanese society, and which constitutes also the central problem of our analysis—namely what kind of capitalism, what kind of political democracy, what kind of modern society in general developed in Japan. This and the following three chapters will be devoted to the analysis of this problem.

III   In the following sections we shall examine the major institutional arenas of modern Japan—its political economy, patterns of industrial relations, and educational and political systems—as they developed in the Meiji period, crystallized at the end of the Meiji and the beginning of the Taishō, and developed throughout the (pre–Second World War) Taishō and Shōwa eras. We shall consider also the impact on the shaping of these institutional formations of social, economic, political, and ideological forces from abroad, and of the numerous processes of change and movements of protest that developed within Japan.

Such analysis will throw light on the extent to which the basic policies of the Meiji schoolmaster state—its opening up of new economic and occupational frameworks to large sectors of the society and the concomitant development of far-reaching mobility and of social mobilization into the new institutional framework continuously guided so as to minimize autonomous political expression—continued after the Meiji period to shape the distinctive features of the modern and contemporary Japanese system.

POLITICAL ECONOMY:
THE JAPANESE MODE OF CAPITALISM

IV We shall start with an analysis of modern Japanese political economy. A good way to begin looking at its specific characteristics is by asking to what extent its structure approximates a pure capitalist market—bearing in mind, of course, that no real modern or contemporary society or economy fully replicates this model. We will observe that the Japanese system is characterized by certain features which crystallized, as Andrew Gordon has shown with respect to industrial relations,[3] in the first decades of the twentieth century and which have, in broad outline, albeit with great changes in detail, persisted until now.

The major orientations of the policies that crystallized under the Meiji—the diversification of the economy, the opening up of new economic arenas, and their incorporation of continuously expanding social sectors—were combined at various times with different modes of governmental and bureaucratic guidance oriented toward the implementation of collective goals. These goals included the creation of a strong nation-state, the development of military strength, economic development, and the maintenance of the existing internal political order.

The distinctive characteristics of Japanese political economy developed from the combination or confrontation of the major orientations and policies of the ruling elites with the processes of economic development and social diversification. They distinguish this mode of political economy from other capitalist systems and make it probably the farthest removed from the pure market model.

The most important among these organizational characteristics were the relatively strong guidance of the economy by the government and other "nonmarket" institutions, especially by the various bureaucracies; a concomitant emphasis on planning, already apparent at the beginning of the Meiji regime but especially prominent in the period after the Second World War; and the distinctive, interlocking internal organization of the basic economic production units, that is, the industrial firms, and the closely related, also distinctive pattern of industrial relations.

Let's now examine these general characteristics in somewhat greater detail.

V Guidance by the government, and especially by various sections of the bureaucracy, of the development of economic policy has been characteristic of modern Japanese political economy since its crystallization in the Meiji period. This guidance is closely related to yet another basic characteristic of the modern Japanese economic system, namely planning, albeit a distinctive type of planning that, though characterized by a long-range vision, took a much more flexible approach to the actual implementation of goals than is usually connected with centralized planning.[4] Such long-range planning has deep historical roots; it can be identified already in the seventh century, in the attempts of the state to regulate demographic expansion in relation to arable land. In Meiji Japan it was usually undertaken by governmental units in consultation with other actors, although often without full coordination between the plans of different bureaucrats. Such guidance, already found in the deliberations about the future economic system that took place in the early phases of the Meiji state,[5] became especially prominent after the Second World War.

Governmental guidance in Japan did not entail the development, along the line of the Communist regimes that later developed in Russia and China, of a master plan that would regulate all aspects of the economy and, in principle, obviate the working of market forces. Rather, such planning entailed the crystallization of a general framework and direction for the development of market forces as well as more direct regulation.

> Already in 1884 the Kōgyō Iken (Advice for the Encouragement of Industry) was published. The original Japanese edition consists of thirty volumes of varied qualitative and quantitative information about the economy and society on both a national and a regional basis. It provides us with the most vivid and detailed picture available of economic activity in the beginnings of modern economic growth. Also, as its title suggests, it sets up a program of economic development. Over-all national objectives, targets for a ten-year time span, and a set of recommended policies—all these ingredients of present-day development plans—were clearly set forth in the Kogyo Iken. In this sense, it might be considered the world's first economic development plan.[6]

Harry Rosovsky identifies seven basic orientations in the Kōgyō Iken: (1) orientation toward the long run; (2) emphasis on saving and thrift; (3) concern with quality; (4) suspicion of foreigners; (5) emphasis on knowledge of markets; (6) exploitation of indigenous strengths; and (7) a certain desire for regulation, order, and guidance; or, from an economic point of view, the desire to avoid excessive competition.[7]

Guidance and planning throughout these periods were concerned not only, as after the Second World War, with the promotion of economic growth or, as in the earlier periods, with the combination of economic growth and political and military aggrandizement. They were also oriented toward maintaining support for the political system, whether by taking care of the interests of special groups, like farmers, or by ensuring some minimal social conditions to broader sectors of society, especially those like workers and the peasantry, with potential political power. In the period after the Second World War—but to some extent already before—it was above all, as Johnson has noted, a developmental planning guided by different collective considerations, rather than a totalitarian planning oriented to overall control of the economy.[8]

Within the framework of such guidance and given the emphasis on broad collective goals, purely economic considerations and discrete interests of particular business, labor, or peasant groups were often secondary, although they were usually taken into account in the intensive processes of consultation between the politicians and bureaucrats in other sectors. These interests were, however, continuously gaining autonomy within the general framework of the guided economy.

There also developed throughout these periods policies oriented toward the structuring of industrial relations—a process which started in the beginning of this century[9]—as well as far-reaching distributive policies, whether in the form of subsidies to farmers, potential house purchasers, and the like or of direct welfare disbursements.[10]

Governmental guidance of the economy in turn had several important characteristics: First—in line with basic conceptions of authority and its exercise prevalent in most sectors of Japanese society—such guidance took the forms of consultation and delegation of authority rather than direct commands.[11] Second, as Lincoln has indicated, Japan eschewed government ownership or sponsorship of "national champions": "The more common pattern is encouragement of industrial structures with a relatively small number of firms which may be forced to share technology (to prevent a single firm from gaining an overwhelming position) and in which quasi-cartel arrangements keep domestic prices high, but fully permit ferocious competition over product development."[12] Third, the relatively extensive state direction of investment that developed in the initial phases of the Taishō and Shōwa periods was based to no small degree on capital mobilized from household savings invested in relatively low-interest accounts (such as in the postal savings bank), on a deemphasis of consumers' interests, and on a high level of productive investment. While the specific methods used to mobilize capital have changed over time, these overall tendencies have persisted. It is only lately, under pressure from other countries, especially Japan's trading partners, and to some extent from within Japan, that consumers' interests have come increasingly to the fore.[13]

The government's guidance of the economy has not always taken the form of direct intervention. Indeed, in the first third of the twentieth century there developed in Japan a rather strong emphasis on laissez-faire—but even this was mostly based on considerations of the collective good. Nor does the importance of government guidance mean that capitalist economic entrepreneurs have been passive. There can be no doubt that it was they—both the great and the smaller ones—who were, after the first push to industrialization in the early Meiji era, the most active element in the economic process.[14] The mode of their operation entailed, however, a continual interrelation with the bureaucracy—which took rather distinctive forms.

VI The second major characteristic of the Japanese political economy was the close interlocking of economic units, which initially developed during the Meiji regime. Three major types of such interlocking developed during this period, one in the relations between major firms, another in those between the large firms and their small contractors and subcontractors, and the third, of special importance for the structuring of industrial relations, in those between large companies and their workers' unions.

While the concrete contours of this interlocking changed greatly throughout modern Japanese history, some general characteristics persisted. The notorious *zaibatsu* of the first stages of Japan's modern economic history, up to the Second World War, was, of course, the first well-known illustration of such interlocking between large enterprises. But even after the dismantling of *zaibatsu* during the American occupation, new modes of interlocking, such as the *keiretsu*, continuously developed. Such interlocking is characterized by

> 1) strong affiliational ties, which create vast spheres of economic life intermediate between anonymous markets and vertically interpreted firms; 2) long term relationships . . . relying on defining sets of obligations extending over time; 3) multiplexity, manifest in the overlapping of transaction with equity, in vertical and personal interlocks used to consolidate financial, commercial and other business ties; 4) extended networks, which set up bilateral relationships in the context of a broader framework of related companies; 5) symbolic signification effected through the infusion of intercorporate relationship with symbolic importance, even in the absence of formal legal arrangements or contracts."[15]

On the contemporary scene the most important such interlockings—with strong roots in the past—center around the major banks. These interlockings have, of course, made it difficult for foreign firms to penetrate Japanese markets.

The second type of interlockings has been that between the large firms and their subcontractors—usually small firms, often family ones, which often employ temporary personnel. R. Dore has analyzed some of the most important aspects of these relations:

> Here is another of those timeless generalizations about "capitalist econo-
> mies" about which Japan gives pause. Transaction costs for large Japanese
> firms may well be lower than elsewhere. "Opportunism" may be a lesser
> danger in Japan because of the explicit encouragement, and actual preva-
> lence, in the Japanese economy of what one might call moralized trading
> relationships of mutual goodwill. The stability of the relationship is the
> key. Both sides recognize an obligation to try to maintain it. . . .
>
> It is a system, to use a distinction common in the Williamson school, of
> relational contracting rather than spot-contracting—or to use Williamson's
> more recent phrase, "obligatory contracting." More like a marriage than a
> one-night-stand, as Robert Solow had said about the modern employment
> relation. The rules of chastity vary. As is commonly the case, for those at
> the lower end of the scale, monogamy is the rule.[16]

Gary Hamilton and R. C. Feenstra have aptly characterized these relations in the following way:

> Japanese business groups, the *keiretsu,* represent another type of vertically
> controlled hierarchical networks. In these networks, the large firms at the
> top of the hierarchy are mutually owned through overlapping sharehold-
> ing. Corporate control and economic decision-making, however, is not
> centralized as it is in most family-owned business groups, but rather is
> somewhat decentralized and tends to be co-terminous with production se-
> quences (i.e., commodity chains) leading to the production of a common
> group of products. These very large corporatized and mutually owned
> networks dominate the markets for intermediate inputs, labor intensive
> operations, and services. These networks, therefore, have positions of con-
> siderable economic power vis-à-vis the thousands of small and medium
> sized firms that supply goods and service to them on a long-term non-
> contractual basis under conditions generally favorable to *keiretsu* firms.[17]

Within the small firms, which were for long periods of time nu-
merically predominant in the Japanese economy, there developed very
strong paternalistic-clientilistic relations of the Oyabun-Kobun ("patron-
client") type, which had some common elements with the pattern of corporate paternalism that developed within the larger ones.

VII The last type of interlocking, that between companies and their
workers and unions, is manifest above all in the "company unions" often
singled out as the distinctive feature of the Japanese industrial relations
system. But it is also found in the more confrontational unions in the

public sector, as well as those in the weaker sector of the Japanese economy—the various smaller firms or companies—even if the unions in this sector are much weaker than those in the larger companies or the public sector.[18] In the public sector the unions have tended to be more militant, while in the secondary sector, composed of small companies and a very segmented labor force, appropriate conditions for the development of active union organizations have not existed.[19]

Closely related to this interlocking between firms and their unions is the pattern of industrial relations that has developed in Japan. Among the most important characteristics of this system, especially since the Second World War, are the relative preponderance, in the majority of great companies, of lifelong (until retirement) job security, a seniority-based salary system, and company unions; a relatively low level of unionization in the weaker sector; and a low level of labor participation in economic policy making combined with a strong emphasis on continuous mediation in labor disputes.[20] These characteristics of the industrial relations system give rise to what T. J. Pempel has described as corporatism without labor, a low level of strikes, and a generally low level of autonomous political activity, as against participation in consultative and mediatory agencies, on the part of the unions.[21]

Labor relations have moved from the more principled contestations about citizenship, the right to strike, and control of the enterprise with strong components of class action, especially in the public sector, which characterized many of the struggles until the end of the 1950s, to an accommodation to the management culture, which has seemed, at least to the leaders of the great unions, to be more beneficial to their members.[22]

These varied patterns of interlocking between economic actors, and especially the central role of banks in such interlocking, attest, as R. Dore has lately shown, to one of the most distinctive characteristics of Japanese capitalism (in contrast to American capitalism and to a lesser extent British capitalism): the stock exchange does not play a central, regulative role in Japanese capitalism. It is above all the banks, in conjunction with various governmental bodies, that perform that role. Thus the Japanese capitalist system is closer to the Continental European systems, especially the German or French ones, than to the American. But the regulatory role of the banks and their interlocking with different ministries and various economic actors seems even stronger in Japan than in either France or Germany.

Such interlocking facilitates also one of the most important features of the economic orientations of most Japanese firms—namely their emphasis on growth and market share as against immediate or short-range profits, a feature closely related to the relatively small importance of the stock market.

VIII Out of the interaction between governmental guidance and the activities of the major economic units described above there developed a
division of the industrial sector between the big companies, which employ about 55 percent of the working force, and the small enterprises—
middle-range and small independent enterprises as well as contracting
firms providing various services to the big enterprises—which employ
about 45 percent. The proportional size of the big and small firms has
undergone constant change. In the 1970s the small industry that remained was linked more closely with the large firms, often for the first
time, and the large firms played a strong role in the technical and managerial modernization of the small firms, thus greatly reducing the dis-
parities between the two segments of the industrial sector and within the
dual labor market.

Closely related to this division of the industrial sector was a highly
segmented labor market, the development of which was reinforced and
fostered by governmental and business policies. This segmentation was
along three main, sometimes intersecting, lines. The first was that between the employees of the great companies, organized in company
unions, in which the system of "permanent employment" (usually until
age fifty-five) and wages based on seniority was prevalent, and those in
smaller firms, where these conditions did not pertain.

The second line, which crossed the first, divided the primary labor
force from a large secondary segment composed mostly of women and
retired people. This secondary labor force included employees from both
large and small companies but especially from smaller businesses; a major
characteristic of these workers was their being relatively temporary, with
weak social security or pension arrangements. The third segment was
composed of a marginal labor force, the real underclass—street laborers,
day laborers, and the like, inhabitants of the *yoseba*, the specific slums.[23]

Between the "strong" and the "weaker" sector of the industrial structure and the labor market there developed a plethora of smaller firms
which have greatly contributed to the innovative and dynamic tendencies
of the Japanese economy. According to some scholars it is they who have
been the main props of the Japanese economic miracle.[24]

IX The various features of the Japanese political economy, of Japanese
capitalism, especially the interlocking between economic actors and the
type of hierarchy developed in Japanese firms, indicate two of its most
distinctive and closely interrelated characteristics: the conception, first,
that the economy is in the service of the nation and not an "autonomous
arena" and, second, that the major actors who engage in economic activities and markets do so within frameworks of "social exchange."[25] These
frameworks leave wide spaces for the working of market forces but also

entail attempts to regulate those forces according to some consideration of social exchange.

The combination of the various forms of interlocking between major economic units and the internal structuring of the firms had a very great impact on the patterns of economic behavior that were of crucial importance for Japanese economic development and performance. To no small degree they account for the great sensitivity of major economic actors to the fluctuations of the international markets, the great predilection for innovation, and the overall high level of economic performance.

The common denominator of these patterns of interlocking was the continual availability of information relevant to economic performance, which enhanced the ability of enterprises to adapt to changing circumstances and encouraged innovation. A strong emphasis on the flow of information also developed within most firms. One of the most important outcomes of these arrangements has been, as Michael Gerlach among others has stressed, "the ability and willingness to experiment, to try new things, and to look outside and learn. . . . Japanese industry has been marked by rapid entry into new fields by firms that have the early and continuing support of affiliated companies."[26]

The potentialities of such innovative tendencies were also connected to the internal structures, especially of the great firms, and to the modes of division of labor, authority, and decision making that developed within them. These are characterized, as Masahilco Aoki and Nathan Rosenberg have shown, by reliance upon on-site information, semihorizontal communications, and ranking hierarchies.[27] They have distinguished this mode of organization as the J-mode, as distinguished from the more horizontal and specialized "Western" H-mode.[28] They examined the advantages and disadvantages of the two modes and came up with the following noteworthy proposition: When environments for planning (e.g., markets, engineering processes, development opportunities) are stable, learning at the operational level may not add much information value to prior planning and the sacrifice of economies of specialization in operational activities may not be worthwhile. On the other hand, if environments are extremely volatile or uncertain, decentralized adaptation to environmental changes may yield highly unstable results.

X   The overall outcome of these types of economic policies and of the modes of economic organization was a story of great economic success, of economic development and industrialization, especially after the Second World War. The economy took off in the mid-1950s, grew rapidly in the 1960s, weathered the oil shocks of the late 1970s, and attained economic ascendancy in the 1980s.[29] During these years Japan created its own production technology and became a major, if not *the* major, international economic and financial power. This was the Japanese economic miracle, manifest first of all in the growth—described by Masumi Junnosuke—of the "employment figure from 36 million in 1950 to 56 million in 1980, while the primary sector fell from 48.3 percent to 10.9 percent[,] with Japan growing from a 50 percent agricultural society to a 10 percent agricultural society during those decades. The tertiary sector climbed from 29.8 percent to 55.4 percent; the secondary sector increased from 21.9 percent to 33.6 percent but hit a ceiling in the 1970s, with its highest point, 34.1 percent, in 1975. (This is [in] contrast with the picture in Europe[;] the first French statistics, in 1856, recorded 51.7 percent for the primary sector. Hence a 50 percent agricultural society may have existed in France between the 1840s and 1860s; yet a 10 percent agricultural society was not reached [in Japan] until the 1970s. According to the first statistics of imperial Germany, in 1882, the primary sector totaled 47.3 percent; we may assume that 50 percent agricultural society existed between the 1850s and 1870s. In 1960 the figure for the agricultural sector dropped to 10 percent. Thus the changes that took a hundred years to accomplish in France and Germany took place in Japan in thirty years, and by the 1970s Japan had reached the same level as these two European countries in terms of the population working in the primary sector.)"[30]

This success was achieved, however, at rather heavy cost, borne mainly by temporary workers, women, retired people, and the lower and marginal classes. Priority was given to the construction of industrial infrastructure. Aspects of such infrastructure oriented toward the development of consumption and improvements in the quality of life, such as the provision of residential facilities, environmental protection, and social welfare programs, were relatively neglected—with the exception of a short period in the late 1960s and early 1970s when public protest and shifting political support brought about a burst of concern with workplace safety. However, even at the end of the Shōwa period, concern for public welfare lagged far behind what one would expect given the high level of per capita income. Compared to those in other industrial countries, housing units remained small, sewer systems appallingly limited in coverage, working hours long, prices for food and manufactured goods astonishingly high, and the penetration of imported manufactured goods extremely low.

XI   These characteristics of the Japanese political economy seem to denote an extremely conservative economic system in which business interests are almost totally dominant. Yet such an assertion, while largely true, presents a very one-sided picture. As the preceding analysis of the major considerations in the guidance and planning of the Japanese economy indicates, the policies promulgated in Japan were oriented also toward what may be called "social" goals, giving rise to combinations of characteristics not found in any other capitalist societies—in particular, conservative business policies and orientations; a relatively weak emphasis on welfare; a low level of income inequality (but not of inequality of assets) and of unemployment as compared with other capitalist societies, at least during the post–Second World War period; and a fairly high degree of responsiveness to demands and pressures of broader, even of lower, social sectors.

This unusual combination of characteristics, combined with a high degree of flexibility in concrete policies, was described by T. J. Pempel as "creative conservatism." It was manifest above all in the macroeconomic shift in the mid-1980s from relatively tight government control of exchange and the money supply to a rather more flexible policy. True enough, this creative conservatism is characteristic of the period from the mid-1950s on. In the first decades of the century a more direct business orientation was prevalent, but even then such an orientation was embedded, as we saw in the preceding chapter, in broader national and to some extent social considerations.

Probably of greatest interest is the rather paradoxical combination of features of the Japanese economy from the point of view of the development of welfare policy and industrial relations. Here several facts are of crucial importance; first is the great changeability of welfare policies, which lagged behind in the 1950s and 1960s, developed intensely in the 1970s, and reversed again in the 1980s. In addition, three aspects of Japanese social economic development—the constantly low level of unemployment; a relatively high level, after the Second World War, of income equality (but not of assets); and the relative peacefulness of labor relations, at least since the late 1970s—make it able, as T. J. Pempel has shown, to "defy its own conservative image."[31]

XII The flexibility that Japanese economic arrangements have exhibited in relatively stable environments might become rigid in more volatile ones.[32] Indeed, much of the recent turbulence in the Japanese economy (e.g., in 1992–93) can be attributed to such rigidity, as was done, for instance, in the recent OECD report on Japan:

> In summary, the Japanese economy is undergoing a period of marked cyclical and structural adjustments to the excesses of the late 1980s boom. The adjustment to a more stable growth path seems likely to be accomplished successfully, avoiding too great a fall-out from the asset price

declines. Nevertheless, because current problems are partly structural in origin, relating to inefficiencies in distribution, financial services, agriculture, construction and real estate, the achievement of sustainable growth requires further substantial structural change. The most important single effect of such restructuring would be to raise the welfare of Japanese households.[33]

Yet at the same time there are indications that very serious attempts are being made to overcome such rigidities—paradoxically, again through deliberate consultative arrangements. Examples include the new agency established to bail banks out of financial crises due to bad loans and the watchdog institution set up to monitor the futures market at the Ministry of Finance (but actually controlled by the latter).

It is as yet too early to say to what extent the Japanese economy will be able to take up the challenges of the recent recession, and to what extent its response will be connected with the radical change of the mode of Japanese economic organization, especially the loosening up or restructuring of the various forms of interlocking.

THE EDUCATIONAL SYSTEM

XIII The general orientations that guided the policies of the Meiji schoolmaster state and were so influential in shaping Japan's modern political economy—the breaking down of previous ascriptive arrangements, great openness and mobility together with strongly paternalistic yet flexible guidance by the government—also shaped the contours of its modern educational system.

These orientations were manifest in the educational arena, first, in the centralization of the school system and curriculum; second, in the emphasis on "moral" guidance and supervision, that is, a strong custodial orientation; third, in a high degree of competitiveness based on a combination of egalitarian starting points and a distinctive meritocratic selective system that gave rise to a highly complex, regulated system of differential status and occupational selection; and, fourth, in the formation of relatively cohesive yet often overlapping status groups or sectors on all levels of the social ladder, especially at the elite level.

The first step in the establishment of a centralized system was made in the early Meiji period. After the Second World War, a more decentralized, "democratic" system was enforced under the occupation, to be reversed, in line with the continuity of the conservative government, from the 1950s on.

"The Meiji leaders," as Richard Rubinger has indicated, "set goals and structures for Japanese education tied directly to the interests of the state, and these remained essentially unchanged until the post–World War II period. The goals included raising minimum academic standards, encouraging progress based on merit, and the use of the school as a primary agent of moral and political socialization." [34]

XIV The custodial of the educational system has been prominent from the early Meiji period on:

> Going back to the Meiji period, the school in Japan has been a major agent of moral and religious socialization. Schools became the institutional nexus linking the family with the polity around a hierarchical ideology that sanctified the relationship among children, their parents, ancestors, and the emperor. By means of school rituals, courses of study, and extracurricular activities, principles in the Shinto and Confucian moral order, such as loyalty, filial piety, the discipline of group life, industry, cleanliness, physical strength, and perseverance, were reinforced.
>
> The role of the school is defined so comprehensively and broadly that it extends to supervisory rights over student behavior outside the school. Almost all elementary and secondary schools have prescribed codes over such matters as clothing and places students may go by themselves and with adults. [35]

The pedagogical vision of learning that pervades this educational system is, as Tom Rohlen has pointed out, strongly oriented toward the acquisition of knowledge, seemingly through imitation. It emphasizes memorizing and the acquisition of clinical knowledge much more than individuality and innovation and stresses the development of character features, like perseverance, rather than of specific skills. [36]

This tutelary paternalistic system combines an emphasis on educational equality with a strong meritocratic orientation, an orientation related to conceptions of achievement and universalism based, not on notions of principled individualism, but on their potential contributions to the national community. The emphasis on equality is manifest in the fact that, in principle, education is open to everybody; no legal obstacles exist to the achievement of high levels of excellence. Concomitantly, the educational system serves also as the most important channel of occupational selection, which is characterized by highly meritocratic orientations imbued with very strong elitist ones.

This selection is organized in a track system, with each of the many tracks conveying a clearly visible level of prestige. The various educational tracks are de facto structured at each level, starting in kindergarten or at the latest elementary school, according to a sharply hierarchical order. On each track the levels are strongly interconnected—that is, each grade school is connected with a specific high school and then university—and the standing of each track is determined above all by the rank of the university to which it leads. Each step in a track prepares the student for the entrance examination to the next step with almost no possibility to change tracks. Such close relations between institutions of similar hierarchical standing at different levels of education has tended to generate many distinct vertical status sets with relatively few horizontal connections between people of "objectively" similar economic or occupational standing. To follow Tom Rohlen:

> Schooling in Japan is a huge sorting machine characterized by meritocracy and competition, a hierarchical and pyramidal structure with elite universities on the top, and prestige differentiation on every level. Individuals are identified and defined by their university credentials, which are absolute yardsticks for measuring the achievement of each individual as well as for determining his position in the social hierarchy.
>
> School segregation is effected by this tracking system as against "openly" through direct class recruitment as in many other Western countries.[37]

The close relation between the different educational levels in each track continues in the occupational arena. Close linkages have developed between educational and occupational institutions at corresponding levels of status, thus extending the seemingly informal but in fact very pervasive hierarchy. Such linkages include, as Rosenbaum and Kariya have shown, agreements between schools and employers whereby an employer commits to hiring a school's students. The students' competition for jobs, and the employers' for dependable sources of labor, is thus shifted out of the markets. In this system, desirable jobs are allocated more on the basis of academic than nonacademic criteria, and achievement has a greater effect on jobs with linked employers than on those with nonlinked employers.[38]

XV The combination of the custodial view of education with a system of meritocratic selection premised on an egalitarian starting point, imbued in practice with a strongly elitist orientation, has to a great extent shaped some of the major distinctive characteristics of Japanese elites and inter-elite relations. Among these features the most important has been the formation of highly cohesive networks between the bureaucratic, academic, and economic elites.[39]

One of the important outcomes of such cohesiveness has been the development of common frameworks of discourse between different elites. The interlocking between groups may be seen from the Western perspective as minimizing the autonomy of the various elites—perhaps especially the intellectuals—and is closely related to some of the distinctive characteristics of Japanese society, especially the weakness of civil society and the mode of structuring public discourse to which we referred in our analysis of the Meiji state. This tendency is illustrated, for instance, by the fact that economic and political planning, while undertaken in cooperation with academics, is often initiated by government bureaucracies.

XVI The relationship between the various elites has, however, undergone far-reaching changes from its beginning in the Meiji era. The major direction of this change, which has become especially visible in the post–Second World War era, is the growing diversification of elites—especially the bureaucratic and business elites.

Until the Second World War the bureaucratic elite (and to some extent the political one), with its roots in the top educational institutions, was predominant. After the war business elites "formed" in different educational institutions gradually acquired greater self-confidence in their relations to the bureaucratic ones—even if they themselves did not form one cohesive elite but were rather segmented. The pattern of consultation between different elites remained as the major mode of relations between them, but the relative importance of different elite sectors changed continually.

XVII This hierarchically structured educational system has generated many tensions, as has been emphasized, especially lately, in Japanese educational circles.

The tracking system's starting point is in principle egalitarian; in practice, however, it is continuously and increasingly mitigated by class and income—that is, by the fact that well-to-do parents can invest in their children's education and hence ensure their advancement into the higher academic tracks.

An important illustration of the impact of class and income on the Japanese educational system can be seen in the relations between public and private schooling as they have developed in different periods in various sectors of Japanese society. These relations have been analyzed by G. Benjamin and E. James:

> They found that public education is primarily limited to compulsory, basic schooling up through the ninth grade for the whole population, and beyond that for only a small elite. At the same time, the government, through partial funding, has encouraged private enterprise to respond to demands for schooling that exceed the carefully regulated public supply.
>
> . . . The number of academic track places in public high schools is limited. As a result, they are oversubscribed. This situation tends to favor upper-class children whose families consider expenditures for private education a good investment and can afford the tutoring fees needed to gain a competitive advantage in examinations. . . .

Working urban-class families who prefer more public academic high school places do not have the political power in these prefectures to bring this about. One exception is Tokyo, where the metropolitan government reformed the elitist aspects of the system. The result was a massive flight of "better students" to private schools.

The public schools, which used to dominate the admissions lists for national public universities, have been replaced by private academic schools in Tokyo. Thus, a reform designed to be egalitarian has had the opposite effect and has helped push private schools to the top of the status hierarchy.[40]

Closely related to this growing class bias, as critics of the system have emphasized, is the relative devaluation of academic degrees, the shrinking of the possibilities of mobility, the weakening of the attraction of universities, and a growing dissatisfaction with the strong ritualization and homogenization of the Japanese school system.

There has also developed growing public criticism of one of the darker sides of the Japanese school system, the bullying of "exceptional," nonconventional students by their classmates—bullying that in some cases has resulted in death.[41] But so far there have been few changes within the educational system. Recently educators have pointed to rising tensions in the system, to demands or needs for growing flexibility and liberalization, but it is still probably too early to be able to evaluate their impact or that of the numerous attempts at reform.

SOCIAL HIERARCHIES AND SOCIAL STRATIFICATION

XVIII The interlocking between the educational and economic arenas had a far-reaching impact on the class system, the structuring of social hierarchies, that developed in modern Japan. There naturally developed in Japan some of the major features of a modern occupational and class structure of the type found in other capitalist-industrial societies, with different echelons of upper, middle, and working classes. But although this system is structurally similar to those in other modern capitalist societies, there are marked differences consistent with some of the general characteristics of modern Japanese society analyzed above.

The major features of the status hierarchies that developed in conjunction with these broad characteristics have been an orientation toward achievement; vertical status sets that cut across other occupational categories and share, at least superficially, many attributes of lifestyle, combined with a tendency on the part of large sectors of society to identify themselves as belonging to the middle class; the weakness of political class consciousness; and a strong tendency to status discrepancy.

In terms of many of the dimensions of the structuration of status, Japan is closer to the United States than to Europe. The first major similarity to the United States, in marked contrast to Europe, can be found, as Tominaga and Treiman have shown, in the close relations between educational and occupational systems and the consequent emphasis on achievement, as against ascriptive criteria of status: "From a comparative perspective both Japan and the United States appear to be at the achievement end of an achievement-ascription continuum."[42]

The emphasis on educational achievement as the key to occupational status does not belittle the importance of family background in this process. The upper groups are indeed continuously able to reproduce themselves, but mainly—perhaps only—through investing in their children's education. Indeed the picture of Japan as a pure educational meritocracy has recently been challenged by Hiroshi Ishida, who has shown, in a very detailed and highly sophisticated study of social mobility in the United States, England, and Japan, that class is the most important determinant of educational attainment in Japan—perhaps even more than in the two other societies.[43] These findings are very much in line with the importance of class in determining different schooling patterns, to which we referred in the preceding section.

Yet a closer look at the evidence indicates that, while Ishida's analysis does bring out the overall importance of class background in socioeconomic achievement in Japan, at the same time it emphasizes education as the major simple mechanism through which occupational positions are attained. The advantages of class can be attained only or mainly through education—and to a much lesser degree through more traditional, ascriptive channels, such as the direct intergenerational transmission of occupation, which is to be found especially among the decreasing population of farmers. In Ishida's words: "In particular, the effect of cultural capital is almost entirely mediated by education," even if "the occupational benefit of a BA degree is greatest at the beginning of the career, but thereafter it has an attenuated impact on later occupational attainment in Japan. Japanese higher education does not appear to exert an enduring occupational status effect."[44]

XIX Closely connected to these rather specific relations between class, education, and occupational attainment in Japan has been the development of a relatively strong tendency toward a dissociation between major dimensions of status, wealth, and power; of multiple vertical status sets; and of rather intricate differences in styles of life between such sets, a characteristic also found, as we have seen, in earlier periods of Japanese history.

In measurable terms, a pattern of status inconsistency is evident in the distribution of ownership of such items as homes and stocks. The tendency to status incongruence and inconsistency as measured by these items is widespread—but not uniformly distributed—in most (but not all) of Japanese society. To follow Ishida again:

> At the extremes of the Japanese class structure, the tendency toward status consistency dominates; the employer class is located at the most advantaged positions in the distribution of most status characteristics, while the skilled and the non-skilled working classes are located at the bottom of all status hierarchies. However, classes which occupy partially dominant and "contradictory" locations in the social relations of production tend to show status inconsistency. The professional-managerial class and the petty bourgeoisie are characterized by a combination of high-status scores on some dimensions and low-status scores on other dimensions of status hierarchies. Neither the bipolarity nor the status inconsistency, however, appears to be a generalized feature of Japanese society.
>
> A cross-national comparison of the relationship between class structure and status hierarchies in Japan and the United States suggests that a combination of polarization and inconsistency of status attributes characterizes both Japanese and American class structure.[45]

Yet some distinctive characteristics can be identified on the Japanese scene. Here several aspects of the relation of education to occupation are of great interest. For instance, the fact that the tendency to status inconsistency is smaller at the top is closely related to some aspects of the educational system, especially to the high level of hierarchization of the university system (comparable to that in England), to which we have referred. At the same time, while both in England and in Japan the linkage between top universities and top elite positions is very close—especially in politics and the civil service, and to some extent in management—in England the students of these universities are more likely to come from the upper classes than in Japan. Moreover, in Japan many managerial positions have, especially lately, been recruited from other universities.

The tendency toward status inconsistency is reinforced by the pattern of recruitment by firms as well as by differences in firm sizes. "The differentiation among college graduates begins some years after entry into the firm in Japan. In contrast, American college graduates of elite institutions tend to enjoy initial access to higher-status occupations."[46] "An important cross-national variation is found in the effect of firm size. Status differentiation by firm size among employees is much more clearly documented in Japan than in the United States."[47]

Thus the tendencies to widespread status inconsistencies are closely connected to the specific characteristics of the hierarchical structure of the Japanese educational system, especially its distinctive combination of egalitarian and meritocratic aspects.[48] Despite the strong class dimension of the educational system, meritocratic selection does not generate uniform, horizontal, country-wide strata, each of which encompasses a great variety of occupations, with a distinct class identity and consciousness. Rather, the very complicated and differentiated tracking system gives rise to a series of complex vertical sets, organized in cross-cutting, pyramidal relations. With respect to both the extent of status inconsistency and the development of relatively similar lifestyles, there seems, according to Tominaga and Treiman, to be a rather marked difference between Japan and not only Europe but even the United States, namely that there appears to be much less status incongruence in the United States than in Japan. Moreover in the United States it is not easily accepted, although more so than in Europe, especially in England.[49]

XX The tendency toward status inconsistency as it has developed in contemporary Japanese society goes beyond these relatively easily measurable indices. It can be identified, for instance, in the internal arrangement of firms, where the authority structure is, as we have seen, organized not only in a hierarchical mode, but also in the strong continuous flow of information between different echelons and in the relatively small salary differentials between different echelons. This tendency can also be found in the predominance of the bureaucracy, with its relatively lower salaries, in the process of decision making. It is manifest in the persistence of the strong school ties that cut across occupational sectors, to which we have referred already.[50]

The more intricate manifestations of the tendency to relative status incongruences are closely related to the fact that wealth and conspicuous consumption do not seem to constitute an autonomous criterion and symbol of status to the same extent in Japan as in the United States. Conspicuous consumption, while obviously quite prevalent, is to some degree looked down upon and certainly not encouraged among higher executives, bureaucrats, and the like. Tendencies to ostentatious consumption are in Japan hemmed in within the various contexts in which people in different occupational positions participate.

Also, as we shall see soon, there developed among many—certainly not all—sectors of Japanese society a *relative* uniformity of lifestyle as well as a tendency among those in such sectors to identify themselves as "middle class." But this relative conformity and self-attribution does not mean that the actual styles of life and status of this broad sector of the Japanese population are uniform or homogeneous. True enough, differences in lifestyle—at least in some crucial aspects, such as dress, patterns of consumption, and entertainment—are in Japan relatively small, certainly smaller than in Europe or the United States.[51] But at the same time, as many anthropological studies have shown, finely tuned distinctions do develop between different subsectors—according to occupation, type of enterprise (large or small factories, shops, etc.), neighborhood, level of education, and the like.[52] Different occupational echelons tend to be embedded in some wider, local, social sets, based on the specific enterprise or bureau, and members of the same occupation usually belong to different such sets. Interestingly enough, all these anthropological studies—as well as survey analyses—also indicate the continuity of the culture of deference in many sectors of Japanese society.

Thus, side by side with the widespread identification of many sectors as middle class, there has developed a system of intricate, vertical, somewhat segregated but also overlapping status sectors. The elitist orientation of the educational system does not produce, except perhaps at the very top, a strong cohesion of different functionally specific, relatively autonomous technocratic and occupational echelons. But the significant thing is that all these finely tuned nuances are indeed very dispersed, the criteria according to which they are constructed (occupation, education, place of employment) very often cross-cutting; they are strongly embedded in very different yet overlapping contexts structured according to multiple social criteria. Moreover, some reference to middle-class status constitutes an important component of many, if not most, of these contexts.

While, needless to say, the concrete ways in which different occupational and ecological sectors formulate concerns about their lifestyles vary greatly, yet they share to a great extent a common framework of social and cultural discourse. They seem to share (as manifest, for instance, in the new local festivals) an emphasis on reconstructing tradition—both their distinctive tradition and the relation of this local tradition to some wider national one—out of a seemingly similar reservoir of themes. This emphasis on the reconstruction of tradition is promulgated both by the authorities and by the media, but it seems to find rather strong resonances among wide sectors of the population.[53]

Closely related to this mode of structuring status was the definition of the major arenas of social interaction. Contrary to the tendency prevalent in modern Western societies to define discrete arenas of life, each with relatively clear boundaries, the definition of arenas of social interaction in Japan has been structured in terms of continuously changing contexts, defined in some combination of sacral and primordial or natural terms and connected through indexical topological metaphors.

The boundaries of these contexts have not combined in the same ways as in Western societies. Family life, occupational life, the distinction between private and public, the relations between genders, while relatively clearly defined in particular contexts, have not been packaged according to local and class relations as has been the case in the West. They can be combined in different ways in different contexts, and while the hierarchical structuring of such contexts is very pronounced, it is mostly structured vertically, in a series of overlapping status sets, giving rise, as we have seen, to rather weak class consciousness.

This mode of structuring different arenas of social life seems very similar to what has been developing in so-called postmodern societies. Hence it is but natural, even if not necessarily correct, that many scholars—Japanese and Western alike—should have begun to look at Japan as a possible model of postmodern society and that the problem of postmodernity should have become a very hot issue in contemporary Japanese intellectual discourse.[54]

XXI Tendencies to status inconsistency and its concrete manifestations are closely related to the relative weakness of politically oriented class consciousness among the middle and the working classes (characteristic also of the United States, in distinction from Europe, although the reasons in Japan, with one exception, differ considerably from those in the United States) and the connected tendency, much stronger than in the United States, of large sectors of Japanese society to identify themselves as middle class.

These traits are related to several aspects of Japanese social structure that we have discussed, particularly the strong connection between education and occupation; the concomitant emphasis on achievement, combined with meritocratic orientations based on country-wide examinations; the highly segmented labor market; the segmentation between large and small business enterprises; the segmentation within the large companies between permanent and temporary workers; and the relatively low incidence of income inequality in Japan as compared with other industrial societies.[55]

This tendency toward weak class consciousness has been reinforced in Japan by several specific historical occurrences. First, owing to the abolition of the status distinctions that were prevalent under the Tokugawa and to the widespread adoption of Western patterns of dress, there did not develop in daily life easily discernible differences between different, especially salaried, sectors of Japanese society—a situation that was further reinforced after the Second World War.[56] Second, "a highly developed 'demographic identity,'" to use Goldthorpe's terminology, extends to the Japanese petty bourgeois class but not the unskilled workers.[57] Third, most occupational sectors seem to share frameworks of cultural and social discourse, one focus of which is their concern about defining their lifestyles as combining elements of both tradition and modernity.

Fourth, the relatively—indeed only relatively—uniform pattern of life was reinforced by exposure to the relatively homogeneous "popular" culture that developed from the end of the Tokugawa period on and increased with growth in the standard of living and the ever greater orientation toward consumption. As Hidetoshi Kato has put it:

> Of course, either implicitly or explicitly, class distinctions in terms of behavior patterns, artistic taste, kinds of magazines read, wardrobe, or use of language can be discovered if the public is carefully examined. However, everybody in Japan today is the recipient of and audience for popular culture. For instance, baseball, *sumo*, and other sports are enjoyed and appreciated by millions of people regardless of their social status or educational background.
>
> Interestingly enough, in Japanese society intellectual snobbery is almost nil. Of course, there are the minority who have high artistic taste, that is, are "high-brow." But "high-brows" in this country are also very knowledgeable about popular culture. It is a commonplace scene, at a bar at midnight, for a university professor or a high court judge to sing a popular song with a carpenter or taxicab driver.[58]

It is indeed the combination of self-identification of large sectors of Japanese society as middle class, the tendency to status inconsistency, and the development of multiple, often cross-cutting status sets that indicates the nature of the difference between Japan and the United States with respect to the weakness of political class consciousness. In the United States such self-identification is strongly rooted in an emphasis on the autonomy of the individual and on the metaphysical principles of equality and individualism. In Japan, on the contrary, it is much more rooted in the concept of equality in performance of service to society through various group networks.[59] Accordingly, it is not connected, as it is in the United States, with strong antistate orientations. It is also this basic conception of the relation between individual and society that explains one of the basic characteristics of the modern and contemporary Japanese social structure—the combination of egalitarian starting points and highly meritocratic orientations in the educational arena, with the very weak autonomy of the various elites and status groups and their embedment in broad, elite networks.

The weakness of class consciousness is also attested to by the fact that, on the local level, few organizations can mobilize people around symbols of class consciousness, but at the same time it is at that level that some of the most effective protest takes place.

THE POLITICAL SYSTEM

XXII The political system that developed in modern and contemporary Japan was, despite far-reaching changes in regimes, characterized by the relative continuity of some basic institutional features that crystallized in the Meiji period, informed by the premises of the schoolmaster state.

Needless to say, the political system has undergone many changes since the Meiji period, and not only with the marked constitutional changes after the Second World War. It had already changed with the opening up and attempts at constitutional government in the Taishō period and the military regime of the 1930s, transitions A. Gordon described as from imperial bureaucracy to imperial democracy and then to imperial fascism—and all these periods were characterized by intensive elite struggles.[60]

While Japan's pre–Second World War political history was very tumultuous, its post–Second World War politics—especially as it crystallized after 1955 and persisted until 1993, when the hitherto continual hegemony of the Liberal Democratic Party (LDP) was challenged—has often seemed immobile, especially in contrast to its social and economic dynamism. The most important manifestations of political immobility were the predominance of the LDP and the concomitant seeming inability of opposition parties to participate in the government; as the ruling party from 1955 to the early 1990s, the LDP promulgated economic and social policies that shaped the overall mode and characteristics of the Japanese political economy and of capitalism, with no apparent responsiveness to movements of protest or to demands by oppositionary groups. However, as we shall see in greater detail in chapter 6, beneath this seemingly complacent, unresponsive surface were continuous negotiations and accommodations between different, including oppositionary, groups.

Important characteristics of the political system seem to have been continually reproduced, albeit in changing concrete forms. The most important of these have been the conflation of state and civil society; the weakness of a public arena autonomous from and with access to the state; and a relatively diffuse pattern of decision making, in which it is often difficult to pinpoint the locus of such decision making due to the great, sometimes dominant place of the bureaucracy relative to the politicians, parliamentarians, organs of public opinion, and especially movements of protest—though in some periods, including the contemporary one, the last has become more important.

The constitutional-democratic system also has had many restrictive or repressive aspects, such as the weakness of judicial review, the weakness heretofore of protection of human rights, and the persistence of bureaucratic censorship—as for instance over textbooks—the combination of which led, for instance, Peter J. Herzog to call Japan a "pseudo-democracy."[61] The primary, perhaps the most outstanding, feature of this system was the relative secretiveness of decision making, most fully evident in the bureaucracy, which was often seen as the most important actor in the Japanese political system—so much so that the shift to a relatively greater importance of politicians that took place in the late 1970s was sometimes heralded as a major change in the Japanese system. A further shift in the direction of greater openness in decision making has come about as a result of the 1993 election and the establishment of the new coalition government—the first non-LDP government in almost four decades.

THE CULTURAL ARENA

XXIII   It would of course be beyond the scope of our endeavor here even to pretend to survey the cultural scene, the burgeoning of different types of cultural creativity, ranging from "high culture"—literature, the arts— to popular culture. In chapter 14 we shall analyze briefly some aspects of these developments as they bear on the problem of distinct patterns of cultural creativity in Japan. Here I would like only to make a few observations on the frameworks of the cultural discourse that has developed in modern and contemporary Japan.

Under the impact of the West, new types of creativity developed in many arenas—in literature and the visual arts, in "high" and "popular" or "mass" culture, in newspapers and subsequent forms of mass media, and in new types of entertainment. Many of these new forms of creativity—as well as their contents—were indeed shaped according to Western models. Yet, as we shall see in greater detail in chapter 15, they did evince some distinctive characteristics, not just in terms of their portrayal of local situations and the influence of local color, but above all in their choice of themes and modes of structuration of literary and artistic discourse.

It is important to again point out that these new forms emerged within the framework of the broad cultural discourse that developed in Japan from the Meiji era on. The central poles of this discourse were the orientations to modernity and to tradition, their relation to the continuity of Japanese collective consciousness and identity, and the search for Japanese authenticity in the modern setting.

The articulation of these problems in Japan was greatly shaped by the fact that Japan, unlike other Asian civilizations, became successfully modernized and industrialized very quickly. Hence it faced the cultural challenge of modernity not only or mainly from the outside, but also from within, from the social and cultural consequences of the processes of modernization and industrialization initiated by the Meiji state, which promoted new, modern types of knowledge along with its distinctive, tradition-oriented civic theology.

The search for the authenticity of Japanese collectivity and the evaluation of modernity in relation to such authenticity moved between two poles. One was the attempt to overcome modernity, to present modernity as undermining the true Japanese spirit. The other was the appropriation of modernity by Japan and the attempt to identify true Japanese modernity, as against other, Western types of modernity. These two tendencies sometimes reinforced and sometimes opposed each other. The attempt to overcome modernity emphasized the uniqueness of the spiritual essence of the Japanese people or collectivity. This direction was, needless to say, susceptible to extreme nationalistic manipulation; in its less virulent manifestations, it was at the roots of the development of the *Nihonjinron* literature.[62] The other major direction—the search for an authentic "natural" essence beyond the artificial contrivances of political, social, or even linguistic constrictions—can be identified in such "utopia" as those of Andō Shōeki.[63]

However different the two orientations toward modernity and the constitution of the Japanese collective identity—which we shall analyze in greater detail in the last chapter of this book—the common core of this discourse comprised strong immanentist and inward-looking orientations and a concomitant disregard or even negation of universalistic values rooted in transcendental visions or orientations directed beyond existing mundane reality, beyond the "times."

The oscillation between negation and affirmation or appropriation of modernity developed in somewhat different, even if closely connected, ways in the realm of the high ideological discourse and that of the construction of daily cultural life. While the high-cultural discourse on the ideological affirmation or negation of modernity was often couched in highly confrontational terms, such confrontation did not easily spill over into the cultural construction of social life on either formal or informal levels. The immanentist, this-worldly orientation that influenced this search for authenticity entailed a great flexibility in the construction of new social spaces and in their cultural constitutions and definitions.

The structuration of the major arenas of social life and interaction that developed in modern and contemporary Japanese society—which facilitated great openness to fads and fashions, to consumerism—entailed a distinctive mode of continual shifting and code-switching between different contexts and social roles, especially between "modern" and "traditional," "Western" and "authentically Japanese" ones.[64] The designation and construction of different styles of life or patterns of consumption as Western or Japanese was on the whole affected not in antagonistic terms (Japanese versus Western) but in a series of complementary contexts.[65]

A central part of the search for authenticity—and of the mode of structuration of social roles and relations in modern and contemporary Japan—was the strong tendency to define such authenticity in terms of tradition. The problem of the traditionalism of different aspects of life has constituted a continuous focus of debate and discussion in Japan. But such discussion has often been combined with a certain looseness and ambiguity in the concrete specifications of tradition; traditionalism constitutes a sort of general orientation in the name of which many activities and organizations, old and new, have been legitimized, a canopy under which many new developments could be brought together. Such a canopy provides a general orientation to the construction of one's social world, to the modes of social discourse, but it does not create sharp boundaries or breaks between the traditional and the nontraditional arenas or levels of life.

The reconstruction of different dimensions of tradition in Japan did not necessarily entail a narrow "traditionalistic" stance—a stance of "closure" or hostility to all innovations. On the contrary, it allowed a great openness to new influences, but tended to legitimize them as traditional. Tradition or traditionalism, as defined in many sectors of Japanese society, tended to become a crucial, albeit often consciously constructed, symbol of legitimation for new patterns of behavior, organization, cultural creativity, and discourse.[66]

The themes that have developed around these poles of modern Japanese cultural discourse have of course come in different combinations, and the concrete problems on which they have focused have of course continuously changed. Thus for instance in the 1920s and 1930s, along with "patriotic," "traditional," and "nationalistic" themes there developed a strong antiforeigner stance, proclaiming a total disruption between materialist, "Western" technology and the "essence" of Japanese culture. Later, with the great upsurge of development starting in the late 1950s, many would emphasize this economic success as rooted in distinctive characteristics of Japanese culture. Similarly the internal political discourse that developed around Japan's international relations—concerning, for instance, the security treaty with the United States—was often closely related to the different perceptions of Japanese collective identity.

Whatever the concrete problems around which the modern cultural discourse has focused in Japan, these themes have constituted its most continual parameters, with only a few individuals or groups going beyond them. But this discourse, as well as the continual construction of different roles and contexts, was indeed, as Sheldon Garon has recently shown, a thoroughly modern one.[67] Most of those emphasizing tradition and Japanese authenticity did so as part of the construction of Japanese modernity—at best on the level of daily life and on the whole not in antagonistic terms.

These frameworks were shared by many sectors of Japanese society to an extent seemingly greater than in many other modern industrial societies—thus reinforcing the picture of relative homogeneity and the emphasis on consumerism.

NEW RELIGIONS

XXIV One of the most important social arenas in which the distinctiveness of Japanese modernity stands out is that of the so-called new religions. The emergence of different religious groups with sectarian characteristics is not a new or modern phenomenon—they have abounded throughout Japanese history. But such new religions have especially burgeoned since the advent of modern times in the Tokugawa period, through the early Meiji and up to the contemporary scene.[68] Some of these new religions have developed a clearly political orientation, especially the Sokagakkai, which is associated with the founding of a specific political party, the Kōmeitō.

The efflorescence of these religions under the impact of modernization has often been compared to the burgeoning of millenarian movements in the third world under the impact of colonialism. More contemporary movements, especially the Sokagakkai with its strong fundamentalist and political orientations, have sometimes been compared to the fundamentalist and religious movements that sprang up in the 1860s and 1870s in the United States, as well as in the twentieth century in various Islamic societies.

The earlier movements did exhibit strong millenarian orientations, yet their basic character differed greatly, as Carmen Blacker has persuasively analyzed, both from such movements in the third world and from the more messianic ones in the monotheistic civilizations. The core of what distinguished the Japanese millenarian movements from parallel movements in other civilizations was their strong affirmation of the given, mundane world. To follow Blacker:

> The general forward-looking character of the Japanese movements is further borne out by their vision of the future earthly paradise. . . . None of the Founders should have felt moved to identify the earthly paradise they announce with one which once upon a time existed. The answer may lie in the fact that their paradise is unequivocally identified with the "image" of the modern world. . . .
>
> . . . It is relevant perhaps to remember in this connection that the millenarism of the *shinkō shūkyō* is not directed against any specific enemy. The *shinkō shūkyō* feel no hatred towards Western culture. Hence the Enemy or Tyrant, whose destruction is necessary before the millennium can come to pass, is neither a specific hated race nor a specific class. It is simply, and a little undramatically, "wrong thinking." To bring the earthly

paradise into being we must simply learn to think aright. First and foremost, of course, right thinking implies devout faith in the principles and program of the cult.[69]

Different cults differ with respect to how actively they promulgate the "salvation of works," with the Sokagakkai being probably the most prominent among them.

XXV　The this-worldly orientation of these new religions is not, as indicated by Carmen Blacker, a simple acceptance of the given material world. Rather, it emphasizes moral self-cultivation and purification, a much more open attitude to others, and a change in the moral quality of the community. In most if not all of these groups purification, as Helen Hardacre has shown, entails a reconstruction of one's worldview—cutting across the multiplicity of dogma. The new worldview conceives of the individual, society, nature, and the universe as an integrated system vitalized by a single principle on a larger scale. The relations among the levels, however, are not static. They must be maintained in balance, harmony, and congruence, qualities manifested in happiness, health, social stability, abundant harvests, and the regular succession of the seasons (and the absence of such calamities as flood, drought, and major earthquakes).

> Since self-cultivation is the primary determiner of all human affairs, notions of fate or divine wrath (karma or bachi, for example) are reinterpreted, ignored, or denied. In like manner, because of the primacy of self-cultivation, the concept of pollution cannot be fully credited, and this opens the door to greater participation by women than is the case in the established religions. . . .
>
> . . . All problems can be traced to insufficient cultivation of self. Thus it is misguided to expect fundamental social change from political ideology. Instead, society can be improved only through collective moral improvement, the doctrine of meliorism.[70]

Such cultivation involves far-reaching changes in social relations and interactions. It also often gives rise to the feeling of exclusiveness among the members of the sect and may entail aggressiveness toward outsiders, who then reciprocate with hostility toward the group. At the same time it attests to the fact that most of these new religions confirm the existing mundane world by imbuing it with new spiritual values, even if such values are often presented as traditional. As Shigeyoshi Murakami has put it, "Objects of worship, sacred sites, beliefs, and practices are 'traditional' elements whose modification and incorporation within the larger context of *Gedatsu-kai* enable members to 'go back' into their old tradition and at the same time to 'go forward' into the new tradition they are creating and transmitting."[71]

The attempts to imbue city life with what seems, to members of many of these religious groups, to be the "old village" spirit are also connected with an emphasis on magic and exorcism, as Winston Davis has shown in his analysis of one of these new religions, the Sūkyō Mahikari.[72] The same combination—mundane orientation with a quest for a highly immanentist spirituality with universifying tendencies—can be also found in more recent, highly commercialized religious developments, such as the Agonshū. Thus, to follow Ian Reader:

> Like Mahikari and others of the latest wave of religious movements in Japan, Agonshū uses folk concepts from the Japanese tradition and appears to have its roots in that particularized and localized religious environment. However, it has not merely flourished in a modern, urban setting but has taken great pains to adopt the most advanced aspects of modernity available to this society while expressing concepts of universality that appear to transcend the limitations of the localized environment.
>
> It is my view that this apparent dichotomy between an anti-modernism centered in one localized tradition, and a modernity that points towards universality, is an important key for understanding such religious movements. Such elements form a continuity, working together to create a whole, a world view which provides such movements with a sense of legitimation, identity, and centrality in religious terms.[73]

Thus these new religions, while attempting to change the quality of social interaction, do not change the basic premises of the social order. Rather they create spaces of social interaction, imbuing them with the new moral principles. Even the more politically oriented new religions, while ambivalent toward the political arena, aim, not to transform it, but rather to imbue it with a new moral dimension—thus differing in their goals from the fundamentalist movements of the monotheistic civilizations.

THE INSTITUTIONAL CONTOURS OF MODERN AND CONTEMPORARY JAPAN

XXVI These characteristics of the major institutional arenas of modern Japan do not stand alone. They are closely interconnected and attest to the development of a distinctive mode of organization radically different from that of other—especially Western—societies. Such differences are not just local variations; they pertain to the basic ways in which the various modern institutional arenas are defined and regulated, and the broader social and cultural contexts in which they operate.

The common denominator of these characteristics is a high level of structural differentiation, mobility, and openness and a dynamic grounded in conceptions of service to social contexts, ideally (as promulgated in the Meiji ideology) to the national community. Neither the emphasis on equality nor the strong emphasis on achievement are grounded in any conception of principled, transcendentally oriented individuality or of transcendental legitimation of different functional (e.g., political or economic) activities.

Accordingly, no social, economic, or political sector could easily develop a principled autonomy or autonomous claims to access to the center, and it was very difficult for autonomous public spaces to develop. In contrast to the potential autonomy, there developed a strong tendency to conflate different occupational or class sectors within various social contexts—be they enterprises, neighborhoods, new religions, or, above all, the overall national community. Within such contexts there developed a very intensive dynamic, the best-known outcome of which were the educational and economic miracles. It was in many ways a regulated dynamic, though regulated in a rather distinctive way.

It is indeed the combination of such regulation with very dynamic situations that constitutes one of the major puzzles for Western scholars—namely, how Japan can be a highly controlled, yet nontotalitarian and continually innovative society.[74]

This puzzle is closely connected with that of the seeming consensus pervading, at least after the Second World War, all sectors of Japanese society. It has, of course, been increasingly recognized that such a consensus is much less pervasive than was assumed in the *Nihonjinron* literature, in the group model of Japanese society. Yet it seems to be much more pervasive than, and possibly even qualitatively different from, whatever consensus and dissensus can be identified in other modern societies. The tendency in the earlier literature, as well as much contemporary popular literature, to attribute this consensus, whatever its exact scope, simply to Japanese culture or tradition has been challenged on many fronts. One of the most important challenges is the one made by many scholars that whatever the scope and strength of this consensus there is nothing "natural" about it. It is not an emanation of Japanese culture or tradition but a consensus manipulated by the elite, by the ruling class. There is indeed an element of truth in such an assertion, but only to the degree that such an assertion would be true of any consensus in any society. Hence it tells us nothing about the specific characteristics of the Japanese case. Above all, it does not tell us enough—possibly it tells very little indeed—about why the Japanese elites have been relatively successful in manipulating large sectors of Japanese society into this type of consensus.

The difficulty in understanding this combination of a highly controlled yet nontotalitarian (indeed formally, and to some extent actually, democratic) society that remains highly dynamic and imaginative touches on some of the central premises of modern Western social science and analysis, and of the understanding of the dynamics of Japanese society. In the following chapters we shall explore the meaning of this system, and shall attempt an explanation thereof.

Tribulations of
Modern Japanese Society

I The picture that emerges from the preceding analysis of the major institutional arenas in modern and contemporary Japan seems to offer a
clear answer with respect to the central problem of what distinguishes
this state and society from others. It depicts Japanese society as a highly
regulated, closed system, changing and modernizing very successfully in
a very distinctive way, under the direction of the center, especially the
bureaucracy.

According to this view, while Japan has all the paraphernalia of a constitutional system—and since the Second World War of a democratic
one—their function is mainly cosmetic. Behind the facade is a basically
authoritarian system, which succeeds in its operation through the manipulation of consensus—through the creation, that is, of an image of
social harmony that belies its scant responsiveness to the demands of
various groups or movements of protest. It is of course fully recognized
that continuous changes, attendant on the processes of modernization,
have been taking place in Japanese society, but these changes have been
seen as directed and regulated by the "system" or by the elites.

This impression is seemingly borne out by the fact that most of the
distinctive characteristics of the institutions analyzed can be identified in
all periods of modern Japanese history, at least until the very recent past,
even if their concrete specifications—the details of the organization of
firms and trade unions; the relations between bureaucrats, politicians, and
the media; the specific contours of the school system—have changed continuously. This picture does not, of course, deny the dynamism of Japanese society, especially in the economic arena. But it presents this dynamism as generated and above all channeled by the center—with the

broader sectors of the society having but little impact on either the course of change or the mostly unresponsive center.

There can of course be no doubt that this picture contains elements of truth; but is it the whole truth? We shall address ourselves to this question in the following way. First, in this chapter we shall analyze some of the periods of "opening" and intense change in modern and contemporary Japanese history, periods in which Japan appeared to move closer to the social and political patterns of other—especially Western—industrialized capitalist democracies. Second, in chapter 5, we shall analyze in some detail various manifestations of "disharmony," that is, patterns of behavior that run against the premises of this presumably regulated and controlled, seemingly consensual society, considering the impact of these patterns on Japanese society, as well as the responses to them. In chapter 6 we shall bring together the main threads of the analysis and explore what they tell us about the distinctive features of modern Japanese society.

We shall start with the analysis of the periods of opening, of intense change in modern Japanese society. The most important of these were the early Meiji period, the Taishō period, the emergence of the military regime in the 1930s, and, perhaps most significantly, the first decade after the Second World War.

In all of these periods of transition and social turmoil, far-reaching changes took place in Japanese society and culture and many new ideological and institutional possibilities seemed to open up. The question of the extent to which new modes of social organization, with novel structures and values, could develop in modern Japan looms large in both public and academic discourse in and about Japan. Concomitantly, in all these periods there appeared intensive movements of social protest: campaigns for citizens' rights in the early Meiji period, the rice riots in the 1920s, and the appearance of radical political organizations—on both the right and the left—which sometimes developed close, even if not continuous, connections with popular movements and more established political organizations.

The developments in these periods have been compared, both in Japan and abroad, with similar or parallel ones in other modern societies—constitutional, authoritarian, and totalitarian alike. Development in the Taishō period has been compared with the establishment of liberal democratic regimes in Europe, the military regime with the fascist, totalitarian ones in European countries, and the period after the Second World War with the establishment of fully fledged constitutional-democratic regimes in Western European and the United States.

In all these periods the intense social, economic, and demographic changes that accompanied urbanization, industrialization, and the extension of education, literacy, and the media—all processes either initiated or fostered by the Meiji regime—were intensified, culminating in what seemed to be challenges to the original premises of the Meiji state. The later developments of these premises were challenged, and some indeed appeared to have been transformed. But what was the nature of this transformation?

In each period of transition, too, there arose the question of the extent to which the changes occurring in Japan were patterned according to the principles and orientations of other civilizations, the extent, in other words, to which Japan was converging with other, Western industrial societies. As the analysis that follows will show, such convergence was only very partial; we shall then attempt to analyze the differences between the Japanese and other modern industrial societies, as well as the implications of Japan's distinctive characteristics for the understanding of the impact of structural and ideological changes on the dynamics of Japanese society.

It is of course wrong to speak of the "usual" pattern of modernity—which presumably exists in "the West"—from which Japan differs. Among the Western countries themselves there developed many distinct patterns of modernity—as, for instance, our comparison of stratification patterns in Japan with those in the United States and Europe, especially England, attests.[1] Thus the Japanese pattern of modernity has to be seen, not as the "deviant" case, but as one among numerous modern patterns;[2] in the preceding chapters we have analyzed some of the major characteristics of this pattern.

But even accepting these premises we have to explore the nature of the distinctive characteristics of the modern and contemporary Japanese system. Do these characteristics reinforce the view that Japan has been a highly regulated society, based on a seemingly harmonious consensus manipulated by the elites in a basically repressive, nonresponsive way?

THE TAISHŌ REGIME
AND LIBERAL DEMOCRACY

II   We shall begin our examination of the periods of intensive change and opening in modern Japanese society with a brief consideration of the Taishō period—from the death of the Meiji emperor in 1912 to 1926, including in our discussion also the first years of the Shōwa period, into the early 1930s—and of the failure of the democratic regime that took place in this period.

In the late Meiji, Taishō, and early Shōwa periods, far-reaching social and economic changes attendant on urbanization and industrialization opened up the oligarchic Meiji regime: growing dislocation in the countryside, the development of an urban proletariat—a more diversified educated and professional class—and an increasing emphasis on consumerism gave rise to a growing awareness of the internal contradictions of the Meiji state ideology. Social protests—the Hibiya Park riot against the Portsmouth Treaty in 1905, the rice riots of 1918—took place, and new economic and professional organizations, labor unions, and many new intellectual groups challenged the hegemony of the dominant institutions.[3]

For the first time in modern Japanese history, parties seemed to become the predominant political force and the cabinet, composed of members of these parties, contributed to some extent to challenging the Meiji oligarchy. It was a period in which liberal and democratic ideals were internationally very popular, and it seemed as if Japan was heading in a somewhat liberal-democratic direction, even if the changes in the political arena—especially the development of party cabinets and the general increase in power, if not prestige, of the oligarchs and bureaucrats—could be seen as the continuation and intensification of previous developments, not necessarily as radical innovations.

> During the decade and a half following World War I, the political parties emerged as the hegemonic elite in the political system, dominating the cabinet, the formulation of national policy, and, to a lesser degree, the execution of policy. With the exception of three short-lived "transcendental cabinets" in 1922–24, party leaders served as premiers and cabinet ministers until 1932. By contrast, the civilian and military bureaucracies saw their influence, though not their prestige and popular status, dwindle. A token of this shift was the increasing number of officials who allowed themselves to be coopted by the political parties.[4]

And yet, despite this seemingly organic development toward a constitutional party regime, such a regime did not fully crystallize in Japan during the Taishō and early Shōwa periods. The explanation of the ultimate failure of this presumably or potentially liberal-democratic regime has since been a focus of scholarly Western and Japanese debate. Some explanations, as for instance that offered by Taichirō Mitani, focus on the conditions for the establishment of the body politic in Japan within the political arena itself:

> (1) the establishment of superiority of the House of Representatives over the House of Peers, (2) the emergence of Minobe's constitutional theory as orthodox, (3) the political neutralization of the Privy Council, (4) party penetration of the civil bureaucracy, (5) party accommodation with the

judiciary accompanying the introduction of the jury system, and (6) party rapprochement with the military. None of these conditions was irreversible, however. If any or all of them were altered, then the party cabinet system would be faced with a crisis. In other words, the system was a fragile one.[5]

Other explanations looked for the social bases of the new military regime, finding them, as seemed to be the case with the rise of the fascist or totalitarian regimes in the West, especially among rural or lower-middle urban classes displaced by developing capitalism.[6]

Slowly the focus of the debate about the reasons for the failure of the democratic-constitutional regime in the 1920s shifted more towards the question of whether there existed in principle in Japan the basic conditions and real potentialities for the development of a liberal regime.

Several contrasting views were developed with respect to this problem, as can be seen in a book edited by Harry Wray and Hilary Conroy.[7] Some scholars viewed the Taishō democracy as a continuation of liberal trends that had started in the Meiji period, and the military regime of the 1930s an aberration. Others claimed that the parties were self-centered and opportunistic, that they did not work for structural changes in the polity, and that there were few genuine liberals among the Taishō intellectuals:

> It is my general argument that while there were doubtless many temperamental liberals in Taishō Japan (although no more, surely, than in eras before or after), there were very few ideological Liberals: neither freedom nor individual has ever been an overriding political ideal in Japan and the Taishō period is no exception. On the contrary, Taishō society was conspicuous for a variety of non-liberal trends. [The most important of these were] nationalistic non-liberals, socialist non-liberals, bureaucratic non-liberals, grass-roots non-liberals—all of which fed, in one way or another, on the growing "statal" democratization of Japanese society. . . . Taishō Liberalism as a significant political movement was very short-lived.[8]

III   The upshot of all these analyses—and controversies—is that posing the question of whether there was a potential for "real" liberalism in the Taishō period is somewhat misleading. The reason is not the absence in Taishō Japan of individuals, groups, and movements promulgating ideologies close to Western liberalism, especially the European variety,[9] nor of new economic organizations and intellectual groups articulating new interests—the numerous movements of protest make the Taishō and early modern period one of the most tumultuous in modern Japanese history. Rather it is misleading because Japan's ideological and institutional framework, the premises within which these themes were promulgated, differed greatly from those of the West within which the terms of the question originated. Hence the meanings of these terms as used in Japan necessarily greatly differed from their meanings in different Western countries.

This was true of both the ideological and the institutional dimensions of the modern Japanese polity. The ideological premises, which crystallized during the Meiji period with its distinctive patterns of legitimation, were based, as we have seen, on assumptions that differed greatly from those of Western constitutional—or even absolutist—regimes.[10] Of special importance in this context was the strong tendency to conflate state and civil society, their embedment in the national community, and the consequent weakness of an autonomous public space. Accordingly, principled individualism, the concomitant distinction between state and civil society, and the conception of an autonomous civil society had weak roots, as Peter Duus has shown, in the Japanese conception of political and social order.[11]

Germaine Hoston has followed this line in a recent article:

Japan's liberals were few, and none fundamentally challenged the interventionist role of the state in Japanese society or the position of the emperor at its apex. . . . As Japanese liberals, these thinkers shared the discomfort of more left-leaning intellectuals, such as Kawakami Hajime, concerning the disruption of Japanese life by the Meiji industrial revolution. A liberalism founded on an abstract conception of natural rights vested in atomistic egos could no more diminish their pain than the equally alien and traumatic conception of class struggle espoused by Marxists. With the advent of war, their liberalism, as *Japanese* liberalism, had to accommodate disparate notions of self and modernity that ultimately came into such intense conflict that it was either extinguished or transmuted into its opposite.[12]

As Duus observes, "The operative element in all these terms was jointness or commonality (do), which the parliamentary mechanism provided. Constitutional government was less the apotheosis of political individualism than the pursuit of collective harmony."[13]

Thus many liberal or even protest groups shared the basic premises of the modern Japanese polity and the institutional patterns that developed under the Meiji regime, especially the relatively diffuse pattern of decision making, the weakness of open, autonomous public spaces, and the weakness of conceptions of the accountability of rulers—all of which were closely related to the nature of the legitimation of the modern Japanese political system.[14]

It is these basic premises and characteristics of the modern Japanese polity and the modes of regulation they entailed that explain the specific fate of Taishō liberalism. This is not to say that no important social or political changes took place in these periods; as we have seen, far-reaching changes, in many ways similar to those in other industrialized capitalist societies at similar stages of economic development in this period, did indeed take place.[15] Moreover, among many sectors of the population there developed a new, wider democratic consciousness that fed on growing demands—directed against the oligarchic big-business coalitions that dominated the Meiji era—for broader participation in the political arena. But the ultimate outcome of these developments was, in the words of A. Gordon (who is critical of the critics of Taishō democracy), "Imperial democracy."[16] Not only did many of the labor and socialist groups support the expansionist politics of the regime, on the whole they also embraced the emperor system with its basic conception of civil society. The new associations were not organized with a view to changing the structure of the center in the name of principled ideological visions—such as those of Western liberalism—but rather sought to influence the center, to construct for themselves broader living spaces away from the central political arena, or to open the existing imperial system to broader participation. They demanded for themselves the possibility of greater participation in this political framework but not necessarily basic changes in its premises.

Many struggles, some quite fierce, developed between various political groups and factions, belying any claim of harmony. These struggles developed, not according to formal constitutional rules—as between open, public representatives of different interests or views—but according to more informal ones, operating through the various network organizations, which were much more forceful and pervasive than the formal arrangements.

True enough, many politicians, in contrast to the more articulate intellectuals, attempted to promote local autonomy or to base political action on locality; but only rarely did they succeed. While many of them were looking for more diversified bases of knowledge on which consideration of the common good could be based, most—with the partial, paradoxical exception of some of the extreme nationalistic groups—did not go beyond the overall general parameters of the relatively loose Meiji ideology and the basic rules of the political game that guided the Meiji polity.[17]

In other words, the processes of control, regulation, and guidance that characterized the Meiji era, and above all the basic premises of its hegemonic ideology and their institutional repressions, proved to be more powerful than the new political forces and formations seemingly cast in the mold of Western modernity. As we shall see in greater detail later on, however, part of the strength of these processes lay in their responsiveness to the processes of change and the demands of various groups and protest movements—even if this response was structured in a way different from those prevalent in modern Western societies.

THE MILITARY REGIME OF THE 1930S AND FASCISM

IV   The paradoxical mirror image of the failed liberalism of the Taishō period is that of the military regime of the 1930s. Of special importance in this context is the question of the extent to which it was similar to fascist or totalitarian regimes of the kind that developed in the same period in Italy, Germany, and elsewhere in Europe—with which it was closely allied and by which it was clearly influenced.[18]

There can be no doubt whatsoever that there were many features common to both the European fascist and totalitarian regimes and the Japanese military regime. First, as was the case with respect to earlier historical periods, there were great similarities, in some regards, in the antecedent conditions of the regimes—such as rising social and economic unrest and a fragile international system. With respect to the latter there was one very important difference: the element of national defeat, especially crucial in Germany, was missing in Japan.[19]

There can also be no doubt that many of the ideologies and practices of the Japanese regime, especially the repressive ones, were very similar to and strongly influenced by those of the European fascist regimes.[20] Similarly, many of the new types of regulation that were promulgated in this period, such as "corporatist" economic policies and the tendency to overall economic mobilization, were influenced by similar ones in the fascist totalitarian societies and, during the Second World War, in the United States. Moreover the Japanese regime shared with the European movements strong exclusivist tendencies and a strong opposition to the constitutional state.[21]

However, as Duus and Okimoto showed in the late 1970s and others have since elaborated, measures undertaken by the military regime did not share some of the basic characteristics of the European fascist regimes, namely a strong, cohesive ideology, leadership recruited from marginal social and political groups, and, perhaps above all, mass mobilization of the population through new political parties.[22] Elise Tipton, in her dissertation "The Civil Police in the Suppression of the Prewar Japanese Left," elaborated on these points, challenging Maruyama Masao's conclusion that the military regime was a "fascism composed from above," above all on the basis that it lacked the basic organizational and ideological component of European fascist movements.[23]

In a similar way Ben-Ami Shillony discusses whether the military regime could be analyzed as totalitarian:

No new party emerged to take the place of the ones which have been disbanded, and the former politicians remained in their parliamentary Diet seats, passing laws, approving budgets. . . . Nor did a new political doctrine or "ism" arise. As at the time of the Meiji Restoration, the goals continued to be pragmatic and rationalistic, not messianic or universal.

The only supernatural ideal was the liberation of Asia from domination by the white race and even this was quickly eroded by the desire to set up an East Asian empire. . . . According to Talmon's definition of totalitarianism, that it is a school of thought claiming to possess the sole and exclusive truth in polities and bent on realizing a messianic paradise on earth, totalitarianism did not exist in wartime Japan, despite the alliance with Hitler and Mussolini.

Interestingly enough, Shillony points out that

the same tradition, which has been faulted for obstructing true democracy in Japan, turned out to be even more effective in obstructing totalitarianism.

Thus the major characteristics of the military regime lack the crucial ideological elements of totalitarian democracy, namely: the ideology and practice of the total regulation of society by the center, do not require destruction of the traditional form of society and creation of new anti-traditional national symbols.[24]

Many characteristics of the Japanese regime may seem close to Franco's regime in Spain, yet with the significant difference that the latter, although in practice much more authoritarian than totalitarian, emerged from a bloody civil war in which ideological contestation played a crucial role.

These rather distinctive characteristics of the military regime in Japan are admitted even by those scholars who emphasize—often following the recent, rather intensive discussions about fascism in Japan by Japanese scholars—the similarity of the regime in Japan to the European fascist (but, significantly, not "totalitarian") regimes.[25] Thus, for instance, Andrew Gordon coins the terms "Imperial Fascism," a continuation of "Imperial democracy," to designate the nature of the Japanese case.[26] In doing so he follows to some extent both Maruyama Masao and Yamaguchi Yasushi, who, while emphasizing the fascist elements in the Japanese case, do not ignore the specific characteristics of "Japanese" fascism.[27]

V   Thus there emerges, with respect to the military government of the 1930s, a picture paradoxically similar to that of the democracy of the Taishō period. Many of the organizational structures were similar to those found in Europe but their overall dynamics were different, and they can only be understood within the framework of the overall characteristics of the Japanese modern political system. As Shillony has alluded, the reasons for the failure of the liberal tendencies in the Taishō era and the development of the specific *nontotalitarian* characteristics of the military regime overlap.

The root of the paradox, at least from a Western point of view, lies in the fact that the forces that explain the failure of the Taishō period's would-be liberals or democrats—namely the strength of the various ideological and informal controls rooted in, or closely related to, the basic ideological premises and institutional features of the modern Japanese political system, which crystallized in the Meiji period—also worked against the possibility of totalitarian tendencies becoming predominant during the period of the military regime. The characteristics of the military regime in Japan that distinguished it from the totalitarian ones of the West are closely related to the conflation of the state and civil society and their embedment in the overall national community. Just as the absence of a principled ideological confrontation between state and civil society made it difficult to institutionalize a liberal party regime, it also explains the weakness of the totalitarian elements in the authoritarian regime of the 1930s. This regime repressed oppositionary groups and movements, but it did not confront an autonomous social society in the name of a "state," and hence was not bent either on its destruction or total transformation.[28]

One interesting manifestation of these relations, in the Taishō period, between wider sectors of the society and the state, or rather within the broader national community, which encompassed both the state and civil society, is, as Patricia Steinhoff has shown, the relatively widespread responsiveness of members of oppositionary groups to the policy of *tenkō*—though reform—employed by the authorities.[29] This policy will be discussed in greater detail in chapter 15. This responsiveness was rooted—according to Steinhoff, as we shall see yet in greater detail later on—in the strong predisposition of many "leftist" intellectuals or activists to become reintegrated in the moral consensus of the broader sectors of Japanese community, in the fact that their radicalism was more often based on commitment to a group than to abstract principles. Certainly not all sectors of former political activists responded to these policies, yet such responses seem to have been widespread enough to represent a very strong trend.

VI These characteristics of the military regime are closely related to the distinctive features of the Japanese collective identity and consciousness to which we have already referred. Japan can be seen as the model nation-state, as indeed it has always been, in one way or another, coterminous with the Japanese collective identity, which was constructed—as we have seen—in terms of "sacred particularity." Yet this specific mode of Japanese collective identity and consciousness evinced significant differences from the premises of the European nation-state. Two closely interconnected facts are of special importance here, in the context of the analysis of the military regime of the 1930s.

First, this political and ethnic or national identity or collective consciousness, couched in sacral-primordial terms, developed early in Japanese history—even if, for long periods, it was limited to some elite groups—and did not constitute a point of continuous internal ideological or political struggle. Second, unlike in Europe, this collective consciousness did not develop within the framework of a universalistic civilization with strong transcendental orientations. Even if its development was greatly influenced by its encounter with Chinese Confucianism and Buddhism it refused, as it were, to cope with the problem of the relation of its primordial "ethnic" symbols to membership in such universalistic civilizations. The confrontation with universalistic ideologies, as we shall see in greater detail in our discussion of the transformation of Confucianism and Buddhism in Japan, was seemingly resolved by the denial of these ideologies—albeit a highly principled, ideological denial of their universalistic and transcendental components—and not by any attempt to specify their relative importance in relation to the primordial ones.

At the same time this concept of nationality entailed a very strong tendency—which has played an important role in Japanese society from the Meiji up to the contemporary period—to define the Japanese collectivity in terms of incomparable uniqueness, couched very often in semi racial, genetic terms, or in terms of some special spirituality. Some such emphasis on Eastern or Asian spirituality—as against Western materialism—could be found among intellectuals, including Marxist ones, in most Asian civilizations, in their confrontation or encounter with the West. But while, in most other Asian countries, such spirituality was defined in universalistic "Hindu," "Buddhist," or "Confucian" terms, in Japan it was presented in terms of the unique spirituality of the Japanese collectivity or nation, often defined in highly exclusive, particularistic terms.[30]

This attitude, asserting the distinctiveness of Japanese nationhood, could easily develop in extreme nationalistic directions—and was indeed characteristic of nationalistic trends throughout the modern era—but in some form it was probably prevalent in much of Japanese society. It was also central in many discussions, especially the more contemporary ones, about the nature of the Japanese language; in the development of the Nihonjinron literature; and in many discussions about the direction of Japanese policies in international affairs.[31]

The European tendency to ideologize the nation-state in universalistic terms and toward totalitarian democracy was to no small degree rooted in the specific European background. These tendencies were closely related to the prevalence, in all monotheistic civilizations, of a perception of the political as one of the major arenas for resolving the tensions or overcoming the chasm between the transcendental and mundane orders, and of the closely related development of the state as a distinct total entity. The absence of the consciousness of such chasm or tensions in Japan helps to explain the differences between the Japanese authoritarian regime of the 1930s and European fascism and totalitarianism.

VII These specific conceptions of Japanese national distinctiveness also had important repercussions on the pattern of the Japanese military expansion. Here again a comparative approach is revealing.

As L. H. Gann has succinctly shown, both Japanese and Nazi military expansion in and prior to the Second World War were initiated by injured pride or negative attitudes toward Western dominance—by a strong orientation toward expansion, grounded in conceptions of *Grossraumwirtschaft* (economy of great spaces) and the like.[32] In both cases it was the army that constituted the bearer of such expansionist attitudes, but the two states differed greatly in their ideological premises. Both engaged in unspoken atrocities; nonetheless,

> The fact remains that the Japanese did not engage in ethnic mass extermination for the sake of creating a better world.
>
> Nazism, by contrast, was a millennial creed that sought to establish a millennial empire . . . ruled by the Aryan race, the noblest of human stocks. In practice, the Japanese might treat Chinese and Philippinos with brutality. The wartime drive for "the imperialization of subject peoples" rested on the assumption of Japanese superiority. But no Japanese theoretician regarded fellow Asians simply as sub-humans, fit only to work for the victor or starve. . . .
>
> . . . The Japanese and German empires differed in another fundamental sense. Germany was a *Führerstaat*. Until late in the war, Hitler represented to the majority of his people both a legitimate monarch and a revolutionary leader—king and *sanculotte* all at once.[33]

THE POST–SECOND WORLD WAR PERIOD
AND THE INSTITUTION OF A DEMOCRATIC REGIME

VIII The picture that emerges in the period after the Second World War, when there began a new era in Japanese modern history, is more complex—yet in some basic features it remains similar to those of earlier periods. The period after the war witnessed the most far-reaching changes in modern Japanese society and polity, creating the conditions for an almost total transformation of the Japanese political system in a democratic direction, and seemingly also for the development of an autonomous civil society.[34]

As Robert Ward has aptly pointed out, "The new constitution substituted popular for imperial sovereignty, . . . provided extensive and detailed protection for civil and human rights, minimized, if not eliminated, the role of the military, . . . reduced the ages for voting and office-holding," extended suffrage for women, opened up the political arena to the opposition, legalized trade unions, and promulgated a civil code that "specified the equality of women, favored nuclear rather than extended families, and instituted equality of inheritance among the children of a nuclear family."[35]

Given all the discontinuities analyzed above, Japan's becoming more like other industrialized countries and constitutional democracies seemed, in the period immediately after the Second World War, quite feasible. Japan seemed ready both to become a modern democracy and to develop a modern economy. It took up both these challenges, becoming in a period of about two decades a highly developed modern economic society and a constitutional democratic system.

But while the formal institutional and constitutional frameworks, as well as the entire ambiance of political life, indeed changed after the Second World War, becoming much more open and flexible, they continued to exhibit some very distinctive characteristics. This could be seen in the constitutional system, set up under the American occupation, which abolished the imperial system, with the emperor renouncing the traditional claim to divinity and becoming "only" a symbol of a new order. This naturally denoted a marked change in the basic legitimacy of the political order, as the locus of sovereignty moved from the emperor to the people—but only a partial change. Indeed, as Kyoko Inoue has argued in her fascinating linguistic analysis of the drafting of the constitution, in their negotiations with the American occupation authorities and in the Diet debates, Japanese leaders manoeuvered sinuously to avoid the idea that sovereignty under the new constitution would reside solely with the people. "By arguing that the Emperor was a *kokumin*, they were able to claim that sovereignty resided both in the Emperor and the people," she writes. "This enabled them to maintain that the fundamental character of the national polity remained, because the Emperor was the center of adoration, even though he would not have political power."[36]

But, as Peter Duus has shown,

> As a result the imperial symbol lost its legitimizing function, and the emperor was placed at an even further remove from politics than he had been

in the prewar period. On the other hand, no new legitimizing symbol replaced the imperial institution.

Consequently, Japan may be the only contemporary democratic polity lacking a widely accepted myth of legitimacy. The notion of *kokutai* has disappeared but the notion of "popular sovereignty" has not quite superseded it.[37]

Indeed, in all institutional arenas, it became quite clear that modern Japanese society evinced some very distinctive characteristics or premises—the very characteristics that we analyzed in the preceding chapter. The same was true of the cultural arenas. Not only were many of the "templates" guiding various patterns of cultural creativity very similar to those of earlier periods; the same is true of the very modes of organization of cultural creativity, in which, as Havens has shown, the network structure, organized in principle around one master, has been predominant. This was even true with regard to sports.[38]

The growing awareness of this fact, connected as it was with the growing economic success of Japan, entailed also a shift in the questions that were asked about the nature of the modern Japanese experience. In the 1950s the major question asked by Western and Japanese scholars alike was, What in the Japanese tradition and social structure may facilitate modernization and economic development and help Japan become similar to Western countries? By the 1970s the question was on the whole a different one: What are the distinctive, possibly unique characteristics of the modern Japanese social and political system?[39]

It was probably in the 1970s that there emerged in the scholarly and more general discourse the picture of Japan as a repressive, highly controlled society. (It was also, significantly enough, in this period that *Nihonjinron* literature burgeoned and became more and more widespread.) It was above all the political system that was seen as epitomizing these distinctive institutional patterns, whose major characteristics were repressiveness and immobilism—manifest above all in the seeming immobility of Japan's contemporary political system, usually contrasted with its social and economic dynamism. The Japanese political system was often portrayed as basically unresponsive to the demands of various broad social sectors and movements of protest, promulgating such collective goals as national-military aggrandizement in the first part of the twentieth century and economic development after the Second World War as "institutional" rather than "participatory" programs.[40] In the latter period, the most important manifestations of political immobility were the predominance of the LDP from the mid-1950s to the early 1990s and the seeming inability of opposition parties to participate in the government; the nature of the economic and social policies promulgated by the ruling party in Japan since 1955, which shaped the overall mode and characteristics of the Japanese political economy and of capitalism; the ruling party's apparent lack of responsiveness to the demands of protest movements and opposition groups; and the closely related secretiveness and diffuseness of its decision making.

IX The mode of response of the modern Japanese political system to movements of protest provides one of the best ways to understand its specific characteristics. Indeed, numerous movements of protest have emerged in the period after the Second World War; it was only natural that, given the democratization of the regime, many oppositionary movements would spring up. Many of these, protests by various labor or local groups, built on the organizational and symbolic foundations of their predecessors in the Meiji and Taishō periods. The most intensive development of various protest movements took place in the late 1940s and early 1950s.

It was also in this period that many such movements—especially labor—became both radical and relatively widespread, in ways reminiscent of European socialist and labor movements; labor and socialist parties not only became fully legalized, but also began to signal the possibility of a social-democratic, if not socialist, order in Japan. This was, of course, a new development. Socialist and communist groups had arisen in Japan, beginning in the late nineteenth century, but only after the Second World War did relatively large socialist parties develop. In the later Meiji state, in the Taishō period, and up to the Second World War, such parties— small groups of intellectuals and radical workers with strong sectarian tendencies and relatively weak appeal to broader sectors of the population—were persecuted, often brutally, by the government. But even these, however weak, contributed new elements to the political scene, diversifying the range of political discourse.

It was, however, only after the Second World War, under the impact of the loss of the war and of the American occupation—when, as we have seen, the old premises of the political order lost some of their legitimacy and a major upsurge of new forms of political and industrial organization took place—that the socialist party emerged as a strong and potentially innovative force, seemingly moving in a social-democratic direction that paralleled developments in Europe during that period. In the public sector, relatively strong connections between socialist politicians and intellectuals and working class organizations emerged, class consciousness among industrial workers increased, and political class movements developed with some trade unions playing an important role.[41]

But these developments were rather short-lived. In about the mid-1950s the socialist and labor movements split, and the socialist party, having lost its original impetus, became seemingly domesticated by the evolving Japanese political system. Leftist parties—the Marxist and socialist parties and a fairly radical communist party—were more prominent than their counterparts in the United States and were able, partially due to the differences between the Japanese and American electoral systems, to mobilize throughout the postwar period around a third of the votes (36 percent in 1958, 32 percent in 1992).[42] But in the 1993 election the Social Democrats were able to get about half as many votes (16–17 percent)—and certainly did not follow the European pattern. Above all, they were not able to attain any prominent role in restructuring the premises of the political center, as socialist movements were able to do in Europe, where they imbued the center with their symbols and participated directly in the formulation and implementation of policy. Thus Werner Sombart's famous question can be paraphrased here—Why is there (almost) no socialism in Japan?[43]

X At the same time, the immediate postwar period—until about the mid-1950s—saw a significant opening up of the basic parameters of public discourse. This tendency was reinforced, first, by the fact that the close cooperation between academics and the bureaucracy, which developed in the early Meiji era but started to disintegrate at the end of the Meiji and during the Taishō era, was further undermined and, second, by the more general and continual diversification of elite groups.

There developed highly diversified academic, journalistic, and literary organizations, many of them constituting important arenas or enclaves of distinct (for instance, Marxist) intellectual and academic activity and discourse. The members of these groups were active participants in public discussion and exerted considerable influence, as Herbert Passin has shown, on public opinion and policy.[44]

There developed also among these groups a wide range of protest activities, critical social discourses, and artistic activities—with the emergence, for instance, of new "proletarian" theater and "critical" films. In many cases, intellectuals participated in protest movements or demonstrations, such as those connected with the peace treaty and, much later, those opposing the elimination of Toshiba University, the creation of Tsukuba University and the International Center for Research in Japanese Studies, or the behavior of the Meiji Gakuin University on the occasion of the death of the Shōwa emperor, which initiated a series of open lectures and discussions on the emperor system and did not fly the flag at half-mast.[45] Some of the most important works of contemporary Japanese literature—as, for instance, the novels and stories of the 1994 Nobel laureate Ōe Kenzaburō—strongly espoused oppositional terms.

But there was a marked change in the nature of this discourse between the first postwar decade and what followed. In the immediate postwar period, up to about 1955, one of the foci of this discourse was the possibility of continual transformation—denationalization—of Japanese society, the creation of a "truly" modern society based on "real" individualism, breaking through the constraints of the preceding authoritarian and military regime. True, these debates were at times highly abstract, their concrete relations to the emerging social and political reality not always clear, and the emphasis on subjective autonomy that characterized large parts of this discourse not easily translated into realistic political action— but at least they signaled the search for ways of changing this reality. This discourse was continually interwoven with the perennial problems of the relation between Japan, the West, and modernization—and as in preceding periods the themes of social or political transformation were in a way subsumed under those of Japan's relations to modernity and the war.

The relative political weakness of this discourse became apparent in the debate about the peace treaty, again when the intellectual discourse shifted, to follow Victor Koschmann's analysis, to the problems of the revision of the U.S.-Japan Security Treaty and the growing criticism of mass society and technological capitalism, and later on in postmodernist discourses.[46]

Multiple discourses of protest against the managed society—for instance, ecological movements and women's groups—thrived, often connected with intellectually oriented peace or antiwar ideals and proclamations.

Common to all these debates—which were continuously interwoven with those about Japanese authenticity, Westernization, and modernity— was the tendency of the intellectuals to promulgate stands with respect to the principled issues that, while extremely radical, were difficult to translate into concrete political actions that might indeed influence or transform the premises of the system they so strongly criticized.

XI Throughout this period there also developed, on the local and to some extent, the national scene, many other movements—citizens' and ecological movements, women's movements, and numerous movements of local opposition. In the late 1960s and early 1970s, the worldwide wave of student unrest swept through Japan, giving rise to intensive student radicalism.[47] Such movements have continued to sprout and have become an integral part of the Japanese political scene. Some of these movements were connected with oppositionary political parties, which were often very prominent locally.[48]

These movements, like the peasant uprisings of earlier periods, were triggered by causes not dissimilar from those which account for the development of movements in other modern societies, and they also seemed, on the face of it, to challenge the salient characteristics of the existing political order. Collectively these movements promulgated a great variety of new concrete demands in many areas of life, including the arenas of local government, housing, and the environment; egalitarian and communal themes also often surfaced. Many of these movements espoused new, sometimes radical themes and raised new issues in the public arena, continuously contributing to the widening of the range of public discourse in Japan.[49]

And yet, however prevalent these movements and their concrete successes—which were sometimes indeed spectacular—they were not able to change some of the core characteristics of the political regime.

Within many of these movements—especially perhaps among the student radicals and later among the extreme terrorist groups—there developed also a growing tendency to confrontation, sometimes violent, with the authorities, and to litigation, undermining the picture of a society based on harmonious consensus. Such movements usually expressed their positions in terms of the denial of the moral legitimacy of authorities, who were said to have abandoned the trust with which they had been endowed.

The burgeoning of confrontational situations and litigation in the post–Second World War period may have been due, first, to the growing complexity attendant on continuous economic development. It was also due, as Ishida Takeshi has suggested, to the fact that after the Second World War, with the abolition of the imperial system and the promulgation of a democratic constitution, the apex of the vertical hierarchical arrangements was taken away, making for greater difficulty in resolving conflicts between actors in various layers of the vertical hierarchies that abounded in Japanese society.[50]

What is important here is not only the failure of the more radical opposition, especially the socialist and communist parties,[51] either to form a government or, after 1955, to participate in one and shape its policies; nor is it that these movements, especially the socialist party, failed to undermine, at least until 1993, the hegemony of the LDP—and even in 1993 the LDP lost its majority through the defection of many groups from within, not through the challenge of the socialists. What is probably of greater importance is that they were unable to change the modes of decision making and public political discourse or to give rise to a more autonomous civil society and public arena—even though they certainly broadened the range of public discourse.

Cutting across, or in parallel with the political developments, or the social movements in the political arena, was the continual development of new religions, referred to in chapter 3, and the creation of new cultural and social spaces and new themes of discourse. None of these, however, had much direct impact on the prevalent premises of the Japanese social and political order.

XII Thus, with respect to all these periods of change and openness, a rather complicated pictures emerges—a picture which bears very closely on our central question about the specific nature of the modern and contemporary Japanese social and political systems. We have seen that—as was the case with respect to the specific type of capitalism that developed in Japan, and in close relation to that development—Japan's modern constitutional democratic regime, and indeed its overall modern social structure, developed according to a very distinctive pattern.

A good starting point for the discussion of the specific characteristics of this modern society is the analysis of the structuration of the major institutional arenas, considering especially the extent to which the various universalistic, egalitarian, and individualistic premises and principles presumed inherent in modernization (like the universalistic premises inherent in Confucianism and Buddhism) became predominant in Japan and shaped the major institutional arenas of Japanese society.

On the one hand, many arenas of social life were restructured according to universalistic and achievement criteria. This was especially true, as we have seen, in the occupational arena—in marked contrast to the rigid official stratification system of the Tokugawa—and in the educational arena. In most of these arenas there developed far-reaching extensions of the range of universalistic principles or criteria, as can be seen, for instance, in the growing importance of the examination system in the educational arena. Closely related was the fact that the modern organizations that developed in Japan came to resemble those in other, especially Western societies; their basic organizational frameworks and their nomenclature were usually, especially in the political and scholarly literature, taken from the West as well.

On the other hand, however, many of the frameworks within which these educational and occupational roles and activities were integrated differed from those prevalent in other modern societies, especially with respect to their organizational rules and goals, their modes of internal integration, and their interaction with their relevant environments. They were organized, as we have seen, in strongly vertical, particularistic modes, and within them these vertical hierarchical orientations persisted—even if in continuously restructured ways. Indeed some of the most crucial organizational aspects of Western modern societies—the open public legal system or the universalistic bureaucratic one—were rather weak on the Japanese scene. Moreover, the ground rules according to which these modern organizations were structured and regulated strongly resembled those that were operative in the respective sectors of Japanese societies in other periods. The application of universalistic principles prevalent elsewhere was hemmed in through the reconstruction of social networks in various sectors of Japanese society, even in seemingly "nonnetwork" organizations, such as political, ideological, or sectlike religious groups.

A similar picture emerges with respect to the political arena. The democracy that was ultimately established in this period was certainly much more an "institutional" than a "participatory" one. It was not only that the opposition parties were unable to form a viable alternative to the LDP, or that the socialist or social-democratic alternative had not become a viable option. Perhaps more important was the ambiguity with regard to the basis of its legitimacy, the continuation of secretive and diffuse patterns of decision making with weak accountability of the rulers to constitutional principles, and the weakness of civil society.[52] The conflation between national community, state, and civil society seemed to continue, even if the number of participants in the public arena and the disputes between them greatly increased. At the same time there seems to have developed, at least from the 1960s on, an even greater consensus than before, around the emphasis on economic growth, which, together with the seeming lack of success of the movements of protest and other oppositionary polities, appears to bear out fully the perception of the Japanese system as a closed immobilist one.

It is clear that, in all these periods of transition, the possibility of institutionalizing radically new premises constituted a very real goal for many intellectuals and some political actors. However, this seems to have remained true only for relatively short periods of time. Then other premises—usually newly reconstituted versions of the ostensibly traditional emphasis on sacral, natural criteria, with a very strong orientation toward collectivity—quickly became institutionalized.

The single most important illustration of this tendency is, of course, the instituting of the emperor system as against a constitutional or liberal one in the Meiji state. Similarly, toward the end of the Taishō era in the early 1920s, it became clear that the attempts to institutionalize a more liberal political system were not going to be very successful. But neither, paradoxically, were the extreme right-wing ideologies in the 1930s able to institutionalize a fascist or totalitarian regime, giving rise instead— again following Gordon's nomenclature—to "Imperial democracy" and "Imperial fascism."[53] A similar picture emerges in the post–Second World War era with respect both to the development of what has been called an institutional rather than a participatory democracy and to the crystallization of the Japanese collective consciousness and its definition in relation to broader international settings—yet another problem that has constituted a continuous focus of debate in Japan. There can be no doubt that after the Second World War the Japanese collective consciousness and identity shed its more "archaic" mythological components, as formulated in the Meiji ideology. Yet the basic inward-looking, particularistic dimensions of this identity, of the civil religion or theology initially promulgated under the Meiji, continued to predominate—even if they also became in many ways rather empty.[54] It was also in this period that the *Nihonjinron* literature burgeoned.

The picture of modern and contemporary Japanese society is, on the one hand, one of turbulence, of very dynamic changes—many in directions suggesting the high degree of innovation and entrepreneurism presumably predominant in other modern industrial societies. Yet at the same time the overall pattern of Japanese institutional dynamics differs in some crucial aspects—those that touch on the very central dimensions of modernity—from those to be found elsewhere, attesting to a rather distinctive pattern of modernity, indeed to a rather distinctive modern society.

XIII It is these distinctive characteristics of modern Japanese society, especially as manifested in the political arena, that gave rise to the perception by Japanese and Western intellectuals alike of especially contemporary Japanese society as highly regulated—not by any center, as was the case in the Meiji state, but by a repressive, nonresponsive, immobilist "system."

The analysis of the numerous movements of protest—and of the fate of the major oppositional groups—seems to reinforce the picture of a largely unresponsive system. Indeed, the upshot of the preceding discussion seems to be that, despite the far-reaching changes that have taken place since the Second World War, which created many institutions similar to those of Western democracies, the contemporary political system in Japan has not developed in the direction of either the European or the American democracies, just as in the 1930s the military government did not develop in the direction of a totalitarian system. Instead, it seemed to exhibit several of the characteristics identified as central in the Meiji period and before—particularly with respect to the prevalence of guidance by the center in most arenas of social life, the narrowness or weakness of autonomous public space, and the pattern of decision making—even if their concrete contours changed greatly.

Thus, the preceding analysis seems to reinforce the picture of modern and contemporary Japan as a highly regulated and repressive homogeneous society or system based on images of harmony and consensus manipulated by the ruling elites and a highly repressive system. But is this the whole picture? Are nonresponsiveness, repressiveness, and immobility inherent characteristics of such a system or such regulation?

Such conclusions not only present a very static picture of Japanese society; they are also very similar, even if in a paradoxical, "mirror image" way, to some of the more extreme and ideological pronouncements of the *Nihonjinron* literature, which presented a very harmonious picture of Japanese society. Such conclusions would seem to indicate, as does the *Nihonjinron* literature, that these precepts and ground rules were continuously and "happily ever after" observed in most sectors of Japanese society almost as if they were naturally given, even if, contrary to the Nihonjinron literature, more critical appraisals of these situations saw the apparent consensus as the result of manipulation by elites.

The preceding discussion of the different periods of "tribulation" in Japanese modern and contemporary history indicates that such a simplistic picture is wrong, that it is false and misleading. Indeed, throughout Japanese history, including the modern and contemporary eras, and in most sectors of Japanese society, there have continuously developed varied and numerous manifestations of dissatisfaction with these precepts and ground rules—constituting the other, disharmonious side of the popular picture. Japanese society has continuously been ridden by attempts to escape the confinement of its predominant rules; by deviant behavior and personality disorders; and—like any other society—by conflict and protest, especially but not only among the lower or marginal groups. These ambivalent, even rebellious attitudes toward the basic precepts or ground rules of social interaction can also be found in different arenas of cultural activity—in literary and artistic creations and activities, in "high" and popular culture alike, in formal and informal occasions, and in a great variety of liminal situations in all arenas of life.

It is impossible to understand the nature of modern and contemporary Japanese society without analyzing the impact of all these manifestations of disharmony. Let us proceed now to have a closer look at this problem.

"Disharmony," Conflict, and Protest and Their Impact
Regulation, Control, and Responsiveness

THE INCIDENCE AND CAUSES OF "DISHARMONY"

I Let's proceed now to a closer examination of the numerous manifestations of "disharmony," of deviant behavior and personality disorders that have developed in modern and contemporary Japanese society; of their impact on the Japanese social and political system; and of what light their analysis may throw on the picture of the Japanese system as repressive and unresponsive.

If there is something specific to Japan, as opposed to any other society, it is not the existence of deviant or conflictual behavior and of protest, but particular aspects of their occurrence: their incidence, their scope, institutional locations, their specific manifestations, the ways in which they have been defined in different sectors of Japanese society and the modes of regulating or resolving them, and the impact of all these factors on the structure and dynamics of Japanese society.

Hence, in our quest to understand the specific characteristics of modern and contemporary Japanese society, we shall have to analyze the impact of the various manifestations of disharmony—of protest and conflict and the numerous changes that have taken place in Japanese society—on the basic premises and ground rules of social activity.

II Most manifestations of disharmony in Japan—personality disorders, criminal behavior, suicide,[1] conflict, and movements of protest—seem to have several things in common: First, all have been relatively widespread in most sectors of Japanese society, belying the "harmony-conflict" model; second, many are rooted in seemingly harmonious aspects of Japanese society; third, they have relatively little visibility, either in statistical data or in public awareness; and, fourth, the specific modes of defining them and coping with or regulating them are similar, as compared with other industrialized countries.

It is not our intention to present here a full-scale analysis of all these processes. In any case, the evidence about these different manifestations of disharmony is, of course, very uneven; in some cases we have reliable statistical data, in others mainly historical sources or ethnographic data of uneven reliability, and we shall have to make the best of them as we go along. Accordingly we hope only to provide some general indications which are of interest from the point of view of our analysis.

We shall start our exploration with a brief examination of patterns of personality disorders and therapies, above all in contemporary Japanese society. The available data indicate that the extent of such occurrences is not negligible but may be smaller than in other industrialized countries. Thus, for instance, by 1975 there were about a thousand mental hospitals of over twenty beds each, providing around a quarter of a million psychiatric beds, served by approximately six thousand physicians, fewer per capita than in most Western countries.[2]

A similar picture can be discerned with respect to delinquency and criminal behavior in Japan. Contrary to the harmony model, delinquency and crime do exist and they are indeed "caused" by some of the oppressive dimensions of the Japanese social structure.[3] At the same time, however, their incidence is much lower than in other industrial countries.[4] A few figures will suffice to show the dimensions of that difference.

In 1977 for every 100,000 people, there were 20.8 murders in New York, 1.7 in Tokyo; New York had 994 robberies, Tokyo 3.1; there were 6,525 burglaries in New York, 576 in Tokyo. Only in the rate of assaults on the person do the two cities come even close: 652 to 148. The contrast is stunning, but it is not central to my purpose to compare our two societies. The extraordinary thing about the Japanese figures is that they represent either substantial declines since the 1950s or at worst a steady rate over the past twenty-odd years. It should not be forgotten that it is in that very time span that the massive migration of the rural population to the cities of Japan has occurred.[5]

Although overall crime rates in Japan have increased since the mid-1970s, serious crime (murder, robbery, rape, arson and felonies) have continued to decline—a trend that is characteristic to Japan since the early 1960s. Except for traffic violations fewer crimes were committed in 1980 than in 1950. Furthermore, the clearance rate for major crimes lies consistently above those of other advanced industrial states—even if their low crime rates are results of non-comparable crime statistics.[6]

There seems to be a rather widespread opinion among scholars that by world standards, Japan does not have a crime problem and that its criminal justice system is performing with remarkable efficiency. This is decidedly the case in comparison with the United States.

> Contrary to what Americans tend to think, Japan's low crime rate cannot be attributed to stiff sentences. Compared with the U.S., in fact, Japan's sentences are lighter in every category of crime, with one exception: Japan does provide capital punishment for homicide (Penal Code, Articles 199 and 200).[7]

> Similarly, the serious crime rate in the United States is over four times the total crime rate of Japan. Only 1.1 per 100,000 of the Japanese population were victims of murder in 1989, compared with 8.7 Americans; for rape the variations were 1.3 and 38.1. The 1989 data were even more striking for robbery: 1.3 cases per 100,000 population in Japan, contrasted with 233.0 in the United States, while for larceny they were 1,203 and 5,077.[8]

Another side of the criminal scene in Japan is the prevalence of highly organized crime—the Yakuza. The development of organized crime is, of course, not unique to Japan, but some characteristics of its Japanese manifestation are rather specific, as we shall see later. Here suffice it to point out that the strongly symbiotic relations between the Yakuza and the police may also explain the relatively low level of crime in Japan.[9]

III It is not only personality disorders, criminal behavior, and suicide that indicate the prevalence of often deep dissatisfaction with the existing social order in Japan.[10] Japanese historical and contemporary society has also abounded in both conflict and highly articulated movements of protest, political violence and terrorism both on the right and the left, to which we have already referred.

Conflict has recently surfaced as a major theme in studies of Japanese society, largely in reaction to the group-harmony model. Often attributed to Chie Nakane, this model was in fact already promulgated in the early Meiji era and seems to have been prevalent in studies for two or three decades.[11] A survey of these studies and the controversies they have engendered is beyond the scope of this chapter. Suffice it to point out the rather obvious fact that Japanese society has never been without conflict. It is enough to peruse any book on Japanese history—ancient, medieval, or modern—or the continuously expanding literature on conflict in Japanese society,[12] to recognize the ubiquity of conflict throughout Japanese history and in all sectors of society, especially in periods of intensive social change.[13]

Whatever the exact incidence of conflict, which is in any case difficult to measure, its very ubiquity belies the implication of the consensus-harmony model that Japanese society is basically conflictless.

The same is true of the most extreme, or at least the most visible, manifestations of disharmony, namely protest movements. As we have seen, a great number of movements of protest arose in the period after the Second World War.[14] Many of these movements, involving various labor or local groups, built on the organizational and symbolic foundations of their predecessors in the Meiji and Taishō—and even the Tokugawa—periods.[15] It was only natural that, given the democratization of the regime, many oppositionary movements would spring up in this period. The most intensive development of protest movements took place in the late 1940s and early 1950s.[16] Also in this period many such movements became both radical and relatively widespread in ways reminiscent of European socialist and labor movements. Later on, in the 1960s and 1970s, political demonstrations and terrorist activities abounded.[17]

Rebellious and subversive attitudes also developed, as in other societies, in various arenas of cultural creativity, in literature and in the arts as well as in popular culture and in the "worlds of fantasy." Indeed, as David Pollack has recently shown, even some of the greatest works of modern Japanese literature—by Natsume Sōseki, Tanizaki Junichirō, Kawabata Yasunari, Abe Kōbō, Mishima Yukio, and others whose literary works have been seen either as affirmations of the new order or escapes from it—contain multiple themes and can be read as radical criticisms of this order.[18]

I V Whatever the exact incidence of these manifestations of disharmony in Japan, their causes are connected to specific points of stress and structural tension in Japanese society.[19] For instance, the causes of many of the personality disorders seem to be closely related to the specific burdens of life in Japanese society—to overwhelming feelings of inadequacy in social relations, in living up to the levels of performance and achievement expected in many social contexts; to the tension between such expectations and the demands of group harmony; to feelings of inadequacy and shame, instilled through socialization, toward sacrificial parents; or to anxieties about disclosing inner feelings in inappropriate situations or being odious or unpleasant to others.[20]

Whatever the deeper psychological causes of personality disorders in Japan, many of their symptoms become especially acute in situations of social transition or times of stress in school, career and work, and the like—when the pressures characteristic of Japanese social structure become more intense.[21]

V Similarly, the occurrence of protest was not external to the basic characteristics of Japanese society. True enough, many such conflicts, as for instance industrial ones, were similar to those in other industrial societies; yet several bases of conflict were built into the structure of Japanese society, the characteristics of which explain the specific locations of conflict in different sectors of Japanese society.

The most important root of conflict was the organization of any group according to hierarchical principles, as represented by its designated (ascriptive or elected) leaders and the more egalitarian, horizontal tendencies within it. There was conflict with respect to the concrete application of such principles between the internal solidarity and interests of various subgroups—family, village group, or company—and those of their broader settings, necessarily extensions of the family or the village and usually defined in terms of hierarchical, vertical order.[22] And there was conflict focused on specifying the exact locus of vertical networks and the mutual obligations of lower and higher echelons within different such organizations.[23]

True enough, the overt ideology of organizational obligations tended to stress mutual harmony and benevolence—themes that became especially predominant with the infusion of Neo-Confucianism into Japanese life—yet acute dissensions often developed around these foci, especially in periods of intensive change when these sensitive points of Japanese social structure became very visible. Indeed, the very emphasis on harmony could exacerbate confrontational situations; because conflict could not be admitted to exist, there were few institutional mechanisms to cope with and contain it.

Moreover, the fact that continuity of social interaction depended to such an extent on vertical pyramidal coalitions meant that when these broke down—or were not yet crystallized in any given situation—quite intensive confrontations could emerge that could not easily be dealt with or regulated. The combination in some situations—for instance, in the student uprisings of the 1960s, during a period of severe confusion in the political arena—of the weakening of vertical links with the ideological emphasis on harmony and conflict avoidance could exacerbate the confrontation and promote breakdown *within* the existing framework without the hierarchical framework as such being broken down.

The preceding analysis certainly indicates that Japanese society is not the harmonious, consensual society depicted in much of the Nihonjinron literature—and, in a sort of mirror image, in some of the "radical" literature, which depicts Japan as totally regulated. Yet the apparent failure of protest movements to significantly influence the "system" may indeed reinforce the picture of Japanese society as a highly regulated and repressive one, in which the elites create and manipulate an illusion of harmony and consensus. Few manifestation of disharmony, of protest, have had far-reaching, transformative effects on the overall social structure; many of them have been segregated in newly created—ecological or institutional—social spaces, seemingly without having affected the broader contexts and premises of the society.

ORGANIZATIONAL AND IDEOLOGICAL CHARACTERISTICS OF DISHARMONY AND PROTEST

VI How can we explain the seemingly scant impact of the various manifestations of disharmony? We shall address this question in several stages, beginning with an exploration of the extent to which there developed within most oppositional movements the organizational and ideological potential for transformative impact. Let us first examine some organizational characteristics of these movements—starting with various terrorist and criminal organizations—and their mode of interweaving with the broader society.

The internal structure of many of the protest movements, even of the most extreme ones, like the terrorist Red Army *(Sekigun)*, has been characterized, as Patricia Steinhoff shows, by an organization which, in terms of authority and status, is very conventional:

> For all its innovations in action and its revolutionary intentions, Sekigun turns out to have been surprisingly conventional in both its organization and its social assumptions. Its members may have rejected corporate Japan and the Japanese government ideologically, but they could have fit right into either institution as well trained employees. That should not be surprising because that was where their educational achievements would have directed them had they not become involved with Sekigun.[24]

Such conventionality can be seen in an even more far-reaching way in the structure of the Yakuza.[25] Organized crime, as we have noted, is not unique to Japan, but its Japanese form does manifest some rather specific characteristics. Yakuza organizations are structured very much according to the prevailing Japanese pattern of group relations—with strong internal control—with an ethic not dissimilar from that of other sectors of Japanese society. Through various arrangements with the police, these organizations also become tightly interwoven with the overall network structure of Japanese society.[26] They lead a semirecognized existence as a sector of Japanese society, semilegitimized and publicly quite visible. They exhibit some distinctive Japanese characteristics, such as emphasis on personal loyalty and connection, as compared with organized crime in other countries—such as the Cosa Nostra, with its greater emphasis on loyalty to the organization.[27]

Such similarity between the broader structure of a society and that of its deviant and criminal organizations is not in itself unique to Japan.

Indeed, the comparison between the Yakuza and the Cosa Nostra points to the affinity of the latter with the American (and to some extent southern European) social structure.[28]

What is, however, rather distinctive about the Japanese scene is the close interweaving of the various manifestations of disharmony—be they deviant or criminal groups or various types of popular culture—with the hegemonic cultural and social sectors. As a result, there develop within the former but few points that can serve as levers for going beyond the hegemonic premises of the given culture. Thus, for instance, the Yakuza's close relation to—indeed, its identification with—the broader Japanese society is also manifest in the fact that the Yakuza, while portraying themselves as partial outsiders with respect to the mainstream of society, at the same time present themselves as the bearers of positive Japanese virtues—loyalty, perseverance, and the like.[29] Interestingly enough, they also often serve as socializing agencies for marginal or Korean populations, imbuing them with the basic orientations of Japanese society and giving them an accepted collective identity within that society.[30] Their self-presentation could be—and has been—interpreted as filling some of the mediatory roles between polluted spaces and pure spaces performed by strangers or artists in the ancient mythological and folkloristic conceptions (see chap. 14).[31]

VII A similar picture emerges with respect to the organization of most of the movements of protest to which we have referred.[32] It is very interesting to examine the structure and ideological orientation of one of the most spectacular new movements—namely the Sanrizuka movement, which opposed construction of the new airport at Narita. As David Apter and Nagayo Sawa tell us, it differed from the "usual" environmental movements:

> It was more than a farmers' movement, although farmers were and must be at the core of it. If it has involved whole families in the community, it has also served as a lightning rod for protest movements all over Japan: anti-nuclear, environmental, and peace groups, groups protesting discrimination against a pariah caste like the *burakumin*. It had direct links . . . with those fighting against the presence of American forces and nuclear ships.[33]

In the concluding chapter of their analysis, they tell us something about the fate of the movement:

> Nevertheless, although it is a movement with a farm base, that base is small and shrinking. This is a protest by people becoming marginalized, their way of life rendered functionally superfluous; that is what gives the movement its special quality. It suggests, too, that it would have failed without

the support of the militants seeking an AMPO 1960 [the demonstrations calling for the revision of the security treaty with the United States] on a larger and more permanent scale. Bringing in the many citizen protest groups transformed the fight over land into a fight over the nature of the state, a rural-based class struggle that would envelop the trade unions in a total mobilization for revolution. Exactly what kind of revolution might occur no one was quite sure; in any case, perspectives varied with ideological preference and between sects and individuals.[34]

Thus even the Sanrizuka, one of the most spectacular new movements of protest, was able to reach beyond its specific domain only for a relatively short period of time; was successful only with respect to other protest movements, such as antinuclear groups, religious sects, and some student groups; and scarcely affected broader sectors of Japanese society.[35] Such movements did not tend to come together in a broad programmatic framework and were characterized by strong sectarian tendencies, which often constituted the major causes of their disintegration.[36]

The momentary success of this movement in overcoming the inability to generalize its concrete grievances and reach out to a wider public seems to have been at best transitory, its great visibility owed largely to the media.

VIII Most Japanese protest movements have also been characterized by a continuous interplay between confrontational outbursts and accommodation to the existing political formations, usually contingent on the authorities' acceptance of some of their demands. At the same time the authorities have been left in control, not only of the regulating agencies and mechanisms, but above all of the power to provide the ultimate definition and legitimation of the demands of the needs of the different groups.

Most of these movements have evinced interesting organizational similarities to the movements of protest of earlier times—especially those that developed, as we shall see, in the Togukawa regime. They have been relatively enclosed in their own domains—finding it difficult to extend their appeals even to groups with seemingly similar interests or to transform their concrete demands into broader political goals acceptable to a wider public. Even movements that seem to succeed in effecting such a transformation, as we have seen with respect to the Sanrizuka movement, have done so for only a brief period of time.

The various types of citizen revolt that have emerged in the modern period have evinced, as a 1973 editorial in the *Japan Interpreter* pointed out, four basic characteristics, similar to those of early peasant uprisings: "They are desperate struggles by local people in defense of their basic right to live; they are non-ideological; they are monolithic; and they are often characterized by the escalation of tactics from peaceful petitions and appeals to direct forceful actions."[37]

Of special interest is that, in these modern movements as in the earlier ones, very few autonomous intellectual or professional groups have taken part; it has mostly been highly sectarian and isolated intellectuals who were active. This has lately changed, but only to a small extent—in some recent cases litigated against the authorities, relatively independent lawyers have helped greatly.

Many extremist groups—be they radical, leftist, or rightist intellectuals or activists, or various terrorist groups—have been active only in small, segregated sectors, even if their activities have become very visible. They have not usually been able to mobilize wider support; once they start to reach out for such support, and insofar as they discontinue their sectarian disputes, they tend to become domesticated or co-opted by the hegemonic sectors and structure. At the same time, however, they have greatly changed some of the parameters of the political and social discourse and created spaces for new social and cultural activities.[39]

IX   A closer look at the reasons why Japan's Social Democratic Party has failed until now to become part of the ruling coalition, or to influence policy significantly in line with its principled declarations, is also very instructive. This lack of success, as Stockwin among others has shown, has been due to several factors—especially the internal structure of the socialist movements, their relations with the trade unions, and their attitudes toward industrial disputes and the broader public. These characteristics have been greatly reinforced, as we shall see later, by structural conditions generated by conscious policies of the authorities and business leaders. It is, however, important for our analysis to note that these policies were successful.

From the late nineteenth century until the Second World War, the socialist movement in Japan was comprised of a number of intellectual groups—various moderate ones and more extreme ones, which were suppressed by the police. No unity ever developed among these groups. Their various ideological legacies reemerged—albeit in different guises—after the Second World War, when the socialist party consisted of a right-wing faction, which included the moderate trade unions; an extreme left wing; and several factions in between. Ideological disputes among the factions, fueled by the Korean war, greatly contributed to the weakness of the Japanese Socialist Party. This weakness was reinforced by the JSP's dependence on the trade unions, especially the Sōhyō. These ideological and organizational factors—above all the continuous factionalism and the vertical hierarchical relation to predominant unions, yet without the flexibility typical of such relations elsewhere in Japanese society—explain the weakness and idiosyncracies of the Japanese socialist movement in comparison with its European counterparts.

In the political arena, these movements were characterized by factionalism, with a bifurcation between extreme ideological, sectarian disputes, on the one hand, and attempts at pragmatic politics, on the other. They also developed rather special relations with the trade unions and with the conduct of industrial relations. Throughout most of their history they were not as closely related as their European counterparts to the organization of the working class and the waging of the industrial struggle; articulating the concrete demands of the workers was not (with the partial exception of the late 1940s and early 1950s) related to the socialist ideologies. The ideology of class consciousness expressed in political terms was not politically very effective either among the working class or among wider sectors of the society, from which the socialist parties would have to mobilize support in order to gain political prominence.[40]

The upshot of these developments, from at least the mid-1960s, has been a far-reaching domestication both of the ideology of the Socialist Party and of its mode of political operation, which has veered between accommodation and participation in the parliamentary arena, on the one hand, and symbolic oppositionary declarations, on the other (see chapter 6 for greater detail), but on the whole has left behind specific class symbolism and more confrontational modes of political activity.

The leaders of the socialist and labor groups have oscillated between spouting radical slogans and playing according to the accepted rules. Because of this and the concomitant tendency to factionalism along ideological lines that has characterized the Japanese socialist (and communist) movements, they have been unable (except during relatively short periods of economic crisis after the Second World War) to appeal to the wider electorate, to withstand the outcomes of the repressive measures and policies directed against them by business leaders and the authorities, and to incorporate the demands of such wide groups in their program. Their successes have come mostly on the local level or through indirect influence on policy (see chap. 6)—often based on pragmatic appeals to larger sectors of the population, usually about specific issues.[41]

When, in 1989 in the aftermath of the Recruit scandal, which shook the standing of the LDP, the Socialist Party emerged—if only for a short period—as a possible alternative, it was already highly domesticated, with a rather weak program of its own. It was found also to be rent by corruption and sectarianism and was indeed the greatest single loser in the 1993 elections; even though it joined the new coalition and a socialist later became prime minister, the government continued to be composed mainly of LDP members.

X No less important than the organizational characteristics of the movements of protest are the basic themes they have promulgated. These have been characterized by the relative—needless to say, only relative—weakness of principled oppositional themes couched in universalistic terms; by the emphasis, to use Thomas Smith's felicitous expression, on "the right to benevolence,"[42] which leads to difficulty mobilizing other groups in the name of class consciousness; and by their similarity with various liminal situations—be they pilgrimages or popular festive events—which have abounded in Japanese society throughout its history and in which similar themes have often been promulgated. As Winston Davis and others have shown, in all these events there developed a strong emphasis on communitas,[43] and all entailed a very high level of social disorder, but they had but few politically radical, transformative, or revolutionary potentials.[44]

The specific characteristics of many of these liminal movements with their great disruptive potentials have also been manifest—as, we shall see, was also the case with respect to movements of protest under the Tokugawa—in the weakness of political utopianism, as against millenarianism, in Japanese society. The directions and limits of Japanese utopianism can perhaps be seen in one central theme which has been voiced by many of these movements—namely, that of autonomy, which was usually defined in terms of oppositionary withdrawal, of finding some arena of activity independent of political control.[45]

Indeed many of these movements of protest have been characterized by the predominance within them of what Koschmann has called "expressive protest." To follow Krauss's exposition of Koschmann's view:

> Active forms of protest that have occurred tend to be of the expressive rather than instrumental kind. Expressive protest brings outward behavior in conformity with internal belief, but more for the sake of provoking one's sincerity of commitment than for accomplishing a particular end through rational, organized action. Thus only the release of frustration is attained by meaningful social change. Although Koschmann believes such patterns of authority and protest remain influential through contemporary times, he sees more recent forms of dissent like citizens' movements as possibly breaking through the mold of Japanese political ethos.[46]

XI An important aspect of the relations between, on the one hand, the orientations and activities of the various movements of protest and, on the other, both the broader sectors of Japanese society and the more hegemonic elites is manifest in some aspects of the ideologies and patterns of behavior which have developed among many potentially oppositionary intellectuals in the periods of change, of seeming openness. At the beginning of the Meiji era, in the Taishō period, in the 1930s, and perhaps above all in the post–Second World War period, intellectual reformers promoted the institutionalization of a variety of universalistic or "liberal" approaches or principles.

In almost all these cases, they failed to have their proposals accepted or implemented, and many if not most seem to have given up their aspirations. Some indeed elaborated justifications for the impossibility of institutionalizing such principles, basically accepting the primacy of some version of the "natural-primordial" approach, as institutionalized in the emperor system, and of national considerations. Indeed, one of the most interesting aspects of the intellectual discourse in Japan in the Taishō and early Shōwa periods was the facility with which critical evaluation of modernity couched in seemingly radical terms oscillated between the denial of modernity or attempts to overcome it and the extolment of technological modernity as the fullest manifestation of the Japanese spirit. In contrast to this discourse, with its veering between affirmation and denial of modernity, stood, for instance, Maruyama Masao's not very successful attempt to develop a distinct critical evaluation of modernity on the basis of universal values.[47]

Similarly, these reformers were not successful in opposing either the attempts of the elites to "tame" individualistic orientations or the strong emphasis on economic achievement. The achievement orientation that developed in many sectors of Japanese society was set within a collective framework and did not develop in the direction of a principled individualism, which would have defined the individual as an independent unit with a right to autonomous access to the center of the respective collectivities. The same has been true of the communitarian or egalitarian themes found in the various popular movements and social and economic activities, as well as of the different expressions of popular culture to which we have referred. Both the achievement and egalitarian orientations have been channeled toward functional service to the collectivity or have developed in autonomous, segregated spaces of social consciousness.[48] Those intellectuals who have continued to uphold seemingly unconventional liberal or communist views have tended to coalesce into small, usually sectarian groups, which have often become objects of repression or social ostracism.

Even many radically heterodox intellectuals, especially the Marxists, who often denied the legitimacy of the imperial system, have not only had to attempt to explain its prevalence in terms of their analysis, but have tended to particularize, to "Japanize," the more universalistic components of, for instance, Marxism; they have oscillated between particularistic and universalistic orientations without finding a way to interweave them in a common cultural or political union.[49] Many of the themes developed in modern Japanese literature have also moved in this direction.[50]

The fate of many Marxist intellectuals and scholars—who were very prominent on the intellectual scene—is indicate of this basic tendency. Of special importance was the way in which these scholars addressed the problem of explaining the specific characteristics of the modern Japanese experience. Many of them tried to put this experience into the framework of universal Marxist categories—feudalism, the petite bourgeoisie, and the like—without critically examining to what extent these categories were adequate. Others—or often the same individuals later in their lives—searched for Japanese uniqueness in terms of some "group" spiritual qualities. Others, like Nakano Shigeharu, developed a critical stance in which the development of Japanese capitalism, which encompassed also the creation of mass consumption, was taken as being against culture in general.[51] Paradoxically, some of these concepts of culture seem to be not far removed from Yanagita's folklore conception of the Japanese community.[52] Common to all of them was their inability to develop any common ground between their use of universal categories and the particular Japanese reality—to develop a discourse that would enable them to participate critically, in an autonomous way, in the political arena and to transcend the basic premises of the hegemonic Japanese political discourse.[53]

The other side of this failure in the public realm has been the retreat of many intellectuals into the private arena. This phenomenon—which also has its roots in the early Meiji period but became especially prominent in the Taishō and post–Second World War eras—entails a far-reaching "privatization" of culture, an almost total depoliticization of the intellectual discourse.

At the same time many sectors of society tended to develop new spaces of leisure time and activities closely connected with the growth of a consumer society. Within these new spaces developed many themes subversive of the hegemonic culture. Many of these arenas were imbued with communitarian and egalitarian themes, building, as we shall see, on traditions of protest from the late Tokugawa and the Meiji Ishin. These themes and orientations continuously confronted the state, but on the whole they tended to separate themselves from any political activities and hence did not greatly challenge the basic institutional premises of modern Japanese society.

These characteristics were probably most visible in the new religions, which constitute, as we have seen, one of the most important developments in the modern and contemporary Japanese cultural scene.

XII Parallel tendencies developed in many arenas of popular culture. Popular culture—be it in the form of public entertainment or popular literature, such as, in modern times, science fiction,[54]—has abounded in Japan. In its varied expressions it has spawned many irreverent themes and cynical observations about the authorities and the social order, not dissimilar from what may be found in other societies. What has, however, been rather distinctive in Japan is that—as with the great pilgrimages of the Tokugawa and earlier periods—the great potential for rebellion inherent in all these patterns of expression has not given rise to "real" rebellion, the construction of new modes of social and political organization or the transformation of central aspects of the social order.

Indicative from the point of view of the psychodynamics of protest is the mode of channeling frustration and aggression that is evident in those aspects of contemporary (but not only contemporary) popular culture promulgated in films, comics, and the like—themes of sexual violence and aggression. In such different types of popular culture many relatively segregated arenas are constructed, in which vent can be given to unregulated expressive—be it sexual or aggressive—behavior and to a variety of aesthetic sensibilities, to various manifestations of spontaneous or inner-oriented *Ki* energy.[55] Sometimes, as in some works of art, in classical or popular theatrical performance, and in some of the best known Japanese films the embroiled sexual or aggressive impulses can become closely connected with more artistic aesthetic expressions.[56]

Subversive and cynical themes have abounded in popular culture as well as in the ways in which multiple life spaces have been continuously constructed by different social sectors—middle-class and working women, youth and "marginal" artistic groups. Within such sectors various patterns of life, including numerous instances of "code switching"—between "modern" and traditional, Japanese and Western modes of behavior—have developed.[57] Many of these patterns have certainly gone beyond the cultural models promulgated by official ideologues. Indeed many of them, building on themes and activities developed toward the end of the Tokugawa period and in the early Meiji period, have developed new patterns of economic and social activities and strong communal, egalitarian, and antistatist orientations, with an emphasis on the autonomy of nature against the politically imposed restrictions. But they seem not to lead to many new modes of social or political organization. Similarly they have but rarely *directly* challenged the hegemonic models and premises. Rather, within these patterns there has developed a strong inward-looking tendency segregated from the official models.

A parallel picture, although of course much more complicated and variegated, can be seen in the art world. The theme of "the nobility of failure," to use Ivan Morris's felicitous expression, of supporting a losing cause and thus proving one's moral sincerity, runs through Japanese history and literature and is indicative of this mode of rebellion—

and fantasy: "Though Michizane's style of life differed diametrically from that of Japan's military heroes, the pattern of his failure was remarkably similar. By doggedly supporting a losing cause, he proved his moral sincerity."[58]

XIII The common denominator of the various manifestations of disharmony seems to be their inability, despite many attempts, to break through the basic ideological and organizational premises of the hegemonic system of the center, and above all their failure to change those premises—and this despite their harboring radical themes and orientations and great potential for rebellion. The distress and discontent which gave rise to them have not given rise to the types of rebellious, potentially transformational attitudes that have been most influential in other civilizations. George De Vos has succinctly analyzed this point:

> As a country of over one hundred million inhabitants, it is the utmost presumption to suggest that this normative orientation represents the inner experience of most Japanese. Many are aware of this pattern and manipulate it cynically. Others submit to expectations, resigned to the insurmountable difference between the ideal and real in the behavior of others. Yet others are aware that they are caught by a necessity to orient their behavior in conformity with this pattern, whatever their personal experience to the contrary, including their primary family experiences which may be far from the ideal of nurturance and legitimately functioning authority.
>
>   . . . There are, indeed, many introspective Japanese who are acutely aware of the difference between the social person—of the mask they wear protectively—and the inner being guarded from exposure to others. . . . But what is most often depicted in this material is that one continues to behave self-protectively, in socially expected ways—whatever the hidden aspects of the self.
>
>   There is, however, relatively little recourse to universalist religious beliefs to assuage or to compensate for needed benevolence or loving concern. A personally related deity is unavailable. Instead, the illusion of having these needs filled is reaffirmed by some Japanese who manage to distort their past family experiences so as to feel gratitude directed toward their parents and mentors.[59]

Before explicating the implications of this fact for the understanding of the Japanese social and political system, we shall first analyze the other side of the coin, namely the distinct ways in which manifestations of disharmony are coped with—the modes of treatment, regulation of conflict, and response to protest that have developed in Japanese society—and examine whether they share any distinctive characteristics.

MODES OF REGULATION AND CONTROL

XIV Let us start with the treatment of personality disorders in Japanese society. Most such treatment is neuropsychological with a strong emphasis on pharmaceutical intervention, in line with a basic conception of illness as rooted in the natural tendencies or weaknesses of the body.[60] In general there has developed in Japan, as Margaret Lock has shown, a distinctive germ theory rooted in a dualistic worldview, a cultural predilection to indulge minor illnesses and endemic physical weaknesses, a preference for somatizing etiologies of illness, and a tendency to minimize mental forces as causal factors.[61] To follow William Kelly's analysis of one of the major researchers in the field, M. Lock:

> In this work she tries to distinguish the real and often acute frustrations from the medical and mass media labeling of conditions such as "school avoidance syndrome," "high-rise apartment neurosis," and "moving-day syndrome." The cultural construction of such pathologies is a conjunction of the medical establishment and a conservative political agenda. It reasserts a Confucian "socio-somatics," whose imperative to lead a well-ordered life produced a healthy body and insured a harmonious social order.[62]

Of special interest, from the point of view of our discussion, are those therapies that seem to be specific to Japan. Even if used only by a small number of people, such therapies may highlight—as psychoanalytical treatment does in the West—some specific premises of the culture in which they have developed. Two such therapies are Morita psychotherapy and Naikan therapy, which Lebra describes as follows:

> Morita therapy, like Naikan, is a distinctly Japanese creation, and has two features in the therapeutic process which stand out. The first is the initial confinement of the patient with bed rest, isolation and without verbal communication (even contact with the physician is by means of a diary). The second feature is that cause of or elimination of symptoms does not figure in the treatment; life history analysis does not take place, and the unconscious is not probed, quite contrastive to Western psychoanalytic thinking. Rather the patient is enjoined to accommodate, to adjust, and to accept. Parenthetically, it should be noted that Freudian psychoanalysis has found little favor in Japan. . . .
> Naikan (inward-looking) therapy reorients clients from the interactional to the inner self through a period of isolated, concentrated self reflection. Its purpose is to arouse and maximize guilt consciousness by "piercing" the innermost "kokoro" [heart] with a mental drill so that the peak intensity of guilt will serve as a level of self-transformation. This interiorization does not entail an alienation from the interactional

dimensions as a whole; rather it means a rededication of self to others, through emphatic realization of others' sacrifice of self.[63]

These therapies emphasize "overcoming the contradiction of thought between idea and fact," "emphasis on realization, i.e. on participation in actual situations" as against "abstract thought," and "obedience to nature,"[64] to cite some of the major characteristics of Morita therapy: "The moral burden is placed fully upon the patient. Attempts to blame a neglectful mother or a self-centered father are brushed aside, and instead the patient is persuaded to acknowledge his or her failure to recognize the benevolence bestowed by others. Not uncommonly, tearful confessions of guilt occur. Ideally, the patient should emerge more selfless, more ready to live for others."[65]

The fact that Morita therapy is basically a psychophysiological method with a strong emphasis on the reembedment of the patients in the prevalent social contexts—in marked contrast to the basic premises of Western psychoanalysis—gave rise to intense controversy between Morita himself, various Morita therapists, and the few adherents of psychoanalysis who had emerged then in Japan. It is interesting to note that in the early 1950s (the rather few) Japanese psychoanalysts were criticized by Western psychoanalysts for employing methods of treatment that were basically, above all in their presuppositions, alien to the original intent of psychoanalysis.[66] Significantly, a rapprochement developed when Japanese psychoanalysts became influenced by Karen Horney's emphasis on interpersonal relations and Zen-like meditation and, later, when many Western psychoanalysts announced a growing interest in, and affinity with, different schools of Buddhism.[67]

It is not, however, only in the types of therapies relatively exclusive to Japan that distinctive premises and orientations can be identified. They can be also found in the more widespread therapeutic activities of the new religions, to which many people in transitional situations—taking high school or university examinations, experiencing problems of career development, and the like—turn.[68] These activities are based, as Lebra has shown, on the "'therapeutic self-reconstruction' of members which involved four aspects: self-accusation (I am to blame for whatever ails me), allocentric attribution (I owe you for the benefit I am enjoying), identity interchange (I am you, and you are me), and expurgation (cleansing of self, physically and mentally)."[69] Kelly comments on the similarity of this process to Morita and Naikan therapy:

> Their [Naikan's and Morita's] striking parallels with the New Religious are hardly coincidental, especially their penchant for simultaneously blaming and empowering the patient-client. All presume the essential benignity of the human condition, and share certain idioms such as "focusing on the

moment," "unblocking the flow," and "accepting the world as it is." What they offer are coping strategies for learning to live with oneself, rather than radical therapies to change the self one lives with or the society in which one lives.[70]

XV Another parallel pattern of "treatment" can be found in the control of criminal behavior, which is guided in Japan by a strong emphasis on the embedment both of potential criminals and of forces of control, of "law and order," in existing social frameworks. Japan's relatively very low incidence of criminal behavior has usually been attributed to informal social pressures—from family and workplace, for instance—and to the modes of behavior of the law-enforcing agencies—above all the police— especially their strong embedment in the various informal social settings, such as neighborhoods.[71]

In the period before the Second World War, the police were highly repressive, perceiving themselves as custodians protecting the public realm from subversive elements acting against growing liberal and democratic trends[72]—and at the same time expanding continuously the scope of the political and military police.[73] Since 1945 with the growing democratization, many concrete aspects of police behavior have indeed greatly changed, due in no small part to

a very self-conscious policy of the police to cultivate public opinion and not to act against public sentiments.

. . . Based on three national surveys conducted in 1983, Kabashima concluded that among eight major public institutions, the police was rated most favorably, ahead of the big newspapers, big business, and government. Significantly, public support for the police did not differ among respondents who had conservative or progressive political preferences. . . .

. . . Several recent studies of police behavior have emphasized the paternalistic guidance role of the police towards the public; the rather informal behavior of police, rooted both in the strong position of the police and the seemingly high level of trust of the public in the police, all of which are also very closely related to the way in which the system is structured and operated in Japan. This indeed a rather far-reaching shift from the earlier period.[74]

All these changes notwithstanding there is remarkable continuity in some of the basic relations between the police and the community.[75] While many aspects of Japanese police behavior developed fully in the post–Second World War period and contrast with earlier, more brutal or coercive patterns of behavior, even these more coercive patterns were often seen as closely embedded in their community or national contexts, and they also employed the guidance metaphor or orientation—as can be seen in the "thought control" techniques of the 1930s and early 1940s.[76] Moreover, many of the concrete techniques of the police—surveillance of neighborhoods, organization of very detailed registers, and the like— developed in the Meiji or Taishō era and have been unabashedly, possibly even effectively, continued in the contemporary scene.[77]

"The social norm relevant to Japan's internal security policy has been that crime is a community phenomenon. Government officials, such as policemen . . . are agents of the community's moral consensus as well as its statutory prescriptions."[78]

Interestingly, John Braithwaite, who refers to this system of criminal control as "reintegrative shaming," also extols it as the most efficient in controlling crime.[79]

XVI A similar pattern can be identified with respect to the mode of management, regulation, or resolution of conflict—and of protest—which have naturally been closely related to the specific modes of defining conflict.

The definitions of conflicts and of conflict resolution prevalent in Japan have been characterized by, first, the view of conflict as something that is not natural but rather an embarrassment, second, the strong tendency to minimize the legitimacy of direct, open confrontation, third, the tendency to minimize the definition of differences of interests and opinions in terms of outright conflict or confrontation, and, fourth, the tendency to resolve differences in seemingly informal ways based on presumptions of solidarity and harmony between the contestants.[80]

> Persuasion and joint problem solving are expected where common objectives are readily acknowledged. Since the assumption of conflict and disagreement over goals is more common within Western organizations and the ideology of community is more common in Japanese organizations, it follows that bargaining is the prevalent mode in the West, whereas problem solving and persuasion are more common in Japan when it comes to serious internal conflicts. . ."[81]
>
> . . . In the West, because of the high reliance on formal and impersonal mechanisms, the most problematic conflicts are those in which the mechanisms themselves become part of the struggle or in some other manner lose legitimacy—as when the equity and fairness of the law or the courts are questioned, for example, or when favoritism or corruption is reported in high office. Around the established formal mechanisms are fought the greatest symbolic battles.
>
> In Japan, the most unmanageable conflicts are the ones unresponsive to personal conflict management. Among conflicts of this type we include those involving ideological extremists, mass protests, and situations with

a history of interpersonal hostility—in such circumstances, face-to-face resolutions and go-betweens are not very effective.[82]

In many cases the main processes through which conflict is seemingly avoided are those which direct and facilitate a person's movement from one context to another—as we shall see in greater detail in our analysis of processes of socialization and of personality formation.[83]

XVII Similarly, the modes of definition, legitimation, and, hence, also of regulation of protest in Japan are greatly influenced by what Susan Pharr has called the "moral economy" of conflict and protest in Japanese society. In Japan, with its particular tradition of protest and dominant social values, the ideal model of social protest appears to have at least five characteristics. To follow Pharr's analysis:

> 1. *Only the most extreme situations of injustice or deprivation should give rise to protest.* . . .
> 2. *Protests (other than those over survival issues) ideally are guided by a high moral purpose.* . . .
> 3. *Commitment to the protest should be total.* . . .
> 4. *Protesters ideally demonstrate a spirit of self-sacrifice.* . . .
> 5. *The protesters' chosen "repertoire of collective action" should be at a lower level of conflict than that used by the opposing party.*[84]

Pharr continually emphasizes that given these models of "ideal conflict" in Japanese society, it is not surprising that the most difficult conflicts to manage and regulate are those she has called "status conflict," that is, conflict in which "concrete," "discrete" demands or conflicts are subsumed under contention about the respective status of the participants. As such they can be best resolved through some mediation—but when such mediation is lacking or unable to overcome a strong incompatibility in the respective status implications of the different contestants, the rupture may be total:

> None of these features of the ideal model of protest is unique to Japan. In combination, however, what emerges is a set of standards that asks a great deal of protesters; full commitment, a willingness to engage in self-sacrifice for the cause, high moral purpose, and selfless goals for protest. And protests that do not meet these conditions encounter serious difficulties in the winning of public support, difficulties independent of the actual issues at stake in the protest.[85]

This analysis of the moral economy of Japanese protest may seem to be too "harmonious." There have certainly developed throughout Japan's modern and contemporary history many confrontations involving outlooks and attitudes that do not seem to adhere to the tenets of this moral economy.[86] Yet confrontations have usually taken place when the contestants felt that the premises of the moral community had been ignored by the authorities, and their claims have often been made in terms of such premises.

MODES OF CONTROL:
LAW AND LITIGATION

XVIII   Many analyses of Japanese law have been very strongly influenced by some of the implicit assumptions of the group-harmony model and the closely related assumption about what has been called the "myth of the reluctant litigant," that is, the assumption that the Japanese— apparently because of the strength of the themes of harmony and consensus—are on the whole unwilling to engage in formal litigation.[87]

This claim seems to be supported by such data as the small number of lawyers in modern Japan as compared with other capitalist industrial countries and, closely related, the small number of cases brought to court; or by the fact that before the Meiji period Japan did not have a system of courts—or of codification—distinct from various administrative bodies or decrees of administrative regulation.[88]

A closer examination of the data shows that the assumption that the Japanese are nonlitigious is simply wrong. A strong tendency to litigation has been fully documented for long periods of Japanese history. Many cases have been brought before authorities—and codified as "customary" agreements. The prevalence of litigious behavior has naturally tended to increase in periods of turmoil, of intensive social change, and its scope has increased with growing economic development.

But whatever the scope and intensity of such litigations, their definition and mode of resolution, as they have developed in Japan, have exhibited several distinctive characteristics that seem to have persisted—if necessarily in reconstructed ways—side by side with far-reaching changes in the formal structure of legal institutions throughout most of Japanese history. These modes of regulating litigious behavior have been closely interwoven with certain basic conceptions of law that have been predominant in Japanese society through many centuries.

In Japan, as in China, "formal" law was the law imposed by the rulers—but in Japan it also encompassed customary law to a much greater degree than in China. Moreover, unlike in China and to an even greater degree unlike in the West, law was not seen as representing some higher or transcendent vision; accordingly it did not acquire any institutional and symbolic autonomy.[89]

The main role of law was the upholding of the contexts and bases of social life and the restoration of whatever social harmony might have been destroyed by contention, conflict, or criminal behavior. Law was embedded, both institutionally and symbolically, in the basic premises of the community or nation, or of the numerous social contexts of different sectors of Japanese society. It exhibited throughout most of these periods the major characteristics of what John Haley has called "authority without power."[90] It is this basic conception of law that seems to have persisted, despite all the great changes in the organization of law that have taken place, especially in the modern period.

The entire structure of the Japanese legal system changed in the modern period when, under the Meiji, a fully fledged system of modern courts with a degree of judicial independence was established and distinct, formal laws and codices were promulgated. Yet even in this period some basic premises and conceptions of law seem to have persisted, or, to be more precise, to have been reformulated, under the impact of the encounter with Western legal philosophies, which emphasized the autonomy of the legal system. Many Meiji legal philosophers—for instance, Hozumi Yatsuka—developed conceptions of law based on Meiji premises of the nature of Japanese nationhood and of the emperor symbolism—emphasizing the embedment of the legal system in the national imperial order—which were inimical to Western conceptions of autonomous formative law.

Even in the post–Second World War period, when a new democratic constitution and legal institutions were established, some of these conceptions of law and premises of legal thinking continued to be both strong and pervasive.[91] Changes in the structure of the legal system naturally gave rise to changes in the patterns of legal behavior—the number and variety of litigations, and general recourse to the different legal practices, have greatly increased.[92] Still, however, certain characteristic conceptions of the contemporary Japanese legal system, especially with respect to the place of law and social order,[93] distinguish it from the Western legal systems from which its institutions and frameworks were "borrowed" and recall earlier Japanese conceptions of law.

While the formal structure of the legal institutions in Japan is a mix of different legal traditions—various European ones, the American, and the traditional Japanese—the actual practice in most legal circles in Japan seems to have been influenced by many of the premises that shaped the premodern Japanese legal system, as reformulated and reconstructed under the impact or challenge of changing conditions.[94] These basic assumptions of Japanese law, articulated and formulated by most modern and contemporary legal commentators, are summarized by Frank Upham:

For such commentators, the ideal legal system must fit their perception of Japanese society as based on consensus, the denial of individually defined self-interest, and the acceptance of a benevolent hierarchy. Such a legal system would not emphasize the legal function of individuals, since taking individuals as the elemental social unit denies that society is composed of groups each of which is greater than the sum of its members and which together constitute a society that is similarly greater than the sum of its constituent groups. Nor would legal rights and duties, even if wielded by groups rather than individuals, play a large role. . . . This view of society and law is hostile to abstract rules serving as a guide to social action, but it is the abstract nature of the rules and the procedural formality and rationality of their application through litigation, more than the content of any given rule that is anathema. . . .

The ideal characteristic of a legal system under this view of society is informality. Informality allows the control of social interaction, whether by private groups, the bureaucracy, or the judiciary, to be particularistic, so that consensus can form the basis of dispute resolution. . . .

Informality also confirms the Japanese people's view of their society as harmonious and conflict-free. . . . Without a formal and open policy making process, government policies can appear as the inevitable and natural results of custom and consensus rather than as the conscious political choices among mutually antagonistic interests that they actually are.[95]

These conceptions of law are closely related to those of justice prevalent in many sectors of Japanese society. Lee Hamilton and Joseph Sanders, in a recent comparative survey of a Japanese and an American city, have explored some of the differences between the two societies with respect to conceptions of justice. They show that, significantly:

Japanese tend to emphasize role-based expectations, whereas Americans tend to emphasize the actor's concrete needs. Although differences are invariably a matter of degree rather than of kind, the pattern of findings is consistent with the idea that the responsible actor in the United States is a more isolated individual. This pattern in turn, is consistent with the more tightly woven web of hierarchical and solidary relationships that characterizes Japanese social life.[96]

XIX Given the persistence of these basic assumptions about the nature and function of law, it is no great surprise that they have informed legal activity in contemporary Japan and given rise to rather specific modes of juridical behavior and conflict resolution. This is the case despite the similarity of many organizational aspects and formal contents of the contemporary Japanese legal system to those of Western ones. Among the most important manifestations of these premises are a very strong custodial conception of the law, an emphasis on conciliation and minimization of litigation, and a reluctance of the juridical body to challenge the authorities.[97]

The emphasis on the custodial role of law, embedded in the conception of the group or society as a self-enclosed moral community, is manifest above all in the very strong preference for conciliation as the central focus of and meaning of law.[98] Judges themselves have tended to prefer conciliation and mediation;[99] when semijuridical, mediatory institutions, such as the *kankai* and the *chotei*, were instituted in the modern period, judges referred many of the cases brought before them to these institutions. In addition to this there is the long tradition of police intervention in disputes between citizens to which we have already referred. Moreover, many semiformal arrangements have been created through various informal agencies—for instance, the appointment of mediators through such agencies by the family court system, the purpose of which is to mediate and to minimize direct litigations and to diffuse their potential impact.[100]

This conception of law is also manifest, among other places, in the emphasis Japanese criminal law lays on educating the perpetrator of a (potentially) criminal act, on bringing him back to the fold of the community or social context—rather than on punishment.[101] This conception is closely related to the widespread practice of the police working for a confession, which may result in their not bringing the (would-be) criminal into court or in his receiving a very light sentence.[102]

Also closely related is the reluctance—which has to some small extent recently weakened—to challenge the authorities.[103] Such reluctance naturally entails a very strong acceptance of the legitimacy of their decisions—as evident, for instance, in the fact that, in judicial reviews, Japanese courts seem to uphold the decisions of administrative bodies, based on their discretion, to a much greater degree than parallel courts in Western countries.[104] This conception of law is also manifest in the *relatively* weak stands of the Supreme Court as a constitutional or law-generating institution,[105] although lately some minor shifts in these directions can be identified.[106]

XX These conceptions of law also greatly affect the ways in which various bodies of law derived mostly from the West are transformed or applied in Japan. In the application of the law of contracts, for instance, it was found that Japanese agreement behavior diverges from the formal rules included in Japan's civil code.

Wagatsuma and Rosset have analyzed parallel premises in American and Japanese contract law and relate these discrepancies to some basic premises of Japanese culture and behavior—especially to the tendency to maintain ambiguity and tension between "stated reasons versus felt reasons for interpersonal behavior," between a person's stated reasons or opinion (*tataman*) and inner feeling (*honme*); the strong distinction between one's inner circle and strangers, as against the Western tendency to emphasize universalistic criteria applicable to all; and the well-known emphasis on group harmony.

Takeyoshi Kawashima suggested that these divergences are due to the facts that

> the formal system found in the code implies that in the event of a dispute there will be an adjudication of rights and wrongs leading to the vindication of the correct position, while Japanese practice seems to prefer compromise and mediation resulting in the accommodation of conflicting claims; and that the Code tends to see each contract between two parties as a distinct and isolated transaction, while in practice the Japanese tend to behave as if each contract transaction is merely an integral segment of an ongoing relationship that has duration and significance beyond the life of any particular transaction.

> In contrast with Western individualism, Japanese corporatism emphasizes: 1) interdependence, the notion that social life is based upon mutual help and interdependence among the people; 2) mutual trust, the expectation and conviction that one's trust in others is reciprocated; and 3) a tendency to view interpersonal relationships as an end in itself or valuable in its own right, deserving of people's efforts to maintain it.[107]

XXI One of the most interesting manifestations of the custodial conception of law and its implication for social control in Japanese society can perhaps be seen in the role of apology in that system,[108] as compared with both Western and Chinese law.[109]

To quote Wagatsuma and Rosset:

> We said earlier that there are real differences in apologetic behavior in Japan and the United States. We are even more confident that there are differences in the significance that is attached to such behavior or to the failure to apologize in each nation. Americans attach much greater significance and legal consequence to the perceptions of autonomy and internal coherence, thus making apology important as an expression of self. This leads apologetic behavior to be accompanied by a justification or an emphasis on the acceptance of liability along with responsibility. . . .
>
> . . . In contrast, the Japanese concept of apology attaches primary significance to the act as an acknowledgement of group hierarchy and harmony. Less concern is expressed for paying the damages and more on repairing the injured relationships between the parties and between the offending individual and the social order that has been disturbed. Sincerity therefore becomes less a function of the internal mental state of the person apologiz-

ing and more a matter of performing the correct external acts that reaffirm submission to that order. The presence of internal ambivalence is expected and accepted as not threatening.[110]

TENTATIVE CONCLUSIONS: THE METALANGUAGE OF DISHARMONY AND REGULATION

XXII The picture emerging from analyses of the manifestations of disharmony and dissensus—personality disorders, deviant behavior, movements of protest, and other forms of conflict—and above all of the modes of coping with them in Japanese society, indicates that they all share some distinctive characteristics.

The very ubiquity of these patterns attests to the fact that in Japanese society, as in any other, there develop continuous tensions, dissatisfactions, and conflicts. Moreover, as in any other society, these conflicts evince rather specific characteristics—especially, in the case of Japan, with respect to their extensiveness, structural location, and visibility and society's definition of the phenomena—and arise from specific structural tensions, contradictions, and "ambivalences" prevalent in the society. The location of "disharmonious" social processes is closely related to those structural locations in which such ambivalences are most visible or pressing.

But it is above all with respect to the modes in which disharmony is coped with, managed, or regulated in Japanese society that specific characteristics stand out. The most important characteristics of such regulation are, first, the strong tendency to minimize the extent of such manifestations of disharmony and, above all, the extent of their definition as distinctive discordant patterns of behavior openly contrary or in direct opposition to the established, hegemonic ones. Second, there is a strong preference for coping with them as far as possible in informal ways and not through frameworks governed by distinct, especially formal and abstract, criteria. Third, there is a strong tendency, as Susan Pharr has emphasized, to privatize social conflict.[111]

Fourth, and in close relation to the third point, there is a strong preference for coping with them within the framework of existing institutions and groups, such as family, neighborhood, and religious or cultural sectors, or, if that is impossible, for connecting the agencies that deal specifically with them with the existing institutions. Thus, for instance, it has been observed that families of psychiatric patients attempt to minimize the patients' visibility by treating them as far as possible within the families, and only in extreme cases deferring to specialized agencies—although here again the small numbers of such agencies leave the families little choice. More specialized agencies, such as hospitals, police, and other agencies of law enforcement, tend to behave according to the premises prevalent in the broader context, as can be seen, for instance, in the many informal roles—local social worker, teacher, neighborhood friend—played by the contemporary Japanese policeman. Agencies tend, as far as possible, to emphasize guidance rather than formal directives— the latter often serving mainly as a sort of background for the more informal rules.

Fifth, there is a strong tendency to resolve the problems inherent in any deviant or disharmonious pattern of behavior by returning the "culprits" to the antecedent situation, and especially to the basic premises of that situation, in which the existing norms are seemingly upheld and no new ones created. This is often true even if the settings themselves have been changed by the numerous new social spaces that result from these patterns of behavior.

Accordingly, innovations, be they in the treatment of personality disorders or in legal arrangements, tend to be defined as technical and not as new principled ones, which would create new types of norms or institutions. They are brought, as far as possible, under the canopy of the existing settings and norms—even if in fact they effect far-reaching changes.

As we have seen, the potentially new themes that have been incorporated into the existing frameworks have not given rise to a restructuring of such organizations according to new principles (especially communal, individualistic, universalistic, or transcendental criteria), despite the fact that many demands and protests have been couched in such terms. Even when the tension between confrontation and the ideals of harmony seemed to intensify, as was the case in some situations of intensive change or of great historical openings—as for instance in the Taishō period, or in the student rebellion of the late 1960s, in which the scope and intensity of conflicts combined with protest did greatly increase—the outcomes or resolution of conflicts were apparently (but, as we shall see, only apparently) very similar to those during more typical times; that is, they did not establish any institutional arrangements based on the different premises— whether individualistic, egalitarian, or communal—that they seemed to promulgate. It was this fact that constituted the central concern of some of the liberal-individualistic post–Second World War intellectuals, of whom Maruyama Masao is probably the most outstanding illustration.[112]

Sixth, in many of these therapeutic or controlling settings, special new spaces are created in which vent can be given to various patterns of expressive, emotional, or aesthetic behavior—often very much in line with basic ontological assumptions about the forces that motivate Japanese individual behavior and expression—to be analyzed later.[113]

Thus all these processes of control are not oriented to the elimination of the symptoms of dissatisfaction or to the changing of contexts or their basic premises. Rather they are oriented to the reembedment of the individual, often within new or newly created contexts.

XXIII   The common denominator of these manifestations of disharmony and patterns of dissonance, of the ideological orientations promulgated by many oppositional movements, and of the means by which they are regulated has been the acceptance—or rather the taking as given—of what E. Ben-Ari has called the basic metalanguage of Japanese discourse and reflexivity, the metalanguage of group-orientations;[114] of themes, discussed by E. Hamaguchi, of group context and moral consensus; and of closely connected assumptions with respect to the moral economy of protest, as analyzed by Susan Pharr.[115] Many of the demands of the various groups and movements—as well as the principled promulgation of policy—have been couched in highly moralistic terms based on the ideology of communal solidarity and harmony.

Underlying all the conceptions of this metalanguage are certain assumptions about group or community cohesion. As H. Befu has put it,

> What is important is to see the group or the community as a moral unit, as a unit espousing a common moral value. When some members of the community start claiming a different moral value or disagreeing with the moral value of the group, that's when there is conflict. For example, when presidents of polluting companies refuse to admit their wrong, when people in the community were dying due to pollution, these presidents placed their company profit above community life. But when they finally broke down and visited the homes of the pollution victims, and prayed before the family altar, where the victims are memorialized, the community saw this action as sharing the moral value of the community and as an act recognizing the value of the community life in the way others did. These presidents were not criticized afterwards.[116]

This metalanguage of the community as a moral unit is very often expressed in terms of symbolic purification, of ritual cleansing of the pollution inherent in disharmonious acts.[117] The central focus or message of this metalanguage as applied to the manifestations of disharmony and to their control was the continuous extension of trust into broader contexts and the continual reembedment of various forms into these contexts.

In all these manifestations—whether of deviance, protest, peasant rebellion, or other conflict—and their regulation; in the worlds of fantasy and of artistic creativity; in high culture as well as popular entertainment, in which many potentially subversive themes are promulgated, it is the establishment or reestablishment of linkages of trust extending beyond the immediate social setting and toward wider networks and contexts that is of crucial importance. In many of these situations, especially in the movements of protest and in many arenas of popular culture, it is the loss of the trust inherent in such linkages to broader settings—possibly its betrayal by leaders or would-be leaders—that has been emphasized.

Linkages of trust may indeed break down—as they do in cases of mental breakdown or intensive conflict—but, significantly, such breakdowns are usually connected with the quest to reestablish them, even if in a new form. Thus the search for the reestablishment of trust in broader settings can facilitate the reconstruction or reconstitution of those settings—including the incorporation of many themes promulgated by the movements of protest or in popular culture. This has indeed diversified the social consciousness and discourse that have developed in these settings. But such reconstitution has usually been effected in terms of an inherent trust in the setting and not in terms of principles going beyond it—even if such principles (for instance, communal, individualistic, or universalistic principles) have been implicit in the themes of protest and popular culture.[118] When reestablished, whether through old or new networks, it is the extensions of trust and solidarity and their symbols that is crucial. This is true also of many of the liminal rituals of rebellion in which the existing social order is upheld through the denial of the value of alternative solutions.

It is this fact—that the reestablishment of trust does not lead to a radical reconstruction of the center—that constitutes one of the distinctive characteristics of the Japanese social and political system. The exploration of this fact constitutes one of the most important challenges for the analysis of Japanese society, and, especially in chapters 6, 12, and 15, we shall attempt to take up this challenge.

XXIV   The characteristics of the major agencies of control that we have examined, especially their tendency to become embedded in the more informal modes of interaction and the overall moral fabric of the community, may seem to be—and are often presented as—benign. Yet these elements of social control in Japan have, as do all systems of control, a strongly repressive side. The concrete manifestations of this repressive aspect in Japan include not only the use of outright coercion and oppression—as used, for instance, by the military regime—but, possibly more importantly, the more informal types of repressiveness.

Thus for instance the repressive aspect of police behavior in Japan has been not only or mainly direct coercion or repression—although these were also employed—but the "hemming in" of those perceived to be *potentially* guilty within the existing network of social relations, leaving them little autonomous space of action. Thus, even when some action was legally available—as, for instance, litigation or procedures to uphold the rights of citizens against arrest—it was not often used.

One manifestation of this repressive side of the Japanese police can be seen in the high rate of confessions by the accused—sometimes even for crimes that were not committed. Those who confess have a "benevolently" low rate of conviction, those who refuse to do so may meet with attempts to deny them even a hearing, although on paper defendants in Japan have the various procedural rights familiar to Europeans and Americans (the right to consult an attorney immediately upon detention and to receive counsel at trial, the right to be informed of the charges against them, freedom from search or arrest without a judicially issued warrant, the right to a speedy trial before an impartial judge, the opportunity to confront prosecution witnesses and to present witnesses of their own, and the right to remain silent). This repressive behavior by the police is often the other side of the informal, seemingly lenient and open, attitude. Both are visible in the friendly yet custodial interweaving of police activities with those of the various informal local or family networks, in the police's seemingly acting as social workers.

It is not only in the behavior of the police that repressive dimension exists. It can be found also in all other modes of regulating the manifestations of disharmony—indeed foremost in the application of the law. As we have seen, the conception of law prevalent in Japan entails a strong acceptance of the legitimacy of the decisions of authority, coupled with a reluctance—which has recently weakened, but only to a small extent— to challenge the authorities.[119]

The legal system, like the police strongly embedded in the broader community, also interweaves formal and informal modes of control, in pursuit of much the same general preferences as the other processes of coping with manifestations of disharmony—namely, a strong preference to cope with such problems in informal ways, within the framework of existing institutions and groups, such as family, neighborhood, and religious or cultural sectors; a tendency to privatize social conflict; and a strong tendency to resolve the problems in behavior by returning the "culprits" to the antecedent group framework.

Indeed this combination of seemingly benign and repressive aspects of social control is characteristic of the structuration of all major arenas of life in Japan. A critical aspect of this mode of control is the high mutual visibility to which, as Michael Hechter and Satoshi Kanazawa have shown, the Japanese people are exposed—in the family, in school, in neighborhoods, in the workforce, and in public. Such high visibility, effected through the numerous dense networks that are the characteristics of all arenas of social interaction in Japan, is indeed closely related to the dimensions of social control—one of the extreme manifestations being the bullying of "unusual" students in schools.[120]

One of the most important aspects of such repressiveness on the macrolevel is the attitude towards minorities—the indigenous *burakumin* subcaste[121] and the more recent minority of Koreans, as well as to the Ainu in the northern Hokkaidō area. Given the closed definition of the Japanese collectivity in primordial-sacral terms and the weakness, if not the total absence, of universalistic orientations within this definition, there is almost no place for minorities within it. These minorities—even if very small by comparison with those in other modern industrialized societies—have had relatively few acceptable ideological recourses against their exclusion and concomitant repression.[122]

XXV These multiple modes of control, with their benign and repressive modes or aspects alike, seem to be rather effective in Japan, as can be seen, for instance, in the relatively low level of crime or, to come back to the starting part of our discussion of the legal system, in the comparatively low incidence of formal litigation—as against various tactics of conciliation between would-be litigants or between the authorities and would-be criminals.[123]

It would, however, be wrong to assume that, as was sometimes claimed in the Nihonjinron literature, these characteristics of the system of control and regulation have developed in some natural way from the depths of Japanese culture and tradition. They are not natural emanations of the basic conceptions and premises of the social order and of the place of law; rather, they developed out of an interweaving of such cultural themes with very specific structural characteristics and are propped up by very distinctive institutional processes. They have developed through a continuous interaction between conscious policies and institutional arrangements undertaken by the elites and cultural predispositions that seem to be prevalent among large sectors of Japanese society. Thus, for instance, these characteristics of the modes of litigation and of the legal system in Japan have developed—and been continuously reactivated—through policies and modes of control employed by the authorities, which in turn have built on and activated predispositions rooted in the basic cultural orientations of large sectors of Japanese society. These policies have not, as it were, left these predispositions to generate by themselves patterns of behavior that would reinforce the various "consensual" arrangements and institutional frameworks.

For instance, some of the reasons for the scarcity of lawyers in Japan provide a good illustration of the pressures and institutional arrangements employed by the authorities:

There are approximately 11,000 attorneys available to serve a population of over 113 million, or about one attorney per 10,250 people. By contrast, the per capita population of lawyers in the West ranges from a high of one lawyer for every 5,900 citizens in France. The scarcity of Japanese lawyers is not a matter of chance or the result of supply and demand, but a conscious governmental policy. To become a lawyer in Japan, one must receive two years of training in the official Legal Training and Research Institute. To enter the Institute, applicants, typically graduates of an undergraduate law faculty, must take the National Legal examination. This examination is extremely difficult to pass. In 1975, for example, 472 out of 27,791 passed, a rate of 1.7 percent. In 1977, the rate fell to 1.6 percent. The successful applicant has on the average taken the exam five times. These figures should dispel any preconception that Japanese do not want to be lawyers. The number per capita of Japanese taking the judicial examination in 1975 was in fact slightly higher than that of Americans taking the bar examination. The difference of course is that 74 percent of the Americans passed.[124]

A similar picture of structural conditions that tend rationally to minimize litigation has been presented by J. M. Ramseyer and M. Nakazato.[125] Many characteristics of the legal system, especially its conformism and political docility, have been very convincingly analyzed by Ramseyer and Frances Rosenbluth[126] as attributable to the basic structure of the judiciary—the strong hold of the Ministry of Justice over appointments, the placement of justices to different courts and positions, and the promulgation of the ideological framework—as well as to the strong interlinkage between the bureaucracy and judiciary personnel.

It is such combinations of cultural premises with manipulative policies and institutional arrangements implemented by the authorities and the responses to them that shape many features not only of the Japanese legal system but also of modes of control in other arenas.

XXVI As with respect to the small number of lawyers, it would be wrong to assume that the characteristics of the various citizen's, labor, and socialist movements analyzed above were only natural emanations of Japanese tradition or predispositions. These characteristics too have been generated to no small extent by structural conditions created by deliberate policies on the part of the authorities.

This can best be seen with respect to the workers' and socialist movements; indeed, the internal characteristics of the socialist movements were reinforced by several structural tendencies, as well as by the policies of the authorities. They were first of all reinforced by the segmentation of the labor market, which was, as noted in chapter 3, of four main, sometimes overlapping, types: first, a division between the employees of the great companies, organized in company unions, and those of the smaller firms; second, a large secondary labor force composed mostly of women and people who retired from the large companies;[127] third, the employees, relatively temporary, of the smaller businesses; and, fourth, the marginal labor force of street laborers, day laborers, and the like, the inhabitants of the *yoseba*, or slums.[128] This segmentation was, as we have seen, related to the weakness of class consciousness among large sectors of the Japanese population, as well as the relative predominance of company unions and the very weak involvement of the (radical) trade union federations in daily industrial bargaining.

The socialist movements were also greatly weakened by the "reverse trend" of the American occupation, during which socialist leaders were purged from positions of political power. Yet another reason was the successful gerrymandering of election districts after the Second World War when the repressive measures employed in the earlier periods were no longer available. At the same time, the response by the center to the demands of various movements was usually effected by practical negotiation between different groups, their leaders, and the elites. These manipulations by the elites, through which distinctive patterns of control were instituted, were closely interwoven with the basic premises of social order, of state-society relations, and of the conception of law—the two continuously reinforcing one another.

Indeed, these policies, together with the actions of business leaders and governmental sectors, defined some of the radical orientations that developed among workers in the first decade after the Second World War. In this period, the labor union movement grew rapidly, from about six hundred thousand members at the end of 1945 to about six million in 1947. In the large enterprises, especially in heavy industry, the labor movement rapidly became radicalized.[129] Most of the local unions affiliated themselves with labor federations—and many to a confederation—that were under left-wing influence (communist and socialist parties). There thus developed a class movement that insisted on class positions and on worker cooperation across companies, which contradicted the idea of the company as the focus of worker identification. The demands of the new labor movement were far-reaching: no layoffs, job security, maintenance of production, wages according to individual needs, abolition of the clear distinction between workers and office employees, chances of promotion for all regular employees and workers, and finally, in many companies, creation of management councils composed of equal numbers of unionized workers and management people, to run all the aspects of the company (financial, personnel, marketing, and so on). To obtain what they were asking for, unions had to strike, to occupy plants, even to sequester high administrators. Many won all these demands, except the one about pay according to needs; a compromise was reached setting wages according to age and seniority, considered by labor as acceptable indices of family needs.

This union expansion was at first encouraged by the American occupation administration. But soon, it seemed to have gone too far. Many Americans in Japan thought that labor and especially the Communist Party was going over the line of what was acceptable and they pushed for a rollback. For many, the idea of worker participation in management was anathema. Moreover, the cold war was on and the idea was to weaken the communists in Japan in order to transform the wartime enemy into a useful ally. In order to do this, the American administration asked the American Federation of Labor to show Japanese how to establish acceptable labor unions. Japanese company administrators and management associations were in agreement with the Americans. From 1946 to 1948, administrators who judged that the main management association, Keidanren, was not aggressive enough, created two new associations, Nikkeiren and Keizai dōyōkai, in order to develop and apply a new (class) policy, with the goal of reestablishing management rights in companies. At the same time, especially after the end of the short-lived socialist minority government in 1948, the Japanese government wanted to crush the Communist Party.

From 1947 on, there was a policy of containment of the labor unions, devised in cooperation by the occupation administration, the Japanese government, and management associations. This policy was applied all the more strictly after the deflationary Dodge Plan of 1948, which forced companies to fire employees in order to eliminate company deficits. Many unions struck against these firings, but the government sent the police to break these strikes. At the same time, company management fostered the creation of so-called second unions, most of the time by middle-management personnel paid by the company. In the auto industry, Nissan had the most militant union, and the three major auto companies agreed to cooperate, with the help of bank loans, to eliminate it. (What this means is that management considered interenterprise cooperation on a class basis as more important at that time than company goals.)

The many-sided offensive by management and government succeeded in crushing the militant labor union movement. The outbreak of the Korean war in 1950 forced many companies to make some compromises in order to promote production and profit from wartime sales. But by 1954, most militant workers were fired or put in jail, labor federations were eliminated, and the insistence was on company identification. It is at that time that most of the practices now common in large Japanese companies were established: hiring of new employees at the same time in March each year, selection of employees according to their ability to accept management-imposed rules, entrance ceremony on the first of April, and job security for regular employees.

It is thus evident that processes of control, the promulgation of themes of harmony, and the denial of conflict can be used by the authorities—in Japan, as in all other countries—to maintain their position and the status quo. There can indeed be no doubt that such arrangements by the authorities—including the special organizational aspects of the legal system to which we have referred—have often been used by the powers that be, especially various echelons of the bureaucracy, against potential threats from different, usually underprivileged, groups: peasants in previous epochs, outcast groups like the *burakumin* or the Koreans in more recent ones, as well as radical workers' unions.

Thus this analysis seems to reinforce the overall picture of the modern and contemporary Japanese social and political system as highly regulated, repressive, and unresponsive. But as we shall see in the next chapter, this is not the whole story.

The Political and Social System of Modern and Contemporary Japan
A Dynamic, Controlled, but Not Totalitarian Society

I The analyses in chapter 5 of the basic characteristics of various modes of control indicate that there is another side to the story of the modern and contemporary Japanese social and political system beyond the emphasis on repressiveness and nonresponsiveness. The starting point for understanding this other side lies in a closer look at the metalanguage shared by manifestations of disharmony and modes of control alike—with its emphasis on the reembedment of the "deviant" into the community, couched in terms of the moral consensus of the community and the reestablishment of trust.

Attempts at reembedment can be—and often have been—unresponsive, even coercive. But an extension of trust cannot be built on repression and coerciveness alone. It necessarily entails also different modes of accommodation and response to processes of change and movements of protest.[1] Significantly, many of these movements use the predominant themes of harmony, loyalty, or, to use T. Smith's felicitous expression, the right to benevolence against the authorities to point out the necessity for the rulers to accede to their demands, in order to maintain such harmony.

Such demands may be made not only in ad hoc outbursts, but also through the use of more formal frameworks of control. This can be seen in the place of litigation in these processes. Despite the generally low level of litigation, quite confrontational litigation, like that which took place in the severe antipollution cases in the 1970s, sometimes does take place. While not common, such confrontational actions by protesting groups and movements are very visible and not without results.

These movements' operations are in many ways similar to those of peasant rebellions in former times—but there are also, as Upham has pointed out, some important differences:

> If we . . . seek a more general perspective on the role of litigation in contemporary Japan, a number of observations can be made. First, litigation raising highly charged moral issues can serve the role historically played by peasant rebellions—that is, it can be a vehicle for popular protest against a neglectful regime. In circumstances where plaintiffs can demonstrate that they have been excluded not only from the political process but also from a fair share of social benefits, litigation can provide a forum for the dramatic presentation of their plight to the nation. . . . In this type of litigation, the prime examples of which are the early pollution cases, process and form are all-important, and the role of the judge and substantive legal norms is secondary. . . . If the cases become part of the successful political and social movement, however, the judges' role can acquire great social importance, and morally powerful opinions like those in the *Minamata* and *Kawamoto* cases can embody and declare the existence of a new social consensus that is politically binding on the society as a whole as well as the specific defendants.[2]

Thus, these movements indeed often succeed in getting some important redress or concessions from the authorities. The possibility of such success is rooted in the fact that conceptions of loyalty and harmony not only define the obligation of the subjects, the criteria of legitimation of elites, but also both limit and direct the ways in which the elites exercise power and give rise to the demands made on them. Accordingly such litigation of protest can be most successful when it upholds the models of "proper" protest, as defined by Pharr,[3] and may even constitute the seeds of innovation and change.

True enough, in the legal system—as in the treatment of personality disorder and as in police behavior—innovations tend to be defined as technical rather than principled ones, which would entail creating new types of norms or institutions. They are usually presented as being under the canopy of the existing settings—even if they have effected far-reaching changes, brought out new themes, or transformed the settings themselves.

The possible effectiveness of litigation attests to the fact that the role of formal law, as against the more prevalent informal modes of conflict resolution in Japan, is not just cosmetic. The threat of formal legal action may serve as an important backdrop not only for the effective implementation of official guidance, but also for demands that the "guides," the various bureaucracies and other authorities, take into account the claims of various sectors of the population—that is, it also promotes informal consultation and mediation. True enough, such claims and especially the responses to them are not necessarily or usually made in principled political or ideological terms, but rather in terms of the upholding of the moral order of the community; nevertheless, such responses may entail the redefinition of components or dimensions of the moral order—and hence also of the political arena.

One repercussion of the conceptions of law prevalent in Japan—and of the fact that, while they are upheld first of all by the authorities, they also find some resonance among wider sectors of the population—is the relatively low level, as compared especially, but not only, with the United States, of political engagement of the legal profession, and the scarcity of legal institutions providing an arena for political context. This low level of politicization of legal activities—probably the lowest among modern, industrialized nations—has been, of course, continuously reinforced by the various restrictions on the number of lawyers, to which we have referred, the relatively great number of other certified legal practitioners (such as, for instance, tax agents and patent agents), and the high level of administrative control over the lives of juridical personnel, such as their seconding to different parts of the country. It seems, however, that these restrictions were to a relatively high degree accepted, or at least not contested, by large sectors of the population—including, above all, the lawyers.

It is only lately that some lawyers have become more involved in political activities—or in litigation with political implications, or in opening hot lines for people suffering from harassment—but this is as yet a very unusual phenomenon.[4] Similarly, protests have developed from statements by some groups of civil rights activists publicly pointing out the not so beneficial aspects of certain police practices—the great pressure to admit to a crime one may not have committed and the difficulties of appeal. While these protests will probably eventually have some impact on the scope of these practices, as of now they do not seem to have changed overall either the characteristics of the Japanese legal system or the patterns of police behavior.

Yet the courts—and the cases brought before them, even litigation that has no chance of succeeding—may perform an important function in the articulation of new, broader social and cultural tendencies and themes in many arenas of law. Such articulations are not, however, formed in terms of principled political contestation but rather in terms of finding the proper common norms for the guidance of the collectivity—and hence for redefining its moral order or consensus, which necessarily entails different modes of response and of accommodation to processes of change and movements of protest. In constitutional law, for instance, the articulation of new norms may signal an emerging consensus as to different proper forms of behavior. Something of this kind may have been happening when in 1993 the courts upheld the first sexual harassment case against a woman worker in a Japanese company, and when in 1994 the court ordered the authorities to reveal to the residents of a middle-class neighborhood in Tokyo the reason for their plan to create an elevated railway passing above their neighborhood (see *International Herald Tribune*, 16 May 1994). Even more radical perhaps is the more recent decision of the Tokyo High Court (20 May 1994) that found the municipality of Tokyo and one of its wards responsible for the suicide of the boy who was bullied at his school.

In more general terms, Yui Kiyomitsu has pointed out (private communication) that Japan, especially when compared with other Asian societies, such as China, "is a very law-oriented society and that for Japanese bureaucracy, law is above all a supreme device to manage the state." Because of this—and "despite the tendency to the mutual embeddedness of judicative administration and legislation, and the relative weakness of the judicature"—it does also contain kernels of a more autonomous stance towards the bureaucracy.

Thus, the analysis of the Japanese legal system clearly indicates that it—like most other systems of regulation and social control that have developed in Japan—exhibits a specific combination of repressive and more benevolent, "harmonious" aspects, those which emphasize the reembedment of "culprits" in the groups or within the new social spaces created through the impact of the various manifestations of disharmony. Of special importance here is the fact that these processes of reembedment in existing contexts often coincide with these contexts' being redefined or made to incorporate new themes, and with the creation of spaces in which new activities can develop and crystallize.

II   The preceding analyses have far-reaching implications for the evaluation of the modern and contemporary Japanese political system as a basically repressive, unresponsive, militaristic or technocratic system. Indeed, a close analysis of various aspects of the political system indicates that this picture is one-sided, and hence distorted. Already the indications provided in chapter 5 have shown that it would be wrong to assume that processes and movements of protest have had no far-reaching impact on the Japanese political and social scene. In the following sections we shall further explicate their impact.

It is indeed true that few protest movements in Japan have achieved all of their broader goals. But this is true of most social movements and does not mean either that they have achieved none of their concrete goals or that they have not made the authorities more wary of imposing unpopular decisions and hence more sensitive to public opinion. This has been especially true of many of the movements at the local level, and of some of the potentially society-wide ones, such as the environmentalists.[5]

But the impact of these movements—as well as of the manifold structural changes that have continuously taken place in Japanese society—has gone much further. Not only have they sometimes achieved their concrete aims—they have also opened up new spaces of public discourse and new types of associations, lifestyles, and policy; constituted a reservoir of cultural themes; and served as important components of collective action, which could later come to the fore.

The various movements of protest—including the new religions, especially the more radical ones, and many women's movements—whether organized on the basis of ideology or of status, have been instrumental in the construction of spaces of social action and cultural creativity—albeit spaces segregated from the center—in which the hegemonic rules were not predominant and within which new types of sophisticated discourse and new levels of reflexivity were generated. Within these life spaces, many seemingly repressed, rebellious, and subversive themes, like equality and commonality, have found expression and new lifestyles with some liminal potentialities have developed.

These movements have indeed greatly broadened the scope of the political agenda and discussion in Japan. Even when, at the end of the different periods of opening—whether in the Meiji or Taishō eras or in the mid-1950s—many themes or demands were suppressed in the public arena of discussion, they did not go into total oblivion.

III To take only the case of the various themes promulgated by the Taishō liberals, these themes did not go into oblivion. On the contrary, as Sharon Nolte has shown in her recent study of liberalism in Japan, they had far-reaching implications.[6] Nolte's and many other studies have shown that these intellectuals and the political groups influenced the political discourse in several ways. First, they opened up new frameworks of discourse on culture, on societal relations, and on their relations to Japanese collective self-consciousness. Themes of liberalism, freedom of the press, women's rights, social problems, and the like, and a general, if diffuse emphasis on equality, remained on the public agenda in one way or another and were not entirely taken out of the political, literary, or ideological discourse.[7]

Second, many of these themes were incorporated into the predominant ideology, the carriers of which often portrayed themselves as having resolved the issues raised by the themes in the "proper" Japanese way. Throughout these periods new types of discourse and social activities continuously developed, including potentially subversive themes promulgated in the name of an "autonomous," mature, antistatist view.

Some of these merged with the romantic stances of the folklorists—others with more "natural" or humanistic positions. Even during periods of repression, these themes can be seen to have been stored, waiting as it were for more appropriate circumstances. Such conditions indeed arose after the Second World War—but again in a fashion that differed greatly from what happened in Western countries.

Third, it was not only on the intellectual level or that of public discourse that these themes were later taken up. Many of the social and political movements that developed after the Second World War built, as A. Gordon has shown in great detail, on the organizational and symbolic foundations of earlier movements.[8]

Thus many of these themes and the groups that promulgated them would come to the fore, not necessarily, or even primarily, by directly achieving their goals or by reconstructing the center, but rather by being incorporated into the more central arenas of discourse as constructed by the hegemonic groups within the center or by creating new social spaces relatively segregated from the center.

One of the most fascinating illustrations of this process is the development of the many new religions, which burgeoned starting in the late Tokugawa period, were to some extent suppressed in the early Meiji period and during the military regime, and have again burgeoned after the Second World War. Many of these have become engaged in politics, but rarely have they challenged the existing order; they have evinced strong this-worldly orientations without developing critical orientations rooted in universalistic visions or principles that would transcend the given order. At the same time they have all constructed spaces in which new, potentially subversive types of activity and modes of discourse have developed that allow their members to escape, as it were, the restrictions of the existing order and to develop lifestyles of their own. The transformation of the cultural orientations of the Rastafarian movement in Japan—in itself not a very important one—is indicative of tendencies common to many of these religions. As D. W. Collingwood and Kusatsu Osamu have shown, the Japanese Rastafarians paid no attention to the cosmological and theological dimensions of the original Rastafarian movement, adopting instead only its ritual and artistic dimensions.[9] This enabled them to create a new life space for themselves that did not challenge the hegemonic mold—but provided a space to escape from it.

IV   Demographic and structural changes in modern and contemporary Japan have also contributed to the continuous creation of spaces for new, often subversive activities and modes of labeling activities and roles that nonetheless impinge on the center only indirectly. The creation of such spaces can be identified in the continuous construction of different lifestyles and of status distinctions within the broad general category of the middle class. Significantly, as we saw in chapter 3, such life spaces are often constructed and legitimized in traditional terms.

Several recent developments illustrate the creation of such spaces. For instance, the difficulty of integrating the *kikokushijo*—Japanese children who return to Japan after having been abroad with their parents—in the current school system has led to the establishment of *kikokushijo* schools, which both incorporate and separate these people, creating a fully sanctioned space for them but distinguishing them from the larger community.[10] A similar trend seems to develop in some of the new international centers at top academic institutions, in which Japanese who have completed their university education abroad and have difficulty finding a place in the usual departments may be incorporated. The networks constructed in such new spaces may become interwoven with older ones, even while remaining separate.

Of broader importance are changes in the development and definition of leisure activities and, above all, in women's lifestyles. For instance, as Sepp Linhart has shown, the highly regulated leisure-time activity typical of modern and contemporary Japan evinces some distinctive characteristics: First, the boundaries between work and leisure time are less tightly drawn than in other industrial societies. Second, and closely related to the first point, the "contents" of leisure activities have often changed—new types of activities have been relatively easily incorporated.[11]

Women's life patterns have also changed dramatically in the last two decades or so, influenced to a great extent by women's movements and the increase in women's levels of education.[12] Some women have attained highly visible managerial executive positions, and others have become prominent in cultural life—in landscaping, architecture, and the like—but these very substantial changes have necessarily affected only a small number of women. In terms of overall occupational status women, perhaps above all educated women, continue to be discriminated against. Yet at the same time far-reaching changes can be discerned among wider sectors of women in Japanese society. To quote briefly from Iwao Sumiko's recent analysis of these developments:

> The past fifteen years have been an era of profound change—a time of what I call inconspicuous revolution—for Japanese women. While the central organizations and groups that make up Japanese society are still almost exclusively staffed and controlled by men, opportunities for women to work and seek fulfillment outside the home have increased, giving them a whole new range of freedoms.
>
> This development has led to a reversal of freedoms, as it were. . . . Now men have become increasingly chained to the institutions they have set up,

with their commitment to long-term employment and the promotional ladder rigged to seniority. Their wives, on the other hand, have been set free by the development of home appliances and other conveniences, and now their ability and energy is being absorbed by a waiting labor market and a broad range of culturally enriching activities. Not only can they work outside the home, but they have great freedom to decide how, where and under what terms they will work. The female side of society has become extremely diversified, while the male side, trapped by inertia and peer pressure, has grown more homogeneous.[13]

First, there are changes in attitudes to work. Such attitudes have slowly started to affect many practices in the workplaces,[14] as well as the patterns of marriage and family life. These changes may raise among women new expectations with respect to marriage—expectations that may give rise, when unfulfilled, to growing tensions in the family.[15]

The principled resistance of members of women's movements has served as symbol and model for many Japanese homes in creating new life spaces for themselves. But the development of such spaces does not do away with women's occupational inequality, or with their "principled" embeddedness in the family.[16] Again we see the tendency to status incongruency prevalent throughout the structuration of Japanese social life. Indeed, the construction of such spaces is encouraged, as Higuchi Keiko has shown, by certain tax policies; these same policies, however, by encouraging women not to work full-time (because they would then be assessed according to their own wages) and to stay married, bind women to the family nexus and make their freedom dependent on their husbands' earnings.[17] Similarly, the relatively few women who have attained top positions in politics or in academic life have been single; they did not develop "usual" families, which would entail giving up their careers during the time they would have had to take care of their children. Thus they were able to act, as Elizabeth McSweeney has put it (private communication), as "men" rather than women.

The constitution of such new spaces does not necessarily mean that those participating in them will see them as entirely positive developments. Such new spaces generate strong ambivalences to the existing order, but at the same time they provide arenas in which these ambivalences may be accepted without challenging the mainstream hegemonic institutional arrangements.[18]

But it is not only in the social or religious arena that new spaces and new types of activities have developed. The same is true, as we have hinted at, in the central arena of the modern Japanese miracle—the economic one. It has not only been the great companies, the conglomerates, and the segmented labor market that have generated this miracle. Of no smaller importance—according to some, of even greater importance—have been the many small firms established by entrepreneurial individuals, who have evinced a great ability to adjust to changing internal and international mores. It is within these new enterprises that many innovations have recently developed—but, again, without challenging the overall frameworks of Japanese political economy.[19]

V The impact of the movements and processes of change and the prevalent modes of regulating disharmony in Japanese society is manifest also in the patterns of policy making and of response by the political center to demands of various groups and movements. Examination of the process of decision making and of the policies developed by LDP governments in the last thirty years or so indicates that the view that stresses the technocratic orientation of these policies, the secretiveness of decision making, and the government's seeming unresponsiveness to opposition demands not only is exaggerated but overlooks some basic characteristics of this system.

Many recent analyses of these policies—by Kent Calder, T. Pempel, Gary Allinson and his colleagues, and many others—clearly indicate that many policies have developed in response to processes of change and the demands of various movements of protest—and have sometimes even anticipated such demands and protests.[20] The upshot of these analyses is that decisions are made, not solely by bureaucrats or by the anonymous system, but through multiple networks composed of bureaucrats, politicians, and sometimes even members or representatives of various pressure groups, including some oppositionary ones.[21] The relative importance of the different elements in such networks has varied greatly; there can be no doubt that during long periods of time some sectors of the bureaucracy—for instance MITI, the Ministry of International Trade and Industry—have been predominant in many of these networks, although the situation is probably changing in favor of various groups of politicians. It may even be, as Sasaki Takeshi suggests, that the role of politicians in guiding the system will have to increase.[22] But the crux of the system is indeed this type of network consultations and decision making.[23]

Indeed, as Gary Allinson, Michio Muramatsu, and Margaret McKean, among others, have shown, the seemingly unresponsive political system of the modern and contemporary—especially post–Second World War—periods has been characterized, to use Muramatsu's expression, by "patterned pluralism."[24] This implies a relatively weak state—a state which does not command but bases its working on continual consultations with various groups, with various consultative bodies playing a crucial role.[25] Thus the political system has had available several modes of response to the demands of various social sectors and protest movements. One is a sort of delayed response; another is the incorporation of demands into official policies, albeit with the claim that the decisions were undertaken voluntarily by the authorities, or at least that the authorities retain the right to make these decisions. These two types of response have been especially important, in the postwar period, on the local level. In other cases groups and networks themselves have been co-opted into the central frameworks.

In general, the processes of control effected by the authorities have been based on the restructuring of markets and status hierarchies (evident, for instance, in the clear lines of promotion within departments of industries or firms) and on the relative dissociation between status and wealth. Concomitantly, the processes of suppression have usually combined, to different degrees in different periods, with the tendency to leave some living space to the loser.[26] Coercion and repression, according to many scholars, have not been as prominent as in other societies. But patterned pluralism and a weak state have not necessarily entailed an open public arena. They are based, as Gary Allinson has written, on a fragmented citizenry, on multiple consultative bodies, and on contests between different groups and the authorities.[27]

This type of decision making and responsiveness, with its requirement of continuous negotiations between different participants, makes it difficult to identify the one person or group responsible for a decision. Moreover, discussions and deliberations are not easily brought out into the open; the relation between open discussions, for instance in the parliament (Diet), and any concrete decision is rather tenuous—even more so than in other modern political systems. Similarly, changes in policies, even when undertaken in response to various demands, need not be directly connected with broad, principled, political issues; more often they are connected with breakdowns in relations between different networks.

The ruling party's accommodative stance and the concomitant weakness of the opposition are also rooted both in the structural conditions and rules of the parliamentary game and in cultural norms. The rule of procedural unanimity, promulgated in the Japanese Diet already in the 1930s, has continued to be operative and has naturally led to greater accommodation on substantive issues. This accommodative tendency is reinforced by the fact that the weak ideological dimension of the ruling party has enabled it not only to accommodate the demands of various oppositionary groups, but also to adopt their policies as its own without acknowledging their sources. This was the case with respect to the disarmament treaty and in many other, less dramatic areas.[28]

As T. J. Pempel has pointed out:

The behavior of the opposition oscillated between participation in such accommodative policies and more "principled" oppositionary gestures which symbolized its seeming refusal to participate in consensual policies. While they were but rarely able to defeat the government, these attempts of theirs in the parliamentary arena very often had remarkable effects, forcing the government to withdraw or change many of its proposals, or even to adopt new ones—without however ever admitting being influenced by the opposition. This often enabled the opposition to maintain its "ideological purity"—although it could also give rise to internal disputes about the mode of participation in the parliamentary game.[29]

This process of decision making has often brought governing and oppositionary groups together in common, semiliminal situations—new spaces of discourse that seem to transcend the existing orientations have been created, even if they do not change the overall rules of the Japanese political discourse. Indeed such liminal elements seem to constitute a very important component of the Japanese political system.[30]

Significantly, this pattern of networking is characteristic not only of the upper echelons of the bureaucracy and parties, but of almost all the levels of political organization in most parties. It is the numerous networks, often focused on the party candidate, that have been the most influential on all the levels of the political process—and on voting.[31] Such continuously changing oppositionary constellations have been effective both in presenting political demands and in creating spaces in which new types of lifestyles or organizations could develop—not only on the local level, but also in the central political arena.[32] It is significant that in June 1993 it was the breakdown of internetwork relations *within* the LDP— and not a confrontation between the LDP and the opposition—that necessitated the calling of new elections that threatened the dominance of the LDP.

VI   These modes of decision making also explain the impact—discernible not only in modern and contemporary Japan but throughout most of its history—of the various political, ideological, and protest movements in the Japanese political and social system. It is these modes of regulation that explain the other side to this continuous creation of new spaces—the common perception of modern and contemporary Japanese society as an immobilist, repressive, and manipulated system. This view is based on the fact that these movements have not, despite great success in attaining some concrete goals (or procuring "rectifications" from the authorities) and creating new spaces, been able to generalize their concrete grievances into broader themes, so as to radically transform the basic premises of the political system. Even those movements that seemed to articulate broader ideological themes, such as those of communalism or of egalitarianism, have not usually been able to make these themes legitimate in the central political discourse or to obtain autonomous access to the center.

The various confrontational situations in which these movements have been highly visible have not led to the institutionalization of new modes of conflict resolution—of, for instance, more formalistic legal or universalistic directions—or to the reformulation of the basic premises of the social and political order, even if they have provided for the re-interpretation and reconstruction of many of these premises. The openings that have developed relatively quickly in these situations have been closed up by coalitions of elites, influential persons, and even counter-elites, coalitions structured according to some recombinant version of the primordial-sacral or natural symbols and achievement orientations embedded in solidary frameworks. But at the same time the new formations created by these elites have entailed more diversified activities than before.

The mode of conflict resolution that has emerged in such situations has instead reconfigured existing vertical hierarchical principles, broadening the scope of these networks and incorporating new ideological underpinnings and definitions. These new definitions, though often imbued with themes of protest, have been set within the established hegemonic framework. Thus, the more successful movements have been effective with respect to various concrete demands, but not with respect to more general principled orientations.

Here again the new religions provide an example. On the one hand they were imbued with strong communal, and to a lesser extent egalitarian, orientations and themes. On the other hand, their this-worldliness was not rooted in a transcendental vision that could confront the given reality, nor did they serve as starting points for radical reform or transformation. Hence in these religions, as in most other movements, the more radical democratic, egalitarian, or communitarian themes were readily hemmed in by the hegemonic frameworks and usually not allowed to challenge directly the premises or symbols of those frameworks. Whenever such challenges have been attempted, as for instance in the discussions, depicted by Norma Field, of the Shōwa emperor's role in the Second World War, they have been either suppressed or disregarded.[33]

In other words, these movements have not given rise to a civil society that could either impose its own criteria of legitimation on the state or promulgate principles that would transcend the state and the national community, and in which different minority groups could ground their claims for inclusion. The most telling illustration of this failure is to be seen in the still restrictive and repressive Japanese attitudes toward those outside of the pure national community—the Koreans and the *burakumin*.

Thus the impact of these movements has been, like that of Confucianism, Buddhism, and many Western ideologies, double-pronged. On the one hand, they have opened up new spaces, generated new modes of reflexivity and discourse, moved toward the reformulation of the core premises, and promoted the construction of new symbolic and institutional frameworks in which these new spaces, modes of reflexivity, and discourses could exist. On the other hand, they have not changed the basic premises of Japanese society and the patterns of conflict regulation. This is, to some extent, true of protest movements in all societies—but the concrete contours of their relative successes and failures vary greatly.

VII The Japanese response to movements of protest or opposition is characterized by the combination of great flexibility in the extension of networks and consultations and the weakness and ineffectiveness of more principled, ideological, potentially confrontational stances.

The crux of the Japanese modern and contemporary system has indeed been an open network of consultations, "contracts" of co-optation into the networks, and the continuous creation of new networks, often overlapping with the older ones. Co-optation has been effected by the activation of various vertical hierarchical ties and appropriate contextual orientations.[34] But even if the structure of such ties and networks has become more dispersed, they remain the major channels of decision making. Not only have such networks continuously expanded and diversified; the policies promulgated within them have been very responsive to changing circumstances and to the demands of various groups, and have evinced on the whole the major characteristics of "creative conservatism" as analyzed by Pempel.[35]

At the same time, however, more principled or ideological demands have rarely been politically effective. They have instead remained on the purely symbolic level, and even on this level have rarely led to the restructuring of the premises of the center. They have not given rise to the sort of challenge that has characterized, for instance, class-conscious European political movements in general and socialist ones in particular. This relative ineffectiveness of the "extreme" ideological movements can be seen also in the development of women's associations—most of which, as Sheldon Garon has shown, were highly oriented toward the state and did not attempt to transcend the parameters of discourse set up by the authorities.[36]

Similarly, policy shifts have but rarely entailed basic ideological changes. Indeed, practical demands and ensuing policies alike have generally been framed in terms of the basic "moral economy" of conflict and protest in Japanese society, as analyzed by Susan Pharr.[37] Both the demands of various groups and movements and the subsequent policy announcements have often been couched in highly moralistic terms based, not on the universalistic premises of autonomous individual access to the center, but on the ideology of communal solidarity and harmony.

It is the prevalence (even if rather precarious at times, as, for example, in the period after the First World War) of these basic patterns, this moral economy of protest, that explains the impact as well as the limits of protest and indicates that the common denominator of the Japanese system of decision making is the weakness of open, principled, political discourse and the continuous tendency to conflate the public arena with such networks.

VIII Patricia Steinhoff has succinctly analyzed some of the most pertinent aspects of this picture:

> It can be argued that while the major public protests of the post-war era did not necessarily achieve their specific goals, they did serve to temper the ambitions of conservative politicians and thus helped to keep the country on a moderate course. As public officials have become sensitive to the concerns of protesters, or to the potential of an issue to provoke public protest, they have sometimes supported policies which had the effect of resolving or circumventing the problem. This is the essence of the Japanese style of conflict management. It represents neither altruism nor spontaneous consensus, but rather a strong desire to avoid direct conflict. Protest, or the threat of protest, thus may have genuine policy consequences that are very difficult to document.
>
> . . . From this perspective, the peace movement has had some modest success, but the student movement has been less successful.
>
> Farmers and labor unions achieved their political incorporation through the 1946 constitution, though they continue to engage in ritualized protest as a symbolic gesture. Women's issues are being taken more seriously in Japan today, and much of the credit must go to a very broad range of pressures brought to bear by women's organizations. Only a fraction of that activity could be called protest, however.
>
> The major beneficiaries of this process have been the environmentally oriented citizens' movements, which began to emerge just as the student movement was entering its most violent phase of activity in the late 1960s. And that, after all, is what protest in a democracy is all about.[38]

IX The combination of policies, decision making, and responses to protest is among the reasons the LDP's one-party hegemony lasted for almost forty years.[39] Several comparative analyses of dominant party regimes point out reasons for the relative success of the LDP as against the dominant parties in Sweden, Israel, and Italy—all emphasize its relatively successful and flexible policies and its nonideological and nonprincipled stance toward the various sectors of the electorate.[40] Pempel concludes:

> If one major source of flexibility by a dominant party involves the overt switching of support groups, there is a second dimension of flexibility that is also possible for the dominant party. This involves less overt betrayal, requiring only that the party, while continuing to make appeals from a clear ideological position, and with due respect to well-entrenched political values and norms, in fact govern far more pragmatically from the political center.[41]

Indeed, the combination of a nonideological, accommodative stance with an emphasis on consensual politics, often implemented in liminal modes, has characterized the LDP from the very beginning. These characteristics are themselves closely related to the conflation of state, civil society, and national community and to the lack of autonomy in civil society (and state) and the public arena.

Needless to say this does not mean the LDP could remain in power forever—and indeed in July 1993 it was ousted from power. It is, however, significant that the threat to its hegemony—the need to call for elections in July 1993 and the consequent formation of a government by various former opposition parties along with groups that left the LDP—came about through the defection of groups from within the LDP and the breakdown of networks within the party. One may suggest, however, that the LDP's loss of hegemony did not change some of the most distinctive characteristics of the contemporary Japanese political scene, especially the relations between state and society.

A rather different problem is that of the efficiency of the pattern of politics and of policy making. This pattern has often been called conservative, immobilist, resistant to reform or restructure—as, perhaps above all, attempts at reforming education attest.[42] There can be no doubt that the tendency to extension of networks and to co-optation into them creates vested interests that make systematic, "rational" reform difficult. The preponderant modes of administrative reform take, in Japan, the form of opening new spaces or new types of activities, or of reorganizing the principles that regulate the working of the different networks. Changes, such as those undertaken in the economic arena in 1992 and 1993, usually come in response to radical pressures from within the system and above all from the outside. Whether this is more true of Japan than of other bureaucracies may be a moot question. It is the extent to which such changes can be effectively undertaken in potentially critical situations that constitutes the major challenge before the Japanese system.

But the regulation of responses to these challenges is also reflected in a distinctly "Japanese" way. The new banking agency created to bail banks out of a financial crisis caused by bad loans and the watchdog institution set up to monitor the futures market and the Ministry of Finance—but in fact controlled by this ministry—are good illustrations of administrative guidance and the incorporative nature of the bureaucratic/political power structure. The extent to which such reforms will succeed as responses to the challenges Japan faces now has yet to be seen. This question is at the very core of the analysis of Japanese society and polity. Do all these changes—in that they do not alter the core characteristics of the Japanese political system—signal only, in van Wolferen's terms, a nonrevolution,[43] or will even such a nonrevolution be able to take up the new challenges Japan faces today?

X It is these rather unusual (from a Western point of view) modes of decision making and of incorporating protest and oppositional demands that make it difficult to classify the Japanese political system in the prevalent terms of political science. This difficulty has been very aptly analyzed by J. A. Stockwin, in his introduction to a series of discussions among Australian scholars.

> In the Japanese case, the model is rather like that of a patron-client system, where some of the clients reside within the patron's house, and others (the larger number) live outside it. Still others refuse to have much to do with the patron, but their success in exercising influence is generally slight, though they can be annoyingly disruptive and he may on occasion have to make significant concessions to them. . . .
>
> In practice, of course, the "patron" is a combination of the government party and the ministries and agencies of the government bureaucracy. Many of its actions will not clearly or demonstrably be related to overt interest group pressure, either from within or from outside the system.[44]

XI The combination of these characteristics of the political arena, which explains the distinctive flavor of the contemporary Japanese political system, is an outgrowth of the interaction or confrontation between the original Meiji model and the continuously changing economic, social, political, and international forces. As a result of these confrontations, there has developed in Japan since the Second World War a political system that has recently been judged by a variety of Japanese and Western scholars to be clearly democratic, in which some of the major components of democracy—rule of law, freedom of assembly and of the press—have been continuously expanding.[45]

Concurrently this system has continued to exhibit some very distinctive characteristics. It is not only that many components of a "full" liberal democracy have been underdeveloped, as manifest for instance in the limited effectiveness of movements of protest.[46] Especially important in the context of our discussion are the reasons for such underdevelopment, which is due, not only to the presumed autocratic or repressive components of the regime, but also, perhaps above all, to some of the basic premises of the mode of legitimation of this system as it developed under the Meiji—especially the narrowness of the autonomous public space, or civil society independent of the state organs, and the concomitant legitimation of the state in terms of its embeddedness in the national community.

The processes of democratization and of the continual diversification of sectors and elites that took place after the Second World War have expanded the access of broader sectors of society to the organs of government and imbued these organs with a greater respect for the legal specification of the rights of citizens and for legal procedure. They have not, however, greatly expanded the capacity of an autonomous civil society to promulgate its own criteria of legitimation and impose them on the state in the name of principles that transcend the state and the national community alike.

The specific type of civil society that developed in Japan is perhaps best illustrated by the continual construction of new social spaces. This process provides semiautonomous arenas in which new types of activities, consciousness, and discourse can develop without, however, impinging directly on the center; participants in such spaces do not have autonomous access to the center and are certainly not able to challenge its premises. The relations between state and society are, rather, effected in the mode of patterned pluralism, of multiple dispersed social contracts.

This weakness of civil society and the concomitant development of what Peter J. Herzog calls "Japan's pseudo-democracy" was due, not to its suppression by a strong state, but rather to the continual conflation of state and civil society with the national community.[47] While it is those close to the center—oligarchies, bureaucracies, politicians, and even heads of economic organizations—who have on the whole shaped the contours of this community, they have not done so in a continuous confrontational response to the demands of other sectors of civil society. The constitutional-democratic system that has developed in Japan has not been grounded in the conceptions of principled, metaphysical individualism or in a principled confrontation between state and society as two distinct ontological entities.[48]

Thus there has developed the paradoxical situation—in usual Western terms—of a relatively stable constitutional-democratic regime in a society with a very weak civil society, of a highly regulated but not totalitarian society. It is this combination that explains some of the specific characteristics of the Japanese political system.

XII These characteristics of the Japanese political system are closely related to the most pertinent features of the specific type of social order to develop in contemporary Japan, which have been very aptly analyzed by W. W. Kelly:

> In both historical and comparative context, postwar Japanese society is characterized by a wide subscription to ideological and institutional standards and by the perpetuation of significant, antagonizing differences. I have argued elsewhere that a loose set of typifications about social relations and personal goals in the home, at school, and in the workplace has given a cultural reality to claims of postwar Japan as a "New Middle Class" society.
>
> Consensus and coercion poorly describe such a social order, which is better formulated as cooptive, contested, and complicit. It is cooptive, in that predominant ideologies and institutions have been remarkably inclusive, embracing much of the population and regularizing their lifeways. In so doing, they have defused much potential conflict, and infused widespread commitment. Nonetheless, the ways in which public theories and societal institutions shape and constrain ordinary lives are neither direct nor mechanical. Within and between these arguments and tensions, the people of the postwar decades have acted, effectively and creatively, to construct and lead their lives.[49]

This rather unusual combination of consensus and coercion—of "cooptive, contested, and complicit" features—is closely connected to the most distinctive and specific characteristics of modern and contemporary Japan—namely its being a highly regulated but nontotalitarian and highly innovative society. It is, as we saw in chapter 3, best understood in terms of the discourse of modernity that has developed in Japan, with its oscillation between negation and affirmation or appropriation of modernity in the realm both of high ideological discourse and of the construction of daily social life.[50]

These characteristics of the discourse of modernity developed in close relation to the fact that the social and cultural consequences of modernization and industrialization were generated not by outside forces but by the Meiji state—which at the same time espoused a distinct ideology, appropriating to itself both instrumental modernity and the definition of Japanese authenticity—as well as to the strong immanentist orientation of this discourse.[51] Of special importance in this context have been the construction of new spaces; their cultural embeddedness in the contextual mode of structuration of the major arenas of social life and interaction; their combination with a tendency to status inconsistency; and the central place of a traditionalism grounded in a flexible definition of tradition.[52]

XIII Most modern Western scholars seem to have difficulty understanding the basic cultural and institutional features of modernity as it developed in Japan, especially its status as a highly controlled yet nontotalitarian, indeed formally and to some extent actually democratic society. This combination of characteristics touches on some of the very central premises of modern, Western social science and analysis, and it comes to the fore, as we alluded to in the first chapter, in some of the trenchant scholarly and ideological criticisms of the *Nihonjinron* literature. Indeed this puzzle, of a highly regulated yet nontotalitarian society, touches the central nerve, as it were, of the modern Japanese social system.

How can we then explain these characteristics of modern and contemporary Japanese society—the modes of regulation of behavior, of structuration of the major arenas of social life, of the overall cultural program of modernity that has developed in Japan? How can we explain this rather unusual combination of features specific to the institutions of modern and contemporary Japanese society? Are they to be explained in terms of "culture," social structure, historical contingencies, or some mixture thereof? Before engaging these questions—and in order to facilitate their exploration—I shall first make a historical detour. I shall examine, as I indicated in the first chapter, several aspects of the Japanese historical experience in which this distinctive combination of similarities and differences with Western societies will come up again, as it has with respect to modern and contemporary Japan.

This analysis does not of course pretend to be a comprehensive history of Japan. I shall concentrate on particular aspects of Japanese history, such as feudalism, the Tokugawa state, patterns of rebellion and reform leading to the disintegration of this state, and patterns of urban development. In all these cases, unlike the modern period, there was little contact between the West and Japan; hence this combination of similarities and differences is even more surprising. I will explore in what way Japanese institutional formations, despite many similarities, differ in some dimensions from those of Western Europe, and how these differences are also evident in the processes of change that have been taking place in Japanese history.

At the same time, however, Japan has been in close contact almost from the beginning of its history with China and Korea, and more recently with India. It was from these countries that two of the most formative influences on Japan, Buddhism and Confucianism, came. There were also threats of invasion—possibly the first settlements in Japan came from Korea. And China has always been much in the minds of the Japanese, at least up till the modern period. One interpretation of the Meiji Ishin (offered by Ben-Ami Shillony) is that it aimed, by creating a new imperial order, to establish Japanese hegemony against China.

But although the influences of China, of Confucianism, and of (Mahayana) Buddhism were paramount in shaping Japan, Japan has never become part of these universalistic civilizations. Concomitantly, Confucianism and Buddhism have been transformed in Japan in radical ways. These transformations, and Japan's relations to these civilizations, constitute a crucial dimension of the Japanese historical experience—yet another illustration of a combination of similarities with and differences from other civilizations. I shall accordingly analyze these problems in the last chapter of the historical part of our analysis. As was the case in the preceding analyses of modern and contemporary Japan, I shall focus only on the features of these institutions, regimes, and processes that are of central importance to an understanding of the specificity of the Japanese historical experience in a comparative framework. We shall first inquire as to whether there are any similarities between, on the one hand, Japan's modern and contemporary experience and, on the other, its historical experience. We shall then ask whether the distinctive characteristics of the Japanese historical experience that constitute the major challenge for comparative analysis can be explained in "cultural" or "structural" terms or whether they call for elements of both the cultural and the structural research perspectives.

In order to explore this problem we shall analyze some central aspects of Japanese culture, then consider whether there is any relation between these aspects and some of the specific characteristics of the Japanese historical experience and how such relations can be explained. Finally, on the basis of these considerations we shall present some summary conclusions on the nature of the Japanese historical experience, and only then shall we analyze the specific characteristics of Japan as a distinctive modern civilization—the specific cultural program of modernity that has developed in Japan.

Part Two

ASPECTS OF

JAPANESE

HISTORICAL

EXPERIENCE

Feudalism in Japan

I The first institutional complex that we shall discuss is that of Japanese feudalism, which is similar in many ways to its Western European counterpart. Japanese feudalism crystallized from about the end of the eleventh century with the disintegration of the early clan-based, centralized Ritsuryō monarchy, which had attempted to create an imperial state fashioned after the Chinese (Tang) model. This historical background was, as Otto Hintze and R. Coulborn have pointed out, very similar to the one that gave rise to European feudalism—namely the decline of central imperial authority, the continuity of an imperial ideal, and the disintegration of relatively wider tribal units, including kinship organization.[1]

The similarity between European and Japanese feudalism is not restricted to their respective origins. It extends also to their development, as Durkheim noted at the beginning of this century and as P. Duus and A. Lewis have shown, from the beginnings of feudalism in Japan (A.D. 794–1185) through what has been called formative feudalism and the first feudal age (1185–1334) to the flowering of feudalism (1334–1568) before the absolutist stage (1568–1868)—or according to some interpretations in Japan during it.[2] Moreover, some of the core characteristics of feudalism in Europe and in Japan are similar.

Japanese feudalism developed over a longer period than feudalism in Europe, continuing until at least 1598, when under the Tokugawa family (which ruled as shoguns until 1868) the feudal order was superseded by a highly centralized one—albeit with many important feudal features.[3]

Japan has been singled out by scholars old and new as having developed a feudal economic-political system very close to the European one. Marc Bloch, in his classic *La société féodale*, pointed to Japanese feudalism as closest to the European model, although he also recognized some important differences, to which we shall return later.[4] Before him Hintze had also indicated, in a more general way, the existence of such similarities.[5] Jouon Des Longrais made a much more detailed comparison of European and Japanese feudalism, as did several other scholars,[6] especially R. Coulborn, who took the question up in the framework of a broad comparative study of feudalism in different historical settings, and Peter Duus, the first Western historian of Japan to analyze Japanese feudalism in a systematic and comparative way.[7]

More recently, Jean Baechler has studied this theme of the similarity between European and Japanese feudalism and used it to explain why capitalism and economic modernization have developed in both cases,[8] while Johann Arnason has shown how Japanese feudalism explains both Japan's strong tendency to modernization and the specific trajectory of this modernization.[9] As these studies have shown, the Japanese political and economic scene, like European feudalism, was characterized by a combination of claims by various would-be lords to the produce of peasants, which later developed into a full manorial organization of land, with some devolution of political authority and of land rights as a compensation for military service, and the consequent emergence of various military groups as the central stratum in society.

II   Its similarities to European feudalism notwithstanding, Japanese feudalism until the Tokugawa age (which some have claimed was still basically a feudal period) evinced, as Bloch noted in his analysis, several very important distinguishing features, which attest to a distinct mode of historical dynamics. First, formalized legal, contractual, mutually obligatory relations between lords and vassals were weaker in Japan than in Europe (although there naturally existed an implicit mutual obligation). Second, multiple lordships were absent, or at least uncommon, in Japan and the distance between the upper lords and the larger sector of samurai relatively great. (This was connected with the continuous expansion of the samurai class, particularly from the Muromachi period on, through the incorporation of large numbers of petty local proprietors and villagers into the armies of competing warriors.)

Third, political institutions comparable to the various representative institutions of medieval Europe, in which vassals could exert some concrete autonomous rights vis-à-vis the center and within the center, did not exist in Japan. Fourth, the distance between especially the higher samurai and the peasants was far greater than in Europe; this gap came to its fullest fruition in the Tokugawa period and was closely connected to the fact that the lords were on the whole much more interested in controlling products from the land than in controlling land itself.[10]

Fifth, the continuous centralization of feudal authority, combined with a framework of national unity, pervaded the Japanese system much more than that in any early medieval European case, with the possible partial exception of England. Sixth, that central authority in Japan was bifurcated between the emperor and the shogun, or the *bakufu*. Seventh, and closely related to the sixth point, the structure of relations between power and status that developed within Japanese society, which can probably be historically traced to the beginnings of Japanese feudalism, differed from that in Europe, at least from the Kamakura period (1195–1335 c.e.) on.[11]

Let's analyze these distinctive characteristics of Japanese feudalism in somewhat greater detail. In contrast to the European case, feudal relations and obligation between vassal and lord were in Japan sharply asymmetrical. They entailed, as Bloch has noted, much greater submission on the part of the vassals—a tendency reinforced by the fact that, contrary to Europe, a vassal could, in principle at least, have only one lord at a time. In fact many vassals did change lords, especially in periods of turmoil, as for instance in the fifteenth century.[12]

In Japan relations between vassal and lord were generally couched, not in contractual terms based on fully formalized mutual legal rights and obligations, but in terms of familial or filial obligations.[13] Within this structure vassals exercised no principled legal rights vis-à-vis their lords—there was no formal mechanism for appealing, in the name of the lord, either to a higher authority within the feudal hierarchy or to an institution such as the king's court, the parliament, or an assembly of estates, although warriors did have the right of remonstrance.[14] This was closely related, as Joseph R. Stayer and many others have pointed out, to a conception of authority rooted in a familial ethos of obligations reinforced by Confucian precepts, and not—despite the influence of the Chinese legal system—in legal rights and obligations as was the case in Europe.[15]

In practice, of course, lords had to take the interests of the vassals into account, and there existed a strong presumption—usually embedded in customary provisions—that they were responsible for their vassals' welfare. The lords would not usually risk alienating their vassals unless they thought they could get away with it, but unlike vassals in Europe, those in Japan had little legal protection and no legitimate right to principled autonomous, independent participation in the councils and other centers of power of their respective lords.[16] Hence, paradoxically, conflicts between them and betrayals of the lord by his vassals erupted more frequently, were extremely confrontational, and could lead, as in the fifteenth century, to very intensive struggles and semianarchic situations—a fact which is of central importance for the understanding of conflict and conflict resolution in Japan.

The second distinctive aspect of Japanese feudalism was that, in principle, a vassal could have only one lord at a time. Vassals did change lords and transfer their allegiance, especially in periods of turmoil; moreover, in such periods loyalty to groups of samurai, always potentially in competition with loyalty to the lords, could largely supersede the latter. But in principle at least, a vassal's allegiance at any given time would be undivided.

Indeed, Japanese feudalism is characterized by the extension of strong familial obligation to frameworks broader than the nuclear family, replacing any wider kinship organization, and by the vesting in the lord of control over such frameworks and the use of and access to their resources. In Europe one became a vassal of a lord through the acquisition of rights to a certain piece of land; thus a vassal who acquired parcels of land belonging to different lords would have several lords. In Japan, by contrast, vassal-lord relations were not mediated by possession of land but were direct personal ones—land or produce were given by the lord to the vassal by virtue of their personal relations.[17] True enough, the initial feudal ties as they developed under Yoritomo and in the Kamakura period did have a strong component of "rights in land," interests that frequently accrued to local warriors for the role they played in developing cultivated land. As time went on, however, the relation between lord and vassal came to be conceived of increasingly in personal terms as the lord extended his authority over his vassals by rewarding them with additional land grants. This led eventually to the emergence of the fief (over which the lord retained residual authority) and, in the Tokugawa period, to the conversion of the fief into a stipend or, in the case of larger vassals, to the clear assertion that the fief is held entirely at the grace of the lord.

III   The absence of fully autonomous legal rights in Japanese feudal relations and the constant emphasis on the seemingly absolute—if in principle benevolent, "familial"—authority of the lord, were of course closely connected to the third major difference between European and Japanese feudalism, namely the absence in Japan of any institutional arena within which the vassals (or other groups, such as the merchants or the peasants) could express as a group their political views independent of the will and sufferance of the sovereigns. To quote Marc Bloch:

> It was assuredly no accident that the representative system, in the very aristocratic form of the English Parliament, the French "Estates," the Stände of Germany, and the Spanish Cortes, originated in states which were only just emerging from the feudal stage and still bore its imprint. Nor was it an accident that in Japan, where the vassal's submission was much more unilateral and where, moreover, the divine power of the Em-

peror remained outside the structure of vassal engagements, nothing of the kind emerged from a regime which was nevertheless in many respects closely akin to the feudalism of the West.[18]

This does not mean, of course, that in Japan there were no de facto modes of consultation among vassals and between vassals and their lords. But such consultations were ad hoc, structured according to situational exigencies and custom, not according to any conception of the inherent rights of vassals either individually or as a body. Whatever corporate or semicorporate relations did develop were based on series of vertical ties founded by particular lords. The lords always attempted to minimize the possibility of the vassals presenting themselves as a corporate unit with autonomous rights and to control the access of the vassals to the central consultative bodies.

The resulting dependency of the vassal on his lord was closely connected to the structuring of access to resources that had developed in Japan, manifest in the late Sengoku and early Tokugawa periods in the lords' strong tendency to provide economic rewards (stipends) to their vassals.[19] This practice was intended to sever as far as possible the previous direct relation between vassals and the land, as was the absence of specifically individual property rights, an absence which deprived vassals of any potentially autonomous resource base.[20] Thus land was not the major link between lord, vassal, and peasant; as John Hall has put it, the main concern of the lords was man and his labor rather than land as such.[21]

This fact gave rise to yet another difference between European and Japanese feudalism, again especially in later periods, namely the great distance between peasants and the samurai class. This led, especially in the Tokugawa period, to a relatively high level of autonomy in the village supervised by the lord and to a much greater differentiation within the samurai class between the higher and lower samurai.

IV The fifth major institutional difference between Japanese and European feudalism was the relatively strong centralization within the former, and the bifurcation of this central authority between the emperor and great military lords—since about the eleventh century, the shogun. Both these characteristics were closely connected to the fact, emphasized by Bloch, that the emperor stood outside the feudal nexus; he legitimized this nexus but did not play an institutional role in it—vassals, for instance, were not able to appeal to the emperor. In a way, by standing outside this nexus, he often constituted a symbol or signal of other institutional possibilities.

Indeed, the central framework and rule were never as weakened in Japan as they were in Europe; there was only one such framework, within which stronger bureaucratization of central rule developed in Japan, as can be seen, for instance, in Mass's comparison of the ninth-century European count with the Japanese *shugo*.[22] Even in periods of disorder, internal war, and decentralization—as in the last decades of the Kamakura, again in the Muromachi age (1392–1573),[23] and during the transition to Tokugawa—the scope of the centralization and bureaucratization, especially within the shogunal *bakufu*, as well as in many of the estates of the various lords (daimyō), was much greater than anything achieved in Europe in parallel historical periods.[24]

The two components of this centralization—the emperor in the earlier periods of predominance of the aristocratic families, until about the eleventh century, and the shogun, or *bakufu*, since then—persisted with great variations in their relative strength, until the Meiji Restoration.

Several aspects of the shogunate component require comment. First, it succeeded—even if with varying degrees of success in different periods—in limiting attempts by social groups, such as peasants or even provincial lords, to gain independent access to its center. This was true to no small degree even in periods of disorganization, when the *bakufu* was not able to exert direct control over many of the provincial lords or sectors. Second, the Japanese (especially shogunal) center was able to concentrate in its hand the regulation of legal adjunctions and adjudications. Such concentration tended to emphasize the "ratification" of existing agreements and arrangements; it was often predicated on the acceptance of the customs of regional groups, and it certainly did not entail a fully fledged codification of existing laws. It did, however, ensure a degree of central regulation of these different jurisdictions and assert the primacy of central adjudications. Third, the development and persistence within the framework of the *bakufu* of relatively strong bureaucratic organizations and procedures constituted an important factor in limiting the power of vassals and provincial groups and helped in the effective exercise of control by the *bakufu* over them. Similarly, in periods of turmoil and decentralization—above all in the fifteenth century—the tendency to centralization developed mainly in the domains of the great daimyō and was used to control the smaller vassals.

One very important ramification of such control by the *bakufu* was the fact that the cities in Japan, however strong and economically developed they were, never attained the principled autonomy of cities within the framework of European feudalism. This is very much in line with the nonexistence of any principled autonomy among the vassals—however strong they might have been in any given situation.

V Through all these periods, up to the Tokugawa era, the most consistent aspect of the imperial component of the center was the very unusual combination of, on the one hand, an almost complete loss of effective power over the country, with only short-lasting and unsuccessful attempts to recapture such power, and, on the other hand, a continuous monopoly over the central symbols of collective identity and prestige— that is, it constituted the major fountain of legitimation, prestige, and status. This monopoly was exercised above all through the granting of court titles, usually regarded as the most (if not the only) legitimate and prestigious ones. True enough, in some periods, especially in the fifteenth and sixteenth centuries, many magnates overlooked the emperor in their quest for land, power, and hegemony. But they did not claim for themselves the right to legitimize the overall political system.

The effectiveness of the emperor's legitimizing function was manifest, not just in the court's natural attempts to maintain this function and monopoly, but in its success, in its continuity—a continuity unusual in the annals of history—and above all in the fact that all the effective rulers (the shoguns and the *bakufu*) and their subordinates had continuous recourse to this symbol in their attempts to legitimize themselves and only very rarely (and always unsuccessfully) challenged the validity of this legitimization. "This dual governmental system at the heart of Japanese life and in its provincial centers had no counterpart in Carolingian domains after Pepin became King of the Franks."[25]

The emperor continued to constitute the major legitimizing institution and symbol of Japanese political and sacral order, with far-reaching effects on its working and dynamics. How crucial and central it was can be seen in the failure of Tokugawa statesmen, Arai Hakuseki in particular, to endow the Tokugawa shogun with all the symbols and prerogatives of royalty;[26] in the fact that the great unifiers of the sixteenth century, Hideyoshi and Tokugawa Ieyasu, the first of whom (Hideyoshi) came from peasant stock, strove to legitimize themselves in terms of the imperial aristocratic symbols and culture;[27] in the fact that toward the end of Tokugawa rule even members of senior branches of the Tokugawa clan turned to the emperor as the major source or symbol of potential reformation; and in the central role of the emperor symbolism in the Meiji restoration.[28]

One of the most important aspects of the relation between emperor and shogun was that, as W. G. Runciman has indicated,

> once the emperor had abdicated *de facto* sovereignty in favor of successive shoguns, the ties between ruler and subjects in the ideological dimension ran separately from those in the coercive dimension of power.
>
> . . . Fission, however, was never an option. No Japanese magnate ever repudiated allegiance to the emperor or sought to establish an autonomous principality of his own.[29]

Moreover, however weak in fact the emperor has been in most periods of Japanese history since the ninth century, his very existence has imposed a serious limitation on the power of the military magnates and, later, the shogun. The limitation was not purely imaginary; the possibility of an attempt at imperial restoration was always present—though until the Meiji regimes such attempts usually failed. But even when no such possibility was evident, the shogun had to decide, for instance, where to establish his court in relation to the imperial court and how to assure the loyalty of the latter in any actual political struggle.

VI The bifurcation between the emperor and the *bakufu* and the symbolic importance of the former—the fact that the emperor was outside the feudal nexus but retained the ultimate legitimizing function—also had far-reaching consequences on the relations of cultural activity (with its civilizing functions, to use Norbert Elias's terms) to the feudal framework.

The imperial court constituted in most periods of Japanese history a center and model of "high culture," often in sharp contrast to the "barbaric" life in the periphery, including sometimes that in the shogunal courts. Even when the shogunate also became an important center of cultural activities, as it did under the Tokugawa, the role of the imperial court as a central locus of high culture remained—a role reinforced, of course, by the fact that it was the fountain of prestige, of the honorific titles sought by the great barons. Thus the court provided a focus and a continuous framework of cultural activity and identity, to some extent outside the changing fortunes of different sectors of society—a function performed in Europe by the Church. The continuity of the imperial court as a center of high culture was to have far-reaching consequences for some central aspects of the absolutist feudal regime of the Tokugawa, and for the entire course of modern Japanese history.

As Johann Arnason has written:

> The autonomous development of feudalism in Japan gave free rein to its self-transformative and self-transcending tendencies. The processes of centralization, pacification and bureaucratization changed the feudal basis so radically that the final outcome—i.e., the Tokugawa regime—is best described as a combination of feudal and post-feudal elements.
>
> On the level of legitimation, there was—in contrast to the European situation, as described by Parsons—only one alternative instance that could "appear both older and newer": the imperial institution.
>
> Moreover the fact that the court's hegemonic cultural role anteceded the development of military rule, and did not, as in Europe, grow out of the

subjugation of the military, enabled the court to serve, both as an institution and as a symbol of natural unity.[30]

The continuity of relatively stronger centralized control in Japanese feudalism was facilitated by several facts. One was that military groups were not identical and continuous from one period or state to another, so that there developed a much more intensive social and ecological mobility, which tended to weaken the continuity of local groups.[31] At the same time Japanese feudal structures were characterized by the persistence of family networks and connections, seemingly much stronger than in Europe. These networks were reorganized and restructured through a much closer linkage between clan kinship and the feudal nexus, thus enabling a high degree of structural continuity among the groups and sectors of society—a continuity which was basically bound by, or predicated on, the existence of the central framework.

Yet other factors that contributed to the centralization of Japanese feudal society were the much greater continuity (compared with any European country) of national boundaries and national identity; the existence of only one national framework; and the ability of the central powers, especially of many of the shoguns, to ward off threats of external interference—up to the attempt at almost total isolation from the external world under the Tokugawa.[32]

VII   The central place of the imperial institution and the separation between the imperial and shogunal centers have also influenced the overall structure of social hierarchies and of the relation between wealth and status in Japanese society. The most important aspect of this structure was a pattern, which emerged early in the Kamakura period, of dissociation between power, status, and wealth—a predisposition to what, in sociological parlance, has been called status incongruence.

John Hall, addressing the nature of the relationship between the imperial family, the Fujiwara regent family, and the several levels of families of lower rank that served as retainers to the high aristocracy, observed that one of the most fundamental principles of late-Heian court politics was that "title to authority and the power to administer it were permanently separated and kept within distinct lines of succession."[33]

Arnason discusses these relations as follows:

> This pattern of association between superior and inferior status individuals within a given structure is found in many contexts: in political factions, warrior bands, and systems of land management. In the *shōen* system, the hierarchy of rights and obligations involved several distinct status levels: (1) the court-based proprietary lord, (2) the local estate custodian, (3) the

heads of village communities, and (4) the cultivators of the land. Within such a hierarchy of differentiated statuses no individual of lower status could compete to displace someone of higher status so long as the overall structure remained intact.

Thus, "effective" power was separated from ultimate legitimacy; the latter was relegated to the sacral sphere and definitively vested in the imperial dynasty as the recipient of the "services and offerings," whereas the former was delegated to lower instances and thus laid open to competition and usurpation. On the other hand, there was an emphasis on joint rule (or, as Maruyama puts it, the "plural nature of ruling"—within varying limits) on both levels: the dynasty as a collective entity was more important than the person of the emperor, and the exercise of actual power was supposed to involve consultation and collective decision making. Joint rule and competition were complementary effects of the delegation of power. A more long-term and destructive consequence was a spiraling devolution: "Power developed downward at the same time as it became more informal and private."[34]

VIII It was natural that, especially among the high echelons of society—as for instance the great daimyō—strong tendencies to status congruence developed. These were reinforced to some extent by the rigid regulation of status relations under the Tokugawa—but even then the shogun's political power mitigated such tendencies. Status congruence probably expanded among the higher echelons mainly in times of great disorder, but it was always mitigated by the fact that whatever status symbols were acquired had to be legitimized by the (powerless) emperor. The close relation of the tendency to differentiate between power and authority to the specific character of Japan's feudal period indicates that the Japanese tendency to status inconsistency has its roots in the specific pattern of state formation of an early Japan, in the distinctive way in which the earlier monarchical clan society disintegrated and new state formation developed.

Needless to say, the concrete constellations of the different groups—which groups had access to power or status, how status and power were defined—has greatly varied throughout Japanese society. But the pattern itself, with its limitations on status congruence and on the freedom of convertibility of different types of resources, persisted throughout the Tokugawa period. Indeed Hall has claimed that the Tokugawa regime is best explained as a status society.[35] This pattern continued, if in a transformed way, into the modern, especially industrial, setting and has proved to be of great importance in shaping processes of change within Japanese society, as we shall see in greater detail in chapter 12.

On the one hand, because of this pattern's inherent flexibility and its close relation to the especially flexible kinship structure, many structural opportunities for change, wide institutional "empty" spaces, were created which could be filled in different ways. On the other, the fact that any such recrystallization was guided by continuous orientations to the prestige vested in the imperial center, and was usually interpreted in terms of the basic symbolism of the centers or subcenters with its strong primordial-sacral and collective "national" components, provided one of the major mechanisms of the rather specific type of continuity that developed in Japan and constituted one of the main characteristics of the Japanese historical experience.

The feudal period was of crucial formative importance in Japanese history, not only with respect to the bifurcation between power and authority, but also in terms of the characteristics analyzed above—especially the continuous civilizing influence of the court and the predominance of familial as against contractual relationships.[36]

IX The comparison of Japanese and Western feudalism indicates the existence of two distinct patterns of feudal institutional complexes or formations. These formations evince some remarkable structural similarities, but the similarities are superseded, as it were, by different modes of institutional integration and different patterns of overall dynamics.

The characteristics that distinguish Japanese from European feudalism—the tendency toward centralization, the bifurcation of central authority between emperor and shogun, and with the noncontractual nature of the vassal-lord relationship—are not so much matters of economic structure (although many differences in this respect can also be identified between Europe and Japan) as differences in the overall social and political mode in which these relations were structured and legitimized and consequently in the specific political dynamics that developed within each of these societies.

Of special interest from this point of view is that this type of feudal institutional nexus as it developed in the Kamakura period[37] (as against the older, clan-based *uji* system, which did however persist in parts of the country)[38] was closely connected with a conception and organization of kinship that comes very close to what Murakami, Sato, and Kumon have identified as the basic characteristics of the *ie* society.[39]

Some of these differences between Japanese and European feudalisms were probably rooted in the different modes of disintegration of tribal-class, semiimperial models and of the concomitant state formations—as was suggested long ago by Asakawa Kanichi and elaborated much more systematically by Johann Arnason.[40] The upshot is that the prefeudal state in Japan was a more elaborate and resilient structure than that in Europe; it originated in a much more systematic effort to learn from a more advanced civilization, and its decline was a more complex and prolonged process. For our present purposes, it is most important to note that both the initial role and the long-term trajectory of feudalism within this process differed from the European situation. But whatever the exact origins of these feudal systems, their distinctive modes of integration had a great influence on the later historical dynamics of each society, as we shall see in the following chapters.

Urban Development and Autonomy
in Medieval and Early Modern Japan

I Another institutional arena, the contours of which in Japan seem to parallel those in Europe, is that of urban development—the institutional and cultural formation of cities in medieval and early modern times, their crucial role in economic development, and their relative autonomy. But again, as with respect to feudalism, there are differences that attest to a distinctive pattern of institutional dynamics. The development of cities was closely related, in Japan as in Europe, with that of feudalism—and Japan's success in economic modernization has sometimes been attributed both to the very development of cities and to their relative autonomy in the pluralistic feudal structure.[1]

It was in the high medieval period (twelfth to sixteenth centuries) that the great spurt of city development took place in Japan. This period was characterized not only by increasing decentralization but also by the growth of relatively new autonomous social and economic forces, which gave rise to a wide variety of rural and urban forms and tendencies toward urban autonomy.[2] It was during this long period, while the basic characteristics of Japanese feudalism evolved and crystallized, that far-reaching urban developments, generated mainly by merchants and artisans, occurred.

The cities that emerged between the decline of the earlier aristocratic regime and the end of the civil wars reflected changes in political-military leadership, the evolution of strong religious factions, and the economy of a decentralized feudal order. The most important changes were the expansion of domestic and foreign trade, which led to the emergence of the genuine commercial city; the emergence, in the Muromachi age, of a highly developed economic sector in the region around Kyoto; the shift, later on, of political-military control to the northeast, away from imperial and aristocratic rule, evidenced in the establishment of Kamakura as a shogunal capital; and the growth of important religious communities, which manipulated significant economic power in the form of feudal fiefs.[3] These changes influenced the process of urbanization in the direction of greater diversity and even, to some degree, greater autonomy.

II   During this long medieval period, the stimulus provided by foreign trade, together with the development of intensive domestic trade, made the commercial city a strong rival to the political, administrative, and religious centers, which had until then been the largest, most dominant cities.[4] The inhabitants of most commercial cities exercised a hitherto unknown degree of self-government and judicial autonomy, which extended even to the maintenance of their own military forces. The merchant classes enjoyed a measure of political and economic autonomy unprecedented in the history of Japanese urban life, utilizing wholesale and retail monopoly systems, guilds, and other economic devices to generate and maintain effective control.[5]

In addition to these commercial cities, new centers of local political and military control flourished. Seeking to avoid pressure from the older imperial and aristocratic factions, the first shogun, Yoritomo (1192–1197), made Kamakura his capital and thus enlarged the effective boundaries of Japan to the north and east, into the Kanto region. This created a new urban focus removed from the traditional area of city life dominated by Kyoto and Nara, although for a long time other regions lagged behind the Kyoto-Osaka center. Except for the period under the Ashikaga *bakufu* (1336–1573), when the political bureaucracy returned to the Kyoto area, the Kanto region has remained the seat of political administration since the twelfth century. Present-day Japan's national capital and largest city, Tokyo, commands the Kanto region and owes its dominance to this early shift of national control to the northeast.

Influential religious centers such as Uji-Yamada and Ishiyama also arose during this period. At the same time, the administration of large rice-producing fiefs by religious factions led to the growth of towns that served as centers of secular commercial activities in addition to their more sacral functions.

III   A new type of city, the castle town (*jōkamachi*), appeared around the sixteenth century and became the major type of urban development during the Tokugawa period.[6] Although the rise of castle towns was initiated, to no small degree, by the political authorities, it was also often based on earlier, diversified processes generated by various autonomous social forces, such as movements of population and trade. The development of these cities, perhaps more than any other phenomenon of the period, illustrates the major characteristics, problems, and vicissitudes of urban development in late medieval and early modern Japan.

The growth of internal commerce and the weakening of central or regional power naturally led to greater self-regulation sometimes verging on a limited form of autonomy, for market centers.[7] From fortified strongholds, initially built to resist enemy attacks during the civil wars of the fourteenth and fifteenth centuries, the castle towns gradually became centers of control and of resource mobilization in the lord's domain. Urban activities, previously scattered over the domain, were increasingly concentrated in the *jōkamachi* of the primary lord.[8] The control of the absentee lords waned, and their former supporters strengthened independent local bases of power.

These institutional changes strengthened the hold of the daimyō, or feudal barons, on their vassals and fostered the development of the castle towns. By the end of the sixteenth century the daimyō held direct economic and political control over entire domains; the lands of absentee lords were largely confiscated and the samurai gradually removed from the villages and restricted to a fixed stipend.[9] Given the intense economic development that took place in this period, the castle towns became great commercial centers and, at the same time, centers of a very intensive and distinctive urban culture.

IV The economic strength and the extent of internal autonomy of the commercial centers and castle towns in the sixteenth century were, however, insufficient to withstand the pressures of a reunified national political authority. The process of unification, which started in the sixteenth century, culminated with the reestablishment of effective national unity under Tokugawa Ieyasu in the early seventeenth century. Once this authority was directed against the cities, as potential centers of independent power, the latter, after often fierce struggles, either declined rapidly or were absorbed into the new administrative structure. The imperial court, the powerful Buddhist hierarchy, and the merchant class of the cities all came under the authority of the powerful Tokugawa shogun, who then instituted highly controlled urbanization programs, above all in the castle towns.[10]

The numerous castles, built at strategic points during the civil war and in the period of unification on the orders of the Tokugawa rulers, became nuclei around which cities and towns sprang up. In order to tighten administrative control, the Tokugawa rulers decreed, in 1615, that all but one castle in each fief should be destroyed. The impetus to urban growth inherent in the Tokugawa political structure was then mainly focused on a limited number of locations. The consequent expansion of these castle centers meant the decline of previously existing towns, except where they could be incorporated into new defense or communication systems.[11]

Although the geographical distribution of cities was such that no region was without an urban center, the urban population was not equally distributed throughout the country. Areas to the south and west of Edo, encompassing Nagoya and Kyoto and the regions bordering the Inland Sea, were the most heavily urbanized. Edo was the nation's largest city with the largest population, over a million inhabitants at its peak, somewhat more than twice the population of Osaka or Kyoto. Osaka, with its great merchant houses, and Kyoto, the imperial capital and handicraft center, were never completely overshadowed by Edo in either size or function.

V   At the same time, a number of secondary population centers developed in addition to the castle towns. The constant travels of the lords and their retainers, demanded by the Tokugawa rulers, required the construction and maintenance of a nationwide network of roads. The service, posting, and market towns that emerged along these routes, especially those that were also castle towns, grew to appreciable size. Like the post stations a few centers specialized in the production of textiles and handicrafts. Some, such as Osaka (the second largest city in Japan of that period) and Nagasaki (the major port city, from which Japan's contacts with China were maintained for two hundred years), grew into important commercial centers, constituting a secondary but very prominent branch of urbanization alongside the major building of castle towns in Tokugawa Japan.[12] Sakai, which enjoyed great autonomy before the Tokugawa, lost it during the Tokugawa period and declined economically relative to the newly risen Osaka, but it continued to be an economic center.

The pattern of urbanization in Tokugawa Japan reflected a consolidation of the political and military power in the castle towns; it also led to changes in the nation's economic structure and created opportunities for the development of an influential merchant class. As population concentrated around the permanent residences of the lords and their retainers, the castle towns assumed growing importance as commercial and consumption centers. Merchants, who served as the commercial link between the city and its hinterland, then moved in increasing numbers to the castle towns rather than remaining in older trade settlements. They were joined by the lower samurai, who engaged in artisanal activities—such as various types of piecework—and to a lesser extent commercial activities. The peace and prosperity enjoyed during the Tokugawa period rendered the military services of the warrior class superfluous, and the lower samurai found it increasingly difficult to maintain themselves on fixed rice allocations. But throughout this process the merchants came more and more under the control of the Tokugawa, and above all of the daimyō, who were controlled and supervised by the Tokugawa *bakufu*.

What distinguishes Japan's process of urbanization from those elsewhere is the creation of a social structure within which urban-oriented commercialism took precedence over feudal agriculture but still depended on it.

VI All these developments—the growth of new commercial activities and of strong urban groups, the development of strong cities—are indeed similar to those of medieval and early modern Europe. Yet these processes did not give rise in Japan to the development of autonomous cities, even if they generated forces which ultimately helped to undermine the Tokugawa regime.

The kernels of autonomy that developed in the period of decentralization, although not the distinctive pattern of urban cultural life, were suppressed by military force during the period of unification, from Nobunaga (1534–1582) on up to the Tokugawa, and became thoroughly weakened under the Tokugawa regime. The commercial communities that had emerged in several ports, among them Sakai—which even had its own armed force, having become an essentially autonomous town— were brought under centralized control.[13] Nobunaga suppressed the various rebellions, led by merchants, in Sakai. True enough, the marked growth of trade in the Tokugawa period produced a stronger merchant stratum; the "townsmen" (*chōnin*) became steadily more prosperous, and the more affluent among them, working closely with the government as its economic agents, sometimes received semisamurai status, bore family names, and even wore swords.[14] Merchants were allowed some degree of self-regulation, mainly in managing the internal affairs of the cities' commercial quarters, but the extent of their independence never approached that achieved by the "free" cities of feudal Europe, and the commercial sector remained largely dependent upon *bakufu's* and daimyō's support.[15]

This was so for several reasons. First, divisions within the urban population—reinforced by the authorities' methods of controlling the urban strata—prevented the development of a common urban political consciousness. Second, although some sectors of the urban population developed modes of self-regulation, such self-regulation was actively supervised by the authorities, an exercise of control rooted in basic conceptions of social and legal order prevalent in Tokugawa Japan. Third, the Japanese cities, unlike those in Europe, were not part of a wider, international network.

Perhaps even more than the rural sectors, urban Japan was characterized by strong divisions among the various strata and status groups and by the latter's relatively extensive self-regulation, usually vested in the

leaders of the respective groups and tightly controlled by the higher echelons in the social hierarchy.[16] Although Japanese historians sometimes
maintain that the merchants of the Tokugawa period lived under a system
of local self-government, this actually consisted of little more than the
privilege of managing certain private aspects of their activities under the
supervision of headmen who themselves operated under the control of a
high samurai assisted by a low samurai.[17] The privileged merchants and
artisans who had been active in the original construction of the commercial blocks (*chō*) could pass their hereditary administrative posts in the
chō on to their descendants, but most of the new headmen were elected,
thus preventing the entrenchment of political power in the hands of the
more affluent and well-established merchants.[18]

Administrative control of the various social strata was quite strict in
the cities, as was especially evident in the restrictions on residence of the
different classes, the unification of weights and measures, the limitations
placed on guilds and Buddhist sects, and the legal decrees. City laws (usually unwritten) and customs differed from locality to locality and were
overlaid by a countrywide, political-legal tradition based on Confucian
social stratification, family hierarchy, feudal devices of ownership of ten-
ants and servants, and the symbolism attached to the imperial court at
Kyoto.[19] Except in cases in which disputes transcended feudal boundaries,
the law of Edo did not reach deep into society, nor did the shogunal civil
law extend beyond its own territory.[20] At the same time, a degree of self-
regulation was vested in the vertically organized leadership of different
sectors of society.

The predominance of the political over the economic order and the
control of the latter by the former were prescribed by Confucian ideology—even when the services of merchants and artisans were needed
by shogun and daimyō. The nobility and the center controlled merchants
and artisans in two ways: by forbidding them to buy their way into an
official title, thus preventing them from becoming a threat to the politicians in power, and by limiting their contacts with other sectors of the
population, especially the peasants. These attempts at control were facilitated by the fact that the bulk of government revenue came from
land taxes.[21] In the rare cases when the central administration borrowed
money from rich traders, this was considered a compulsory loan, and the
merchants' lender status did not give them any real leverage. The merchants therefore had no firm basis for demanding concessions and no
means of exerting pressure to obtain them.

At the same time, a degree of self-regulation was vested in the vertically organized leadership of some sectors of society. Nevertheless, no
concept of urban citizenship could emerge because such self-regulation

did not ultimately create fully autonomous units, within which the members had rights of access to internal centers of power or cities autonomous access to the central political arena. For all these reasons the Japanese city was never considered as an independent unit and never developed a distinct corporate or civil consciousness.[22] In addition, as already indicated, Japanese cities were not part of an international network, and their confinement to one country made it easier for the political center to control them.

VII   The distinctive characteristics of Japanese urban development— especially the combination of a high degree of economic development and a vibrant urban life with severely limited corporate political autonomy— are, of course, closely related to some of those of Japanese feudalism, especially the absence of representative institutions and of concepts of rights and contracts in lord-vassal relations. These characteristics also reflect a more general lack of political autonomy and the particular mode of structuring social hierarchies that developed in Japan, especially under Tokugawa rule.

The official system of stratification that developed under the Tokugawa designated urban groups (merchants and artisans), following the Confucian classification, as entirely separate and distinct categories. These categories became in Tokugawa Japan much more rigid than in China. While in China the children of merchants could study for the Confucian literati examinations—in Japan there was no way in which a member of the merchant (or artisan) class could become a samurai. Thus, as R. Sieffert has pointed out, in contrast to the French case, no bourgeois could become ennobled, even if only into the *noblesse de robe*, and become a member of the rulers' advisory body.[23]

Merchants and artisans were in most periods of Japanese history, and especially under Tokugawa rule, effectively deprived of autonomous access to the major centers of political power. This was not in itself different from the situation in many other countries including, of course, China. What distinguished Japan, however, was that merchants and artisans could develop open institutional spaces within which innovative activities were possible without developing as an independent social stratum. This possibility was closely related to the relative dissociation between status, wealth, and power in large sectors of Japanese society.

This development of relatively open spaces, concurrent with relatively rigid stratification in the Tokugawa period, explains the development of what, from a Western perspective, appear to be contradictory tendencies: on the one hand, the very high level, not only of economic, but also of cultural and intellectual activity; on the other, the relative lack of radical activities and of direct participation in the political process and confrontation with the authorities.

Unlike the European bourgeoisie, Japanese urban groups did not become active autonomous actors in the political process that toppled their country's regime. Indeed, they did not directly contribute either to the toppling of the Tokugawa regime or, in any distinctive way, to the political agenda of the Meiji Restoration. Neither they nor the intellectual actors connected with them participated significantly in shaping the ideology of the Restoration or determining the contours of the subsequent political system—although they did open up, as through their many cooperative ventures, new worlds of discourse and activity.

The absence of any fully fledged urban autonomy is also closely connected to the distinctive role that the Japanese middle classes played in the development of capitalism in Japan. There can be no doubt that the growth of commercialism and of the market economy—both in the countryside and in the cities—greatly contributed to the disintegration of the Tokugawa regime and constituted an important background factor in Japan's quick industrialization under the Meiji. Yet the overall picture is here quite different from that in Europe—even in Germany, to which Japan has often been compared.

The view, which was for some time quite prevalent in the literature, that it was mainly selfless, patriotic ex-samurai, some of them turned bureaucrats, who presided over the economic modernization of Meiji Japan has been proved to be at least exaggerated. Many ex-samurai captains of industry were not, of course, that selfless; it was the premodern merchant entrepreneurs, with their know-how and experience, who performed the central roles in Japan's development of modern enterprises. Nonetheless, it is true that the initial impetus to economic modernization and, above all, the basic contours of economic modernization were generated, not by these merchants, but first by the Meiji oligarchy and later by the bureaucracy. The bureaucracy did take the interests of the higher urban and commercial classes into account, but it was the oligarchy and bureaucracy that guided the economic development of Japan, promoting an energetic entrepreneurial capitalism that—although it continued to be guided by and closely interrelated with the major governmental bureaucratic sectors—did not entail the development of state capitalism.

All these constitute different aspects of the basic fact that in Japan and in Europe (and even more so in the United States) the development of capitalist-industrial systems was not connected with the emergence of an autonomous bourgeoisie. This is but a part of the general picture that developed in Japan—namely the seemingly paradoxical combination of intensive activity in commerce and culture with relatively muted autonomous political activity, especially in the central political arena. This combination indeed constitutes one of the distinctive characteristics, not only of the urban scene, but of most sectors of Japanese society. It attests yet again to the specificity and distinctiveness of Japanese institutional dynamics and historical experience. These specific dynamics and experience are most fully manifest in the development of the Tokugawa regime.

Tokugawa State and Society

THE TOKUGAWA REGIME AS AN ABSOLUTIST FEUDAL STATE

I The specific dynamics of Japanese feudalism and urban development can be better understood within the framework of the development and working of the Tokugawa regime. That regime, which unified Japan from 1600 till 1868, has lately been compared with the European absolutist states of the sixteenth to the eighteenth century; its breakdown led to the Meiji Restoration, which ushered in Japanese modernization and modernity. We shall begin by considering the debate as to whether this regime was a feudal or an absolutist one.

The picture of the Tokugawa regime as a purely feudal state was prevalent in studies of Japanese society from the 1940s and 1950s.[1] It was presented in Herbert Norman's *Japan's Emergence as a Modern State*,[2] in which feudalism is defined in several different ways, and later on by such scholars as Reischauer.[3] Peter Duus designated the Tokugawa regime as the last phase of Japanese feudalism but pointed out that while it was feudal at the top, it was more bureaucratized at the bottom.[4] The regime was also termed feudal by Perry Anderson; in his comparative analysis of the origins of absolutism Anderson analyzes the rise and fall of the Tokugawa in terms comparable to those applied to the European feudal experience and focuses on the decline of the Tokugawa feudal system as leading to the modern absolutist regime of the Meiji. He does, however, note the more centralizing dimensions of the Tokugawa regime.[5]

It has always been recognized that however feudal—in whatever sense—the Tokugawa regime was, it was also highly centralized, and it was indeed its centralization, with the consequent central political control by the Tokugawa *bakufu* of the powerful daimyō and of the broader groups of samurai, that distinguished it from former periods of Japanese history. The fact that these groups were partially depoliticized, or at least highly controlled, by a system that required them to leave their families in Edo as hostages when away from the capital; that they were shorn of the relatively autonomous bases of power they had had before; and that they could be deposed by the shoguns make this regime easily comparable to many of the European early modern absolutist states, perhaps above all to the French system under Louis XIV, in which the nobility had no effective political power.[6] This line has indeed been taken by several scholars, including Umesao Tadao[7] and the organizers of a 1986 conference on Japan's transition from medievalism to early modernism, which emphasized the similarity of the Tokugawa regime to the absolutist regimes of modern Europe.[8]

That the Tokugawa regime can be defined in such seemingly contradictory ways, as both feudal and absolutist, indicates that it evinced a rather unusual combination of characteristics. This unusual mix to some extent attests to the difficulty of applying terms derived from the Western historical experience to another setting, but above all it attests to the distinctiveness of the overall characteristics and dynamics of this regime, which go beyond its structural and organizational similarities to other regimes, especially Western European absolutist ones. In the following section we shall analyze the specific features of this combination.

II The Tokugawa regime arose as the last and most enduring of the attempts to unify Japan in the sixteenth century. Tokugawa Ieyasu came after the other two great unifiers, Oda Nobunaga and Toyotomi Hideyoshi, and established the most enduring regime in Japanese history.[9] This regime arose against a background of anarchy and internal war, together with the development of more productive forces in the countryside and cities alike. Both the disintegration of the feudal order and the new economic and social processes were, as Michael Birt has forcefully indicated, similar to those which facilitated the rise of the absolutist states in Europe—as was the growth of the centralizing powers of the state.[10]

This transition to what can be—and often has been—designated as an early modern society and state, and the concrete policies through which state power was centralized, were not, as Kozo Yamamura has shown, an automatic process of transition from one stage of economic development to another.[11] While the changes in the structure of economic and social forces did indeed provide the background for such centralization, the fact and manner of its development were the result of the specific policies undertaken by Tokugawa Ieyasu and his followers, and to some degree by his predecessor and rival Hideyoshi and the preceding great "feudal" unifier, Nobunaga.[12]

It was indeed not foreordained that something like the Tokugawa system should evolve. Other apparent possibilities arose from the numerous *ikki* rebellions[13] or, as we shall discuss below, from the different type of unification that seemed to emerge under Nobunaga. But ultimately it was the policies set in motion by Hideyoshi, then taken up and more fully developed under Tokugawa Ieyasu, that prevailed. These policies resulted in a degree of centralization of power unprecedented in the history of Japan. As Mary Elizabeth Berry has put it:

> The governing elite of the Tokugawa period (1615–1868) could fully assemble, with some crowding and rumpling of robes, in a suite of expansive reception rooms within Edo castle. Neither the composition nor the encompassing authority of this elite—a group embracing the shogun himself and roughly 250 daimyō—was a matter of question . . . .
>
> . . . The shogun and the daimyō of the Tokugawa period collectively monopolized a previously dispersed authority over land and its resources, military force, law and judicature, cities and commerce.
>
> . . . Japan's passage from the medieval to the early modern eras appears to mimic, in respect to the contraction in size and significantly expanded prerogatives of the elite, the passage of western European countries.

Of special importance in this context were

> the "meta-texts" of the time: the cadastral registries which accounted in detail for the nation's resources and the agrarian population; the administrative and commercial maps which portrayed cities, domains, and the country itself as integral units with clear centers of authority; the bukan, or registries of military households, which—with their lists of the daimyō, their heirs and major retainers, their revenues and castles—served, too, as maps of power. The explosion and control of knowledge, the objectification and textual representation of political relations—these were the hallmarks of an apparent revolution.[14]

III   The Tokugawa policy of unification and control was also very much evident in the religious arena, especially with respect to the Buddhist monasteries which were reformed and largely depoliticized under the Tokugawa, losing the more or less autonomous status they had enjoyed in the preceding, semianarchic period.

It was during this period that some of the most severe persecution of religious institutions and groups took place in Japan, as for instance when Oda Nobunaga wiped out the great concentration of Buddhist institutions on Hieizan, slaughtered thousands of monks and priests, and razed the temples. The Maeda, when they took over the domain of Kaga in the late sixteenth century, were given the task of subduing the Ikkō sect of Buddhism.

These persecutions of Buddhists were motivated above all by political considerations—that is, by fear of the growing political independence and insubordination of Buddhist groups and abbots, rather than by doctrinal war or confrontation between orthodoxy and heterodoxy. Political and doctrinal dimensions were, however, closely interwoven; the groups' moves toward independence were often driven by religious considerations and loyalty to their respective abbots. Memories of these persecutions have persisted for generations and centuries.

Similarly, persecutions of Christians by Japanese rulers were probably motivated, not by doctrinal disputes, but by fear that the expansion of Christianity, especially in periods of internal turbulence, might undermine the moral bases of the Japanese social order or even create a distinct state or region. This fear gave rise to some of the most far-reaching measures of centralization, as well as the prohibition and persecution of Christianity. The destruction of Christianity was indeed a case, as George Elison has put it, of "Deus destroyed." But the fear of this Christian Deus was based more on the recognition of its constituting an authority beyond the existing political structure than on deep theological disputes.[15] The anti-Christian measures, which intensified after the Shimabara revolt of 1637, gave rise to requirements that Buddhist temples carry out regular censuses of communicants and that all daimyō send the resulting registers to Edo.[16]

IV   The Tokugawa regime, with its unique combination of "feudal" and "absolutist" characteristics, crystallized out of these efforts at unification, intensive processes of centralization that evince similarities to the formation of the absolutist states of early modern Europe. Indeed, in some respects, these measures—the efficiency of the control over the daimyō, the possibility of confiscating the holdings of samurai—were probably more far-reaching than those employed by many of the absolutist states of Europe.[17]

Yet other features of the Tokugawa regime distinguish it from these regimes. Some of these differences seem at first glance to be mostly of an organizational nature, for instance, the reach of the new bureaucracy, which in contrast to most of the European absolutist states, was mainly limited to the Tokugawa *bakufu* and did not on the whole extend to the daimyō—although bureaucratic organizations, manned by impoverished samurai, also developed within many of their domains. The reach of the *bakufu* was also relatively limited, as John Morris has shown, with respect to the *hatamoto* (direct retainers of the shogun), who maintained throughout most of Tokugawa rule a relatively widespread seigneurial system.[18]

These organizational features, as well as the distinctive characteristics of the juridical system, which we shall analyze in greater detail later on, already point to certain more principled characteristics and dynamics of this regime—indeed, to the very paradox of a centralized feudal regime. The crux of this paradox, which was at the core of the debate as to whether the Tokugawa regime was feudal or absolutist,[19] was, as John Hall put it, that "the 'feudal' class consolidated its rule over Japan at a time when the mechanisms and institutions through which it exercised authority became less feudal."[20] This paradox attests to the specificity with respect to this regime of the structure and modes of legitimation of political power, the basic conception of the political realm, the basic characteristics of the prevalent ideology, and the very dynamics and the processes that led to its breakdown, which ushered in the modern period in Japanese history.

The most important specific characteristic of this regime was, of course, the fact that the daimyō were not deprived of political power in their domains, as were, for instance, most of the French nobles under Louis XIV—if anything their power was reinforced and assured by centralization under the Tokugawa. They continued (when they were not deposed) not only to own their domains but also to administer them— even if they were very closely supervised and controlled by the Tokugawa rulers.

The Tokugawa instituted a basic segregation of daimyō into categories called Tozama and Fudai. Tozama were those daimyō who had been enemies or at least not subordinates to Tokugawa before the final battle of Sekigahara, which ended the period of war and established a kind of peace league among daimyō. Fudai were those who had been supporters or subordinate to Tokugawa prior to the battle. When the Tokugawa regime was established, the domains of Tozama daimyō were located farther from the city of Edo, and those of Fudai nearer to the city as protection for the Tokugawa. Thus *sankinkōtai*, the annual travel between the domain and Edo, imposed a much heavier burden on Tozama daimyō, who were required to travel a greater distance; that expense, and their geographically peripheral position, made it difficult for them to challenge the power of Tokugawa. Only at the end of the Tokugawa period did such challenges arise—from two domains, Satsuma and Chōshu, far from Edo but, significantly, close to the imperial center in Kyoto.

This centralization and control ended any possibility of extending one's domains by means of internal warfare; Tokugawa supervision entailed a marked change in the daimyō's political power vis-à-vis the shogun, amounting practically to a loss of the daimyō's independent political power—most fully manifest in the fact that their domains could be confiscated by the shoguns. Yet, in contrast to the situation in France or other European absolutist states, not only did the daimyō maintain their autonomous superior status in the social hierarchy, but they also continued to constitute the major *political* elite. One of the most significant indications of the relatively autonomous status of the daimyō is the fact that each of the 250 or so lords or princes was called by a court title which matched his *bakufu* title. Indeed, as H. Bolitho has shown, even the *fudai daimyō* who staffed the central government were subject to the preoccupations and responsibilities of the daimyō class as a whole. Disputing the conventional portrayal of these men as paragons of fealty to the shogun, Bolitho describes the competing claims upon their loyalty and their self-interest. These claims, he argues, compelled the fudai daimyō to stand in the way of centralization. In the final years of conflict that led to the Meiji Restoration they refused to jeopardize their positions by fighting for the Tokugawa house that had raised them up nearly three centuries before.[21]

In France Louis XIV, the first nobleman of the realm, depoliticized the *noblesse d'epée* (the nobility of the sword) by divesting it of most political and administrative duties and by making attendance at the court of Versailles the epitome of its status, but no longer of power. This was not the case in Japan, where Tokugawa Ieyasu and his successors did not themselves come from the upper noble court families, or even directly from upper aristocratic ones. It was the major daimyō, together with members of the Tokugawa family, who constituted the major political elite, what could be seen as equivalent to the council of the state, although—and this is in itself very significant—no such formal body existed. This council, although not an autonomous body like the European assemblies of estates, was one of the major organs of government, and one the shoguns could not dispose of, despite the growing bureaucratization of their own organs of government. There was basically no other political elite in Tokugawa Japan—although internal tensions did develop between those close to Tokugawa and their ministers and the various daimyō and samurai retainers.

Beyond the maintenance of peace and order the Tokugawa *bakufu* was not very active in organizing public life—courts, police, codification of laws—or in the establishment of a countrywide judiciary to provide proper channels for appeal against "private" justice. But perhaps of greatest importance for understanding the specificity of this regime was the fact that, as Berry has shown, the new policies of unification were not effected through centralized nationwide bureaucratic organization, but rather through the reinforcement of existing practices—gift exchanges, adoption, interfamilial alliances, the taking of hostages, and the like.[22]

Moreover, the Tokugawa regime based itself on the older warrior ethos of the samurai and did not promulgate a new status or ethos of its own. Yet at the same time, by pacifying the country and isolating it from foreign involvements, the regime brought about the weakening of the military and the extension of the civilian duties of the samurai. This situation undermined the objective basis of the "warrior" ethos and gave rise to manifold attempts, evident in the burgeoning *bushido* literature, to domesticate this ethos, to reapply it to civilian endeavors, and hence necessarily to transform it.[23] The elaborate rituals established at the shogunal court, and to some extent in those of the domains, served the same purpose.[24]

A similar pattern developed with respect to the attitude of the *bakufu* to other strata. True enough, the Tokugawa regime established a highly formalized status system, based on Confucian precepts, which aimed at the control of the major strata. Yet at the same time its rule did not permeate deeply, beyond sumptuary and general status legislation and the keeping of peace, into the internal life of the various strata. Rather, it encouraged, subject to close supervision, their self-regulation.[25]

V   The distinctive characteristics of the processes of centralization that developed under the Tokugawa and the general features and orientations of the regime were manifest also in the legal system, which, while building on earlier developments, crystallized and became more fully systematized in this regime.[26]

The first such characteristic of this system was the absence, until the modern period, of any definition of law as a distinct symbolic and institutional arena—such as was the case in Rome, later in the Byzantine empire, and in Jewish halakha and the Islamic shari'a. Second, there did not develop in Japan the strong emphasis on criminal law as part of the imperial (or shogunal) administration that could be found in China— although some kernels of such law could indeed be identified. Third, and closely related, was the absence of what D. F. Henderson called justiciable law. This absence was closely related to the tendency in Japanese society and culture to subsume ethics under the overall moral structure of the community—a tendency central to the transformation of Confucianism, and to some extent also of Buddhism, in Japan.

A fourth distinctive characteristic of the Tokugawa legal system was that there was no court system apart from various administrative bodies, that

for successive generations of Tokugawa, bureaucrats and "judges" were synonymous, and all was now administration; there was no political activity worth noticing. This legal system was informed by a very distinct conception of law.

... The natural-law order of the Tokugawa shogunate represented quite a different conception of the nature, sources, purposes, and efficacy of law than our current concepts of justiciable, "made" law, or even the nineteenth-century concept of law as social excreta.[27]

The basic legal ideology of the Tokugawa regime could be summarized in Tokugawa Ieyasu's pronouncement in the "Rules for the Tokugawa House" as the basis of social order: "Reason may be violated in the name of law, but law may not be violated in the name of reason."[28]

A fifth characteristic of the Tokugawa legal system—which epitomizes as it were the essence of Tokugawa centralization—was the combination of a high degree of regulation of interstrata relations with a relatively low level of interference in the internal life of each stratum or domain. Henderson terms this pattern of regulation and segregation of the different status groups "status law."[29] These tendencies to regulate on the basis of hierarchical status and to keep different status groups separate were manifest in the multiple sumptuary laws, which extended to all areas of life, including architecture, the structure and organization of cities, and the like.[30]

In line with the basic orientation analyzed above, *bakufu* law put great emphasis on upholding the jurisdictional hierarchy within the daimyō's estates. The *bakufu* also claimed authority over cross-jurisdictional cases involving more than one daimyō or *hatamoto* and directed the daimyō to seek its advice and generally to follow its lead on certain cases involving capital crimes—but it did not act as a court of first resort for those under daimyō jurisdiction or as a court of appeal unless the appeal was endorsed by the authority with immediate jurisdiction.

Closely related to these concepts of law and to the characteristics of the legal institutions was the fact that most of the judicial functions performed by the administrative bodies consisted of ratification of agreements between different parties, presumably arranged according to customary laws, and not of adjudication according to "objective," clearly enunciated legal principles or precedents. Indeed in many cases the central legal presumptions were semisecret, known only to the officials.

Such various customs, as well as the numerous administrative regulations or laws on which agreements between different parties were based, were often codified in corpuses unrelated to one another. Such situations can, of course, be found in many historical empires. But unlike most such empires these codes of customary law were not in principle conceived or organized as distinct from the law of the central government.

VI   These characteristics of the process of centralization in Tokugawa Japan, as well as the distinctive pattern of distribution of power between the shogun and the daimyō, are closely related to the specific conception of the public realm and of statehood that developed in the Tokugawa regime, which again shares some characteristics with absolutist and imperial regimes, but also exhibits some very striking differences.

As in the absolutist states of Europe there developed in the Tokugawa regime—to a degree probably unprecedented in Japanese history—new, broader concepts of legitimation, and a new mode of ideological-political discourse focused on the problem of such legitimation, the definition of Japanese collective and cultural identity, the construction of clear geographical boundaries of the state, and the relation of state boundaries to those of the Japanese ethnic or national collectivity.[31] Words like *kuni* (country), *kokka* (state), and *kōgi* (public realm) denoted new concepts of such collective entities.

Such new conceptions of the public realm of the daimyō's domain as "kokka country" (country of the state), developed first among the various warlords, the daimyō of the Sengoku period of unification, who were trying to justify their attempts to establish direct control, unmediated by lower samurai, over their domains.[32] These concepts denoted a new and distinctive conception of public good and were oriented against the weakening shogunal powers, as well as against the lower samurai, who could claim multiple loyalties to different lords, and above all to their own groups[33]

These conceptions of the public realm were elaborated in different directions by the two great unifiers, Nobunaga and Hideyoshi. Nobunaga developed them not only in the direction of a broader public political realm, but also in the direction of an entirely new, "rational" conception of political authority, heralding a severe rupture with the preceding ones. But under Hideyoshi this rupture was not further elaborated, and the new concepts were reembedded into the symbolic, "imperial" framework. As Katsumata and Collcutt put it:

> For Nobunaga the equivalent of the Sengoku daimyō concept of kokka was undoubtedly the ideal of *"tenka."* Nobunaga's concept of tenka has been defined by Asao Naohiro in these terms: "Nobunaga conceived of 'tenka' both as a sphere of political control and as a universal principle (dōri) transcending social status, and he sought to instill in his followers the recognition that he was the tenka. . . .
>
> . . . It was to the concept of tenka, not to Shogun Yoshiaki, that he consistently looked for the source of his political authority. Nobunaga's evasion in 1582 of the proposal by the imperial court to appoint him to the offices of *daijodaijin, kanpaku,* and *seiitaishōgun* demonstrated his conviction that his authority over the country was sustained by the tenka he was trying to create for himself and not by any imperial court of shogunal office.

... Nobunaga's tenka was a rationale for rule created as the sole source for the legitimation of his authority over the country. Hideyoshi based his claim to rule the country on his appointment to the office of kanpaku by the emperor. Thus, in form, at least, tenka became the object of the authority exercised by the kanpaku.[34]

While the concepts of *kokka* and *tenka* as they developed in the period of unification were rooted in the preceding historical periods, their meanings were reconstructed in line with the new problems and possibilities specific to this period. But on the whole even these concepts did not entail a view of the state as an entity distinct from the community or country. Similarly, the concept of *kōgi*, with all its novelty, was not only rooted in older conceptions, but in many ways did not go beyond them. As Berry observes:

> It has come to signify a new principle of legitimacy, and hence a consequential change in consciousness, that identified rightful authority with service to the "public interest." Supplanting claims to power grounded purely in office holding or religious sanction or the like, kōgi has implied the ascendancy of the common good as the proper source and measure of legitimate rule. . . . [Yet] certainly the term is misconstrued insofar as we associate it with a public body, a collective citizenry. . . . If the "public" good had become one of the pillars of power, it was a good defined and benevolently bestowed by the powerful upon a subject public.
>
> As a paradigmatic description of Japan's transition from the medieval to the early modern eras, then, kōgi traces not the revolutionary ascendancy of a public domain over the ruler but the evolutionary absorption of privilege and alliance into the compass of the ruler.[35]

VII The common denominator of these processes of centralization was the conception of the political realm of the state as embedded in the broader national community. From a comparative point of view it is this absence of a concept of the state as a distinct ontological entity—in the sense, for instance, of the French concept of *l' état*—that is most striking. This conception of the political realm was fully elaborated in the ideology spawned by and within the Tokugawa regime, which introduced a broader political discourse focused on new modes of legitimation, the definition of Japanese collective and cultural identity, and the geographical boundaries of the state.

As the Tokugawa regime solidified, a far-reaching and fully articulated political ideology arose, probably for the first time in Japanese history, that in many ways paralleled developments in early-modern Europe. As we have seen, the establishment of the regime—built on the heritage of the preceding, anarchic period in which multiple centers of power had competed for authority—resulted in the centralization of power, the emergence of new sophisticated social forces, and the beginnings of economic development. It was the Tokugawa shoguns' awareness of the need to convert, as it were, their power into an authority acceptable to sectors of society that no longer took any central power for granted, that made them very interested in legitimizing their power in terms that went beyond the exigencies of battle and even beyond the general quest for order, which was quite prevalent in many sectors of the society.[36]

VIII The crystallization of this ideology developed within a broader public discourse in which neo-Confucianism as well as the schools of nativistic learning play an important part.

The ideological discourse that developed under the Tokugawa regime passed, to follow P. Nosco, through several stages.[37] In the first period, until the end of the seventeenth century, its major contours crystallized, bringing together neo-Confucian, Buddhist, and nativistic "Shinto" themes. The second period—the eighteenth century—was characterized by greater popular interest in intellectual discourse, the growth of urban population, and a growing split between neo-Confucianism and nativistic schools. This split greatly contributed to the growing intellectual ferment that was generated in many sectors of Tokugawa society—among the samurai, the merchant groups, and even some upper groups of the peasantry—by the internal crises of the regime (the Tempō Crisis of 1730–43);[38] the continuous demilitarization, bureaucratization, and impoverishment of the samurai; and the growth of private schools and academies. This ferment spilled over into the last phase of Tokugawa ideological discourse, which developed in the late eighteenth and the nineteenth centuries and was much more directly connected with social and economic upheavals and with various protest movements.

The basic framework of the Tokugawa discourse, especially its ideological or political dimensions, nourished a mixture of Confucian, nativistic (or Shinto), and Buddhist components. While each of these components had its own specific institutional niche—autonomous schools, temples, and the like—they acted primarily within this common framework of discourse. The neo-Confucian scholars and schools set the major parameters of the philosophical discussion, while the Buddhists played an increasingly secondary role.

IX The specific ideology that developed within the framework of Tokugawa discourse addressed itself to the problems posed by the constitution of Tokugawa rule and society, especially the problems of legitimizing the regime and interpreting the collective national identity—particularly, as

Kate Wildman Nakai has shown, in relation to the Sinocentric civilization and "world order."[39]

This ideology, slowly and intermittently promulgated, was oriented against the general openness that prevailed in the period of disorder and to some extent, as Herman Ooms has suggested,[40] against the growing self-consciousness, often imbued with Buddhist themes, of many sectors of the peasant society, who confronted the power of the new warriors.

The upshot of all these developments was the crystallization of certain ideological patterns which were to be characteristic of Japanese public discourse even beyond the Tokugawa period, and which were characterized above all by the "reduction of the multiplicity of continuously changing affairs to a synchronicity and immediacy that partakes of the mythical and eternal" and a consequent sacralization and cosmologization "of the constituent elements of a new structure of domination." Ooms further notes that "this ideology was not clearly doctrinal. Its neo-Confucian components were interwoven with the native traditions, especially Shinto."[41]

Indeed, in many ways the neo-Confucian elements were overlaid, or rather channeled, by the Shinto ones or, to be more exact, by underlying native orientations that were sometimes designated as Shinto, especially by promulgators of the nativistic learning (I owe this formulation to Kate Wildman Nakai). Their central import, as manifest in the construction of the Tokugawa ideology, was to construct both the legitimation of the regime and the collective Japanese identity by minimizing the transcendental and universalistic components of "classical" Chinese Confucianism.[42]

X The construction of such a societywide, relatively articulate political ideology was, on the face of it, very similar to what happened in the absolutist regimes of Europe in the seventeenth and eighteenth centuries, as well as in the Chinese empire, at least during the Sung period. Yet in several crucial aspects this ideology evinced very distinctive characteristics—again attesting to the *comparative* specificity of the Japanese historical experience—not only with respect to the specific conceptions of the public good and statehood to which we have referred, but above all in the grounding of the legitimacy of the Tokugawa regime.

In this respect the most important characteristic distinguishing the Tokugawa regime from the absolutist or imperial regimes of Europe and China is the fact that the Tokugawa were only shoguns and not emperors.[43] The Tokugawa regime, the most centralized in the history of premodern Japan, continued to be characterized by the bifurcation between authority and power, which emerged, as we have seen, in the early periods of Japanese feudalism. The emperors were, in fact, deprived of almost any real power; what power they had was confined to their own estates, and they were supervised more closely by the Tokugawa than in any other period of Japanese history. Moreover, the emperor symbolism, which played an important institutional role in the Meiji regime, did not occupy a very central position in the political consciousness of wide sectors of Tokugawa society.[44]

However, among at least some sectors of the population, above all the higher ones, some components of such a political consciousness did exist—as portrayed, for instance, in the very popular Chikamatsu puppet play about Coxinga (Kokusenija), first performed in Osaka in 1715, in which the theme of Japanese patriotism, of Japanese spirit as against Chinese technique, is prominent—and the emperors or imperial symbols often constituted a minor component of such consciousness.[45] Not only did the emperors never give up their central legitimating functions (nor were they deprived of them), but even in popular culture or folklore the emperor's persona played a continuous role—even if only as the *kami*, or rather ambivalent stranger, of many theatrical performances.[46] The imperial symbolism constituted a very important component in the reservoir of themes of Japanese tradition and collective consciousness. It was one of the few, if not the only, symbol of collective identity common to most sectors of the society—even if for large sectors of the society it was dormant and not fully articulated.

The importance of this imperial symbolism is manifest in the fact that the relation between the shogunal and imperial authority constituted a focus of political concern and discourse throughout the period of unification in the sixteenth century—and beyond, throughout the Tokugawa regime. The great daimyō, and the great unifiers—first Nobunaga, then Hideyoshi[47]—established their authority against the background of the decline of the power of the then shoguns, whose appointments were officially given by the emperor. Hence, potentially at least, the unifiers' conception of their own power and legitimacy could lead to the disregard, if not to the outright abrogation or denial, of imperial authority. Their interpretation of such concepts as *kokka*, *kōgi*, and *tenka* were, as we have seen, informed by conceptions which at the very least were not grounded in imperial legitimacy, and could also become oriented against that legitimacy. Yet, as we have seen, this possibility did not materialize; Hideyoshi reverted to grounding his authority in imperial legitimation, and the same was true of the Tokugawa regime.

Even in earlier times, during the period of the warring emperors when shoguns tried to appropriate to themselves imperial status, the *office* and symbols of the emperor were not abolished. Indeed the struggle over the imperial regalia, and the attempts of each contending emperor and shogun to portray himself as bearer or "proprietor" of the authentic regalia, constituted one focus of these struggles.[48] Nevertheless, the emperor's place, couched within a divine paradigm, remained predominant, however strong the attempts of the shoguns were to attain semidivine or sacral status—as in Hideyoshi's last megalomaniac year, or in the so-called deification of Tokugawa Ieyasu after his death. This deification did not imply, contrary to what has sometimes been proposed, more than the comparatively conventional religious transformation of a person into a *kami* and the promulgation of a new divine conception of shogunal rule, except that the ceremonies attendant on the constitution of Ieyasu's shrine and his deification were of an unprecedented scale and magnificence.[49] Moreover, the Nikko shrine dedicated to Ieyasu required an imperial decree to obtain the status of *miya*, hitherto reserved for the Sun Goddess's shrine at Ise.

This grounding of shogunal authority in that of the emperor was not merely a symbolic exercise—it was strongly connected with some concrete aspects of the political process. In the first years of Tokugawa rule, the court could still intervene to some extent among the different warring factions, through the use of appointments to court offices—but this potential power of the court was by that time considerably curtailed. Not only was Ieyasu officially appointed as shogun, but his son Hidetada implemented his father's plan to marry his daughter (Ieyasu's granddaughter) to the *tennō* (emperor). The actual powers of the court, especially with respect to the appointment of shogunal officers to court offices, were purely symbolic—yet this symbolic function remained relatively strong, however much the authority of Tokugawa was grounded in the new, "autonomous" conceptions of public realm and good. Not only was the shogun unable to abolish the court, but it was the emperor who constituted the overall foundation of the legitimacy of the regime and of its social arrangements.[50] Many aspects of the structure of the social hierarchies of the upper strata, such as the relative status of different daimyō families, were defined in terms of titles conveyed by the imperial court—and the Tokugawa shoguns always stressed that their own legitimation, and that of the Japanese polity in the East Asian international order, were focused on the symbolism of the emperor.

Concomitantly, as Bob Tadashi Wakabayashi noted in his recent discussion of the dimensions of court influence throughout the Tokugawa period, shoguns did not treat the traditional *ritsuryō* rank and title system as a "crusty relic that the shogun had to tolerate and work around. Instead, they shrewdly exploited it to consolidate their power over the realm."[51]

XI The unbreakable strength of the imperial legitimation is perhaps best attested to by the failure of the attempts to invest the Tokugawa ruler with all the powers and symbolism of a king. An attempt was made in the name of pure Confucian principles by Arai Hakuseki, an advisor to the sixth and seventh Tokugawa shoguns in the early eighteenth century (especially 1709–1716). Kate Wildman Nakai has shown in great detail that Hakuseki's efforts ran into insurmountable difficulties inherent in the Tokugawa state and ideology. Probably more important than any conceptual obstacles was the fact that any attempt to make the shogun into a full-fledged independent ruler would undermine the status of the daimyō, which (like that of the shogun) was legitimized by the emperor. Thus the daimyō naturally opposed any attempt to invest the shogun with the monopoly of allocation of status.

Similarly, the attempt to enthrone the shogun on the international scene would have to face the fact that any attempt to legitimate Japan as the center of the East Asian international political system (based on Confucian principles, with a strong Sinocentrism) could only be upheld—if at all—on the figure of the emperor or *tennō*.

Only by relying on the Tennō, who historically had claimed to be equal in stature to the Chinese *huangdi, the focal point of the Sinocentric order upheld by Korea, could Hakuseki attempt to present Japan as the new apex in the hierarchy of nations. Such a strategy necessarily compromised Hakuseki's primary endeavor to consolidate the authority of the shogun as an autonomous national monarch.*[52]

XII Thus it was, first, the conception of the public realm as embedded in the context of the domain and of relations between domains and formulated in the idiom of the family, and second, the grounding of the legitimation of the social and political order in the archaic symbolism of the emperor, that constituted the common denominator of the major distinctive characteristics of the Japanese collective consciousness as it crystallized—even if in a rather loose way—under the Tokugawa. Both of these conceptions were clearly different from Western European absolutist, as well as from Chinese, conceptions of statehood and national community.

Moreover, the construction and promulgation of this ideology were not directly undertaken by the state, that is, by the shoguns or on their instigation, to the extent as they were in Europe, and even more so in China. The initial push to construct this ideology was given by neo-Confucian scholars like Razan, most of whom came from dispossessed samurai families, rather than by the shoguns themselves. The interest of the shoguns was mostly in attaining some semisacralization or mythologization of their status, rather than in highly sophisticated ideological-political discourse. They naturally tried to keep the range of this discourse within limits acceptable to them, but within such limits they did not tend to give any group or school continuous standing.

As a result this ideology was not as fully integrated as has sometimes been suggested; there developed within it an intellectual and ideological discourse that went far beyond a simple legitimation of the status quo.[53] Moreover, this relatively loose ideology and its social consequences were not connected, as was the case in Europe, with the efflorescence of a new court society that would promulgate a new cultural program, a "civilizing process," to use Norbert Elias's phrase,[54] or a new cultural hegemony.

The Tokugawa shoguns initiated a very elaborate court ritual, and they and various daimyō cultivated cultural activities at their respective courts. They also emphasized the promulgation of the samurai ethos, which they attempted to channel into more "civilian" applications without, however, losing its military basis.[55] But the tradition of courtly high culture was more centered on the imperial court in Kyoto than on the shogunal court. Hence the civilizing process that developed in Japan gave rise to what Johann Arnason has aptly described as a trajectory of pacification, urbanization, bureaucratization, and intellectualization that differed radically from the transition from military aristocracy to court society that was characteristic of Europe.[56]

THE INTERNAL CONTRADICTIONS OF THE TOKUGAWA REGIME, THE REFORMIST AND RESTORATIONIST VISIONS

XIII   The specific combination of absolutist and feudal features, the process of centralization, and the conceptions of statehood and collective consciousness that were spawned by the Tokugawa regime generated structural and ideological contradictions, starting from about the eighteenth century, that contributed to the decline of the Tokugawa regime and affected the direction of post-Tokugawa developments. We shall begin with an examination of the relations of these contradictions to the processes of status dissociation that developed in this regime.

Paradoxically, the Tokugawa regime continued and even intensified the dissociation between power and authority, the roots of which John Hall has identified, as we have already seen, in the feudal period. But it was not only in the central arena of the relations between the *tennō* and the shogun that this dissociation between power and authority took place. No less important was the way in which the relations between power, status, and wealth developed in other sectors of Tokugawa society.

On the face of it Tokugawa society was highly stratified and the divisions between strata strictly observed, probably to an unprecedented degree in Japanese history (possibly with the partial exception of the failed attempts of the *ritsuryō* system in the eighth century). In reality, the situation was much more complex and even within the formal system some very important aspects of status incongruency developed. The official status division did not reflect the situation with respect to actual control over resources. The great bulk of the samurai were deprived of any autonomous access to the centers of power—whether in the Tokugawa *bakufu*, in the domains, or in the smaller seigneurial domains of the *hatamoto*—or to the fountain of honor and prescript of the emperor. Their land was taken away from them and instead they were granted rice stipends, making them even more dependent on the central authorities and the daimyō.[57] Due to pacification of the country, the domestication of the samurai, economic development, and the monetarization of the economy, large sectors of the samurai became impoverished and their chances of mobility blocked.[58]

A parallel but obverse situation developed within the merchant classes. The growth of trade and the monetarization of the economy greatly enriched them, and their economic activities became highly diversified. As a result of all this

> things were fuzzy at the top levels of the non-samurai status groupings as well as at the lower end of the samurai ranks. In early Tokugawa decades many of the large merchants who had played quarter-master roles were absorbed into the samurai class. As commercialization advanced in the countryside class differentiation became conspicuous as well, and large land-owners like the Honma in Shōnai became figures to reckon with, and even to court, for local daimyō. In metropolitan centers wealthy and cultivated chōnin mixed easily with samurai peers, and the groupings of artists, writers, and aesthetes that included figures like Watanabe Kazan were a far cry from the rigid social structures shown in the sources for Satsuma.[59]

Throughout the society—among the samurai, the merchants, and many sectors of the peasantry—this intensification of status inconsistency created wide open structural spaces in which new types of activity could be attempted; it made members of these social sectors available to explore new institutional and cultural avenues; and above all it gave rise to a far-reaching expansion of, especially Confucian, education—as is evident in the growing number of schools, academies, and literary activities. These schools, most of them manned by dispossessed samurai and not controlled by the *bakufu*, were part of a great educational expansion that made Japan under the Tokugawa probably the most literate premodern society.[60]

Thus a situation developed, not unlike the one at the end of the absolutist regimes in Europe, in which a new common discourse—a new ideology—could potentially develop, new modes of knowledge could become connected in frameworks that cut across major sectors of the population, and common political action could develop. Such possibilities would have been reinforced by some characteristics of discourse and education as they developed in Japan, as compared, for instance, to China. In China, Confucian education was relatively limited, mostly to those aspiring to office. In Japan, on the other hand, where offices on the whole were hereditary, education and the public discourse that developed in its wake were available to wide sectors of the population—samurai, merchants, and to some extent even peasants—contributing greatly to the ideological-political ferment that developed in the last decades of the Tokugawa rule.

Similarly, as in Europe, these processes generated a potential fiscal crisis for the shogunate. The increasingly uneven distribution of the growing national economy threatened the *bakufu*'s revenues. Attempts by the *bakufu* to raise the "easiest" taxes available to it—those on peasants—faltered due to numerous rebellions, which made it clear that any taxes beyond a certain level would be resisted; gradually, then, the shoguns gave up these attempts, thus weakening the center by diminishing its revenues and its ability to support the impoverished samurai.

In general the responses of the *bakufu* to these rebellions were characterized, especially from the early nineteenth century on, by an oscillation between repression and accedence to some demands—or simply ignorance of some rebellions—which generated, as in Europe, an intensification, through mutual feedback, of contentions and protest. (I owe this observation to J. White; see also note 78.) Yet, as we shall see in greater detail later on, while a revolutionary situation did indeed develop toward the end of the Tokugawa regime, it went its own way and differed markedly from the prerevolutionary situations in Europe.

XIV The rather distinctive structural contradictions that developed in Tokugawa Japan were closely related to the specific symbolic ones within the Tokugawa ideology, which constituted also the basic framework of the intensive ideological discourse that developed especially from the end of the eighteenth century on.

The root of these ideological contradictions lay in the fact that, while most of the constructs promulgated by the ideologues of the period attempted to glorify and justify Tokugawa rule, to attribute semisacral status to the shogun, and to equate the hierarchical arrangement of the Tokugawa regime with the way of heaven or of nature, they did it mostly in terms of Chinese neo-Confucian tenets, which had originally been set within the framework of a centralized empire. While some of these scholars and ideologues tended to gloss over the differences between the

Tokugawa regime in concept and in reality—and the ultimate legitimation of the regime by the emperor—these differences constituted the foci of far-reaching intellectual and ideological discourse.

This contradiction, rooted in the legitimation of the shogunal regime by the emperor, was in a formal way parallel to the one that developed in absolutist European regimes between the traditional, "religious" component (divine right of kings) and those components rooted in the ideologies of the Enlightenment. But the concrete contents of these contradictions moved in opposite directions in Japan and Europe. The ideological discourse that developed in Europe (and, in a different mode, in China in the second half of the nineteenth century) focused on the inability of the monarchs to live up to universalistic conceptions grounded in transcendental—religious or secular—visions and in ideals of accountability, and often also on the practical inefficiency of the monarchs, which was often attributed to this inadequacy. In Tokugawa Japan, the *bakufu* was also found wanting in efficacy, as well as in adherence to the Confucian precepts of proper rule. But in Japan, unlike in China, such precepts were rooted in moral visions of the existing community, which could be symbolized in the figure of the emperor who affirmed and legitimized the community in, above all, immanentist terms.

It was the combination of these ideological and structural contradictions that developed in the Tokugawa *bakufu*, rooted in the basic characteristics of the regime, that explains the direction of the various reform and protest movements that developed within it.

PROTEST AND IDEOLOGICAL AND SECTARIAN MOVEMENTS IN TOKUGAWA JAPAN

XV All these characteristics of the Tokugawa regime influenced the structural and ideological processes leading to its breakdown, but the numerous movements of protest and seemingly heterodox movements, which developed, especially in the last century of the regime, to a degree unprecedented in Japanese history, were of special importance. Such movements multiplied especially under the impact of the increasing centralization of the regime.[61]

Among the movements of protest and opposition that developed were some four thousand peasant rebellions, which took a variety of forms. There were also numerous movements of ideological reform among samurai, the most important, or at least the most spectacular, probably being the one that developed in the Mito domain.[62] Many discourses developed in the various Confucian academies (whether those of the samurai or, such as those in Osaka, of the merchants' groups);[63] there developed groups promulgating nativistic learning and various "religions of relief."[64]

In many ways these trends constituted the last phase in the unfolding of the Tokugawa ideology, or, rather, of the intensive philosophical and ideological discourse that developed under the Tokugawa, the general contours of which we have discussed above. They were part of much wider, more encompassing cultural and ideological trends that developed from about the middle of the eighteenth century. Their common denominator was a growing nonacceptance of the existing social, political, and hierarchical order promulgated in the Tokugawa ideology—in sacral, natural, and mythical terms—and the concomitant growth of reflexivity concerning the bases of social order. Even the Mito ideology, which promulgated and sanctified such sacral and mythical terms, developed out of the growing awareness that these terms and symbols were no longer accepted by many sectors of the society as naturally given. Concomitantly there developed a variety of discourses, all of which challenged the holistic view of society that constituted the early stance of the prevalent ideology. To follow Koschmann:

> In the Bakumatsu period the Tokugawa leaders began to see themselves and the bakufu in a new way. Rather than being representatives of "Japan" as a whole they were now mere "parts"—"domestic institutions among other such institutions." From that newly relative position, moreover, they finally proceeded via the mediation of European models to redefine the public realm as a "structurally unified nation." By redefining it, of course, they sought to reestablish over it their own firm control. For Mito activists the public was synonymous with *kokutai* (the national body), a mystical paradigm of government without politics in which order would be maintained through the sustained epiphany of Amaterasu Ōmikami.[65]

All the popular rebellions, as well as the various movements of reform, were part of the general background to the downfall of the Tokugawa regime. Their very development in so many sectors of the Tokugawa society contributed to an atmosphere in which "Tokugawaism" was no longer taken for granted, and to the mounting concrete problems faced by the *bakufu*. The various ideological and opposition movements that developed toward the end of the Tokugawa regime are probably more closely connected to the downfall of a regime than any other movements of protest in Japanese history. Hence, the analysis of their ideologies, structural characteristics, and impact is of special interest with respect to the nature of dissent in Japanese history and society and its similarities and differences from activities and organizations in other societies.

In the following pages we shall analyze briefly some aspects of these uprisings—of the peasant rebellions and the Mito reform movement—as well as the merchants' academies in Osaka and the religions of relief.

Peasant Rebellions and Social Protest in the Tokugawa Era

XVI Peasant rebellions have been a subject of great fascination and scholarly controversy among students of Japanese history and society. One can discern three phases in the analysis of peasant rebellions, especially by Western scholars.

In the first phase, best exemplified by the early works of H. Burton and E. Norman, the importance of peasant rebellions—and of their suppression—in Japanese history, in general under the Tokugawa and more particularly in the early Meiji period, was strongly emphasized.[66]

The second phase of research, in the 1950s and early 1960s, was characterized by a lack of interest in agrarian turmoil—or at least a disregard for it. The scholarship of that period tended to emphasize the consensual aspects of Japanese society—the internal cohesion of its communities, especially in the rural sector—and to minimize the conflicts between different strata of peasantry. There was also an emphasis on the paternalistic mode of relations between the government, the landlords, and the peasants and on the ideology of "benevolent rule."

While, needless to say, scholars of this period did not deny the obvious existence of peasant rebellions, the analysis of protests was no longer a priority in studies of rural life. The rebellions were not seen as being of crucial importance for the understanding of Japan's modern development. Instead emphasis was laid, for instance in T. H. Smith's well-known book *The Agrarian Origins of Modern Japan*, on the great potential for modernization that developed in the Tokugawa agrarian structure.[67]

Starting in the mid-1970s, a new wave of scholarship set in, again focusing heavily on peasant uprisings and rebellions, especially, but not only, in the Tokugawa period, and on their importance to an understanding of the downfall of the Tokugawa regime, the Meiji Restoration, and the turbulence of the early Meiji era. One of the forerunners of this new approach was Irwin Scheiner, whose investigations culminated in the essay "Benevolent Landlords and Honorable Peasants: Rebellion and Peasant Consciousness in Tokugawa Japan."[68] Since then numerous studies on peasant rebellions in Japan have been published.[69] All these studies contradicted the view, attributed perhaps unjustly to the modernization school (see chap. 1, n. 20), that such rebellions were of but little importance in the texture of Japanese society. At the same time, their analytical emphases put the study of Japanese peasant rebellions directly into a comparative framework.

Most of these studies were torn between two theoretical or analytical stances, which are of great interest with respect to the basic comparative orientations of Japanese studies in the West and in Japan. On the one hand, they emphasized the importance of various economic and political conditions in the genesis of these rebellions—conditions in principle very similar, or at least easily comparable, to those which gave rise to peasant rebellion in other (especially, but not only, Western) societies: rising rates of taxation, growing economic insecurity, especially in years of bad harvest or in periods of turmoil, and the increasing marketization of agriculture were often singled out. Many of these studies also stressed the difference between the earlier rebellions, which were reactions to exploitation by landlords and by the state, and those in the last decades of the Tokugawa regime, which were much more connected to the inroads of capitalistic modes of production into the villages and to the general weakening of the Tokugawa regime. Some studies, as for instance that of Herman Bix, were undertaken from an explicitly Marxist point of view— building to no small degree on the burgeoning Japanese Marxist scholarship and rebelling against the harmonious view of village life in Japan; these studies often argued that peasant uprisings erupted as a result of growing class conflicts and sentiments within the villages. In general they reinforced James White's assertion that the very centralization of the regime had contributed to the intensification of these rebellions.[70]

On the other hand, given the revisionist—sometimes radical—Marxist stance of many of their studies, it was natural that these researchers should also look for the emergence of a distinct peasant consciousness— opposed to the "official," hegemonic emphasis on harmonious relations between rulers and ruled and the ideology of benevolent rule—a consciousness with some revolutionary potential that could perhaps be compared with those of various European (and Chinese) peasant uprisings. The discussion of the revolutionary potential of these movements was closely connected to the question of how the new modes of discourse that developed in Tokugawa society affected, first, the processes that led to the downfall of the regime and, subsequently, the transformation of Japanese society under the Meiji.

XVII More recent and more detailed studies of peasant rebellions under the Tokugawa elaborate but do not greatly change the import of Scheiner's earlier analysis.[71] In general, these researches emphasize that many of these rebellions denied the validity of the existing social order and promulgated semiutopian or millenarian egalitarian and communitarian visions combined with an emphasis on arbitrary social arrangements. At the same time the researchers stress that these visions were not transformed into countrywide consciousness and organization or into revolutionary ideologies and activity.

Thus these studies indicate that many of the peasant uprisings, especially those in the early periods of the Tokugawa regime, were continuations of "traditional" types of peasant uprisings found throughout Japanese history. As such they spawned a dramatic discourse on what Thomas Keirstead described as "the theater of protest", the major characteristics of which he presented in the conclusion of his analysis of the protracted and violent struggles that developed between peasants and overseers on the Yano estate in 1377 and in 1393–94.

> In the well-rehearsed forms of the theater of protest, one can detect a relationship between cultivators and proprietors that was mutually constitutive and confirmed again and again in a flow of communication that presupposed the very categories it has created.[72]

This type of discourse was not confined to any single movement or set of events. The general outlines of such discourse could be identified in many of the *ikki* movements of medieval and early modern times, which had quite far-reaching impact on the changing political and economic scene.

Yet much of this research also emphasized three additional important aspects of these movements: First, the fact that toward the end of the Tokugawa regime, in the late eighteenth century, a much more radical stance developed within many of these rebellions. This was manifest in the appearance of a distinct peasant consciousness, related to the broadening scope of popular participation and imbued with strong nonhierarchical (if not necessarily antihierarchical), sometimes millenarian orientations. As Scheiner indicated in his pioneering essay on some of the later rebellions, some far-reaching transformations of the traditional themes of rebellion took place:

> Doctrines which in the past had been passively enjoyed, such as Maitreya, and ideas which had been celebrated as part of a compact of owed duties and received grade, now became foundation principles for rebellions that challenged the assumptions on which society was ordered. None supplied a political principle which directly assailed the political authority of the shogunate, but they represented, at the least, a major disintegration of the beliefs that supported it.[73]

Second, these studies showed that, as the preceding quotation states, very few of these movements developed far-reaching revolutionary orientations or capabilities, even when the awareness of the decline of the regime had become widespread. Third, some of the studies emphasized the fact that, however limited their revolutionary potential or impact, the social and political symbols and themes espoused by these movements contributed greatly to the development of a reservoir of symbols and modes of discourse in Japanese society that could be—and were—reactivated, reconstituted, and reconstructed in future historical situations.[74]

XVIII The search for explanations both of the prevalence and intensity of these peasant rebellions and of their revolutionary limitations, even when they were more radically transformed at the end of the Tokugawa, has preoccupied many scholars—especially those with Marxist orientations.[75] They noted that the various peasant communities in Japan were relatively isolated and embedded in a distinctive cultural world in which traditions of protest (like the medieval *ikki*) upheld prefeudal ideals of equality and justice but rarely developed into political action. To follow Bix:

> But it was at the local level, in the culture and folk beliefs of the village community, that peasant consciousness received it strongest impressions. Here beliefs and symbols of medieval provenance operated from within to limit the growth of peasant class consciousness, just as feudal repression acted on peasants from without.
> ... So the *ikki* was not only a habit, a defense, and a right to be exercised by peasants in times of acute crisis. It was also a ritual for keeping alive prefeudal ideas of impartial justice, equality, and equity in a society dominated by kinship, hierarchy, and fixed statuses.[76]

Most such explanations, as White showed in a review of four major recent books on peasant rebellions,[77] refer to the fact that the basic orientations of the peasant movements were closely related to their particular organizational and structural characteristics—especially their tendency to look inward, a marked ability to manipulate different levels of local authority, and a weak connection with potentially rebellious groups in different parts of the country, such as various samurai groups or religious sects.

In a recent book, White elaborates systematically and in great detail on the origins and mode of confrontation and protest that developed in the Tokugawa period, reinforcing and refining these earlier general conclusions. Among other factors he stresses the absence of strong religious themes capable of supporting rebellion and countering the hegemonic ideology.[78]

XIX These analyses, concerned with the weakness of class consciousness and of revolutionary occupations within the peasant rebellions, are cast in a comparative framework perhaps to a greater degree than other parts of the literature on Japan and can be seen, paradoxically, as a sort of "inverted orientalism." This may be due to the radical orientations of many

of the scholars concerned. However, in searching for revolutionary potential according to the Western model, they often do not do justice to the
impact of these movements of protest on Japanese society.

This problem was touched on by Scheiner and has been taken up in
several more recent studies, of which Ann Walthall's analysis provides a
good illustration. Walthall has shown that whatever the limitations of the
peasants' rebellions from the point of view of class struggle and political
action, they were of great importance in creating, maintaining, and promulgating social and political themes and symbols, as well as patterns of
collective action and conflict. These themes and symbols constituted an
important part of the cultural reservoir of many sectors of Japanese society and could be reactivated—and often reformulated—in many different historical situations.[79] These were not just recapitulations of older,
"traditional" themes; they often denoted new modes of discourse and
patterns of activities, often connected to the underground literature that
constituted part of a broader development in the last century or so of
the Tokugawa regime, challenging the hegemonic holistic and sacral
view of social order and broadening the symbolic reservoirs of Japanese
society—even if the social groups promulgating these themes were not
able to overcome the organizational and ideological limitations of these
movements.

Heterodox Movements—Mito Ideology; New Religions; Religions of Relief; Merchant Academies

XX Protest movements under the Tokugawa regime were not, as we
have indicated, confined to peasants or other "lower" classes, but also
became more common among the upper and middle classes. In some of
these movements, which became most conspicuous toward the end of the
Tokugawa regime among the shogunal loyalists, loyalty to superiors and
to the existing order was upheld through heroic, unredeemable, non-
practical acts, manifest in some form of retreat or in the ultimate withdrawal of ritual suicide—the "nobility of failure," to use Ivan Morris's
felicitous expression.[80]

But beyond this seemingly traditional type of protest, which has been
closely related to political struggle throughout Japanese history—especially among samurai and some religious groups—there developed in the
second half of the Tokugawa regime, among the higher or middle classes,
many movements with highly articulated protest ideologies that changed
the mode of cultural discourse in major sectors of Japanese society.
Among the most important of these heterodox ideologies were those connected with the upsurge, in the eighteenth and especially in the nineteenth centuries, of neo-Confucian and nativistic schools of thought, as
well as of numerous new religious movements, the "religions of relief."[81]

All these movements attest to the intensity of the new modes of discourse that developed in this period—all searching for greater self-understanding, all questioning the "natural" bases of the existing order, all looking for new bases for its restructuring. Although each of these movements was based in a different social stratum or sector and went, on the whole, its own way, there were many contacts between them, as well as between them and peasant rebellions.[82] Among their common characteristics was a nonacceptance of the ideology that depicted the Tokugawa society as a natural, sacred whole, combined with a certain retreat from the center; with a search for new modes of knowledge, and possibly for some union between such knowledge and politics; and sometimes with attempts to create the basis for a new center. The quest to unite knowledge and politics was often imbued with communal, hierarchical, or egalitarian visions with some millenarian or semiutopian components, yet with strong this-worldly orientations—even within the religious movements.

XXI Among the most important and ideologically articulate movements among the samurai was the Mito one.

> Between the 1830s and 1850s a group of Mito retainers closely associated with the ninth daimyō, Tokugawa Nariaki, carried out a series of reforms with far-ranging implications. Their avowed aim was to strengthen the existing social and political order by rectifying it, thereby enabling Japan to meet the growing threat from without. The reforms they pushed through included a comprehensive resurvey of domain lands meant to restore peasant morale and economic health by redistributing the burden of taxes. In addition, the reformers attempted to return domain *bushi* to the land so as to revitalize them spiritually and make them the foci of a defense structure that, incorporating the lower classes, would permeate the countryside. The reforms also aimed at a spiritual and mental mobilization that may be summed up as a commitment to the various ramifications of the principle of *sōnno jōi* (lit., "honor the emperor, expel the barbarians"), two concepts that were formulated in their combined form by Mito thinkers.[83]

The Mito vision was informed by a strong millenarian stance, couched in terms of an "inverted utopianism," of imperial restoration—even if they attempted to incorporate pseudohistorical themes.[84] The nature of these inverted utopian themes, in Mito and in many of the movements influenced by it, could perhaps best be seen in their vision of the ideal community and government: "The ideal toward which 'utopian' restorationism tended may be summed up as government by rites and music. . . . The qualities of imperial 'government,' the behavior of the court in Kyoto, made it a perfect concrete image of government by rites and music."[85]

Such conscious promulgation and semiideological sanctification of the archaic mythical symbols entailed a recognition by the Mito ideologues that these symbols and policies were no longer accepted by wide sectors of the society. This recognition explains a central theme of the Mito ideology, namely the fear of history as a locus of corruption rather than the upholder of absolute moral norms, a fear, as Koschmann put it, that "history may take over." "The antihistorical, representational thrust of the Mito project may have been responsible in part for the widespread reading its texts received."[86]

On the more realistic political level the Mito ideology was continuously caught up in the contradiction of its dual commitment to the *bakufu* and to the court; in this way it is important as an extreme representation of the tensions in the Tokugawa polity and ideology.

Some of these major contradictions in the ideologies of protest can also be identified in the discourse of the merchant academies, such as those in Osaka, which constituted a central part of the new philosophical and ideological modes that developed in the later parts of the Tokugawa regime.[87] In philosophical terms this discourse emphasized the givenness of nature and its importance as the basis of moral discourse—thus potentially emphasizing the autonomy of different social groups and creating new spaces in which they could undertake technological activities attuned to nature or to the well-being of the community. However, as in Mito and in most of the peasant rebellions analyzed above (though in different ways), the political demands of the merchants were limited, inward-oriented. They focused on raising their status in the existing social and political frameworks, extolling their contribution to the welfare of the community without, in principle, making far-reaching demands for autonomous political access to the center. Nor did they tend to establish continuous organizational links with other social actors or sectors.

Yet at the same time certain themes, especially those of equality and communality, became central in many new activities in the rural and urban arenas—the formation of credit cooperatives, protoindustrial activities, and the like.[88] Similar overall orientations can be identified among the new religions that developed in this period, especially the "religions of relief." These religions emphasized equality and community, couched in specific religious terms but with strong this-worldly, practical orientations and only weak challenges to the center. They created new spaces of social and cultural activity, but not of direct political activity, and made no attempt to displace the center.[89]

XXII All these ideological movements and movements of reform constituted, as we have seen, part of the new broader discourses that developed in all sectors of Japanese society. All of them questioned the existing order and presented an important challenge to the center, and they were all of crucial importance in the delegitimization of the shogunal rule.[90]

Even the Mito ideology, which ostensibly sought to strengthen the shogunate, challenged, with its strong communitarian orientations (albeit with hierarchical overtones), the horizontal arrangements of Tokugawa society. Similarly, the millenarian themes promulgated by many movements had, as George Wilson has indicated, significant political implications. Their impact on the fate of the Tokugawa regime can only be understood if we also take into account some of the structural characteristics of these movements.

XXIII The rebellions and movements of reform discussed above evinced specific structural similarities, with respect to their "causes," to those that developed in the various absolutist and imperial regimes in Western Europe, Russia, and China before the great revolutions. But at the same time they too attest to the specificity of the Japanese historical experience. This specificity is manifest in some very distinctive organizational and ideological features, in the relations between structure and ideology, and in their overall impact on the Tokugawa political regime.

Among the characteristics that led to the organizational self-closure of these movements was the weakness of the interlinkages that developed among them. True enough, toward the end of the Tokugawa period the range of contacts between different regions and even between movements increased to a degree unprecedented in Japanese history. Moreover, as Nakai has shown, there developed broader movements, which cut across many sectors of Japanese society and aimed at removing Confucian studies from the hands of a narrow group of specialists and making them part of the wider public discourse.[91] But such linkages were tenuous and did not coalesce into enduring frameworks in which different movements or sectors of the society could be brought together. The dislocated samurai and Confucian scholars, for example, did not tend on the whole to establish continuous linkages with the merchants or the peasants—even though some tenuous linkages did develop.

The contacts between different samurai groups—especially the more pragmatically oriented ones, such as those in Chōshū and Satsuma,[92] and those for whom the millenarian themes of the Mito ideology were a crucial point of reference—were naturally much more continuous. A very intensive discourse developed between these different groups and it was this discourse which in many ways constituted the crux of the ideological ferment of the Meiji Ishin. But even among the samurai no continuous framework for common political action developed.

The major reason for this was that the processes of change and movements of protest generated by the pattern of status inconsistency did not, until the fall of the Tokugawa regime, displace the prevalent symbolic status restrictions that regulated the lifestyles and occupations of the different strata. Most samurai, however much economic circumstance might have pushed them toward mercantile activities, could not and would not, given the strict status prescriptions and their own status perceptions, engage *openly* in such activities, even though many children of the samurai were adopted by merchant families.

Similarly, neither the increase in the economic power of the merchant and upper-peasant sectors, nor their cultural activities could break through the status restrictions imposed on them by the Tokugawa regime. They did not question the right of the center to regulate the status system of the society or ask for autonomous access to the centers of power. Rather they asked for their work and their contribution to the common good to be recognized by the center and their status changed or reformulated.[93]

The processes generated by internal contradictions and status inconsistencies in Tokugawa Japan were on the whole contained within distinct social strata and did not create—with the partial exception of some of the academics—common frameworks cutting across different status groups. Even the spread of education and the fact that the students in many— certainly not all—academies came from different strata did not give rise to many groups of autonomous intellectuals capable of mobilizing those different sectors of society and breaking through the traditional restrictions. Thus, all in all, the processes of change generated by these status inconsistencies did not give rise to new strata with a distinct political program focused on demands for autonomous access to the center.

Of special importance in this context is the fact that in all these movements there were few autonomous religious or cultural groups, and very few autonomous cultural leaders or ideologues who could provide such links. The few influential people who did promote more universalistic or communitarian themes were not able to create autonomous followings and social bases. It was—rather paradoxically—within the Mito groups that there developed nuclei of such autonomous tendencies, but these were restricted by their inward-looking tendencies and their ultimate embeddedness within the Mito domain.

This compartmentalization of protest movements, of the general structure of the intellectual world, was indeed very much in accord with Maruyama Masao's metaphor of the "octopus pot" in which different parts are connected by a rope but otherwise enveloped within themselves. This metaphor indicates that these various groups constituted (as Peter Duus has suggested in a private communication) an aggregate but not a countrywide community, lacking strong linkages—even if of opposition and conflict—between its parts.

Parallel to these common organizational features there developed some distinctive ideological orientations. First, most of these movements evinced a strong tendency to secede from the center, which in their eyes had lost its capacity to represent the entire nation. They looked for ways of "world renewal" and new types of knowledge that would help to reconstitute the whole. At the same time, however, they lacked a clear vision of the whole, and thus of how to reconstitute the nation; each group rejected the older conception of the whole, but then withdrew into its own separate shell. Although concerned with the fate of the country they were all inwardly oriented.

It may well be (again I owe this suggestion to Duus) that the West generated so many more alternative utopian models in part because of Europe's diverse cultural roots (Jewish, Christian, Hellenistic, pagan, and so on) and its encounter with the Orient and the Americas during the period of its expansion. In contrast the Japanese had a more restricted repertoire of models of social and cultural order and of protest based largely on Japanese Confucianism and Buddhism, with some leanings toward their Chinese antecedents. Be that as it may, such restricted and inward-looking orientations were characteristic of most, if not all, Japanese protest movements.

The second ideological tendency common to many of these movements concerns the relation between the different types of new knowledge that they promulgated and their overall political visions, as well as their practical politics.[94] Many of these movements, in a way modeled after the earlier Mito secession, sought to promote a close relationship between merit, ability, and leadership, making knowledge of a certain kind a prerequisite to leadership, the basis of the entitlement to power, equivalent to or indeed more important than the achievement of mere moral rectitude. This new knowledge emphasized practicality, utility, and instrumentality as the necessary preconditions for leadership and the attainment of power, and the identification of ability as a manifestation of such knowledge functioned as a universal criterion for political recruitment.

The more pragmatic orientations emphasized technical innovations aiming at the administrative strengthening and reorganization of the government—possibly in a conciliary direction. These attitudes toward political and administrative reform abounded among many groups of samurai and among some groups of officials in the *bakufu* and in the different domains, but were not easily connected with the millenarian, semiutopian or inverted utopian, and communitarian themes promulgated by many of these movements. These themes were, by contrast, inward-oriented, with a strong emphasis on secession from the center; in general they could not provide an overall new political vision capable of encompassing the more pragmatic orientations.

Many of the reformers were also caught, as was the case in Mito, between loyalty to the *bakufu* and to the emperor; it was those who could overcome the former that later succeeded in the Meiji Ishin.

Hence the new knowledge sought by many of these movements was not easily translated into political action or any vision that could deal with the concrete problems confronting the Tokugawa *bakufu*—especially the problems arising from the impact of external forces and the consequent need to reorganize the government.

XXIV   This dissociation between different kinds of knowledge facilitated the superimposition of the restorative, inverted utopian themes within different movements and communities of discourse—in the philosophical and the more egalitarian, communitarian, and horizontal ones, in the discourses that developed in the merchant academies, in Mito, in the schools of nativistic learning, in the religions of relief, and in the peasant rebellions. The egalitarian and communitarian themes (sometimes connected with a denial of hierarchy) and the strongly antistatist views that developed in many of these movements were not rooted in a transcendental, universalistic vision.

The same was true of the emphasis on achievement, or merit, that developed among the samurai. The emphasis on merit became, as Thomas Smith showed long ago, a basic ideological theme especially among those who saw their mobility blocked and questioned the efficiency of the older, hereditary status on which the organization of the *bakufu* was based. But this ideology was based, as Sonoda Hidehiro has pointed out, on the functional contribution of such achievement to the needs of the community or the nation rather than on any universalistic or individualistic conceptions.[95]

Hence neither achievement orientations nor tendencies toward egalitarianism were channeled so as to establish new universalistic principles that would transcend the existing settings; because of this, public space was easily monopolized by "inverted utopian" restorative themes. At the same time these themes were promulgated in many new social spaces and in the new cultural activities that abounded in these spaces, creating new forms of social consciousness which would later continuously confront the state.

XXV   The tendency of these movements to withdraw and the lack of continuous linkages between them limited their *direct* impact on the fate of the Tokugawa regime. In Koschmann's words, "Despite the debilitating impact of their rebellion on the bakufu, the political actors formed in Mito did not themselves overthrow the old regime or establish the Meiji state. Instead, their activism was fated to dissipate in internecine battles and to play itself out in what is best understood as a dress rehearsal for revolution."[96]

Many of these movements were characterized by distinctive liminal features, exemplified in the many "traditional" pilgrimages that have abounded throughout Japanese history.[97] Such pilgrimages, especially the *okage-mairi*—the popular pilgrimages to the Grand Shrine of Ise that took place throughout Tokugawa Japan—evince many liminal characteristics, giving rise, to follow W. Davis, "to far-reaching confusion and social unrest with high potential for social, political disruptions." Yet these political potentialities did not materialize. "They were curtailed by (*a*) government policies of repression and/or compromise, (*b*) the sagacious charity of the upper classes, (*c*) the guidance provided by the priests from Ise, and ultimately (*d*) the unrevolutionary, ritual nature of pilgrimage itself."[98]

Significantly, Satsuma and Chōshū, the daimyō of Tozama and the main actors in the Meiji Restoration, were located farther from Edo than from the emperor's court, in Kyoto. Thus, in the final period of the Tokugawa regime, these daimyō appealed to the emperor's court, the cultural center (and center of legitimation) to which they had access, orienting themselves toward the other center in an explicit challenge to the centrality of Edo. (I owe this remark to Yui K.)

XXVI Thus, while all these processes of change and movements of protest set the stage for the downfall of the Tokugawa regime, the actual toppling of the regime was brought about by the activities of various groups of samurai, such as the *shishi*, the pragmatic reforms of the different domains, and the like. The roots of these groups' discontent lay, as we have seen, in the fact that the mobility of many sectors of the samurai was blocked, and many of them, as Sonoda Hidehiro has shown, came to perceive that there was a dissociation between their estate and the performance of their functions, and that the older modes of performance of these functions were not adequate to cope with the new challenges Japan faced.[99] This contradiction provided the structural roots of the discontent of many samurai groups, which led to the downfall of the Tokugawa regime; the bifurcation between the authority of the emperor and the power of the shogun provided the ideological roots. This combination of structural and ideological contradictions also explains the direction of the samurai's efforts and reforms.

Similarly, while all these movements were characterized by a search for new types of knowledge that could provide guidelines for action in the new open situation, these new modes of knowledge did not—as was the case in Europe, in America, and later in Russia and China—become closely interwoven with countrywide encompassing political programs and frameworks.

It was probably the weakness of autonomous cultural links between these different groups that made it difficult to bring them together around the innovative communitarian, egalitarian, and universalistic themes that constituted their major common focus. Their inability or unwillingness to enunciate principles of political action that would transcend any single sector of the society, or any single movement, reinforced the tendency to emphasize and respond to restorative themes rather than legitimizing reform in the name of some new, transcendent principle; ultimately it was only the restorative symbols that provided such vision.

Thus the critical discourse of the period, which focused on the existing shogunal rule and the failures of the regime as it succumbed to foreign influence, developed in the direction of rediscovery or reinforcement, indeed of reinvention of the archaic imperial legitimation. The emperor was made into a symbol of collective identity to what probably was an unprecedented extent—a symbol around which, under conditions reflecting the breakdown of the regime, forces opposed to the Tokugawa *bakufu* could rally without seeming to challenge the basic legitimacy of the Japanese collectivity.[100]

Hence, the outcome of all these movements was the construction of an entirely new center, the symbolism and legitimation of which was couched in inward-looking, restorative principles, but which was in fact guided by more pragmatic considerations.

It is these features of the Japanese scene at the end of the Tokugawa regime that explain the specific outcomes of the breakdown of the Tokugawa, as compared with that of the European—and Chinese—absolutist and imperial regimes. In Japan the combination of millenarian, restorative themes and inverted utopian themes predominated among the movements of protest, while in Europe, China, and Russia these movements were characterized by a vision of historical progress involving a break with the past and justified by universalistic-transcendental orientations—orientations that also shaped the outcomes of the breakdowns of their respective regimes.

XXVII   It might be worthwhile to address briefly one of the most important problems for research on modern Japan—namely, the conditions that allowed Japan to industrialize so quickly and successfully, to become the first and, until recently, only non-Western nation to become fully industrialized. However great the differences between different scholars with respect to which details of the Tokugawa economic structure facilitated this economic development—for instance, the relative importance of developments in the agricultural sector as against those in the urban one—there seems to be a consensus that the causes or processes or conditions were mostly internal, "native sources" to use T. Smith's expression.[101]

The process of industrialization in Japan shared numerous structural characteristics with that in Europe. The most important among these were the development of structural pluralism, of a multiplicity of centers, and of economic power; the breakdown of narrowly segregated ecological frameworks; the opening up of family structure, especially in the rural sector, which generated many new resources; and widespread, cross-domain marketization.[102] Of no small importance also were the high levels of literacy and urbanization, and extensive economic integration.

Needless to say, there were also many differences in the push to economic development in Japan and in the West, one of the most important of which was the relative timing in terms of the development of the international capitalist system and the concomitant necessity to find appropriate niches in this system.

Whatever the details, there can be no doubt that there is a strong convergence between the structural conditions that were conducive to such economic development in Western Europe and in Japan. But this structural similarity highlights even more the distinctive features of the Japanese and European paths. One distinguishing characteristic has been the greater importance of the political realm—the state—in the Japanese development. This was not only a "technical" or organizational feature but is attributed by Alexander Gerschenkron to all "late developers."[103]

In Japan, the role of the state was much greater than in, for instance, Germany or Russia, an indication of the weakness, in terms of their social and cultural autonomy, of the major actors—the peasant sector, the various urban groups, and the potentially aristocratic samurai entrepreneurs with their embedment in broader ascriptive frameworks and settings—with respect to the social forces that were crucial in this process. Thus, while it is likely that "modern" capitalistic enterprises would have developed within Tokugawa society on the micro level, it is not certain that they could have given rise by themselves to an overall new mode of political economy conducive to the creation of an autonomous capitalistic system and society.

While such considerations are necessarily conjectural, there can be no doubt that the social characteristics of the various sectors of Tokugawa society, and of the early Meiji one, explain many of the contours of Japanese capitalism.

XXVIII   From all these points of view we find a marked difference between the processes of change generated in Japan and those in the modern European absolutist states—despite many similar underlying causes. The structure of the Tokugawa regime exhibits—as does the development of Japanese feudalism, and of early modern cities—a distinctive form of institutional dynamics.

These differences had far-reaching implications for the nature of the revolutions that toppled the absolutist regimes of Europe, on the one hand, and the absolutist Tokugawa regime, on the other. The combination of ideological and structural characteristics of the various movements of protest and modes of ideological discourse also explains some of the basic characteristics that distinguish Meiji Restoration from the great modern European revolutions (see chapter 11).

TEN

Some Aspects of the Transformation of Confucianism and Buddhism in Japan

I In the preceding chapters we have compared Japan with Western European societies and civilizations—even in periods in which there were no continuous and massive contacts between these societies and Japan. But throughout its history Japan was in continuous contact with other major Asian civilizations, above all with China and Korea, but also, through the impact of Buddhism, with India. It is impossible to understand the dynamics of the Japanese historical experience without taking into account the ways in which aspects of these civilizations—especially Confucianism and Buddhism—contributed to shaping the cultural and social life of Japan. For our immediate purpose the central question is the precise nature of this impact and of the ways in which Buddhism and Confucianism were transformed in Japan and, in their turn, transformed Japanese society—how they contributed to the cultural and religious-cultic life in Japan, how they influenced the patterns of creativity in these areas, and how they transformed the general cultural climate.[1] Under the impact of Confucianism and Buddhism, and contrary to the situation prevalent in many non-Axial civilizations (e.g., ancient Egypt, Assyria, Mesoamerica), highly sophisticated intellectual, philosophical, ideological, and religious discourses developed in Japan. Central to this development in the Tokugawa period was the intensive debate between different neo-Confucian schools and the schools expounding "natural" learning, to which we have briefly referred above.[2]

It would be beyond the scope of our endeavor even to pretend to analyze all, or even most, of the influences of Confucianism and Buddhism in Japan. Our more specific questions concern, first, the basic "principled" difference, if there is any, between the way Confucianism became institutionalized and incorporated in the imperial order in China (and later in Korea and Vietnam) and the way it was incorporated in Japan and between the way Buddhism was institutionalized in Japan and in mainland Asia, and, second, the measure of the impact of Confucianism and Buddhism on Japanese society and culture. To be more specific, what were the ways in which Confucianism and Buddhism transformed the basic ontological conceptions and conceptions of social order, together with their basic institutional derivatives, that were prevalent in Japan, and conversely to what extent were the conceptions prevalent in mainland Asian Confucianism and Buddhism transformed in Japan?[3]

It is of course simplistic and dangerous to talk about the patterns of transformation of Buddhism and Confucianism in Japan across different historical periods. The concrete details of their development have of course differed greatly between various periods, and we can refer here only to some of the most general aspects of this development. It seems, however, that some common general tendencies can be discerned, and it is these tendencies that are of special interest from the point of view of our comparative analysis. The identification of such tendencies does not explain the patterns of transformation of Buddhism and Confucianism in Japan—and it should not be taken to mean that some basic Japanese "essence" effected this transformation. Rather, such tendencies, once identified, call for an explanation.

Some decisive *institutional* differences between the incorporation of Confucianism in China, Korea, and Vietnam and in Japan are easily identifiable, as are some aspects of the impact of Confucianism (and Buddhism) on the basic institutional premises of these societies, especially with respect to the structure of their centers, the legitimation of their regimes, and the composition of their ruling strata.

Under the impact of Confucianism both Korea and northern Vietnam developed new types of centers, new bases of legitimation, and new ruling elites and systems of stratification—and even of family structure. These new institutions were imperial rather than patrimonial or patrimonial-feudal (such as persisted, for instance, in southern Vietnam).[4] This change was effected by the transformation of feudal-patrimonial ruling groups into something similar to the Chinese literati, that is, an autonomous, bureaucratic-cultural elite, recruited according to distinct, independent criteria and organized in relatively autonomous frameworks.

True enough, in Korea, Confucian elites never achieved the level of autonomy and independence that characterized the Chinese empire, especially after the Tang dynasty. Aristocratic and patrimonial tendencies remained very strong; the Confucians encountered a vigorous Buddhist opposition, which was allied with much of the older aristocracy and some of the rulers. Once the Confucian institutions and elites became predominant, however, even the aristocracy became "Confucianized." Aristocratic families and lineages continued to be much more important in Korea than in post-Tang China, but their importance was manifest in their at least partial monopoly over Confucian bureaucratic literati positions, rather than in any reversion to distinct "semifeudal" aristocratic policy. In other words, they played their game according to Confucian rules, even if they manipulated those rules to their advantage.[5]

In northern Vietnam the Confucian state was even more coercive than in China and Korea and in some ways more truly "imperial" in its permeation of the periphery than the Chinese model.[6] In all these countries, Confucianism radically changed the mode of legitimation of the regime and of the rulers—moving from some type of divine, usually patrimonial kingship, toward some conception of rule under the "mandate of heaven," according to which the ruler was called upon to uphold Confucian principles and could be held accountable expressly to Confucian scholars and officials, often located in the so-called censorial bureau, which had to edit and formulate imperial edicts.

II The development of Confucianism and Buddhism in Japan differed from that elsewhere in Asia in a radical way. Their overall cultural influence was immense, yet its general institutional and symbolic direction was different from that of Confucianism in China, Korea, and Vietnam and of Buddhism in all Southeast Asian countries and China—although there were of course many similarities in concrete details.

Confucianism first came to Japan in the seventh century, when the imperial court looked to China for an example of a centralized regime and established the Ritsuryō system after the model of the Tang emperors.[7] (It is interesting to note in this context that Prince Shōtoku's "Buddhist" constitution (604 C.E.) has as its first sentence a literal quotation from the Analects of Confucius.) Its influence as a model of social and political order and as a focus of philosophical discourse was much weaker during the long feudal period, when Buddhism provided the major framework of cultural creativity and discourse, but even then it continued to serve as an important component in the imagery and legitimation of the political system. The Confucian influence became much stronger under the centralized regime of the Tokugawa, when neo-Confucianism constituted a major focus of philosophical and political discourse—although there is still much debate concerning its extent. But whatever its influence and extent, its institutional and cultural impact in Japan differed greatly from that in China itself, in Vietnam, and in Korea.

Confucianism in Japan did not change the basic structure and premises of the center or of the ruling elites. Despite some attempts in this direction in the eighth century, its importation did not give rise to the institutional structures that developed in China, Korea, and Vietnam—namely the examination system and the crystallization through this system of a stratum of literati. Thus, while the famous Confucian saying that one should have educated rulers implied in China (and to a smaller degree in Korea and northern Vietnam) the crystallization of entirely new autonomous ruling classes, in Japan it entailed attempts to educate the existing rulers.

True enough, during the Edo period there developed, in fiefs of the various daimyō and in that of the shogun himself, many groups of people who would play important roles in the subsequent overthrow of the Tokugawa regime. Most were educated in the numerous Confucian academies that were founded in this period—some by the shogun or the daimyō, some as private enterprises drawing members from different classes, especially from the two ends of the spectrum, samurai and merchants. Many of them performed important bureaucratic functions in the courts of the shogun and of the daimyō. A relatively strong common consciousness certainly developed among them, but they did not constitute a countrywide, autonomous stratum that could control its own recruitment to official positions. Rather, they remained almost entirely dependent upon the various lords in whose service they were employed. As Watanabe Hiroshi has put it, possibly by way of deliberate exaggeration, their functions did not differ greatly from those of doctors, surgeons, or other specialized functionaries.

Confucianism did not transform the basic premises of Japanese society, but it did have a far-reaching cultural impact on many aspects of institutional life and behavior, especially during the Tokugawa period. Rather than giving rise to a new institutional format, it became "Japanized." It also created new institutional spaces and modes of social consciousness and philosophical discourse, which constituted a basic dimension of Japanese institutional formations and cultural dynamism. Thus, Confucian themes, such as discipline, loyalty, and harmony, were continuously selected and incorporated into the symbolic perspective or repertoire of the different sectors of society—samurai, merchants, and peasants.

Later, under the Meiji regime, some of the "classical" Confucian views of education and officialdom provided background or general orientations for the establishment of the modern bureaucracy. It was in this context that Confucian ethics—or what was seen as the major component of these ethics, namely the emphasis on hierarchy, harmony, and discipline, but not the study of Confucian texts—were promulgated by the educational elites in their attempts to create the new national ethos.[8] If this selection was made in ways that tended to reinforce the basic premises of

the still-crystallizing social and political order, it also entailed the continuous generation of new social and cultural spaces amid new modes of
discourse.

III A parallel development took place in Japan with respect to Buddhism, which also developed characteristics that distinguish it from the
mainland Asian varieties of Buddhism. Buddhism was introduced into
Japan in the fifth century, probably from Korea. Yōmei (r. 585–587)
was the first emperor officially to accept Buddhism, but it was his son,
the prince regent Shōtoku (574–622), who was responsible for creating
Japan's first great age of Buddhism.[9] Throughout its history in Japan,
Buddhism has undergone important changes in its social organization, in
the nature of the audiences to whom it addressed itself, and in its religious
doctrines and practices.

A crucial step in the development of Buddhism in Japan occurred at
the end of the eighth century, at the beginning of the Heian period, when
the imperial palace was moved from Nara first to Nagaoka and then, in
794, to Heian-kyo, present-day Kyoto.[10] This was done, among other reasons, to escape the growing influence of the senior Buddhist clergy, who,
so close to the political center, were generating a far-reaching transformation, effected above all by two monks, Saichō (767–822) and Kūkai
(774–835).[11]

Until the late Heian period, Buddhism was confined to aristocratic and
court circles, although it also enjoyed wider influence. From the late tenth
century, especially during the Kamakura period (1185–1333) and later
during the Muromachi period (1338–1575), Buddhist groups addressed
themselves to much wider sectors. It was also in the late Heian and early
Kamakura period that Buddhism began to crystallize into distinct sects,
or rather, as there was no unified church, into distinct schools, each with
its own doctrine and audience, even if their boundaries were quite volatile, not as firm as they would be portrayed in late Tokugawa and Meiji
retrospectives. This growing denominational or sectarian development
was greatly influenced by the prevailing modes of political economy.[12]

Each of the new schools or denominations—as well as the older,
"traditional" Buddhist groups or schools—became organized around
monasteries and temples, often ruled by lineage groups related to their
founders, which became very powerful, both economically and politically,
especially in the period of late semianarchic feudalism in the fifteenth and
sixteenth centuries. With the ascent of the Tokugawa, and already before
that under Hideyoshi, they were brought under strict central supervision.
In this period, Buddhism became something close to a state religion, for
it was more than merely a state-controlled one. Since every Japanese

family had to be registered at some Buddhist temple, the temples functioned also as population registers, though at the same time they lost some of their wealth and almost all of their political autonomy. As a result of these developments the various schools became even more sectarian than before in their mutual relations, each segregated in its own domain or temple.

Throughout this period Buddhist and Shinto rituals were continuously intermixed, the shrines or altars of both often found in the same temples, as well as in many households, which in this period had become the major foci of religious worship.

IV   The critical period in the development of Japanese Buddhism was the late Heian and Kamakura periods, when Buddhism reached beyond aristocratic and court circles to wider sectors of the population and became an integral part of Japanese society.

The most important of the denominations or schools that emerged in the Kamakura period were the Pure Land school, which originated in the sixth and seventh centuries but was transformed in the twelfth century, by Shinran (1173–1262) in particular; the closely related but distinct sect organized by Nichiren (1222–1282); and the various Zen schools or sects. All these originated in China, often with very strong roots in India, as had the earlier Buddhist groups, but were transformed in Japan. The Zen schools were mostly oriented toward various aristocratic, samurai, and intellectual sectors; the Pure Land sects addressed themselves to traditionalistic rural and urban sectors; and the Nichiren groups addressed themselves above all to displaced, especially urban, sectors.[13]

It was in this period that the impact of Buddhism on the institutional and cultural formations and dynamics of Japanese society became fully crystallized, following a pattern similar in outline, but obviously not in detail, to that of Confucianism.

V   The nature of Buddhism's impact in Japan can best be understood if it is compared with the development of Buddhism in mainland Asia. As indicated above, all these schools or denominations were of external origin—Chinese, in some cases Korean, or more indirectly Indian.

Many of the developments in Japanese Buddhism evince interesting parallels or similarities with the developments of Mahayana sects in India, with which they had indeed many contacts. I shall mention, at this stage of our discussion, only two such similarities: on the organizational level there was a multiplicity of dispersed sects, each focused around a specific sutra; closely related to this, on the level of religious practice, there was a strong emphasis on the recital of such sutras and on other, "this-worldly" ritual activities. Later, especially after the Kamakura period—when, as Frank Reynolds and Charlie Hallisey have pointed out, Buddhism became transformed from a "civilizational," transnational religion upheld through intensive contacts between monastic institutions into a more closed, cultural national religion or religions[14]—Japanese Buddhism also developed institutional formations and religious practices strikingly similar to those that developed in other Asian countries.[15]

Yet despite these similarities—of which we shall come across many more in the course of our discussion—the overall formation, dynamics, and impact of Japanese Buddhism differed greatly from that of the Mahayana sects in India. This was due to two facts. First, however strong the direct contacts between Indian and Japanese Buddhist sects, Chinese and Korean Buddhism probably constituted the main reference points for large sectors of Japanese Buddhists. Second, and possibly more important, Buddhism in Japan had to adapt itself to the relatively compact political and national setting within which it developed; interestingly, because of this there developed within Japanese Buddhism some similarities with the other compact Buddhist theocracies—Tibet and Mongolia.

As we have already indicated, it was in the late Heian and Kamakura periods that the development of Buddhism in Japan and its impact on Japanese society came to parallel in many ways those of Confucianism. Given the fact that Buddhism was a religion, it became organized, unlike Confucianism, in distinct organizations, sects, schools, temple establishments, monasteries, and the like. Yet, as with Confucianism, even when these groups were very powerful, they did not create radically new forms of social organization distinct and autonomous from those of other social or political groups, which evolved in a very familistic and factionalistic direction consistent with the existing frameworks of political struggle. On the contrary, tendencies toward greater autonomy, inherited from their mainland Asian precursors, were usually radically changed, and ecclesiastical structures were instead modeled after "native" Japanese patterns. Indeed, as W. Davis has pointed out, although many of these sects began by transcending local communities, they tended to be coextensive with such communities and even subsumed by them. Even those that were not subsumed did not attain much distinctiveness or autonomy, because they were organized according to the existing principles of social organization prevalent in most sectors of Japanese society.[16]

Buddhism, like Confucianism, did not transform the basic premises of the Japanese social organization, nor did it create, even in its own sphere, distinctly new modes of social organization. The institutional and ideological adaptations of Japanese Buddhism were thus significantly different from those in mainland Asia—especially in Korea and the Southeast

Asian countries. Among the most important differences was the fact that in Japan there developed, instead of a central church, many sects or schools.

VI Japanese Buddhism's combination of strong familistic organization with active participation in the existing spheres of political struggle can be clearly seen already in the ninth and tenth centuries, when the different types of court patronage and participation in court rituals were of paramount importance to the various Buddhist monasteries and their leaders, abbots, and members. This combination continued from the Kamakura period on, in spite of the fact that—with the development of new, popular sectarian schools—conditions developed which seemingly could have enhanced the Buddhist groups' social and political autonomy.

Closely connected to the tendency toward groupism structured according to prevailing familistic principles were the transformation of monks into priests, their abandonment of the rule of celibacy, and the blurring of the distinction between priests and laity—all of which attest to the strong embeddedness of Buddhism in the prevalent social structures. The progressive blurring of the distinction between monks and laymen in many Buddhist denominations in Japan particularly reinforced these familistic tendencies. This combination of tendencies toward groupism and involvement in the existing political frameworks became even more pronounced in the late medieval, and especially Tokugawa, periods.[17]

VII The structural characteristics of Japanese Buddhist organizations also greatly influenced their "sectarian" features, which developed in ways markedly different from those of most groups in mainland Asia. Many disputes developed among the various sects, especially the Pure Land groups, each of which presented its own teaching or dogmas as the only real truth; but only rarely were such claims intended to convert other groups or to eradicate "heresies" on theological or dogmatic grounds (Nichiren being probably the most important exception, and still probably a partial one). Such groups did not in general aim to impose their own doctrine as *the* doctrine of the realm, independent of the existing rulers, to impose it on the rulers, or even to establish, as many South Asian groups sought to do, the predominance of their specific monastic lineage, its ritual, or its exposition of the canon. The fact that there was no countrywide church or overall Buddhist organization facilitated the development of sectarian disputes into something resembling family feuds or disputes between feudal groupings, rather than theological or doctrinal disputes aiming at religious conversion—although they could lead to the execution of "defeated" opponents.

Some characteristics of the Japanese schools were reminiscent of the

Indian Mahayana sects from which they descended. But many of their more outstanding characteristics, such as their embeddedness in the existing political arena, developed more fully in Japan. Especially in late medieval times, the various Buddhist sects and monasteries developed into very powerful political and economic forces; many of the shoguns and daimyō attempted to control them, but in periods of disintegration they often enjoyed considerable autonomy and power vis-à-vis the shoguns—themselves becoming daimyō-like units. They engaged in continuous struggles among themselves, with the various feudal lords, and with the shoguns. While specific religious disputes and controversies were of great importance in the relations between groups, most struggles with the powers that be concerned economic resources and political or patronage power. As indicated above the Buddhist groups made few attempts to impose their particular dogmas on the entire land or to make acceptance of them a precondition for the legitimation of the rulers.

The leaders of some sects, especially the Zen schools, attempted to distance themselves from the more syncretistic features of most religious practices in Japan, for example, pilgrimages to the Ise shrine. But such attempts did not have strong appeal to the wider membership of these groups. At most they were confined to select groups of religious cognoscenti.[18] The familistic character of sectarian identities weakened the development of boundaries between schools—contrary to what has been suggested through the lens of later Tokugawa experience. Indeed, it was under the Tokugawa, when growing state supervision of the temples imposed such boundaries, that the various Buddhist schools or sects became, as we have seen, more self-enclosed, with little mutual interaction.

VIII Buddhist themes and symbols also became closely connected with the various popular rebellions, such as the medieval *ikki*. The infusion of such themes into these rebellions imbued them with new symbolic and spiritual dimensions and probably intensified the various communal and millenarian themes, but only rarely did they generate new types of political ideology, as was the case, for instance, in the Yellow Turban rebellion in China. The use of the symbolism of rice—which, as Emiko Ohnuki-Tierney has recently shown, was indeed taken up seriously in the *ikki* rebellions—is indicative of these tendencies:

> The world they envisioned and hoped for emphasized a low price for rice and an abundant rice crop; their songs and dances often derived from harvest songs and dances. . . .
>
>   . . . The utopian vision portrayed in the rebellions and millenarian movements testifies to the acute shortage of food, especially rice. It is highly significant that the people who participated in these movements not

only upheld the symbolic importance of rice but, in fact, intensified it by using symbols made from the rice plant, rather than challenging or subverting the cosmology based on rice agriculture.[19]

Thus indeed the political themes and activities generated by various Buddhist groups, with the partial exception of Nichiren, did not involve any attempts at the transformation of the basic premises of the Japanese political order. The major new sectarian orientations, most clearly manifest in the Pure Land sect, were in principle directed toward the perfection of the individual, seemingly without the development of any new political premises. This led to political passivity or withdrawal, or to participation in the political struggle according to the prevailing rules, imbued at most with highly moralistic and millenarian dimensions. In Nichiren's case some more active political overtures, beyond simple struggle for power, could indeed be identified, but significantly these were also basically contained within the framework of the prevalent premises of the political order, which they undertook to purify and strengthen.[20]

IX Thus the common denominator of the institutional or organizational transformation of Confucianism and Buddhism in Japan was the farreaching de-autonomization of their respective organizations and activities and their becoming embedded within existing social frameworks. Moreover, Japanese Buddhism was characterized by the relative weakness or total absence of distance and autonomy from the authorities and other social and political groups; such relative distance and autonomy were characteristic of most Buddhist groups and sects in mainland Asia, with the exception of the theocratic regimes in Tibet and to some extent in Mongolia. In the latter cases, however, it was the Buddhist groups that were the dominant partners in the ruling coalitions.

All these tendencies to familism and to the blurring of the lines between monks and laity also developed in Buddhist communities on the Asian mainland—in China and Southeast Asia—especially after the "civilizational" dimensions of Buddhism were weakened around the eleventh century. But their development there differed, in overall impact as well as in significant details, from the Japanese case. In most of these other Buddhist communities such tendencies were usually manifest in the emphasis on genealogical relations to some founding father or great figures. Indeed, as Bechert and Gombrich have shown, what have often been designated as Buddhist sects were in most Asian countries groups focused on monastic (not familial) lineages;[21] given the relatively sharp distinction between monks and laymen and the preponderance of celibacy among the monks, temples could not easily, as they did in Japan, develop into familial estates.

Lay Buddhist groups also developed in China, and even more so in Tibet, where the creation of a Buddhist theocratic state gave rise to a basic redefinition of laity. But the major difference between all these (with the partial exception of Tibet) and the Japanese case was that they were viewed by the more orthodox, or by the self-proclaimed guardians of orthodoxy, such as the kings in Southeast Asia—Burma, Thailand and especially Sri Lanka—as deviations from the true doctrine. Furthermore, they would often try to reform the Buddhist establishment. This was not the case in Japan, where the familistic tendencies and the blurring of the distinction between monks and laity became the hegemonic mold, and where the would-be reformers had to enclose themselves within monastic enclaves.

X Parallel to the organizational development of Buddhism in Japan were changes in its religious, ideological, and philosophical orientation—transformations which also had a far-reaching impact on conceptions of the national collectivity, of authority, and of the legitimation of the political system.

The word "transformation" may seem to some extent to be too strong here, as in many ways the Japanese Buddhist sects continued the teachings and practices of the various Indian Mahayana sects from which they originated. But whereas in India, and especially later on in China, such Buddhist sects were only some among many and had to contest with other, more hegemonic sects, in Japan it was these orientations, borne by relatively powerful organizations, that became hegemonic. The discourse with which Mahayana sects elsewhere confronted the more canonical Buddhist orthodoxy became in Japan the almost undisputed hegemonical mode.

These transformations took place against the backdrop of Buddhism's close association with magic and its special sort of syncretization with Shinto (in which again some similarity with Indian Mahayana orientations and practices, especially the tantric ones, can be discerned)—in the context, that is, of what Joseph Kitagawa has called the Ritsuryō synthesis:

> What happened in Japan during the fifth and sixth centuries was the coming together of several—rather than only two—semi-independent traditions, none of which was a fully self-sufficient, comprehensive system, for example the indigenous "animistic" (for lack of a better word) beliefs and practices inherited by a number of semiautonomous *uji* (lineage groups), which in part informed the later government-sponsored Shinto; semi-established shamanistic traditions; strong streaks of Confucian, Taoist, Yin-Yang, and other Chinese-inspired systems; and the newly

introduced Buddhism, which also penetrated Japan together with Sino-Korean civilization. All these semi-independent traditions, systems, and schools were influenced by others while modifying others simultaneously, as constituent elements of Japan's first self-conscious religious-cultural-social-political synthesis, the seventh-century Ritsuryō (imperial rescript) system, an immanental theocratic state, in which the sovereign functioned simultaneously as the living *kami*, the reigning monarch, and the chief priest.[22]

It was against the general background of this symbiotic synthesis that the major tendencies to the immanentization of the transcendental components or orientations of classical Buddhism and of the particularization of its universalistic ones developed in Japanese Buddhism.

The major manifestation of these tendencies in the realm of religious belief or doctrine was to be found in the emphasis on the shortening of the way to salvation, and on the potential openness of the access to salvation—to the realm of the sacred—to everybody. In the realm of religious-philosophical discourse, this tendency was evident in the weakening or even denial of the logocentric characteristics of classical Buddhist discourse in favor of what Thomas Kasulis felicitously described as "philosophizing in the archaic."[23] With respect to conceptions of authority and the definition of the national collectivity, it was manifest in the minimization of the emphasis on the accountability of rulers and of the collectivity to a universalistic vision grounded in transcendental conceptions. Let us now explicate these general statements.

XI   In the arena of religious belief, practice, and discourse, the immanentization of Buddhism was manifest above all in the growing emphasis on faith and on personal enlightenment, as against the combination of contemplation, study of the proper texts (even if the sects disagreed as to which texts), and adherence to the precepts of behavior and discipline regarded as appropriate for monks and laymen (as promulgated by the various texts), that was characteristic of most mainland Asian Buddhism, especially in Theravada Buddhist countries, but to a large extent also in China and Korea.

This tendency, once again closely related to Mahayana (especially Indian) and tantric traditions, can be identified throughout the history of Japanese Buddhism. It had already appeared early on when, for instance, Heian "theology" criticized Chinese thought for its preference for "principle" (*li*), or theory, over "phenomena" (*shih*), or practice. This critique became a theoretical justification for Japanese preference for ritual over reason. An immanentist tendency could also be seen in the great popularity and influence of Indian tantra and the development of the so-called original enlightenment doctrine (*hongaku*), both of which emphasize the absolute value of the phenomenal world and the ethic of ritual expression (rather than transcendental knowledge) of the absolute. Mark Wheeler MacWilliams identifies this tendency in the very early model of indigenization of Buddhism in Japan, as shown, for instance, in his analysis of the Kannon *engi*.

> One major chrono-topical way of configuring the divine/human *do ut des* relationship in Kannon *engi* is to show how, throughout the Kannon temple's history, the locale is venerated as a *yuen no chi* where everyman can come to make karmic causal contact (*kechien*) with that divinity. With a topographical karmic strategy such as this, the Kannon cult was able to localize itself within the particularistic *kami* cult centers of the preexisting system, entering into "communication" and "association" with it.[24]

This tendency to immanentization, with its implied incipient this-worldliness, is also to be found, from the early Heian period on, in Saichō's as well as Kūkai's concern with the rapid realization of enlightenment, a concern which had already been a matter of debate in early China. The debate about sudden, as against gradual, attainment of enlightenment was also taken up by the Zen school. Similarly both Kūkai and Saichō taught, at least partly, Tantric Buddhism, which was becoming important at that time in India and which was concerned with the rapid realization of enlightenment and did not neglect mundane matters.[25]

XII The immanentist transformation of Buddhism in Japan became even more evident—in a way that may seem paradoxical given the tendency toward transcendental and inner-worldly orientations that developed concurrently—in some of the basic characteristics of Buddhist sects or schools, especially as they developed in the Kamakura period. It was in this period, as we have seen, that Buddhism was transformed from a mainly, if not exclusively, aristocratic religion with strong connections to the ruling sector into a series of sects or schools oriented toward broader sectors of the population. This was tantamount to a rebellion against the earlier religions and institutional character of Buddhism, and it denoted in principle a more inner-worldly, transcendental orientation. This orientation complicated, but did not obviate, the basic immanentist ideological transformation.

The immanentization of Buddhism's transcendental orientations was especially evident, as has already been noted, in an emphasis on shortening the path to salvation through direct access to the Buddha or to a Buddha-like state. Such access could be attained either through direct personal enlightenment, often achieved through a personal relation to the leading figure of the appropriate school, or by the practice of appropriate rituals, as opposed to continuous disciplined contemplation and behavior and the exposition of classical texts. This faith could easily become focused—as is also the case in many of the contemporary "new religions"—on one person, teacher, or exemplary figure, who would thus become semisacred. Here again, in contrast to the situation in Southeast Asia and China—and to a lesser extent India—such conceptions of personal relations with the Buddha were embedded in a concrete social nexus, in groupism, closely connected to the tendencies to hereditary transmission of leadership roles. The emphasis on direct contemplation and faith and on performance of rituals reoriented the practices of many Buddhist sects in rather this-worldly directions, promising shortcuts to salvation and conflating such salvation with mundane, daily reality.

Most of these sects (especially the Pure Land and some of the Zen schools) emphasized salvation through faith over discipline and enlightenment. The doctrines and teachings of the Pure Land sect were, in principle, oriented to the perfection of the individual, often attained through an emphasis on ritual:

> One of the most fundamental doctrinal problems in Pure Land Buddhism was whether the nembutsu—the calling upon Amida to be saved—should be recited once or many times and the same applies to the lotus equivalent of the Nichiren schools. [This could perhaps be formulated in Christian, especially Protestant, terms: *nembutsu* is salvation and faith; repetition of its name turns it into "works."]
>
> . . . It was Hōnen's disciple, Shinran (1173–1262) who finally resolved this problem by asserting that Amida promised salvation unconditionally to all who sincerely called upon him once, whether or not they actually pronounced the nembutsu aloud.[26]

XIII A similar tendency to redirect Buddhism toward an immanentist orientation emphasizing this-worldly possibilities can be identified in some of the Zen schools in Japan, even though they have seemed to emphasize total detachment from the world. Dōgen, as well as many other Japanese Zen schools, emphasize "reflective nonthinking" and "action performs man"; the definition of "nonaction" as the major context defining personality in Japan, is one indicator of this immanentist tendency.[27] Some aspects of Zen soteriology, especially its teachings on faith and on the abandonment and commitment that flow from it as they were interpreted in Japan, also point in such directions.[28]

This immanentist, this-worldly tendency, which developed on the philosophical level, could also be interwoven with the emphasis on ritual that developed in the practice of many Buddhist sects or schools, including Zen. While the traditional emphasis on discipline was maintained, it was necessarily weakened by the shortening of the path to salvation. It is indeed with respect to the emphasis on ritual that the forms of devotion prevalent in Japan differ most from those of the various sects of mainland Buddhism. To quote Carl Bielefeldt's concluding remarks in his interpretation of *Dōgen's Manual of Zen Meditation:*

> The ancient "mind seal" (Shin'in) transmitted by the Buddhas and Patriarchs seems here to have become a seal (mudra) of a distinctly corporeal sort . . .
> . . . If the model for Zen practice here is still the enactment of enlightenment, it is no longer simply the psychological accord of the practitioner's consciousness with the eternally enlightened mind; it is now the physical reenactment by the practitioner of the deeds of the historical exemplars of enlightened behavior.[29]

XIV The concern with the possibility of sudden enlightenment, of subitism, as against a gradual process was of course not confined to Japanese Buddhism. It constituted a central problem and focus of discourse in Chinese, especially Ch'an, Buddhism. Indeed, as Peter N. Gregory has put it, "The sudden-gradual polarity not only reflects the uniquely Chinese historical circumstances in which Buddhism, and especially Ch'an, came to define itself in China, it gave also form to a preexistent tension within Chinese thought."[30] Such a polarity also developed in Tibet in the eighth century, where significantly enough the gradual approach was accepted and became hegemonic.

This discourse was conducted by various scholars, in China, India, and Japan, in highly sophisticated terms. At the same time the emphasis on the possibility of sudden direct enlightenment also served as a powerful means for popularizing Buddhism among wider sectors of the population—making it easier for them, as it were. Although such popularization seems, as we have already suggested, to have been quite widespread in mainland Asia, especially in some Mahayana and tantric traditions and above all in China, it was never fully accepted by the different schools there, and it never weakened, let alone obliterated, the distinction between monks and laymen. The situation in Japan seems to have been different. While the problem of sudden versus gradual constituted here also a focus of philosophical discourse, it was not as central as in China. But what especially distinguishes the Japanese scene is both the very wide spread of the more popular, seemingly "easy" ways of enlightenment and their acceptance by many (though certainly not all) of the leaders of the various sects. Such acceptance was also closely related to the blurring of boundaries between monks (who had been transformed, as we have seen, into priests) and laymen.[31]

XV These developments attest to the fact that at least in Zen, Buddhism in Japan was in many ways more creative than that in India and China, where it originated. Indeed, the tendencies to immanentization and to a more this-worldly emphasis extended beyond doctrinal matters and ritual practices to more general cultural orientations and themes with which Buddhism imbued the general Japanese cultural climate. They expressed themselves, among other things, in the sacralization of nature, especially, as A. Grappard has shown, of landscapes.[32] They can also be detected in the way in which the general tendency, prevalent in East Asian Buddhism, to invest nature with inherent religious value, became intensified in Japanese Buddhism, and in a way even transformed it. One forceful illustration of such tendency to the immanentization of values is to be found in the poetry of Saigyō (1118–1190), a Buddhist monk whose poetry, as W. R. La Fleur has shown,

> historically fixed a lasting nexus between Buddhism and nature in the popular consciousness of the Japanese people. . . .
> . . . For the phenomenal forms that are in complete realization of the truth are more than symbols of the way; for Saigyō they are the essence of the Truth itself. Contact with them is to be in the presence of the absolute. The things of nature became, in this attribution of value, not only mediators of Truth, but its very being.[33]

Such immanentist orientations, with a very strong affirmation of nature and of this-worldly attitudes, could also be identified in the attitudes toward sex in Japanese Buddhism. The problem of sexual activity and desires constituted a very important focus of religious discourse throughout most of the history of Buddhism. On the one hand there developed a puritanical-ascetic denial of sex; on the other many attempts to affirm sexual activity in terms of transcendent religious experience, even of detachment from the world. Such a discourse developed also in Japan. Significantly, there developed in Japanese Buddhist sects, even in various Zen schools, a much more direct affirmation of sex as a set of natural givens, together with a rather weak emphasis on its problematization in transcendent terms. This attitude was closely connected to the affirmation of married life for monks, which in its turn contributed to the blurring of the distinction between monks and laity.[34] In general the emphasis in Japanese Buddhism on rituals or "attainment through the body" attests to its strong this-worldly orientation.

Yet another illustration can be found in the mode of reception in Japan of one of the most widespread Buddhist cults, that of Maitreya, the future Buddha, which was transformed, as Helen Hardacre has shown, in a very earthly, millenarian direction—attesting to the strong indigenization of this cult.[35] A concomitant indication of the transformation of the Maitreya cult in Japan can be seen in the relatively quiet role played by Miroku—one of the Japanese designations of Maitreya—as compared to that of Milo (a Chinese designation) in rebellious movements, such as the White Lotus movement in China.

XVI   The tendency to this-worldliness and the immanentization of Buddhism (and later on of the so-called new religions) also explains one of the most puzzling aspects of the Japanese religious scene, namely, its tendency to syncretism and, above all, the nature of that syncretism. This tendency has been especially evident, as we have seen, in the relation between Buddhist and Shinto patterns of worship in the early and medieval periods, and Shinto, Buddhist, and Christian patterns in more modern times.

A central aspect of the syncretistic process was that no sharp demarcation of the symbolic boundaries of the religious collectivity (in this case of the Buddhist one, but the same could apply to Confucianism) and of the theological domain of doctrine developed. It is significant that this syncretistic tendency reasserted itself, above all but not only in many of the new religions, after the Second World War, that is, after the abolition of the violent post-Meiji "desyncretization." This fact provides the most important key for the understanding of the specific type of syncretism that developed in Japan.[36]

These syncretistic tendencies were often attributed to the relative openness of the "older" Shinto to Buddhism; Shinto's lack of any general or universal concepts has been presumed to make it susceptible to the "universalizing" principles or orientations of Buddhism.[37] This is not in principle very different from the presumed impact of "great" religions on various "pagan" and polytheistic ones, especially on various smaller traditions.[38] Nor is the adaptation of Buddhism to local circumstances, its de-Axialization, very surprising.[39] What is, however, unique in the case of Japan is that its pagan premises, a basically this-worldly religious outlook, have transformed those of a "great" religion in shaping the tradition of an entire civilization, bracketing out, though certainly not obliterating, its more transcendental or other-worldly premises. It was this relatively strong "de-theologization" of Buddhism, and the concomitant weakening of religious discourse, that constituted one of the foci of the process of transformation of Buddhism in Japan and of the syncretism that developed there.

This mode of transformation and the syncretism it entailed pertained to many concrete ritual practices, literary works, and works of art of Buddhist origin, which collectively seem to have superseded, or at least overwhelmed, Shinto tradition. Buddhism had greatly "aestheticized" these works and imbued them with a deeper spiritual dimension. But at the same time some of the Shinto templates, or native orientations, modeled the mode of reception of these Buddhist works, giving rise to a far-reaching transformation of the classical Buddhist premises.

The editors of a recent work on the impact of Buddhism on Japanese art[40] provide the following summary analysis of Japanese Buddhist conceptions of heaven and hell:

> [Barbara Ruch] demonstrates that for Japanese the understanding of the Buddhist *rokudō* (Six Realms) afterlife structure—especially its ideas of Heaven and Hell—became something other than the expression of an approved theological exegesis of formal Buddhism. She argues that while Japanese culture adopted the language of the scriptural understanding, the actual internalized interpretations of the *rokudō* structure departed considerably from orthodox norms; instead of seeing the six realms as a primarily vertical structure of highly compartmentalized cosmic realms, Japanese assimilated the *rokudō* schema into the old horizontal cosmologies of *yomi no kuni*, "the land of gloom," and *tokoyo no kuni*, "the land over there."
>
> In pressing for validity of this thesis, Ruch argues that a careful distinction must be made between self-consciously didactic literature whose expression of orthodox values may be largely conventional lip-service, and the less self-conscious—and therefore more telling—expressions found in what Ruch calls the "intimate" literature.[41]

Similarly they summarize, basing their argument on Royall Tyler's analysis of Buddhist influences on Nō, some of the enduring Shinto-Buddhist elements:

> The importance of numinous places (ubiquitous in Japanese religion), themes of nondualism, the intertwining of aspiration and "grace," transcendental worldliness, and a number of similar motifs are exposed as powerful lineaments of the Buddhism of Nō, a Buddhism that is syncretic, diffuse, more attitudinal than doctrinal, largely asectarian, and in most ways very close to the archaic values of pre-Buddhist Japan.[42]

In general the impact of Buddhism on the development of ritual and art in Japan provides some very interesting illustrations of the double-pronged development of Buddhism in Japan. As Michele Marra has shown, Buddhist monks spiritualized many Shinto cults—especially cults of purification—adding to them a new spiritual and reflexive dimension. But at the same time the emphases of the Shinto cults greatly immanentized these rituals, minimizing or bracketing out the more transcendental Buddhist orientations.

Structurally the Buddhist temples organized and took in various marginal elements—vagabonds, thieves, courtesans—who served as mediating figures in many rituals of purification. By organizing these people, the temples institutionalized or domesticated whatever liminal and subversive potentials they had. Such institutionalization—which was, of course, very convenient for the powers that be—could also be found in many of the more refined arts, as for instance in Nō plays, in which potentially subversive themes became aestheticized and embedded in existing "hegemonic" institutions. In all these ways the potentially radical and subversive themes contained in many Buddhist works of art were politically neutralized—"aesthetized" and privatized, as it were—to a higher degree than in many other Buddhist countries.[43] The same is true of the transformation of Taoism in Japan.[44]

XVII All these tendencies attest to a paradoxical situation in the development and transformation of Japanese Buddhism, especially after the Kamakura period. First, there developed within these sects strong transcendental, other-worldly, inward orientations; one might have doubts, such as those raised by La Fleur, about the attractiveness of Buddhist universalistic tendencies in Japan,[45] but there can be no doubt that the widespread reception of Buddhism in Japan gave rise to a deepening and diversification of religious consciousness and discourse. This deepening was usually connected with an emphasis on inner experience and an apparent move from more "canonical" interpretations to a "semi-Protestant" position, giving rise, in the words of R. N. Bellah, to "moments of transcendence."[46] At the same time there developed a strong this-worldly, immanentist orientation that hemmed in such fleeting transcendental moments and became predominant on the ground. Such "hemming in" was also manifested in the privatization of the potentially politically radical dimensions of transcendence. Thus, while the reinterpretations of many aspects of Buddhist doctrine and practice that developed in this period can be seen to emphasize "inner," transcendental experience, they could, and did, also easily move in a more immanentist, this-worldly direction. This is of crucial importance to our analysis.

The overall tendency to immanentization in Japanese Buddhism minimized the emphasis, found both in many mainland Buddhist orientations and later in European Protestantism (to which Kamakura Buddhism is often compared), on the gap between the transcendental and the mundane and the assertion that this gap cannot be easily bridged—certainly not by ritual activities. Thus, while in the more "catholic" Buddhism of mainland Asia the attempts to jump this gap usually started from the top (that is, with the transcendental realm descending toward the mundane world), attempts at closing this gap in Japan usually went from the bottom to the top—in a sense taking the mundane into the transcendental, thus further facilitating the immanentization of the transcendentalist orientations.

The tendency toward immanentization was also reinforced by the fact that, although the development of Kamakura Buddhism constituted a reaction against the overritualized tantra and hongaku of the Heian, the emphasis of the reformers (in Pure Land, Nichiren, and Zen) was, as we have seen, on self-transcendence through submission to a master, lineage, tradition, community, temple, or ritual form.[47] Yet the development of such this-worldly orientations did not necessarily obliterate the new transcendental consciousness and orientations. Buddhist priests and sages never gave up the basic other-worldly and transcendental premises of Buddhism. What took place was rather a process of selection and interpretation of Buddhist themes, especially as promulgated to wider audiences; religious practices tended to move in directions that lent themselves to this-worldly interpretation more readily than did similar practices generated in many of the Mahayana sects. Transcendental orientations were continuously bracketed out of large parts of daily religious practice, and removed to the more private or "esoteric" arenas of philosophical speculation.[48] Concomitantly, symbols and interpretations with stronger immanentist emphasis were continuously selected from within the Buddhist repertoire.[49]

XVIII   Collectively these developments distinguish the so-called Kamakura Buddhist Reformation from the Protestant Reformation in Europe. As has often been noted, the two reformations shared many characteristics, above all the emphasis on direct unmediated relation to the sacred and the minimization, and sometime total denial, of the importance of canonical worship as vested in the hands of divinely ordained mediators. No doubt the orientations that developed in the various Kamakura schools were markedly transcendental, stressing individual inner experience in ways reminiscent of the Protestant Reformation. Yet, as James Foard has suggested, the differences from the Protestant case are equally evident and probably more significant.[50]

In particular, the emphasis on self-transcendence through submission to a master, community, or the like has no counterpart in Protestantism. It minimized the emphasis prominent within Protestant sects, on the immediate access of all members of the community to the sacred. Moreover, no autonomous lay religious organizations or leadership capable of transcending the existing social nexus developed, as in Kamakura Buddhism.

This strong this-worldly orientation may help to explain why Buddhism in Japan was more conductive, as Nakamura Hajime has suggested, to the development of mundane, including economic, activities than was the case in mainland Asia.[51] But, again contrary to the example of the Protestant Reformation, these developments did not entail a reevaluation of the economic area as an arena of salvation or the implementation of a strong transcendental vision. Thus, no new types of economic motivation, modes of economic rationalization, or types of political economy developed in conjunction with these this-worldly orientations.

XIX The tendencies toward the immanentization of the transcendental orientations of Buddhism and the de-autonomization of its social organization did not, of course, detract from the far-reaching impact of Buddhism—and later of Confucianism—on the general cultural and spiritual climate of Japan. However much Buddhist organizations became embedded in the existing—usually hierarchical—feudal structures, the very permeation of Buddhism and Confucianism into wide sectors of Japanese society imbued these sectors with the ethos of equality and community—even if this ethos did not give rise to a transformation of the political and organizational settings in the way Buddhism and Confucianism did in mainland Asian settings.

Similarly, Buddhism generated spaces in which cultural activities containing themes and orientations subversive of the existing order could develop. The most striking illustration is probably the way in which Buddhist themes were infused into some of the masterpieces of Japanese literature—among others, the *Taketori monogatari*, the *Ise monogatari*, the code of *miyabi* (courtliness), Yoshida Kenkō's "Essays in Idleness" (the *Tsurezuregusa*), and Bashō's poetry—in a way that entailed a strong element of political criticism.[52]

In all these works new cultural spaces and themes, distinct from the center of power, were created in which a new type of aesthetic and moral sensibility could be generated. This sensibility entailed, as Michele Marra has shown, the creation of an "aesthetics of seclusion," basically a depoliticized aesthetics, leading, as in the "Essays in Idleness," in a highly utopian, restorative direction, creating the vision of an imaginary pure court, uncorrupted by history or power, curiously reminiscent of some of the images found in the aesthetics of techno-ideology (i.e., an ideology emphasizing the purity of technological arrangements). Thus while many of these works of art presented critical and subversive themes, their aestheticization, or privatization, effectively neutralized any political potential.[53]

All these developments illustrate the double-pronged transformation of

Buddhism in Japan. On the one hand, it was increasingly domesticated—its transcendental orientations immanentized and its social structure made less autonomous. On the other hand, the transcendental orientations were channeled into special niches, in which innovative types of cultural creativity with new spiritual dimensions and new types of social consciousness and themes were made available to broader sectors of society. These developments were *potentially* subversive of the hegemonic premises without *directly* challenging or threatening to transform them.

XX Such double-pronged developments also took place in the religious and philosophical discourse that developed in Japanese Buddhism, and even more so in Confucianism. The tendency to immanentization in this discourse was evident in the transformation of the logocentric nature of classical Buddhist discourse, with its emphasis on proper understanding and interpretation of canonical texts, in the direction, to use Thomas Kasulis's felicitous phrase, of "philosophizing in the archaic."[54]

Concern with exposition of the proper doctrines was indeed central to Japanese Buddhism, as it was to other branches, and this concern was reinforced by the tradition of disputation, which was also imported from China. The exposition of dogma constituted a key function of the sect leaders, but the mode of this discourse differed greatly from the classical Buddhist logocentric one, especially in so far as it went beyond the restricted scholarly arena and became concerned with the promulgation of basic ontological conceptions and more popular exposition, thus moving in the direction of "philosophizing in the archaic." The core of this discursive practice was the emphasis on the centrality of mythic, nondiscursive components or premises—as against logocentric ones—in its ontological conceptions and on the centrality of indexical nonlinear modes of structuring discourse.

Contrary to their role in, for instance, Confucianist China, Buddhist India, or the monotheistic civilizations, myths and mythological exposition served in Japan not only as starting points but also, and above all, as the ultimate legitimation of the philosophical and aesthetic discourse. Such discourse was not seen as moving away from the mythological, as subsuming the mythological under a discursive canopy. On the contrary discourse was taken, as it were, under a canopy of "mythological," nondiscursive tenets and ontological conceptions. It is this subsumption that constitutes one of the most important manifestations of the "Japanization" of Buddhism and Confucianism, especially in the neo-Confucianism and nativistic discourses of the Tokugawa period.[55]

These conceptions of ontological reality and the weakness of a logocentric orientation have been, as Nakamura Hajime has shown, closely connected with the specific semiotic structuring of discourse, as well as of modes of thought that have been prevalent in Japanese society.[56]

XXI The tendency to immanentization in the exposition of Buddhist doctrine, practice, sensibility, and discourse can of course also be found in mainland Asia, in India and in China, yet its cumulative effect seems to have been much greater in Japan. In China, Korea, and Vietnam, however, this tendency never attained the hegemonic standing that it enjoyed in Japan, and whatever its significance in the high (as distinct from the more popular) manifestations of Buddhism, it was hemmed in by the more transcendental orientations—or at least held in constant tension with them. In Japan, however, the transformations that resulted from this tendency became predominant, providing the major, hegemonic framework of Japanese Buddhist discourse. Within this framework many classical modes of Buddhist discourse developed and flourished—but on a secondary level.

The difference between, on the one hand, the hemming in of the more immanentist orientations of Buddhism in mainland Asia and, on the other hand, the immanentization of the transcendental ones in Japan can be seen, for instance, in the way the attitude to space and place in the Chinese Ch'an Buddhist tradition differed from that in the parallel Japanese tradition.[57] Many Ch'an masters struggled, not always with success, against the more popular interpretations of or attitudes to space and time, the tendency to the sacralization of space or the mediation of the sacred through space. Such interpretations, however, became the predominant mode in Japan.

In Japan the *Aufhebung* of the mundane space into the transcendental was emphasized. The same seems to be true of various tendencies to bring the Buddha down to earth, in the genre of recorded sayings that developed in China and in Japan.[58]

XXII The specific developments and transformations of Japanese Buddhism have also influenced the ways in which major cultural and religious roles were constructed in Japan. Perhaps the central transformation was that of the Buddhist monks, implicitly assumed to be at a distance from the laity, into priests who served the laity directly. This transformation went so far in Japan, especially after the Kamakura period, as to blur the ideological, and even to some degree the organizational, distinction between priesthood and laity.

Similarly, the semiprophetic components of Buddhism became transformed into the role of the "seer," as illustrated, for instance, by the famous poet Bashō. This transformation is evident when the seer is compared with the prophets of monotheistic religion, on the one hand, and the Romantic poets, on the other. Some similarities clearly suggest themselves, but the differences, as analyzed by La Fleur, are even more revealing:

> It is clear that in some important sense the poet is to receive and revive religious functions from an archaic past.
>
> . . . Therefore, even when these millenarian expectations were disappointed, "Romantic thinking and imagination remained apocalyptic thinking and imagination, though with varied changes in explicit content." . . .
>
> The role of the Buddhist seer, by comparison, is less related to the events of a specific epoch. In the case of Gyōhi clairvoyance was thought to extend into the past so as to see the natural things near at hand and before our own eyes. Being attached to "the world" leads to such occlusion of the eye and mind.[59]

XXIII   A parallel double-pronged transformation developed within the ideological, political, and philosophical discourse of Japanese Confucianism—especially neo-Confucianism, which flourished in Japan under the Tokugawa. Here also the major trend was in the immanentist and particularistic direction, but at the same time there developed new spaces of cultural creativity and new modes of discourse. One of the most important indications of this tendency in the highly sophisticated discourse that developed in Japanese neo-Confucianism was the minimization, weakening, or bracketing out of the transcendental orientations that existed in classical Confucianism, especially the emphasis on the distinction between the realm of the transcendental and that of nature. Instead there developed a strong move in the immanentist direction, in which nature was given a more autonomous standing, sometimes even in sacral terms, and accordingly had to be taken on its own terms.

These developments were part of the intensive intellectual discourse that developed during the Tokugawa regime, and to which we have already referred. In this discourse's first period, until the end of the seventeenth century, its major contours crystallized, bringing together neo-Confucian, Buddhist, and nativistic Shinto themes. The second stage, in the eighteenth century, took place with the growth of urban population and was characterized by greater popular interest and by a growing split between neo-Confucianism and nativistic schools that contributed greatly to the intellectual ferment that developed in many sectors of Tokugawa society. This ferment spilled over into the last phase, which developed in the late eighteenth and the nineteenth centuries. This last phase was much more directly connected with social and economic upheavals and with various protest movements.[60]

The problems the discourse addressed were, as we have seen, those posed by the constitution of Tokugawa rule and society, particularly the problems of the legitimation of the regime and of the interpretation of the collective national identity—especially in relation to the Sinocentric civilization and order.[61] The answers to these problems, as well as to more purely philosophical ones, were shaped by premises that differed greatly from the original Confucian or neo-Confucian ones, above all by the underlying nativist orientations of the Shinto templates. These orientations directed the construction both of the legitimation of the regime and the collective Japanese identity in terms that minimized the transcendental and universalistic components of classical Chinese Confucianism. They also minimized the logocentric aspects of the discourse; the logocentric tendency of Confucianism and especially of neo-Confucianism went in many ways against the grain of the more mythocentric, nondiscursive orientations, seemingly rooted in the "archaic" Japanese culture, that were prevalent among many Japanese intellectuals and throughout much of Japanese society.

Such mythocentric tendencies could be identified already in earlier periods of Japanese intellectual history—beginning probably with Kūkai, the great religious teacher of the eighth and ninth century. As Thomas P. Kasulis has shown, "Kūkai philosophized in the archaic. . . . He sought to give the archaic a philosophical expression and participation, . . . thus giving rise to Japanese philosophy which developed in the context of justifying rather than overpowering the archaic world view."[62] The tendency to "philosophize in the archaic" was prevalent throughout most of Japanese history, but only in the Tokugawa period did it become both widespread and consciously ideological—no longer confined to small sects of cognoscenti, but promulgated by many scholars and teachers who reached out to wider publics in schools and academies.[63]

In the first phase of Tokugawa discourse, the logocentric tendencies inherent in neo-Confucianism did find some autonomous space—but even then they were hemmed in by the more central, mythocentric, Shintoistic tendencies. In the eighteenth century an open rift took place between the nativists and the neo-Confucians, with the nativist ideology, or confrontation, promulgated by such scholars as Keichū, Kada No Azumamaro, Kamo No Mabuchi, and, probably the most famous, Motoori Norinaga.[64] The development of the nativistic school took place against the backdrop of the ideological symbiosis that characterized the earlier stage of Tokugawa ideological discourse. In this symbiosis the Confucian discourse was, as we have seen, redirected to the problems of legitimating the Tokugawa regime and the Japanese collectivity, which was often portrayed as the purest bearer of the pristine human values promulgated by Confucianism. The nativist scholars, especially Motoori

Norinaga, basically turned the tables on this attitude. They extolled the uniqueness of the Japanese way, its distinctiveness, ultimately rooted in some quasi-genetic qualities of the Japanese people. This emphasis on the uniqueness of the ancient Japanese way became connected with the negation of other ways, "especially of the Chinese way, leading to the assertion that this pristine Japanese way was corrupted by the intrusion from the outside of Confucianism—and of 'book learning.'" [65]

This ideological turn entailed a *principled* negation—stated, paradoxically, in terms derived from logocentric discourse—of the strong logocentricity of classical Confucianism and Buddhism. [66] The nativist school spawned widespread and intensive scholarly activity—above all philological activity, directed to the study of the classical Japanese Shinto texts, such as the *Kojiki*, and of the great literary classic *Tale of Genji*. The aim was to distill from these texts the pure Japanese essence and meaning, as against the polluted meaning of the external philosophical discourse. It thus superimposed the orientation to the archaic myth with the nondiscursive approach as the major foci of scholarship and of philosophical and philological—indeed textual—inquiry.

There was, however, a highly paradoxical element in this process, namely, as Kate Wildman Nakai has put it (private communication), "that some of the key Confucian figures who incorporate what they term Shinto (like Yamazaki Ansai) and many kokugaku scholars, are fascinated with the mystique of the word, and much of the exegesis of their position is done through philological analysis of the *Kojiki* and *Nihon shoki*."

XXIV It was within the framework of this discourse that the transformation of neo-Confucian discourse took place in the Tokugawa period. One of the most important tendencies in the development of Japanese Confucianism was a rather strong devaluation of the major motifs of Mencius, a Confucian thinker who emphasized the metaphysical dimensions or orientations—a devaluation that indeed greatly facilitated the move in an immanentist direction.

The most important respect in which neo-Confucian thought was transformed in Japan was through the attempt to dissociate its discourse from the metaphysical, transcendental orientation of classical neo-Confucianism—to "materialize" and immanentize it. This tendency was closely related to the transformation of the conception of man and to the strong tendency to emphasize the naturalness and autonomy of politics, aesthetics, art, and poetry.

The most encompassing transformation of the basic tenets of Japanese neo-Confucianism took place with respect to the conception of the principle of *li* as an ultimate reality that encompasses both the transcendental and the sociopolitical realm. This conception was rooted in a dualistic conception of the world, in which the transcendental and the mundane are distinct entities or realms which can be unified only through the metaphysical conception of the *li*: "Such 'desynthesization' of Confucianism called for a theoretical re-definition and reduction as to what 'remained.'"[67] Here there developed different solutions, all of which entailed a concern "with providing a theoretical underpinning for an action ethic—*jissen rinri*—that would lead to saving other people—kyūmin, saimin—in the actual world of existence. In other words, what kind of action might be undeniably 'truthful.' This is the problem of *makoto* that permeated eighteenth century Tokugawa thought."[68]

The tendency to immanentization and particularization can already be identified in the work of Hayashi Razan, who tried, as Watanabe Hiroshi has shown, to explain neo-Confucian concepts in accord with Shintoist theology.[69] A later illustration of this tendency can be found in the work of Kaibara Ekken, one of the most prominent neo-Confucians of the late seventeenth and early eighteenth centuries. The principled philosophical implications of Ekken's transformation of classical neo-Confucianism have been aptly analyzed by Tetsuo Najita:

> Whereas Neo-Confucianism proceeded from distinctions based on dualism to a unified and integrated view of ultimate reality, Kaibara started with a unified view of physical reality to suggest necessary distinctions in different spheres of knowledge. In short, he replaced dualism with monism as the principle conceptual apparatus with which to work.[70]

Mary E. Tucker has elaborated on this aspect of Ekken's thought.[71] In her analysis of Japanese neo-Confucianism she writes:

> Ekken did not want to articulate his cosmology from a dualistic metaphysical basis. He wished to avoid a bifurcation in which a transcendent principle (*li*) was regarded as prior and superior to an immanent force which was both matter and energy (*ch'i*). In doing so, Ekken affirmed the absolute, or the origin of life, as existing within the phenomenal order rather than separate from it.[72]

Here a comparison with the development of neo-Confucianism in Korea can be, as Park Choong-seok has shown, very informative:

> Chason Chu Hsi-ism [the Korea development of neo-Confucianism] was mainly inclined towards universalist norms and traditions, while Tokugawa Chu-Hsi philosophy centered around objective aspects—a trend that was not limited to the Chu Hsi school—with emphasis upon particularism, situationalism and realism.[73]

Within this context of the desynthesization of Confucianism, most Japanese thinkers moved in a direction that emphasized the relative autonomy of different spheres of human activity—politics, art, aesthetics, and the like—and a basically commonsense, almost materialist character to these various aspects of social and cultural life and creativity.

One of the most forceful exponents of this conception was Motoori Norinaga, who stressed the autonomy of aesthetics, of art, and of poetry—liberating them as it were from the constraints of the Confucian metaphysical-transcendental conception. Art and poetry were seen as legitimate for their own sake, for the sake of natural enjoyment, and not just as ideological means for the cultivation of the mind and of moral character. This liberation from metaphysics of the major arenas of life had, first of all, far-reaching repercussions for the conception of the nature of man—a philosophical transformation that also had important political implications.

The autonomization of different spheres of human activity could move, from the point of view of moral and political implications, in two different, almost opposing directions—which nonetheless shared strongly immanentist orientation, and both ran contrary to the classical conceptions of (Chinese) neo-Confucianism, rooted in a metaphysical transcendental vision of innate human goodness and of the need to cultivate this goodness through rites and learning. One such direction, best represented by Ogyū Sorai, denied the (neo-)Confucian conception of the inherent goodness of human nature and its emphasis on the individual as the primary unit, instead emphasizing the sociability of human beings and positing a social-totalistic view of social order.

This social-totalistic view of social order was opposed by a new, natural egalitarian humanism and utopianism, best represented by Andō Shōeki.[74]

> The contrast here between Shōeki and Sorai is striking. For Sorai, little human virtues are realized from within the individual, but the conditions for this realization are provided by mediating political constructs dedicated to human nourishment—yashinai no michi. Shōeki rejected such a theory of "nourishment" as discriminatory interference from above, the source of exploitation of the natural work of the populace. In his insistence that there is no hierarchic priority in nature beyond "oneself doing," Shōeki theorized an egalitarian philosophy of existence devoid of elites providing "nourishment" for the people. Without the exploitation from above that is endemic to hierarchic systems, the people would nourish themselves through the fruits of their own natural labor.[75]

XXV   This transformation of the conception of the innate nature of man, when combined with the tendency to see various arenas of life as autonomous or dissociated from the overarching metaphysical vision, had also far-reaching implications for political discourse:

In this process of erosion, discordance and contradiction supplanted harmony as a central assumption about the nature of reality; the needs of particular history and of society replaced ideology and the Sino-centric conviction in universal history; and politics assumed primacy over the belief in a constancy of ethics.[76]

Indeed Ogyū Sorai was one of the most important exponents of the principle of the autonomy of the political arena in Japanese neo-Confucianism. Maruyama Masao presented him in his classical exposition of Tokugawa thought as the Japanese Machiavelli. Maruyama's interpretation of Sorai has been challenged by, among others, Tetsuo Najita and Harry Harootunian, both of whom claimed, though in different veins, that Sorai's ultimate conception of society was indeed informed by a strong moral vision.[77]

Significantly, however, these correctives to Maruyama's classical exposition of Sorai point to major differences of Japanese conceptions from those of both classical neo-Confucianism and Western thought. These "modern" Japanese conceptions differed from Western ones in that they denied or at least minimized the continuous tension between the transcendental and the mundane orders. The emphasis on the autonomy and naturalness of the various arenas of human endeavor, did not imply, as in the West, a continuous confrontation with a transcendental vision. Hence Sorai's conception of politics as natural differed from that of Machiavelli; it could easily be encompassed in a broader moral, historical vision, as Najita has indicated—a basically immanentist vision, however, which could be combined with a very pessimistic view of human nature. It could also easily be combined with an overall communal, natural vision which—contrary to that of Machiavelli and to much of Western, Islamic, and Chinese thought—did not allow for individual autonomy rooted in strong conceptions of basic transcendental orders. Indeed as Yui Kiyomitsu has recently shown, Sorai's emphasis on the naturalness of politics had distinct technocratic-totalitarian overtones.[78]

Against this view, a radically critical, egalitarian, communal, antistatist orientation with strong utopian components, as espoused by Andō Shōeki, proved to be very forceful and generated new levels of critical social consciousness, but it did not lead to direct political action. This view was in many ways diametrically opposed to those promulgated by Sorai and the nationalistic thinkers. Potentially very subversive of the existing and emerging hegemonic themes, it would reappear in different veins in many sectors of Japanese society. It shared, however, with Sorai and the nativists the denial of transcendental principles beyond nature—and this had, as we shall see later, some important repercussions for the impact of these oppositionary views or themes.[79]

In this sense both tendencies differed greatly from the parallel developments in the West—whether in the thought of Machiavelli or of the Romantics, all of whom took the predominance of a strong transcendental vision as given and continuously confronted this vision. Hence these transformations, which implied an erosion of the original transcendental neo-Confucian orientations, tended to minimize the politically—at least potentially—activist, radical, and critical tendencies implicit in transcendental orientations that went beyond the existing order.

All these transformations did not mean that the transcendental and universalistic orientations inherent in classical Confucianism, and especially in classical neo-Confucianism, disappeared in Japan—or that Confucianism only had a shallow impact on Japanese society, merely reinforcing prevalent ontological conceptions and conceptions of the social order. Rather, the transformation and impact of Confucianism developed, as was the case in Buddhism, in a double-pronged manner. On the one hand, there developed a strong tendency toward the immanentization of the transcendental premises of classical Confucianism and the particularization of the universalistic ones. But on the other hand, the very process of Japanization gave rise to new spaces in which new modes of discourse, of collective consciousness, developed, and to the consequent bracketing of the transcendental and universalistic orientations into specific, relatively segregated arenas.

XXVI It is probably with respect to the conception of the national collectivity and its relation to the broader Buddhist or Confucian civilization—as well as to conceptions of authority, especially imperial authority and its legitimation—that the ideological transformation of Buddhism and Confucianism is most fully manifest.

The challenge of defining the Japanese collectivity, especially in relation to other collectivities and broader civilizational frameworks, has loomed large whenever Japan has felt the impact of outside religions or civilizations—in response to Confucianism and Buddhism in the eighth century, to neo-Confucianism in the Tokugawa period, and to Western ideologies in the late Tokugawa, modern, and contemporary eras. In these contexts two central, closely interconnected problems arose. One concerned the extent to which universalistic orientations inherent in classical Confucianism, and especially in neo-Confucianism ontology, could be incorporated as components of the definition of Japanese collectivity. The other was the question of how the relations of the Japanese collectivity to the broader, external civilization would be conceptualized.

Here yet again a double-pronged development took place. Confucianism, like Buddhism, had a powerful impact on the definition of the Japanese community and on the formulation of the premises of authority. Its

redefinitions of the national polity and reformulations of the basis of social and political legitimacy did not, however, change the basic conceptions either of the Japanese collectivity as a primordial, sacral community
or of sacral kingship and authority. Rather, Confucianism and Buddhism
cast their formulations in these very sacral-primordial or natural terms,
if anything, strengthening them. Buddhist and Confucian discourses in
fact imbued these definitions, especially the emphasis on commitment to
the center—on loyalty to one's lord, hierarchy, and group solidarity—
with strong moral and metaphysical dimensions. Nonetheless, they went
far beyond what were probably these definitions' and symbols' original
formulations, reconstructed them in a highly reflexive way, and generated new types of discourse and collective consciousness.

XXVII Japan's first encounter with Buddhism transformed the older sacred kingship into a particularistic, sacral, liturgical community rooted in
the older Shinto conceptions, and all subsequent reformulations of the
nature of this community have only strengthened this core conception.
This conception of collective identity crystallized, as Joseph Kitagawa has
pointed out, in an immanentist-theocratic model in which the idea of a
liturgical community (which to some extent could also be found in China)
became combined with strong soteriological components and the conception of the sacred kingship:

> These conceptions of state and kingship in ancient Japan have provided for
> Japanese society a structural continuity that has never been lost, though
> the society has undergone various historical changes and transformations
> from archaic times down to the present.[80]

This continuity has been evident less in the actual position of the emperor
than in his symbolic standing. The emperors, however powerless, have
been, as we have seen, the ultimate legitimators of the sacral and political
order—even if they have often not been central figures in the national
consciousness. The latent, symbolic importance of the emperor, however,
made it possible for the imperial symbol to be drastically reconstructed
and reinvented in the Meiji period as the central symbol of the new political regime.

The Japanese conception of sacred particularity was also reinforced by
a tendency that developed in Japanese Buddhism toward the sacralization
of locality as loci of Japanese collectivity—as can, for instance, be seen,
as Allan Grappard has shown, in the way a specific mountain or region in
the Kunisaki peninsula was "textualized" in the interpretation of the
Lotus Sutra in the nineteenth century.[81] The sacralization of specific
places also developed within Buddhism in other countries, for instance in
India, where the Kailari, the source of the four rivers, was considered to

be Mount Meru, or in Tibet, where all snow mountains were sacred. But in Japan this tendency moved easily into the identification of any such sacral place with the country as such. The sanctification or sacralization of Mount Fuji—especially in later medieval Tokugawa and to some extent also in the Meiji period—not only as a symbol of Japan but also as the symbol of overcoming the foreign, the other, is very indicative of this.[82]

XXVIII A similar pattern developed with respect to the definition of the Japanese collectivity in relation to other, broader civilizational frameworks. The conceptions of the Japanese collectivity that developed in periods of change entailed very intensive orientations toward others— China, India, the West—and an awareness of these civilizations' claims to universal validity constituted a continuous focus of Tokugawa neo-Confucian discourse. This awareness, however, did not give rise to a conception of the Japanese collectivity as part of such broader frameworks. Rather, the universalistic premises inherent in Buddhism, and latent in Confucianism, were subdued and "nativized." A relatively early formulation, in the Heian period, had already combined such orientations with a definition of Japan as a divine nation (*Shinkoku*)—a nation under the protection of the deities—a conception that developed in close relation to the elaboration and promulgation of Shinto and of imperial ritual.

Such a conception was couched, to follow Werblowski's felicitous expression, in terms of sacred particularity.[83] Yet contrary to the Jewish conception of a chosen nation, for instance, and its later transformation in Christianity, sacred particularity in Japan did not entail the conception of a responsibility to God to behave according to any specific precepts or commitment. This conception of a divine nation, while it obviously emphasized the sacrality and uniqueness of the Japanese nation, did not characterize its uniqueness in terms of a transcendental and universalistic mission. As such, it stands in rather marked contrast, for instance, to Sri Lankan Buddhist tendencies toward national sanctification, which posited, as Michael Carrithers has put it, "no Buddhism without the Sangha, and no Sangha without the Discipline. And indeed Sinhalese historians, who were always monks, tended to add—no Sri Lanka without Buddhism."[84]

The Japanese conception of sacred particularity usually held its own when confronted with universalistic ideologies, be they Buddhist, Confucian, or various modern ones—liberal, constitutional, progressivist, Marxist, and the like—all of which seemingly called for a redefinition of the symbols of collective identity in some universalistic direction. Except among small groups of intellectuals, such redefinitions did not take root in the Japanese collective consciousness; some version of the liturgical, sacral, primordial, "natural" collectivity ultimately prevailed—albeit in continuously reconstructed forms.

Claims about the superiority of Japan—that the Japanese collectivity embodies the pristine virtues proclaimed by "foreign" universalistic religions—were promulgated especially under the early Meiji, in tandem with calls for Japanese hegemony in East Asia. These claims did not entertain the possibility that Japan was one—even if the leading—country in a civilization constituted in transcendental and universalistic terms, in which all other countries could participate equally. Rather, they were based on the assumption that the primordial Japanese character in fact represented these universal pristine values. The pronouncements of imperial loyalists denoted, as Hershell Webb has observed, the development of a universal ethic focused on a particularistic frame or object.[85]

The Japanese rhetoric of sacred particularity differed significantly from the official Chinese Confucian one. Particularistic components, with an emphasis on China as the center of the central kingdom, had been, of course, quite prevalent; yet officially at least these particularist components were subsumed under the universalistic ones. It was the strength of these components that enabled the Chinese to view the Korean, Vietnamese, and Japanese kingdoms as members, even if politically subordinate ones, of a broader civilizational framework, a potentially universal one.

The claim of many Japanese scholars that it was in Japan—or at least not in China—that the pristine vision of the sage promulgated by Confucius and Mencius was realized, was perhaps not entirely misplaced. The view that the very institutionalization of Confucianism as a state-bureaucratic mold could perhaps be seen as a perversion of this original ideal was to some extent also to be found among some of the Chinese neo-Confucians. (I owe this observation to Peter Nosco.) But whatever the "objective" validity of such an assertion, it is of course a major historical fact that Confucianism in China went in a distinctive direction, becoming closely interwoven with the imperial-bureaucratic state. The leading Japanese historians of the period developed a strategy to show differences between Japan and China—and to limit or eliminate the revolutionary potentialities of Japanese Confucianism; parallel tendencies can be identified, already in early medieval Japanese Buddhism.[86]

As in the political arena, with its definitions, influenced by neo-Confucianism, of the national community in relation to broader civilizational frameworks, the religious or cultural community that developed within Japanese Buddhism did not emphasize strongly the universalistic dimensions found in most other Buddhist communities. Indeed, the awareness of such international community was often very muted among Japanese Buddhists, especially in the late medieval period under Tokugawa.

Yet at the same time Japan's continual confrontation with universalistic civilizations and the problem of how to define Japanese collectivity in relation to them continuously generated new dimensions of collective consciousness and other levels of highly sophisticated discourse.

XXIX   The Confucian conceptions of political authority, of its legitimation, and of the accountability of rulers that were prevalent in China and later also in Korea and Vietnam underwent a far-reaching transformation in Japan—as can be seen in the very conception of sacral kingship and immanentist theocracy analyzed above. Chinese concepts of authority, especially that of the mandate of heaven, became a focus of intensive intellectual and ideological discussion in the Tokugawa period. This discourse touched not only on the definition of the national community, but also on the core of political ideology—the conceptions of the legitimation of authority and of the accountability of rulers.

The outcome of these discussions was the transformation in Japan of the political implications of Chinese Confucianism an neo-Confucianism, such that they came to reinforce the basic premises of liturgical-primordial legitimation, that is, to minimize the principled accountability of rulers and the transcendental and universalistic dimensions or principles of legitimation. Unlike in China (and Korea and Vietnam), where in principle the emperor, though a sacral figure, was under the mandate of heaven, the emperor in Japan was seen as the embodiment of the gods, as in direct contact with a transcendent but not transcendental heaven, and could not be held accountable to anybody. Shoguns and other officials *could* be held accountable, but in ways not clearly specified and only in periods of crises. As Peter Nosco has put it:

> For example, in a Confucian-inspired history of Japan, Hayashi Razan's (1583–1657) son, Hayashi Gahō (1618–1680), cast Tokugawa Ieyasu in the classical guise of the newly appointed recipient of the mandate of heaven, equipping him both morally and spiritually for the task of human rulership. However, the obverse side of this issue—that heaven might withdraw its mandate from any specific regime—was of necessity skirted by all the Tokugawa Confucian thinkers until the very last years of the Tokugawa era.[87]

These thinkers also emphasized, until the last decades of the regime, the upholding of the existing hierarchical order.

Closely related to the transformation of the concepts of authority in Japan was that of the concepts of loyalty, especially of the relation between loyalty to one's father and loyalty to one's lord. The problem of the relative priority of filial and institutional piety indeed constituted one of the major issues in the intellectual debate that took place among neo-Confucian scholars as they confronted the nativist schools and Chinese Confucian scholars. Some Japanese scholars opted for the classical Chinese Confucian emphasis on filial piety—which was justified in terms of transcendental evaluation of the place of the family. But most stressed the priority of loyalty to the existing social nexus—to the family, to the head of the family, to the lord, and ultimately to the emperor. This emphasis on loyalty to one's lord was also related to the acceptance in Japan of non-agnatic adoption—that is, the adoption as sons of people who had no blood or kinship relation to the adopting family. While such adoption seems to have been rather common in various sectors of Chinese society, it was on the whole seen by Chinese neo-Confucian scholars as wrong, as undermining the conception of Chinese family and kinship and of ancestor worship.[88]

At the same time, loyalty to the lord—and ultimately to the emperor—and to the group or collectivity of which one formed a part (or with the fate of which one was embroiled) could not be questioned in Japan, as it could in China, in terms of universalistic principles or a higher, transcendental authority; nor was the lord's authority legitimized by such principles.[89] The nativist scholars presented the very possibility of such questioning as anathema to the Japanese spirit or culture.[90]

True, this reformulation of the concept of loyalty contained within itself possibilities for the extension of family loyalty beyond any given setting, possibly in a universalistic direction. But in fact such extensions always took place within the confines of the Japanese collectivity and the existing authority structure. In China the emphasis on filial piety was not usually extended beyond the kinship frameworks, but given the relatively strong transcendental justification of such piety, especially in neo-Confucianism, it could also become a potential basis for challenging existing authority structures. This possibility was less feasible in Japan—and when it developed there it went, as is well known, in a distinctive restorative direction, that is, toward a generalization of particularistic loyalties.

This transformation of the basic conceptions of the accountability of rulers inherent in classical neo-Confucianism was closely connected with a more general transformation of Confucian political ideology and with the crystallization of a distinctive conception of the legitimation of the state, of the political community. This conception of legitimation developed yet again in a double-pronged manner, entailing on the one hand, as Herschell Webb has pointed out, the particularization of the potentially universalistic dimensions of such legitimation and, on the other hand, a close connection with restorative orientations rooted in the immanentist-soteriological-liturgical conception of the Japanese collectivity:

> In the hands of its truly articulate formulators of a Confucian persuasion, and as addressed by them to rulers, it was a true universalism—an ethic that stressed values that were conceived to be independent of time, place, or social status—but one that appeared to be particularistic, for it seemed to pivot the ruler's duties on the variable will of a superior person in the authority structure. Furthermore, the generalized duty asserted for the ruler himself seemed to be similar to that obligation of obedience to an external human authority that was at the heart of the political ethics of the Tokugawa period. In this sense, loyalism may be called "pseudo-particularism."[91]

Bellah speaks of loyalty to a figurehead emperor or shogun as a "generalized particularism which was a functional substitute for universalism in the extension and rationalization of power." Elsewhere he speaks of imperial loyalism as "pseudo-universalism."[92] This loyalist conception was often closely connected, as was the case in Mito, with a distinctive cosmological-historical vision as well as with strong restorative ones.[93]

XXX　These basic attitudes to the national community and to authority greatly influenced the political orientations and activities of Confucian and Buddhist groups in Japan, which also developed in two directions.

Embedded as they were in the existing social and political frameworks, the Confucian and Buddhist groups tended to minimize their involvement in the political arena in a radical way. In mainland Asia—in China, Korea, and Vietnam—Confucian, and especially neo-Confucian, sects and literati participated in the political arena as relatively (often very relatively) autonomous agents. Many noteworthy attempts at reform in China were grounded in Confucian and neo-Confucian visions, especially from the Sung period onward. Neo-Confucian groups were much concerned with the reconstruction of the imperial order in accordance with the metaphysical and moral visions they articulated, and these had a far-reaching impact on certain aspects of policy, such as land allotment and taxation, and to some extent on the details of the examination system itself. These groups were continually politically active and often critically engaged in the political discourse.

Unlike the sects and heterodoxies of monotheistic civilizations, the Confucians rarely challenged the basic political premises of the regimes, the very foundation of the imperial order. This was probably due, to no small extent, to the fact that they conceived the political-cultural arena as the main, if not the only, institutional ground (as distinct from the more private, contemplative one) for implementing the Confucian transcendental vision. But they did constitute, at least potentially, a challenge to the existing political regimes—even if in modes that differed greatly from the pattern of relations between orthodoxy and heterodoxy in the monotheistic civilizations.

Similarly, Buddhist sects in South Asian countries—and until their partial suppression also in China—participated in the political arena, thus constituting, at least potentially, a challenge to the existing political regimes—even if, again, in ways that differed greatly from those prevalent in the monotheistic civilizations. Within Buddhist and especially Taoist groups in China there developed tendencies to millenarian rebellions.

This strong, relatively autonomous, often critical political involvement, however, almost entirely disappeared in Japan. Here most Buddhist sects and Confucian schools became either supporters of the existing political order—performing religious or cultural functions for the existing powers, imbuing the political process with proper ethical values and orientations—or politically passive.

The major new sectarian orientations that developed in Japanese Buddhism, most clearly manifest in the Pure Land sect, were in principle inclined toward the perfection of the individual—seemingly without any direct political change, certainly without any change in the premises on which the political realm was based. They were also strongly inclined toward strengthening the national community, but this could, contrary to Confucian teaching, lead to a certain political passivity or withdrawal. It was only in Nichiren's case that some more active political overtures—beyond the simple struggle for power—could be identified, but even these were entirely embedded within the prevalent Japanese political order. There did not develop among these groups in Japan—as there did in at least some neo-Confucian groups in China and, in a different way, in Theravada countries—a specifically sectarian political dynamic.

Of course, the various Buddhist sects and monasteries in Japan, especially in late medieval times, developed into very powerful political and economic forces, and many of them enjoyed great autonomy and power vis-à-vis the shoguns. They engaged in intensive struggles among themselves and with the feudal lords or the shogun. But most of these battles were fought over economic resources and political power; the religious dimension was quite weak.

Yet this was not the whole story. Japanese Confucian and Buddhist groups also contributed to the opening up of the range of political discourse in radical critical directions. They channeled their discourse, however, into restorative, inverted utopian directions that only rarely challenged the basic foundations of the imperial regime. Nonetheless, the strong critical potential of this discourse, which developed to some extent in Confucian learning and academies, especially in the late Tokugawa period, made several Tokugawa shoguns rather suspicious of some Confucian scholars, as well as of some Confucian academies, especially those which catered to common people.[94]

These groups and scholars could challenge the actual shogun regime in situations of grave crisis, but not in terms taken from outside the imperial system or premises—hence they could not envisage revolution:

> Generally speaking, the concept of revolution was often troublesome for Japanese Confucianists. Unlike Chinese emperors the Tenno was not the adopted son of heaven by the mandate, but—according to Japanese myths—the real son of heaven, as it were. Therefore, it was logically unthinkable to expel a Tenno. All Shintoists were adamant against any theory of revolution. Some people did not hesitate to call the ancient sages the criminals of high treason.
>
> This situation naturally influenced Confucianists. Some contrived to make the Confucian teaching coexist with such feelings by various feats of acrobatic logic. Some rejected the idea of revolutions flatly.[95]

XXXI Buddhism did not promulgate, on the whole, an explicit conception of political authority. True, distinctive forms of political authority, especially of theocracy, developed in some Buddhist schools. Yet in most Buddhist societies, no clear overarching conception of political authority developed, as was the case in Confucianism. Hence, it is more difficult to point to the transformations of such conceptions in Japan. Yet even here some indications are of interest—one of them being the Confucianization of the Buddhist conception of authority. The earliest illustration of the way in which Japanese Buddhism was Confucianized is provided by Prince Shōtoku's famous Seventeen-Article Constitution. This "Buddhist" document is in reality the most Confucian document imaginable. Article 1 begins with the sentence "Harmony is to be valued"—a literal quotation from Analects 1.12.

A parallel development can be seen in the early middle ages when the imperial system was also legitimized in Buddhist terms, emphasizing the concept of "the mutual dependence of Buddhism and Imperial law," and the enthronement ceremony was imbued with Buddhist rituals—although the ceremony was carried out by the emperor himself. If the emperor were to received the transmission from a Buddhist monk, they would establish a master-disciple relationship that would involve the emperor in one of the factions of the temple social structure. The actual performance of *sokui karys*, however, assumes that it is the emperor who is at the apex. "Therefore, the mundane and the sacred are not confused by Buddhists, and even the presence of a monk was not allowed during the actual endowment ceremony."[96] No less indicative of possible directions of the transformation of Buddhist political conceptions in Japan is the strong tendency to reconstruct religious authority as familial succession.[97]

It is above all the mode of involvement of the Buddhist groups and sects (and, as a matter of fact, also of Confucian scholars) in the political process, which we have analyzed above, that is most indicative of such transformation—especially the fact that Buddhist (as well as Confucian) groups participated in political struggles from the very beginning of their penetration into Japan, but they did so within the existing rules of the game—with almost no attempts to change these rules. The overall tendency of Buddhist monks, artists, poets, and seers—as well as of Buddhist organizations—was to reinforce the existing political order. The potentially more critical stances that did from time to time develop in mainland Asia were in Japan thwarted or minimized.[98] The rejection or dilution of Taoism in Japan, to which we have already referred, is very much in line with these developments.

XXXII   The Buddhist and Confucian groups' mode of participation in the social life and political process of Japan was closely related to the fact that neither Japanese Buddhism nor Confucianism ever became full autonomous orthodoxies; hence neither could give rise to far-reaching, fully crystallized heterodoxies. Some neo-Confucian scholars, like Razan, attempted to present themselves as the bearers of the official ideology, to have their schools approved by the authorities and their teachings declared orthodox. Some of these attempts succeeded—but only to a limited extent, in periods of turmoil in the late eighteenth and early nineteenth century.

Yet given the basic premises of the Japanese political order and its legitimation in some combination of sacral and primordial terms, even when the rulers were interested in promulgating their own legitimation in Confucian terms, they were less concerned with the promulgation and imposition of orthodoxy than was the case in China. Accordingly, although the academies and religious institutions indeed performed useful functions for the regime, their overall dynamics differed from those to be found in mainland Asia. While the rulers' supervision of these academies and of Buddhist monasteries was often stronger than in China, it was also much less concerned with issues of doctrinal differences.[99]

Each Buddhist and Confucianist group or school claimed to be the bearer of the undiluted truth, and in this sense it could indeed be described, as Dobbins has suggested, as promoting an orthodoxy.[100] But sectarian or school disputes did not develop, as we have seen, into the confrontations between orthodoxy and heterodoxy characteristic of the monotheistic civilizations or of Confucianism in China or Korea. The Japanese did not aim to impose their own doctrines as *the* doctrine of the realm, independent of the existing rulers, or to impose them on the rulers. The struggles among them resembled much more those between familial and feudal groups, which were characteristic of the Japanese scene in that period.

True enough, some of the Buddhist discourses, like some of the neo-Confucian discourses, developed in a critical direction; such was the case with Nichiren. But these critical orientations tended to reinforce the conceptions of the sacred particularity of the Japanese collectivity and not to judge this collectivity according to transcendental, universalistic criteria, as was the case with many Buddhist sects in mainland Asia. Although the Japanese authorities looked askance at such political activities, these activities were oriented toward the spiritual strengthening of the Japanese collectivity and above all the reaffirmation of its sacredness. They aimed to purify the collectivity and to imbue it with spiritual dimension—but not to go beyond it, to judge it in terms of broader, transcendental criteria.[101] Any ideological formulations that seemed to have transcendental groundings usually entailed the claim that the Japanese collectivity embodied in a unique way the universalistic values enunciated by other civilizations—and which these civilizations wrongly attributed to themselves. Significantly, this nationalistic emphasis of Nichiren Buddhism has recently been reemphasized.[102]

XXXIII These far-reaching transformations of the political conceptions and orientations of Confucianism and Buddhism were closely related to the internal structure of neo-Confucianist and Buddhist groups in Japan and to their relations to the powers that be, some aspects of which we have already referred to. In these respects they again differed greatly from developments elsewhere in Asia, with the possible partial exceptions of India and, in different ways, of the Buddhist theocracies of Tibet and Mongolia.

In Japan, both the Confucian scholars and the Buddhist sects were deeply embedded in the existing power, kinship, and family settings. While the Confucian academies in Japan were often relatively independent, their members—teachers and "graduates" alike—were highly dependent on the rulers for any offices. This was in rather sharp contrast to China, where the Confucians constituted an autonomous political-cultural stratum recruited in principle, even if not always in practice, through the examination system, the basic contents of which they promulgated and set up themselves. It was also in contrast to Theravada Buddhism in Southern Asia, and to a lesser extent to Buddhism in India or China, which were not embedded in the existing power or family structures and were, at least in the religious arena, relatively autonomous. In Japan Confucian scholars served at the courts of the rulers according to criteria set up by the rulers, and they served at the rulers' will. The Buddhist sects became, as we have seen, strongly embedded in the familistic settings predominant in most sectors of Japanese society and, with the partial exception of Nichiren, did not develop new types of political organization or orientations aiming at the transformation of the political system.

In China, except for a short period under Tang, Buddhism did not become a major component of the center and, even more importantly, the Buddhist establishment did not become part of the hegemonic ruling groups. Paradoxically this gave Chinese Buddhist groups some internal autonomy—not only organizationally but ideologically—although it also isolated them from the central arenas of Chinese culture, as distinct from the more "folk" or "daily" ones. In Japan the situation was, in a sense, the opposite. There Buddhism became a key component of the general culture and of the center. Buddhist monks, or rather priests, became interwoven into the ruling coalition and major countercoalitions—but on the existing terms according to which these coalitions were structured. This very fact minimized, weakened, and almost obliterated their ideological and institutional distinctiveness, especially in the political arena. This mode of participation in the political arena was also related to the tendency in Japanese Buddhism to blur the boundaries between laity and monkhood, a general tendency, as Helen Hardacre has put it with respect to the modern period, to "lay centrality."

In the South Asian Theravada countries, the Buddhist Sangha usually constituted a rather ambivalent component of the hegemonic coalitions. The Sangha was highly dependent on the political elites, but its organizations were *relatively* autonomous; the distance between monks and laymen, and between at least some sectors of the Sangha and the political elite, was on the whole upheld, and some radical political tendencies would from time to time develop within it. In the Tibetan (and to a lesser extent Mongolian) Buddhist theocracies, it was the Buddhist groups that, to a great extent, became the ruling class, controlling, incorporating, or dispossessing the older or lay groups.

XXXIV Let us now bring together some of the main lines of our discussion about the transformation of Buddhism and Confucianism in Japan and their impact on the Japanese social and political systems. The major point of our analysis is that this transformation was a double-pronged one, manifest, on the cultural or ideological level, in the weakening of transcendental and universalistic orientations and their channeling into an immanentist, particularistic, primordial direction and, on the organizational level, in the relatively low institutional autonomy of the major Confucian schools and scholars and of the Buddhist sects' leaders and seers, who remained embedded in the prevailing social settings and networks—be they familial, regional, or political.

Such Japanization did not, however, result in a simple disappearance or weakening of the transcendental and universalistic orientations that were central to classical Confucianism and Buddhism, but rather in their being bracketed into special, segregated arenas. These transcendental and logocentric dimensions constituted a continual challenge to Japanese scholars and gave rise to a highly sophisticated and reflexive philosophical, religious, and aesthetic discourse, the like of which could not be found in any other non-Axial civilization. But this discourse was consciously constructed in the direction of the "archaic," with the paradoxical result of a highly sophisticated textual exegesis denying in principle its own logocentric focus. The rather paradoxical attempt to de-ideologize, in reflexive, ideological terms, the logocentric orientations of classical Confucianism and Buddhism did, however, continuously generate tensions between the discourse and the prevailing intellectual hegemony and thus constituted one of the major moving forces in the development and diversification of this discourse.

A large part of this highly developed ideological discourse has been the conscious and highly reflexive denial of the type of ideologies grounded in the premises of Axial civilizations; but at the same time it has usually been couched in terms derived from these ideologies, and the confrontation between them has constituted a continuous focus on reflexivity.[103] Contrary to the situation in many other non-Axial civilizations (e.g., ancient Egypt, Assyria or Mesoamerica), there evolved in Japan a highly sophisticated intellectual, philosophical, ideological, and religious discourse, as for instance in the development of different neo-Confucian schools, which confronted and debated the so-called nativist learning in the Tokugawa period.

All these developments attest to the fact that the transformation of Confucianism and Buddhism, and later of Western ideologies, in Japan in the Meiji, Taishō, and post–Second World War periods constitutes the de-Axialization of Axial religions, ideologies, and civilizations, not in the local or peripheral arenas of "small traditions" but in the very core of the "great tradition." This de-Axialization has taken place on a societywide level, effected by the elites at the very center of the civilization and combined with continuous openness to outside influences and the development of highly sophisticated discourse—a combination which cannot be found in any other great civilization.

These basic parameters of the ideological and organizational transformation of Buddhism and Confucianism also shaped the concrete impact of their teachings and practices in Japan. This impact naturally varied among different sectors of Japanese society and at different periods of Japanese history; throughout Japanese history groups have selected themes from within the Confucian and Buddhist traditions according to their own major cultural orientations and interests. Thus in the Tokugawa period such selection was above all interwoven with the goal of legitimizing the regime, while in the early Meiji period several statesmen, especially educators, attempted to imbue the new polity with the Confucian values of hierarchy, loyalty, and discipline.[104] But whatever the variations across different historical periods, these selections of Buddhist and Confucian themes reflected a general inclination toward the immanentization of transcendental orientations and the particularization of universalistic ones.

One important aspect of this Japanization of Confucianism and Buddhism was, as Harumi Befu has shown, that quite often it was the various social messages of these religions that were accepted—as, for instance, in the responsiveness even to some of the social messages of Christianity—but not their ontologies, basic religious tenets, or premises.[105]

XXXV Such double-pronged transformations of Buddhism and Confucianism also took place on the organizational level, as well as with respect to their broader social impact. Thus, on the institutional or organizational level the transformation of Buddhism and Confucianism in Japan entailed, on the one hand, a relative de-autonomization of the major Confucian schools and scholars and of the Buddhist sect leaders and seers, their being embedded in the prevailing social settings and networks—be they familial, regional, or political. On the other hand, however, because neither Confucianism nor Buddhism served as channels for recruitment to political or social positions, and in close relation to the ideological tensions mentioned above, there developed within this framework new cultural activities, and new social spaces were constructed within which new types of social relations, social consciousness, and discourse developed.

Indeed, one of the paradoxical results of the fact that Confucianism did not become in Japan—in contrast to China, Korea, and Vietnam—the main channel for the recruitment of officials was that it gave rise, as W. T. de Bary has pointed out, to the development of a widely educated public in Tokugawa Japan, and in this way had a far-reaching impact on the cultural and social ambience of Japan.[106] Within this public manifold, diverse and highly sophisticated forms of cultural and public discourse developed—as well as the reconstruction of the realm of private meanings of many sectors of Japanese society. There developed also a broadening of the scope of participation of various sectors of Japanese society in cultural creativity and in political and ideological discourse, as well as an elaborate redefinition and symbolization of the ideological political discourse.

All of these developments gave rise to the construction of new social spaces in which various transcendental, logocentric, or utilitarian orientations could be played out. Buddhism and Confucianism also continuously imbued such discourse with new components and dimensions. Buddhism imbued many new areas of social relations and individual consciousness with an ethos of equality and communalism and generated a great reservoir of such themes, which were available and could be picked up, selected, and activated in many situations, as for instance in the various manifestations of the "aesthetics of seclusion."[107] While Confucianism was much more attuned to the hierarchical tendencies of Japanese society, it also generated, especially in the Tokugawa period, new consciousness and new modes of discourse—and the very expansion of Confucian education generated intense new ideological discourses.

XXXVI   The combination of these ideological and organizational aspects of the transformation of Confucianism and Buddhism in Japan explains also the double-pronged nature of their political impact. On the whole both Confucianism and Buddhism in Japan reinforced the prevalent political orientations, premises, and symbols both of the legitimacy of authority and of "customary" rebellion against authority. This ran counter to some of the basic "original" tenets of Chinese Confucianism. Neither Confucianism nor Buddhism undermined the core ontological and social premises prevalent in Japanese society—even if they gave rise to their continuous reformulation and imbued them with new moral and metaphysical dimensions.

The tendencies to immanentization and particularization of the transcendental and universalistic orientations of classical Buddhism and Confucianism also generated the potential for a critical political discourse and for a certain type of political activism. Throughout most of their history, these potentials were hemmed in and accommodated within existing ideological frameworks, but in times of great crises, as can be seen especially in the late Tokugawa period, they could undermine or challenge the existing frameworks. Such challenges did not, however, change the immanentist and primordial framework of the Japanese political discourse and of the legitimation of the regime. Most of these politically subversive potentials instead developed in restorative and nativist terms—even if these terms were continuously reformulated in more and more sophisticated ways.

Accordingly, however great the impact of the spread of Confucian education and learning on the dynamics of Tokugawa society may have been, neither Confucian nor Buddhist groups were autonomous participants in the toppling of the Tokugawa regime. They did not perform the sectarian political roles that, for instance, the Puritans did in the English Great Rebellion. It was various groups of disenchanted and rebellious samurai who toppled the *bakufu*. They were greatly influenced by the development of new modes of public discourse—but the more intellectual groups were not active, autonomous participants in this process of rebellion, nor in the working out of the tenets of the Restoration. At the same time, given that the concept of loyalty as promulgated in Japan and reinforced by the Confucian discourse was not, as we have seen, tied to any fixed context, loyalty could be transformed and channeled by different elites. This is what happened in Meiji Japan; this emphasis on loyalty, together with that on education, was channeled by the Meiji elite in a new direction of modernization.[108]

The Meiji Ishin
The Revolutionary Restoration

I The analysis in chapter 9 of the distinctive characteristics of the To-kugawa regime—and above all of its various contradictions and the processes of change and movements of protest that developed within it—brings us to the Meiji Ishin, or Meiji Restoration, that series of dramatic events which culminated in 1868 in the abolition of the Tokugawa *ba-kufu*, the old "feudal" or "centralized feudal" regime, and ushered in the modern era in the history of Japan.[1]

The Meiji Restoration has often been compared with the great European revolutions that preceded it—the English Great Rebellion and Civil War, the American and French revolutions, and the subsequent ones in Russia and even China. The long-range processes and causes that led to the downfall of the Tokugawa regime were indeed similar to those associated with the great revolutions, just as the processes and causes of the rise of the Tokugawa regime resembled those of the crystallization of the early modern European absolutist regimes. To repeat briefly some of the major points made in the preceding chapter—the most important among such causes were the disintegration of the old political economy through the development of new economic forces and the consequent undermining of the bases of control of the ruling groups;[2] the spread of education and the increasing marketization of the economy, two processes that cut across multiple domains; the deterioration of the economic situation of the lower samurai and much of the peasantry; and the improvement of the economic situation of the merchants and of other peasant groups. Last but not least were the struggles within the central elite—in various samurai groups in the *bakufu* and in the domains.

The late Tokugawa period—from the Tempō reforms of the early nineteenth century on—abounded in peasant rebellions, in rural and urban movements of protest,[3] and in continuous struggles within the shogunal court and between the *bakufu* and the great lords, the daimyō. Extensive struggles also developed with the growing dissatisfaction of many of the lower echelons of samurai within the domains of the daimyō. It was the cooperation between groups of upper and lower samurai in several domains, especially Chōshū and Satsuma, with some connivance from the imperial court, that toppled the Tokugawa regime.[4] In the last decades of the Tokugawa regime—as in those of the absolutist regimes in Europe—there also developed, as we have seen, far-reaching changes in the cultural scene. New modes of intellectual and ideological discourse—influenced by both neo-Confucian and nativist schools—called into question many of the basic premises of the Tokugawa ideology. There developed also, as in Europe before the great revolutions, a general consciousness of the disintegration of the center.[5] All these processes contributed to the backdrop against which the movements that toppled the *bakufu* developed: "Thus in late Tokugawa times there existed a revolutionary situation among the Japanese peasantry that, far from being incidental to the collapse of the Tokugawa, provided the occasion and the energy by which others were to carry out the seizure of the central control apparatus."[6]

It is difficult, as in any potentially revolutionary situation, to estimate to what extent these processes of change and movements of protest could have been contained, as it were, within the framework of the ancien regime; some kind of external trigger usually has to give the final push. It is conceivable that without such an external trigger, the Tokugawa regime could have developed in a more conciliar, bureaucratized direction—and a more capitalistic one—but as with any such exercise, this is mere speculation. In the Japanese case the final push was given by the threat of Western invasion, which forced the opening of Japan, ending the closure that had been imposed by the Tokugawa rulers.

II The Meiji Ishin also shared some important characteristics with the European revolutions in terms of its outcomes. Like them it deposed an existing, "traditional" ruler, in this case the shogun, and changed the composition of the ruling class entirely. The old feudal warrior class, which by then had become highly domesticated, was displaced by a new oligarchical, political, bureaucratic elite. Initially this elite was recruited mostly from the samurai, but later it drew, to some extent, from wider strata. Although some members of the older ruling class also belonged to the new elite, the overall result was a far-reaching change in the composition of the ruling class.[7]

The institutional effects of the Meiji Restoration, in terms of structural change and modernization, are also easily comparable to those of Western revolutions—but in Japan, unlike in the first European and American revolutions, these processes were the result of conscious policies. The tempo of urbanization, of expansion of education, and of commercialization (the high level of which, especially from the end of the eighteenth century, contributed to the erosion of the Tokugawa regime) was rapid, and the process of industrialization and of crystallization of a modern capitalist-industrial system proceeded relatively quickly.[8] In many ways these changes were quicker and more intensive then parallel processes in many European countries. Japan's international orientation—that is, its commitment to attaining an independent, possibly major standing in the new international order dominated by Western European and American economic or political and colonial orientation—was also more pronounced.

As did the great revolutions, the Meiji Ishin ushered in not only a new mode of legitimation of the political system—albeit a new mode presented as a restoration of an old one and legitimized by a combination of restorative terms and new, pragmatic knowledge—but a new, essentially modern overall cultural program that encompassed most arenas of life. It was indeed a modern program, even if it differed in many crucial ways from that of modernity in the West, and it constituted a total change of Japanese society.[9]

III   Yet from the very beginning the Meiji Ishin differed in certain crucial aspects from the European, American, and later the Russian and Chinese revolutions. The first such difference is manifest in its very name—the meaning of "Ishin" is possibly closer to "renovation," or being pulled in a new direction, than to "restoration," as it has been rendered in Western literature.

Before analyzing in greater detail the implications of this distinctive feature of the Meiji Ishin and of the cultural-political program promulgated by its various participants, it might be worthwhile to recapitulate the structure of the major groups that were crucial in deposing the Tokugawa *bakufu* and bringing about the Restoration. The literature has often emphasized the central importance of various secondary samurai groups in the struggle against the *bakufu*, a participation that seems to justify designating the Restoration as a "revolution from above." The widely accepted view that it was mostly territorial subgroups—the Chōshū and Satsuma—that toppled the Tokugawa regime has, however, been challenged by Thomas M. Huber, who has attempted to portray the revolutionary groups more in terms of class divisions within the samurai.[10] This view—which tends to idealize these revolutionary groups—has not been widely accepted.[11] But even if there is an element of truth in Huber's assessment—in the sense that these were mostly secondary samurai groups with relatively extensive Confucian education—it would still not invalidate the more general fact that the Restoration was in fact effected from within the broad stratum of the samurai, with relatively little *active* participation from merchants, peasants, and the like.

At the same time the participation of members of these other social sectors, especially in various crowds and crowdlike situations—for instance, the widespread *Ee ja nai ka* dancing groups in 1867—provides another indication of the weakness of the center as it was faced with various economic upheavals, as well as a further series of events contributing to the demise of the *bakufu*.[12]

Indeed the toppling of the Tokugawa *bakufu* was the culmination of many processes of rebellion, disaffection, and withdrawal from the regime.[13] But organizationally, the Meiji Ishin was characterized, in contrast to the Western and Chinese parallels, by the relative segregation of the different sectors that participated in it; as in the peasant rebellions and movements of reform that we have discussed, the various groups of actors—whether peasant groups, dissatisfied merchants, or samurai—each remained relatively self-contained.[14] Most of these actors evinced strong secessional tendencies, tendencies to withdraw from the center, and only relatively weak connections, and relatively few continuous frameworks of common action developed between the different actors.

Nonetheless, widespread contacts, unprecedented in Japanese history, developed in this period between the various regions and even between different social classes, contacts which were greatly reinforced by the expansion of education through the numerous Confucian academies. Many ad hoc contacts also developed; the *shi shi* groups, for instance, although predominantly samurai, also include merchants, peasants, and a few women. But significantly enough there did not develop any continuous organizations or frameworks within which the political struggle in the center and the popular rebellions or movements of protest could be continuously linked. The latter constituted a very important component of the backdrop to the toppling of the Tokugawa regime, but they did not play a major political role in the Restoration. There developed no new types of political organization—except for various types of crowds—in which such different groups could be held together in common action, nor did there develop any political leadership capable of mobilizing the disparate social forces.

The new types of political organization that developed—such as the various semiconciliar meetings—were mostly confined to samurai, and were often further restricted to specific regions, very much in line with Maruyama's metaphor of the octopus. From this point of view it is important that in many ways the goals of the *bakufu* and of the rebels and reformists were not entirely different—both wanted to pursue *Fukoku kyōhei* (rich country; strong army).[15] The major bone of contention, at least initially, was with respect to the efficacy of various measures and groups in implementing this goal and, of course, with respect to control over such implementation.

Some incipient tendencies toward more diverse intersectorial contacts did develop, especially among the more popular sectors, but they certainly were not encouraged by most of the more central actors. Similarly, many of the themes of popular culture—above all its millenarian orientations and its emphasis on communal equality and autonomy and on direct, unmediated relations to nature (which flourished in the late Tokugawa and early Meiji period and were also manifest in *Ee ja nai ka* dancing)—were not on the whole taken up by the more central groups. Some of the samurai groups—especially those who promulgated the millenarian, nativist, communal, or "reverse utopian" vision—did have close contacts with some of the popular groups and took up some of the themes of popular culture, but they were not very central in the revolutionary process and especially not in the institutionalization of the new regime.

Of special importance in this context is the fact, which we have already mentioned, that close and continuous contacts did not develop between the major actors in the Restoration and religious or cultural sectarian groups or autonomous religious leaders. The numerous Confucian academies that sprang up from the eighteenth century on greatly contributed to the development of such political consciousness and to the undermining of the legitimacy of the Tokugawa rule. So did the many new religions, the "religions of relief," which were so widespread in the last decades of the Tokugawa rule.[16] Moreover, many of the themes of protest that developed, whether in the periphery or at the center, were imbued with relatively recently constructed ideologies—whether Confucian or "nativist." But despite all these developments there were few independent Confucian scholars or Buddhist monks who played an autonomous role or attempted to construct the basic framework of the revolutionary discourse.

What is indeed perhaps most distinctive about the Meiji Restoration as compared to the great revolutions was the almost total absence of distinct, autonomous religious or secular intellectual groups among the *active* participants in the political process. This was in marked contrast to the involvement, for instance, of the Puritans in the English Revolution and their descendants in the American one, the ideologues in the French Revolution, or the intelligentsia in the Russian one.[17]

It was above all the samurai, some of them learned in Confucian lore, and the *shi shi*, who were most active in the Restoration—but on the whole they acted, not as scholars bearing a distinctly Confucian vision, but as members of their respective social and political groups. It is possibly this near absence of autonomous groups of the ideologues—of intellectuals independent of other social sectors and cutting across them—that explains the fact that there developed in the Meiji Ishin few new, relatively continuous political frameworks capable of bringing different social groups together, molding them according to an overall political-social vision, and allowing for the development of common discourse and political activism.[18]

Some additional aspects of the revolutionary process of the Meiji Ishin are interesting from a comparative point of view. The violence that marked the events leading to and following the Restoration was, above all, elite violence, especially on the part of Tokugawa loyalists, often manifest in rebellions by samurai groups, who engaged in violence in order to "restore" the shogun. This was very much in line with the more traditional type of violence, with the "nobility of failure" that was sanctified among at least some of the elite groups.[19] But no such sanctification was accorded to popular violence, unlike the situation in the great revolutions, nor even to the violence employed by those samurai groups that toppled the *bakufu*. Such violence was not seen as the expression of the search for a new overall social order.

Similarly, while liminal situations abounded, of course, among the various rebellious groups and movements of protest, the central political areas did not become—as they did in the great revolutions—arenas of liminal experience, with the constructive and destructive aspects of the yearning for a charismatic experience.

Of special significance is that fact that some of the most spectacular new liminal types of behavior, such as *Ee ja nai ka* dancing, shared many of the characteristics of the earlier pilgrimages, such as the apolitical, visionary—or, as Wilson has put it, filmlike—type of behavior.[20] They were infused with very strong millenarian orientations, which were also shared by many samurai groups and probably prompted many of them into the activities that toppled the *bakufu*. But these orientations did not combine with the more pragmatic considerations and did not crystallize into full-fledged political programs.

IV Thus the revolutionary processes that toppled the Tokugawa *bakufu* are distinguished from those of the great revolutions by the relative weak connections between different rebellious groups, their relative segregation, the almost total absence of sacralization of violence, and the lack of a center constructed in a liminal mode. This does not mean that the Meiji Ishin was a purely political event, as has been sometimes alleged. Like the great revolutions, its process was one in which, out of the numerous strategies of action that developed as reactions to events and broad visions, there gradually crystallized a new cultural and political program— a vision of the total transformation of society. But this program, the discourse that developed during the revolutionary process, was characterized by some distinctive features, which bear on its being called a "restoration" or a renovation rather than a revolution.

As we have already indicated, "restoration" is not an accurate translation of the term "Ishin," although some of the early ideological foundations legitimized the Ōsei fukko (act of restoration) in the principled terms of restoration. Tetsuo Najita has pointed out that the term's real connotation is to "pull together the disparate trends of society in a new direction." The discourse of the Ishin, the debate over Keisei saimin (the oral bases of political economy) implied the search for some basis of knowledge for ordering society and saving people, for the reexamination of the principles of reconstruction of social order.[21] But this discourse evinced some very distinctive characteristics, closely related to those of the late Tokugawa discourse analyzed in chapter 9.

The basic framework of the philosophical-ideological discourse was formulated, as Tetsuo Najita has shown, in terms of a dispute between empirical and idealistic interpretations of nature and history and of the search for universal truth about them.[22] Within this general framework, the discourse that developed during the revolutionary process leading to the Restoration veered between two poles. The first was the more millenarian or "inverse utopian" pole, which set its no-place in the past as opposed to the future, aiming at the restoration of an "original," "pristine" native national community; the second was the more pragmatic attitude promulgated by various groups, some of which focused on the reconstruction of political organizations, some on new legal constitutional arrangements—above all on some type of conciliar government. Groups at the second pole did not connect these arrangements with an overly social-political utopian vision.[23] This more pragmatic view was based on the assumption that some such rearrangement would make for a more efficient government that would be able to deal with the new problems confronting the nation, especially the ones stemming from the need to adjust to the new international situation. Other groups were learning how to organize the Japanese economy and polity in appropriately modern ways.

Both discourses focused, above all, on how to save the Japanese state or collectivity, and later possibly on how to save Asia, ultimately legitimizing the Meiji Ishin itself in terms of what Herschell Webb has called the "inverted utopia" of restorative imperial symbols, which was, as we have seen, central in the Tokugawa intellectual and political discourse.[24]

Within this discourse, as it developed in the movements leading to the Meiji Ishin, there arose a dissociation between various millennial and communitarian visions and the search for new types of knowledge, on which we commented in the preceding chapter. This dissociation also shaped the critical discourse that developed before and during the Meiji Ishin.

Thus the orientations and considerations on which the new social order was to be built were mostly pragmatic ones guided by the attempts to make Japan into a viable modern state. Many of the leaders of groups active in the Restoration emphasized the importance of learning and of promulgating universal knowledge, but very few of them translated this into principles of overall political action, of ways to reconstruct the Japanese policy and collectivity—and these leaders lost out very early in the game. Ultimately these attempts were legitimized by means of highly restorative terms and symbols. Such restorative terms also seemed to many of these leaders to be able to stem the purely hedonistic, utilitarian tendencies which they saw as developing among large sectors of Japanese society with the downfall of the Tokugawa regime.[25]

True enough, what this Restoration "restored" was a regime—based on an ideology or mythology of the divine origin and rule of the emperor—that had never existed in this form before in Japanese history. Yet, the very insistence on such terms or symbols indicates some very crucial differences from the ideologies of the great revolutions. The restorative themes developed in the direction of the backward-looking inverted utopia, or in a strong millenarian direction, and not, as in the other revolutions with which it is often compared, in the direction of the construction of a social order based on new principles that override the existing order and its basic principles of legitimation.

The Meiji Ishin was oriented inward, toward the Japanese people; it aimed at the revitalization of the Japanese nation, at making it capable of taking its place in the modern world, but it made no pretense of "saving" the entire world—mankind as a whole—through the promulgation of a new, universalistic, future-oriented utopian vision.

It is this combination of characteristics that makes the designation "revolutionary restoration" or "revolutionary renovation" the most appropriate one to describe the Meiji Ishin. It was indeed—because it envisaged a new type of society, a new modern cultural program—a revolutionary transformation, more than just a violent change of regimes, and more than just a political event. It espoused a totally new vision of society.

V It is in the cultural program that gradually crystallized in the Ishin, and above all in the Meiji state regime—which entailed, as we saw in chapter 2, the change in the role of the emperor and the choice of Shinto as state religion—that the major characteristics which distinguish the Meiji Ishin from the great revolutions are to be found. The new cultural vision out of which this program developed, the cosmology and ontology entailed in it, were promulgated as the renovation of an older, archaic system—which in fact never existed—not as a revolution aimed at changing the social and political order in an entirely new universalistic direction. Utopian orientations, with strong emphasis on the future, rooted in universalistic, transcendental visions, were, in contrast to the other revolutions, almost nonexistent, although millenarian restorative themes were prominent in some sectors of the uprisings before and during the Restoration, as they had been in some of the peasant rebellions that erupted during the Tokugawa period, especially toward the end of the regime, and in some of the important ideological schools of the Tokugawa era—especially the Mito one.

True enough, among some of the would-be reformers of the Meiji Ishin and, perhaps above all, among some of the reformers of the 1870s, there developed strong emphases—derived to some extent from neo-Confucianism, but above all from orientations toward the West—on universalistic as well as egalitarian themes. But these were later suppressed or, rather, submerged in the new hegemonic restorative mold.

Concomitantly, in the Meiji Ishin there did not develop, as there had in the revolutions in Europe, the United States, Russia, and China, a universalistic, transcendental missionary ideology, or any components of class ideology—two elements which were also very weak in the peasant rebellions and movements of protest of the Tokugawa period. Some elements of a universal civilizing mission developed in late Meiji, in attitudes toward Korea and China, but these did not entail the conception of these societies constituting, with Japan, a broader, universal civilization.[26] Similarly, explicit social symbolism—especially class symbolism—was almost entirely absent and was certainly not incorporated into the major symbols of the new regime, not even in connection with the semiutopian or, rather, inverted utopian restorationist themes.

The cultural program that crystallized in the Meiji Ishin and was promulgated in the various imperial edicts mentioned in chapter 2, combined the restorationist, nativist vision with a pragmatic emphasis on what may be called functional prerequisites of modern society, such as efficacy, achievement, and equality. These later themes were indeed very strongly emphasized, but mainly, as Sonoda Hidehiro has shown, in terms of their functional contribution to the organization of a modern society, that is, to Japan's adaptation to the new international setting.[27] At least in the hegemonic mold of the new ideology they were not grounded in any metaphysical or transcendental principles—such as, for instance, those of principled individuality—which went beyond the existing order. As

Sonoda puts it, "Functionalistic egalitarianism was not the recognition of 'equal' human rights as a political ideology which was of European origin and played a significant role in European history, but was the unintentional outcome of the samurai's thorough pursuit of practicality in service to the state."[28]

Only among small groups of intellectuals did there develop a tendency to ground these functional prerequisites in principled metaphysical or transcendental orientations, but they were not successful in changing the hegemonic orientations and premises. The message promulgated by the Meiji Restoration was oriented to the renovation of the Japanese nation—and had almost no universalistic or missionary dimensions. During the Ishin, and especially after the Restoration, numerous scholars engaged in the pursuit of knowledge from abroad and promulgated various new ideas at home, including strongly universalistic ones, but ultimately it was the so-called Meiji oligarchs, the leaders of the different rebellious factions in the Restoration, that molded the Meiji regime.

VI Thus the crux of the differences between the Meiji Ishin and the great revolutions lay in the fact that the Meiji Restoration ultimately legitimized itself in terms of seemingly backward-looking, "inverted" utopianism; the new direction was legitimized in some combination of purely pragmatic terms and restorationist claims, in contrast to the utopian, future-oriented, universalistic ideologies of the great revolutions. Even the Meiji insistence on progress and on learning from the West—especially but not only with respect to technology—were couched in terms of Japan's need to adjust itself to the modern world and not in terms of the implementation of general, universal values.

Many Japanese ideologists would later claim, as was claimed in earlier periods, that Japanese culture and society represented the purest, best synthesis of the different ways of life of other civilizations. But such statements were usually of an apologetic nature, part of the process of legitimization of the Japanese identity in a modern world, or they were directed against claims of Western superiority based on universal visions. They resembled the claims made in earlier periods with respect to Chinese civilization. The Japanese leaders who made these claims did not see themselves as missionaries of a universalistic way of life. Such statements, when made in connection with military encounters—after the Russo-Japanese and Chinese-Japanese wars, during the occupation of Korea, and especially during the military expansion of the 1930s and in the Second World War—often sought to legitimize Japanese conquests in terms of the superiority of their way of life. The missionary themes that appeared in this context were anti-Western, oriented toward saving Asia from the West—a process which Japan claimed to be called upon to lead.[29]

But the Japanese way of life was not seen as part of some universalistic vision, to be shared equally by all humanity. When Japan conquered other countries and ruled over them for any length of time, as in Korea or Taiwan, it attempted, often through very repressive measures, to Japanize them, but not to make them partners in any universalistic framework. No missionary element capable of overriding national identity—such as the emphasis on Islam that overwhelmed any regard for the Iranian state in the Iranian Revolution of 1979—could be found in the Japanese case.

VII Closely related to the other characteristics of the Meiji Ishin was the way in which the old ruling class—the daimyō and the broad samurai class—became dispossessed. Unlike most other aristocratic classes it went into decline not because of attacks from other classes; rather, its dispossession was effected from within the class itself—giving rise to what T. Smith has termed an "aristocratic revolution." [30] This self-dispossession was rooted, as Sonoda has shown, in the contradictions inherent in the structure and self-legitimation of the samurai class, that is, in the separation of the samurai functions from the samurai estate, which developed gradually but continuously, especially in the second half of the Tokugawa regime. [31] The samurai class, as Jansen and Rozman have put it, "dominated the early government, but its members also paid the highest price in loss of income, prerequisites, and honor. The leaders of that class, the former daimyō, were pushed aside—the most eminent into affluence, but a good many into genteel poverty." [32]

VIII The Meiji regime crystallized as a result of the victory of the more pragmatic leaders of the rebellion, those who emphasized the reorganization of the government in a conciliar direction, over the more millenarian nativist ones, the "pure" restorationists of the various *shi shi* groups. The pragmatic groups won probably because, in a sense, they were the least secessionist and least radical. [33]

But pragmatism could not provide its own legitimation, so those who promulgated it had to legitimize their preference in broader terms. The major such terms available to them in the dominant conceptual frameworks of the time were those of imperial restoration. Thus, their legitimation was highly influenced by the restorative ideology—but without its millenarian components and with a strong emphasis on merit and practicality.

The analyses in this and the preceding chapters should not be interpreted as implying that these various movements and organizations and the innovative themes they articulated had no impact on Japanese society beyond providing a framework for the toppling of the Tokugawa regime.

Many new institutional spaces were opened up through these movements and many new contacts between different sectors of society developed, often initiated by various "Confucian" schools or by such groups as the *shi shi* on the eve of and during the Restoration.

Indeed many of these uprisings and protests, especially those that took place in climates of great historical upheaval, such as the late Tokugawa period (from which most of our illustrations are drawn), introduced new themes of discourse. Under the impact of these movements, the basic premises of Japanese collective order and consciousness were reconstructed, reformulated in new and more sophisticated ways, incorporating many new conceptions. Of special importance in this context were, of course, the themes of individualism, equality, and achievement, as well as the new, "secular" definition of nature and the search for laws of nature—all of which were indeed incorporated into the universe of Japanese public discourse, expanding its conceptual range with respect to issues of ontological reality and national identity.

Many of the ideological themes espoused by these movements were also later incorporated into the ideology of the Meiji Restoration, just as the utopian millenarian and nativist ones were. Such incorporation minimized the relative autonomy of these themes—whether they concerned the moral worth of merchants or communal solidarity—and subsumed them under the canopy of the overall Meiji ideology of national solidarity and distinctiveness. Thus, new themes and orientations were subsumed under the reformulated premises but did not break through them. As Harootunian has put it,

> The price paid for this conception of authority (which in its original formulation was mediated by strong horizontalist links) was the installation of a new program of knowledge and power that valorized merit, ability, and practicality over mere status ascription; equality and utility over inequality and propriety as enduring evaluative criteria in the management of state and society. The communitarian and human impulses would have to find new modes of expression. Once more they would seek roots and power in the hidden world of rural Japan, which offered, too late, this frayed promise in folklore studies, romanticism and nostalgia, and the rantings of the radical right.[34]

But all these themes of protest—as well as those of the "nobility of failure" and of "men of high purpose," which so fully epitomized the loyalist rebellions in the Meiji Restoration—did not just disappear or become suppressed. These themes, often building on older themes of rebellion, protest, and popular culture, were incorporated in the repertoire of themes of protest in modern Japan and around the many new cultural activities and new types of discourse.

IX The awareness among scholars of these special characteristics of the Meiji Restoration has given rise to its designation—especially in the 1970s, together with, among others, the Kemalist Revolution in Turkey—as a "revolution from above," a revolution not initiated by middle and lower classes but imposed on the society by some (usually bureaucratic or military) part of the upper strata or of the "state," even if such imposition is connected with the ousting of the previous ruling elite.[35]

In many works published in the 1950s and earlier, the similarities of Japanese modernization under the Meiji with the more autocratic patterns of European modernization, especially those in Germany, were also emphasized—a comparison that seemed natural given the fact that the Meiji constitution was modeled on the German one.[36]

There is, of course, quite a lot of truth in both of these designations—above all in the emphasis on the relative weakness of the peasant and urban middle classes as autonomous social forces in the central revolutionary processes of these revolutions from above. And yet the weakness or lack of autonomy of these social groups was not the same in all these cases; significant differences can easily be identified between the Japanese, the German, and the Turkish cases. Unlike in Turkey, in both Germany and Japan there existed relatively strong urban, professional or semiprofessional groups, and their relative political passivity cannot be taken for granted: it has to be explained.

The German middle and, later, working classes engaged in quite extensive political activities intended to assert their political autonomy—and these attempts were supported by some of the basic premises of their political systems and of their modes of legitimation. Even in the Turkish case the basic legitimation of the regime—however inwardly, nationally oriented—was also couched in the terms of universal citizenship espoused by the Enlightenment. The story was different in Meiji Japan, despite some important similarities, especially with respect to statist orientations.

To reiterate, in conclusion, some points made above: the Meiji Ishin was not—as has sometimes been implied—a purely political coup without wide social or cultural implications. It was proclaimed as a renovation of an older archaic system, which in fact had never existed, and not as a revolution aiming to reconstruct state and society according to new principles. But not only did the new regime totally change Japanese society; this change was informed by a very distinctive cultural-political vision, a clearly modern cultural program. This program differed greatly, as we have already seen above, from that of most of the great revolutions; it was in a sense the mirror image of their programs, although in many ways it was no less radical.

In fact a radical reconstruction of state and society took place; there can be no doubt whatsoever that the Meiji Ishin constituted a sharp break with the immediate past and pushed Japan in a new modern direction, yet a very distinctive one couched in terms of a revolutionary restoration. It was in the Ishin, grounded as it was in specific Japanese historical experience, especially the Tokugawa one, that the roots of modern and contemporary Japan analyzed in the first part of the book were planted.

Part Three

THE FRAMEWORK
OF JAPANESE
HISTORICAL
EXPERIENCE

Japanese Historical Experience
Distinctive Characteristics
of Japanese Social Formations

JAPANESE COLLECTIVE CONSCIOUSNESS
AND PREMISES OF SOCIAL ORDER

‖ In the first part of this book, we explored some distinctive characteristics of modern and contemporary Japanese society, and in the second
part some institutional and cultural patterns in premodern—that is, pre-
Meiji—Japanese history. We were especially interested in finding out
what features, if any, can be identified throughout the Japanese historical
experience and what major changes and transformations have occurred in
these features in different periods. We will now attempt to bring the different threads of this analysis together. Accordingly, we shall first summarize some of the basic features of the Japanese historical experience
and then look for explanations of these features. This discussion will be
undertaken in a comparative framework, in line with the preceding analysis, which examined the similarities and differences between Japan and,
first, Western European societies, then—especially in the chapter on
Confucianism and Buddhism—that of China.

One of the most important problems to arise from our analysis is the
question of whether there exist any common elements in the *differences*
between Japan and each of these other societies—and if so, how these
recurrent differences are related to the continual changes that have taken
place in Japanese society throughout its history. The starting point for
this comparative foray is the fact, mentioned in chapter 1, that the institutional history and dynamics of Japan have been very similar to those of
Western Europe, as Emile Durkheim remarked at the beginning of this
century. Japan and Western Europe alike have undergone transitions from
semitribal monarchies through some type of feudalism to more centralized, seemingly absolutist states; they have experienced continuous economic development, the growth of cities and commerce, multiple economic

development, the growth of cities and commerce, multiple peasant rebellions, and the processes of modernization, along with generally high predispositions to continuous institutional restructuring. The preceding analysis also indicated that the *causes* of many of the major transformations in Japanese history—the disintegration of the feudal system and the rise of the semiabsolutist Tokugawa regime, the numerous peasant rebellions, the downfall of the Tokugawa regime and the success of the Meiji Restoration—could easily be compared with those of parallel processes and events in the West. Yet at the same time the overall institutional formations that have developed in Japan have differed greatly, as we have seen, from their closest structural analogues in Europe.

Is it then possible to identify some common elements among the basic characteristics of the Japanese historical experience that distinguish it generally from other civilizations? There is of course a danger in posing the question in this way: one may fall into the trap of either essentialism and simpleminded "Orientalism" or their mirror image, which is evident in the *Nihonjinron* literature. This is especially true insofar as any similarity in Japan's distinguishing characteristics across different periods of history may easily be taken for a "natural" construct that need not be explained. But such similarity or continuity—insofar as it exists—must be explained, and it is such explanation that constitutes the major challenge for comparative analysis.

We shall first consider some of the distinctive parameters within which the major social actors, the major institutional arenas and the Japanese collectivity were defined, the conceptions of authority that developed within most sectors of Japanese society, and the impact of such definitions and conceptions on the functioning of institutions throughout Japanese history. Second, we shall analyze some characteristic patterns of cultural creativity in Japan. On the basis of these analyses we shall examine some of the main features of the Japanese historical experience, especially the patterns of continuity and change in the major arenas of social and cultural creativity.

II   The analyses presented in the preceding chapters indicate that the prevailing definitions of the major arenas of social life in Japan have in common a strong embeddedness in contextual frameworks and a concomitant weakness of rules demarcating different arenas of action and defining them in abstract formal terms as separate, even autonomous, ontological entities. Every institutional arena we have considered—whether political, economic, familial, or concerned with cultural creativity, whether individual or collective—has been defined in terms of its relation to the social nexus in which it was embedded, which was in turn defined in some—continuously shifting—combination of primordial, sacral, natural, and ascriptive terms. The distinctive characteristic of these terms was that they were not defined in relation to principles that transcended them.

Above all, the major arenas of social action have been regulated, not by distinct autonomous, legal, bureaucratic, or voluntary organizations—even if such organizations have developed within them—but mostly through less formal arrangements and networks, which were in turn usually embedded in various ascriptively defined—and continuously redefined—social contexts.

III The emphasis on the embeddedness of the major arenas of action in contexts defined in some combination of natural, sacral, and primordial terms can be identified in the construction of the symbols and boundaries of the Japanese collectivity, which we have discussed in connection with both the transformation of Buddhism and Confucianism and the development of ideology in the Tokugawa, Meiji, and contemporary Japanese states. Some of the basic components of this distinctive definition—especially its construction in terms of a sacral-liturgical community with an emphasis on sacredness or divinity and on uniqueness—have developed, as we have seen, throughout Japanese history.[1] Such was the case in the early formulation, in the Heian period, of Japan as a divine nation (Shinkoku)—a nation under the protection of the deities—a conception that developed in close relation to the elaboration and promulgation of the imperial ritual and of what could be defined as Shinto.[2]

This conception of a divine nation, of sacred particularity—to follow Werblowski's felicitous expression—did not entail, as was the case in the monotheistic religions and civilizations, the connotation of being uniquely "chosen" in terms of a transcendental and universalistic mission. Nor did it entail the conception of responsibility to God to behave according to particular precepts or commitments.[3] Nevertheless, this conception of sacred particularity held its own when confronted with universalistic ideologies—Buddhist, Confucian, or, in modern times, liberal, constitutional, progressivist, or Marxist—all of which seemed to call for a redefinition of the symbols of collective identity in universalist directions. Except among small groups of intellectuals, however, universalist redefinitions have not taken root in Japan. Instead the premises of these religions or ideologies have been reconstructed in Japan in a combination of sacral, primordial, and natural terms. At the same time, they have been continuously reformulated in ways that allow for the incorporation of new themes and tropes. Thus, for instance, Japan's particularity and territoriality has often been sanctified, as for instance in some interpretations of the Lotus Sutra, and reinforced by being imbued with new spiritual dimensions.[4]

An interesting illustration of the persistence of such conceptions of the Japanese collectivity can be found in the attitude toward Marxism of some very distinguished Japanese leftist intellectuals in the twentieth century. In common with many such Chinese intellectuals, these Japanese scholars, such as Kōtoku Shūsui or Kawakami Hajime, attempted to deemphasize the materialistic dimensions of Marxism and to infuse them with values of spiritualistic regeneration. But while most of the Chinese intellectuals emphasized the transcendental and universalistic themes of "classical" Confucianism, the Japanese ones emphasized the specifically Japanese spiritual essence.[5]

One crucial derivative of the weakness, even lack of universalistic components in such definitions of the Japanese collectivity has been the impossibility of becoming Japanese by conversion. The Buddhist sects or Confucian schools—the most natural channels of conversion—could not perform this function in Japan. True enough, in the pre-Heian period and in later times, Koreans, as well as members of other groups, became assimilated into various regional Japanese settings. But these earlier experiences of assimilation did not entail a *principled* acceptance into a common collective entity sharing a specific transcendent vision. When more articulated conceptions of such collective consciousness developed in modern times, they excluded even the possibility of such assimilation. Lacking strong universalistic references, this exclusiveness could be formulated in terms of the genetic ("racial") purity of the Japanese collectivity—a formulation that easily led to the exclusion of nonpure minorities, such as the Koreans or the *burakumin*, as well as non-Yamoto groups, such as the Ainu[6]—or of social purity, unique spiritual essence, or the uniqueness of the Japanese language. All of these formulations, however, shared the core notion of sacred particularity, which provided the background to the numerous modern "schools" and promulgations of Japanese uniqueness and to the later development of *Nihonjinron* literature.[7]

The extent to which these formulations were articulated and their concrete institutional implications varied greatly in different periods of Japanese history. In the medieval period they were not necessarily of central concern to wide sectors of Japanese society, but were confined to various groups of *Kulturtraeger,* among whom Japanese identity—of a highly particularistic sort—was probably conceived above all in terms of political allegiance to Japanese warrior lords. In the Tokugawa period the construction of collective identity became closely connected to the political program of creating relatively clear state boundaries, while in the Meiji period it was closely interwoven with the construction of the new modern state and national community.[8]

Yet at the same time Japan's continual confrontation with universalistic civilizations continuously generated new dimensions of collective consciousness and highly sophisticated discourse. These conceptions of the Japanese collectivity entailed very intensive orientations toward "others"—China, Asia, the West; an awareness of other civilizations that did claim universal validity; and a continuous comparative attempt to place Japan in a (Buddhist, Confucian, or modern-Western) world scheme. Such comparisons usually emphasized Japanese uniqueness or its purported status as predominant bearer of universal pristine values. But they did not envision Japan as a part, not even the center, of a universalistic civilization.[9] Nor did they entail the participation of the Japanese collectivity in such civilizations or its reconstruction according to their universalistic premises. At most they asserted that the Japanese collectivity embodies the pristine values enunciated, and wrongfully appropriated, by the other civilizations.

It is the negation or bracketing out of universalistic components in the definition of the Japanese collective identity that makes it so difficult for most leaders in Japanese society to apologize for Japanese behavior in the Second World War toward Koreans, Chinese, and other Asian people—a response in marked contrast to that of many, if certainly not all, sectors in Germany.

The emphasis on the "purity" of the Japanese collectivity could also give rise, as in prime minister Nakasone Yasuhiro's famous speeches in the mid-1980s, to criticisms of Western societies, especially of the United States, based on their being racially mixed and hence unable to stand up to the standards of achievement presumably set by the "purer" stock.

These definitions of collective identity were not just naturally given—even if they were perceived to be so by large sectors of the population throughout much of Japanese history and seemed to persist in some natural way. Rather, such definitions have been continuously and consciously reconstructed by many groups of Japanese intellectuals, *Kulturtraeger*, elites, or other influentials who have felt the need to define themselves and their own collectivity in relation to others. Insofar as they have been concerned with such issues, these definitions have become relatively predominant in Japanese society.

The fact that there has been some continuity in the conceptions of collective identity does not mean either that the concrete definitions of such identity have not changed or that they have been of any salience for large sectors of the population. It was probably only in the Meiji or late in the Taishō and Shōwa periods—although there were strong antecedents in the Tokugawa era—that such collective consciousness, above all through intensive promulgation by the various political and cultural elites, pervaded wide sectors of the society. The upsurge of the *Nihonjin-ron* literature is probably the most recent widespread manifestation of these tendencies.[10] But even in periods of transition, marked by the spread of new options, and in sectors of Japanese society for which such consciousness was not very salient, definitions of collective identity, insofar as there was any interest in such definitions, were mostly expressed in terms of the sacred particularity analyzed above.

IV   Definitions of the major arenas of activity in Japan have been closely interwoven with the basic conceptions of social order and authority and the definition of the ground rules regulating institutional activities. Tom Rohlen has succinctly summarized this conception of authority:

> There is no insistence that governmental institutions solve problems by removal from society and objectification. A structural approach that equates hierarchy with power is somewhat misleading. Normal, everyday order itself stems from sources of group involvement, it appears, rather than distancing being a key maintenance mechanism, as in a utilitarian market rational world, attachment and interdependence are emphasized. Authority seems to depend in part on inclusiveness and patience in some fundamental way. Delegation within organization does not seem to threaten authority, because it does not undermine compliance or imply independence. Power is not basically assumed to, and apparently does not generally, lead to corruption and misuse. Social borders and informal processes of management appear much more important than public formal institutions or universal principles of reference.[11]

The full import of these conceptions of authority can be understood only if we take into account the concept of loyalty as it developed in Japan.[12] Such loyalty focused on the "lord," and by extension the emperor, and on the group, collectivity, or context of which these figures formed the apex or in the fate of which they were embroiled. Such loyalty could not be questioned, as was the case in various Axial civilizations, in terms of principles promulgated by a higher, transcendental authority standing outside the given social nexus, nor was the lord's authority legitimized by such principles.[13]

Thus, in general, social order, authority, and power have, like the major arenas of social interaction, usually been defined as embedded in different contexts, which are themselves defined in primordial, natural, and sacral terms and not as entities regulated by abstract rules and distinct from the people participating in them. These conceptions of authority and loyalty have tended to reinforce the tendencies to situational morality that were identified already by Ruth Benedict as a basic component of Japanese conceptions and behavior.[14]

Needless to say not all Japanese have adhered to the norms implicit in or derived from these conceptions, nor have they necessarily "believed" in them; but these conceptions have constituted the guiding templates for most patterns of behavior. Moreover, they have often been taken for granted, even if disregarded in some details or even openly contravened. Thus, as Befu and Manabe have shown, the prevalence of conceptions of sacred particularity did not necessarily entail a firm belief among wide sectors of Japanese society in all the tenets of the *Nihonjinron* literature. What is significant, however, is that no widespread counterconception of collective consciousness has developed in Japanese society.[15]

V As we have indicated, conceptions of social order and of authority in Japan have been closely related to the definition of the major institutional arenas and to the regulation of social activities within these arenas. The various institutions and the actors within them have been defined in terms of their relations to the social nexus in which they are embedded— a nexus defined in some combination of primordial, sacral, and ascriptive terms, together with strong achievement orientations, and not in autonomous terms derived from some conception of natural law or from what is perceived as the organizational needs of the specific arenas.

Thus the conceptions of social order, authority, and power analyzed above have been closely related to the basic rules of political organization and behavior—what Maruyama Masao called the "basso sostinato" of Japanese politics[16] and analyzed with special emphasis on the transformation of Chinese conceptions of authority in Japan:

> The separation of the level of legitimacy from the level of actual political power—this particular bass note—influenced the large-scale adoption, both theoretical and institutional, of the Chinese system of centralized bureaucracy by the *Yamato* court in the seventh century. What was noteworthy was that a new institution was interposed between the emperor and his ministers. It was called the *dajōkan*. The *dajōkan*, literally translated, was a council of great government and became the highest organ of the Japanese state. In China there was no counterpart to the *dajōkan* since it was taken for granted that the emperor was both the source of legitimacy and the holder of supreme power.
> . . . In all of these cases, the relationship between power and legitimacy is the same, always separate and distinct, whether between the *dajōkan* and the emperor, or between the regent (sesshō) or kampaku and the emperor, or between the shogun and the emperor, or between the shogunal regent (shikken) and the shogun.
> The two trends mentioned above converged: power developed downward at the same time as it became more informal and private. The climax of this convergence was *ge-koku-jō*, or inferiors overpowering their superiors, a phenomenon which characterized the fifteenth and sixteenth centuries when powerful local warriors rose to power and chaos prevailed. The

remarkable thing, however, is that no matter how extreme *ge-koku-jō* may have been, it never led to any change in the level of political legitimacy in Japan as a whole. Toyotomi Hideyoshi, one of the great unifiers of the late sixteenth century, was symbolic of his age. He rose from the peasantry to the highest level of political power; and yet only the title of kampaku (regent to the emperor), conferred on him by a powerless emperor, could legitimate his supreme position.

This paradox is revealed in modern history as well. In what is known as *ge-koku-jō* within the military in the 1930s, power devolved downwards from the general staff to low-ranking field officers.[17]

One interesting outcome of this mode of devolution of authority has been the fact that, throughout Japanese history, Japanese political regimes have veered between the development of a centralized framework and branching into a seemingly multiple-states system.[18] This has also given rise, as Murakami Yasusuke has pointed out, to the relatively weak legitimation of any concrete (especially shogunal) regime. Thus while the dissociation between the authority of the emperor—and later of the shogun, with the vesting of the right to legitimation in the emperor—and that of the powerful military families has assured the continuity of the national collectivity, it has never provided a strong enough basis for legitimation of the various regimes, as the attempts to promulgate the Tokugawa ideology, and even the modern Meiji ideology, attest to.[19]

VI In close relation to these basic premises, there have developed several features of the structuration of the political arena that are significant from a comparative point of view: the development, first, of a weak concept of the state as distinct from the broader, overall, (in modern terms) national community (defined here in sacral, natural, and primordial terms) and, second, of a societal state characterized by a tendency to emphasize guidance rather than direct regulation and permeation of the periphery by the center—in D. Okimoto's term, "a weak state."[20]

This view of the state is connected with the fact that power in Japan is not conceived as an independent entity to be applied to different arenas of life according to "objective" criteria. Rather, it is embedded in a structure of interdependent relationships that operate on the basis, not of coercion from above, but of dispersed action and coordination within vertical hierarchical networks. It is based on fine tuning, consensus building, and continual adaptation; hence, government could be compared to an "orchestra conductor,"[21] and there has developed a marked tendency—to use a term proposed by Victor Koschmann[22]—to "soft rule," the rule of a given authority not grounded in any transcendental vision.

Such conflation of the national community and the state, and the concomitant weakness of distinct conceptions of the state and of civil society, had developed already in the Sengoku and Tokugawa periods, in the concept of *kokutai*, and is manifest in the modern and contemporary periods in the concept of *kunmin dōchi* (united monarch and people) and the closely related distinction between *kokutai* (national structure) and *seitai* (political structure), which makes the latter inferior to the former and embedded within it.[23] One of the most interesting corollaries of this embedment of the political arena and of civil society within the overall community has been, as we have seen, the absence in the feudal and early modern periods of conceptions of autonomous legal rights and representative institutions. In Japan, however, unlike in many absolutist or totalitarian systems, the absence of such institutions was not concerned with a strong symbolic distinction of the center, of the state, or with strong efforts by the center to restructure and mobilize the periphery according to a new vision.

VII Throughout Japanese history, from at least the Kamakura period to the Meiji constitution and, especially, the Japanese defeat in the Second World War, the Japanese had very great difficulty in admitting the accountability of rulers to any concrete institution or institutional process. The concept of the emperor as the sacral embodiment of primordial, cosmic moral virtues and attributes—not as one to be judged by any institution or social actor—along with the concept of the absolute obligation of the subject to the ruler or of the vassal to the lord, made it difficult to specify any institutional process through which rulers could be held accountable. At the same time the importance of the ruler's or the lord's benevolence toward their subjects was strongly emphasized. This emphasis on the right to benevolence was often linked to the premise that the rulers are required to rule according to the way of heaven. But the conception of rule under the Mandate of Heaven as it crystallized did not specify any process to ensure institutional accountability.

Significantly, most Japanese scholars, as we have seen, had difficulty with the potentially revolutionary implications of Confucian ideology. They could not direct such ideology against the emperor; at most they could direct it against the shoguns, but even then mostly, possibly only, in the periods of their decline. In general the shogun also enjoyed a semiabsolute or sacral standing—even if this standing was ultimately legitimated by the emperor. It was only during periods of turbulence, toward the end of the Tokugawa regime and in the Ashikaga period, that shogunal authority could be challenged in principle. But even this disavowal of the shogun's authority was made in the name of the emperor's authority as defined in sacred-primordial and restorative terms—and it was these terms, however reformulated, that constituted the basic parameters and framework of the ideological-political discourse in most periods of Japanese history.

Given the bifurcation between authority and power, only lesser officials could be, under some circumstances, called to account when they seemed to transgress the moral balance and rhythm of the community. Such calling into account was not, at least until after the Second World War, vested in any specific institution or exercised according to any clearly stated rules. Rather, it could be expressed either through rebellions and protest or through communal public opinion, which would attest to any disturbances of group harmony. The first move toward institutionalized accountability was of course the Meiji constitution, but given the ambiguous place of the emperor in the consciousness and political process of the Meiji regime, the means of enforcement with respect to the misdemeanors of those in power was not very clear.

Even in the post–Second World War era, when constitutional democracy and fully fledged elections were institutionalized, persons in positions of authority were more often called to account, not through constitutional and legal procedures (though some politicians were indeed sent to jail), but by the pressure of public opinion or through the zeal of particular legal officials. Public pressure, as before, emphasized the disturbance of the community's harmony, consensus, or moral ambiance rather than the nonadherence to legal rules, and the culprits were pressed to offer public apologies. While such pressure is crucial in calling authorities to account in all modern (and many nonmodern) regimes, what was distinctive in Japan was the relatively limited extent—at least till very recently—of recourse to the legal arena. Many of the public apologies made by leaders in such situations bore the characteristics of rites of purification, of shredding the pollution accumulated through "deviant" activities—still defined in terms of personal or interpersonal, not universalistic moral, norms.[24] In situations of communal moral crises, for instance, superiors might take indirect responsibility for the transgressions of those under them—but there were no clear institutional ways to hold them to such a standard of accountability.

Thus, for instance, the dramatic toppling of the forty-year LDP hegemony in the 1993 elections was due more to the combined effects of accumulated corruption scandals and the secession of several groups from the LDP coalition than to either strong ideological confrontation (the socialist opposition was, in both absolute and proportional terms, the main loser in these elections, but by August 1994 there was a new LDP-dominated government headed by a socialist!) or confrontation over social and economic policies—although some indications of the latter conflicts did develop in these elections. In many ways these elections bore the character of a collective purification rite.

These conceptions of political authority, accountability, and "soft rule" have given rise to specific modes and ideologies of protest, for which Koschmann coined the term "expressive protest." (We have discussed these characteristics in the preceding chapters and shall come back to them later.) The most general manifestations of such expressive protest have been, as defined by Koschmann,[25] either separation of oneself from the community, "retreatism," or private dissent coupled with outward obedience and "ritualistic conformity."[26] Such protests need not be totally ineffective. The cultural emphasis on benevolence and on the upholding of the moral consensus of the community creates the possibility for strong claims to be made on the authorities to uphold the ideals. While such claims have not usually succeeded in breaking through the hegemony of the authorities, they have often been acceded to, even if in an indirect way, and have also generated new social spaces and modes of discourse.

VIII The conceptions and ground rules of the political arena have also to a great extent shaped the relations between center and periphery that have crystallized in Japan throughout its history. No sharp distinction has developed between the societal and the cosmological orders represented by the center and those represented by the different sectors of the periphery. Concomitantly, a relatively close relationship has evolved between the symbols of the center and those of the various peripheral groups, with the orientation of the former constituting an important component in the collective consciousness of the latter.

Although weak in certain historical periods, this symbolism has been embodied, in principle, in the figure of the emperor as the main mediator both between the cosmic order and the mundane world and between the collectivity—however defined—and natural forces. However weak the emperor's figure or symbol may have been during much of Japanese history, it has remained, as we saw in our discussion of the Meiji Ishin, the only symbol that has significance for most—not only the higher—sectors of Japanese society.

Accordingly, in structural-organizational terms, the premodern political systems that developed in Japan can be regarded as similar to various patrimonial systems, in which relatively little distinction existed between center and periphery, and there was little permeation of the center into the periphery or impingement by the periphery on the center. In Japan the centers have continuously attempted to permeate the periphery, but this permeation has been less oriented to the ideological restructuring of the periphery than in other imperial systems. Rather, it has focused on mobilizing the economic, political, and military resources, as well as the loyalty and strong commitments, of different groups of the periphery for the benefit of the center. Such attempts by the center (or in the feudal periods, by different, "decentralized" centers) to permeate and mobilize the resources of the periphery have been based on the strong emphasis in Japan on group commitment, as well as on the identity of the center's and of the periphery's cultural parameters.

This emphasis on the symbolism of the periphery has not, on the whole, entailed a romantic stance or glorification like that in Europe, in which the periphery has been glorified against the modern rational, secular center. Rather, it has emphasized the common and continuous participation of the various sectors of society in the primordial and sacral attributes of the collectivity—thus reinforcing the conflation of any public sphere, of any potential civil society, with the overall community and with the weak state.[27]

IX   Throughout the Japanese historical experience, however much various technical, utilitarian, or aesthetic aspects of economic or cultural activity may have been appreciated, the arenas within which these activities are undertaken have been defined contextually, in terms of their embeddedness in various social frameworks, and only to a very limited extent in autonomous functional terms specific to a given arena. Thus, definitions and modes of structuring social interaction in the economic and cultural spheres parallel those in the political realm.

This tendency can be identified in the conceptions of political economy, which is seen as embedded in the community and in the polity, its emphasis on economic achievement and performance set within the context of collective goals—whether those of the basic family unit (that is, the village manor), of the company, or of the nation—and of moral obligation to the community.[28] The merchant academies that developed in the Tokugawa period, for instance, emphasized the moral significance of mercantile activities because of their contribution to the welfare of the community, and many statesmen and industrialists of the Meiji and later periods made similar ideological pronouncements. The frequency of such declarations does not, of course, mean that such merchants or industrialists acted in a disinterested way, motivated by purely patriotic or "moral" reasons. It does mean, however, that in pursuing their economic goals they had to take such considerations into account, and that these considerations may have influenced some aspects of their economic activities. Indeed, as David Williams has very persuasively shown, the basic conception of economy from at least the Meiji period on has been that it should be in the service of the nation—its development, its growth, its ability to withstand the force of Western powers—and not an autonomous arena propelled mainly by the utilitarian goals of individuals.[29]

While modern Japanese economists have, of course, been influenced by Western economic thought—indeed, most of their work is couched in terms derived from the West—there runs throughout the development of Japanese economics a strong tendency to emphasize the contribution to the well-being or goals of the collectivity as against purely individualistic-utilitarian considerations.

At least three important derivations of such conceptions of political economy can be identified; although they are probably best documented for the modern period, kernels of them can be identified in earlier periods. First is the tendency to establish relatively long-term connections between different economic actors, such as producers, suppliers, "extractors," and subcontractors, seemingly disregarding the pull of direct market forces. Second is the closely related tendency toward a relatively long-term view of economic activities—which can be found already in the seventh century in the attempts of the state to regulate demographic expansion in relation to arable land. Third, there is a strong tendency among heads of many economic conglomerates to act on guidance received in consultation with officials of ministries.[30]

Very much in line with this approach to economics is the attitude to work that can be found among many Japanese employees, who, to paraphrase Jeremiah J. Sullivan, tend to view work not in instrumental, goal-oriented terms, but rather as part of the process of participation in their social setting.[31]

Significantly, many new types of activities developed in Japanese institutions—one of the most famous of which is the quality control that developed in Japanese industries—have been legitimized in terms of their contributions to the welfare of the community, not only in more specific, functional terms.

X Some distinctive characteristics, parallel to those of the political arena, can also be identified with respect to the structuring of social hierarchies as it has developed throughout Japanese history. Even in periods such as the early monarchical or the Tokugawa ones, when Chinese Confucian hierarchical classifications—in which power, authority, and wealth were combined in relatively uniform, homogeneous patterns—were imposed in Japan, the actual concrete hierarchies tended to be localized or sectorialized, and organized vertically in multiple, often cross-cutting networks, especially at the macro level. These networks have tended to converge, but only rarely have they been connected in terms of overarching, countrywide strata.[32] While horizontal status arrangements and consciousness have not been lacking, they have rarely been articulated on a countrywide, or even sectorwide, scale.[33]

One of the central aspects of this mode of structuration of social hierarchies is the relative looseness of many of the relations among power, wealth, and status within any given setting or context. The specific structural manifestations of this pattern of status incongruence have naturally differed in different periods of Japanese history. In the medieval, "feudal" period, it was manifest, first, in the multiple types of relations within the center; second, in the bifurcation between emperor and shogun; and, third, in the great urban developments, above all those of castle towns. The relation of status incongruence to the process of change was also clearly evident in the Tokugawa period. The Tokugawa regime attempted, as is well known, to impose rigid forms on Japanese society, and it developed the most stringent modes of control to achieve this. But this control was based, as we have seen, on the perpetuation of some discrepancy between status, authority, and wealth—which indeed intensified toward the end of this period.[34] Such incongruence was seemingly taken for granted, and the few attempts to change it, as for instance to make the Tokugawa shoguns into kings, failed. In the Meiji, Taishō, and Shōwa periods this mode of status incongruence was again manifest—in the composition of the new ruling and bureaucratic classes and in the pattern of advancement in the public sector and in large private industrial companies, where education played a crucial role in the crystallization of yet more new patterns of status incongruence and institutional formation.[35]

The relatively loose relations between the different major status dimensions can also be identified in many micro situations, for instance, in the tridimensional spatial structuring of hierarchy in the houses of Japanese nobility or in the structuration of neighborhood groups in suburban Tokyo.[36] Several studies of such neighborhoods have shown that people from different occupations and of different economic standing may participate in the same neighborhood groups or festivities, that different associations cut across economic or professional categories, and that older inhabitants, even those whose economic standing is not very high, often occupy positions of influence in such associations and activities. Such status discrepancies are also visible with respect to women's lives, especially in the relation between their education and occupational achievements (see chapter 6).

The combination of strong disassociations between status, power, authority, and wealth—closely related to the basic characteristics of Japanese kinship, which we shall discuss in chapter 14—with a relatively decentralized pattern of political rule has created wide institutional "empty spaces," which could be filled in various ways. It has also provided strong institutional incentives and new structural opportunities for change, creating the possibility of many new types of activities and organizations. The creation of such empty spaces, and of closely related free-floating resources—that is, economic or manpower resources—could and did lead to the development of groups competing, sometimes fiercely, with each other. But however bloody such competition might have been, it rarely led to principled confrontations with the premises of the center. Power and wealth had to be legitimized in terms of symbols borne by a center. Accordingly, the dissociation between different dimensions of status has combined with far-reaching restrictions on conversion of resources and on autonomous access to the centers of relevant contexts. Innovative arrangements have ultimately been legitimized in terms of ascriptive criteria or by a charismatic representative of the particular group, for instance, the head of the family or the leaders of the village. Innovation has accordingly been guided by the prestige vested in the center or centers and interpreted in terms of the basic symbolism of the center, with its strong primordial-sacral and collective components.

The patterns of dissociation between the major dimensions of status and the continuous reconstruction of networks have also facilitated the continuous development of spaces in which new types of social activities, consciousness, and cultural creativity, many espousing subversive themes, have been able to develop without necessarily coming into open confrontation with the basic premises of the centers or with the hegemonic conceptions of the social order.

Which groups have had access to power or to status has naturally greatly varied throughout Japanese history. But the pattern of limited status congruence and restricted convertability of resources has persisted, up to the Tokugawa period, which John Hall claims is best explained as a status society, and beyond.[37]

XI   Japanese conceptions of authority, loyalty, and morality and the tendency to status incongruence have influenced the structure of authority in most sectors of Japanese society, including the economic arena: in corporations, small businesses, public bureaucracies, and even many informal encounters, in historical and contemporary settings alike.[38]

First, in most institutional arenas authority has been dispersed and there has tended to develop, as we have seen, what John Hall called a dissociation between power and authority.[39] Second, there has developed within most organizations a combination of hierarchical and collective orientations with a relatively strong emphasis on long-range, largely (although not exclusively) collective goals, and a yet stronger emphasis on obligation and commitment of members to the goals of their respective collectivities. Third, given that social order, authority, and power are usually perceived in Japan as embedded in contexts defined in primordial, natural, and sacral terms and not as regulated by abstract, formal, universalistic rules, there have developed several structural characteristics of the exercise of power and authority, including a strong tendency to informal arrangements and networks; the construction of continuous relations and crossings between different networks; a predisposition to consultation; and a tendency to concentrate different types of functionally specialized activity within a common framework.

Concomitantly, most organizations or arenas of social interaction have not been structured according to formal, abstract rules or "substantive rationality." Not that abstract rules and agencies have not developed in Japan—they have always existed and naturally burgeoned in the modern era, especially pursuant to the great centralization under the Meiji—but they have usually been thoroughly embedded in the background, as it were, of various social networks. Formal and informal rules continually reinforced each other and the former were not usually seen as distinct from the latter. It is the continual density of such networks that has assured the great extent of mutual visibility of their members—this greatly facilitating the implementation of intensive and extensive processes of social control.[40]

The concrete forms of these networks have, of course, greatly varied between different periods of Japanese history and different sectors of Japanese society. The more overarching ones, those that cut across and combine many organizations to broad, flexible frameworks, have become more important with growing modernization and economic development. But throughout Japanese history these networks have retained some basic characteristics—such as the emphasis on moral guidance and consultation rather than formal, abstract rules or direct force.

As Hamaguchi Eshun and his collaborators,[41] as well as Murakami, Rohlen, Kumon, and Imai have recently indicated,[42] such relations have been based on the existence of autonomously distributed hierarchic systems, the different units of which are coordinated by networks that give rise in Hamaguchi's words to a "multi-layered complex insider society." In such a society the more formal rules are embedded in tacit understandings, which are promulgated and continuously renegotiated in the various networks. Given the crucial importance of such tacit understandings the transmission of information plays a crucial role in these networks.

These arrangements have also facilitated, under appropriate conditions, the development of patterns of interaction affording widely dispersed, nonhierarchical access to information. Information is not stored in different, technically specialized compartments, but spread among different compartments, between which there exists some tacit understanding. At the same time these arrangements facilitate more hierarchical decision making.[43]

This mode of hierarchical arrangement gives rise to two seemingly (especially from a Western point of view) contradictory tendencies with respect to the dynamics of authority. One is the tendency toward relative—indeed, only relative—equalization of the lifestyles of different echelons, especially within given frameworks, organizations, or sectors. The relatively lower degree of income inequality in modern Japan, as compared with other advanced industrial countries, is one indication of this tendency; other illustrations can be found in other periods in Japanese history. The second is the tendency toward supervision and regulation by the authorities of such frameworks, which minimizes the possibility of the egalitarian tendencies' becoming the bases of autonomous political activity or of the restructuration of the basic premises of authority.

The prevalence of these conceptions of authority and organizational patterns does not, of course, mean that governance in Japan has been peaceful or without conflict—rather it indicates that the numerous conflicts that have arisen in Japanese society have been defined and coped with in rather specific ways.[44]

CHANGE AND CONTINUITY IN JAPAN: CHANGE, PROTEST, AND EXTERNAL INFLUENCES

XII The preceding chapters have emphasized the seeming continuity of some major aspects of Japanese social formations in what is—probably unavoidably—a rather simplistic and exaggerated way. Assuming, however, that there is some merit in this picture, the discussion sheds some light on one of the most important aspects of the Japanese historical experience, namely the question of what has changed and what has persisted or been continuously reproduced. What patterns of continuity and change characterize this historical experience, and how do they compare with those in other societies?

What has been changing seems rather obvious. Japanese history has been characterized by continuous change in most concrete institutional formations—in the forms of families and villages and the patterns of economic and ecological status, political and religious organization—as well as in the major arenas of cultural creativity—in modes of artistic and intellectual discourse, which have developed to a great extent under the impact of foreign influences. Not just concrete details but some of the basic organizing principles of these arenas have changed, as for instance in the development of new economic systems (different types of feudalism; commercial and market networks before and during the Tokugawa regime; a capitalist system in the Meiji period) or the constitutive principles of the political systems that have developed in different periods.

Moreover, throughout Japanese history, new social spaces have continuously developed, in which new cultural and institutional patterns not guided by the hegemonic definitions have crystallized and thriven.

As we pointed out in the first chapter and in the beginning of this one, the tempo and variety of these changes have been very high, probably comparable only to those in Western Europe. But alongside these far-reaching changes, some core symbols of the Japanese collectivity and basic conceptions of social order and its legitimation have maintained a marked continuity, or at least a similarity between different periods.

Within the more hegemonic discourse that has prevailed in Japan there has developed a relatively weak consciousness of ideological or symbolic discontinuity, of ideological transition or breaks between different periods. Japanese historiography has tended in all periods to emphasize continuity, especially that of the imperial line (see chapter 16). Some changes—for instance, the transition to Tokugawa rule, the Meiji Restoration, and the Second World War—have indeed been conceived as great breaks. But such breaks have not on the whole been conceived in overall metaphysical or cosmological terms, in terms of the unfolding of some cosmic vision. Rather, they have mostly been conceived in terms of the impingement of some—often external—events. The emphasis on continuity has been helped to no small degree by the continuity of the imperial symbolism and of the court and by the fact that the basic mode of legitimation was not radically changed.[45] Almost all such changes have been perceived as severe outbreaks disrupting—albeit seemingly for a short period—the usual smoother continuity.

Closely related to this weak consciousness of symbolic or ideological discontinuity has been Japan's relatively low level of ideologization—and of principled, ideological struggles guided or legitimized by principles lying outside the existing reality. This has been one of the most distinctive characteristics, as compared with the Axial civilizations, of the intensive mode of institutional changes that has developed in Japan. The intensive struggles that have developed in connection with many of the changes in centers, organizations, and roles have not been connected with strong ideological contentions, as was generally the case in Europe. Concomitantly, no sharp demarcation of the symbolic boundaries of these collectivities and centers has emerged.

The embedment or incorporation of new activities within existing settings was facilitated by the fact that such settings were themselves to some extent continually redefined; for instance, new urban settings were defined as traditional. Significantly, such redefinitions were effected, not in new terms opposed in principle to the old ones, but rather in some combination of sacral, primordial, or natural terms. The same applies to the structuring and definition of new activities, roles, and organizations.

The many new roles (be they entrepreneurial-economic or bureaucratic-political), the related organizations (industrial enterprises, political parties), and the ground rules that evolved to regulate them, while necessarily defined in new technical terms, have not been legitimated in entirely new or autonomous ways. They have been legitimated neither in terms of their functional prerequisites (that is, in terms of the exigencies of power or of economic performance), nor as autonomous manifestations of some higher, transcendental order (for instance as signs of grace), but rather in terms of their contribution to the contexts in which they were embedded—contexts defined in some version of primordial, natural, or sacral terms.

Most of these activities and organizations have been embedded or re-embedded and seemingly easily incorporated in the prevalent social settings or, to be more exact, in the continuously redefined and reconstructed social settings and contexts with their flexible and shifting boundaries—without, however, principled changes in their basic premises.

The common denominator of the patterns of change that have developed in Japan has been the continuity of symbols, such as those of family or community, that have allowed for extensive changes in a familiar symbolic context, thus softening the sense of rupture and avoiding the need to address change ideologically.

XIII Such relative continuity, and the consciousness thereof, does not mean that the basic conceptions of social order and the ground rules of social interaction have been formulated in the same way throughout Japanese history. On the contrary, the concrete forms of these social definitions—their literary expression, the ideological language in which they have been couched, their specific intellectual contents, and the discourse that has developed around them—have been, as we have seen, continuously changed and reconstructed. Nor have such reformulations been simply cosmetic; rather, they—and the problems they have engendered—have continuously changed the frameworks of the ideological, philosophical, and aesthetic discourse that has developed in Japan. These changing definitions, interwoven with an emphasis on achievement and performance and with strong utilitarian considerations, have also often been connected with the development of new, usually relatively segregated arenas or social spaces in which new themes and new modes of activity have been able to develop. One of the most interesting manifestations of this segregative approach to the impact of external influences is the development, in the early Meiji and Taishō periods, of two schools of painting: Yōga, painting in the Western style, and Nihonga, painting in the old "traditional" Japanese style.[46]

It is especially in periods of rapid historical change and intensive encounter with other civilizations, and probably in situations of personal or of group crisis—some of which we have analyzed—that new definitions of social activities have been considered within Japanese society. Such openings have also taken place in connection with the numerous movements of protest, or in variegated forms of popular culture, which have spawned egalitarian, communitarian, and other themes opposed to the hegemonic premises. These situations of rapid change, conflict, protest, and exposure to external influences have usually crystallized in a double-pronged manner such as we have already analyzed with respect to the transformation of Confucianism and Buddhism in Japan, as well as some of the major developments in the modern era.

On the one hand, there have developed throughout Japan's history new modes of discourse and social spaces in which new types of cultural and social activity—newspapers, journals, avant-garde theater, and popular culture, for example—have flourished. Many of the most dynamic enterprises and entrepreneurs have emerged in such arenas. On the other hand, such spaces and activities have been incorporated into the overall framework of Japanese society, not by changing the basic rules or definitions of the major institutions, but rather through the construction of separate social categories, for instance, those assigned to priests or monks in ancient and medieval times or that of the *kikokushijo*, the Japanese children who have come back to Japan after having been abroad with their parents, on the contemporary scene.[47] In such new, partially segregated, partially incorporated settings, new networks have often been constructed which could become interwoven, by co-option or by incorporation, with older ones, as we saw in chapter 6.

Concomitantly, there has developed a continuous redefinition and restructuration by various intellectuals, influentials, and elites of the various arenas of action in terms of the new discourses. The concrete definitions of the different social contexts have been continuously changing, as have the ways in which their sacral, liturgical, primordial, and natural attributes are deployed and the relative importance of these attributes in the new definitions. These changing definitions have usually incorporated themes promulgated during the periods of change, as was the case with the incorporation in the late Tokugawa and early Meiji periods of components of historical orientations into the prevalent mythical templates. At the same time there have developed many new, relatively segregated but more autonomous discourses focused on such themes. Moreover, many changes have taken place in the definition of concepts central to the social order—for instance, the more independent, rational concepts of *tenka* promulgated by Nobunaga. The promulgation of such concepts has entailed, potentially at least, the possibility that the core definition of the social order would be radically redefined, going beyond the primordial-social-natural order.

Such radical reformulations have not, however, taken place on the level of the hegemonic discourse. New themes either have been incorporated into the discourse without fundamentally changing it or have become foci of intensive discourse in relatively segregated spaces. The basic framework of such a discourse is usually formulated, all these changes notwithstanding, in terms of some combination of sacral, liturgical, primordial, and natural terms, of "philosophizing in the archaic," of some social nexus—together with a strong emphasis on obligation, duty, and achievement as set in the framework of these nexuses. The sacral-primordial-cultural premises and themes have been selected, by large numbers of influentials, intellectuals, and leaders, from the available cultural repertoire and reformulated to become the guiding templates of a new, diversified discourse.

Between these two prongs there have naturally developed continuous tensions and areas of ambiguity. It is probably these tensions and ambiguities that have generated Japan's highly sophisticated modes of reflexivity and discourse, as well as the specific characteristics of this reflexivity. This reflexivity has been structured, as Murakami Yasusuke has indicated, in a "hermeneutical" rather than "transcendental" mode, that is, it has been oriented much more inwardly, toward the continuous exploration of the Japanese cultural mode according to its contextual contents, than toward transcendental, universalistic principles, thus reinforcing the general direction of intellectual discourse in Japan.[48] Such hermeneutical reflexivity is not "simple," habitual, commonsensical, inward-looking. It constitutes a highly sophisticated reflexivity that developed to no small extent out of confrontation with other, universal, transcendental civilizations—China and the West—to which the Japanese appeal in delineating themselves and their activities. (I owe this observation to B. Silberman.)

XIV A double-pronged response is also clearly manifest in the regulation of various manifestations of disharmony, be they deviant behavior, conflicts, or protest. On the one hand, the regulatory processes attempt to reembed potentially disharmonious activities within prevailing frameworks. On the other hand, they permit the development of spaces, such as those generated by the various movements of protest, especially the more radical ones; the broader processes of change (for instance, those that have influenced the status of women in contemporary Japan, which we discussed in chapter 6); or, earlier, the impact of Confucianism and Buddhism. These new social spaces, even if segregated from the central ones, are arenas in which the hegemonic rules and topics of discourse are not necessarily predominant, and within which sophisticated discourses and new levels of reflexivity have developed.

The most continual carriers of subversive themes throughout Japanese history were the various *hiteijūmin* (nonsettled people), intensively investigated by Amino Yoshihiko, as well as nonagricultural population.[49] These groups dominated the early literature and performing arts; their voices could be continually heard, even if they were often tamed by the hegemonic institutions, particularly Buddhist monasteries, which incorporated them into their frameworks. But such taming did not obliterate these voices, which instead blended with those of other marginalized groups, often emphasizing the importance of marginality in Japanese culture and even, as we shall see in greater detail in chapter 13, the close relation of such marginality to the feminine aspect of the emperor figure.

Not only have the various movements of protest sometimes achieved their concrete aims, influencing the policies initiated by the authorities; even when, in the various periods of opening, their demands were suppressed in the public arena, their subversive themes and the new areas of public discourse they generated contributed to the reservoir of cultural themes that constituted the collective consciousness and at times led to action. They came to the fore, not primarily by achieving their goals or reconstructing the center, but by either being incorporated into the more central arenas of discourse or becoming foci of new, relatively segregated spaces.

Such spaces may become reconnected with the center in different ways. Some, as for instance that of the kamikaze bikers,[50] allow an avenue to blow off steam in direct reaction against the mainstream, but amount to no more than a hobby, and often a transient one. Others, like the schools for Japanese children educated abroad, became an avenue to reintegrate marginal groups into the system.[51]

The strong tendency to reembed "deviant" or protest activities—processes of change—within existing social frameworks and the upholding of the prevalent hegemonic premises is manifest in the fact that the confrontational situations in which movements of protest have been especially visible have not usually led to the institutionalization of new modes of conflict resolution. In such situations new ideological and institutional options—many of them rooted in potentially universalistic, transcendental conceptions—have surfaced, often promulgated by groups of potentially autonomous intellectuals. The leaders of protest movements have also often stressed communitarian themes, or horizontal ("class") as against vertical solidarity—themes also often articulated in popular culture.

But despite the many demands couched in such terms, these movements have not given rise to a restructuring of organizations at the center according to entirely new—especially universalistic or transcendental—criteria. They have not, for instance, led to the full institutionalization of more formal legal activities grounded in universalistic principles, or to the reformulation of the basic premises of social and political order, even if they have provided for the reinterpretation and reconstruction of many of these premises.

Even when the tension between a confrontational stance and the ideals of harmony has intensified—as was the case, for instance, in the Taishō period or during the student rebellion of the late 1960s—the conflicts have seemed to be resolved by means of familiar, "routine" processes. Sometimes, however, far-reaching concrete changes have taken place.

The various openings, which have developed relatively quickly, have usually been closed up—albeit in more diversified modes in the modern period—by coalitions or countercoalitions of elites, influentials, or even counterelites. The mode of conflict resolution or management that has emerged has emphasized reestablishing the vertical hierarchical principles, even if in new organizational or institutional configurations and with the addition of new themes of discourse and social consciousness.

XV Numerous external influences—ideas, artifacts, technologies, styles of dress—have been incorporated into Japanese culture, so much so that Japan has often been called a country of imitations and imitators. But such a designation is misplaced, because a central aspect of Japanese historical experience has been that most such borrowings, while very influential, have been thoroughly "Japanized," that is, organized or structured according to principles specific to the Japanese experience or modes of life.

This capacity of the Japanese to absorb, in their own way, many external influences, has been vividly described by Endō Shūsaku, in his novel *Silence*, in the powerful metaphor of the Japanese swamp.[52] This "swamping" capacity can be identified in many arenas—those we have analyzed above, as well as the transformation of Christian beliefs and sects analyzed by Robert N. Bellah and recently by the eminent Japanese Jungian psychoanalyst Kawai.[53] On a more mundane level this capacity for Japanization can be seen in the transformation of baseball practice—vividly described by Robert Whiting—or of the basic premises and organization of the Jamaican Rastafari movement in Japan.[54]

But the Japanization of foreign artifacts, ways of thought, and patterns of behavior has been carried out, as is the case with regard to processes of change and movements of protest, in a double-pronged manner. On the one hand, these foreign influences, insofar as they are incorporated into Japanese life, are often consigned to segregated areas; at the same time, their basic premises are radically transformed on both an institutional and an ideological level, so they become congruent with the basic ontological vision and conceptions of social order prevalent in Japan. On the other hand, under the impact of these foreign influences, new, highly developed modes of discourse and collective and cultural consciousness have developed in Japan.

Among the most important and dramatic such transformations were, as we have seen, the Japanization of Confucianism and Buddhism—two major Axial civilizations. We noted the transformation of orientations that stressed the chasm between the transcendental and mundane orders in a more "immanentist" direction, and the parallel transformation of some of their basic premises and concepts of the social order—manifest, for instance, in the change from the concept of the Mandate of Heaven, a remarkable change in view of the obvious dependence of the Japanese *tennō* emperor (ten = heaven) on the Chinese model, but without the Chinese version's conception of authority and implication for the accountability of rulers. Unlike China, where the emperor was, in principle, "under" the Mandate of Heaven, in Japan he was seen as in close touch with heaven—and heaven itself was on the whole conceived in sharply transcendental terms—and not accountable to anybody. Similarly, the strong universalistic orientations inherent in Buddhism, and more latent in Confucianism, were subdued and "nativized" in Japan.

Thus, the Japanization of Buddhism and Confucianism entailed, not just the addition of local color, but the transformation of their basic conceptions in line with the basic premises of Japanese civilization. The same processes have been operative in the modern period with respect to Western ideologies and forms of social organization. One interesting aspect of the Japanization of Buddhism, Confucianism, and various Western universalistic ideologies has been that the Japanese bearers of these ideologies have not attempted to reexport their versions; this in itself attests to the weakening of their universalistic, often missionary orientations. Japan has, however, attempted in modern times to put itself at the head of an Asian counteroffensive against the West, which has entailed an expansionist turn. This constituted, as Johann Arnason has observed (in private correspondence), "a radical transfiguration of particularism, in which Marxism played a very ambiguous, complex and intriguing role: on the one hand, Marxism was—as Maruyama has argued—the symbol of consistent and uncompromising opening to the West, but on the other hand, it was indirectly instrumental in the radicalization of particularism."

Nevertheless, it is probably Japan's continual encounter with China, with Confucianism and Buddhism, and later with the West, and the continual necessity to distinguish itself from China and the West without either denying the outside values or admitting their superiority, that has led to the development of the intense, complex, and sophisticated mode of ideological discourse that distinguishes Japan from most other non-Axial civilizations. This highly developed discourse has paradoxically constituted a conscious and highly reflexive denial of the type of ideologies grounded in the premises of Axial civilizations; but at the same time it has been couched in terms derived from these ideologies.[55]

XVI The double-pronged mode of response to change and to external influences can be seen most clearly in the development of intellectual and public discourse in Japan. Throughout Japanese history, and especially in periods of rapid social change or intensive impingement of foreign influences, many Japanese intellectuals and artists have sought, not only to develop new forms of artistic creativity and philosophical discourse, but also to break through the hegemonic premises and templates. Some have succeeded, but usually only in the confines of their own endeavors.

In each of these periods many intellectuals—religious or secular—have espoused oppositionary views, views usually derived from foreign universalistic conceptions—Chinese and Indian Confucianism, Buddhism, or, in modern times, liberal or Marxist ideologies—which could in principle negate many of the basic premises of Japanese traditions. Such tendencies can be identified in almost all periods of Japanese history, as, for instance, in the discussions of the Taishō era on the nature of the state and in the many ideological formulations developed in this era, which, while in some ways opposed to the hegemonic premises, in fact accepted and even reinforced them, often because their promulgators were unable to apply their potentially radical or revolutionary intellectual stances to concrete political issues.

The pattern of the construction of new spaces within a relatively continuous mode of discourse is also to be found, as it was in the preceding discussion, with respect to the definition of the Japanese collectivity. Many of the concrete details of, for instance, the sacral or archaic definitions of the early Meiji ideology, would be shed with the "secularization" that set in after the Second World War, and some new components, such as the growing emphasis on knowledge, developed already in the early Meiji, would be added, but without changing the core definition of the collectivity and without becoming the foci of intensive political and ideological struggles. This situation seemed to change in the post–Second World War period after the democratization effected under the auspices of the American occupation. Indeed, the immediate postwar period—until about the mid-1950s, saw a significant opening up of the basic parameters of such discourse. This tendency was reinforced by the fact that the close cooperation between academics and the bureaucracy that developed in the early Meiji era, and which started to disintegrate or at least weaken at the end of the Meiji and during the Taishō era, was even further undermined.

Especially in the modern and contemporary periods, the Japanese public has been exposed to many foreign influences—in literature, the arts, and films—and many imitations have developed. Moreover, throughout these periods there developed many activities and groups imbued with the more egalitarian and communal vision of people like Andō Shōeki.[56] Yet in these cases too a double-pronged process developed. On the one hand, new activities and modes of discourse—many with highly subversive themes—emerged and became institutionalized in continuously expanding new spaces. The range of discussion in the press was very wide, and the press emerged as a powerful force. New academic, journalistic, and literary organizations and settings were established, many of them serving as enclaves for distinctive (for instance, Marxist) intellectual and academic endeavors and discourse. The members of these groups were active participants in public discussion and exerted considerable influence, as Herbert Passin has shown, on public opinion and policy.[57]

There developed among them many highly critical discourses and artistic activities promulgating themes of protest—as, for instance, in the new "proletarian" theater, which developed especially in the period after the war, or the many "critical" films. In some cases, intellectuals participated in movements of protest; their protest activities included, for instance, opposition to the elimination of Toshiba University; the creation of Tsukuba University and of the International Center for Research in Japanese Studies; and the response of Meiji Gakuin University on the occasion of the death of the Shōwa emperor, when it initiated a series of open lectures and discussions on the emperor system and did not fly the flag at half-mast.[58]

On the other hand, these activities did not do away with the dominance of the hegemonic modes of structuration of cultural creativity and their basic premises. Most of them did not come into full, ideological confrontation with the central, hegemonic system in an open public arena. Most of the public discourse did not break through the framework of the basic conflation of society and state, with the concomitant weakness of civil society. However far-reaching the reformulation of these premises may have been on some occasions, the changes were usually couched in nondiscursive, quasi-mythical terms rather than logocentric ones. Thus, for instance, writers who challenged the major modern developments promulgated by the ruling elites, such as industrialization and urbanization, often did so in terms that valorized nature and folk images, in line with the folkloric studies of Yanagita Kunio.[59]

It is some combination of the mythical primordial-sacral-liturgical or natural social nexus that has ultimately constituted the framework even of many of the sophisticated new formulations that have emerged in the philosophical discourse. This nexus has provided the basic codes, parameters, or templates for these formulations, giving rise continuously to the immanentization of potentially transcendental orientations and the particularization of universalistic ones. Even many of the highly opposition-ary themes increasingly promulgated by various groups—Andō Shōeki being yet once more a crucial illustration—emphasize the givenness of "nature," as against the artificiality of any political or even linguistic con-struction, and do not go beyond such givenness. The specific mode of Japanization of external influences is, of course, but the other side of this mode of continuity.[60]

XVII Domestication of foreign influences (or of internal protest) is not, of course, unique to Japan. It happens all over the world, in many societies and civilizations. The specific aspect of such domestication in the Japanese case has been the strong, and rather paradoxical, tendency to de-Axialize Axial influences on a societywide level, combined with a continuous openness to outside influences and the development of highly sophisti-cated discourse—a combination not found in any other great civilization.

De-Axialization denotes the muting, segregation, or bracketing out of specific Axial orientations—above all the transcendental and universalis-tic ones. This often takes place when a "great tradition" reaches the pe-ripheries and "small traditions," as it were, within itself, losing contact with its original center. The transformation of Confucianism, Buddhism, and Western ideologies in Japan, however, constitutes the de-Axialization of Axial religions, ideologies, or civilizations, not in local or peripheral arenas, but in a total society in the very core of the great tradition. This transformation has given rise, as analyzed in chapter 10, to a reconstruc-tion and reformulation of the basic ontological conceptions and premises of social order prevalent in Japanese society, but not in the transcendental and universalistic directions implicit in the original ideologies.

In Japan, unlike many non-Axial civilizations that were also pre-Axial—for instance, ancient Egypt, Assyria, or Mesoamerica—there evolved sophisticated intellectual, philosophical, ideological, and religious discourses, as for instance in the development of different neo-Confucian schools, which confronted and debated the so-called nativistic learning in the Tokugawa period. Much of this discourse has been a conscious and highly reflexive denial of the types of ideologies grounded in the premises of Axial civilizations; but at the same time it has usually been couched in terms derived from these ideologies, and the confrontation between them has constituted a continuous focus of reflexivity.

The process has been, as Johann Arnason has put it, one in which "con-tinental (i.e., mainland Asia) cultural orientations were—selectively— incorporated into the Japanese civilizational complex, whose indigenous component was at the same time reconstructed in relation to—and with more or less identifiable inputs from—these Chinese models. They entailed a continual deradicalization and transfiguration of the Chinese Confucianism and Buddhism—Axial premises" (Arnason, private correspondence).

At the same time, Japan has never become, in its own collective consciousness, an integral part of other, broader civilizations, even if it has continually been oriented to them and lived with them or under their shadow, and even if the comparison with other civilizations and the search for a place in the world order they constructed has constituted a continual concern of many Japanese *Kulturtraeger*. Japan has always lived with these other civilizations but never been one of them—continuously maintaining its conscious collective distinctiveness and the distinctiveness of its civilizational premises.

XVIII   This specific pattern of de-Axialization also explains the special mode of rationality, of "secular" thought and reflexivity, that has developed in Japan. Indeed, Carl Steenstrup has pointed out a preference for rationalistic as against metaphysical (Buddhist and Confucian) orientations, manifest in the examples of Ogyū Sorai and other thinkers of the Tokugawa era, who rebelled, as we have seen, against neo-Confucian metaphysical trends building on earlier tendencies.[61]

This secular or rationalistic orientation has, however, several features which distinguish it from the major rationalistic trends in the West, to which Steenstrup compares it. This rationalism has been highly pragmatic and has emphasized the natural characteristics of society, as against its being constructed by social and political agents. This emphasis has been oriented not only against "magical" or traditional beliefs but also against metaphysical principles, transcending the mundane reality. But just because such pragmatic and secular thought, with its *Zweckrationalität* orientation, has been free from metaphysical grounding does not mean it has given rise to a critical *Wertrationalität* discourse, and it has been the nondiscursive "philosophizing in the archaic" that has become predominant in Japan.

The predominance of this mode of discourse has not meant that no reflexive discourse has developed in Japan. On the contrary, Japanese philosophical discourse has entailed an intensive, highly sophisticated reflexivity and self-contemplation—especially with respect to Japanese society and culture. The continuous confrontation between nativist orientations (usually, as we have seen, dubbed Shinto) and the Confucian and Buddhist discourses has generated such self-reflexivity in many circles of Japanese society. Such reflexivity has indeed entailed, to use B. Schwartz's expression, the "standing back and looking beyond" that has developed in Axial civilizations.[62] But this mode of reflexivity, this discourse—the like of which cannot be found in most pre-Axial civilizations—has developed in a very distinctive way. It is, in Murakami Yasusuke's terminology, a "hermeneutical," self-referential discourse rather than a transcendental one that judges reality by principles beyond it. At the same time this discourse has been shaped by continual confrontation with the transcendental, universal orientations of China and of the West.

XIX The continuous reconstruction and reformulation of basic social conceptions would probably not have been possible in the intellectual and artistic realms without parallel developments in the institutional arenas. Such changes first took place with regard to the Tang models of government imported from China in the eighth century and later with regard to Confucian and Buddhist institutions brought over from Korea, China, and more indirectly from India.

Such transformations have perhaps been most visible in the modern era, when many organizations have been patterned after Western models and many arenas of social life have been restructured according to universalistic and achievement criteria. This has been especially true of the educational and occupational arenas. However, the modus operandi of these organizations has differed in crucial organizational details from those of their counterparts in the West—especially with respect to their internal integration and their interaction with their environments, as manifest in their prioritizing of goals or in their hierarchical structure. They have been set, as we have seen, in contextual, particularistic frames organized in vertical hierarchical networks. Their goals have to some extent differed from those of firms in other modern societies, as for instance in their greater emphasis on long-term planning, assuring a share in the market rather than short-term profits, and in their orientations toward the well-being of the collectivity within which they operate. Similarly, in most such situations of change, far-reaching reconstruction of the relevant social networks has taken place; often seemingly nonnetwork organizations—for instance, radical, political, ideological, or religious sectlike groups—have appeared. Yet, only rarely have these groups been able—unless they give up their sectarian characteristics and integrate themselves into the particularistic, vertical networks—to mobilize wider sectors of the population. Moreover, as we have seen, sectarian and rebellious groups have often themselves been organized according to the hegemonic principles of the center.

XX Thus, in the realms both of discourse and of institutional transformation themes adopted from external sources have been filtered through specifically Japanese codes or templates—as, for instance, those suggested by Nakamura Hajime.[63] Through this process, the basic conceptions and premises of ontological and social order prevalent in Japan have been both reaffirmed and continuously reconstructed, their specific formulations changing greatly over the years and becoming more and more reflexive.[64] In other words, it is the nondiscursive, sacral-primordial premises that have been continuously selected and reformulated as templates for the new discourse.

At the same time, oppositionary intellectuals have tended to retreat, as it were, into private spaces—academic or literary—as did many Buddhist scholars and monks in earlier times. Within these enclaves they have engaged in various innovative activities, deepening and diversifying the major modes of discourse and the basic problematic of such discourse.[65] But only rarely have they gone beyond the premises of the hegemonic mold—at least in public ideological discourse—even if these premises have been reformulated through their discussions. When intellectuals have challenged such premises, they have rarely succeeded in mobilizing broader sectors of the public and have more often coalesced into small, segregated, sectarian groups. Their attempts at mobilization have been more successful when they have used traditional symbols—such as those associated with rice—but the use of these symbols already entails going beyond their sectorial confines.[66]

The prevalence of these templates does not mean—as Fosco Maraini has correctly pointed out with respect to the importance of the Shinto myth in contemporary Japan and as Paul Veyne has shown with respect to the ancient Greeks[67]—either that most sectors of Japanese society have been aware of the more sophisticated formulations as promulgated by the *Kulturtraeger* or that they have necessarily "believed" in these promulgations. What it does mean is that these orientations have provided—or have continuously been chosen to provide—the basic premises, templates, or master codes that have formed the framework, often taken for granted, of the universes of discourse that have developed in Japan.

XXI The combination of far-reaching changes and the construction of new social spaces with the prevalence of some basic organizational premises can be illustrated in many arenas of contemporary Japanese life. Among the most important new spaces are the numerous new religions analyzed in chapter 3. Another concrete illustration is to be found in the modern, highly commercialized marriage ceremony. As Walter Edwards has shown in his illuminating analysis, all the major organizational details differ greatly from traditional marriage. Yet at the same time these ceremonies are symbolically structured so as to convey certain "traditional" premises.

> The emphasis in marriage has shifted to the needs of the principals rather than those of their families. Nevertheless, it is not as individuals that their

interests hold priority, for the conclusion of this work can only be that the individual has not replaced the *ie* as the fundamental unit in cultural values, despite the legal changes. Rather the *katei* has become its successor—particularly in its minimal form as the husband/wife relationship, for here we seen most clearly the *katei* meeting the two criteria set out earlier; it is the smallest viable social unit, and a microcosm for the larger society.

Moreover, the husband/wife unit as depicted in the wedding is both hierarchically ordered—again because of differences ascribed to men and women—and harmonious.

Thus while the legal form of the *ie* has been abolished, underlying principles of hierarchy and harmonious interdependence—principles that inevitably deny the autonomy of the individual—survive in its successor as basic unit. If this continuity shows a remarkable conservatism in the values of contemporary Japan, it is surely because the coherence of those values constitutes an argument for how life ought to be lived that is as compelling in the modern world as it was in the past—an argument that is no less Japanese today for all its modernity.[68]

Thus we see that while the concrete organization of these ceremonies differs greatly from older ones—attesting to the great capacity of the Japanese to incorporate new patterns of action and to create, as it were, new customs—the new customs have been put in the framework of traditional, albeit highly reconstructed, themes and premises. Needless to say, in such modern settings many individualistic subthemes do develop, but they seem to remain subordinate, possibly generating more flexible contexts and spaces, but seemingly not changing the core premises.

Of special interest here is the fact that the promulgation of these themes has not necessarily been instituted by the authorities. Rather, entrepreneurs who organize these ceremonies seem to have presumed that these themes would find wider responsiveness within the society and have organized the ceremonies accordingly.

TRADITION AND CHANGE

XXII Our discussion now brings us to the problem of the place of tradition in Japanese society, especially in shaping the processes of continuity and change. As we noted in the first chapter, there has developed a tendency in many scholarly works on Japan to explain specific phenomena in terms of Japanese tradition or culture. Against this, institutionalists of various persuasions have totally denied the validity of such explanations.

As the cases already considered indicate, including that of modern marriage ceremonies, the situation is more complex. "Tradition" is not just a static, homogeneous set of symbols or themes that automatically shape institutional contours or patterns of behavior. Rather, tradition has to be viewed as a heterogeneous and often contradictory reservoir of usually polysemic themes, which are continuously selected and reconstructed on different levels of social life through the interactions between influentials, elites, and broader sectors of society.

Robert Cole's discussion of the lifelong employment system is relevant in this context:

> A close examination of the emergence of the permanent employment practice reveals that innovators were both able and constrained to draw heavily from the stock of traditional values and practices. Indeed, the borrowing and use of native cultural resources is so pronounced in the case of permanent employment, at both a structural and symbolic level, that its emergence may be seen as a recrystallization of similar types of norms and structures that were operative in Japanese society. Japanese leaders were adept, on both a conscious and unconscious level, at using traditional symbols to secure the legitimation of the new institutional arrangements associated with permanent employment (e.g., payment by age and length of service) and to motivate new kinds of behavior. It is in these terms that the practice may be described as having traditional elements.[69]

Such reformulations have often entailed the incorporation of new themes, such as the growing historical consciousness or the emphasis on universal knowledge, which have changed the modes of public discourse. While the successful institutionalization, in each of these cases, of the hegemonic ideology has entailed a continuation of the predominance of the primordial and sacral premises and themes of Japanese tradition, it has also given rise to transformations of some of the bases of legitimation of these premises—and generated new problems and new tensions.

Thus it is not a simple, automatic unfolding of primordial, sacral, or natural premises of social order that explains the continuity of traditional themes and symbols in Japanese society. Such continuity, to the extent that it can be identified, is the result of complicated social processes, undertaken not only by different elite groups but also by broader sectors of society or nation, which entail the continuous selection of particular symbols, tropes, and patterns of behavior.

The fact that tradition is in all societies continuously reconstructed does not mean, however, that its reconstruction is haphazard. The concrete modes of the reconstruction of tradition—the selection, reformulation, and invention of themes from the reservoir of tradition, the addition of new themes, and the definition of what constitutes tradition and how binding it will be—develop in different directions in different societies, although similarities also develop. The specifically Japanese mode of reconstruction of tradition has developed on three levels. First, the symbols of collective identity have been constructed in restorative terms; the continuous reproduction of such symbols has been legitimized as traditional and it has been their "traditionality," even in the case of newly constructed symbols, that has constituted the core of their legitimacy.

Second, there has been a tendency also to legitimize new developments and customs as traditional or as expressive of tradition. Tradition, as defined in many sectors of Japanese society, has tended to become a crucial, albeit often consciously constructed, symbol of legitimation of new patterns of behavior, organization, cultural creativity, and discourse, as well as of their broader, continuously changing contexts defined in particularistic, primordial, sacral, and natural terms.[70] Moreover, the very problem of the traditionality of different aspects of life has constituted a continuous focus of debate in Japan. Such discussion has to a great extent taken the legitimizing nature of tradition as a given. Indeed tradition, and the search for tradition, have often been tantamount to the search for the "authentic" Japanese, as against the alien, the Western. In various situations this search for tradition has been couched in either antimodern or authentically modern Japanese terms.

Third, the construction of traditions in Japan has been marked by the continuity of the main components—the natural, social, and primordial ones of the basic ontological conceptions of social order—combined with a certain looseness in their concrete specifications. Such looseness, as well as the great openness to foreign influences, has been rooted to no small degree in the lack of any explicit dogma and logocentricity in the hegemonic Japanese discourse.

Thus, the preceding analysis indicates that the modes of reconstruction of tradition in Japan have been characterized by openness to the development of new patterns of social organization, cultural creativity, and discourse, combined with the continuous reproduction of some basic definitions of these activities and of the modes of their legitimation.

The combination of all these modes of reconstruction of different dimensions of tradition in Japan has not necessarily entailed a stance of "closure" to all innovations, of denial of anything new. Tradition and traditionalism have constituted a general orientation in the name of which many activities and organizations, old and new, have been legitimized, a canopy under which many new developments could be brought together. This canopy has provided the general orientations for the construction of social discourse, but it has not created sharp boundaries or breaks between the traditional and the nontraditional arenas or levels of life.

Even potentially subversive themes have been incorporated in the new spaces, as was, for instance, the case with some of the themes that developed, under the influence of Buddhism, in medieval Japanese literature. Some of these were subsequently crystallized into the more formal tea ceremonies and became seemingly legitimized in some traditionalistic terms.[71] Such legitimation has always entailed an implicit assumption that these subversive themes would not become openly confrontational. When they have become so, as in three incidents described by Norma Field—the harassment of the mayor of Nagasaki after he talked about the emperor's involvement in the Second World War, the prosecution of a citizen of Okinawa who put the Japanese flag down at a baseball game, and the failure of a Japanese woman's protests against the interment of her husband at the Yasasuki shrine as a war hero—at least a partial clampdown has usually followed.[72]

XXIII The preceding analysis of Japanese institutional formations highlights some of the features that distinguish the Japanese historical experience from those of other civilizations—both those in Western and Central Europe, with which Japan shares many institutional features, and that of China, with which it shares many cultural and intellectual traditions. Thus, the Japanese historical experience has been framed within institutional structures similar to those of some Axial Age civilizations, but has been defined in contextual terms through modes of ideological discourse that, although continuously reformulated in encounters with Axial civilizations, are unlike those found in most Axial civilizations. Within this framework of ontological conceptions and structural characteristics intense internal changes, reflecting both an openness to foreign influences and a tendency toward their Japanization, have developed, generating the distinctive combination of continuity and change that we have analyzed above.

These characteristics have given rise to a specific mode of social and cultural dynamics, which comprises, on the one hand, vigorous changes in concrete organizational and institutional formations, in ideological discourse, and in cultural creativity and, on the other hand, the apparent continuity of the basic symbols and premises of the social and cultural order and of the Japanese collectivity, and a double-pronged mode of responding to and at least partially incorporating foreign influences, structural changes, and movements of protest. This seeming continuity or reproduction of basic premises—of the ground rules, as it were, of social action—and of cultural themes consonant with such premises was not foreordained. Indeed, at several points of Japanese history there have developed openings toward other possibilities. In addition to the circumstances already discussed—the Meiji, Taishō, and post–Second World

War periods and the impact of Confucianism and Buddhism—Johann P. Arnason points out (in a private communication) the following:

> The initial seventh-century attempt to combine Chinese bureaucratic institutions with direct imperial rule, rather than with the aristocratic regime which eventually prevailed (Temmu and some of his successors); the fourteenth-century Kemmu restoration; the abortive attempt of the first Ashikaga shoguns to absorb the imperial institution into the new military state; the fifteenth- and sixteenth-century alliance of a part of the Buddhist establishment with popular movements; and the state-building strategy characteristic of the first phase of unification (especially Nobunaga), which would seem to have differed significantly from the later Tokugawa pattern.

In each of these situations, as in the medieval and early-modern era at the time of the impact of Confucianism and Buddhism (the era of unification before Tokugawa), other options seemingly opened up.

Thus, for instance, it might well have happened that the process of unification under Nobunaga or even Hideyoshi could have weakened or even abolished the traditional imperial legitimation and ushered in a more "rationalized," unified bureaucratic state. This might also have happened with respect to the earlier periods mentioned above. But such possibilities did not materialize—such alternative ideological and institutional arrangements did not become fully crystallized and hegemonic. Nonetheless, these openings, these periods of possibility that did not achieve their aims, had far-reaching effects on Japanese history. They created not only new spaces, but also reservoirs of continuous alternative configurations and nonhegemonic traditions.

This combination of the institutionalization, and of the repeated contextualized production, of specific symbolic and institutional patterns of continuity and change with the emphasis on immanentist and sacral premises, and cultural themes consonant with such premises, calls for an explanation.

IN SEARCH OF AN EXPLANATION

XXIV These distinctive characteristics of the Japanese historical experiences are central to the "enigma of Japan," the explanation of which constitutes the major challenge for comparative analysis. Are these characteristics truly unique to Japan? Are they to be found in all sectors of Japanese society and in all periods of Japanese history? Are they best explained in cultural or structural terms or as matters of historical contingency?

With respect to the first question, the thrust of our analysis—with its emphasis on the comparison of Japanese institutional formations with those in Western Europe and in Confucian and Buddhist China—has been that Japan's seeming uniqueness can and should be analyzed in a comparative framework. With respect to the second question, it seems, at least at this stage of our analysis, that these features have been characteristic of the hegemonic sectors of Japanese society throughout most of its history.

The third question is in a way the most difficult one and has constituted the focus of both scholarly and broader public controversies. An emphasis on culture could, especially on the ideological level, be identified with many of the characteristics of Japanese life as portrayed in the more extreme versions of the *Nihonjinron* nationalist literature. As we have seen, several very serious arguments have been proposed against the cultural or culturological explanations. One is that culture and tradition are not static entities but are continuously reconstructed. A second, closely connected but probably less forceful, argument is that what has often been identified as culture or tradition is a relatively new construct. The third, and possibly most important, criticism is that many patterns of behavior often explained in terms of "traditional" groupism—whether factionalism in politics or issues of loyalty in labor relations—can be explained equally well in terms of rational behavior in given frameworks.

Yet at the same time, the structuration in any given period of Japanese history of the major arenas of social life—the definitions and other parameters regulating the behavior within them—has been quite similar to that in other periods. We find that throughout Japanese history, when changes have taken place under the impact of external forces, many new options have developed but the response which became hegemonic has included similar patterns of what we call Japanization. The same is true to no small extent of the modes of coping with internal protest or conflict, which have also emphasized either isolating or co-opting their subversive potentials.

These two sides to the argument attest to the validity of the major analytical assertion presented in chapter 1—that posing the question of how these characteristics should be explained in such dichotomous terms is erroneous, and that we should look instead for the specific modes in which cultural and structural dimensions of social action are continuously interwoven in any particular society. In the following analysis we shall spell out this assertion in detail.

Thus, we now face the challenge of analyzing the ways in which "culture" and "social structure" have shaped the major characteristics of the historical experience of Japan. In order to do so we have first to examine more closely what we mean by culture, or rather what aspects of what has been called culture—often a broad residual category with few explanatory powers—may be most relevant to understanding the major characteristics of the institutional formations and patterns of cultural creativity that have developed in Japan. The preceding analysis of the various aspects of modern contemporary and historical Japan, and above all the transformation of Confucianism and Buddhism in Japan, has indeed pointed to the importance of one such dimension or aspect of culture, namely of various ontological and cosmological conceptions—of the nature of the cosmos and man's place in it, of nature and culture, of time and space, and of personality and interpersonal relations. The de-Axialization of Axial civilizations or religions that has taken place in Japan, has indeed entailed the transformation of such basic ontological conceptions, as well as conceptions of societal order. It might therefore be worthwhile to analyze in a more systematic way the basic ontological conceptions that have been prevalent in Japan.

There is an obvious danger in looking for such basic dimensions of Japanese culture: such analysis can easily fall into the essentialist trap of assuming the existence of eternal, transhistorical, ontological conceptions, immune to historical change and the impact of concrete social forces and struggles. Much of the literature on Japanese culture and tradition has indeed fallen into this trap. There may be no easy way to avoid it—except perhaps to be fully aware of its existence. Bearing this in mind, let us stress two points. First, as Fosco Maraini has indicated, it is not the possible continuity and impact of fully articulated cosmological and ontological conceptions that are critical here, but rather "modes of thinking, attitudes to the world."[73] Second, however correct, at least in broad outline, is the assumption of the similarity, possible continuity of basic cosmological conceptions and definitions of the social order, the major problem is how such conceptions and their institutional repercussions are reproduced—and possibly changed and transformed, at least in some of their dimensions—through the processes of such reproduction.

We shall proceed in the next chapters to explore these problems.

Japanese Culture or Cultural Tradition

BASIC ONTOLOGICAL CONCEPTIONS AND THEIR IMPACT

Nature and Culture, Vitalism, Purity and Pollution

I Like any other cultural tradition, Japanese culture can be defined in many different ways: in terms of its great variety of customs; of what is designated as tradition, which in fact often consists of rather recent innovations; or of pure, pervasive, guiding conceptions of *Weltanschauung*, or, to use Kate Wildman Nakai's term (private communication), underlying native assumptions or orientations. Among the many aspects of what is called culture, two of the most continuous, it seems to me, are also of particular importance for understanding Japanese institutional formations. These are, first, the basic ontological conceptions and conceptions of social order and, second, the basic definitions of self and personality.

The most distinctive Japanese conceptions of ontological reality, as identified in the relevant historical, anthropological, and philosophical literature, are first, a high degree of mutual embeddedness of what in Western parlance are called nature and culture, that is, a strong sense of the interrelations between the transcendent and the mundane worlds and of their immanentization, as against the emphasis on a chasm between them in the Axial civilizations; second, and closely related, an emphasis on gods as the continuous regenerators of the world, but not as its creators; third, a dualistic conception of the cosmos that strongly differentiates between purity and pollution, order and its inverse; fourth, a commitment to the cosmic and natural (including social) orders, and the concomitant structuration of various arenas of action according to, above all, these basic dualistic categories; fifth, a highly vitalistic conception of life, combined with an activist-pragmatist attitude to the world; and, sixth, an emphasis on mythical time conceptions as the most important temporal dimension of the collective and cosmic rhythm, and a closely related mythocentric, as against logocentric ontological discourse.

This approach to natural and social reality has been interwoven with a distinctive mode of semantic structuration of the major arenas of discourse. This mode is characterized by the minimization of the importance of the subject relative to the environment and emphasis on relational and indexical criteria (as against abstract, linear principles) as the regulating principles of the discourse.

The common denominator of these basic ontological conceptions and of the semantic structuration of discourse is an emphasis on reality as structured in terms of shifting contexts rather than discrete, enclosed ontological entities or absolutist, dichotomous categories. Reality, in this view, is conceived of, not in terms of relations involving "things" on an objective horizon, but rather as something that is constructed or defined by these very relations.

II The first fully articulated formulations of many of these conceptions of ontological reality can be identified in ancient Japanese texts such as the *Kojiki* and *Nihongi*, which already constitute elaborate cultural constructions probably built on earlier, less formalized formulations.

John Pelzel's analysis of these texts is very pertinent; we may follow here the Lebras' exposition of his major points:

> John Pelzel in his analysis of the myths that appear in the Kojiki and *Nihongi* has recently summarized some of these major themes, what may be called the major transformation rules which define the nature of ontological reality in the Japanese tradition. . . .
>
> Some of the most important characteristics of Japanese thought, especially as contrasted with the Chinese and Western ones, are the relative lack of opposition between (in addition to those mentioned above) gods and humans, life and death, mortal and immortal, order and disorder, blessedness and misery, wild and tamed, nature and culture. Between these, there is no gulf, no confrontation, no dominance, no contradistinction; instead, one finds continuity, compromise, fusion, and duplication. So too is the relationship between good and evil. Hence we come to learn that the gods do not play the role of exemplary moral actors nor do they take full charge of maintaining a moral order. Moral standards are more or less relative and lack the kind of didactic assertions that feature in the rationally oriented Chinese myths and philosophy. If there is anything close to an ultimate standard, it is, we are led to believe, the cleanliness of the actor's heart.
>
> The world of *Kojiki* and *Nihongi* does not exhaust the Japanese sense of morality or worldview, however. Undeniably, Confucianism and Buddhism have had overwhelming impact upon Japanese culture and behavior, and

the Japanese sense of morality cannot be captured without considering these. The point is that the long history of religious and philosophical transfusions from the Sinified continent and of the conglomeration of newer beliefs with the earlier "native" cult (which came to be known as Shinto) has not replaced the pre-Confucian, pre-Buddhist intuitions and sentiments symbolized by the myths. Not surprisingly then, we read about "the principle of harmony that admits no distinction between good and bad as operating in today's Japan."[1]

This Japanese basic ontological conception can be characterized, as Munakata Iwao has done, as symbolic immanentist thought or cognition (*"Symbolische Immanezdenken"*).[2] Or, in the words of Augustin Berque:

> In the Japanese tradition it is impossible to envisage either logos or the subject independently of the world. There is no principle which transcends reality. And reality is the word of appearances [Erscheinungen] which we have to accept as it is contingent, in the given place and time.
>
> For the Japanese, thus, the world is not something the subject has to impose his logic upon; he has to adapt himself to it. Anyway, both the world and the subject are perpetually changing.[3]

III   The "primitive" or archaic mythological conceptions analyzed by Pelzel changed greatly in later times, especially through the impact of Confucianism and Buddhism. This is true both on the purely "academic," intellectual or philosophical level and on the level of prevalent common-sense definitions, conceptions, and discourse. The definitions of ontological reality that developed in the various Buddhist and Confucian schools in Japan transformed the formulations presented in the ancient myths. At the same time, many of the Buddhist and Confucian formulations originating from mainland Asia were transformed in Japan—again, not only on the philosophical level, but especially on the level of public discourse, whether that determined by ideology or that regulated by unconscious assumptions regulating daily commonsense discourse. The transcendental orientations of these religions were increasingly immanentized and the universalistic ones particularized. Yet the impact of the transcendental orientations was indeed very great—transforming what could be called, in Munakata's terms, an archaic worldview into a symbolic immanentist one.

Such a worldview or ontology entailed a very high degree of spiritualization and aestheticization of the world, creating many spaces in which dimensions of human sensibility could be articulated, while incorporating these spaces within the basic immanentist frameworks.

IV   The persistence of these conceptions of ontological reality has often been identified—rightly or wrongly—with Shintoism, that is, with basic ontological beliefs or assumptions that could be better called underlying native orientations. These orientations were not necessarily identical to the more formal aspects of the continuously changing organization of Shinto shrines, or even to what was from time to time represented as the true Shinto doctrine—almost a contradiction in terms—rooted in the conception of gods as generators but not creators of the world.[4] As Fosco Maraini has indicated, this conception—in contrast to that of God as creator, who is outside the world and who created it "in a silent and terrifying act of the mind"—"establishes a relation which is fundamentally biological, therefore intimate, simple, warm. . . ."

> . . . Creation establishes clear-cut oppositions, of which God and the world, spirit and matter, soul and body, eternity and time, supernatural and natural, are some examples, and is therefore necessarily accompanied by transcendency in religion and by dualism in philosophy. Generation on the other hand is more naturally connected with synthesis and harmony, with immanence and pantheism in religion, with forms of monism in thought, be it explicit or not. In the West terms such as "immanence" or "monism" refer to ideas which are essentially bookish, academic, scholastic; in Japan they refer to the stuff of everyday life, to ideas and attitudes which are so ubiquitous and obvious that one hardly talks about them, they are folklore and common sense, festival and proverb.
>
> If gods beget the world, then nature is somehow sacred, nature is the ultimate criterion of truth, of goodness and of beauty.[5]

This basic attitude to the world entailed a certain sanctification of the phenomenal world, of nature, the possibility of sanctification of almost any object. Throughout Japanese history there developed on different levels of discourse, but especially on the more implicit level of common discourse, a tendency to conflate the divine sacred spirits (*kami*) with the phenomenal world.[6]

V   The Japanese emphasis on the mutual embeddedness of nature and culture does not entail the perception of reality as homogeneous. On the contrary, it entails a perception of reality as structured in multiple, continually shifting contexts, between which it flows—contexts organized above all according to a basically dualistic cosmology.

Dualistic distinctions are of course not unique to the Japanese worldview. In Japan, however, first, there is basically no attempt to subsume these dualistic categories under overarching abstract unitary principles and linear conceptions of reality. Second, the dualistic principles are not defined as contrasting, but rather as flexible, complementary categories, the movement between which is structured in definite contexts which themselves may be continuously reconstructed, in topological and not in linear modes. As Emiko Ohnuki-Tierney has put it:[7]

> The basically dualistic Japanese universe is a universe that constantly ebbs and flows between two opposite principles: purity and impurity—or according to a different interpretation a state of full vital energy and the waning thereof; good and evil; order and its inversion. With opposing forces simultaneously present, it is a universe in which the negative elements are as integral as positive elements.[8]

Third, and derivative of the first point, distinctions between the different dualistic principles refer to different social and cosmic arenas or spaces and the interrelation between them rather than to different dimensions of the cosmic reality and of the world conceived as distinct ontological entities.

Thus such dualistic differentiation entails a rather weak distinction between transcendent and mundane reality but is rather strong with respect to zones within which "natural" and "supernatural" are interwoven. The distinction between the dualistic principles—between good and evil, purity and pollution, order and its inversion, full energy and its waning— is conceived in Japanese culture, not in terms of transcendental absolutes, but in terms of continuously changing contexts. Again in Emiko Ohnuki-Tierney's words:

> Purity and impurity are classificatory principles that govern a particular context rather than absolute properties. Thus, the classification of an object or being in the universe as pure or impure depends upon what it is being contrasted with. Therefore, while both deities and humans are characterized by the dual qualities of purity and impurity, when deities as a category of beings in the Japanese universe are contrasted with humans, the former become pure in contrast to the latter, which become impure. By the same token, when boundaries are contrasted with the structure consisting of the deity-human dyad, the structure is pure and the boundaries impure.[9]

VI These basic conceptions gave rise to Japan to the construction of many arenas of reality regulated by a variety of dualistic principles. The most important among these are, as we shall see in greater detail in our discussion of the Japanese concept of personhood, those of *omote* and *ura* (front and back), *honne* and *tatemae* (inner feeling and formal pretense), *uchi* and *soto* (outer and inner).

Such distinctions, between contexts or forces defined according to dualistic principles, especially according to conceptions of purity and pollution, are closely related to distinctions between insiders and outsiders— the relations between whom have also to be bridged.

Thus a state of pollution is believed to bring danger, adversity, and misfortune to human beings and a state in which pollution has been entirely removed to bring public peace and prosperity. The belief that purification from pollution can be achieved by the repetition of rituals can be discerned in the Japanese belief system from the time of the *Kojiki* and *Nihonshoki* to the present. It is not too much to say that Shinto places this ritualism at the center of its belief system, and the usual Japanese interpretation of Buddhism is that it brings salvation to the spirits of the dead, that is, purifies them from the pollution of death. . . .

. . . This ritualism can easily be used in support of political manipulation—for example, to explain a class structure with the imperial court, the utmost in ritual purity, at its apex [and] as a rationale for discrimination.[10]

In such a universe the transition from one arena or context to another is of crucial importance. Pollution and purity, like good and evil, are conceived, not as abstract absolutes, but in contextual terms. Transitions, especially those from pollution to purity, are of very great importance and are effected by a great number of mediatory figures and forces—gods, spirits, strangers, and others.[11] Many patterns of ritual behavior focus on taboos, many of which can be violated so long as appropriate rituals restore the original state. The pertinent mediating figures effect this restoration by connecting between arenas of the universe, of reality, regulated by different dualistic principles.

Among the many mediating figures, strangers and visitors are, as Yoshida Teigo has shown, of special importance. They are often seen as godlike, creatures who are both gods and men and who appear especially in in-between situations—such as at twilight.[12] Such figures range from the highest to the lowest insiders and outsiders in any natural or social context. Many figures—for instance, the monkey, as well as clowns, murderers, slaves, courtesans, and the like—may perform such mediating functions as deities or ritual scapegoats.[13]

Such attempts at mediated redemption, at bridging the gap between inside and outside, are effected not only by foreigners or outsiders, but also by other marginal elements, above all by artists. Many artists, especially the itinerant ones, were indeed strangers to the closed villages, but at the same time constituted a constant component of the Japanese cultural arena. Interestingly, as we saw in chapter 5, the *yakuza* also sometimes portray themselves as mediators—as outsiders who claim to be the bearers of the most pristine Japanese values.[14]

The potentially redemptive qualities of such marginal elements have also been articulated in the development of certain traditional forms of theater, especially the Kabuki, and even, as Yamaguchi Masao has shown, in the conception of the imperial house as it developed under the Tokugawa and was portrayed in many Kabuki plays.[15] Indeed the continuous, in a way central, place of the emperor within this mediatory universe is one of the most significant features of the Japanese cosmology.[16]

> The emperor was referred to in ancient Japan as Sumemima-no-mikoto (divine messenger's sacred body). He was believed to be charged with the spirit of emperorship, which entered his body in the inauguration ceremony. This spirit ensured the timeless continuity of emperorship, assumed to have existed since the creation of the world and to lie beyond the order of everyday life, essentially wild and untamed. What was essential was the spirit; the emperor remained at the center of authority as long as his body remained the receptacle of that spirit. If the spirit left him, he could be banished or killed.
>
>   . . . After the failure of the Kenmu Restoration at the beginning of the 14th century, the emperor became a largely insignificant and marginal figure. It is of great interest here that the closeness of the emperor to the itinerant entertainers once again became evident with the demise of his political influence. . . . The emperor became the central figure in ritual activities that were basically not much different from performances of other kinds. . . .
>
>   . . . Thus, ironically, the structure of the relationship between the emperor and the aristocrats was repeated in the organization of these lower-class entertainers and beggars.[17]

VII This conception of the givenness of reality, of the mutual embeddedness of its various dimensions, and of a continual shifting between the different contexts within which it is structured, has been continuously promulgated in rites and rituals that have prevailed, in one form or another, throughout Japanese history. It also permeates many aspects of life and behavior in Japanese society. First of all, it permeates the basic attitude toward nature—the perception of nature and of culture—embracing social life as on a continuum of sorts with nature.[18] One interesting and, from the Western point of view, astonishing illustration of this attitude has been provided by P. Asquith, a British primatologist, describing an event she witnessed involving a group of Japanese colleagues. To follow the Lebras' account of Asquith's report:

> Describing a memorial service for dead monkeys, this short essay reveals the status equivalence (or lack of opposition) between human and animal life which entitled the "souls" of monkeys to the same Buddhist rite as for the human dead. Something more may be read into this chapter, although it is not the author's point. While showing such humane compassion for the dead monkeys, the Japanese mourners apparently are not opposed to lethal experimentations on live monkeys. In other words, the Japanese,

while holding a belief in the sacredness of all life, are not as extreme as antivivisectionists found in the West. Nor do they find suicide morally abhorrent. Their regard for life does not reach the dogmatic extreme "absolute."[19]

Yet another very pertinent illustration of this conception of life and death—in recent times but building on earlier Buddhist conceptions—is the burgeoning around major temples, as for instance in Kamakura, of memorials for aborted children, thoroughly analyzed by R. J. Zwi Werblowski and William LaFleur, among others.[20]

One of the most important manifestations of this conception of life and nature may be the Japanese attitude toward suicide, which has baffled and fascinated Westerners. Not only is suicide not abhorred and "altruistic" suicide—suicide in service of the collectivity—fully accepted, but even nonaltruistic suicide is often perceived as a legitimate means of protest or of resolving in an ultimate way the dilemmas and contradictions one is caught in. This legitimacy distinguishes the attitude toward suicide in Japanese society from that in other societies; in Japan, as elsewhere, suicide often constitutes an escape from such situations, but in Japan it is a particularly honorable way out of such contradictions, especially those between intense internal feelings and social and group pressure, and is seen as a very legitimate culmination of one's life.

The legitimacy of certain types of suicide is rooted in the positive attitude toward nature—the immanentist, as against the Western transcendental orientation—in which nature is not conceived as totally opposed to life, as Pinguet has pointed out.[21] It is also probably connected to the special place of violence, especially ritual violence, as one way of overcoming the boundaries between different contexts or spaces of life and nature.

Such attitudes and patterns of behavior have not always been universally accepted. Indeed they often constituted foci of public controversies.[22] But even the controversies attest to the fact that such attitudes constitute a continual theme within the Japanese cultural repertoire. Thus, immanentist premises are to be seen also, for instance, in the emphasis in many Buddhist rituals on "attainment through the body."

VIII The conception of continuity between the mundane and the spiritual worlds is manifest in many aspects of life in Japan, for instance, in the important place of ancestor cults and the continuity between family cults, those of the wider communities, and possibly even that associated with the imperial ancestors, which again emphasizes the central place of the emperor in the Japanese cosmology (see chapter 15).[23]

The idea of the mutual embeddedness in different contexts of nature and culture, and of the continuity, through various mediating figures, between them, can also be found in many Japanese folktales, which are thus distinguished from similar tales in other, closely related civilizations.[24] For instance, the ending of a folktale brought over from China, about a love affair between a hare and a woman, is tragic in China, where the classical Confucian conception with its strong emphasis on the discontinuity between nature and culture prevailed: the fox ("nature") dies and the woman ("culture") is separated from it forever. In Japan, however, the fox, after its death, is incorporated in the form of a shrine into the woman's household.[25]

In daily life, such conceptions of nature, of natural reality, pervade, for instance, attitudes toward food, the partaking of which is often seen even in daily life as a partaking in the sacred;[26] the modes of wrapping various objects; and various patterns of behavior which seem intended to prevent or neutralize pollution.[27] The basic attitude toward nature also gives rise in daily discourse, in daily artistic activities as well as aesthetic discourse, and in the construction of gardens or homes to a strong emphasis on proximity to nature, on being at one with nature. This attitude is not of course something "natural," but rather something culturally constructed—but it is a construction that emphasizes the quest for unity with nature.[28]

Similarly, the attitudes of Japanese patients and doctors alike toward health and illness are greatly influenced, as Ohnuki-Tierney has shown, by conceptions of the body as defined in terms of the embeddedness of people in nature in a dualistic universe, as well as in terms of the danger of pollution—conceptions of the fragile boundaries between purity and pollution, "us" and "them," inner and outer space—and of the necessity to circumvent pollution by series of ritualized actions.[29] These conceptions also inform in many ways the aesthetic sensibility and modes of artistic creativity in Japan that we shall analyze in chapter 15.

The dualistic conceptions, the contextualized conception of purity and pollution, and the emphasis on overcoming pollution through appropriate rituals also pervade the basic ethical conceptions and conceptions of conflict resolution prevalent in Japanese society. As Robert J. Wargo has shown, acts of conciliation on the part of Japanese companies or of the Japanese government toward Americans or Europeans are not based on conceptions of absolute good or evil, but rather are performed as sincere acts of purification (and hence are often misunderstood by Westerners).[30]

IX Conceptions of the mutual embeddedness of nature and culture, of the continuity between them, and of a dualistic cosmogony went together, in Japan, with a strong vitalistic conception and an active-pragmatic attitude toward life, and with the potential sanctification of everything pertaining to life.[31] This combination of vitalism and pragmatism, together with a commitment to the natural, cosmic, and social orders, distinguishes the definition of ontological reality prevalent in Japan from those in many so-called pagan or non-Axial religions, with their emphasis on the basic homology between the transcendental and the mundane worlds.

Reality in its multiple facets was not conceived in Japan as just a given to be passively accommodated. Rather it called for continuous activity, an ongoing process of adjusting to the world that gave rise to what may be called a utilitarian ethic, as well as to an emphasis on acquiring technical skills. These orientations allowed Japanese to break through the limitations of various relatively narrow contexts and indeed helped in their continuous restructuring.

Such utilitarian orientations, emphasized in the practical rationality that developed throughout Japan's history and the ideological discourse that developed especially in the Tokugawa period, continuously confronted the strong emphasis on one's obligations to the natural, cosmic, and social worlds. Attempts were made to contain the utilitarian and achievement orientations within the framework of such obligations, even if the frameworks were continuously reconstructed, often through the impact of such pragmatic orientations. These reconstructions, however, tended to be based on reformulations of the natural, primordial, and sacral premises, the first relatively unsophisticated versions of which could be found in the ancient myths.[32]

X A final component of Japanese ontological reality was a conception of mythical, cyclical time combined with a linear dimension similar to what could be called duration (*mono no aware*). Time was thereby defined as flowing, basically not in a historical or progressive-lineal direction, but rather in a natural-temporal (above all annual) cycle, conceived in terms of the dualistic principles, combined with a more linear conception of duration. As Jane Bachnik has put it:

> The Japanese conception of annual time, such as it is, is based upon these natural and social realities, the harmony of which the calendar expresses. Yet this harmony does not seem to be realized by a regular mathematical symmetry, but rather by the constant relations between human and divine worlds. . . . It might also be the constant infusion of the divine world into human activities that originated the cobweb-like structure of annual time.
>
> The Japanese attitude, as it expresses itself through the annual conception of time, does not require that a central subject compose the unity of time; it is, on the contrary, quite satisfied with the extreme mobility of the subject on the surface of time. Note the fact that the only purely Japanese word for time is toki. This word is often used with the same meaning as

the term jikan, which is originally Chinese and literally means "intervals between toki"; but toki is above all a word close in meaning to the French quand.[33]

As with respect to utilitarian conceptions, there developed in Japan a far-reaching openness with respect to seemingly incompatible conceptions of the temporal and the ability to contain them within the framework of continually reformulated and reconstructed mythical premises. Thus, for instance, in the Tokugawa period, and even earlier, intellectuals increasingly emphasized conceptions of linear, historical time, always set, however, within the basic framework of the eternal and mythical, which was in turn set within the periodic cycles of nature. Throughout Japanese history linear conceptions of time—often connected with utilitarian conceptions—were predominant in various sectors of the society.[34] But these arenas were relatively segregated, did not spill over into others, especially into the central ones, and were on the whole hemmed in by the mythical, nondiscursive templates. Moreover, the linear conception of time that developed was more one of duration than of movement in some specific direction.

XI The persistence of these basic conceptions of ontological reality in Japan does not mean that their concrete formulations did not change. On the contrary, these formulations were, as we have seen, continuously reconstructed, especially under the impact of other cultures or religions. Such reformulations did not, however, entail the abandonment of their basic parameters, templates, or master codes, which continued to frame the discourses, attitudes toward the world, and modes of thinking that developed in Japan. That these premises were often taken for granted made them even more powerful. They also greatly influenced, as we have seen, the semiotic rules regulating the major arenas of social and cultural activity and were of crucial importance in shaping the various manifestations of dissatisfaction with the existing order, the modes of protest and rebellions.

These fundamental premises, first promulgated in ancient myths, were elaborated under the impact of intensive internal changes and external stimuli, giving rise in some periods of Japanese history, especially but not only the Tokugawa period, to a highly sophisticated philosophical discourse that at the same time denied its own logocentricity.[35]

As we saw in our discussion of the transformations of Buddhism and Confucianism in Japan, no overarching dogma developed, nor did any series of canonical texts present a framework for the construction of cosmological reality or a starting point for continuous philosophical or artistic interpretation. Accordingly, it was not continuous exposition and construction of textual pronouncement, as in China and Korea, but mythic conceptions and nondiscursive premises that served as the framework or starting point for the construction and interpretation of ontological reality in Japan—a discourse on the whole based on "philosophizing in the archaic."[36]

Conceptions of the mutual embeddedness of nature and culture, of the continuity between them, and of their coming together in different ways and different contexts, combined with the weakness of logocentrism, explains some of the most crucial aspects of the so-called religious syncretism in Japan. That Japan absorbed, as it were, many aspects of Buddhism, Taoism, and Confucianism is not in itself unique. What is unique is that, first, components of the beliefs and practices of Shintoism, Buddhism, Confucianism, and Taoism were consciously combined in different ways in different periods, seemingly without great concern for their respective boundaries; second, a sort of mirror image of the previous point, whatever principled differences—couched in metaphysical and transcendental terms—had existed between these religions, especially Buddhism, Taoism, and Confucianism, were successfully diluted. The theological or ideological boundaries *between* these religions were, to a great extent, blurred; the intergroup boundaries that were constructed in Japan were mostly those *within* each religion—especially within Buddhism.

Semiotic Structuring, Relational Orientations, Indexing

XII The prevalent conceptions of ontological reality and the weakness of a logocentric orientation in Japanese society were closely connected with specific modes of semiotic structuring of discourse and of thought. The most important characteristics of these modes are their relative devaluation of the subject vis-à-vis the environment—the construction of a topological-metaphorical relation between subject and environment, as against one of active ordering, structuring, or "mastery" and their emphasis on indexical rather than referential and relational rather than dichotomous parameters of discourse.[37]

Augustin Berque has succinctly analyzed the relation between subject and environment in Japanese discourse:

> In many respects, the subject in general is less important in Japanese culture than in European culture. It is the environment, in the Japanese case, that is more important. This tendency has been aptly defined as contextualism (jōkyōshugi). The Japanese language, for instance, does not need to distinguish the subject from its environment in a statement like samui (both "I am cold" and "it is cold"). Nor does it distinguish the subject from the object in a statement like suki ("(I) love (you)" or "(I) like (it)").[38]

In this conception the relations between the subject and the environment are mediated above all by topological metaphors, not linear conceptions.[39]

At the same time, this environment is conceived as decentered and polysemic, ambiguous:

> From a medial point of view, the way Man feels about his environment bears a close link with the way he acts upon it. Indeed, just as Japanese culture does not favor intelligibility over experience, it dislikes symmetry and general orientations in the organization of space.[40]

These spatiotemporal conceptions—like the ontological ones discussed earlier—found their expression not only in works of art but also in many seemingly mundane matters. The symbolic arrangements of households, the relations of nobles and "simple people," and the spatial organization of cities, for instance,[41] were all rooted in distinctive conceptions of the environment, based on an immanentist and topographic orientation toward nature and space, with a relative deemphasis of the center; of space, seen as embodying the interweaving of nature and culture and as having potentially liminal characteristics;[42] and of order, understood in situational, topological terms as implicit in actual position and movement from one place to another.

XIII The second major feature of the structuring of the modes of discourse in Japan is a strong emphasis on (performative) indexing, as against referentiality; on a relational, as against a dichotomous, orientation toward reality; and on lexical literacy, as against grammatical compositions. To follow Jane Bachnick, who has analyzed these orientations in great detail:

> I will focus on indexing, and indexical meaning, as relevant for approaching Japanese social life. Thus the objectified poles of self/other can be related to reference—and a focus on what the participants say. The continuum between self and other can be related to index—and a focus on how the participants anchor and index the "world" both of reference and of social ties (the other) in relation to themselves. Yet in approaching language, as well as social life, we in the West have focused predominantly on the poles rather than the continuum; on reference rather than index; and on what rather than how.[43]

The common denominator of these various modes of semiotic mediation is, as we have already mentioned, an emphasis on reality as constructed in a multiplicity of settings in contextual rather than absolutist, dichotomous modes, and on the importance of the relations and transitions between different contexts.[44]

These numerous contexts, between which people constantly move, are not constructed in terms of general, abstract principles beyond or outside of reality. Rather, they are constituted in some combination of sacral, primordial, and natural terms, which are seen as embedded in the reality they construct and are rooted in the conception of the mutual embeddedness of nature and culture and in the dualistic world conception.

The differences between various contexts of action are usually relatively clear; at the same time, however, there has developed in most sectors of Japanese society an emphasis on the interrelatedness of different contexts and on the importance and possibility of shifting between them according to the inherent parameters of each and not according to "objective," formal, linear, or dichotomous principles. Hence the great importance of liminal situations, which structure the transition from one context to another.

These same principles also provide the basic framework of reflexivity in Japanese culture,[45] which is based, not on an evaluation of existing reality in terms of transcendent principles, but rather on the continuous and rather complicated "mirroring" of the different principles inherent in the construction of reality. It is no accident that the mirror plays a central role in Japanese rituals—from the imperial rituals through those in religious settings to those in daily life.[46] Ohnuki-Tierney discusses this point as follows:

> In my interpretation, the reflexive structure consists of the self, spatially expressed as "inside," and the other, spatially expressed as "outside." The self may be humans or the Japanese as opposed to the other represented by deities and foreigners.
>
> The nature of Japanese deities provides us with an important clue to the structure of reflexivity. They are "divine strangers" who visit humans periodically from outside and are endowed with dual qualities. Harnessed through ritual, their positive quality is the energy source for revitalizing the lives of people in a settlement. Their negative quality, if uncontrolled, looms as a threat to life. The Japanese self is the mirror image of these deities; it too consists of dual qualities and powers. Or, more accurately, the deities, which are symbolically represented by a mirror, represent the transcendental or elevated self. The transcendental self, which mirrors the other, is equated by purity. Thus the structure, comprised of a set of relations—in:out; human:deity; self:other; secular (ke):sacred (hare)—is assigned the character of purity and the boundaries of impurity.[47]

These basic conceptions of ontological reality and modes of structuring discourse in Japanese society have been closely connected to the templates or codes regulating the construction of modes of thought in Japan, such as those proposed by Nakamura Hajime.[48] The preference for indexical over referential and topological over linear conceptions of time and space, along with the ability to shift from one context to another, to cross boundaries relatively easily, also has far-reaching implications for the modes of construction, in much of Japanese society, of the conceptions of personality and selfhood, and of social interaction, to which we shall turn in greater detail in the next part of this chapter.

CONCEPTIONS OF SELF AND PERSONALITY

XIV The basic conceptions of ontological reality prevalent in Japanese society, with their far-reaching consequences for the construction of social interaction, also provide the framework for the prevalent definitions of selfhood and personhood. Several major characteristics of these definitions have been identified by researchers and in Japanese literary works: first, individual personality is conceived in Japan as embedded in social relations or contexts and is to a great extent defined in terms of its place in such contexts; second, persons are seen to move continuously between such varied contexts; third, emotion, or emotional sensibility, is regarded as a basic component of personality, and "inner" feeling and outward behavior are clearly differentiated; and, fourth, there is a strong achievement orientation set within expressive solidary settings.

This definition of personhood, prevalent in large sections of Japan, is distinct from the prevalent Western definition, in which individual personality is defined as a discrete ontological entity or monad. Rather, personality in Japan is defined as basically interactive, shaped by the contexts within which it acts and by its obligations in such contexts. This does not, of course, entail—as some critics have claimed—the denial of individual personality. Rather, it denotes a specific mode of formulation of the basic parameters of selfhood and of human relations.[49]

One of the first modern scholarly formulations of these characteristics of Japanese selfhood and personality is found in Nakane Chie's well-known book *Japanese Society*.[50] In this book she presents, to follow the Lebras' exposition,

> a bipolar typology of "attribute" and "frame" as criteria for group formation and group identity, and she characterizes the Japanese case as frame-oriented in contrast to the attribute-oriented Westerners and Hindus. Frame is rooted, Nakane argues, in the traditional structure of the *ie*, the household, which she defines as a corporate residential group apart from kinship. The *ie* as an archetype is replicated, the author claims, by all Japanese organizations, and notably by modern enterprises and companies.[51]

Subsequent research has gone beyond these formulations and moved from emphasis on the group to emphasis on context, as Hamaguchi Eshun and Thomas Kasulis have put it, to emphasis on the orientations to contextual frameworks as the basic constituent elements in the formation of Japanese personality and selfhood: "In the Japanese version the emphasis is on the relationship, not on the people who created the situation. . . . The individual becomes meaningful insofar as he or she is an outgrowth of the relationships established by the operative context, not vice-versa."[52]

Such contextual orientations entail the conceptualization of the relations between self and others, and self and environment, in terms, not of polar opposition, but of a continuum. Whereas conceptions of personality prevalent in the West emphasize the independence of the self and its potential for confrontation with environment and society, the Japanese emphasize the continuous interrelation and interweaving between them. Neither self nor environment can be defined without reference to the other, and the relations between them are redefined according to the numerous specific contexts of action.[53]

XV The contextual embeddedness of personality, with its strongly vertical-hierarchical overtones,[54] finds possibly its clearest expression and corollaries in the linguistic structuring of interpersonal discourse and relations.[55] This structuring is closely related to the general characteristics of the semiotic mediation of discourse, analyzed above, and to the ways in which the personal referent is structured.

The central place of different personal referents in Japanese discourse has been succinctly analyzed by R. J. Smith.

> It is impossible to speak or write Japanese without employing keigo [register]. The level is chosen by each speaker, who is compelled to make a calculation of social distance, largely conceived in terms of a complex combination of age, sex, social position, nature of previous interactions, and context. For any given person, then, it is always the context of interaction that determines the level of speech opted for.[56]

An analogous decision must be made when using what in English are called personal pronouns.

> Japanese has historically used an enormous variety of words to refer to speaker, persons spoken to, and persons spoken of. . . . Japanese has this enormous lexicon of "personal pronouns" because it never really had "personal pronouns" at all. What I will call Japanese personal referents are in point of fact nouns that indicated categories and degrees of communicative distance. The selection of one from among the great array of such referents will reflect the human and social relationships that exist between the two parties. There are no fixed points, either "self" or "other," and as I have already remarked, it is of the utmost significance that designation of the other invariably precedes designation of the self in any interaction.

Another quite remarkable feature of personal referents in Japan is the great rapidity with which they have changed historically.

. . . By the age of three, children in the United States have generally mastered the distinction between "I" and "you," two personal pronouns that will serve them throughout life in all interactions with others. Furthermore, in the daily speech of the American child, these two terms are heavily favored over all other possible personal referents, such as name, kin, term, and the like. The Japanese male child, for his part, by the age of six must master the use of at least six terms of self reference; girls of that age will employ five.

. . . What is more, the acquisition of personal referents does not end in childhood in Japan, but instead continues throughout adult life at least into middle age. . . .

Smith stresses that "there is little need to resort to profanity in a language where the use of an inappropriately high or low referential term is quite enough to inflict a grievous insult" and offers the following example:

During the upheavals on Japanese university campuses in the 1960's, this was a tactic employed brilliantly by the students. In meetings with members of the faculty, the students bent every effort to demolish the linguistic markers of relative status by using styles of address and reference of the most demeaning sort. The more senior the faculty member, the more devastating the effect of this deliberate leveling or inverting of status indicators. Toward the end of a round table discussion held in 1968 between striking students and a group of professors of Tokyo University, the novelist Mishima Yukio, who as an alumnus had been invited to participate, burst out impatiently and demanded of one of the faculty: "Why don't you speak on equal terms with them? If they use insulting terms, you should reply in kind!" There was no answer. The professor could neither tolerate the humiliation nor summon the wrath required to destroy the habit of a lifetime.[57]

These referents, as indicated above, have changed continuously according to historical situations, above all with the processes of urbanization, industrialization, and democratization. In many areas, including family relationships, somewhat more egalitarian conceptions started to intrude and, in general, flexibility in the application of the various registers has tended to increase. But such changes imply, not the decontextualization of these modes of address, but rather greater flexibility in the structuring of the different contexts and of the movements between them.[58]

XVI The commitment to contextual and relational interpersonal or group frameworks can be identified in most of the great works of Japanese literature, in popular literature and art, and in the activities of great political personalities, as Albert Craig has shown with respect to some of the leading personalities of the Tokugawa period and I. Morris has shown with respect to many tragic rebel heroes.[59]

But it is in research on contemporary settings that Japanese conceptions of selfhood and personality have been most fully documented and analyzed. Dorinne Kondo's summary of the major features of the Japanese definition of selfhood, based on her analysis of a personal relationship in a factory, is one of the best such exponations:

> It is impossible to attempt definition of Japanese "selfhood" in vacuum, in vitro, so to speak, for the very essence of the Japanese self is that it takes on meaning through living, through interaction with others in specific contexts. And the understanding of this fundamental connectedness to others is shaped in multiple ways and in various arenas of life. Among the most important for the people who were my friends, neighbors and co-workers in Shitamachi, were the arenas of family and work. Here one can most fully realize what it is to be human: to feel deeply, but to be simultaneously suspended in webs of duty and obligation.
>
> To be a member of a household is to feel a double connectedness, first to the living members of one's uchi, a unique group that defines primary emotional ties as well as one's social universe, and to the ie, the household's ancestors and descendants. Belonging means far more than mere passive existence; it requires active participation and responsibility in group life. Moreover, this is not a static sociological model, but a dynamic process created and recreated in the actual fulfilling of roles: in "work," [broadly defined].
>
> Similarly, the company is conceived as both a universe of belonging on the one hand, and a hierarchical set of roles and duties, on the other.[60]

XVII But the Japanese, as do people in every society, live and act, of course, not in one context but in many. What is distinctive in Japanese society is the modes in which such contexts are constituted.

Such contexts are constituted according to several axes or dimensions. The first such dimension is what may be called the functional one—i.e., the institutional or organizational *locus* of the context—whether it is, for instance, located mostly in economic, military, family or some ecological frame. The second such axis relates to basic concepts of human energy and human sensibilities. The most important of such conceptions to the constitution of "Japanese" selfhood or personhood, are, to follow Nancy Rosenberger:

> . . . The Japanese self is posited in movement between categories. The vehicle of movement is the ki energy, which is considered to be the basic

energy of the human being—mind and body. Traditionally, it was the basic energy of the whole universe of which the human being partook. Japanese conceive of the ki energy as moving in two ways within the self: (1) from inner sanctums of the self to outer contact with others' ki and the ki of the universe; and (2) from a fluid, spontaneous expression of ki energy to a directed, disciplined expression of ki energy.

. . . The movement of self in terms of ki energy along two axes (inner/outer, spontaneous/disciplined) results in four representative modes of self in which all Japanese are expected to participate: inner-oriented, spontaneous ki energy; inner-oriented disciplined ki energy; outer-oriented spontaneous ki energy; and outer-oriented disciplined ki energy.

These modes are representative of the varieties of modes through which the self moves, and thus are suggestive rather than definitive. Any specific situation may not fall neatly into any one mode. . . .

Their occasional contradiction is recognized, but the mature person is able to control—and profit from—that contradiction by negotiating movements among modes. . . .

. . . Central to movement among modes of self is the principle of contextualization; by moving among contexts, Japanese can shift among modes of self-presentation. Contexts can change according to place, time and/or social group. As we shall see later, movement among modes can take place without any contextual changes, but contexts provide clarity.[61]

XVIII The third axis according to which any context is constituted is the concrete relation, the mode of the interweaving of any such context with other contexts. It is the continuous shifting between contexts, above all the way in which the relations between these contexts are conceived and constructed and how they are connected to the different concepts of human energy and strategy, that is, as Nancy Rosenberger has shown, of crucial importance for the understanding of Japanese personality and behavior.

As with the construction of reality in general, social interaction is framed in terms of multiple, continuously shifting contexts defined according to a basic dualistic conception. These definitions generate the major distinctions relating to behavior referred to above—namely, those between outer and internal space, front and back (*omote* and *ura*), inner and outer (*uchi* and *soto*), and inner reality and facade (*honne* and *tatemae*).[62]

Such contexts are integrated by way of basically topological metaphors and by the continuous play of "mirror images." While the parameters of these contexts are relatively clear, their boundaries and, above all, the movement between them are very flexible. The shifting between them is not random or accidental, but well structured—albeit in topological rather than linear ways—and grounded in a dualistic conception of the world.

Here we may follow Ishida Takeshi's formulation of the nature of *omote* and *ura*.

> Omote-ura can be defined only in relative terms; hence the border between the two remains flexible. Let me illustrate by giving a concrete example. When there is a gathering of the people in a hamlet, this means more omote compared with the personal discussions that take place between individual members of the hamlet, but more ura compared with the official discussions that take place in the village assembly.[63]

Coinciding with but also crosscutting the *omote-ura* distinction is that between *uchi* and *soto*, "inner and outer," and between the inner state which emphasizes the individual's integrity and group conformity. Similar considerations apply to the distinction between *uchi* and *soto*.

> What is uchi or soto differs from one context to another, not according to some general principles but according to changing contexts of interaction. Not only does the same person behave on the omote level in one situation and on the ura level in another situation, but sometimes even the same behavior may be considered ura from one angle and omote from another, as the sample of the gathering of people in a hamlet indicates.

This is part and parcel of a more overarching concept of relativity, situationality, contextuality, etc. ("Reference" vs. "index" also falls in this category.)[64]

These movements between different contexts include the shift from "hard work" to "home," to the sweet pleasures of life, as John Pelzel has succinctly analyzed. The ability to shift between such different contexts, *kejime*, is of crucial importance in the structuration of Japanese personality. Such ability entails continuous movement, constant transformations.[66] It is closely related to the mastery of various rituals of purification through which the pollution attached to unsuccessful transactions can be nullified, and it lies at the heart of the interpersonal conceptions prevalent in Japan, namely the continual reinforcement and extension of trust.[67]

These abilities to shift between different contexts are closely related to the basic emphases on adapting to the environment, as against mastering it, on changing the self more than the world, and on indirect secondary as against direct primary control.[68]

XIX The distinctions between different dimensions of one's external role and internal feelings, which are central in regulating transitions and shifts between contexts, attest to a very strong emphasis in the Japanese conception of personality on emotional sensibility—but a sensibility related in a rather distinctive way to performance of social roles.

The emphasis on emotional sensibility, or, to follow John Pelzel's formulation, "the strong tendency to equate human nature with emotions," entails, as we have seen, the importance of inner feelings, of the search for authenticity.[69] This search is manifest in the close relation to nature, in the quest for fusion of the human and the natural, and in the emphasis on aesthetic sensibility.

One of the most important manifestations of such sensibility is *seishin:*

> Seishin connotes an individualistic streak focusing on a strong sense of obligation, emotional sensitivity, as against more utilitarian or instrumental motivations: it is seen by Japanese as the opposite of materialism and easygoing self-gratification. It involves a single mindedness of purpose and often has practical aims: a strong-willed person can conquer physical illness, selfish desires and can accept whatever comes, including unreasonable demands by superiors and the pressures of group life.
>
> . . . In this respect the role of the Japanese hero who persevered against all odds has been described by Morris (1975) in his book *The Nobility of Failure: Tragic Heroes in the History of Japan.* Notoriously misunderstood in this respect are the kamikaze suicide pilots of World War II. . . .
>
> Naturally, in this respect there are also cultural differences, even if the amount of seishin has been the same: suicide for a "good" cause in Japan is regarded as laudable and even heroic at times, while it is basically sinful in the West, owing to the Christian teaching. But it is finally not so much the flamboyant aspect of seishin which should concern us here rather than its appearance in Japan in many humdrum situations: workers taking greater pride than workers in the West in carrying out routine tasks which are basically boring; or the persistence shown by the traditional daughter-in-law who had to cope with the demands of her husband's mother until the latter's retirement, if they resided together.[70]

The complement of *seishin* is *jinkaku*—or personal character—to be respected for your virtues.

XX   The combination in many sectors of Japanese society of contextual orientations, emotional sensibility grounded in the dualistic conception of the mutual embeddedness of nature and culture, and the linguistic modes of discourse referred to above has entailed some very important behavioral and attitudinal corollaries or consequences. One of the most interesting of these is the development of an emphasis on nonverbal communication—on body motions and tones of voice—as well as on the central importance of silence as a distinct, evocative mode of communication.[71] Nonverbal communication is, of course, also used extensively in other societies—even in the highly vocal American one. It seems, however, that the emphasis on silence as a major evocative mode of expression is, if not unique to Japan, certainly much more central there than in other cultures.

Another important consequence of these orientations is a strong emphasis on achievement—but one which differs from the parallel Western one, and which is closely related to the concept of *seishin*. The distinctive feature of this orientation in Japan is that it is rooted in participation in the various social settings and not adherence to universalistic, transcendental principles or emphasis on individual autonomy. It is characterized, as Robert N. Bellah has put it, as particularistic goal achievement. Within, for instance, the work settings analyzed by J. J. Sullivan, there develops a strong emphasis on obligations derived from participation in the setting and on cooperation with others, and a certain deemphasis of personal autonomy.[72]

Closely related to this achievement orientation is an emphasis on the importance of developing and nurturing the capacity to undertake a given task, against the much sharper emphasis on appropriate motivation in the West. The specific attitude toward achievement in Japan, when set in the context of the contextual and group orientations, also generates a predisposition toward long-range goals and commitments.[73]

Japanese attitudinal and behavioral patterns are also marked by an emphasis on "sincerity," on the correspondence between mental states and actions, sometimes designated as *makoto*. This emphasis tends to conflate ethics and aesthetics:

> On the aesthetic side, makoto in Onitsura points to the fundamental truth contained in the essence of things and self, and their ultimate unity. On the ethical side, makoto (ch'eng) is a metaphysical principle which focuses precisely on the relationship between human nature and the Way of Heaven; it has the additional element of creativity.
>
> . . . Makoto is considered to be much more than a state of mind or even a character trait of an individual. When the individual is makoto it is as if the genuine self has been realized (and this implies a unity with things or the Way of Heaven).[74]

Closely related is the positive attitude prevalent among many Japanese toward the small pleasures of daily life—sleeping, eating, having sex, contemplating nature, and the like—which may seem very hedonistic from a Western point of view:

> Compared to Western ideas of basic sinfulness which inhibit the full enjoyment of many pleasures, Shinto as well as Japanese Buddhism encourage

the enjoyment of simple things in life. It may be this positive attitude which Shinto has towards creation (and thus sexuality) and living things; and the quiet, sad realization (through Buddhism) that nothing is permanent, which makes for a heightened appreciation of the here-and-now.[75]

At the same time the Western emphasis on uprightness, on principled consistency, may be seen by the Japanese as very serious, hectic, and unrelenting.

Brian Moeran has captured some central aspects of Japanese morality by selecting two key words, "*seishin* (spirit) and *kokoro* (heart), which together embrace many Japanese concepts. Moeran presents a semantic analysis that demonstrates how *seishin* and *kokoro* mingle to make group ideology compatible with individual character and spontaneity, or to reinforce the Japanese tradition of morality while at the same time "smuggling" in Western ideas. All this is accomplished, without capitulating to Western individualism, which remains anathema in Japanese eyes.[76]

XXI The combination of all these factors—the contextual embeddedness of personality; the differentiation between inner and outer space, between *honne* and *tatemae;* and the mode of movement between different regions or contexts—also gives rise to what has seemed to many Westerners, starting with Ruth Benedict, one of the great puzzles of Japanese behavior.[77] This is the strong tendency to situational as against principled morality, in other words, to behavior regulated by the norms intrinsic to each situation rather than universal, formal norms that transcend any given situation. Hence the very strong tendency to conformity to situational or group norms, and the great unruliness in nonstructured, unknown situations.

The sense of selfhood prevalent in Japan has had important implications for the basic conceptions of justice and morality—at least in the contemporary scene. Thus, for instance, an analysis by T. S. Lebra of the results of sentence completion tests administered to adult residents of Tokyo, Hong Kong, and Seoul, focusing on compensatory justice and purposeful moral actions, showed no cross-cultural differences in the respondents' expectations of rewards for "perseverance" and "kindness" and retribution for "wrongdoing," but found that

> the kinds of rewards and retributions are remarkably varied. Japanese surpass Chinese in stressing the human, subjective, inner consequences, while Chinese are more disposed to strive for success and goal attainment and to anticipate objective, external consequences. Koreans generally, if not always, stand in between. When the respondents articulate what sorts of resources are to be mobilized to attain a goal like "to build an ideal

home life," Japanese and Koreans paid attention to cooperation and family relations, whereas the Chinese emphasize difference, nationality and economy.[78]

XXII Within the framework of these general, above all attitudinal, corollaries of the definitions of personality there developed some more specific behavioral tendencies. The most important of these are an emphasis on perseverance, on role perfections and personal responsibility (which may manifest itself, for instance, in leaders resigning, or in extreme cases committing suicide, because of faulty performance of the organizations under their control), and on strong mutual obligations.

The emphasis on mutual obligation or debt is closely related to the emphasis on responsibility and to the fact that a person has meaning only in relation to others. To follow Harumi Befu:

Such sense of debt is rooted in the fact that any interpersonal relation is a moral one, entailing mutual responsibility, and that a person's identity consists of his/her relationships with others to whom he/she is related. . . .

The three basic value concepts critical in understanding human relationships in Japan are *on, giri* and *ninjō. On* is indebtedness, which one incurs when others have done what Japanese culture has defined as a "favor" or "gift." One owes, for example, life to one's parents and by extension to one's ancestors. One is indebted to whomever—usually one's parents—is responsible for one's material well being. Before Japan's defeat in World War II, this idea was stretched to include the emperor in the sense that since the emperor was the ruler and the symbolic father of the country, and since the country's well being was thought to be possible only because of the imperial reign, all Japanese subjects owed *on* to the emperor. The sense of indebtedness extends to everyday life in Japan. One owes a debt to teachers for the knowledge and wisdom they impart. One owes the employer for the salary and other, intangible benefits one receives. . . .

It makes sense in this context that in the Japanese value system one's duties or obligations to others come before one's right or claim of duties of others to one.

In Japan, too, of course, decisions are made in self-interest, but these decisions are tempered by other-interests, that is, by consideration of how self-interested decisions affect others. Moreover, while decisions are made by the individual, there is greater awareness that one's destiny is influenced by forces other than one's own volition.

In the scheme of things Japanese, such debts, whether they are called *on* or not, need to be repaid. Repayment of debt, especially those heavier debts called *on*, is one of the most serious social obligations.

The normative value which binds Japanese to repay their debts is called *giri*. As such, *giri* is a moral concept. One has *giri* not to just anyone, but to those who are "significant," that is, to the people with whom one has an ongoing, give-and-take relationship.

The concept of *giri* is different from the Christian concept of "love they neighbor," in which "neighbor" is used metaphorically to refer to anyone. The latter is a universalistic concept, as opposed to the particularistic concept of *giri*. Also, in contrast to the Christian concept of love, which is God-ordered, the Japanese concept of reciprocity is a *social* contract.

In addition to the obligatory relationship imposed by *on* and *giri*, Japanese human relationships are also motivated by the concept of *ninjō*, generally translated as "human nature" or "human feeling." It is human feeling unfettered by social obligations and normative duties. . . .

One should not go against *ninjō*, but if *giri* requires one to do so, *ninjō* must be subordinated. Obligation takes precedence over human feelings. Normally, however, one's feelings and social norms go hand in hand.

These reciprocal obligations are structured in a complex way in which hierarchical and egalitarian emphases, as well as the distinction between formal social obligation and their feeling are continuously interwoven.[79]

Such interpersonal relations are rooted in long-range mutual obligations between people interacting in different contexts. Obligations are often symbolized in an almost ritual exchange of gifts—one of the most important aspects of Japanese social behavior. While the range of obligations differs between different contexts, most enduring social relations are based on some sense of obligation. Loyalty to such contextual interrelations and settings best explains what has been noticed as one of the most important characteristics of Japanese behavior—namely group loyalty. It is not, however, that the Japanese are bound in groups; it is rather that many sets of such interrelations take place within groups and that groups provide some of the most important contexts.

XXIII   All these definitions of personality and selfhood, and their normative and behavioral corollaries, constitute an ideal that, needless to say, has not always been scrupulously observed. The prevalence of contextual definitions of personality should not be interpreted to mean that the Japanese are motivated exclusively by altruistic considerations and that they cannot be selfish, egoistic, or self-centered. Nor does it mean that the behavior of all Japanese is identical; as has been abundantly illustrated, there exists a great heterogeneity of behavior patterns throughout Japanese society.[80] What it does mean is that all the selfish, egoistic, and self-centered, as well as deviant, modes of behavior develop within the broad framework of these basic cultural definitions of personality. The very definitions of deviance—and the attempts to control it—are shaped by these basic conceptions.

That many of these conceptions have been changing in recent years and probably loosening up does not necessarily mean that new, purely individualistic conceptions have developed. It rather means a shift in the importance of different contexts—for instance a greater shift to those contexts in which hedonism and/or the emphasis on sensibility are emphasized, and some weakening of resilience in the adherence to the more formal or arduous norms.

These tendencies are also manifest in the basic poles of reflexivity prevalent in Japanese society, in the construction of the metalanguage of metacommunication in Japan, which can perhaps be best observed in the different attempts to escape from the limitations of daily discourse.

It would be, of course, wrong to assume, as has been sometimes stated or implied in the literature, that the average Japanese is totally bound in given groups or contexts and is not capable of going beyond them. Most Japanese evidence not only the capacity but also the tendency to move away from at least some groups or contexts; yet they move on the whole either into tragic isolation, as is depicted in many literary works, or into some other group or context, and not to arenas of social interaction that are structured according to other (for instance linear, universalistic) principles.

Even the fantasies of many Japanese are, to no small extent, regulated by such orientation and metaphors.

> Dreams of escaping from this society sometimes lead to utopian ideals where, however, a new exclusive group will be set up, such as in the fantasy found in a Japanese adolescent's Future Autobiography:
>
> "First of all, I will buy an island in the Pacific where nobody lives, and build my ideal country there. The conditions to be an inhabitant there are, firstly, to be a good man, not to betray other people's trust, and to be of above 120 IQ. I will gather the inhabitants by using my subordinates. I will gather poor orphans and able people from everywhere in the world, build a great research institution on the island, and then do experiments I want to do. There I will teach knowledge to children and create geniuses, and accomplish my life's ambitions with the people's love and respect, as a king of the country. I hate to live with the stupid of the world throughout my life . . . and what I want to do finally is to kill all politicians on earth, and to destroy all weapons. The world is uninteresting only because of stupid politicians and stupid people."[81]

Similar pictures can be found, as we have seen, in both popular and high culture; in literature and the arts and in folklore; and in films, plays, sports, and the like, in which common, potentially subversive themes are presented as being ultimately brought under the canopy of such hege-monic Japanese values as group solidarity or samurai perseverance.[82]

XXIV Thus we see that basic conceptions of selfhood and personality, strongly embedded as they are in the conceptions of reality and modes of discourse prevalent in Japanese society, share with those framing conceptions an emphasis on the mutual embeddedness of cultural and natural orders and on active attitude toward a world conceived in dualis-tic terms, which gives rise to a structuring of multiple arenas of reality and interaction. The relations between these arenas are effected across, not clear linear boundaries and unbreakable taboos, but much more flex-ible structures of ritual and liminal activities, organized in overlapping, hierarchical-vertical modes.

Jane Bachnik has, in a private communication, summarized these basic principles of the construction of social reality and of selfhood in Japan:

> "Relationships" are crucial to the paradoxes Japan poses for the West, which involve a shift in basic perspectives of the individual self and social order. At one level, the shift perspective is toward the process of producing the social context (rather than toward the context as product). In *Situated Meaning* Charles Quinn and I argue that the range of formal/informal and polite, or deferential distinctions revolving around "relationships" is the organizing parameter in Japanese language, self and society.
>
> These distinctions have significance beyond a single context, since they also delineate an organization for social life that focuses not on "structural" constants (abstracted from time), on ideological principles, or "social or-der" as an abstraction. Rather they revolve around the process of producing the social order itself, and the relationship of that process to structural con-stants, ideological principles, and "order." In other words, this is a focus on the relationship between social participants in time (and in social context) and the continuity of social life over time. It involves a kind of double per-spective; of the process of a social order being produced, and the social order itself, which is part of the process of its being produced (but not entirely). It's like a snake eating its tail. It's this same process that delineates the "re-lational" or situationally defined self, and the "situated" or "organic" so-cial order. These are simply two sides of the same coin; that is, the self in time produces the social order over time.[83]

Culture, Social Structure, and Process in the Formation and Reproduction of Japanese Institutional Dynamics

I Did the conceptions of reality, the social order, and personality analyzed above—dimensions of culture that presumably shaped the perceptions of large sectors of Japanese society throughout much of its history—have any impact on the main feature of the Japanese historical experience, especially its institutional formations and dynamics? Here the central analytical problem of the relations between culture, social structure, and historical contingency arises. (We shall address the same problem, with respect to the relation between these premises and patterns of cultural creativity, in chapter 15.)

It is indeed possible to point out close elective affinities or homologies between, on the one hand, the strong immanentist ontological conceptions and the indexical mode of semantic structuration and, on the other, the contextual mode of definition (in some combination of sacral, primordial, and natural terms) of the major social actors, the arenas of social action, and the Japanese collectivity.

Similarly, the social and ontological conceptions that have been prevalent in Japan evince several distinctive characteristics, which seem closely related to the combination of a predisposition to change and openness to external influences with a double-pronged response to such changes and influences—their Japanization alongside the creation of new social and cultural spaces.

First, there seems to exist a strong elective affinity between, on the one hand, predispositions to change and openness to external influences and, on the other, the flexibility or openness of Japanese ontological conceptions, with their strong vitalistic and activist components—a strong orientation toward the mastery of the natural order and a feeling of obligation toward the basic frameworks of that order. At the same time, such activism was in a sense contentless, a sort of context without text. As such it could be directed toward many different contents. The metaphor of the "empty center," so often used with respect to Japan, is very suggestive in this respect—emphasizing that such contents, the focus of such obligation, could be defined and formulated according to changing circumstances and contexts in a very flexible way. Indeed, the lack of any transcendental specification of the contents of the potential foci of obligation could drive a search for new and diverse arenas of activity; this also explains the great openness to external influences.

Second, there seems also to exist an affinity between the centrality of mythic, nondiscursive—as against logocentric—orientations and of indexical, nonlinear, topographical modes of structuring discourse (which are closely related to the "Japanese way of thinking" as defined, for instance, by Nakamura Hajime) and the strong tendency to channel in a contextual direction the intensive changes generated in prevalent ontological conceptions by the openness to external influences—thus minimizing the possibility that they might break through the core premises of Japanese culture and social order.

Third, a close elective affinity can also be identified between, on the one hand, the emphasis on the flexible movement between different contexts and, on the other, the openness to change and to external influences. The combination of the creation of new spaces with their subsumption under the prevalent basic premises recalls both the general dualistic cosmology, with its emphasis on inner experience and aesthetic sensibility, and some of the major modes of structuration of artistic activities, especially the search for transcendence in the rules of form.

Fourth, there seems also to exist an affinity between the vitalistic ontological conceptions and the degree of activism and pragmatism characteristic of much of Japanese society throughout its history. Moreover, as Fosco Maraini has emphasized, there seems to be an affinity between the emphasis on the acceptance of the phenomenal world and the great pleasure associated with the small details of life.

True enough, the basic ontological conceptions and definitions of personality provide a framework for the conceptions of reality and the constitution of meaning in various arenas and activities. Yet the existence of affinities or homologies between these ontological conceptions and the characteristics of the Japanese historical experience does not "explain" the crystallization and reproduction of the distinctive institutional features of the latter. Nor does it indicate through which social conditions and processes the impact—if any—of these ontological dimensions on the patterns of behavior and social organization occurs. The affinities do not in themselves indicate who are the bearers of these conceptions and how these bearers influence behavior within specific organizations in particular directions.

For such conceptions to influence patterns of concrete behavior and of institutional frameworks, they must first receive some motivational push. But such a motivation can be transformed into specific patterns of behavior only insofar as there exist social structural frameworks to facilitate the development of such patterns. Even the combination of such motivational predispositions with appropriate social structural frameworks is not enough, however, to explain the crystallization—and above all the continual reproduction—of distinct behavioral and institutional patterns. Here some additional social processes—"exchanges" between different sectors of society and on all levels of social life, especially between elites and broader sectors—come to be of crucial importance.

Let us now explore these problems and processes in greater detail. We shall first consider the processes through which institutional and behavioral patterns are reproduced and changed through time, then proceed to the exploration—as yet conjectural in many ways—of the historical conditions within which these patterns originally crystallized. We shall start with the analysis of processes of socialization through which motivational predispositions are developed and may be transformed into patterns of concrete behavior.

Processes of Socialization

II   The motivational, behavioral, and attitudinal implications of the conceptions of personality analyzed above are shaped through the processes of socialization that have prevailed especially in modern and contemporary Japanese society. These processes are closely related to, especially, the emphases on the embeddedness of personality in different social contexts and frameworks and on continuous movement between different contexts.

Most of the available systematic data on processes of socialization in Japan are from the modern and contemporary periods, and some of the characteristics singled out in the literature, such as the distance of fathers from family and children, are certainly specific to the contemporary scene. It seems, however, that other aspects of this process—especially its embeddedness in social contexts, the mode of construction of trust, and parts of the concomitant definition of personhood—were also prevalent in earlier times. At least this is not an entirely implausible hypothesis; it is to some extent supported by folklore, by works of literature, and by later historical evidence, especially from the late Tokugawa period on.[1]

Socialization processes in Japan have been characterized—as indicated in the immense literature on the subject—by several features, among which the following are most important: first, the strong dependence of the child on the mother and great initial maternal indulgence, connected with the inculcation by the mother of orientations toward the world outside the family, and of feelings of eternal indebtedness to her (especially under the modern conditions of work in the cities, such dependence may be reinforced by the relative distance of fathers from the actual process of socialization); second, the emphasis in all socializing and educational settings on appropriate behavior and loyalty to the respective groups and contexts, on emotional attachment to and participation in the group, and on the creation of specific symbol systems that invest seemingly trivial matters with great emotional and symbolic importance; and, third, the strong emphasis, in the transition from one setting or context to another, on the combination of achievement with extension of trust.

Tom Rohlen has succinctly analyzed these—mostly modern and contemporary—characteristics of Japanese patterns of socialization.

> Readers will recall the work of William Caudill and his associates comparing Japanese and American mothers' child-rearing practices. They found more physical contact and less verbalization among mothers and infants in Japan and made the suggestive general interpretation that whereas in the United States mothers generally regard the child as born dependent and therefore to be raised to great independence, the Japanese mother is inclined to view the child as born asocial with the implied goal of childrearing to be teaching the child to integrate with others, to become social.
>
> What comes across in these essays is that many Japanese mothers work very hard at seeing to it that their children succeed in school.
>
> In addition they are consistent and clear about the value and behavior they reinforce in their children. In particular, they stress persistence (*gambaru*) and exact, correct forms of behavior in public. . . .
>
> Related to this is the assumption that ability is not inherited, but acquired through effort.[2]

This combination of strong, seemingly unconditional support from mothers with their orienting of the children toward the outside world helps in the transition from the indulgent atmosphere at home to the more demanding and competitive one in the school.

It is this combination—energy driven by guilt, or, to be precise, feelings of debt to the mother, with the continuous search for maternal nurturance and confirmation, that is, the grounding of authority in the maternal, or the group in the mother's absence—that constitutes the psychological backdrop of what to outsiders seems a basic paradox of the Japanese character, namely the combination of "workmania" with an emphasis on pleasure—on the small, daily pleasures of life, for instance, on oral libidinality, as manifested in the tendency toward gluttony or immersion in food so vividly portrayed in Itami Juzo's 1986 film *Tampopo*—but somehow combined, as Fosco Maraini has shown, with a rather melancholy-aesthetic attitude, probably rooted in Buddhism, in which all reality is seen as transient.[3]

III The nature and consequences of continuous maternal authority and support, which at the same time orient the children toward activities in the wider world, manifest themselves in the period of transition from the status of indulged child to participant in the wider society. Mothers, as we have seen, play a key role in this transition, which now starts in preschool day care and intensifies at school, where merit, achievement, and the permeation of the broader society are emphasized.

It is crucial that this transition to the outside, achievement-oriented society not disrupt the solidarity and trust generated within the family. Rather, it must combine its emphasis on achievement with an extension of familial trust, especially that generated in the mother-child relationship, to broader solidary settings. It is within these settings, with their emphasis on symbols of family and community, that the tenuous demands for achievement are set.

Closely connected to this extension of trust is the learning or acquisition of *kejime*, the capacity to shift between different contexts. The range of contexts to which one must adapt becomes more diverse with the passages from childhood to adolescence and adulthood. Indeed it is during these transitions that the child learns the traditional *uchi/soto, tatemae/honne,* and *omote/ura* distinctions.[4] Such transitions are facilitated by the fact that physical separation from the mother does not imply, as it often does in the West, emotional distancing from her. According to Emiko Ohnuki-Tierney, in a private communication, "Japanese young males can openly say that they are looking for someone like their mother to be their wife. No 'killing of the father' is also an important factor in differentiating the Japanese mother-son relationship."

The specific constellation of emotional relations within the family—rooted in the nature of the conjugal bond prevalent in Japan—probably explains the possibility of the continuous transition from one solidary context to another without recourse to criteria and values that are beyond the context.

IV The Japanese emphases on achievement *and* on group harmony, that is, on individual endeavor within a solidary framework and on the extension of trust from the family to broader settings in learning to move between different contexts, is first evident in the transition from preschool to school, the nature of which has been aptly described in a comparative analysis of Japanese, Chinese, and American preschools:

> All this seems to suggest that in contemporary Japan children learn the dyadic relations at home and group relations at school, and that the role of schools is to transform dependent, selfish toddlers into group-minded youngsters ready to function in a group-oriented school system and society. But this is an oversimplification that underestimates the complexity of the Japanese preschool (and, for that matter, of Japanese character and society). To be Japanese is not to suppress or sacrifice the self to the demands of the group but rather to find a balance between individualism and groupism, between giri (obligation) and ninjō (human feeling). The task of the Japanese preschool is to help children find this balance, to help them integrate the individual and group dimensions of self, to teach them how to move comfortably back and forth between the worlds of home and school, family and society.[5]

More specifically, the researchers note: "To prepare children for successful careers in first grade and beyond, Japanese preschools teach not reading, writing and mathematics, but more fundamental preacademic skills, including perseverance, concentration, and the ability to function as a member of a group"[6]—as well as the ability to shift between different contexts.

This complex of attitudes and behavioral patterns is reinforced by various pedagogical devices, found both in classrooms and in many adult settings: "The most important among these are (1) minimizing the impression of teacher control; (2) delegating control to children; (3) providing plentiful opportunities for children to acquire a "good girl" or "good boy" identity; and (4) avoiding the attribution that children intentionally misbehave."[7]

V   Another significant aspect of these processes of socialization is the emphasis on the importance of pleasing people, the satisfaction of being liked, perhaps especially by those above one. These attitudes, inculcated in the various settings in which children and adolescents learn the ground rules of social interaction, spill over and continue into adult life.

These patterns of learning, with their emphasis on learning modes of behavior appropriate to specific contexts, regulate also the many therapeutic situations discussed in chapter 5 and the various adult education retreats (as for instance that described by Dorinne Kondo) in which companies often encourage their employees to participate.[8] Although evidence from former periods is necessarily less systematic, many indications point to the same direction.

In all these settings there tends to develop an emphasis, as Tom Rohlen has shown, on emotional attachment to the group, on participation and inclusion:

> It is compliance with the basic routines promulgated in various groups, which defines one as a social being and a member of a group providing markers for the context in which behavior has been socialized and they define the realm of participation.
>
> . . . The outcome of these practices is that a "society" is not abstraction, but a very tangible, distinctive, largely face-to-face entity with clear boundaries, norms and customs. . . .
>
> . . . Participation thus not only signifies attachment, but represents a form of discipline. . . .
>
> . . . The implicit rule of participation and consensus carries with it the eternal problem that participants have considerable veto power. The legitimacy and eventually the power of those in authority would be diminished. The gloved fist is very real, but it is rarely put to use.[9]

VI It is, as we have seen, essential that transitions from one setting to another, especially from the indulgent familial setting to the school, not entail a total rupture with the solidarity and trust generated within the family, but instead extend that trust to a broader setting while also introducing an emphasis on achievement. This extension of trust is also closely connected with the construction of new spaces and contexts, structured according to the axes of *omote* and *ura*, *tatemae* and *honne*, *soto* and *uchi*—among them outlets for various forms of expressive behavior, ranging from the "small pleasures" of life to often inhibited sexual and aggressive drives to delicate aesthetic sensibilities.[10]

The extension of familial trust is couched in broader, generalized kinship terms and symbols, in an *Iemoto* pattern with strong expressive components, and not in terms of criteria beyond such kinship symbols. These symbols contain strong maternal aspects, which, as we shall see later, are also important components of the emperor symbolism.

The trust generated in all these situations is a generalized trust defined in broad, continually changing particularistic terms. This generalized particularistic trust, which is close to but not identical with R. N. Bellah's generalized particularism,[11] is not confined to narrow settings but is generalized over many different settings or situations. Such generalization is not effected in universalistic terms, but particularistic ones, made possible by the fact that the extension of trust is effected by the continual movement between different contexts defined in the dualistic terms of *uchi/ soto*, *tatemae/honne*, and *omote/ura*.

VII The relative success of these processes of socialization explains also the high level of responsiveness of many sectors of Japanese society to the themes promulgated by elites—such as loyalty, obligation, harmony, and consensus—through which the prevalent patterns of behavior and institutional arrangement in Japan have been legitimized. One of the most interesting illustrations of this predisposition, and of the resonance of the themes of loyalty and harmony, is the use of thought control by Japanese authorities in the 1930s and the concomitant phenomenon of *tenkō*. We follow here Patricia Steinhoff's illuminating analysis:

> The word "tenkō" has been applied at various times to everything from the Meiji intellectual's rediscovery of Japanese culture to the post-war student activist's acceptance of a job with Mitsubishi. It refers to the act of renouncing an ideological commitment under pressure. The current usage of the term originated in the 1930's, when the majority of imprisoned members of the Japan Communist Party publicly renounced their party affiliations. The fact that an ideological commitment was given up, and the fact that the persons involved were in prison because of that commitment, suggests that tenkō is related to thought control. . . .
>
> . . . Several Japanese cultural traditions, undoubtedly shared by court and prison officials, suggest an implicit orientation towards encouraging thought criminals to change their beliefs. . . .
>
> Many said wistfully that they could have maintained their faith with the support of the group, but could not sustain it alone. The silent comrade became less salient over time than the letter from home, or the kind and persuasive chaplain.
>
> The emotional ties which drew the tenkōsha away from the Party and its ideology were the social bonds linking that person to Japanese society. The critical areas were his sense of identity as a Japanese; his sense of belonging within his family; and his sense of connection to social groups through commitment to particular persons. Viewed from the perspective of the individual these three kinds of links constituted the main elements of Japanese social structure. From a societal point of view, these links formed a national political and symbolic structure centering around the Emperor system and resting on a common cultural heritage, a strong family system and a strong group structure based on factional linkages.[12]

The predispositions to such responsiveness were also continuously reinforced by certain characteristics of the Japanese language, especially its contextual structuring, the lack of personal pronouns, and the tendency to indexical structuring of modes of semantic discourse.[13] But while the characteristics of the Japanese language reinforced the potentials for responsiveness to themes of harmony, loyalty, and contextual orientations, they were not by themselves enough to activate these potentialities. Moreover, language itself is not unchanging.

The example of *tenkō*, or any other illustration of responsiveness to the themes of loyalty, harmony, and consensus, does not of course mean that all members of the Japanese society respond identically in all situations of potential conflict. It does mean, however, that responsiveness to such themes is very widespread within Japanese society, and that it is relatively difficult to mobilize wide sectors of Japanese society without invoking some of these themes, at least to some degree.

Aspects of Social Structure: Family, Kinship, and Structuration of Status

VIII   The analysis of the process of socialization has taken us another step in the exploration of the ways in which the elective affinities between the prevalent ontological conceptions and conceptions of self and personality, and the patterns of behavior and institutional formation that have developed in Japanese society may become concretized. The processes of socialization have continually provided the motivational drive and a predisposition toward the development of specific patterns of behavior, such as loyalty or perseverance, but the concretization of such predispositions can take place only within appropriate social frameworks. It is thus necessary to examine the social structure that has developed in Japan in order to see if some aspects thereof may have facilitated the development of such patterns of behavior. We shall not, however, at this stage inquire as to when these patterns developed and became interwoven with the processes of socialization analyzed above.

Structurally, some of the central aspects of the Japanese family and kinship organization and the relative looseness of the relations between status, power, and wealth have been of crucial importance in producing the framework within which the specific patterns of behavior and institutional formations prevalent in Japanese society crystallized and were reproduced.

The most important aspects of the Japanese family and kinship system in this respect have been—as analyzed first by Marion Levy and John Pelzel, then by Francis L. K. Hsu, and more recently by Jane Bachnik and many others—the following: (*a*) the combination, at least from the time of the Middle Ages, of fairly open unigeniture and the relatively widespread practice of adoption of people from outside into the family, a practice that remains prevalent, although in a different form; (*b*) an emphasis on functional adequacy and achievement within the framework of family solidarity; (*c*) the relatively strong emphasis, with regional variations, at least from the medieval period, on the nuclear unit, which in the Edo and

Meiji periods crystallized in the formalized *ie* system; (*d*) the weakness of broader kinship units, as manifest in the absence or vagueness of specific broader kinship terminology (as against such general connotative terms as "uncle" or "cousin"), and the consequent lack of specified obligations to such wider kin categories (similar, as R. Smith has pointed out, to the English and American cases). Of crucial importance is that the *ie*, "the basic family unit," as it probably developed from the Middle Ages, has been conceived,

> [not] as a kinship unit based on ties of descent, but as a corporate group that holds property, land, a reputation, works of art, or "cultural capital" in perpetuity. *Ie* are perhaps best understood as corporate groups which can serve a primary religious function, to provide social welfare and the like. Pelzel succinctly describes the *ie* as "task performance."[14]

The fact that throughout most of Japanese history, rights (especially, but not only, in land) were vested in the family, was of course of crucial importance.

One has to distinguish here between, on the one hand, the formalized *ie* structure instituted, or institutionalized, in the Edo period and made the cornerstone of the Meiji legal family system, but certainly not the only type of family organization in earlier times, and, on the other hand, the more analytical orientations that guided the construction of family relations, cutting across several types of family organization. The concrete forms of family varied greatly even in the Edo period—and certainly earlier—across regions and classes. Indeed, in several regions— and in several sectors of the lower strata—the older clanlike organization continued to be prevalent through the Middle Ages.

It seems, however, that many of the more general principles analyzed above have been of wider importance in structuring family relations. One important outcome of the prevalence of the *ie* has been the relatively great availability within the family of resources that can be freely mobilized as family leaders deem appropriate; such resources have often been redirected into other, nonkinship groups, which nonetheless were organized according to the principles that regulate the family structure. It is these features of the Japanese social structure that make up the "*iemoto* system," a term denoting, according to Francis L. K. Hsu, kinshiplike groups or settings which constitute the core of Japanese social structure.[15]

Whatever the correctedness of Murakami, Sato, and Kumon's characterization of the entire Japanese society as an *ie* civilization, it seems they are correct in asserting that this type of family and kinship organization has been predominant, at least in middle and upper rural and urban sectors, in historical and contemporary periods alike and that in many ways it has served as a model for other patterns of social organization.[16] As Jane

Bachnik has observed (private communication), especially with respect to the contemporary scene,

> The ie itself can be viewed as a contextualized locus with permeable boundaries that is closely connected by a network of ties beyond itself (which are part of its organization). These ties are the focus of the organization for the members, and this kind of a focal organization connected with its ties is actually the model for the large industrial groupings of the keiretsu and kigyo shudan (vertical and horizontal groupings).[17]

The basic characteristics of the family and kinship settings—above all perhaps the widespread practice of adoption, which entailed the total transformation of the identity of the adoptee, who was incorporated, not only into the household, but into the associated ancestry—have limited the self-closure of particularistic family and kin groups and made them open to permeation by outside, more "central" forces. But at the same time society and its center or centers are defined in terms of kinship symbols and legitimized in "internal" terms, in terms of their own existence. Hence the family and kinship units have been open to permeation by almost *any* power that was ultimately legitimated by the "familistic" social order ultimately symbolized by the figure or trope of the emperor or of the collectivity. Thus, any victorious leader could occupy this position without reference to any criteria beyond the given social nexus—and especially without reference to transcendental criteria. One manifestation of this openness, defined in terms of loyalty to any occupant of the relevant center, is the primacy in Japanese—as distinct from Chinese—neo-Confucianism of loyalty to one's lord over loyalty to one's father, to which we have already referred.[18]

A second central aspect of Japanese social organization has been the relative—obviously only relative—flexibility with which the relations between power, wealth, and status have been structured in any given setting. The mode of status incongruence that developed in Japanese society early on in the crystallization of the state—the bifurcation of power and authority between the emperor and the military leader, later the shogun—has probably been of crucial importance in generating the strong predisposition to change found in large sectors of Japanese society, and in shaping the specific processes of change.[19] The flexibility built into this pattern, when connected with the family and kinship structure, have created wide institutional "empty spaces," that is, spaces the concrete contents of which are not predetermined, which can be filled in different ways. It has also provided strong incentives and structural opportunities for change. The combination of this relative disassociation between status, power, authority, and wealth with a relatively decentralized pattern of political rule has generated continuous processes of ecological, economic, and social mobility and a wide range of possible combinations between them—thus creating continuous possibilities for institutional innovation.

IX   It is these "empty spaces," spaces with no predetermined contents, that have provided the arenas in which the orientations to activism and obligation, rooted in basic ontological conceptions and reinforced by the processes of socialization, have been activated, especially in conjunction with the free resources generated by the organization of family and kinship frameworks. It is also within these empty spaces that many of the new, semisubversive activities and attitudes have been able to develop. These developments are connected in particular with the inculcation of the ability to shift between different contexts, between *uchi* and *soto*, *tatemae* and *honne*, *omote* and *ura*—an aspect of socialization that is critical in the transitions, for example, from home to school and from school to adult life.

At the same time, the Japanese scene is characterized by the combination of the openness of family nuclei—their orientation toward and permeability by outside forces—with the fact that such outside forces are themselves constructed and legitimated in terms of family and kinship symbolism. This combination is closely related to the tendency to channel the intensive changes that take place in different arenas, and the achievement orientations connected with them, toward the reconstruction of contexts defined in sacral, primordial, or cultural terms, often in a kinshiplike, *iemoto* structure.[20] Such channeling has been guided by an orientation toward the prestige vested in the center, usually defined in terms of a basic symbolism of the center with strong primordial-sacral, collective-national, and kinship components. The kinship components of this symbolism are closely related to the maternal grounding of authority, to which we referred while analyzing the processes of socialization.

The overall symbolization of this pattern of maternal grounding of authority in Japan can be found in the emperor figure, as analyzed by Shigeru Matsumoto and R. N. Bellah.[21] To follow Bellah:

> But of course the emphasis on the feminine side is not something recently discovered by social scientists. Who is the most important figure in Japanese mythology? Of course the sun-goddess, Amaterasu ō mikami. Not only is she female but, unlike some more Amazonian types in other mythologies, her influence is exercised in a very feminine way. She is no patriarchal despot like Jehovah. She is often portrayed as confused; she relies on the advice of her counselors; she asks the will of higher gods through divination. She is often shown as relatively weak and defenseless, for example, as compared to the willful Susa no o no mikoto. She is a peacemaker, conciliator, mediator, not a despot.

It is my contention that through Amaterasu we can understand the emperor in Japanese ideology, the very emperor who is the focus of the whole austere Confucian family-state unit.

. . . But not only was there a base in the family (the mother) which provided emotional security for breaking with all traditional identifications of status and occupation, there was also an external base, namely the emperor. All kinds of aggressive and innovative behavior could be legitimated if it were for the sake of the emperor. . . .

. . . The emperor, then, both in recent times and in the far distant past, has been primarily an emotional point of reference. He stands for no policy, no rules, no institution and no constitution. The men who rule and who build institutions may come and go. The imperial house is unaffected. This pattern has had the function of providing what Maruyama has called an empty envelope or empty bag. Anything can go in—there is almost infinite receptiveness and flexibility—yet also a stable point of reference unrelated to the particular cultural content of the moment. The difficulty is that this pattern makes it extremely difficult to establish higher order universalistic cultural controls.[22]

This centrality of the emperor figure can be seen, for instance, in the fact that the specific pattern of ancestor worship that developed in Japan, especially in the Meiji state but building on earlier dispositions, promulgated the idea that imperial ancestor worship encompasses, to a very large extent, the ancestor worships of different households—very much in line with the basic characteristics of adoption in Japan. As a 1920 teachers manual in history stated, "Amaterasu Ōmikami is not only the ancestor of the Imperial House, but also of all Japanese." It is this maternal grounding of authority that generates the combination of the openness of the family to outside, society-wide force—which constitutes the basis for extensions of trust beyond the family—with the couching of such extension in generalized family and kinship terms and symbols, in a *iemoto* pattern and not in terms of criteria extrinsic to kinship. Through these processes the framework of generalized particularistic trust is generated.

REPRODUCTION AND TRANSFORMATION OF INSTITUTIONAL FORMATIONS AND PATTERNS OF CONTROL IN JAPANESE SOCIETY AND OF SOCIAL INTERACTION; EXTENSION OF TRUST; HERMENEUTICAL REFLEXIVITY AND LIMINALITY

X The preceding analysis of the sources of the strong predisposition to change that has characterized large sectors of Japanese society indicates that these sources are not distinct from those aspects of Japanese culture and social structure seen as important for the understanding of the processes of continuity. There seems to exist an interesting homology in Japan between, on the one hand, the openness that developed in the family, kinship, and status systems and in the prevalent ontological conceptions and conceptions of social order and, on the other hand, the relative openness to change and external influences, accompanied by a tendency toward the Japanization of these influences. The specific combination of open spaces and the ways in which this openness was brought to closure are characteristic of the ontological conceptions prevalent in Japan, as well as of the social structure, and also explain to some extent the predisposition to change and movements of protest, the openness to outside influences, and the specific directions in which such influences and protests were channeled.

Moreover, the analysis of the processes of socialization has identified the motivational forces that give rise to these patterns of behavior, while the analysis of the openness of the social structure and of the maternal grounding of authority has pointed to the social frameworks within which such behavior is implemented.

But the specific type of institutional formations and dynamics that has developed in Japan, the coming together of these various components of culture and social structure, is not a natural outcome of the homologies or affinities between them and the ontological conceptions, definitions of personality, patterns of socialization, and types of social structure, or of the broad cultural framework figured in the symbolism of the emperor.[23]

It is in principle possible to envisage the combination of such ontological conceptions with some (even if not all) other types of social structure—or vice versa—and hence also with other types of institutional formations and dynamics.[24] In other words the preceding analysis cannot and should not be interpreted as supporting the simple "culturologic" view that it is these basic ontological conceptions that explain the major dimensions of the Japanese historical experience which we have analyzed—and especially the similarity or continuity of these dimensions through different periods of Japanese history.

It seems that, as we shall see in greater detail later, the bringing together of these ontological conceptions, basic family and kinship structure, and looseness of status dimensions, and the concomitant establishment of specific types of formations and dynamics in the central regions of Japan as the hegemonic institutional patterns, took place around the Kamakura period and was effected by coalitions of aristocratic and clan families, peasant groups, and religious groups that came together by virtue of contingent historical processes. But whatever the historical details and contingencies, only a few of which have been fully investigated, this institutionalization cannot be considered as a natural outcome of the homologies analyzed above.

It is not just that the bringing together of these components of social structure and culture—however long a process that might have been—is not foreordained by the existence of such homologies. These affinities, even when reinforced by the processes of socialization and the maternal grounding of both personal and societal authority prevalent in Japan, cannot explain the seeming continuity of the definitions of major arenas of action and of the major social actors, their institutional repercussions throughout many periods of Japanese history, and their continuous reproduction and transformations in the directions specified above. These phenomena should not, however, be taken for granted. The continual reproduction, transformation, and reconstruction of both basic conceptions and major institutional and cultural formations should be explained, and the processes through which they are effected should be identified. Neither the illustration of the *tenkōsha* nor any other case that emphasizes the widespread responsiveness to themes of harmony and loyalty promulgated by elites and influentials explains the continual construction, in a double-pronged way, of new contextual frameworks, defined in sacral, primordial, or natural terms, to encompass new types of organizations and cultural activity, or the reproduction of the modes of regulating the manifestations of disharmony, conflict, and protest endemic in Japanese society.

Indeed, the emphasis on the continuity of basic ontological conceptions and ground rules of social life and cultural creativity present what appears to be a very static picture of Japanese society—like some of the more extreme and ideological pronouncements of the *Nihonjinron* literature, portraying an overly harmonious picture of Japanese society—as if all these precepts and ground rules had been given naturally and observed happily ever after in most sectors of Japanese society.

This is obviously a false and misleading picture. Throughout Japanese history and in most sectors of Japanese society there have developed, as we have seen, manifestations of dissatisfaction with these basic precepts and ground rules—constituting another, disharmonious side to the picture of Japanese society. Japanese society has been, as we have repeatedly stated, continually ridden by attempts to escape the confinement of the predominant premises and ground rules and, like any other society, by conflict and protest, especially but not only among the lower or marginal groups; by deviant behavior and personality disorders; and by the persistence of "secondary," nonhegemonic traditions of protest and communality.

Neither can the continual reproduction of institutional formations be explained by military victories, the repressive measures often employed by the ruling strata, or other applications of brute force. Military force was of crucial importance in shaping some of the features of the major regimes in Japan—notably the Muromachi, Tokugawa, and Meiji ones— and repressive measures were employed, as we have seen, to maintain them. But the use of force and repression—like the existence of conflict— has not been unique to Japan. What are distinctive in any given society are the specific institutional contours that crystallize and are reproduced in the wake of such uses of force. These contours are not explained by the use of force as such but by the interweaving of its use with other modes of interaction and control. Here we come back to the problems of the nature of the patterns of interaction that developed in Japan and the reproduction and reconstitution of its specific institutional formations.

XI   The reproduction and reconstruction of the basic institutional formations of Japanese—as of any—society is contingent on the structuration of the interactions between the major social actors and agencies, above all those between influentials and elites and broader sectors of the society; on the modes of control and regulation effected by the elites and influentials; and on the patterns of empowerment of the broader sectors.

Our starting point in analyzing these processes is indeed the ethic of loyalty, consensus, and harmony promulgated by the elites—which built on predispositions inculcated through processes of socialization and which legitimized the hegemonic institutional pattern common to most sectors of Japanese society—and the concomitant widespread sharing of metalinguistic assumptions. But even the broad acceptance of these assumptions does not explain the high degree of acceptance by large sectors of Japanese society of the predominant modes of coping with conflicts, the consequent upholding of the major ground rules of different arenas of interaction, or the creation of new social and cultural spaces. The crystallization of such institutional and behavioral patterns can be only assured insofar as the interactions between different social sectors are constituted in a mode that is resonant with such basic presuppositions.

Of critical importance is the fact that this metalanguage, with its themes of loyalty, obligation, and the like, not only provides a sort of "opium for the people," it also constitutes the basis of legitimization and self-legitimation of the elites and authorities. Hence, it limits and directs the ways in which these elites exercise power and also influences the demands made on them. These metalinguistic themes have indeed often been used by the broader sectors of society or by counterelites, by the leaders of the various movements of protest, to justify demands made on the elites. Within many movements of protest and of rebellion, there developed an emphasis, often connected with communitarian and millenarian themes, on the right to expect benevolence from the authorities. These expectations are generated by the symbolism of authority, symbolized in the emperor figure, and by the continuous extension of trust between diverse contextual settings, often defined in familial or semi-familial terms. In many of these movements rice, as symbolic of plenitude, was employed.[25]

The prevalence of this type of demand implies that the institutionalization and reproduction of the basic features of social formations and of patterns of behavior and response to change and protest is contingent on the authorities' continual engagement in distinctive modes of control, interaction, and exchange with broader sectors of the society that are in some way compatible with the premises of harmony and consensus and with the moral economy of protest prevalent in many sectors of Japanese society.

It is only insofar as the elites and influentials exercise their power according to these premises, engaging in specific modes of control and acceding to some extent to the demands made on them in terms of such expectations of benevolence, that the predispositions of the community to respond according to the themes of loyalty and moral consensus may be successfully actualized in concrete situations, especially situations of change and conflict.

XII An analysis of various situations in which control has broken down indicates some of the most important components of the processes of social control, regulation, and interaction between various sectors of the population. One such component is the relatively (indeed only relatively) smaller scope of the coercion employed by Japanese elites as compared to those in other societies. Elites in Japan, like those in all other societies, have used coercion to resolve conflicts in the direction most convenient to them.

In most periods of Japanese history—even those characterized by intensive strife and violent conflicts, such as the early feudal period and the Tokugawa regime—coercion has usually been closely interwoven with other modes of social control, with their emphasis on the self-control of seemingly autonomous groups. Thus, processes of repression have usually combined—albeit in different measures in different periods—with a tendency to leave some living space to at least some of the losers. Even if individual losers were executed, the groups with which they were connected were left some space. To this day the Japanese police suffer from a negative reputation inherited from the post-Meiji period, but even the violent suppression of conflicts, in which there was much bloodshed and in which losers—for instance, Etō Shinpei, a Meiji leader who led a rebellion in 1874—were executed, did not give rise to "regimes of terror."

Closely related to this mode of repression has been the continuous restructuring, by various influentials, gatekeepers, and elites, of networks, markets, and status hierarchies, together with a certain mode of responsiveness to the demands made by different groups and the co-optation of different echelons onto middle and sometimes even higher rungs of the vertical hierarchies. Such restructuring of networks, markets, and status hierarchies, often the result of the policies we have analyzed above, to which we shall turn again shortly, has been closely related to the dissociation between status and wealth.

XIII Such restructuring of networks, markets, and status hierarchies can be effective only insofar as it is interwoven with rather specific patterns of interaction or exchange between different social sectors. The special characteristics of the patterns that have tended to develop in Japanese society do not lie in the nature of the resources—power, trust, prestige, information, or instrumental resources—that are exchanged, but in the modes in which these resources are combined.[26] Of special significance is the prevalence of a certain type of package deal in which solidarity, power, and instrumental resources are continuously interwoven and organized in relatively enduring contexts, oriented toward long-term interaction, as is the case in many other, especially modern, societies. These different types of resources are not organized into discrete, ad hoc activities or within frameworks connected only formally, through legal agencies, bureaucracies, or the impersonal market.[27]

The major characteristic of these patterns of exchange, which Murakami and Rohlen, following Peter Blau's nomenclature, term "social exchange," is the continuous combination of various packages of resources under the canopy of long-range trust.[28] Such packages are channeled through the numerous networks characteristic of Japanese society—and through the continual transmission of information within them. This mode of interaction or exchange is closely related to the far-reaching tendencies to incongruence between the different dimensions of status, and the concomitant limitations of the degree to which the respective resources—wealth, power, and status—can be converted into one another.

The prevalence of this mode of interaction or exchange does not mean that no competition or conflicts develop between different groups in Japanese society or that no coercion is used by the elites to regulate or quell conflicts. What it means is that competition and conflict are regulated in a distinctive way and that even when confrontational situations develop, the reestablishment of trust, of a certain level of predictability within the basic premises of interaction—even if on somewhat altered terms—often constitutes a major objective of the contestants; it is the ability to restructure the networks and trust under conditions of intensive change that constitutes the major challenge for the elites and influentials.

These patterns of interaction have been effected within the numerous densely woven networks that characterize Japanese society. These networks contribute, as Hechter put it, to the high level of mutual visibility to which most Japanese are exposed in most arenas of their lives—in school, family, workplace, neighborhood, or leisure activities—as we saw in chapter 5. This visibility is closely related to the repressive aspect of the modes of regulation in Japanese life that constitutes the other side of the interaction and trust relations analyzed above.

As with all the other patterns of behavior we have considered, many of these patterns of interaction can also be found in other societies—but not to the same extent as in Japan, where they became hegemonic.

XIV Such patterns are prevalent in many arenas of social interaction in Japan, among them the special form of patron-client relations prevalent in many sectors of Japanese society.

> Clientelistic relations emphasize to an even greater degree than those found in other settings the combination of voluntary undertaking of such links with strong elements of inequality in hierarchical standing of the partners, and the recognition by the clients of the patron's rights to control the avenues and terms of exchange and flow of resources. In spite of these similarities, however, and as against clientelistic relations found in Latin America, Southeast Asia or in the Mediterranean, by being involved in oyabun-kobun relations, Japanese "clients" are not only granted a certain degree of security, of control over sources of uncertainty, of protection or of delegation of power, but also have certain obligations that are not typical of other patron-client relations. People attached to an oyabun feel less free to indulge in individualistic behavior and are expected to be more committed to the proper performance of duties, in which they will have greater emotional involvement. In addition, the oyabun is, in some sense, seen as responsible before people higher in the social hierarchy for the behavior of his dependents, since he is supposed to guide and control them on responsible conduct, and their irresponsible acts may therefore endanger his own market position. . . .
>
> . . . The emergence of Japanese hierarchical links has been fostered and reinforced, to a greater extent, by the widespread acceptance of certain cultural orientations, among which stand out the recognition of authority, commitment to it, and to the norms upheld by its strong emphasis on seniority, on harmony and on giri obligations, and the high value placed on filial piety and paternalism. It is therefore the oyakata (oyabun) who seem

to invest time and resources in maintaining the kokata's (Kobun's) long-term commitment. This is done by renouncing in the short term the use of the differential ranking advantages they have, and by stressing the highly expressive content of the relationship, shaped around values of long-term recognition of paternalistic authority. This phrasing of the relations confers expressive gratification upon clients and an egalitarian aura, despite their hierarchical inequality.

. . . This translation of monetary advantages into long-lasting power domains in the institutional markets is, indeed, not peculiar to oyabun-kobun relations but is shared with other types of clientelism in other societies. What is peculiar to Japan is the enforcement of these links—of the submission to a superior, as prescribed within the framework of a strong social consensus by the cultural outlook of this society.[29]

XV Beyond such informal settings, such modes of exchange, based on package deals combining (as illustrated, for instance, in Harumi Befu's description of the relations between different echelons in Japanese bureaucracies) instrumental, affective, solidary, and power resources, are to be found in all sectors of Japanese society and in all arenas of social life—in micro and macro situations alike, in the centers and at the periphery, in primarily individual relations and in those between organizations.[30]

In micro situations in which the amount of instrumental exchange is limited (in contrast, for instance, to buying in department stores), there tends to develop a very strong symbolization—usually highly ritualistic—of range commitments and objectives. In macro settings there usually is a stronger, more continuous combination of all types of resources. In both micro and macro situations the flow of resources emphasizes long-range commitments and investment in modes of behavior that symbolize such commitment and the concomitant extension of trust. These modes of interaction can be identified in many arenas, among them that of contemporary industrial relations—in the "welfare-type" organization of the large Japanese firms—or in the structuring of the political process, that is, the processes of mobilization of votes. As has been noted, this type of relation is also closely tied to the emphasis on vertical hierarchy, to the comparatively weak horizontal job differentiation in quality circles (i.e., in circles of workers in factories or offices that are hierarchically looser and in which everybody learns to perform all the tasks), to less formal delegation of authority but a greater de facto participation in decisions at lower levels of management, and to the high mutual visibility of the Japanese in many arenas of life.[31]

Within this context certain repercussions of the tendencies to status incongruency—for instance, the bringing together of different status activities within common organizational frameworks—become very important. Such activities have often been regrouped and connected in patterns that reinforce, within the framework of multiple solidary relations, the tendencies to the limitation of status congruence. This gives rise, on the one hand, to a weakening of various manifestations of inequality, a certain equalization of the lifestyles of different echelons, especially within given frameworks, organizations, or sectors, and on the other, to far-reaching supervision and regulation by the authorities of the various activities. It is this confrontation that minimizes the possibility of transforming such egalitarian tendencies into a basis for autonomous political activity or for restructuring the basic premises of authority.[32]

Needless to say, such restructuring will not always be successful in terms of the challenges it faces—and the contemporary scene provides from this point of view one of the most challenging periods, at least in modern Japanese history.

XVI The prevalence of institutionalized modes of interaction, exchange, and control in combination with a strong ritualistic emphasis can be identified throughout most of Japanese history. This structuration of social interchange was already very prominent, as we have seen, in the early feudal system. We have also encountered some of these characteristics of the exchanges between different sectors of Japanese society in M. E. Berry's analysis of the relations between the Tokugawa shogun and the daimyō in terms of gifts, a definition that emphasizes the interpersonal and contextual—as against the characteristically abstract nature of these relations in Western, to some extent Chinese (especially neo-Confucian), patterns and ethics.

These patterns of interaction, exchange, and control have been of crucial importance even in periods, such as the Tokugawa period or the 1930s, when coercion and repression played an important role. The same patterns were evident in the restructuring of Japanese society starting in the mid-1950s, and have had, as, for instance, Sheldon Garon has shown, a significant impact on the development of industrial relations in Japan, and on the fate of the socialist party.[33]

Similarly, as Kent Calder, among others, has shown, the combination of relatively flexible policies toward various seemingly politically weak sectors—farmers, small businessmen, the lower middle class—effected through networks cutting across the government, opposition parties, and the bureaucracy, has been the dominant pattern in Japanese policies since the 1950s.[34] Indeed, the capacity not only to co-opt new people or groups into the existing networks, but to extend and adapt such networks, according to the basic premises of the hegemonic system to new environments and to enable the development of new networks in close relation to the existing ones, has constituted the major challenge before the elites and influentials in all periods of social change.[35]

Insofar as the elites have employed these types of social regulation in situations of conflict, they have been able to mobilize the commitment of wide sectors of the population in terms of loyalty, harmony, and group or network obligations. These themes have been interwoven with the relative cohesion of the major social groups and have relied heavily on strong vertical relations between them. Such cohesion and vertical relations, when reinforced by governmental policies—above all in the Tokugawa period—have led toward relatively far-reaching self-regulation and responsibility within many sectors of Japanese society. The control of such self-regulation—associated with honor, family pride, and the like—has been vested in the leaders, hereditary or elected, of collectivities, families, villages, towns, and later, modern occupational groups. Yet, although the vertical lines converge on the center, or subcenters, access to the center is determined, as we have seen, not by the autonomous approaches of members of the group, but by a strong commitment or loyalty to the basic framework and to the authorities, to the gatekeepers of the respective groups of networks.

The Structure of Coalitions and Countercoalitions

XVII The specific characteristics of control, regulation, and interaction between the participants in different, often newly constructed or reconstructed contexts, have been, in their turn, closely related to some basic characteristics of the major elites and influentials, their coalitions and countercoalitions, and the modes of reflexivity that seem to have been predominant in Japanese society at least from the Kamakura period.

The exact composition of such coalitions has naturally varied from place to place and from period to period. The most important among these have been the "functional" elites—political, military, economic, and cultural-religious—as well as representatives of the family, village, feudal, or regional sectors and in modern times different economic and bureaucratic actors.

Yet some common characteristics of these coalitions of elites and counterelites can be identified in most periods of Japanese history and most sectors of Japanese society, the most important of which has been their embeddedness in settings defined mainly in primordial, ascriptive, sacral, natural, and often hierarchical terms, not on the basis of specialized functional or strong universalistic criteria. At the same time such coalitions have evinced a great openness, a strong tendency to co-opt new members and to extend their membership and arenas of activities. They have usually been constructed and effected through vertical rather than horizontal ties and loyalties, although this has not necessarily negated the existence and consciousness of horizontal divisions. Moreover, the concrete composition of these coalitions has often been shifting between different contexts. Nonetheless, the members of the subgroups within any such coalition are not granted autonomous access to the centers of power, just as the members of most sectors of Japanese society have lacked independent access to the centers of collectivities in which they participate. The groups have themselves been supervised by their hierarchical superiors— a strong overlord, the shogun, and in rare cases the emperor.

These characteristics of the major coalitions and countercoalitions and the tendency to extend membership are very close, even if not identical, to those of the *iemoto* system analyzed by Hsu; those of the *ie* society or organization, as defined by Murakami, Sato, and Kumon,[36] and the closely related contextual model of social organization based on interlocking networks in multiple vertical arrangements, which Hamaguchi and associates see as having been predominant in Japan since the early medieval period.[37]

The specialized activities that have developed in various coalitions— economic, cultural, or religious—have also often been combined with strong achievement orientations, but these have ultimately been oriented toward broader contextual settings and imbued with strong expressive dimensions and solidary components. Within each such setting and between different settings, cultural elites have enjoyed only very limited autonomy. Many cultural actors—priests, monks, scholars, and the like and, in the modern age, specialists and scientists—have participated in such coalitions, but with few exceptions their participation has been structured in primordial, sacral-liturgical, or natural terms, in which terms both their achievements and their social obligations have been defined. Only secondarily has their participation been structured according to autonomous criteria rooted in or related to functional needs or distinct definitions of their arenas of cultural specialization. In other words, while specialized cultural activities have been undertaken in continuously constituted and reconstructed social spaces and frameworks, the overall cultural arenas have not been defined as distinct ones, autonomous from the broader social sectors.[38]

Accordingly, the cultural, religious, and intellectual elites, while often engaged in sophisticated cultural activities and discourse, have evinced little autonomy in the social and political realm, that is, as actors upholding values and orientations not embedded in existing social frameworks, but enunciated and articulated by these actors, and according to which they would be recruited. At the same time, the great openness of many such coalitions to new members, as well as their capacity to shift between different contexts, also explains the possibility of the creation of new spaces and of the ability of many people to move between the different spaces—so long as the activities undertaken in these spaces do not directly impinge on or take a confrontational stance toward the centers of the respective coalitions.

This embeddedness of the various specialized and cultural elites in broader social settings has made it very difficult for universalistic criteria based on a transcendental vision or on functional specialization to become predominant. Such criteria have instead tended to be subsumed under the various contextual orientations. The ensuing self-referentiality of the cultural elites has also made it difficult, as we saw in our discussion of the various rebellions late in the Tokugawa regime, for them to become connected with other rebellious groups or with various national or religious elites. The most visible illustration we have encountered of the absence or weakness of such actors has been in the process of the Meiji Restoration, where no such groups—in contrast to the European, Russian, and Chinese revolutions—played an independent, formative role.

The embeddedness of the cultural elites in prevalent social settings is of course closely related to the de-Axialization of transcendental and universalistic orientations, the most important manifestation of which, at the end of the Tokugawa period and in the early Meiji period, was the failure of the enlightenment movement in Japan.[39]

The Structure of Reflexivity in Japanese Society

XVIII The major characteristics of these coalitions and countercoalitions are closely related to some distinctive characteristics of reflexivity as it has developed in Japan, to which we alluded in chapter 12. This reflexivity has been structured, as Murakami Yasusuke has indicated, in a "hermeneutical" rather than "transcendental" mode—that is, it has been oriented mostly inward, toward the continuous exploration of the Japanese cultural tradition in terms of its contextual contents rather than transcendental, universalistic, logocentric principles, and it has thus reinforced the general direction of intellectual discourse. It was the "other"—China, and later the West—that was seen as the bearer of such transcendental visions, which were consciously refused by most sectors of Japanese society, and especially by most Japanese intellectuals.

The most important characteristic of such reflexivity is the continuous and very flexible reflection, in a very rich imagery, of primordial, sacral, and natural principles as they function in the construction of different codes of action and the movement of persons between various contexts. This reflexivity is rooted in indexical as against referential, topological as against linear, conceptions of time and space, in the ability to shift from one context to another, to cross demarcated boundaries. But at the same time such reflexivity is bound by the criteria immanent in it, and does not go beyond them. The metalanguage used in these situations is constructed in these terms, reaffirming their ultimate validity.[40]

Existing reality is thus evaluated, not on the basis of principles that transcend it, but in terms of a continuous and rather complicated "mirroring" of the principles inherent in its construction. Such reflexivity is very much attuned to the extension and reconstruction of trust in internal terms, in terms of the successful movement of persons between different contexts. While a comparative analysis of mirror symbolism in Japan and in Buddhist rituals on mainland Asia is still a desideratum, its central role in Japanese rituals, from the imperial ones to those of daily life, has been often commented upon.[41]

XIX The analysis in the preceding sections indicates that the metalanguage of extended particularistic trust—embedded in continually shifting contexts and combined with hermeneutical reflexivity, as inculcated in the process of socialization and in the maternal grounding of authority in the symbol of the emperor—is shared by both the various manifestations of disharmony and the attempts to regulate them. In most situations of "disharmony"—whether manifested in deviance, protest, or other conflict, in "worlds of fantasy" or artistic creativity, in high culture or popular entertainment, in which subversive themes are often promulgated—the establishment or reestablishment of linkages of trust networks and contexts that extend beyond the immediate setting is of crucial importance. In most of these situations, especially the numerous rebellions and protest movements, the groups acting in a disharmonious manner emphasized the loss of such broader trust—possibly its betrayal by leaders or would-be leaders.

The same features are characteristic of the protests or rebellions that have developed in liminal situations throughout Japanese history, as well as in the liminal "rituals of rebellion," to follow Max Gluckman's famous phrase, that develop in drinking parties at different echelons of industrial enterprise, in which the existing social order is affirmed through the devaluation of any alternatives. Such quests for affirmation and the extension of trust are indeed characteristic of the moral economy of protest to which many of these movements seem to have subscribed—especially insofar as they have tried to reach out to broader sectors of the population. This concern with the extension of trust is also the common denominator of the processes of regulation, as we saw in chapter 5; such an extension allows for the incorporation of new types of activities into the existing frameworks and the creation of spaces for new activities, without changing the basic premises of such frameworks.

The core of this metalanguage of extended particularistic trust consists of certain assumptions about the groups or community and about the construction of trust. To again follow Befu, previously quoted in chapter 5,

> What is important is to see the group or the community as a moral unit, as a unit espousing a common moral value. When some members of the community start claiming a different moral value or disagreeing with the moral value of the group, that's when there is conflict. For example, when presidents of polluting companies refuse to admit their wrong, when people in the community were dying due to pollution, these presidents placed their company profit above community life. But when they finally broke down and visited the homes of the pollution victims, and prayed before the family altar, where the victims are memorialized, the community saw this action as sharing the moral value of the community and as an act recognizing the value of the community life in the way others did. These presidents were not criticized afterwards. (private communication)

Such acts of repentance often bear, as we have noted, the character of a purification ceremony aiming to overcome the pollution brought about by the "deviant" activities.[42]

The focus of the moral consensus of the community—inculcated through the various processes of socialization prevalent in Japanese society—is the search for the maintenance and extension of trust through movements between the numerous shifting contexts, and the embedding of actors in broader frameworks of trust.

XX   One of the most interesting manifestations of the combination of a metalanguage emphasizing the extension of trust with hermeneutical reflexivity is to be found in the numerous liminal or semiliminal situations, ranging from informal company parties, sports outings, leisure activities, and groups that create temporary solidarities among strangers[43]—the various retreats which abound in Japanese society[44]—up to the numerous movements of protest.

All such situations are related to tensions generated by the various modes of control prevalent in Japanese society, especially by the high visibility of people in the various contexts and networks in which they participate. In all these situations such tensions are portrayed, worked out, "reflected upon"—and all contain numerous, sometimes very strong, liminal components. Situations such as these, in which "society reflects on itself," contain a double message. On the one hand, the various tensions generated by the modes of control prevalent in Japanese society are portrayed and many subversive themes voiced. On the other hand, the conceptions of self as embedded in social nexus and the obligation pursuant on these conceptions are strongly emphasized through the processes of symbolizing and extending trust, which are played out often very openly. The pinnacle of such extensions is—or at least used to be—the symbolism of the emperor as the focus of the overarching trust and solidarity of the national community.

It is in such situations that what Ben-Ari calls the metalanguage of group—which Hamaguchi terms its contextual orientations—is continuously promulgated and reinforced.[45] In Don Handelman's words, "The ritual of rebellion reproduces the social order by denying the value of alternative solutions, in comparison to that of the existing order" (private communication).

Needless to say, not all liminal situations in Japan have been "rituals of rebellion." As we have seen throughout our discussion, Japanese history is replete with real rebellions and movements of protest, which were coercively repressed, and with subversive themes containing strong millenarian orientations.[46] But, significantly enough, most of these rebellions and movements, while certainly not accepting the existing social arrangements, did not challenge the core premises and symbols thereof, especially the assumptions of the "right to benevolence" and the basically nonconfrontational egalitarian and communal themes.

This is also true of the new spaces continuously created in Japanese society. Thus, for instance, the liminal, self-referential orientations and themes characteristic of hermeneutical reflexivity are also found in contemporary films, theater and television shows, popular literature, and science fiction. Themes of violence and sex, and potentially subversive criticism of one's self and of society, abound in all the major arenas of popular culture, possibly to an even greater degree than in many Western societies.[47] These themes are, however, usually subsumed under the canopy of the broader themes of harmony and loyalty, and only rarely assume an openly confrontational stance in relation to hegemonic themes. The same is true with respect to the egalitarian and communal themes that have created new modes of discourse and permeated many activities in such spaces.

XXI   The maintenance and extension of linkages of trust constitute the common denominator of the interaction between elites, influentials, and broader sectors of society, of the themes promulgated by the elites and influentials, and of the responses to them in many sectors of Japanese society. Such linkages may indeed break down—as they do in cases of mental breakdown or intensive conflict. When this happens—for instance, during the student outbreaks in the 1960s or in some of the cases of status conflict analyzed by Susan Pharr—an unregulated anomic situation, often with great potential for aggression, may arise. In other cases the breakdown of the ability to move between different contexts and to construct new contexts may give rise to the dissolution of groups or organizations.[48]

Significantly, such breakdown is usually connected with the quest to reestablish linkages, even if in a new form or through new networks. The former lineages of order are often not reestablished—it is the extensions of trust, solidarity, and their symbols that is crucial. In most such situations there develops an intensive search for, or responsiveness to, the reconstruction or extension of trust from the concrete settings in which the crisis occurs to some broader societal context, rather than attempts to institutionalize entirely new, for instance formal, universalistic norms of regulation.

Such reconstruction and broadening of the range of trust in terms of the extension of primordial, sacral, and ascriptive—as against transcendental—criteria is closely connected with an emphasis on achievement defined in expressive and solidary terms and on the movement between contexts of interaction defined in the dualistic terms of *tatemae* and *honne*, *uchi* and *soto*, and *omote* and *ura*. Such reconstruction makes the extension of trust seem to flow naturally from one context to another; trust is conceived as embedded in such settings, not as conditional on adherence to principles that are beyond these settings. It is, as we have noted, self-referential. This reconstruction of trust recalls the strong emphasis on finding transcendence in the rules of form— an emphasis that at the same time allows considerable scope for innovation in contents.

The result of this emphasis on the continuous extension of trust from one solidary setting to another is, as Raymond Grew put it,

> a universal expectation that the behavior of others will be predictable, which reinforces the emphasis upon social form and also what has often been described as a pressure for conformity and an anti-individualistic quality. You can only trust what you know and expect. Recognizing that, the Japanese tend to present innovations in terms of continuity, individual contributions as expressions of the group. (personal communication)

XXII The extension of the range of trust—grounded in the combination of the modes of regulation and control and modes of interaction and exchange; in the continuous kinship-family symbolism, with its strong maternal components; and in hermeneutical reflexivity—provides the crucial key for understanding the dynamics of social interaction in Japanese society. It is this process that explains the relatively successful channeling in a "contextual" direction of the predispositions to change that have developed in Japanese society, that is, the specific patterns of change and continuity that we have analyzed above.

The combination of this extension of trust with the specific type of self-reflexivity analyzed above facilitates the concretization—and above all the continual reproduction and reconstruction—in different institutional settings of the elective affinities between the basic ontological conceptions and the definition of the prevalent institutional arenas and modes of interaction. But the reproduction and success of these modes of regulating the various manifestations of disharmony and changes under the impact of endogenous and exogenous forces is never given naturally. It has been contingent on the continual interaction between elites, influentials, and broader sectors of society according to the specific modes of exchange and regulation analyzed above.[49]

One of the most important aspects of this process is the fact that the modes of regulation employed by the elites and influentials are very similar to those prevalent within families. In other words, it is not just the elites and influentials but the continual interaction between them and the broader sectors that constitute the agency through which institutional formations are crystallized.

Engagement in these patterns of interaction does not mean, as we have stressed above, that force, coercion, and repression have not played an important role in the reproduction and reconstruction of the basic features of institutional formations in Japan. What our analysis implies is that force, coercion, and repression were able to renegotiate and reconstruct these institutional patterns only insofar as they were interwoven with these premises of interaction—and such interweaving greatly influenced the modes of coercion. Another measure of how successfully these modes of interaction have been effected is the degree to which the continuous reconstruction and reproduction of frameworks incorporating both the strong predisposition to action and openness to change and the channeling of such activities in the specific directions analyzed above are also effected.

It is thus through the continual engagement in such modes of interaction in different, large- as well as small-scale social networks that those definitions and ground rules of social interaction that evince elective affinities with conceptions of ontological reality have been continuously reproduced and reconstructed.

XXIII   It is indeed this predisposition to the extension of trust in a flexible but continuously self-referential mode that explains what is probably the dimension of institutional dynamics most specific to Japan, namely the double-pronged nature of the impact of the various manifestations of disharmony, movements of protest, processes of change, and foreign influences on the dynamics of Japanese society.

As we have seen, this process is characterized, on the one hand, by the far-reaching impact of the processes of change and openings to new influences; such processes have generated new modes of discourse, given rise to segregated sectors of action as well as to a growing reflexivity within which new types of cultural and social activity have flourished, and heightened awareness of alternative cultural and social possibilities. The themes promulgated by such movements, by public responses to them, and through the impingement of outside forces have in many cases been incorporated into the public discourse; new, more sophisticated discourses have developed, and many concrete demands have been acceded to. Above all, social spaces have often been created in which new patterns of economic and social activity, modes of cultural creativity, and forms of discourse could develop. On the other hand, the continuous reformulation of the prevailing ontological conceptions and conceptions of social order has been guided and reformulated in contextual settings by templates defined in some combination of primordial, social, and natural terms, and the new themes and orientations have not been, as it were, able to break through the relative hegemony of these themes.

The combination of reflexivity and extension of trust also explains the continual selection of "traditional" themes and modes of constructing tradition in Japan (to which we referred in chapters 4 and 13), the willingness of elites and influentials to incorporate new actors within existing coalitions and networks, and the parallel continual development of new spaces. Taken together, these specific processes of interaction, the modes of reflexivity, and the development of generalized particularistic trust explain the major aspects of Japanese historical experience to which we have referred—namely the great openness to change and to external influences; the distinctive modes of definition of the major arenas of social interaction; the continuous Japanization of the impact of Axial civilizations; the double-pronged mode of response to change and protest; and the combination of a highly regulated yet dynamic and innovative society.

XXIV   The explanation presented above of the processes of reproduction of the major institutional aspects of Japanese historical experience makes it possible to face squarely criticisms such as those arguing that research on Japan uses Western theories which exaggerate the peculiarities of Japanese constitution, while neglecting more universal categories, for instance, those of class. A good illustration of this type of argument is Bowen's criticism of a large part of the literature on conflict in Japan (for instance, the books by Koschmann Krauss, and others). Bowen accuses them "of the use of Western, so-called conflict theory 'to explain how traditional Japanese Confucian values conflict with Western reification of egoistic self-interest.' The result, I believe, is confusion, however well-intended their motives."[50]

Yet Bowen—who extols, for instance, Rob Steven's analysis of Japanese society in terms of class conflict—does not confront one of the most important questions concerning conflict in Japan, that of why, when egalitarian, communal, and confrontational class themes have been promulgated, they have not effected far-reaching changes in the basic premises of the society, although they affected many aspects of life of sectors of that society.

It is not only the relative absence or weakness of egalitarian, communal, or even more radical confrontational themes—such as those of class struggle—that characterizes the Japanese scene and has to be explained. Rather, one must explain several facts: First, that these themes have indeed been important in generating new modes of discourse and new types of activities—for instance, the many industrial cooperatives that burgeoned towards the end of the Tokugawa period and in the beginning of the Meiji.[51] Second, that it was difficult to mobilize wide sectors of the population around these themes in a confrontational stance against the center. Third, that such themes have often been subsumed under those of harmony and loyalty and their bearers segregated in new spaces or embedded in social frameworks defined, even if in highly reconstructed ways, in combinations of sacral, primordial, and natural terms.

Our preceding analysis attempted to explain these facts, as well as the continual reproduction and transformation of the premises, cultural formations, and double-pronged mode of response to change that have been hegemonic throughout much of Japanese history. This explanation brings us back to the important question of whether the emphasis on harmony and loyalty and the relatively widespread acceptance of the hegemonic modes of conflict management and resolution attest to the natural strength and prevalence of such themes in Japanese society or to the success of the Japanese elites in coercing or manipulating the broader sectors of society, in selling their ideas as a sort of "opium for the people"?

There is no doubt an element of truth in both these views, yet both are rather simplistic. Even if there is a relatively wide acceptance of these themes or orientations toward conflict management, it could not be effected merely by the promulgation of such themes by the various elites or by the coercive manipulation of the broader sectors. Even if coercion could explain the passivity of large sectors of the population, it would not explain the relatively high level of motivation many Japanese show in the performance of their tasks, even if they express dissatisfaction with many actual arrangements. The use of coercion as the main means of control would not explain either the continuous development of spaces in which new types of social and cultural activities can develop.

Our analysis has indicated that, instead of assuming that such responsiveness is to be explained by predispositions naturally inherent in large sectors of Japanese population or assured by ideological manipulation or coercion, it would be more useful to look at social processes that—against the background of the responsiveness to themes of harmony, consensus, and loyalty promulgated by elites and influentials, including, of course, the main agents of socialization—facilitate the continual reproduction of the major organizational and cultural features of the Japanese historical experience, without assuming that the activation of such predispositions and responses is naturally assured.

Historical Origins

XXV The question of the "origins" of the processes that produced the major features of the Japanese historical experience has often been posed. But such origins are ultimately relevant only insofar as the historical conditions and processes important at the genesis of these institutions have remained important in later periods, insofar, that is, as they have been reproduced. But the quest for historical origins may, of course, also shed light on the processes of reproduction and change. Two major explanations proposed in the scholarly literature for the historical origins of the specific Japanese pattern of institutional and cultural development are of importance from this point of view.

One, advanced by David Pollack in his *Fracture of Meaning*, attributes some central aspects of Japan's cultural development to the nature of its encounter with China. Johann Arnason has aptly summarized the major points of Pollack's argument:

> Pollack's main thesis is that the fusion of the Chinese cultural model with the Japanese tradition took the form of a "fracture of meaning," or, in other words, "a dialectic, in the ongoing synthesis of whose terms—the fullness, implicitness, and ineffability of native Japanese content on the one hand, the emptiness, the explicitness, and power to signify of alien Chinese form on the other—can be "read" the history of Japanese literature in the broadest sense, and indeed of Japan itself.
>
> . . . Although the model of self-definition included on essential reference to another culture, the emphasis could be shifted towards the native component. Successive—and sometimes ambiguous—steps in this direction culminated in the work of Motoori Norinaga and the school of "native learning" during the eighteenth century. A stronger sense of Japanese specificity or even superiority did not necessarily weaken the interest in China; rather, an "increasing awareness of what was properly 'native' provoked a heightened sensitivity to what was 'foreign,' and vice versa." Most importantly, the very meaning and function of the Chinese component was redefined: the cultural model was gradually dissociated from its territorial and political context, and China thus became "less an actual geographical

entity than . . . a part of the process of cultural self-definition, the archetypal background against which native Japanese patterns of thought and action were felt to attain greatest significance." In other words, the dialogue with China (encapsulated in the notion of *wakan* ("Japanese/Chinese"), tended to become "a Japanese monologue with itself about China." This internalization of the original relationship did not prevent the Japanese from responding to new developments in Chinese culture and translating them into their own terms.[52]

XXVI But this mode of collective consciousness and self-reflexivity could not have been continually reproduced without the development of the appropriate frameworks for the distinctive institutional formations that developed in Japan.

The most plausible attempt to analyze the historical roots of the specific Japanese institutional formations and dynamics is the one systematically presented by Arnason, building on the earlier expositions and insights of Asakawa and Sansom.[53] The focal point of this analysis follows Max Weber's analysis of the modes of disintegration of early clan-society:

> In the case of Japan the focal *historical* points are the Taika reform at the end of the 7th century which attempted to create the first "Imperial" clan state in Japan and which ultimately resulted, as Asakawa underlines: "in the practical isolation, one from the other, of the two principles constituting the reform. The organization of Japan prior to 645 was a fictitious hierarchy, whose foundation, the clan or quasi-clan, was now theoretically destroyed, while the apex, the Emperor, was preserved and elevated. . . . The loss was compensated by the imported conception of the state. How could the two be reconciled with each other? . . . Combined with causes too deep and numerous to be even casually referred to here, the two fundamentally incongruous factors, the Emperor and the state, were gradually pulled apart from one another, until the authority of the former was completely usurped by the high civil officers who surrounded his person and the majority of whom issued from one and the same family, and the state lapsed into the real control of certain new military clans.
>
> "This bifurcation resulted in the crystallization of a specific mode of double, parallel hegemony, that of power and that of authority, which contrasted greatly with comparable developments in Europe.
>
> "The imperial court appropriated the cultural and symbolic hegemony, which was almost never challenged—and which seemingly could not have been effectively challenged. Indeed, it constituted *the* institution epitomizing the collective identity and consciousness, the encounter with the other—especially with China. At the same time political and economic power were continually vested in the various types of aristocratic or feudal

groups. These however lacked any autonomous legitimation distinct from the imperial one. Hence, unlike for instance the Church in Europe, there did not develop any centers or bases of power which were autonomous from the feudal nexus and from the imperial center—nor did the cultural and the power and economic centers compete with each other for both power and legitimation."[54]

It was in this period that the bifurcation between power and authority that was at the root of the specific pattern of state formation that developed in Japan crystallized; it was also within the framework of this formation that the strong tendency to status dissociation developed in many sectors of Japanese society.

The type of institutional development attendant on the disintegration of a clan society is distinct both from that which characterized the development of great pre-Axial patrimonial empires (like those in ancient Egypt) and from the various Axial civilizations. In pre-Axial empires the transition from one stage of political development to another—for instance, from early state to archaic kingdom—was usually connected with the reconstruction and widening of the kinship or territorial elements and ascriptive categories and symbols, with the growing importance of territorial units as opposed to purely kinship ones, and with what may be called the qualitative extension and diversification of basic cosmological conceptions. It was also characterized by the increasing specialization of the elites (who were, however, on the whole embedded in various, sometimes complex and wide-ranging, ascriptive units), by a close correspondence between structural differentiation and the differentiation of elite functions, and by the prevalence of cultural models and conceptions containing relatively low levels of tension between the transcendental and mundane orders. The centers that developed in such societies were ecologically and organizationally, but not symbolically, distinct from the periphery.

In contrast, the Axial Age civilizations were marked by growing distinctions, even discrepancies, between structural differentiation, in the form of the social division of labor, and the differentiation of elite functions. In addition, these societies witnessed the emergence of autonomous elites and concomitantly more radical developments or breakthroughs in cultural orientation, especially in the direction of a radical conception of the tension between the mundane and the transcendental orders. At the same time, different modes of institutional formations appeared, including distinct civilizational or religious collectivities—different types of autonomous centers distinct from their peripheries. There also developed in these civilizations a strong tendency toward ideological politics.

The distinctiveness of the institutional development in Japan lies in its unusual combination of a high level of structural differentiation with low levels of distinction between roles and of autonomy of elite functions, that is, with the fact that in Japan the major elite functions were embedded in ascriptive settings.

The major impediment to the development of autonomous elites was the differentiation in Japan of a clan society into two distinct, noncompeting centers. The absence or weakness of such elites in turn reinforced the continuity of these two noncompeting centers and the bifurcation between power and authority. This mode of differentiation was also reinforced by the changes in the structure of family and kinship connected with the shift from the *uji* (clan) to the *ie* system, which led, among other things, to a growing tendency toward primogeniture around the Kamakura period.

XXVII Let us now briefly recapitulate the argument presented in this chapter. Our starting point was the existence of strong elective affinities between, on the one hand, the ontological conceptions and the conceptions of self and personality prevalent in large sectors of Japanese society and, on the other, major aspects of the Japanese historical experience, especially the mode of defining the major social actors and arenas of action and the double-pronged response to processes and movements of change and external influences.

We addressed ourselves to the problem of the social processes through which homologies and elective affinities become concretized in specific institutional patterns. *Historically* these processes probably crystallized some time between the seventh century and the Kamakura period. *Analytically* the most important such processes were those of socialization, through which the motivations to be responsive to themes of loyalty, consensus, and harmony and to engage in the concomitant patterns of behavior have been inculcated in large sectors of the population. Second was the development of social frameworks, especially family and kinship structures and the status system, that facilitate the concrete channeling of such motivations in the specific institutional directions characteristic of the Japanese scene. In this context we have laid special emphasis on the rather unusual combination of a weak kinship system and strong nuclear families open to penetration by a broader framework and center defined and symbolized in kinship terms in the figure of the emperor.

This analysis implies no chronological or causal hierarchy between these different components of Japanese culture and social structure. The distinction between these components is analytical, and the major thrust of our analysis that there took place, in a certain historical period, a coming together of these components. This analysis does not assume that this was unavoidable or foreordained. On the contrary, it assumes that such coming together was in many ways accidental, historically contingent.

It was these often contingent historical processes that provided the organizational and symbolic frameworks within which the various components of the picture—the homologies and elective affinities between the basic ontological conceptions, the institutional premises, the symbols of loyalty and harmony, the structure of the family, and the structure of the elites—were brought together and crystallized into specific institutional patterns and modes of change. These processes generate both special types of conflicts and the modes of their definition and resolution, as well as possible breakdowns of such resolutions.

The coalescence between the different components of culture, social structure, and the like is not generated by some metaphysical necessity, nor did it imply the continual reproduction of the resulting patterns. Such reproduction was contingent on the development of distinctive patterns of interaction between the major social actors.

We therefore laid special emphasis on the patterns of interaction and exchange between the major social actors, on the interweaving of these patterns with the processes of control exercised by the elites and influentials, and on the underlying premises of such modes of interaction and control, namely the extension of trust and its combination with self-referential reflexivity. These in turn were seen to be closely related to the structure of the major coalitions.

The focus of this analysis was the extension, in flexible, generalized settings defined in primordial, sacral, or natural terms, of a generalized particularistic trust—a trust, that is, that does not rely on transcendental criteria—and the close connection of such extension with an emphasis on achievement set within expressive and solidary settings, with the creation of new contexts and spaces, and with the continuous construction of self-referential reflexivity.

The selection and reformulation of specific cultural themes and symbols; the structuring of control and interaction, especially of the flow of resources and the definition of institutional arenas; and the legitimation of such exchange through the propagation of the reconstructed themes and symbols, taken together, constitute the crux of the process through which culture, tradition, social structure, and behavior are interwoven and shape the continuous reproduction and restructuring of institutional arenas and modes of symbolic intercourse.

The processes of socialization, social control, and above all the control of information, combined with those of interaction and exchange analyzed above, have given rise to a feedback process between the components of "culture" and "social structure" as they were brought together in the initial critical historical situation. The success of such a system of feedback is not automatic. It is, rather, continuously reflexive and may break down precisely because of this very reflexivity. It may also break down when the overall environment in which any concrete institutional patterns that had crystallized at a certain moment changes drastically. The possibility of such breakdown may also be intensified because of the seeming lack of access of the major social actors in this process to symbolic resources beyond the given social nexus, beyond the particularistic—even if generalized—trust. This is probably one of the most important challenges facing contemporary Japan.

XXVIII With respect to the central theoretical problem of our analysis—that of the relation between "culture" and "social structure" in the shaping of institutional formations and dynamics—the preceding analyses have illustrated that research based on the assumption that culture, social structure, and agency are distinct, ontological realities cannot explain certain crucial aspects of human activity, social interaction, and cultural creativity.

Many aspects of institutional formations and dynamics, such as the structure of the centers or the construction of boundaries of collectivities and modes of political protest, cannot be explained entirely in terms of either the "natural," autonomous tendencies of these spheres of activity or "routine," "rational," utilitarian activities. That is, they cannot be explained in purely structural terms—whether of structural differentiation, exchange, or power relations—or, despite the claims of some structuralists, as emanations of certain principles of the human mind. Similarly, the analyses of the transformation of Confucianism and Buddhism in Japan indicated that crucial aspects of the patterns of cultural creativity, such as the various modes of organizing and structuring worlds of knowledge or religious beliefs and their impact on the structure and dynamics of social life, could not be explained only in terms of the inherent dynamics of ideas or symbols.

We have seen, rather, that central aspects of social interaction, institutional formations, and cultural creativity could be better understood in terms of the processes through which symbolic and organizational aspects or dimensions of human activity and social interaction are interwoven—and that culture and social structure are best analyzed as components of social action and interaction and of human creativity, as constitutive of each other and of the social and cultural orders.

Beyond these general indications, these analyses have specified several systematic attributes of such processes of institutionalization, especially those bearing on the relations between culture and social structure: first, the different aspects of the symbolic and cultural dimensions of human life that are important for the construction of the various institutional frameworks or organizational settings, and of daily praxis; second, the patterns of social interaction and especially of macroinstitutional order on which the various aspects of the cultural or symbolic dimension have the greatest impact; third, the social processes, especially those of social control, through which the relations between the cultural and institutional dimensions of social life are mediated; and last, the relations between cultural and power components in the activation of such processes.

The rational-choice approaches, on the other hand, claim that the major institutional formations and behavioral patterns—for instance, juridical behavior—can be best explained in terms of the rational, ability oriented consideration of the actors and not in terms of some inherent cultural belief, predisposition, or tradition. Our analysis has indicated that such an extreme culturological explanation is not valid. At the same time it has shown that central dimensions of "culture" are of great importance in shaping institutional formations and patterns of behavior—but only when effected through specific social processes and institutional frameworks. Such social processes do not shape directly the concrete behavior of different individuals. Rather they shape the frameworks, within which such behavior is undertaken, the institutional ground rules—the "rules of the game"—within which the rational, utilitarian considerations (although not only they) may play an important role. But these considerations explain neither the constitution of such rules nor the social processes through which culture and social structure are interwoven to create such frameworks and rules.[55]

These considerations bear also on the explanation of social change. Such changes are not caused naturally by the basic ontologies of any civilization, or by structural forces or patterns of social interaction in themselves, but rather by the continual interweaving of these two dimensions—the "cultural" and the "social structural."

True, the cultural visions, ontological processes, models, codes, and "ethics" contain within them some of the potential developments that occur in the societies or civilizations in which they become institutionalized. But the types of social formations that have developed in various civilizations have certainly not been located merely in the basic premises of inherent tendencies of any culture. Historical changes and the constructions of new institutional formations have been the outcome, as we have seen, of basic institutional and normative forms, of processes of learning and accommodation, and of different types of decision-making by individuals placed in appropriate arenas of action, necessarily responding to a great variety of historical events. But similar, contingent forces can have different impacts in different civilizations—even civilizations sharing many concrete institutional or political-ecological settings—because of the differences in their premises.

Thus, any concrete pattern of change is to be understood as the combination of historical contingency, structure, and "culture"—the basic premises of social interaction and the reservoir of models, themes, and tropes that are prevalent in the particular society. At the same time, the rise of new forms of social organization and activity entails new interpretations of the basic tenets of cosmological visions and institutional premises, which greatly transform many of a civilization's antecedent tenets and institutions.

In other words, the restructuring of the meaning of situations is in some cases—on both the macro and the micro levels—concerned not only with attributing new meanings to specific actors or actions, redefining concrete arrangements, and selecting different themes and symbols according to the various interests or inclinations of the participants. It may also be concerned with redefining and legitimizing some of the basic premises of action through a redefinition of the ground rules that delineate the frameworks of social interaction and activity—in Carlo Rosetti's words, the constitutional parameters of social order—within the framework of which, and in relation to which, concrete rules and strategies of actions are formed and developed.

The most dramatic such changes are relatively rare in history. When they do occur, as in the crystallization of the Axial Age civilizations, in the great revolutions, or in the Meiji Ishin, their historical impact is enormous. Attempts at such reconstruction may also take place in less dramatic fashion, in various informal or formal situations and organizational frameworks, as well as through long processes on different macro levels, where they tend to become more formalized and more fully articulated. The continuous, less dramatic developments in this direction that have taken place in most societies may be ultimately no less important in effecting changes in the construction of society.

All these processes develop in all societies—but in different ways and constellations. In the preceding chapters we have analyzed these processes in modern and contemporary Japan and in selected other periods of Japanese history. It is now time to put these analyses into a comparative framework.

A Brief Excursus on Patterns
of Cultural Creativity in Japan

I In the preceding chapter we analyzed the relations between, on the one hand, the ontological conceptions and conceptions of social order and of personality that were presumably prevalent in Japanese society throughout much of its history and, on the other, the main features of the Japanese historical experience, especially its institutional formations and dynamics. Above all we were concerned with the processes through which these relations were effected. In this chapter we shall consider how these premises relate to cultural creativity in Japan. Indeed, relations to these basic premises are relatively easier to identify with respect to the central patterns of cultural creativity. These will necessarily be only very preliminary and tentative indications; it would of course be beyond the scope of our endeavor to attempt even a superficial survey of all the arenas of cultural creativity.

Specific characteristics related to the prevalent ontological conceptions can be identified above all with respect to two dimensions of cultural creativity: first, the range of themes that developed as part of the cultural activity of many periods of Japanese history and, second, the modes of cognitive and aesthetic structuration of philosophical and artistic creations.

With respect to the selection of themes of artistic creativity, the relatively great efflorescence of different forms—in, for instance, literary activity, painting, and the performing arts—is of special interest. This is manifest not only in folklore and the cultural creations of the periphery—in the ways of the "floating world"—but also in the central arenas of "high" artistic creativity. This efflorescence is closely related, as Katō Shūichi has shown, to the fact that such creativity was not regulated by cultural and religious elites promulgating transcendental principles, as was the case not only in the monotheistic civilizations but also, very markedly, in China. Such principles usually entailed a clear hierarchical evaluation of different arenas and forms of artistic creativity and, accordingly, strong tendencies toward censorship.[1] It is also probably related to the basically positive attitude toward nature and natural activities—including bodily activities—which can be contrasted with the more restrictive one found at least in the official Confucian Chinese discourse, as well as in the monotheistic civilizations.[2]

Hand in hand with the efflorescence of artistic themes there developed in many—certainly not all—realms of creative activity a distinctive pattern of structuration. This pattern was rooted in certain presuppositions about the nature of reality, of man, and of the cosmos that were inherent in the dualistic cosmological conceptions and modes of semantic discourse analyzed above, especially in the emphasis on context, defined in immanentist terms, as against content; in the aesthetic emphasis on form and on the search for transcendence in existing reality, above all in the rules of form; in the devaluation of the subject, as against the environment defined in topological terms; and in nonlinear conceptions of representation.

In the words of Augustin Berque, already quoted in chapter 13, "In the Japanese tradition it is impossible to envisage either logos or the subject independently of the world. There is no principle which transcends reality. And reality is the word of appearances (Erscheinungen) which we have to accept as it is contingent, in the given place and time."[3] Berque notes elsewhere that "this inclination obviously favors a poetical rather than a rational attitude toward the world."[4]

Some of the implications of these basic immanentist assumptions for the structuration of cultural creativity in Japan have been aptly summarized by Noël Burch:

> Firstly, tradition inclines the Japanese to read any given text (and this may also be a film, as we shall see) in relation to a body of texts. Secondly, the sacrosanct value placed on originality, the taboo placed on "borrowing," on "copying" in the West are as utterly foreign to Japan as are Western "individualism" and the primacy of the person or subject. Thirdly, the linear approach to representation is not a privileged one. Finally, the precedence given "content" over "form," or rather hypostasis of meaning to detriment of its production, is a specifically Western attitude. It has informed all Western methods of analysis, explanation, reading of interpretation; it has also been imported into Japan to fill an undeniable theoretical and instrumental void. It has, however, no place in artistic or other practice that can be identified as specifically Japanese.[5]

II　As indicated above, these modes of structuration could be identified as relatively hegemonic in all arenas of cultural creativity—literature, architecture, and painting, high and popular culture, philosophical discourse as well as the discourse of common sense. These templates and modes of structuration were manifest, as we noted in our discussion of the transformation of Confucianism and Buddhism in Japan, in the prevalence in Japan of mythocentric, nondiscursive—as against logocentric—orientation, that is, in the strong tendency to "philosophizing in the archaic."

This tendency, contrary to the more extreme claims of the *Nihonjin-ron* literature or those attributed to it by its critics, did not entail the nondevelopment of abstract philosophizing or the lack of openness to external influence. On the contrary, it entailed the development of a highly sophisticated philosophical discourse, which, while grounding itself in the archaic, at the same time continually incorporated new themes. It is indeed this tendency to "philosophizing in the archaic" that stands in marked contrast to the mode and premises of philosophy that developed in Greece and the West.[6]

A similar mode of structuration can be identified in the mainstream of the history of Japanese literature, especially perhaps in classical literature and No theater. To follow Tzvetana Kristeva's analysis of the archetypical *Taketori monogatari:*

> A close reading of *Taketori monogatari*, being as it is a moveable aesthetic pleasure, reveals it to be the "ancestor of all *monogatari*" in two respects: its narrative discourse, on the one hand, and its immanent aesthetic nature, on the other.
>
> . . . Now, as I mentioned in the beginning, a close reading of *Taketori monogatari* is of great theoretical interest with regard to the pattern of signification in early Japanese literature, *i.e*, the literature of the Heian period, highly praised for its supreme beauty and subtlety. This is even more important if we consider the facts that, first, in the development of Japanese literature, Heian literature played a role similar to that played by Ancient Greek literature in European cultural development and, second, that its influence was even greater than that of Greek antiquity in the West because its tradition was interrupted.
>
> The essence of Heian literature differs very much from Ancient Greek literature and from the later development of European literature. One of the basic differences derives from the fact that, whereas in Greek antiquity the first literacy genres were the epos and the drama, in Japan the first offsprings of literature were lyrical poetry and lyrical prose, which have long been disregarded in Europe as "lower" genres.
>
> This predetermined the formation of different sets of values and led to different patterns of development. . . . For me one of the essential differ-

ences is that whereas in Europe the pattern of cultural development implied evolution from a "primitive" sensory perception to a mental one, early Japanese culture developed through a sophistication of sensory perception, which was at all times able to adapt to change in a way similar to the adaptations of "primitive" Japanese religion, Shinto. In other words, in Europe it was on a conceptual level that literature defined the stages of its development, while in early Japan the development of literature was accomplished rather through the perfection of form than through the acquisition of new concepts. In semiological terms this means that the signification and the generating of new meanings in European literature proceeded mainly through the changes of the signified, while the pattern of early Japanese literature, being a chain of "reincarnations" of beauty, comprised a refined play of signifiers.

     . . . If the relation between myth and literature in Ancient Greece seems to be vertical, i.e. literature defines itself on the basis of mythology, or is "above" it, in Japan, myth and literature functioned in two adjacent horizontal spaces: the sacred central space of *kami*, and the profane marginal space of *mono*. Or, in other words, the narration of *mono-monogatari* was possible only in the space beyond the borders of the semiotic space of *kami*.

     Another important fact which influenced the formation of Japanese literature was that in *Kojiki* and *Nihongi* the "primacy" of mythology had already been destroyed by its subordination to the needs of politicized history. This predetermined, first, the double taboo of the central space, and second, the obligatory character of the mytho-historical consciousness for subsequent writings. That is why it is only natural that the narration in *Taketori monogatari* should stick to the norms of this politicized mythological consciousness exemplified by one of its major characteristics, i.e., the opposition of mundane versus alien.

     . . . Inadequate as it is, or even possibly a product of "wishful thinking," this pattern of signification does at least point to the differences between early European and early Japanese literature in their quests for the perfection of human nature—the former through the development of moral and ethical concepts, the latter through aesthetic refinement.[7]

Indeed as Hide Ishiguru has shown, the widespread reading in Japan of the *Tales of Genji* has sanctified and sacralized, among wide sectors of Japanese society, this aesthetic refinement—and given rise also to the belief that it is specifically Japanese.[8]

III A parallel pattern of structuration developed in the Japanese classical theater, especially the Nō theater, where again the comparison with classical Greece or Western culture is very instructive. In Masao Miyoshi's words:

The noh is often called the noh-play in English, which is quite inaccurate. Of course, the noh is staged, performed by those who talk, act, and dance, has a chorus that chants with a small orchestra of flutes and drums, and even has a few props. Yet the noh is not dramatic; neither tragic nor comic, neither mimetic nor symbolic, it is not even emplotted.

The story line, if this is a story line, varies from noh to noh, but the fact remains that the main interest of the noh is its unfolding of an unexpected event. Most of the events and characters are borrowed either from such well-known works as Ise or Genji or from public events via Heike, and the audience is presumably familiar with what happens in the play.

The performers, too, are not actors in the ordinary sense. . . .

. . . The main actor sometimes performs two characters in one scene: in the case of noh called Tadanori, the main actor impersonates both the defeated warrior-poet Tadanori and the person who kills him in the murder scene itself.

This denial of a one-to-one correspondence between the actor and the character is even more conspicuously demonstrated by the chorus that often speaks for one character and then for another, as if distinctions among characters were trivial. Unlike the Greek chorus, which sings in its own voice, the noh chorus presents several points of view, often even sharing a line with the main actor.

Thus the noh seems indifferent to dramatic representation of human acts. It is set on presenting a being or doing, a "concrete abstraction," through a complex interrelationship of actors, their masks and costumes (or the absence thereof), music, chorus, stage design, and theater space.[9]

Miyoshi's perceptive analysis, in the same article, of the distinctive characteristics of the Japanese *shōsetsu* (telling tales), as contrasted with the European novel, indicates how this pattern of structuring literary activity, with its emphasis on sensibility and deemphasis of the individual and of "originality," has also greatly influenced some of the most important modern literary forms—which are influenced by Western literature, and often aim at crafting something like it:

The "third person" is a mask the Western novel dons without an exception. The convention demands the distance of the "he" from the author. As man and author gradually work up to be the third person, his "soliloquy becomes a novel."

Against such a victory of the "he" over the "I" in the novel, the defeat of the "he" at the hands of the "I" characterizes the shōsetsu. The shōsetsu is so overwhelmingly marked by the dominance of the "I" form that the shi-shōsetsu ("I-fiction") is the orthodoxy of the convention. Instead of man and author attempting to transform themselves into the third person, they aim at discarding—or at least, concealing—the narrator. The man will speak and write directly. He will not wear a mask, but insists on the first person even to the extent of aggressively reporting his own daily routine (that excludes any formal and artistic intention) and presenting it as an emplottable event. It is the reverse of the novel: rather than a "credible fabrication which is yet constantly held up as false," the shōsetsu is an incredible fabrication that is nonetheless constantly held up as truthful. Art is hidden, while honesty and sincerity are displayed. Distance is removed, while immediacy is ostensive. The rejection of individualism in Japan is thus compensated for by the dominance of the first person. . . . The shō-setsu is thus an art that refuses to acknowledge art.[10]

The prevalence of such distinctive literary forms in Japan does not mean that others similar to those in the West did not develop—they did, just as literary genres similar to those in Japan developed in the West. Kristeva has shown, for instance, that European memoirs seem to stand, in terms of narrative patterns, closest to the Japanese lyrical diaries. It is noteworthy, however, that the relative importance of these literary genres differed greatly in the two civilizations. As Kristeva put it: "There are significant structural differences here as well. European memoirs tend to be socially more involved and historically more reliable; fact prevails over fiction in them. The Japanese lyrical diaries tend to be more fiction-alized and some of them are often even regarded as *monogatari*."[11]

IV The basic modes of literary and philosophic discourse analyzed above evince a rather distinctive conception of representation, certainly differ-ent from that prevalent in the West. As Edmond Fowler has put it:

> The Japanese writer, on the other hand, never had the faith in the authority of representation that his western counterpart had. Rather than attempt to create a fictional world that transcended his immediate circumstances, he sought to transcribe the world as he had experienced it, with little concern for overall narrative design. Unschooled in the notion of telos, he regarded plot as an unnatural fabrication. He therefore limited the scope of his au-thority to his personal realm. . . .

It may well be that it is this prevalent mode of representation that tends to create a situation in which

> writing in Japanese is always something of an act of defiance. Silence not only invites and seduces all would-be artists and writers, but is in fact a powerful resource. To bring forth a written work, to break this silence is thus often tantamount to the writer's sacrifice of himself, one defect and exhaustion."[12]

But this defiance focuses on a rather specific strong tendency of Japanese writers to withdraw "into nature and private space." [13]

The tendency to extreme withdrawal may also explain the prevalence of suicide as a theme among Japanese writers—and the actual suicides of some of the most outstanding among them. [14] But withdrawal need not be purely private and apolitical. Not only have many Japanese writers been politically active—some have even been arrested for their activities. Even those who seem to have withdrawn often, as James A. Fujii and David Pollack have shown, convey strong oppositionary messages. Some of these messages emphasize "natural," egalitarian themes, not dissimilar from the messages of Andō Shōeki; at least kernels of such messages can be identified in the classical Japanese literature and in Buddhist literature, and they abound in the contemporary artistic scene. [15] But these oppositionary messages have developed, as we shall see, in a rather distinctive way, closely related to the double-pronged response to protest and external influences that we previously analyzed.

V   A similar pattern developed in Japan with respect to the structuration of space. It was rooted in distinctive conceptions of environment, based on a immanentist and topographic orientation toward nature and space—with its relative deemphasis of centrality—and in the conception of space as embodying the interweaving of "nature" and "culture" and having potentially liminal characteristics. Such structuration is manifest not only in high art—painting and architecture—but also in such seemingly mundane matters as, for instance, the symbolic arrangement of households, of nobles and "simple people" alike; the organization of gardens; and the spatial organization of cities—in all of which there developed a strong emphasis on proximity to nature, on being at one with nature. [16] This attitude was not, of course, something "natural," but rather was culturally constructed. To follow Berque again:

> From a medial point of view, the way Man feels about his environment bears a close link with the way he acts upon it. Indeed, just as Japanese culture does not favor intelligibility over experience, it dislikes symmetry and general orientations in the organization of space. . . .
>
> A first manifestation of this tendency can be seen in urbanism. Japan has introduced geometrical models twice: once (to simplify) from China and once from America. The imitation of these models gave birth, as is well known, to Kyoto on the one hand, and to Sapporo on the other. These cities display an orthogonal grid of rectilinear streets (there are other cases, such as the core of many a *jōkamachi*). Similar principles were applied at the time to rural land (the *jōri* system in ancient Japan, and the *gobannome*

system in Hokkaido). However, the grid patterns were generally not so uniform as those seen in many other countries. . . . What we find instead is a mosaic of differently oriented grid patches.

Architecture shows similar trends. Here also geometrical principles were applied sporadically, or progressively rejected. . . . But order there is, nevertheless: it is the situational, topological order implied by actual position and movement from one place to another, from one room to the next one. This is a dynamic and experimental organization of space, not a static and abstract one. . . .

This situational bias appears not only in actual settlements, but also in their cartographical representation. For instance, the toponymy of urban maps of the Edo period seems, at first glance, to have been written in every direction. In fact, it relates mainly to two topological references; the effective orientation of the streets and plots which are represented, and the diverse possible positions of the observer looking at the map, unfolded on a tatami.

Traditional painting, too, disliked unitarian perspectives. In some pictures, the same figure can be shown in the different stages of an action, several times within a few centimeters; one has to look at the painting successively, not all at once. This is conspicuously the case of *emakimono* (picture scrolls), where each scene, although not separated from the others, has its own focus or focuses. The respective size of the figures, also, is not determined by their theoretical distance from the eye of a single observer, but by the interest one is supposed to have in them at the particular moment one looks at them.[17]

VI Underlying these modes of structuration of the different arenas of cultural activity is a strong tendency to what may be called sacralization of form, "to look for transcendence not in the content of works of art but in the rules of form."[18]

Dorinne Kondo's analysis of some of the most salient aspects of the tea ceremony is apposite here:

Perhaps the answer to these riddles lies with the Zen masters. For at least in the tea ceremony, and perhaps in other rituals as well, it is by becoming one with the rules that the possibility of transcendence lies. The formality of ritual also enables the participant to forget the contingencies of everyday life and frees the mind for "greater" thoughts. Ritual, then, need not be an ossified form interfering with "true" feeling and spontaneity. In fact, form separates the ritual from the everyday and distinguishes the casual partaking of a cup of tea from chanoyu, the way of tea. By its precise orchestration of sequence and the interrelations among symbols in different sensory modes, the tea ceremony articulates feeling and thought, creating a distilled form of experience set apart from the mundane world.[19]

This dimension of the tea ceremony has been reinforced throughout its history, especially under the impact of Buddhism, which "spiritualized" the ceremony without abandoning the basic emphasis on form. As Katō Shūichi has put it, "The chief characteristics of the aesthetic of tea lies, surely, in the elaborate procedure whereby the denial of pleasure directly related to the senses leads to the discovery of what one might term as spiritualized, internalized pleasures of the senses. Tea is the sensuous expression of the denial of the senses."[20]

The tendency to look for transcendence in the rules of form was probably first manifest in the emphasis on form as authentically Japanese—as against that on content, which is often viewed in Japan as being characteristic of the Chinese—an emphasis closely related with emotional sensibility, with the distances between inner and outer space, *omote* and *ura*, which have pervaded many of these arenas of cultural creativity. It may well be that this distinction developed, as David Pollack has claimed, in the original and continuous Japanese encounter with China, with the imposition of Chinese script on Japan and the consequent "fracture of meaning."[21] Whatever its historical roots, this distinction has pervaded Japanese cultural creativity—above all, but not only, painting and sculpture. It has indeed been often connected, as Jean Stanley Baker has shown, with a confrontation with Chinese art.[22]

The strong, almost transcendent emphasis on form is to be found not only in high art or in rituals but also in a wide range of more "applied" or popular artistic creativity. As Allan Booth has indicated:

> A performance of a noh play today (or a Kabuki or a Bunraku puppet play, for that matter) strives as far as possible to remain true to a style of performance unchanged since its inception. . . . This example of the classical theater suggests two further related tendencies. One is the habit of placing greater emphasis on form than on meaning, a habit linked to the importance of precedent. This is evident in the elaborate tangle of social intercourse that we call etiquette. In Japan, as many visitors have discovered, the forms required by etiquette are often given an unusual amount of significance. How you say a thing is often more important than the thing you say. How and when and how low you bow is, in traditional circles, a mark of your education and of how seriously you take your role in society. The obsessively careful wrapping in which even a commonplace item must be disguised before you can give it as an end of year gift often seems to carry more weight than the choice of the item.
>
> . . . The shape of a piece of origami paper never changes; it is always a perfect square, out of sheer ingenuity and dexterity, an astonishing variety

of animals, plants, and other objects can be formed. . . . The trick—and the secret of much of what the West so admires in Japanese aesthetics—is to see the possibilities in the simple. . . .

. . . Just as Japanese architecture has not often tended toward the monumental (except in periods when Chinese or other foreign influence was fresh and strong) so traditional buildings, and the arts in general, have usually stressed elegance over grandeur and simplicity of line over baroque elaboration. . . .

. . . Brush calligraphy (an art still taught in all schools and regarded at all levels of Japanese society as a serious attainment) provides the classic example of an emphasis on form over meaning. Often, it seems, the more idiosyncratically illegible a piece of calligraphy, the more deeply it is admired. A Western student of the art (who had taken it up partly as an aid to reading) once complained to his Japanese teacher that he could not be expected to write a word satisfactorily if he didn't know what it meant. The teacher was puzzled. "The meaning of the words is irrelevant," he said, "our only concern is with their shape."[23]

VII   These modes of structuration of cultural activities are closely related to the nondiscursive tendencies in the structuring of universes of discourses, and to the major templates or codes regulating the construction of modes of thought—as, for instance, "the Acceptance of Phenomenalism, the tendency to emphasize a Limited Social Nexus and Non-Rationalistic Tendencies," probably still among the most systematic ones, analyzed by Nakamura Hajime. These codes, which shaped the transformation of Buddhism and Confucianism in Japan, could be seen also in the impact of Buddhism in Japanese art and literature, to which we have referred, and *grosso modo* to the incorporation of Western ideologies in Japan.

These modes of structuring discourse did entail the incorporation of many new themes—for instance, as George Wilson has shown, of historical orientations into the prevalent mythical-natural templates. We referred to such incorporations in our discussion of Tokugawa and Meiji periods, but the phenomenon did not emerge only in the modern period. We have already referred to the importance of utilitarian, "rational" conceptions in earlier Japanese thought. Tendencies toward the incorporation of historical consciousness can also be found in earlier times, for instance, in the medieval Hon-Jaku (Buddhist) philosophy on Mount Hiei.[24]

Yet these new options were incorporated both within the high culture of the center and within popular culture in some combination of, on the one hand, sacral-liturgical and natural definitions of social action set in contextual frameworks and, on the other, the basically mythical conception of collective time. Such incorporation entailed the creation of new spaces which could find their place according to the various dualistic principles, especially *omote* and *ura*, in the hegemonic concept of collective time. As Wilson has put it:

> Not merely human nature and individual destiny but history and historicity in Japan also partake of this temporal sense of separate segments rather than sequential series. The emperors reigned, it is said, one after another, but it makes no apparent difference in what order the reigns occurred. The line itself is clear and sharp, a thread running through all the chronicles as well as the more cosmopolitan *Gukanshō*. But its ultimate fate, what will finally become of the imperial line, does not arise as a subject for consideration. Time in the form of existence cannot run out.

In the *Gukanshō* Jien pondered the future of the emperors, reflecting a general fear that only one hundred reigns would be allowed. Originally the phrase "one hundred reigns" indicated an indefinite number extending ad infinitum, but political commotion had changed confidence into anxiety. As he actually plotted the story of the imperial line, Jien never questioned its heroic character—yet he was writing around the time of the troubled year 1220! He hardly expected the emperors to rule without the aid of courtiers, monks, and warriors. It was enough that the imperial line existed and would continue to exist through improvement and replenishment even as the barely perceptible deterioration of the long Buddhist cycle continued.

. . . A later history, more famous but not as sophisticated as the *Gukanshō*, evinces a similar approach but ignores Buddhist fears of decline. *Jinnō shōtōki* (Record of the orthodox succession of divine rulers), written in 1339 by Kitabatake Chikafusa (1293–1354), introduces the imperial line as the hallmark of Japan and the touchstone of its genius as a culture.[25]

VIII The strong hold of some of the basic conceptions of personality, interpersonal relations, and emotional sensibility combined with a very strong embeddedness in social nexus can be also found in most arenas of cultural creativity in Japan—from the highly artistic to the more popular and vulgar, the highly conventional to the marginal or avant-garde, often imbued with strong rebellious or subversive themes.

Whatever the differences between these different types of cultural creativity—and it would be beyond the scope of our analysis to go into any of these—most of them enumerate basic themes of Japanese fiction, such as, to follow Gregory Barrett in his analysis of Japanese cinema, "the Loyal Retainer and the Tormented Lords; the Chaste Warrior, the original Yakuza hero; the warriors; the vengeful retainer; the all suffering Female; the weak passive male; the prodigal son; forgiving parents; self-sacrificing mother and the like."[26]

Continuous changes have of course been taking place, under the impact of broader social and economic changes, with respect to the relative importance of these various themes. Some of them, such as that of self-sacrifice for the sake of the family, have lately been weakened or have entirely disappeared. Interesting changes have also taken place in the connections between personal types and different behavioral stances. But the entire repertoire has but rarely been broken through. Thus, however rebellious or critical of the existing social system some films, for instance, may be, most of their rebellion or criticism is expressed through variations on the themes of the nobility of failure, passive withdrawal, and cynicism toward society. Such attitudes are, of course, to be found in films of all countries, but in Japanese films they are usually played out within the repertoire of these themes.

New repertoires do quite often emerge to some extent in more segregated artistic groups—as, for instance, in the nonorthodox proletarian theater, or in what has been aptly called "alternative Japanese drama."[27] In such groups rebellious, critical, subversive, or cynical attitudes have intensified and diversified, accompanied by attempts to escape from the constraints of the social order, and an emphasis on searching for authenticity beyond it, but they have not broken through the basic social and cosmological premises of this order. Thus many modern Japanese writers, such as Shimazaki Tōson, Natsume Sōseki, and Origuchi Shinobu, have voiced themes highly oppositionary to the hegemonic sociocultural patterns of the Meiji and Taishō periods but have couched their opposition in terms emphasizing nondiscursive themes—the unity of men and culture, the embeddedness of men in a natural environment—very much in line with, for instance, Yanagita's folklorist studies.[28] Similarly, as Brian Moeran has shown, such themes or orientations permeate all arenas of contemporary "popular" culture in Japan.[29] This is true of contemporary literature[30] as well as science fiction and the many subversively themed cartoons.

SIXTEEN

Japanese Historical Experience in a Comparative Framework

I In order to better understand the specificity of the Japanese historical experience, and especially of the pattern of continuity and change that developed in Japan, it might be worthwhile to compare this pattern, even if necessarily briefly and rather schematically, with those that developed in other civilizations, especially those with which Japan has been connected or has shared characteristics—Europe, China, and India. In this short comparative foray we shall focus on some of the major dimensions of change analyzed in the preceding chapters, namely on the extent to which structural, institutional changes, the crystallization of new types of institutional formations, the reconstruction of centers and collectivities, and the development of new organizations and roles were related to the construction of new types of legitimation and new symbols of collective consciousness and identity. We shall also consider the major characteristics of reflexivity that developed in these civilizations; the extent to which each civilization was conscious of discontinuity between different historical periods, and how such discontinuity was conceived; and the impact of the encounter with other civilizations on these modes of reflexivity and on the reconstruction of tradition.

EUROPE

II A good starting point would be, as at the beginning of this book, a comparison with European, especially Western European, experience. With Europe Japan shared, as we have seen, many structural characteristics and even the general contours of institutional change and development. Yet at the same time there developed far-reaching differences in overall institutional and historical dynamics.

One of the most interesting of these differences can be seen in the ways the construction and dynamics of collectivities and centers were connected with the development of collective consciousness.[1] As both Europe—especially Western and central Europe—and Japan were in some crucial phases of their history highly decentralized societies with strong regional organizations and allegiances, there developed within both continuous processes for the reconstruction of various centers and collectivities. But the modes of such construction differed greatly between the two civilizations. Its major characteristics in Europe were the connections of the frequent attempts at such reconstruction, first, with ideological struggles that focused on the relative symbolic importance of the various collectivities and centers; second, with attempts to combine the structuring of the boundaries between centers and collectivities with the reconstruction of the bases of their legitimation; and third, with a strong consciousness of discontinuity between different stages of their development. At the same time, far-reaching institutional, economic, and political changes were in Europe often connected not only with the development of new organizations but also with the redefinition of major roles in terms of new criteria and with their legitimation in terms of new symbolic tropes.

One central aspect of European medieval and modern history was the continuous construction and reconstruction of chiefdoms, municipalities, feudal fiefs, and cities, as well as of tribal or transtribal, regional, protonational, and national communities. Indeed, one of the most distinctive characteristics of European historical experience has been the continual constitution, within the broad flexible frameworks and boundaries of European civilization, of multiple, often competing communities, each claiming to be the best representative of this broader civilizational framework. The various centers and subcenters, as well as the different collectivities that developed in Europe, did not simply coexist in a sort of adaptive symbiosis. They tended to become arranged in a complicated but never unified rigid hierarchy, with no clearly predominant center. Many of them, however, aspired not only to actual but also to ideological predominance and hegemony.

Naturally, the activities of the "higher" centers were wider in scope than those of the local ones, but the former did not have a monopoly over any component of "central" activities. Each type of center claimed some autonomous standing and access with respect to the functions of the others, for instance, the religious vis-à-vis the political and vice versa. Hence, the various centers were never completely separate from one another. This was true not only of the relations between church and state, but also of those between different religious, political, and ethnic centers and subcenters. These collectivities and institutions were legitimized in a variety of terms—in terms of primordial attachments and traditions, of transcendental criteria, and of standards of civic tradition—and their continuous restructuring in Europe was closely connected with the oscillation and tension between these sacred, primordial, and civil dimensions of legitimation. While, for instance, many collectivities were defined mainly in primordial terms and the church mainly in sacral ones, each collectivity and center also attempted to arrogate all the other symbols of legitimation to itself.

Closely related was the structure of center-periphery relations that developed in Western and central Europe. As in the imperial societies, such as China or the Byzantine empire, Western and central European societies were usually characterized by a relatively strong commitment among their more active sectors—both central and peripheral—to common ideals or goals; the center permeated the periphery to mobilize support for its policies, and the periphery impinged on the center to influence the shaping of its contours. Many of these centers aimed at expansion, which would encompass other centers and communities, and such expansion was often legitimated in universal—often religious and ideological—terms, frequently giving rise to religious or ideological wars. But in contrast to purely imperial regimes, there developed in Europe, not only a multiplicity of centers and collectivities, but also a much stronger impingement of the periphery and of various subcenters on their respective centers.

The potential of such impingement was rooted in the combination of structural and cultural pluralism that developed in Europe. The structural pluralism was characterized above all by low but increasing levels of structural differentiation combined with the continuously changing boundaries of different collectivities and frameworks. At the same time, a multiplicity of cultural orientations developed, as did a multiplicity of worldly (political and economic) and otherworldly ways to resolve the tensions between the transcendental and mundane orders. This multiplicity of orientations was rooted in the continuous interaction in Europe between, on the one hand, the secondary breakthroughs of two major Axial civilizations—the Jewish and the Greek—and, on the other hand, numerous "pagan," tribal societies.[2]

This combination of cultural traditions with pluralistic structural and political-ecological conditions explains the fact that in Western and central Europe there developed—more than in other Christian civilizations—continuous tensions between the conception of hierarchy and that of equality as the basic dimensions of participation of different sectors of the society in the political and religious arenas, and between the strong commitment and autonomous access of different groups to the religious and political orders, on the one hand, and the emphasis on the mediation of such access by the church or by political powers, on the other.

III The mode of change that developed in Western Europe, from at least the late Middle Ages on, was characterized by a relatively high degree of symbolic and ideological articulation of political struggles and of movements of protest; by a high degree of coalescence of changes in different institutional arenas; and by a close relationship between such changes and the restructuring of political centers and regimes. As, for instance, the economic or cultural arenas changed, they impinged on one another and above all on the political arena. Such impingement was, as in any society, not only objective or structural, but also often conceived as bearing on the basic premises of these arenas. These changes gave rise to a continuous restructuring of boundaries, which did not, however, obliterate the autonomy of these different arenas. Rather, there developed a strong tendency to define institutional arenas, collectivities, or strata as distinct social spaces with relatively sharp boundaries and to conceive of different arenas of social life, of individuals, and even of roles as distinct ontological entities, often delineated in absolutist ideological terms. The strong tendency toward the ideological demarcation of different arenas of life at times conflicted with the multiplicity of collectivities and centers. In some historical circumstances, as for instance in the period of the Reformation, it gave rise to intensive wars of religion and later, in the modern period, to extreme nationalistic movements. A related tendency toward defining new activities, roles, or organizational complexes and collectivities in relatively autonomous terms also developed.

IV The continuous changes in the structure of centers and collectivities, and the struggle over their relative cultural and institutional standing, were activated in Europe by primary and secondary elites relatively close to the center, among them the major carriers of religious heterodoxies and political innovations. These elites, often closely related to broader social strata, tended to direct their activities toward center formation and to combine them with those of institution building in the economic, cultural, and educational spheres.

It was the various religious orthodoxies and heterodoxies and the secular rulers that promulgated the ideological dimensions of the restructuring of centers and collectivities; protest movements, many of which were oriented toward the reconstruction of the political arena, also played a very important role. It was indeed in close relation to the place of

heterodoxies—and, of course, that of the orthodoxies they confronted—
that the tendencies to universal claims and expansion developed.[3]

V There developed also in early-modern Europe the nuclei of a distinctive type of civil society characterized, first, by the existence of "private"
public arenas distinct from the state; second, by the development within
such arenas of associations that regulated many of the activities of the
major social groups and prevented the civil society from becoming a
shapeless mass society; third, by the relative openness and autonomy of
these arenas, that is, by the fact that they were not embedded in closed,
ascriptive, or corporate groups; fourth, by the multiplicity of such sectors;
and, fifth, by the autonomous access of most of these sectors to the central political arena, combined with a certain degree of commitment to
the center.[4]

These features of civil society in modern Europe were closely related
to the continuous, often ideological confrontation between the construction of centers and the processes of institution building, as well as to the
continuous competition between different groups for access to the construction of these centers. In close relation to such confrontations, there
developed—especially in modern Europe but with roots in earlier periods—the assumption that political elites and the more autonomous
social groups, the state on the one hand and civil society on the other,
were engaged in a continuous, ideological struggle over their relative
importance in the formation of the cultural and political centers of the
nation-state and in the regulation of access to it.

VI The most important institutional changes—especially those from
feudal to absolutist and from absolutist to modern, revolutionary nation-
state—were in Europe connected with marked changes in the legitimation of regimes and with the development of a strong consciousness of
discontinuity, in patterns of legitimation and in the conception of the
cosmic order, which became an integral part of the European collective
consciousness. The most important such shifts were the changes from
social-religious legitimation to the theological principle of the divine
rights of kings, then to the concept of sovereignty and later the patterns
promulgated by the great revolutions and the Enlightenment. The centrality of the revolutions in the European collective consciousness is the
clearest manifestation of this conception of discontinuity. The growing
legitimation of the economic arena in its own terms—especially its definition, in relation to Protestantism, in soteriological terms—is yet another illustration.

True enough, all these patterns of legitimation built on themes and tropes already present in the rich traditions derived from tribal, Greek, Roman, Jewish, and Christian sources. But in many situations of historical change these themes and tropes were reconstructed in a very selective manner. This is, of course, true to a great extent in all societies and civilizations. Beyond this, there developed in Europe a strong tendency to emphasize the novelty of the new patterns of legitimation, even if such breaks were legitimized in terms of older themes (such as the rights of Englishmen, in the Puritan revolution). The various themes and tropes were not only de facto reconstructed but consciously and advisedly so. There developed with respect to the premises of European philosophical and social discourse—especially from about the fifteenth century on—a strong consciousness of discontinuity and innovation and a tradition of questioning these premises in terms of various, often changing, transcendental values and premises, formulated both in "religious" and in "secular" terms.

These changes in patterns of legitimation and this consciousness of discontinuity were also closely related to a mode of reflexivity in which the older order was reflected upon according to new criteria that transcended both old and new orders. Such emphases on discontinuity were, in the European setting, closely related to the impact of Jewish, and above all Christian, eschatological visions, which not only gave rise to a strong historical consciousness but also shaped some very important dimensions of this consciousness. The most important of these, from the point of view of our discussion, was the evaluation of concrete institutional developments in terms of the unfolding of some universal historical plan—not just (as was the case in some Buddhist historiography) the evaluation of a given epoch in general moral or cosmic terms, or in terms of the fate or decline of the universe, but also the evaluation of events and institutional formations in terms of a temporal progression toward a (religious or secular) eschatological end and according to the criteria or values implied in such a vision.

VII From its very beginning European civilization confronted, albeit in different ways, the two other monotheistic civilizations, Jewish and Muslim. While the confrontation with Jewish civilization was mostly a religiously ideological one with but a slight power component, this latter component was of central importance in the encounter with Muslim civilization. Throughout these encounters—and even more so later on, during the age of discoveries and the expansion of Europe—the consciousness of other civilizations constituted a continuous component of the self-definition of European civilization. These encounters, imbued with strong ideological dimensions and often connected with attempts to redefine the very boundaries of European civilization, were usually characterized by an oscillation between a willingness to incorporate and acknowledge the legitimacy of some aspects of the other civilizations and the principled denial of their validity.

Many of the discontinuities and breaks between different "stages" of European society, and above all the consciousness thereof, were related to such encounters with other civilizations. These encounters did of course expose European societies to foreign or alien influences, not only in the technological arena or with respect to various commodities, but also with respect to different conceptions of moral and social order. The absorption of such foreign influences was in many, perhaps most, cases effected according to the premises of the European societies. Yet both the encounters with other civilizations and the absorption of their influences were effected in ways that emphasized the discontinuities and differences within these premises and often gave rise to patterns of reflexivity that tended to question the basic premises of European civilization and its major institutional corollaries.

Hence the concern with defining the "other" constituted a central and continuous component of European civilization. Such concern could easily spill over to the relations between collectivities within Europe itself, each of which sometime portrayed other such collectivities as the "other."

VIII   There also developed in Europe strong competition between different *Wertrationalitaeten* (value rationalities), such as the religious and philosophical ones in the Middle Ages, and between them and different instrumental rationalities, which would sometimes—especially in the modern period, as with science—make claims to be the bearers of ultimate values. These tendencies were closely related to the modes of reconstruction of tradition in Europe, which oscillated between principled traditionalism and the selective incorporation of components of the tradition into new frameworks.[5] Principled traditionalism is not to be confused with a "simple" or "natural" upkeep of a given tradition. Rather, it denotes an ideological stance directed against new symbols; it espouses aspects of the older tradition as the only legitimate symbols of the traditional order and upholds them against "new" trends. By opposing these trends, traditionalist attitudes tend toward formalization on both the symbolic and the organizational levels and toward rather sharp segregation between traditional (ritual, religious) and nontraditional spheres of life without, however, developing any strong connective symbolic and organizational bonds between the two. At the same time, a predisposition toward or demand for some clear unifying principle tends to persist, and uneasiness and insecurity becomes pronounced when it is lacking. As a result, a tendency can develop toward the ritualization of the symbols of traditional life, on the personal and collective levels alike. Relatively rigid, militant attempts to impose traditional symbols on the new, secular world may then alternate with efforts to isolate these traditional symbols from the impurities of that world. This persistence of traditional patterns is often accompanied by an intolerance of ambiguity on both personal and collective levels and by apathy and the concomitant erosion of any normative commitments.

On a macrosocietal level this pattern, most fully manifest in Europe in the Counter-Reformation and its offshoots, has been usually characterized mainly by conservative ideologies, coercive orientations and policies, and an active ideological or symbolic closure of the new centers, with a strong traditionalistic emphasis on older symbols.

A second major pattern of the reconstruction of tradition in Europe yielded a continuous differentiation among the various layers of tradition and between the traditional and nontraditional (or religious and nonreligious) spheres of life. Such differentiation allows for more continuity and greater overflow and overlapping between the different arenas of life, and this continuity does not ordinarily become fully formalized or ritualized. In such patterns there does not usually develop a strong predisposition toward rigid unifying principles, and greater tolerance of ambiguity and of cognitive dissonance is continuously built up. The social groups that develop this pattern tend to distinguish between different layers of traditional commitments and motivations and to draw on them all, insofar as possible, in the development of new tasks and activities.[6] Other flexible relations tend to develop between these different layers of tradition, between certain poles or modes of perception of the cosmic, cultural, and social orders, and between symbols of the collective identities of major subgroups and collectivities. Traditional symbols may be transposed into new broader frameworks by groups or elites with tendencies to innovate, to create new central symbols of personal or collective identity, as well as new criteria of behavior.[7]

INDIA

IX Let us continue our comparative foray with an analysis of some of the most salient aspects of the processes of change and continuity in Indian civilization, within which Buddhism, which influenced Japan so much, originated. There is indeed an interesting parallelism between India and Europe, which is also significant from the point of view of the comparison with Japan. The decentralization common to all three civilizations, however, developed in India over a wider territorial expanse than in Japan or even in Europe.

From a broad comparative perspective, India and Europe share some important characteristics that cannot be found in so pristine a form in any of the other great civilizations in the history of mankind. The most important of these characteristics, which distinguish them also from Japan, is the existence of relatively broad common civilizational frameworks, rooted in basic ontological conceptions, cultural-religious orientations, and a multiplicity of continuously changing political centers and subcenters and economic formations. Islamic civilization, especially in the Middle East, also shared some of these characteristics. But given the continuous expansion of Islam, as well as its continuous confrontation with other civilizations, the sense of a continuous, semiterritorial civilizational framework was not as strongly developed as in either Europe or India. In this sense Islam has been the most universalistic civilization, having, in principle at least, negated primordial-territorial or kinship components.

Many concrete structural or organizational aspects of the political and economic arenas (especially the former) that developed in India and Europe evince similarities, for instance, in forms of political domination; kinship; patrimonial, semifeudal, and semiimperial regimes; and the structures of cities. Given these similarities, the different civilizational dynamics of these two civilizations are indeed very striking. The overall political and economic dynamics, the structure and construction of the centers and of their activities, the nature of the protest movements, their articulation into political conflicts, and the modes of incorporation of such movements and of their demands into the center differed greatly between the two civilizations.

In India, as in Europe (and as in Japan), institutional change has been continuous, entailing the construction of a great variety of economic, political, and religious institutions and organizations. As in Japan, most of these have been embedded in prevalent yet continuously reconstructed broad social settings, above all in what have been designated, without great precision, as countrywide caste orders—which are in fact more local or regional—and legitimized in multiple themes rooted in Hindu ontologies.

The interrelations between castes are constructed according to schemas rooted in some of the basic ontological conceptions prevalent in Hinduism, probably among the most complicated in the major Axial civilizations. On one level, that of the Brahmanic ideology and symbolism, Hinduism was based on what could be seen, among the Axial Age civilizations, as the most radical recognition of the tension between the transcendental and the mundane orders—the perception that the mundane order is polluted in cosmic terms, because its very creation constituted a breach of the original cosmic harmony. This pollution can be overcome in two ways, which are at once complementary and contradictory. One such way is through the faithful performance of the ritual and mundane activities ascriptively allocated to different groups—above all caste and subcaste groups. Such hierarchical arrangement of social ritual activities signifies different degrees of social and ritual purity or pollution and reflects an individual's standing in the cosmic order and his duties with respect to it. Here we encounter the other dimension or level of the ontological conceptions prevalent in Hinduism—namely that in many ways the mundane activities are, perhaps paradoxically from the point of view of the pristine conception of purity and pollution, endorsed with some sacral elements and transcendent orientations.[8]

At the same time, however, the stress on the pollution of the world also gives rise to attempts to reach beyond it, to renounce it; the institution of the renouncer (*Sannyasa*) has been a complementary pole of the Brahmanic tradition at least since the postclassical period.[9] Such renunciation could be the last stage of one's life cycle, but it could also entail the breaking out from this life cycle. Such breaking out was usually manifest not only in purely individual acts, but also in the development of group processes centered around the figure of the renouncer, which could become the starting points of sectarian formations.

The two approaches to mundane arenas were based on two distinct value orientations, two "axes of sacral value"—those of auspiciousness and purity. These axes were always closely interrelated; although purity was hierarchically higher, it could never be concretely realized without auspiciousness, in which other castes, especially the Ksatriya from which the ruler usually comes, predominated.[10] The concrete working out of the tension between the two axes, and between the acceptance of the mundane life in terms of the sacred and the emphasis on renunciation, constituted one of the major motive forces of Indian ideologies, institutions, and history, of the construction of caste interrelations, of political formations and dynamics, and of sectarian activities.

These castes and caste networks were not simple units of the kind known in many tribal or nonliterate societies, defined in terms of relatively restricted kinship or territorial criteria. They were, in fact, elaborate ideological constructions—continuously reconstructed—that imbued such primordial attributes with a more sophisticated level of symbolization and ideologization, giving rise, above all, to broader ascriptive local and regional caste networks, which interacted continuously with the political arena.

The caste networks were characterized by several distinctive features. Organizationally, castes were local or regional units interlocked in a combination of ritual, economic, and political ways. Despite many local variations, the schemata according to which castes and intercaste relations were constructed, and the various networks that bore them, constituted the focus of a broad, potentially continent-wide civilizational identity. Intercaste relations, constructed in terms of either hierarchical principles or center-periphery relations, were usually effected through series of gifts and presentations, often in public displays and ceremonies in which the ritual power and economic relations between the different castes were symbolized.

Within this broad framework there developed no sharp distinction between religion and politics—or economics. Rather all arenas of life, and perhaps above all kingships, were imbued with strong sacral dimensions rooted in auspiciousness. Insofar as a more transcendental otherworldly orientation toward purity prevailed, the Brahman and the renouncers constituted the pivot. Other castes, especially but not only the Ksatriya, were imbued with sacral dimensions rooted much more in the cosmology of auspiciousness, which was very powerful in its own realms, but did not challenge the Brahman's predominance in its own specific context. Nevertheless, the Brahmanic orientations were not the only ones effective in intercaste relations.[11]

X   In close relation to these basic ontological conceptions and the construction of caste networks, there developed in India a rather complex principled definition of the political arena—or rather, as this arena was barely conceived of as an autonomous entity—of political actions.

On the one hand the political arena did not constitute—as it did in monotheistic civilizations or in Confucianism—a major arena of "salvation," of the implementation of the predominant transcendental vision. The major center of Indian civilization was not the political but the religious-ritual one. This center, with its otherworldly emphasis, its wide ecological spread, and its embeddedness in various ascriptive units, was not organized in a homogeneous, unified, organizational setting. Rather, it consisted of a series of networks and organizational-ritual subcenters—pilgrimage shrines and networks, temples, sects, schools— spread throughout the subcontinent, and often cutting across political boundaries.[12]

Yet within this context the king played a central and rather complex role. According to Dumont and to a lesser extent Heesterman, the king's symbolic authority was in principle derived from the overall Brahmanic cultural-religious vision and was symbolized through religious rituals; some degree of authority seems to have been attributed to him independently of religious legitimation, but on the whole his "sanctity" was derivative.[13] Recent revisionist approaches, however, have emphasized the high level of sacral or semisacral status, distinction and honor that accrued to the political ruler. The king was often portrayed as "king of the

universe," his rule extending to the four corners of the earth, his coronation ceremony and annual commemoration and its accompanying horse
sacrifice renewing his powers annually. His claim to universal sovereignty, as "lord of all lords," and the manifestation of his greatness
through temples and monuments attested to the power and distinctiveness of political authority. His symbolic portrayal as king of the universe
also reflected an ever-present desire to extend political domination and
mundane power, primarily through territorial expansion or the encompassing of the loyalty of peoples in the area.

> Recent analysis of the meaning of Hindu Kingship in diverse historical
> contexts have confirmed Gonda's view that to separate the "secular" aspects
> of kingship from the "religious" is to misrepresent the nature of Hindu
> social reality. Or, to put it another way, the dharma or the code-for-conduct
> of the king is as laden and as culturally specific as the dharma of the
> Brahman. . . .
>   . . . As Marriot had earlier suggested, it is not only the Brahman varna
> that is the source of values in caste society. And in the textual discourses,
> these images of lordship are, according to Inden, "the fundamental cate-
> gories of . . . Hindu social thought." Thus, while the Brahman stands at the
> apex of the hierarchy of varnas his "purity" or renunciatory capacities do
> not stand in opposition to a supposedly "secular" Ksatriya power. Both
> exercise lordship and mastery over their respective ritually defined do-
> mains, and caste appears to be organized, in Inden's text, in terms of this
> essentially Ksatriya image of lordship.

In Gallait's words: "My argument, I hope, has shown how little we
would gain in dealing with Indian kingship from a political point of view.
It is a ritual organization which, along with priesthood and the gods, orders the world in a continuous series of transformations."
Goodwin-Raheja resumes:

> To assume that Brahman cannot be hierarchically preeminent while being,
> at the same time, in some ways equivalent to Barbers, Untouchables, and
> other recipients of gifts from the ritually central jajmān, is to fall prey to
> an unnecessarily reified and concretized notion of social structure and so-
> cial order. The order lies not in one fixed or internally consistent ranking,
> but in a pragmatically constituted set of shifting meanings and shifting
> configurations of castes.[14]

The openness of the top of the hierarchy, as Pamela Price has shown,
made this system very flexible[15]—but at the same time this independence, this detachment, allowed different criteria for access to political
power to develop, based on previous regional traditions of kingship or on
mundane criteria of success—military strength, wealth, and articulation

of solidarity of local and regional groups or centers. This created an opening for foreign rulers to be accepted and for rivals to try to usurp power. One manifestation of the distance of the political center from the religious one was that political leaders would take office without the appropriate *varna* qualifications. Chandragupta, for instance, came from obscure origins, yet became one of the greatest emperors.

XI These conceptions of the political arena were closely related to the conception and practice of sovereignty that developed in India. As Wink, the Rudolphs, and others have shown, this concept emphasized the multiple rights of different groups and sectors of society rather than a unitary, quasi-ontological concept—real or ideal—of the state.[16] This "fractured" sovereignty was combined with a tendency to civilizational, universal expansion. The tendency to expansion did not, however, give rise—as in China and the monotheistic civilizations—to autonomous political centers, distinct from the periphery, with strong imperial orientations.

Accordingly, Indian politics developed predominantly patrimonial characteristics, the rulers relying mostly on personal loyalty and ties for recruitment of personnel and for contacts with different sectors of society. True, the political centers that developed—for instance, in the Gupta or Mauryan empires—were stronger, and the territorial scope of the polities wider than those of previous polities. Their central and provincial administrations had strong centralizing tendencies; yet these tendencies retained strong patrimonial characteristics and did not lead to the restructuring of the relations between center and periphery, to the creation of new links between them, or to any break with the ascriptive premises of the periphery. The rulers of these political entities were not able to imbue the political arena with meaning beyond the existing premises. On the rare occasions when they attempted to do so their efforts were successfully counteracted by coalitions of the leaders of various networks. Thus indeed, no imperial or absolutist conceptions developed in the political arena.

Moreover, despite their political distinctiveness, sacral attributes, and drive for civilizational expansion, few polities achieved anything approaching unity of the subcontinent. Although India knew states of different scope, from semiimperial centers to small patrimonial ones, the overall Indian cultural tradition was never identified with any of them.

This organizational picture is, of course, similar to the one that prevailed in Europe throughout the Middle Ages and the early-modern period. The crucial difference is, however, that in Europe the ideal of political unification—manifest in the ideal establishment of the Holy Roman Empire, however fragile its institutional bases were—constituted an ideal model that was later transformed into that of the modern nation-states.

In India—at least until recently—such an ideal was at best very weak. Indian civilization, unlike that of Europe and even more so that of China, did not define itself in political terms, and only lately have tendencies in this direction developed, among political groups promulgating a specific Hindu identity.

These conceptions of the political arena and the concomitant weak tendencies toward "absolutization" have had far-reaching repercussions on the political dynamics that developed in India, two of which are of special interest in the comparison with Europe. The first is that in India—despite all its "empires"—there never developed a conception of statehood as a distinct, absolutist ontological entity. Second, there were not—until modern times—wars of religion.

Political imagery nonetheless played a crucial role in the construction of Indian collective consciousness—especially in encounters with other, above all Islamic, civilizations. Such encounters, as Sheldon Pollock has shown, have intensified the importance of the cult of Rama in large parts of India since about the twelfth century, and that of the political components in the self-definition of both the Indians and the new "others."[17] Significantly, however, even the intensification of this political component did not give rise to attempts to impose one Axial vision (Hinduism) against the other (Islam), that is, to confront the other civilizations with assertions of the universalistic exclusivity of one's own.

XII Accordingly, the principled, ideological reconstruction of the political (or economic) arena according to basic transcendental orientations did not constitute, as it did in Europe and in China, a major focus of the movements of protest or the numerous sects that developed in India— Bhakti, Jain,[18] Buddhism, and other, minor movements within Hinduism—even if in many cases segments of such movements participated in the changes of political regimes and the wars between different kings and princes.

The basic definition of ontological reality prevalent in India did not generate strong alternative conceptions of political order. Many of these visions and movements emphasized equality, but it was above all equality in the cultural arena, in access to worship, and to some extent in the definition of membership in the political community. Similarly, the Krishna and egalitarian orientations promulgated in some of the heterodox movements, which sometimes became connected with rebellions and political struggle, were not characterized by the strong articulation of new political goals, nor were they linked with many attempts to restructure the basic premises of political regimes. Only in some popular uprisings against alien or "bad" rulers did such goals crystallize for a short while.

These movements, oriented toward the reconstruction of ascriptive civilizational symbols and collectivities, could become connected with the extension of the borders of political communities or with the establishment of new ones, with changes of dynasties, but rarely with the reconstruction of the premises of the political centers. Buddhism did give rise to such new premises, but they became fully institutionalized only outside India, in the new Theravada Buddhist polities of southeast Asia and in Mahayana Tibet.

The major thrust of these dynamics was focused on the continuous restructuring of the criteria of membership in ascriptive-primordial and religious-political communities, with the redefinition of the boundaries of these communities and of access to them, and with periodic attempts to imbue them with an emphasis on equality. These characteristics of the major religious and popular movements, their relations to the center, and the institutional and symbolic characteristics of the political arena explain one of the most interesting aspects, from a comparative point of view, of Indian medieval and early-modern history, namely the absence of wars of religion, such as characterized Christianity and Islam, that is, wars in which political goals were closely interwoven with, and legitimized by, attempts to impose a religion.

XIII   In common with other Axial civilizations, but in contrast with Japan, there developed in India specific collectivities with distinctive attributes of membership, constructed and reconstructed by groups distinct from but closely interwoven with the various primordial, ethnic, regional, and political communities. In the case of India, it was the Hindu ritual frameworks and symbols, focused on the specific relations between king, Brahman, and renouncer, and the different intercaste relations, that constituted such a distinctive civilizational framework. Moreover, as in Europe, there took place in India a continuous reconstruction—often effected in highly ideological terms—of the boundaries of different collectivities and centers in relation to the broader civilizational frameworks. Incidences of such reconstruction constituted foci of struggle, with various movements of protest, especially religious sects—the Jains, Bhaktis, and the like—playing an important role in the processes. Again as in Europe, there took place in India a continual redefinition of the basic institutional formations and collectivities, but the arenas that served as the major foci of such struggles and ideological reconstruction differed greatly between Europe and India.

Numerous new entrepreneurial activities were undertaken, mostly within the context of the various caste settings and networks and the intercaste relations. The boundaries of these broad settings—in principle not mutually permeable but in fact rather flexible—were on the whole drawn much more tightly than in Japan but certainly much less so than in Europe or, as we shall see, in the Chinese empire. Within these broad frameworks new types of activities could be incorporated without becoming defined in autonomous terms, as happened in Europe first in the political arena and later in the economic one. Organizational changes in the major institutional arenas, political or economic, did not, in India, either alter their symbolic legitimation or imbue them with new autonomous meanings beyond the sacral components they entailed.

XIV In contrast to Europe, the reconstruction of collectivities and the development of new types of organization in Japan were not, on the whole, connected with shifts in the modes of their legitimation, or with struggles concerning the bases of such legitimation. The bases of legitimation of the various mundane activities—political, economic, and the like—defined in terms of their respective dharmas, were relatively continuous throughout Indian history, even if their concrete applications were often rather flexible.

Thus, throughout its long history India witnessed far-reaching changes in its political and economic organization, in technology, and in levels of social differentiation—redefinition of the boundaries of political units, some restructuring of the economic sphere, and changes in social and economic policies—all effected by coalitions of entrepreneurs rooted in different caste networks. But except for the ultimately unsuccessful attempt of Asoka, most of these processes or movements of change did not succeed in—and possibly did not even aim at—restructuring the basic premises of the political arena or the basic center-periphery relations.

XV The characteristics of political and economic organization and dynamics in India were closely linked to those of the civil society that developed there, the core of which was the *relative* autonomy of the major social groups and elites, the complex of castes and villages, and the networks of cultural, economic, and political communication. The nature of this autonomy has been captured by Ronald Inden, who defines the various local and caste groups as both subjects and citizens, who, although taxed and controlled by the kings were also allowed a high degree of self-regulation: they "had an inherent, but limited and partial capacity (we might call it rights) to combine within and among themselves and order their own affairs."[19]

Accordingly the various sectors of civil society were characterized by a high degree of autonomy—but an autonomy embedded in ascriptive, albeit wide and continuously reconstructed, frameworks. Sectors' place in the social order was in principle prescribed by their ritual standing in the purity-auspiciousness schemes. Hence their autonomous access to the religious and political centers was, in principle, seemingly limited by their prescribed place in the social order. Given these basic characteristics of Indian civil society, there developed no basic ideological confrontation between state and society—until recent times, under the impact of European modernity—and no wars of religion.

XVI The patterns of innovation and change analyzed above are duplicated in the cognitive-symbolic realm and in the concomitant processes of reconstruction of tradition that developed in India. The most important characteristics of these patterns are the low ideologization of the attitude to change; a relatively nontotalistic approach to mundane change; weak attempts to organize the various aspects of reality in a hierarchical way; and the continuous addition and incorporation of new contents and patterns of behavior into the existing tradition, without any great effort to combine them in a clear, hierarchical way.[20]

Concomitantly, there did not develop in India a strong emphasis on principled discontinuity between different political regimes, and usually no new principles of legitimation developed in conjunction with such changes. This deemphasis of the transcendental significance of discontinuity in mundane affairs was connected with a distinctive conception of the relations between cosmic and mundane time. Cosmic time, in Hindu cosmology, was full of ruptures and discontinuities—but it was not directly connected or even interwoven with mundane time or events. Such events were, in principle, bracketed out of cosmic time and were not on the whole relevant to it—and it was cosmic time that was predominant in the collective consciousness of Hindu civilization. Thus there developed a sharp dissociation between ontological time, defined in terms of the different ages of the universe, and mundane institutional change, the importance of which was devalued. Discontinuity between cosmic, as against mundane, ages was much more strongly emphasized.

Historical consciousness, consciousness of the passage of time, was, however, incipient in the Indian tradition; Pollock has shown that "a-historicality" is itself historical, that it develops out of Mimansa's confrontation with history. In other words, we are dealing not with a simple (if puzzling) lacuna in consciousness but with an attempt to deal with the problem of time by deliberately turning away from the historical moment, with all its specificity, in favor of apparently unchanging or eternal prototypes."[21] As Narayana Rao and D. Shulman have shown, such denial of historicity did not impede the development of a rich discourse in which the present is conspicuously preferred to the mythic past, and in which mythology serves not as a way of looking back but of bringing forward into the present various "mythic themes."[22] But such historical consciousness did not develop into the conception of a clear interweaving between discontinuities in cosmic and in mundane time. At most, there developed a conception of the possibility of interweaving the sequence of mundane events with the unfolding of a cosmic order.

A similar pattern can be discerned with respect to the impact of other civilizations in India and the absorption of their influences. Given the flexible relation between arenas of action, especially those concerning mundane activities, many influences from abroad, whether in the form of artifacts or of organizational and institutional patterns, could be absorbed without impinging directly on the basic premises of Indian civilization. The impact of Muslim rule is of course the most extreme illustration of such capacity, but similar tendencies can be identified in earlier times. The impact especially of Muslim and, later, Western civilizations, which led to the transfer of political sovereignty in the Indian territories to others, gave rise to the consciousness of what V. S. Naipaul has termed "wounded civilization." But even such consciousness did not change the more eclectic dimensions of Indian approaches to other religions or civilizations.[23]

CHINA

XVII   We shall continue our comparative excursus with a discussion of China, the Axial civilization that had, in premodern times, the greatest impact on Japan. The closest Axial civilization to Japan from the point of view of territorial and cultural continuity, China also exhibited some striking similarities to Japan in other respects.[24] Indeed, among the most distinctive characteristics of Chinese civilization were, first, its political compactness, a territorial, political, and cultural continuity almost unique among the Axial civilizations (with the partial exception of the Byzantine empire) and, second, its sanctification of the political arena as the major, almost exclusive, arena for the implementation of the prevalent transcendental vision. Moreover, as in Japan, there developed a seemingly this-worldly emphasis. Yet there also developed, in these very same arenas, far-reaching differences between China and Japan. Apart from the obvious difference in size, most of these were rooted in the fact that China was an Axial civilization.[25]

True enough, doubts have often been expressed as to whether China, given its strong this-worldly orientation—emphasized already by Weber—could indeed be designated as an Axial civilization. The starting point for the analysis of this problem lies in the recognition of what is probably the major principled error in Weber's interpretation of Chinese civilization—namely the denial of the existence, within Confucian China, of any transcendental tension.[26]

Contrary to what seems to be the Weberian view, the Chinese—above all in the Confucian tradition—did not deny the existence of this tension.

Accordingly, there developed within Chinese civilization a high level of rationalization of the cultural (or religious) orientations connected with the elaboration and definition of such tension. In Benjamin Schwartz's words, "In the Analects we find considerable emphasis on his [Confucius's] relationship to 'heaven' which is treated not simply as the immanent Tao of nature and society but as a transcendental will interested in Confucius' redeeming mission. . . . Beyond this it is already clear that the word Tao in Confucius refers not only to the objective structures of society and cosmos but also to the inner way of man of *Jen*."[27]

In the classical Chinese belief systems the tension between the transcendental and mundane order was couched in relatively secular terms, that is, in terms of a metaphysical or ethical—and not religious—distinction. Concomitantly there developed a conception of time that was basically cyclical and secular, not historical or eschatological. This secularly defined tension and approach to the implementation of the metaphysical vision, and the rationalizing tendencies they involved, became here connected with an almost wholly this-worldly conception of the resolution of such tension.

The official Confucian position was that the implementation of this vision was attained through the cultivation of the social, political, and cultural orders as the major way of maintaining cosmic harmony. Thus, it focused on the elaboration of what Herbert Fingarette has defined as the cultivation of the "secular as sacred."[28] and stressed the proper performance of worldly duties and activities within the existing frameworks—the family, broader kin groups, and imperial service—as the ultimate criteria for the resolution of the tension between the transcendental and the mundane order and for individual responsibility. Such stress could be seen as a simple, traditional, ritual upholding of the existing social arrangements, and in practice this might have been the case for many Confucians. Yet in principle this was not the case. The major thrust of the Confucian orientation was the conscious taking out of these social relations from their seemingly natural context and their ideologization in terms of the higher transcendental orientations, the proper attitude to which could be only acquired through a largely demysticized and demagicized ritual, learning, and contemplation. This learning and contemplation, paradoxically enough, not only allowed but—as can be seen especially in neo-Confucianism—emphasized a nontraditionalistic, reflexive definition of the nature of the cosmic order and of human existence. This definition contained within itself a principled awareness of the tension between the cosmic ideal and the given, imperfect reality of the mundane order in general and the political one in particular. It was only partially legitimated in terms of the basic cosmic harmony, and great personal tensions were involved both in the attempts to maintain such harmony through proper conduct and attitude, which necessitates a very stringent and reflexive self-discipline, and in the development of a critical attitude toward the existing mundane world—all of which, of course, developed in China among the many Confucian and especially neo-Confucian schools.

But all these orientations had, in comparison with those which developed in other post–Axial Age civilizations and especially in the great monotheistic civilizations, relatively limited institutional effects.[29]

XVIII The structural and organizational changes that developed in imperial China, at least from the Tang dynasty on, like those in the other Axial civilizations tended to incorporate strong ideological dimensions. China underwent changes in all institutional areas far beyond what can be found in non-Axial civilizations—not only dynastic changes and divisions of the empire, but also growing differentiation in the structure of both agrarian and urban sectors of the economy, as well as changes in the importance of cities, in the relative power and standing of different cultural and social groups (such as the aristocracy), and in the predominance of the emperors as against the bureaucracy.

As in Europe, India, and other Axial civilizations, movements of protest and change, popular rebellions, warlord uprisings, and especially different sectarian movements and secret societies developed in the Chinese empire. The various processes of change mentioned above, as well as these movements, rebellions, and uprisings, had a strong impact on the center, often with potentially transformative ideological dimensions—a fact of which the center was not unaware. The symbols and aims of these movements often included strong political, historical, and semimythical or utopian components, seemingly similar to those found in the monotheistic civilizations, particularly in the West.

Unlike what occurred in other civilizations, however, no breakthroughs developed in the institutional realms. From the institutionalization of the Confucian-legalistic imperial system under the Tang and throughout the long period of the empire, the overall political formations and the modes of political economy underwent no far-reaching changes—such as the development of fully fledged feudal economic patterns or the transition from tribal to patrimonial formations—as happened in various ways in Europe, India, and Japan, even if it naturally happened in different ways in each of these civilizations. The breakthroughs that did take place in the cultural arenas—especially those of philosophy, education, and art—were hemmed in by the hegemonic imperial Confucian elites, and this was even more true of potential economic and political breakthroughs.

Thus, ultimately, the rebellions and ideological developments that emerged in China usually provided only secondary interpretations of the dominant value structure—even the development of neo-Confucianism in the twelfth and thirteenth centuries, which may appear to break the existing mold. Most emphasized the ideology and symbolism of the mandate of heaven and did not spawn radically new orientations or institutional patterns, above all with respect to the accountability of rulers. The political orientations of the military governors and warlords were also usually set within the existing value system and political framework. Although they strove either for greater independence from or for control of the central government, only rarely did they attempt to establish a new type of political system. It was only with the downfall of the empire that "real" warlordism developed.

Above all, the movements of protest and religious movements that arose in the institutional periphery evinced little capacity (despite incipient tendencies in this direction) to connect with the central political struggle and to develop new ideologies and frameworks of action, particularly in relation to the definition and structuring of the major institutional complexes. Similarly, few enduring organizational, structural, and ideological connections developed between the central heterodoxies, the various ideologies and policies emanating from the center, and the more popular movements. True, many (usually unemployed) literati and members of the gentry participated in secret societies and rebellions, but those either tended to articulate the ideology of the mandate of heaven or to provide different secondary interpretations of the predominant ideologies.[30] Nor did the relations between the central political struggle and the secondary religions or heterodoxies, like Buddhism and Taoism, exert any far-reaching transformative influences on the Chinese social and political order (except in the T'ang period, when the Buddhists were pushed out of the center), although they brought about many changes in particular institutional arenas.[31] Accordingly, the pattern of change that developed in China was characterized by a relatively low level of coalescence between the restructuring of the political regimes and of the various economic institutions or strata, even if the latter did influence the policies undertaken by the center.

The closest relation that developed in the Chinese empire between changes in political regimes and those in strata formation was that common to all imperial societies—namely, the relation between the strength and standing of free peasants and that of the various aristocratic elements or gentry. But even this connection was manifest in China—as distinct from, for instance, the Byzantine empire—more in the development of the rulers' policies than in the political articulation of the demands of these strata. Similarly, even the great urban and commercial development under the Sung, or the growing differentiation of the economy under the late Ming and the Ch'ing, while connected with changes in government policy, were not as evident in the mode of impingement of the respective economic groups on the center. Changes in political boundaries and dynasties were less strongly connected with changes in the agrarian or commercial economic systems than they were in some other imperial systems, though obviously the need to maintain proper economic conditions and to develop adequate policies constituted continuous challenges for the rulers.

Changes in the cultural arena—above all in the schools and ideologies of Confucianism and in the rise of neo-Confucianism—were indeed closely related to those in the political sphere and led to many political struggles, to changes in the composition of elites, and to policies with a high ideological tone. But these changes were confined to the center—to the literati, the bureaucracy, and the emperor. Unlike, for instance, in the Roman or Byzantine empires, there was little participation by broader strata or secondary elites in these movements, and these changes were, officially at least, not seen as involving far-reaching political ideological standing.

In contrast to Europe but like Japan (and to some extent India), China saw few redefinitions of the major roles and institutional arenas or changes in the bases of their legitimation. The official Confucian evaluation of different patterns of activity continued on the macrosociological level throughout most periods of Chinese history until modern times. Concomitantly, there developed a relatively low level of consciousness of breaks in the historical process. Such changes were mostly perceived in a cyclical mode, and accordingly no consciousness of far-reaching, principled breaks arose.[32]

The conception of time in China combined the perception of cosmic changes with that of mundane changes, but given the cyclical nature of this perception dynastic changes, for instance, were not conceived as breaks or discontinuities, but rather as recurrent modes of relations between cosmic and mundane changes.

The mode of reconstruction of tradition and of response to the impact of other civilizations was closer to that of India than to that of Europe. The development of neo-Confucianism constitutes the clearest illustration of this pattern. While neo-Confucianism, as it developed under the Sung, was greatly influenced by Buddhism—in a way it constituted a response to Buddhism—and incorporated some Buddhist orientations, it did so only within the reformulated and reconstructed premises of Confucianism, and did not quite acknowledge a legitimate place for Buddhism in the hegemonic discourse.

XIX The development of a specifically Chinese historical experience was closely related to the emphasis on a this-worldly mode of "salvation," the implementation of a transcendental vision distinct from that of both pre-Axial and other Axial civilizations, and the modes of legitimation of the social structure, the major institutional arenas, and the hegemonic elites. The continuity of Chinese civilization, in a way the epitome of this historical experience, constitutes a great riddle, the crux of which is China's ability to contain most internal, structural, and ideological changes—which were more far-reaching than those acknowledged by the official Confucian ideology or later by much of Western historiography (itself greatly influenced by Confucian ideology)—within the basic premises of the Confucian-legal system, allowing the premises themselves to undergo continuous processes of reformulation while avoiding radical transformations.

The key to our understanding of this ability lies in the recognition of the fact that China was characterized, not by the lack of a transcendental vision or tension, but rather by a "secular" definition of this tension. Thus, the sanctification of the political arena in this-worldly terms had a different meaning in China than it did in Japan. In China, unlike Japan, such sanctification was effected in transcendental and not in immanentist terms. As a result there developed in China an emphasis on a mixture of civility and sacredness as the central criterion of the legitimation of the sociopolitical order, while purely sacred or primordial criteria were secondary or absent. That is, the tension between different criteria of legitimation tended to be relatively weak in comparison to other Axial Age civilizations. Civility tended to be formulated in a mixture of traditional and legal terms with relatively weak charismatic components focused mostly around the office of the emperor.

This pattern of legitimation had crucial repercussions in the basic institutional formats of Chinese society and civilization. First of all, the political-cultural center was defined and perceived in Confucian-legalist China as the major locus of attempts to maintain cosmic harmony. This autonomous, absolutist center tended, through mobilization and communication, to mold—but only partially—the periphery according to its own premises. This center shared with the periphery, in principle, a common cultural framework, but it mediated access to its sacred charismatic attributes, controlling the orientations of the periphery to the center, if not the material life of the periphery itself.

The basic characteristics of the center, center-periphery relations, and the social structure of elites were finely attuned in the civil society that developed in China. As in Europe and India, there developed wide social sectors that were autonomous from the state; however, in China such autonomy was only de facto—it was not fully legitimated. In principle most arenas of social life were regulated by the state, according to the Confucian-legalist precepts—although in fact many social sectors and spaces had far-reaching autonomy. But the most important difference from India and from Europe was the fact that none of these sectors in China had any autonomous access to the state, to the center. Such access was totally monopolized and controlled by the center.[33]

This structure of the center was closely related to that of the major collectivities and subcenters. This was evident first of all in the ideological centrality and institutional strength of the political frameworks—albeit defined in cultural terms—as against the institutional weakness of the civilizational ones, insofar as they were institutionally interwoven with the political. We find in China, of all the Axial civilizations, the closest interweaving, sometimes verging on identity, between cultural and political collectivities and the concomitant weakness of any distinct cultural or religious centers which might compete with the political one in defining the attributes and boundaries of society.

All these characteristics of Chinese society and civilization, closely related to the specifically Chinese this-worldly orientations, were constructed and effected by the predominant elites. The most important elites and subelites in China were of course the famous Confucian literati and bureaucracy, who were the major bearers of the Confucian-legalistic world order outlined above. As such they were, especially symbolically, relatively autonomous vis-à-vis both the broader strata and the political center, though rather closely related to them. They were recruited, legitimated, and organized according to criteria directly related to, or derived from, the precepts of the Confucian-legalistic canon, and were not mediated or controlled by either the broader strata of society or in principle (if not always in practice) by the emperor himself.

The literati were not, however, just learned men performing intellectual functions. Their stratum constituted a source of recruitment for the bureaucracy, and they exercised at least a partial monopoly over venues of access to the center. Together with the emperors, their entourage, and sometimes the major warlords, the literati were major partners in the ruling coalitions—to the almost total exclusion of other groups or social elements. Their structure and organization were influenced by their predominantly this-worldly orientation. Unlike the parallel European, Byzantine, and Islamic elites, the literati combined both cultural-religious and administrative-political functions, with only a slight degree of organizational or even symbolic distinction between these activities. Their organizational framework was almost identical with that of the state bureaucracy (which recruited 10 to 20 percent of all the literati), and except for some schools and academies they had but little organization of their own. Accordingly, they developed no separate political, administrative, and religious organizations and hierarchies.

At the same time, central administrative and cultural elites, as against the emperors and their entourage, had few autonomous bases of power and resources. Only in the educational sphere did autonomous organizations and structures develop, but even these were usually closely interwoven with and oriented toward the political-administrative setting and rather segregated from the activities of secondary elites in the periphery.

These characteristics of the center, of center-periphery relations, of the structure of the literati, and of civil society in China explain, to some extent at least, the riddle of the continuity of the Chinese institutional structure—a continuity, that is, within an Axial civilization with great potential for discontinuity. Significantly, China was the only Axial civilization in which no secondary breakthrough—such as Christianity within Judaism, Islam in relation to Christianity, or Judaism or Buddhism within Hinduism—took place.

JAPAN

XX We may now return to our point of departure and compare the patterns of continuity and change in the three Axial civilizations discussed above—Europe, India, and China—with those in Japan. We have seen that the patterns of institutional change that characterized the Japanese historical experience were quite similar to those in Western Europe, to a lesser extent similar to those in India, and markedly different from those in China.

The central axis of differentiation between the historical experience of Axial civilizations and that of Japan, however, lies in the strength of the tendency toward the ideologization of changes and struggles in different social and, above all, institutional arenas. The intensive mode of institutional change that developed in Japan entailed a relatively low level of such ideologization and of ideological, principled struggles—that is, struggles defined in terms that emphasized general principles beyond the existing reality. This relatively low level of ideologization was first of all manifest in the restructuring of centers and collectivities. Changes in the structure of regional and urban centers and subcenters continually developed, especially during the monarchical and feudal ages, with the relative strength and fortunes of the various centers changing greatly over time—some even disappearing or becoming incorporated into others. These fluctuations were often closely related to the construction of strong regional identities.

Some such changes—for instance, the move of the imperial court from Kyoto to Edo in the Meiji Ishin, and the establishment of the Meiji state—constituted important symbolic moves, signaling the end of the bifurcation of power and authority between the shogun and the emperor and the creation of a new political system—albeit one legitimized in "traditional," restorationist terms. Most changes in the location, strength, and fortunes of the various centers and collectivities were not, however, connected with strong ideological struggles. Moreover, because the struggles that developed in connection with these changes in Japan were not focused, as was the case elsewhere, on the ideological standing of collectivities and centers, no sharp demarcation of the symbolic boundaries of such entities emerged—even if many such changes were indeed symbolized in distinctive ways.

The various centers were continuously embedded and incorporated within the broad framework of the Japanese collectivity and its central symbols, often epitomized in the symbolism of the emperor. There were no criteria or values beyond those of this framework in terms of which new centers or collectivities could be constructed and their boundaries defined. Accordingly, it was, on the one hand, difficult for those not belonging to the primordial Japanese collectivity to penetrate it. On the other hand, within the boundaries of the Japanese collectivity and the numerous social contexts continuously constructed and reconstructed in Japan, many new and varied activities could be incorporated without ideological struggles and without principled reconstruction of such boundaries.

Of crucial importance in this context was the fact that in Japan the geographical and political boundaries were on the whole continuous with those of Japanese—at least Yamato—civilization, and that Japan did not view itself as part of broader civilizational frameworks (as was, for instance, the case with England—another island to which Japan was sometimes compared—which deemed itself part of the European civilization). Hence, there was little room in Japan for the development of ideological confrontations between different collectivities in terms of their relation to the broader civilizational framework. The various minority people, the Okinawa Ainu, while often attempting to resist the homogenizing tendencies of the Japanese-Yamato collectivity, did not on the whole connect themselves with other, broader civilizations, even if some contacts did develop.

The same applies, as we have seen, to the structuring and definition of new activities, roles, and organizations, and new political and economic formations. These continuously developed in Japan but, in contrast to Europe and much more in line with India and China, were rarely connected with the construction of new principled definitions or new modes of legitimation. The many new roles in both the economic and political arenas—for instance, entrepreneurial or bureaucratic functions, industrial enterprises, and political parties—and the ground rules that evolved to regulate them, were not defined in entirely new, autonomous ways. They were usually legitimated neither in terms of their functional prerequisites nor as autonomous manifestations of some higher, transcendental order, but rather in terms of their contribution to the respective contexts in which they were embedded—contexts defined in some version of primordial, natural, or sacral terms.

Most of these activities and organizations were defined and perceived as embedded in the prevalent social settings or, to be more exact, in the various continuously redefined social contexts. Thus in Japan, new activities and organizations could be relatively easily incorporated without the need for principled changes in the basic premises of these frameworks and contexts.

The same combination of continuity and of construction of new spaces was also to be found, as we have seen throughout the preceding discussion, with respect to the definition of the Japanese collectivity. Many of the concrete details of such definitions—as for instance the place of the different marginal groups like the Ainu, or the weakening sacral or archaic definitions of the early Meiji ideology—could be shed with the "secularization" that set in after the Second World War, and some new components, such as the growing emphasis on knowledge, which had already developed in the early Meiji, could be added without the core necessarily becoming the focus of political and ideological struggles. It is within this institutional and symbolic framework that the dominant mode of struggle developed in periods of transition, with fierce outbursts which yet did not radically change the framework and bases of legitimation.

This low level of ideologization of institutional change and the concomitant weak demarcation of boundaries between the various contexts of social interaction was in marked contrast to the historical experience of Europe, where there developed a strong tendency toward the construction of such boundaries, the construction of which could become a focus of intensive political and ideological contestation. As a result of such struggles, various sectors and activities could be denied autonomy or even the right to exist.

The tendency in Japan toward weak ideological struggle around institutional changes was, to a limited extent, similar to that which developed in India. Japan shared with India the strong tendency to embed new organizational tasks within wider societal frameworks. In India, however, such frameworks, especially the various ascriptive communities, were continuously reconstructed, very often in connection with the activities of sects imbued with a strong transcendental vision.

In China, no principled reconstruction of the basic premises or boundaries of collectivities or centers or of the definition of major roles took place either. Yet in contrast to Japan many of the processes of change and movements that impinged on the centers in China bore within themselves the seeds of strong ideologization and ideological struggle and entailed the potential for such reconstruction; the development of these tendencies could be avoided only through the specific processes of regulation analyzed above. Hence in China, the relatively clear symbolic boundaries of the major institutional arenas seemed to be relatively continuous throughout most of imperial history.

Given the existence within all these Axial civilizations of cultural or civilizational collectivities distinct from primordial or political ones, at least some of these institutional arenas constituted foci of principled ideological struggles and reconstructions. But the intensity of such struggles and their specific loci varied greatly: in India it was above all the ascriptive collectivities (both political and religious ones, such as various sects), in Europe the political and religious arenas, and in China the political-cultural center. In Japan, however, no institutional arena or collectivity constituted, as we have seen, a focus for the implementation of transcendental visions and intensive ideological struggle. Hence, such struggle was very weak—almost nonexistent.

This was closely related to the fact that, in contrast to developments in the Axial civilizations, few principled confrontations between orthodoxy and heterodoxy developed in Japan. The sects that developed in Japan did not, as we have seen, challenge the basic non-Axial premises of the society but rather tended to generate a two-pronged response: the "Japanization" of the potentially universalistic and transcendental orientation combined with the creation of new spaces amenable to "internal spiritualization." Thus certain dimensions of the immanentist-particularized settings would be open to activities regulated by universalistic or transcendental orientations but these spaces were usually segregated from the overall institutional frameworks and centers.

The common denominator of this pattern of change in Japan was a continuity of symbols that allowed extensive change within a familiar symbolic context, thus softening the sense of rupture. Such continuity also shaped the patterns of incorporation of change that characterized Japanese society, especially the construction of new contexts independent of the construction of new roles, modes of legitimation, or boundaries. Once they touched or threatened the central frameworks or symbols, as the cases reported by Norma Field attest to, they were put, as it were, outside the pale.[34] The symbolic impact of changes did not usually go beyond the existing frameworks in the name of any transcendent principles. Rather their impact was manifest in the incorporation of such changes into the existing frameworks and in the reconstruction of these frameworks without reference to such "external" principles.

XXI In all Axial civilizations there developed, as we have seen, conceptions of the existence of discontinuities in cosmic time and of a relation between such discontinuities and those in mundane time—even if the definitions of such relations and the nature of such discontinuities differed greatly in different Axial civilizations. In Japan, given the mutual embeddedness of culture and nature and the topological, mythical, and indexical time conceptions, the situation was markedly different.

There did not develop, in Japan, the emphasis on a *principled* discontinuity between different regimes or "stages" of institutional change. Nor did there develop any strong conception of such changes and breaks as constituting steps in the unfolding of historical programs or cosmic plans with possible eschatological implications. In principle no new modes of legitimation were connected with such changes. The assumed, mythical continuity of the imperial symbolism—often fictitious but continuously emphasized—was crucial in this respect. The bases of legitimation—especially those rooted in the symbolism of the emperor, as we have seen—were continuous and could not, as the illustration of Hakuseki in the Tokugawa period attests to, be dismantled or changed. The epitome of this emphasis on (a reconstructed) continuity could be seen in the totally new construction of the emperor system under the Meiji regime.

The continuity of the major symbols of legitimation in Japan was closely connected with several factors: First, with a reflexivity couched in a hermeneutical mode, which in turn was closely interwoven with Japanese collective consciousness and identity, that is, it was based on looking inward, not beyond the given reality. Second, with the modes of development of rationality that developed in Japan. This rationality was characterized by a continuous extension of the arenas in which instrumental rationality, *Zweckrationalitaet,* could develop without the development of a discourse of *Wertrationalitaet,* of critical reflexivity about the sphere of ultimate values rooted in some type of transcendent orientation. Accordingly the development of instrumental rationality did not become interwoven with such reflexivity. And, third, with the reconstruction of tradition, which was characterized by openness to changes that were then brought under the reconstructed canopy of the existing framework, defined in sacral, natural, and primordial terms as traditional, and legitimated through the indexical, hermeneutical, self-referential mode of reflexivity. Tradition and traditionalism constituted a sort of general orientation, often identified with what was authentically Japanese, in the name of which many activities and organizations, old and new, were brought together and legitimized. This canopy provided the general orientations for the construction of one's social world—toward the mode of sacral discourse—but did not create sharp breaks between the traditional and nontraditional arenas or levels of life.

Japan, however, shared with the Axial civilizations a tendency to develop principled attitudes toward tradition, which in their most extreme manifestations entailed strong fundamentalist potentials, as against principled openness. The development of such differences in attitudes toward change and tradition was especially sharp in the monotheistic civilizations, which emphasized the interweaving of this- and otherworldly orientations and a strongly linear conception of time. In China, where the otherworldly orientations did not seemingly bear at all on the mundane, the differences in attitudes toward tradition were much less sharply drawn.

All these factors also greatly influenced the impact of encounters between civilizations and the modes of incorporation of foreign influences. While the Axial civilizations usually effected such encounters according to their respective basic premises, the extent to which such premises, their major institutional implications, and the consciousness of the continuity of collective identity were transformed through such encounters differed greatly. The most crucial differences resided, first, in the extent to which such encounters were connected with a consciousness of discontinuities within these civilizations and, second, in the extent to which they gave rise to a reformulation of the civilization's premises in terms of new principles that seemingly negated or transcended the existing ones.

Such transformations and the consciousness of discontinuity were strongest in the monotheistic civilizations, weaker in Hinduism and Buddhism, and probably weakest in Confucianism. In contrast, there developed in Japan a double-pronged response to such impingements—an openness to them combined with a tendency to Japanize them with but little effect on the basic Japanese ontological premises and conceptions of social order, even if such premises were continuously reformulated, and with the constant construction of special spaces in which new modes of social and cultural discourse could develop.

Thus the core of the Japanese historical experience, as distinct from that of the Axial civilizations analyzed above, was the marked dissociation between institutional changes and their ideological reconstruction; the weakness of the tendency to define boundaries between different institutional arenas ideologically, combined with the generation of new spaces within such arenas; and the continual shifts between contexts, with the concomitant strong tendency toward self-referential hermeneutical reflexivity.

XXII These constellations of continuity and change in different civilizations were related to different modes of constructing trust, solidarity, power, and the division of labor. The distinctive characteristic of the Japanese civilization was that the broader civilizational framework was based on a continuous extension of trust, symbolized in primordial kinship terms, from the family to the broader institutional formations. In other words, the permeation of the basic family units and the mobilization of family resources by broader institutional formations, by the center, was legitimized in kinship terms.

As against this, in all the Axial civilizations permeation by the center of the family units (and of the periphery in general) was legitimized in terms of universalistic principles. Accordingly, there developed a break and potential confrontation between trust defined in primordial terms and the claims of universalistic principles. In all these civilizations the problem of how to interweave the primordial with the universalistic constituted a potential point of contention. The Confucian controversy over the relative priority of filial piety as against loyalty to one's lord—a controversy which developed in all Axial civilizations—is but one illustration of such contention. Such confrontations were effected, as was the permeation of the center into the periphery and into the various familial settings, by various autonomous cultural and political elites and influentials, who, in their interaction with broader sectors of the society, also constituted, as we have seen, the most active elements in the ideological reconstruction of centers, collectivities, and institutional formations and in the struggles attendant on such reconstruction, struggles to no small extent borne by different sects and heterodoxies.

As against this, in Japan the major elites and influentials were embedded in broader settings, defined in some combination of primordial, sacral, and natural terms in which symbols of kinship were often predominant. Hence the extension of trust from the family units to broader settings, to the centers, did not entail the confrontation with autonomous elites promulgating universalistic principles or the concomitant confrontations between orthodoxies and heterodoxies, and this mode of extension of trust accordingly generated a distinctive pattern of change and of historical continuity.

These characteristics of the historical experience of the different civilizations also had far-reaching impacts on their interactions with processes of modernization and on the cultural programs of modernity that developed within them. Let us now proceed to an analysis of the distinctive experience of modernity that developed in Japan.

SEVENTEEN

Japanese Modernity
Japan in the Contemporary World

I The preceding analysis of the distinctive aspects of the Japanese historical experience in a comparative perspective brings us back to the problem of the specific characteristics of Japanese modernity, of Japan as a modern society and civilization, and of the importance, if any, of these characteristics for the understanding of contemporary changes and possibly of future developments.

One question that preoccupied scholars for a long time—namely, what it is that made Japan capable of becoming a modern industrialized country and a modern state—and the closely related question of the extent to which different aspects of Japanese "traditional" or "premodern" (that is, pre-Meiji) society facilitated or impeded such modernization, no longer occupy center stage in the scholarly discourse. Most scholars now agree that the pluralistic sociopolitical structure, the growing marketization of the economy, the development of protoindustrial enterprises, the strong cohesion of family units and their openness to penetration by the wider society, the combination of *ie* solidarity with an emphasis on merit and achievement, the spread of education, and the like constitute important factors in the successful modernization of Japan.[1]

Whether, given the internal dynamics and contradictions of the Tokugawa regime, a more differentiated social and economic structure would have emerged in Japan even without the impact of external forces is of course a moot question. Given the course of premodern Japanese history, with its continuous institutional changes, it is a good guess that some such structure would have emerged; what its concrete contours would have been is, of course, a matter of sheer speculation.

427

Be that as it may, a "modern" structure did emerge in Japan, and Japan was incorporated into the international economic, political, and ideological systems that had developed in the West from the sixteenth century on. Japan's confrontation with these systems, with Western modernity, and with the "West" constituted a continuous force in the shaping of Japanese modernity.

One of the many paradoxes Japan presents for comparative historical analysis is that this first, and at least until recently only, fully successful non-Western modernization has been that of a non-Axial civilization, a civilization that could not be seen—to use terms employed by, among others, Max Weber—as a great religion or a world religion. Weber's analysis of the civilizational roots of capitalism was based on the premise that all the great religions that he studied contained the structural and cultural potential for the development of capitalism—but that only in the West did this potential bear fruit. In other great religions or civilizations—in what later would be called Axial civilizations—these potentials were obviated by the specific hegemonic combination of structural and cultural components that developed within them—especially by the confrontations between orthodoxies and heterodoxies or sectarianism.

It is here that Japan's status as a non-Axial civilization that has become the first fully modernized non-Western society becomes connected with another interesting comparative paradox, which bears directly on our problem in this chapter—namely that the pattern of economic, political, and cultural modernity that developed in Japan is markedly different from the original Western version.

In the first part of the book we analyzed some specific characteristics of this pattern—especially its being a regulated but not totalitarian society and a highly innovative one. Our analysis indicated that this pattern was the result not only of historically contingent institutional arrangements but also of a distinct cultural program of modernity. In the third part of the book it has been shown that this cultural program is closely related to some of the basic features of the Japanese historical experience, analyzed in the second part of this book.

II This cultural program of modernity, like those that crystallized in various Eastern European, Asian, and later African societies, developed as a continual response to the impingement of the West, which presented its military, economic, and technological superiority as closely bound with its distinctive cultural and ideological program. Japan, like other Eastern European or Asian societies—for instance, the Russian and to some extent even the German one—saw itself challenged by this program.[2] The far-reaching ideological and political implications of Western modernity—manifest in the central dimensions of the modern constitutional nation-state, in the heritage of the great revolutions, in such political and ideological movements as liberalism, socialism, and communism, and in the rationalistic (above all, perhaps, scientist) heritage of the Enlightenment—constituted basic challenges to their self-evaluation. The multifaceted impingement of Western modernity gave rise in all these civilizations, including, of course, Japan, to a search for their own place in a new world dominated by the West. The basic parameters of this search were aptly analyzed by Najita and Harootunian:

> In the twentieth century and especially after World War I, Japan's conceptualization of the West affirmed a theory of militant and articulate revolt against the "other," usually imagined as a collective threat to Japan's national independence and cultural autonomy. The construction of the "other" clarified for the Japanese the essence of their own culture. This reversing of images was no less true in the Tokugawa period, when an idealized China had constituted the "other," than in the twentieth century, when a monolithic West did. If the "other" defined what was exceptional in Japanese culture, it also offered a model of excellence against which such distinctiveness could be measured. Just as Tokugawa writers focused on the world of the ancient sages, changing it into an unhistorical abstraction whose values existed only in pure form in Japan, so twentieth-century thinkers imagined a Japan destined to reach new levels of achievements realized by no single Western nation. Through this doubling of images, they shaped a theory of action aimed at maintaining a pure, indigenous cultural synthesis protected from outside elements that might disturb the perceived equilibrium. It was precisely because Japanese saw the urgency of keeping their culture uncontaminated and hence preserving its essence against the threatened external pollution that many felt justified using militant forms of political and cultural action.
>
> Although desperate and even violent resistance against the West spread among nationalist groups in the 1920s, reaching a climax in the mid-1930s, the concern for keeping Japan's culture pure prompted others to try more moderate ways of preventing Japan from assimilating too closely with the West. The impulse behind these efforts can be traced to the cosmopolitanism in the 1920s and the general conviction that Japan had contributed its own unique voice to a global civilization whose diversity was unified by a broad conception of humanity. Yet the emphasis on Japan's special contribution to world civilization narrowed easily in the political environment of the late 1920s and early 1930s to a preoccupation with the status of Japan's uniqueness. Many believed that by realizing the best of East and West, Japan had achieved a new cosmopolitan culture. . . . Whereas an earlier

cosmopolitanism promoted the ideal of cultural diversity and equivalence based on the principle of a common humanity, which served also to restrain excessive claims to exceptionalism, the new culturalism of the 1930s proposed that Japan was appointed to lead the world to a higher level of cultural synthesis that surpassed Western modernism itself.[3]

III   Najita and Harootunian's discussion points out clearly that the poles of the discourse of modernity that developed in Japan have been the question of the place of modernity and of its perception in the cultural self-definition of different sectors of Japanese society, and the concomitant attempt to define Japanese collective consciousness—Japanese authenticity—in the new international setting, with its transcendental and universalistic claims—a challenge not unlike those faced by Japan throughout its history vis-à-vis Chinese-Confucian and Buddhist civilizations.

This search for self-definition in Japan, as compared to that in other modern non-Western civilizations, was greatly influenced by two factors: First, Japan, unlike most other Asian civilizations (but like Thailand) was not colonized, and, in contrast to Thailand, it very quickly became successfully modernized and industrialized under the auspices of the Meiji state. Hence it faced the cultural challenge of modernity not only from the outside, but also from its own new modern center, from the social and cultural consequences of the modernization and industrialization undertaken by the Meiji state, processes based on new, modern types of knowledge as well as on the state's own distinctive civic theology and ideology, which appropriated to itself both instrumental modernity, or the instrumental-rational dimensions of modernity, and the construction of Japanese authenticity defined in restorative and immanentist terms.

Second, the distinctive Japanese cultural program of modernity was rooted, as we have seen, in the Meiji Ishin. Like the great revolutions, in the framework of which the first Western programs of modernity crystallized, the Meiji Ishin constituted a process which, out of a more fluid vision and the actions of multiple actors, gave rise to a new cultural and political program—a vision of a far-reaching transformation of society influenced to no small extent by the cultural program of modernity the West was seen as promulgating. But this program of modernity, the discourse that developed during the revolutionary process, was characterized by certain features that constituted in a way the mirror image of those of the great revolutions—although it was no less radical. It was proclaimed as a renovation of an older archaic system, which in fact had never existed, and not as a revolution aiming to change the social and political order, to reconstruct state and society alike, according to principles that transcended them. Utopian orientations rooted in a universalistic, transcendental vision, were, in contrast to the great revolutions, almost nonexistent, although millenarian restorative themes were prominent in different sectors of the uprisings before and during the Restoration.

In the Meiji Ishin, unlike the great revolutions in Europe, the United States, Russia, and China, no universalistic, transcendental, missionary ideology developed. The Meiji Ishin was inward-oriented; it aimed at the revitalization of the Japanese nation, at making it capable of taking its place in the modern world, but it had no pretension of "saving" mankind as a whole.

The cultural programs promulgated in the Meiji Ishin—and later by the Meiji state—consisted of a mixture of pragmatic orientations toward the question of how to adapt to the new international setting with strong restorationist components. It combined the restorationist nativistic vision with a strong emphasis on what may be called functional prerequisites of modern society, such as efficiency, achievement, and equality.

IV Thus, in the Meiji state there developed a conception of modernity in Japan as keeping up with the times, adapting to the mastery of Western technology, and finding a proper place in the international arena. "Keeping up with the times" was defined as the verdict of the movement of history, but such movement was not defined—as in the West with its Christian roots, and to some extent in other Asian civilizations with their Axial premises—in terms of a historical progression to be measured in terms of transcendental criteria, values, or vision. It was not perceived as a process beyond existing mundane reality, as beyond the "times" and guiding the construction of the new reality and the "movement of times."[4] Despite the great concern in Tokugawa thought with the problems of the relations between nature and history, this thought nonetheless tended toward the negation of historicity, of the unfolding of history as an autonomous process.[5] This trend became the central concern of some of the liberal-individualistic post–Second World War intellectuals, of whom Maruyama Masao is probably the most outstanding illustration.[6]

Concomitantly, the hegemonic cultural program of modernity that developed in Japan was, as in the case of the earlier encounters with China, with Buddhism and Confucianism, characterized by the negation of the universalistic claims of those civilizations. Moreover, counterclaims that the Japanese collectivity alone actually embodied these pristine universal values were connected at most with only very weak interests in incorporating Japan into the new international systems these universalistic visions implied. When modern Japanese historians developed themes of universal history in contrast to those developed in Western historiography with its Western-centricity, they usually ended up, as Stefan Tanaka has shown, emphasizing, in line with earlier expositions, the exclusivity and particularity of Japanese civilization.[7]

V   One focus of the Japanese discourse of modernity was the search for Japanese authenticity in this new international modern setting.[8] That search oscillated between the negation of modernity—defined mostly as Western modernity—as undermining the true Japanese spirit or pristine nature and the appropriation of modernity manifest in attempts to identify a truly Japanese, as against other, Western, modernity, which sometimes even presented the technological success of the Japanese as proof of the superiority of Japanese spiritual sensibilities. Emphasis of the uniqueness of the spiritual essence of the Japanese peoplehood or collectivity was, needless to say, susceptible to extreme nationalistic manipulation; in its less virulent manifestations it was at the roots of the development of the *Nihonjinron* literature. This literature, especially in its more popular versions, was perhaps the most widespread manifestation of the quest for authenticity among wide sectors of Japanese society. However limited the belief of these sectors in the objective truth of many of the specific tenets of *Nihonjinron*—an issue Befu and Manabe have examined—the extensiveness of this literature and the response to it indicate that it must have struck some chords very close to the search for authenticity among large sectors of the Japanese population.[9]

The other major direction of the search for identity, which could overlap with the emphasis on uniquely Japanese modernity or spirit but could also develop in a contrary direction, was the search for an authentic, "natural," universal essence beyond the artificial contrivances of political, social, or even linguistic construction—a search which could be identified in such "utopias" as that of Andō Shōeki.[10] The emphasis on universal essence was, however, couched in highly immanentist terms. In contemporary Japanese literature Ōe Kenzaburō is probably among the most forceful exponents of this theme or orientation. Thus, however strong were the differences between these different orientations toward modernity and toward the constitution of Japanese collective identity, this discourse was at its core strongly immanentist, bracketing out universalistic values rooted in transcendental visions or orientations perceived as being directed beyond existing mundane reality.

Closely related to these core aspects of the Japanese discourse of modernity was the continual dissociation between *Zweckrationalitaet* and *Wertrationalitaet*. The strong tendency to extol instrumental and technological achievement in a technocratic mode has been manifest in the emphasis on information as the core of a new societal order, an information society of which Japan is presented as the precursor.[11] Japan's claims to leadership in the international arena, seemingly reversing its previous disinterest in a missionary universalistic vision, refer to the economic and technological arenas—the epitome of *Zweckrationalitaet*. There have also developed attempts to negate such *Zweckrationalitaet* in the name of pristine Japanese or "natural" spirituality—with, however, little discussion of the relation of such instrumental rationality with the discourse of different Wertrationalitaeten. Concomitantly, there has developed on the level of ideological discourse relatively little autonomous critical evaluation of the concrete aspects of the modern society that developed in Japan that could guide concrete political programs.

It is these themes, set within the frameworks of the construction of modern self-understanding, that have constituted the parameters of modern cultural discourse in Japan, whatever the concrete problems on which it has focused. These frameworks are shared by many sectors of Japanese society to an extent seemingly greater than in other modern industrial societies, thus reinforcing the highly exaggerated picture of relative homogeneity or consensus.

It is within this common core of the Japanese discourse of modernity that the combination of the non-Axial premises of Japanese ontological conceptions with the fact that the social and cultural consequences of modernization and industrialization were generated not by outside forces but by the Meiji state—which at the same time espoused a distinctive ideology that appropriated to itself both instrumental modernity and the promulgation of Japanese authenticity defined in immanentist, primordial terms—was most clearly manifest.

VI As in all non-Western societies (or, rather, all societies outside of Western Europe, the United States, and Canada), one focus of the Japanese discourse of modernity was the search for authenticity in face of the "onslaught" of the West, especially the exploration of Japanese tradition as a possible repository of such authenticity. Indeed the Japanese discourse about traditionalism was closely connected—possibly even identical—with the discourse on the meaning of being Japanese, that is, the search for modern Japanese identity and authenticity.

What distinguished the Japanese discourse, however, was not the intensity of the concern with authenticity and tradition, but the mode in which tradition and traditionality were defined. Tradition was defined, as we have seen, in relatively flexible terms, which enabled it to encompass many new items and ways of life without presenting them in a highly confrontational way as totally anti-Japanese or antimodern. Thus, there did not develop a sharp confrontation between traditionality and modernity.

Moreover, while the problem of the traditionality of different aspects of life constituted a continuous focus of debate and discussion in Japan, such discussion was often combined with a certain looseness and ambiguity in the concrete specifications of traditionality. Traditionalism constituted a sort of general orientation in the name of which many activities and organizations, old and new, were legitimized, a canopy under which many new developments could be brought together. It provided the general orientations to the construction of one's social world, to the mode of social discourse, but did not create sharp boundaries or breaks between the traditional and the nontraditional. It entailed also a continual reconstruction, not necessarily in antagonistic terms, of Western and "authentic" Japanese modes of life—a reconstruction which itself constituted part of the discourse of modernity in Japan.[12]

These relatively flexible terms were closely related to the concrete modes of the reconstruction of tradition, the definition of what is seen as tradition and how binding it is, as they developed in modern and contemporary Japan. As we have seen, this mode of construction was characterized, first, by the continuous reconstruction of the symbols of collective identity in "restorative," "traditional" terms that constituted the core of their legitimation; second, by a tendency to legitimize many new patterns of behavior, organization, cultural creativity, and discourse as expressions of traditions;[13] and, third, by the continuous reproduction of the basic ontological conceptions and concepts of social order, combined with a certain looseness in their concrete specifications.

The combination of all these modes of reconstructing tradition has not necessarily entailed a closure to all innovations or a denial of anything new. On the contrary, it has allowed for the incorporation of new influences in continuously reconstructed contexts.

VII   The mode of reconstruction of tradition that developed in Japan has also influenced the ways in which the oscillation between negation and affirmation or appropriation of modernity developed, in the realms both of high ideological discourse and of daily cultural life. Ideological discourse seemed often to be marked by extreme antithetical positions—although even here the boundaries were not always clear. But in the construction of daily life there developed, as we have seen, relatively flexible modes of structuration and of code switching between different contexts and social roles—especially between traditional and modern, internal and external ones. The immanentist this-worldly orientations of this program also entailed a great flexibility in the construction of new social spaces and in their cultural constitution and definition. Family life, occupational life, distinctions between private and public, and relations between genders, while certainly relatively clearly defined in different contexts, have not been characterized by the same clear packaging according to local, occupational, and class relations that has been typical in the West. They could be combined in different ways in different contexts, in a series of overlapping status sets structured mostly in terms of vertical hierarchies, giving rise, as we have seen, to rather weak class consciousness.

Indeed, even those groups often seen as obstructionist or conservative in the early studies of modernization of Japan acted, as Sheldon Garon has shown, not only within the framework of Japanese modernity but, often, as "modernizing" forces.[14] Similarly, the continual nonantagonistic reconstruction of different areas of life and patterns of consumption as either Western or Japanese constituted a part of a process of continual modernization—and also shaped the relatively frequent crossings between the boundaries of different ideological ways. At the same time the continually changing ways in which different aspects of Japanese life were constructed, in different periods of modern and contemporary Japan, as representing "authentic" Japanese ways of life were greatly influenced— as among others Marilyn Ivy has shown—by the changing position of Japan in the world, especially *vis-à-vis* the West, and they were fraught, as we have analyzed above, with the continual ambivalence to the West.[15]

VIII This combination of characteristics of the Japanese cultural program of modernity was probably at the root of Kojeve's statement that modern Japan epitomizes the "end of history."[16] It also explains why many scholars, Japanese and Western alike, should have begun to look at Japan as a possible model of postmodern society and why the problem of postmodernity should have become such a hot issue in contemporary Japanese intellectual discourse.

But while many Japanese intellectuals were sympathetic to a conception of contemporary Japan as a postmodern society, some also emphasized that whatever postmodern features now characterize Japanese society existed throughout Japan's modern history and have developed not in contrast to or rebellion against the modern ones. This point was made by Karatani Kojin in his famous discussion with Derrida.[17] The continual, nonantagonistic reconstruction of different areas of life and patterns of consumption, with Western opposed to Japanese, constituted a part of this process of continual modernization.

Hence the validity of Kojeve's claim; this nonconfrontational relation to modernity indeed attests to the distinctiveness of the cultural program of modernity that developed in Japan. The statement that Japan epitomizes the end of history makes sense only insofar as the end of history is defined in terms of a historical movement rooted in some transcendental vision, and not in terms of the more immanentist search for changes from *within*. Indeed, the thesis has recently been promulgated that Japan's mode of national economic development negates Fukuyama's claim, based to no small extent on Kojeve's general argument, that a contemporary end of history has indeed taken place since the decline of the European Communist regimes.[18] Similar arguments applied to the entire East Asian scene have also often been voiced.[19]

IX All these characteristics of the Japanese program of modernity—above all the negation of the universalistic claims of other civilizations, the emphasis on the uniqueness of the Japanese collectivity, the search for the pure Japanese spirit, and the weak interest in becoming incorporated into the new international systems except in terms of pragmatic (that is, power or economic) interests—and its closely related ahistoricity distinguish it not only from the Western program but also from the response of other non-Western societies to the impingement of Western modernity.[20]

As in the earlier encounters with Buddhism and Confucianism the dominant tendency in the Japanese discourse was to claim to represent most fully the universal values claimed by the "other." But such values were reconstructed in immanentist and particularistic terms, bracketing out or negating their original universalistic and transcendental orientations. Interestingly, such claims developed even with respect to modern technology, without attempts at evaluating such technology in transcendental terms—and it is indeed in much more immanentist terms that Japan's recent claims to be an international leader have been made.

These characteristics also explain some of the distinctive and rather paradoxical aspects of Japanese nationalism to which we have referred above—especially the ways in which Japan has continued to exist with other civilizations without being one of them—as well as the attitude toward other nations and toward the international scene. This program, first, emphasized purely pragmatic and instrumental attitudes aiming at the adjustment to the new international reality and, second, oscillated between viewing instrumental relations in power or economic terms and justifying Japanese policies in terms of what were seen as the major Japanese cultural values.[21]

Cutting across these poles was the denial of the claims, especially of Western societies, of the superiority and universality of their policies. Instead the Japanese often portray these policies as guises for imperialistic designs and by contrast emphasize the purity of Japanese activities in this arena. Gavan McCormack has aptly analyzed the connection between the construction of Japanese authenticity from the Meiji period on and the attitude toward other societies:

> The process of critical transcendence that was interrupted early in the wake
> of the defeat of 1945 remains to be carried out by democratic and inter-
> nationalist Japanese. As Tsurumi puts it, what is needed is not so much

"inter-national studies" (*kokusaigaku*, with its implicit centrality to the role of the state) as "inter-people studies" (*minsaigaku*). The universalist civil society prescriptions of human rights, democracy and equality and intercourse continue to be suspect as part of a hegemonic Western imposition. Rejected in 1942 in the name of "transcending modernity" (*kindai no chōkoku*), they are rejected now in the name of affirming a "robust" autonomous "Japaneseness." "Internationalization," by a perverse logic, is defined as the equivalent of "ultra-nationalism" (*kokusaishugi = Kokusuishugi*).[22]

X How do the major characteristics of Japan's historical experience and distinctive program of modernity relate to the changes that have taken place in Japan in the last decade or so? Do these more recent developments point to the possibility of the development of critical transcendence, to which McCormack refers?

Among the most important recent changes in Japan have been the demographic ones: the growth of the older population, reductions in the size of family units, the postponement of marriage, the growing number of single persons.[23] The last decades have also seen the weakening of the permanent employment system, even within the strong companies, as companies and at least some younger executives or specialists have entered into a growing competition for expert manpower.[24] At the same time the political system became increasingly turbulent, culminating in the 1993 election and the loss by the LDP of its hegemony. Closely related has been the growing turbulence of the international system—the breakdown of the Soviet communist regime, the instability of the international economic system, and the growing economic tensions between Japan and the Western countries, especially the United States.[25]

The question again arises as to whether these developments, as well as the apparent weakening of commitment to the emperor symbol—which started already soon after the Second World War—will shake up the Japanese system enough to send it in a new direction. Will Japan become more individualistic, bound less by tradition, at long last more similar to other, that is, Western, industrialized countries? It is, of course, not easy to answer this question, especially given the fluidity of the situation, and it is important to remember that similar questions were asked in the 1950s and 1960s. In any case, some tentative indications are possible and not out of place.

The Japanese social and political system are undergoing far-reaching changes, manifest above all in the opening up of many of the existing networks and the loosening of their interrelations. There can be no doubt that the drastic changes in the political scene attendant on the results of the 1993 elections signal an important shift in the postwar Japanese political system, ending an era of seemingly unquestionable LDP hegemony and heralding a period of instability, reminiscent to some extent of the interwar period. This instability is manifest above all in the fact that, as of August 1994, the government had changed three times since the 1993 election—the last one being dominated by the LDP but headed by a socialist. There are also indications of possible political reforms; indeed after much dispute a new electoral law was enacted in the spring of 1995.

The media have also, as they had formerly, increased the tendency toward consumerism, which can easily be depicted as the strengthening of the tentacles of "late commodity capitalism" and the concomitant intensification of "postmodern" trends. It could at the same time signal a shift from the emphasis on productivity that has characterized the Japanese postwar economy. Many surveys indicate also that extensive changes have taken place in attitudes toward marriage and the relative importance of work and family life.[26]

Within the framework of such developments—in reality starting already in the late 1940s—commitment to the Meiji civil theology, especially to the emperor symbol, has eroded. Although not everybody believed in Hirohito's statement desacralizing the emperor in the aftermath of the Second World War, there can be no doubt that the centrality of the emperor symbolism and its salience for large sectors of the population has decreased. Indeed, as Winston Davis has put it, the original civil theology has become an empty shell.[27]

Does this mean that Japan will become more similar to the Western industrialized countries, especially the United States? Will these changes lead only to a new version of the old pattern, or will Japan come to be based more on universalistic premises, with a pluralistic collective consciousness and an autonomous public sphere and civil society?[28]

XI The available data indicate a complex, seemingly contradictory picture, the major components of which are, first, important structural changes accompanied by some shifts in policy that may seem to indicate a growing opening of Japanese society. But a closer look indicates, second, that these openings are relatively limited and that "older" ways, stronger inward-looking attitudes, and closure are very persistent—even if for pragmatic reasons a more flexible form is often presented, especially in international affairs. At the same time, third, growing political instability, economic recession, and recent attacks by terrorists using various poisons in the subways in Tokyo and Yokohama have given rise to a strong feeling of malaise in many sectors of Japanese society.

Indications of the direction in which these changes will lead can be found on the structural-organizational level and that of policy. On the former level, there can be no doubt that many of the older, closely interlocked networks are loosening and the movement of individuals between them is becoming more frequent and varied. Construction of new, more variegated networks—and of new social spaces—seems to be continually taking place, although networks still constitute the major form of organization of social relations, even in the face of the weakening of the lifelong employment system.[29]

Changes have also taken place with respect to economic policy. Internal economic problems unprecedented in Japan's post–Second World War experience—such as recession and growing unemployment—have given rise to increasing deregulation, a move that seems to be in the direction of the goals stated in the OECD report of 1992 (see chapter 3). There has also developed within Japan a far-reaching discussion among officials, top managers, and bankers of the need for changes in economic policy, especially for greater liberalization so as to be able to respond to the new international situation.[30]

At the same time the themes and intensity of public discourse have been broadened, politicians have come under closer, more critical media scrutiny, and cynicism toward politicians, which has existed in Japan from at least the end of the Meiji era, has increased. This growing distrust of politicians is of course closely connected with their frequent involvement in corruption scandals. At the same time political and corporate decisions have also come under closer scrutiny from the courts, which in 1993 for the first time upheld a charge of sexual harassment against a company and in 1994 declared in favor of the residents of Kyodo, a middle-class neighborhood in Tokyo, forcing the authorities to publish a plan they had to build an elevated railway over the neighborhood.[31] The Tokyo High Court also ruled, on 20 May 1994, that school and ward authorities were responsible for the suicide of a student who had been harassed in a mock funeral at school and ordered the city of Tokyo and Nerima ward to pay 11.5 million yen to the boy's parents.[32]

Officials have also seemingly become more sensitive to international opinion, or, rather, a new way of expressing this sensitivity—especially with respect to Japan's behavior in the Second World War—for instance, in the present emperor's apology to Korea for the Japanese conquest and the resignation from the newly formed government in May 1994 of the minister of justice, who had denied in a public statement that the Japanese had committed any atrocities in China. On the same subject Prince Mikasa, the brother of the late Emperor Hirohito, declared in a dramatic interview—albeit only after the document was made public—that military chiefs suppressed copies of a speech he made in 1943 denouncing Japanese troop atrocities in China. On 10 June 1995 the Japanese government made also a declaration of "deep remorse" about its conduct during the Second World War. This resolution was, however, a compromise between the Socialists, who proposed a full-fledged apology, and the LDP, who at the beginning did not want to issue any statement at all. The discussion also stressed that Japanese behavior was only a part of the general pattern of behavior by many countries in the international field.[33]

Controversies over the portrayal of Japanese behavior during the Second World War in history textbooks have also opened up a bit, even among the officials and bureaucrats.[34] There has also been, for instance, greater positive public acknowledgment of Sempo Sugihara, the Japanese consul in Lithuania during the war who saved thousands of Jews (seemingly against the instructions of the foreign office).[35]

Similarly, among some—albeit small—groups of Japanese intellectuals and academics there has developed a greater openness to the examination of Japanese history and even prehistory—of the construction of Japanese collective identity—in directions that go beyond the older, "orthodox Marxist" critiques. Some of these scholars have been willing to deconstruct the constructs of Japanese collective identity promulgated by the Meiji civil theology in order to address the problem of the collective identity of minority, non-Yamoto groups—the Okinawa, the Ainu, and of course the Burakamin. More Japanese intellectuals, however, seem to be moving in more nationalistic directions.

XII   There is, however, another side to these developments which indicates the persistence, even if in new forms, of many older patterns of behavior and organization and an increase in nationalistic attitudes. A good starting point for understanding this is to look at the reasons for the downfall of the LDP government, which was due, not to any ideological shift in the electorate, but to the struggle between different factions within the party and the defection from the LDP of several networks of politicians. These groups did not—as the instability of the government since then attests to—develop a coherent alternative policy or agenda. Nor did they signal a radical change in relations between the state and civil society. Similarly, the public discourse that has developed before and since the 1993 elections, while it has been more diverse and has created more open public spaces, has not changed the parameters of this discourse.

Thus, the new policy debate has been conducted in rather distinctive terms. To quote David Williams:

> The slow erosion of the old consensus and the gradual creation of a new elite view of Japan's future must be the work of many minds. In the winter of 1992, for example, Morita Akio, the former president of Sony and the deputy head of the *Keidanren*, the Federation of Economic Organizations which represents senior managerial opinion in Japan's largest companies, made a start. He called for a radical rethinking of the post-war philosophy

of retaining capital for re-investment by Japanese firms. Morita's article in the intellectual monthly *Bungei-Shunjū* (February 1992) provoked a wild discussion, not all of it critical, but this dissent from the goals of the Meiji state and its Shōwa reincarnation should be seen as another sign of an emerging Japanese consensus which accepts the view that the trusting nature of the country's GNP machine must be altered.

Similarly, the 1992 *MITI White Paper* (*Tsusan Hakusho*) placed fresh stress on the need to enhance the material well-being of the individual household, rather than the firm, as the future priority of public policy-making in the trade sector at national level. The 1992 *White Paper* was novel in its relative freedom from the complex defenses of industrial policy that have colored MITI's public statements in recent years and in the ease with which it passed through the various screening challenges, at the bureau, ministry and cabinet levels. Here, as in the Morita critique, the emphasis is on raising Japan's standard of living. The *MITI White Paper*, side-stepping, some would say snubbing, the policy pretensions of the Bush administration over the trade question, was also an attempt to finesse the effects of the era of bad feeling in the US-Japan relations with a domestic or national solution to the country's international problems. The suggestion would be that Japan is a nationalist regime that may be turning liberal, but on Japanese terms.[36]

The new 1993 government and the subsequent two governments, which came on the wave of demands for reform, were certainly no less nationalistic than the previous ones; if their nationalism was manifested in a new openness to the international arena, that openness was constructed mostly with the goal of enhancing Japan's standing in the international arena—even if such standing was defined in terms of the performance of peaceful obligations. Thus while apologies were made to various Asian states for Japanese atrocities in the Second World War, the Japanese government did not show a willingness to compensate some 200,000 women from several Asian countries (especially Korea) who were forced to become sex-slaves to Japanese soldiers in the Second World War, and instead recommended that mostly private sources should finance the establishment of educational or cultural centers in their respective countries. Such openness certainly did not entail the acknowledgment of universalistic principles as enunciated by the United States. American demands, couched in universalistic terms, were instead perceived as a cloak for American or Western power interests and often contrasted with the more "genuine" Japanese approach.[37] The declaration about Japanese conduct during the war emphasized, as we have seen, remorse but did not entail an apology.

The range of internal discussion has broadened—but is still confined to relatively segregated spaces. Moreover, as we have noted, more Japanese intellectuals have moved in a nationalistic direction.[38] The statement by Ōe Kenzaburō, a few days after being informed that he won the 1994 Nobel Prize in literature, that in order to understand Hiroshima and Nagasaki the Japanese have to reexamine *their* own history was exceptional, as was his subsequent refusal to accept the Order of Culture from the Ministry of Culture. More characteristic was the fact that his refusal, while reported in the press, gave rise to no far-reaching public discussion.[39] Large parts of the public, it should be noted, opposed issuing the declaration about Japanese behavior in the Second World War.

Suspicion of politicians has increased, but the investigations connected with various scandals—and the bringing of some of the culprits to court—were effected by different branches of the bureaucracy, thus probably heightening the perception of the bureaucracy as the bearer of the pure common will, of *keitai*. The same may happen with respect to the courts. The electoral reform, passed under the recent LDP-dominated cabinet, did not give rise to a widespread belief that political life and corruption will noticeably change, even if some other signs, such as the organization of a wide opposition party and the open election of Mr. Kafu as its leader, were signs of new trends in the political arena.[40]

On the attitudinal level some indication can be found in a rather unusual combination, documented by S. M. Lipset, of traditional and modern attitudes toward major arenas of social life, such as sense of obligation, filial piety, gender roles, and acceptance of hierarchy.[41] Lipset showed that many of the opinion surveys indicate that the more traditional attitudes prevalent in Japan are not just survivals from earlier periods, giving way naturally to more modern, open trends. Rather, they seem to indicate that traditional and modern attitudes will continue to interact in continually changing ways.

Of great interest from the point of view of our discussion are the findings of Wonho Yang about the relation in Japan between the development, to follow Inglehart's nomenclature, of nonmaterialist values and political activity. He shows that in large sectors of Japanese society, especially among the younger generation of affluent, professional white-collar workers, there have indeed developed—as in other industrialized countries—"postmaterialist" values. But the pattern of political activity and orientations found in other countries to be connected with the development of such values has not taken place in Japan. In general this is due, according to Wonho Yang, to the fact that "since Japan has long been a group oriented and authoritarian society, the recent rise in individualism has different characteristics from that of Western individuals. Japanese individualism focuses heavily on escape from social norms and group activities. . . . With an increase in individualism in Japan, group activities will decrease—and hence there will not develop new types of collective political activities or new social movements." [42]

Similarly, however weakened the symbol of the emperor may be, it is the only shell whose strength may be, as Ōe Kenzaburō indicated, even increasing. [43] While this symbol, to follow Harootunian's exposition, has become a "symbol without referent," it continues to be a central symbol of national consensus or collective identity. Moreover, as Norma Field has shown, it is used to set limits to protest. [44] While other components of the Meiji civil theology, especially the mythological archaic grounding of the emperor system, have indeed become irrelevant, the ideology of *kokutai*, as Carol Gluck has put it, remains central and has in some ways even intensified, if only in terms of potentially greater sensitivity and opening to the international scene (a sensitivity that, as we have noted, is perceived at least in the West as being more pragmatic than principled). [45] Thus, on the whole, recent developments seem to reinforce the more exclusionist tendencies, even if these tendencies are connected with a more variegated structure of networks and public discourse and, superficially at least, greater sensitivity to international opinion. In any case, these changes do not necessarily imply a revolutionary change of the system. It seems doubtful that developments could give rise to the opening up of the Japanese discourse in the way McCormack anticipates: "To achieve its true identity, its multiple subjectivities, Japan in the 1990s faces a grand, and yet terrible choice: to renounce the mask of 'Japaneseness' as a unique, imperial essence that it has worn for over a thousand years." [46]

Doubt as to the potential for radical or deep change, as against what might be called organizational adjustments, have been voiced by many people, Japanese and Western alike, including, in a 1994 interview, former prime minister Miyazawa Kiichi:

> To Miyazawa, who presided over the end of the Liberal Democratic Party's 38 years of unilateral rule, only two semblances of change have appeared since he stepped down in August, 1993:
>
> One, political reform has been carried out. And, two, "the Liberal Democrats have come back to power" or at least "half-way back."
>
> "Whether a change has occurred or not is still premature to judge," he added. . . .
>
> But Miyazawa doubted that change would occur at the core of Japan's economic philosophy.
>
> "Talking about easing of regulations has become fashionable . . . but I am skeptical.
>
> "There are 'litigation societies' like the United States in which people act on their own responsibility, and if trouble occurs, file a law suit. Japan is a society that creates safety regulations . . . in a well-meaning way . . . to

ensure that no one has trouble and that litigation doesn't occur. . . . Overall, Japan is that kind of society.

"It's a society that has been shielded. . . . Japan is a safe society because government protection has been broadly extended throughout society. It's a regulated society."

People may bad-mouth bureaucrats but they praise police boxes, he noted.[47]

A similar view was presented some months earlier by van Wolferen:

Cracks in Japan's political edifice have excited hopes in the United States that reforms are on the way. What Americans fail to grasp is that Japanese politicians do not count for much. In the absence of a strong civil society, and protected by the press, Tokyo's government ministries call the shots. Washington should press Japan to write a new constitution strengthening politicians vis-à-vis the bureaucracy. Until Japan reshapes its political system, the split in the Liberal Democratic Party will remain no more than fractures in a facade.[48]

It is, of course, true that lately other far-reaching signs of malaise seem to have been quite widespread in Japan. These signs of malaise built on some earlier developments in the political scene. The "depoliticization" of the emperor that took place after the Second World War, becoming more fully visible in the late Shōwa period and especially after the death of Hirohito, the relative weakening of the bureaucracy as against the politicians, and the growing contestation between different groups in the political arena have to some extent opened up that arena to many social groups. At the same time, however, the developments have left the search for the common good almost entirely bereft of any clear institutional arena, framework, or direction, with some far-reaching anomic potentials rooted in the central feature of Japanese social structure—namely the emphasis on generalized particularistic trust—and in the lack of an external Archimedean point to be used in restructuring society when some of the networks through which such trust is effected break down. The instability of the post-1993 governments and the impact of this instability on the economic policy may be one indication of such potential. The combination lately of economic recession, internal political instability, and poisonous gas attack by terrorists in the Tokyo and Yokohama subways in the spring and summer of 1995 have indeed increased these feelings of malaise.[49] It is probably such feelings of malaise that explain the great popularity of van Wolferen's book *The System That Makes Japanese Unhappy*.[50]

Among the manifestations of anomic "sickness" or "disease," Sugahara Mariko, a cabinet councilor and chief of office for women's affairs in the prime minister's office, has singled out a weakening of the work ethic, excessive homogeneity and conformity, a loss of creativity, a lack of public spirit and civic morals, failure to achieve the productive potential of women, and early retirement.[51]

Interestingly enough, while many younger Japanese seem to embrace "nonmaterialistic" values and a growing emphasis on greater range of individual choice, this does not bring them to engage, as has been the case in the West, in new forms of political activities. Such emphasis on greater individual choice represents a quest for escape from restrictive contexts but not a willingness to engage in new autonomous collective activity.

But does all this necessarily indicate, as van Wolferen implies, that without such change Japan will remain immobilist, unable to live up to the new challenges it faces? The experience until now, as has been strongly emphasized by David Williams, has to a large extent belied this implication.

Until now Japan has been able to adapt to changing circumstances in its own way or ways—without the changes demanded by van Wolferen—and to live with many of its problems. The future will tell us, not whether Japan will change—it has changed continuously throughout the modern and contemporary era—but rather what will be the directions of these changes. First of all it will tell us whether the mode of change that develops in Japan will enable it to face the new internal and external challenges constructively or in more anomic, disintegrative, and probably also extremely nationalistic ways. Second, and possibly more important for understanding the unfolding of the contemporary world scene, it will tell us whether we are indeed witnessing the "end of history," the ultimate convergence of industrial societies and the development of one worldwide, modern civilization, or instead the development of multiple, continually interacting, fluid yet distinctive modern civilizations, of which Japan will continue to be one.

N O T E S

CHAPTER ONE

1. K. van Wolferen, *The Enigma of Japanese Power* (New York: Knopf, 1989).

2. R. Pulvers, "Japan: A Key to Understanding the Western World," *Japan Foundation Newsletter 7*, no. 5 (December 1979–January 1980): 8–12; Kuwabara Takeo, *Japan and Western Civilization: Essays on Comparative Culture* (Tokyo: University of Tokyo Press, 1983).

3. J. Goff, "Recent Publications on Japan," *Japan Quarterly*, January–March 1991, 103–11; E. Dening, *Japan* (New York: Praeger, 1960); A. E. Tiedemann, *An Introduction to Japanese Civilization* (New York: Columbia University Press, 1974).

4. D. F. Lach, *Japan in the Eyes of Europe* (Chicago: University of Chicago Press, 1965); R. A. Rosenstone, *Mirror in the Shrine: American Encounters with Meiji Japan* (Cambridge, Mass.: Harvard University Press, 1988).

For recent analysis of some Western views and studies of Japan see also E. O. Reischauer, *Japan: Past and Present*, 2d ed. (New York: Knopf, 1953); *idem, The Japanese Today: Change and Continuity* (Cambridge, Mass.: Belknap Press of Harvard University Press, 1988); H. Befu, *Japan: An Anthropological Introduction* (San Francisco: Chandler, 1971); J. P. Lehman, *The Image of Japan: From Feudal Isolation to World Power, 1850–1905* (London: George Allen Unwin, 1978); R. P. Norman and H. Norman, *One Hundred Years in Japan, 1873–1973* (Toronto: United Church of Canada, 1981); H. Passin, *Encounter with Japan* (Tokyo: Kodansha International, 1982); Shimbori Michiya, "From Japanology to Japanese Studies," *Japan Quarterly* 32 (1985): 389–95; T. Yokoyama, *Japan in the Victorian Mind: A Study of Stereotyped Images of a Nation* (New York: Macmillan, 1987); S. K. Johnson, *The Japanese through American Eyes* (Stanford: Stanford University Press, 1988); J. Kreiner, "Das Bild Japan in der europaeischen Geistesgeschichte," in J. Kreiner (ed.), *Japan Studien*, Jahrbuch des Deutsches Institut fur Japanstudien der Phillip-Franz-von-Siebold-Stiftung, vol. 1 (Munich: Judicium Verlag, 1989), 12–42; Hans Dieter Olschlegn, "Ethnologische Ansätze in der Japan-Forschung (1) Arbeiten," *Japan Studien,* op. cit., 43–70; B. Moeran, "Introduction: Rapt Discourses: Anthropology, Japanism and Japan," in E. Ben-Ari, B. Moeran, and J. Valentine (eds.), *Unwrapping Japan: Society and Culture in Anthropological Perspectives* (Manchester: Manchester University Press, 1990); H. Befu and J. Kreiner (eds.), *Othernesses of Japan: Historical and Cultural Influences on Japanese Studies in Ten Countries* (Munich: Judicium Verlag, 1992); Ian H. Nish, "European Images of Japan: Some Thoughts on Modern European-Japanese Relations," *Japan Foundation Newsletter* 20, no. 3 (December 1992): 1–5; S. Linhart, "Paradigmatic Approaches to Japanese Society and Culture by Western Social Scientists," *Japan Foundation Newsletter* 22, no. 3 (1994): 7–11.

5. E. H. Norman, *Japan's Emergence as a Modern State* (New York: International Secretariat, Institute of Pacific Relations, 1940); reprinted in John W. Dower (ed.), *Origins of the Modern Japanese State: Selected Writings of E. H. Norman* (New York: Pantheon, 1975), 109–316. See also Norman, "Feudal Background of Japanese Politics," ibid., 317–466.

6. T. Parsons, "Population and the Social Structure of Japan," in *idem, Essays in Sociological Theory* (New York: Free Press, 1949), 275–97.

7. M. J. Levy Jr., "Contrasting Factors in the Modernization of China and Japan," in S. Kuznets, W. Moore, and J. J. Spengler (eds.), *Economic Growth in Brazil, India and Japan* (Durham, N.C.: Duke University Press, 1955), 496–536. See also R. Bendix, "Preconditions of Development: A Comparison of Japan and Germany," in *idem, Nation Building and Citizenship: Studies of Our Changing Social Order,* 2d ed. (Berkeley: University of California Press, 1977), 212–55.

8. J. C. Pelzel, "Japanese Kinship: A Comparison," in M. Freedman (ed.), *Family and Kinship in Chinese Society* (Stanford: Stanford University Press, 1970), 223–49. See also Bendix, "Preconditions of Development."

9. R. N. Bellah, *Tokugawa Religion: The Values of Pre-Industrial Japan* (Glencoe, Ill.: Free Press, 1957).

10. E. Durkheim, "Die gesellschaftliche und wirtschaftliche Entwicklung in Japan" (review of T. Fukuda), *L'annee sociologique* 5 (1900–1901): 342–47.

11. M. Bloch, *La société féodale* (Paris: A. Michel, 1939). (*Feudal Society,* trans. L. A. Manyon [Chicago: University of Chicago Press, 1961].) For a later comparative analysis see F. Jouon Des Longrais, *L'Est et l'Ouest: Institutions du Japon et de l'Occident comparées* (Paris: Maison Franco-Japonaise, 1958). See also A. Gonthier, *Histoire des l'institutions japonaises* (Bruxelles: Editions de la Libraire Encyclopedique, 1956).

12. J. Baechler, *The Origins of Capitalism* (Oxford: Blackwell, 1975).

13. Introduction, Symposium on the Transition from Medieval to Early Modern Japan, *Journal of Japanese Studies* 12, no. 2 (1986): 235–36.

14. B. Moore, *Social Origins of Dictatorship and Democracy* (Harmondsworth: Penguin, 1966); E. K. Trimberger, *Revolution from Above* (New Brunswick, N.J.: Transaction Books, 1978).

15. E. Lederer and E. Lederer-Seidler, *Japan in Transition* (New Haven: Yale University Press, 1938). See also E. Lederer, "Fascist Tendencies in Japan," *Pacific Affairs* 7 (1934): 373–85. On the Lederer analysis of Japan, see W. Schwenk-

ler, "Die Japan studien Emil Lederers," *Rikkyo Economic Review* 44 (1991): 107–27.

16. K. Singer, *Mirror, Sword and Jewel* (Tokyo: Kodansha International, 1987).

17. R. Benedict, *The Chrysanthemum and the Sword* (London: Secker and Warburg, 1947).

18. G. B. Sansom, *Japan in World History* (Tokyo: Charles E. Tuttle, 1977).

19. J. Stoetzel, *Without the Chrysanthemun and the Sword: A Study of the Attitudes of Youth in Post-War Japan* (New York: UNESCO, 1955).

20. In the first stage of those studies the comparision was made mostly with Europe. See R. B. Ward (ed.), *Political Development in Modern Japan* (Princeton: Princeton University Press, 1968); R. B. Ward et al. (eds.), *Political Modernization in Japan and Turkey* (Princeton: Princeton University Press, 1964); M. B. Jansen (ed.), *Changing Japanese Attitudes toward Modernization* (Princeton: Princeton University Press, 1965); R. P. Dore (ed.), *Aspects of Social Change in Modern Japan* (Princeton: Princeton University Press, 1967); D. Shively (ed.), *Tradition and Modernization in Japanese Culture* (Princeton: Princeton University Press, 1971); J. Morley (ed.), *Dilemmas of Growth in Prewar Japan* (Princeton: Princeton University Press, 1971); B. S. Silberman and H. D. Harootunian (eds.), *Japan in Crisis: Essays on Taishō Democracy* (Princeton: Princeton University Press, 1974).

See also I. Hijiya-Kirschnereit, "Vexierspiegel—Einander gegenubergestellt. Zum Japanbild in neuen deutschsprachigen Publikationen zue Japanischen Perspektive," *Leviathan* 14, no. 3 (1986): 418–51; J. Baechler, "The Origins of Modernity: Caste and Feudality (India, Europe and Japan)," in J. Baechler, J. A. Hall, and M. Mann (eds.), *Europe and the Rise of Capitalism* (New York: Basil Blackwell, 1988), 39–65; Shimbori Michiya, "From Japanology to Japanese Studies."

Later on, in the mid-1970s, the comparisons were made mostly with the United States. See, as examples of the vast literature, E. Vogel, *Japan as Number One* (Cambridge, Mass.: Harvard University Press, 1979); J. Fallows, *More Like Us: Making America Great Again* (Boston: Houghton Mifflin, 1989); H. Patrick and H. Rosovsky (eds.), *Asia's New Giant: How the Japanese Economy Works* (Washington D.C.: Brooking Institution, 1976); B. Bernier, *Capitalisme société et culture au Japon: Aux origines de l'industrialisation* (Montréal: Les Presses de L'Université de Montréal, 1988); C. V. Prestowitz, Jr., *Trading Places: How We Are Giving Our Future to Japan and How to Reclaim It* (New York: Basic Books, 1989). For a contrary view see also Bill Emmont, *The Sun Also Sets: Why Japan Will Not Be Number One* (New York: Simon & Schuster, 1988).

For a pertinent analysis of these developments among American and Japanese social scientists, see T. Ishida and P. Steinhoff, keynote addresses in *The Postwar Development of Japanese Studies in the United States: A Historical Review and Prospects for the Future*, International House of Japan Fortieth Anniversary Symposium (Tokyo: 1993), 7–18, 19–35; see also the panel discussion, pp. 36–58.

21. J. C. Abegglen, *The Japanese Factory* (Glencoe, Ill.: Free Press, 1969). For a critical look at this approach see *idem, U.S.-Japan Economic Relations* (Berkeley: Institute of East Asian Studies, University of California Press, 1980).

22. Ward, *Political Development in Modern Japan;* Ward et al., *Political Modernization in Japan and Turkey.*

23. An introduction to a book of photographs from Japan published in 1953 conveys beautifully this view of Japan as a model civilization: Francis Haar, *The Best of Old Japan,* foreword by Antonin Raymond (Tokyo: Charles E. Tuttle, 1953). See also Fosco Maraini, *Japanese Patterns of Continuity* (Tokyo: Kodansha International, 1979); *idem, Meeting with Japan* (New York: Viking, 1960).

For an earlier account see F. H. Harrington, *God, Mammon and the Japanese: Dr. Horace N. Allen and Korean-American Relations, 1884–1905* (Madison: University of Wisconsin Press, 1944).

24. Abegglen, *Japanese Factory.*

25. F. Maraini, in Ronald Bell (ed.), *The Japan Experience* (New York: Weatherhill, 1973), 12–13.

26. A. Carter, in Bell, *Japan Experience,* 24–25.

27. Vogel, *Japan as Number One;* see Befu and Kreiner, *Othernesses of Japan.*

28. Vogel, *Japan as Number One.*

29. C. Johnson, *MITI and the Japanese Miracle* (Stanford: Stanford University Press, 1982).

30. R. Dore, *Flexible Rigidities* (Stanford: Stanford University Press, 1986); *idem, Taking Japan Seriously: A Confucian Perspective on Leading Economic Issues* (Stanford: Stanford University Press, 1987); E. Wilkinson, *Japan versus the West: Image and Reality* (London: Penguin, 1990); J. Fallows, "Containing Japan," *Atlantic* 263, no. 5 (May 1989): 40–62.

31. Van Wolferen, *Enigma of Japanese Power.*

32. J. M. Bouisson and G. Faure (eds.), *Japon, le consensus: Mythes et réalités,* Cercle d'études sur la société et l'économie du Japon (Paris: Economica, 1984).

33. R. Barthes, *L'empire des signes* (Geneva: A. Skira, 1970). (*Empire of Signs,* trans. R. Howard [New York: Hill and Wang, 1982].) For a critical evaluation see Ishiguro Hide, "The Idea of the Orient," *Times Literary Supplement,* 12 August 1983, 853). See also W. Kelly, "Japanology Bashing," *American Ethnologist* 15, no. 2 (May 1988): 365–68.

34. Miyoshi Masao and H. D. Harootunian (eds.), "Post Modernism and Japan," special issue of the *South Atlantic Quarterly* 87, no. 3 (1988); Y. Sugimoto, "A Post-Modern Japan?," *Arena* 91 (1990): 48–59; A. Berque, "French Japanology as an Objective Contribution to a Post-Modern Debate," in Befu and Kreiner, *Othernesses of Japan,* 141–57; D. Pollack, "Modernism Minceur, or Is Japan Postmodern?" *Monumenta Nipponica* 44, no. 1 (spring 1989): 75–97; A. Woodiwiss, "Postmodanizumu: Japanese for (and against) Postmodernism," *Theory, Culture and Society* 8 (1991): 111–18. See also J. Rauch, *The Outnation: A Search for the Soul of Japan* (Boston: Harvard Business School Press, 1992).

35. Benedict, *Chrysanthemum and the Sword.*

36. Z. Brzezinski, *The Fragile Blossom: Crisis and Change in Japan* (New York: Harper and Row, 1972), esp. chaps. 1 and 2. See also Rauch, *Outnation.*

37. Maruyama Masao, *Studies in the Intellectual History of Tokugawa Japan* (Princeton: Princeton University Press, 1974). Also *idem, Denken in Japan* (Frankfurt: Suhrkamp, 1992).

38. Singer, *Mirror, Sword and Jewel.*

39. Sansom, *Japan in World History.*

40. Bellah, *Tokugawa Religion;* J. Pelzel, "Human Nature in the Japanese Myths," in W. P. Lebra and T. S. Lebra (eds.), *Japanese Culture and Behavior: Selected Readings,* 2d ed. (Honolulu: University of Hawaii Press, 1986), 728; Pelzel, "Japanese Kinship."

41. J. M. Kitagawa, *On Understanding Japanese Religion* (Princeton: Princeton University Press, 1987); W. Le Fleur, *The Karma of Words: Buddhism and the Literary Art in Medieval Japan* (Berkeley: University of California Press, 1983); P. Beonio-Brocchieri, *Religiosita e Ideologia alle Origini del Giapone Moderno* (Milano: ISPI, 1965).

42. Bellah, *Tokugawa Religion.*

43. Barthes, *L'empire des Signes;* Ishiguro, "The Idea of the Orient." See also, for instance, Ikegami Yoshihiko, "Homology of Language and Culture: A Case Study in Japanese Semiotics," in W. A. Koch (ed.), *The Nature of Culture* (Brockmeyer: Bochums Studienverlag, 1989), 388–403.

44. Singer, *Mirror, Sword and Jewel.*

45. Van Wolferen, *Enigma of Japanese Power;* F. Maraini, "Japan in the Future: Some Suggestions from Nihonjinron Literature," in G. Fodella (ed.), *Social Structures and Economic Dynamics in Japan Up to 1980* (Milan: Luiggi Bocconi University, 1975); H. Befu, *Symbols of Nationalism and Nihonjinron* (Stanford: Stanford University Press, 1989); *idem,* "Civilization and Culture: Japan in Search of Identity," *Senri Ethnological Studies* 16 (1984): 66–74; H. Befu (ed.), *Cultural Nationalism in East Asia* (Berkeley: University of California Press, 1993). See also Befu and Kreiner, *Othernesses of Japan;* P. Dale, *The Myth of Japanese Uniqueness* (London: Routledge, 1986); and idem, *The Myth of Japanese Uniqueness Revisited* (Oxford: Nisan Occasional Papers Series, no. 9, 1988); R. C. Marshall, review of Dale, *Myth of Japanese Uniqueness, Journal of Japanese Studies* 15, no. 1 (1989): 266–71. See also Bruce Cumings, "Archaeology, Descent, Emergence: Japan in British/American Hegemony 1900–1950," in Masao Miyoshi and H. D. Harootunian (eds.), *Japan in the World* (Durham: Duke University Press, 1993), 79–111.

46. D. Pollack, *The Fracture of Meaning: Japan's Synthesis of China from the Eighth through the Eighteenth Centuries* (Princeton: Princeton University Press, 1986).

47. P. Nosco, *Remembering Paradise: Nativism and Nostalgia, Eighteenth-Century Japan* (Cambridge, Mass.: Council on East Asian Studies, Harvard University Press, 1990).

48. See on this J. P. Lehman, "Mutual Images," in L. Tsokalis and M. White (eds.), *Japan and Western Europe: Conflict and Cooperation* (London: Frances Pinter, 1982), 14–30; Befu and Kreiner, *Othernesses of Japan;* A. Berque (ed.), *Le Japon et son double: Logiques d'un autoportrait* (Paris: Mason, 1987).

49. Nakane C., *Japanese Society* (London: Weidenfeld and Nicolson, 1970).

50. Doi T., *The Anatomy of Dependence* (Tokyo: Kodansha International, 1973).

51. Kawamura Nozomu, "The Historical Background of Arguments Emphasizing the Uniqueness of Japanese Society," in *Social Analysis,* no. 516 (Decem-

ber 1980): 44–62; Y. Sugimoto and R. E. Mouer, *Images of Japanese Society* (London: Kegan Paul International, 1986); *idem, Constructs for Understanding Japan* (London: Kegan Paul International, 1989); Befu, "Civilization and Culture"; *idem, Cultural Nationalism;* Befu and Kreiner, *Othernesses of Japan.* See also Aoki Tamotsu, "Anthropology and Japan: Attempts at Writing Culture," *Japan Foundation Newsletter* 22, no. 3 (1994): 1–6.

52. Abegglen, *Japanese Factory.*

53. E. Vogel (ed.), *Modern Japanese Organization and Decision Making* (Berkeley: University of California Press, 1975), specially the chapters by T. Shirai, "Decision Making in Japanese Labor Unions," 167–84; T. P. Rohlen, "The Company Work Group," 185–209; and G. A. De Vos, "Apprenticeship and Paternalism," 210–27.

54. See for instance the analysis in Sugimoto and Mouer, *Images of Japanese Society; idem, Constructs for Understanding Japan.*

55. R. Dore, *English Factory—Japanese Factory: The Origins of National Diversity in Industrial Relations* (Berkeley: University of California Press, 1973).

56. See, for instance, Sugimoto and Mouer, *Images of the Japanese Society; idem, Constructs for Understanding Japan.*

57. Vogel, *Modern Japanese Organization.*

58. Lebra and Lebra, *Japanese Culture and Behaviour.*

59. Vogel, *Modern Japanese Organization.*

60. H. Befu, "Four Models of Japanese Society and Their Relevance to Conflict," in S. N. Eisenstadt and E. Ben-Ari (eds.), *Japanese Models of Conflict Resolution* (London: Kegan Paul International, 1990), 162–91; Bouisson and Faure, *Japon, le consensus;* Kamishima J., "Society of Convergence: An Alternative for the Homogeneity Theory," *Japan Foundation Newsletter* 17, no. 3 (January 1990): 1–7.

61. E. Krauss, T. Rohlen, and P. Steinhoff (eds.), *Conflict in Japan* (Honolulu: University of Hawaii Press, 1984); T. Najita and J. V. Koschmann (eds.), *Conflict in Modern Japanese History: The Neglected Tradition* (Princeton: Princeton University Press, 1982); M. Granovetter, "Dispelling the Japanese Mystique?," *Contemporary Sociology* 19, no. 6 (1990): 789–92; Eisenstadt and Ben-Ari, *Japanese Models of Conflict Resolution.* See also R. Goodman, "Sociology of the Japanese State, the State of Japanese Sociology: A Review of the 1980s," *Japan Forum* 2, no. 2 (1990): 273–84.

62. M. J. Levy Jr., "Contrasting Factors."

63. F. L. K. Hsu, *Iemoto: The Heart of Japan* (New York: Wiley, 1973).

64. Nakane, *Japanese Society.*

65. H. Nakamura, *Ways of Thinking of Eastern People* (Honolulu: East-West Center Press, 1964).

66. B. Moore, *Social Origins of Dictatorship and Democracy.*

67. Trimberger, *Revolution from Above.*

68. R. J. Smith, *Japanese Society: Tradition, Self, and Social Order* (Cambridge: Cambridge University Press, 1983).

69. For summaries of these approaches see Y. Murakami, "Ie Society as a Pattern of Civilization," *Journal of Japanese Studies* 10, no. 2 (1984): 279–363; Kumon S., "Some Principles Governing the Thought and Behavior of Japanists

(Contextualists)," *Journal of Japanese Studies* 8, no. 1 (1982): 5–28. For discussions of the *ie* society thesis, see R. J. Smith, "A Pattern of Japanese Society: Ie Society or Acknowledgement of Interdependence," *Journal of Japanese Studies* 11, no. 1 (1985), 29–45. See also J. M. Bachnik, "Inside and Outside the Japanese Household (Ie): A Contextual Approach to Japanese Social Organization," doctoral thesis, Harvard University, Department of Anthropology, 1978; S. Kumon, Y. Murakami, and S. Sato, "Japan Viewed as Ie Society: Analysis of Japan's Modernisation Process," *Japan Echo* 3, no. 1 (1976): 16–36.

For a very impressive comparative approach, see J. P. Arnason, "The Modern Constellation and the Japanese Enigma" (parts 1 and 2), and *Japan and the West, Thesis Eleven,* no. 17 (1987), 4–39, no. 18, (1987), 56–84. See also J. W. Hall, *Japanese History: New Dimensions of Approach and Understanding,* 2d ed. (Baltimore: Waverly Press, 1966).

70. Murakami, "Ie Society."

71. K. Jaspers, *Von Ursprung und Ziel der Geschichte* (Munich: Piper Verlag, 1945). See also the issue "Wisdom, Revelation and Doubt: Perspectives on the Fink Millenium B.C.," *Daedalus* (spring 1975); S. N. Eisenstadt (ed.), *The Origins and Diversity of Axial Age Civilizations* (Albany, N.Y.: State University of New York Press, 1986). For a recent critical evaluation see S. Breuer, "Kulturen der Achsenzeit: Leistung und Grenzen eines geschichtsphilosophisches Konzepts," *Saeculum* 45, no. 1 (1994): 1–34.

72. B. A. Shillony, "The Meiji Restoration: Japan's Attempt to Inherit China," in I. Neary (ed.), *War, Revolution and Japan* (Sandgete, Kent: Japan Library, 1993), 20–32; H. Bolitho, "Tokugawa Japan: The China Connection," lecture delivered at the Stirrup, Sail and Plough Conference, Canberra, September 1993.

73. See Dale, *Myth of Japanese Uniqueness; idem, Myth of Japanese Uniqueness Revisited;* and the papers in Befu and Kreiner, *Othernesses of Japan.* See also "The Forum on Universalism and Relativism in Asian Studies," *Journal of Asian Studies* 50, no. 1 (February 1991): 29–83; D. Bashbrook, "South Asia, the World System and World Capitalism," *Journal of Asian Studies* 45, no. 3 (August 1990): 479–508.

74. Dale, *Myth of Japanese Uniqueness Revisited,* 30–32.

CHAPTER TWO

1. M. B. Jansen and G. Rozman (eds.), *Japan in Transition: from Tokugawa to Meiji* (Princeton: Princeton University Press, 1986).

2. J. Baechler, *The Origins of Capitalism* (Oxford: Blackwell, 1975). See also *idem,* "The Origins of Modernity: Caste and Feudality (India, Europe and Japan)," in J. Baechler, J. A. Hall, and M. Mann (eds.), *Europe and the Rise of Capitalism* (Oxford: Basil Blackwell, 1988), 39–65, and, in the same book, J. Mutel, "The Modernization of Japan: Why Has Japan Succeeded in Its Modernization?," 136–58; B. K. Marshall, *Capitalism and Nationalism in Prewar Japan: The Ideology of the Business Elite, 1868–1941* (Stanford: Stanford University Press, 1967); J. Hirschmeier, *The Origins of Entrepreneurship in Meiji Japan* (Cambridge, Mass.: Harvard University Press, 1964).

3. Jansen and Rozman, *Japan in Transition,* 12.

4. Jansen and Rozman, *Japan in Transition;* Tohata S. (ed.), *The Moderniza-tion of Japan* (Tokyo: Institute for Asian Economic Affairs, 1966); A. Iriye, *China and Japan in the Global Setting* (Cambridge, Mass.: Harvard University Press, 1992); *idem, The Origins of the Second World War in Asia and the Pacific* (London: Longman, 1987); *idem, Power and Culture: The Japanese-American War, 1941–1945* (Cambridge, Mass.: Harvard University Press, 1981); *idem, Japanese Culture and Foreign Affairs,* Richard Storry Memorial Lecture no. 5 (Oxford: Saint Antony's College, 1992).

5. Jansen and Rozman, *Japan in Transition;* M. B. Jansen, "The Meiji Restoration," in M. B. Jansen (ed.), *Cambridge History of Japan,* vol. 5, *The Nineteenth Century* (Cambridge: Cambridge University Press, 1989), 308–66; C. Blacker, *The Japanese Enlightenment* (Cambridge: Cambridge University Press, 1964), 109–201; T. Najita and H. D. Harootunian, "Japanese Revolt Against the West: Political and Cultural Criticism in the Twentieth Century," in P. Duus (ed.), *The Cambridge History of Japan,* vol. 6 (Cambridge: Cambridge University Press, 1988), 711–74; D. E. Westney, *Imitation and Innovation: The Transfer of Western Organizational Patterns to Meiji Japan* (Cambridge, Mass.: Harvard University Press, 1987); J. Siemes, *Hermann Roesler and the Making of the Meiji State* (Tokyo: Sophia University Press, 1966).

6. S. Vlastos, "Opposition Movements in Early Meiji, 1869–1885," in Jansen, *Cambridge History of Japan,* 5:369–431; E. Torozen, *Takaino Village and the Nakano Uprising of 1871,* doctoral dissertation, Columbia University, 1981; Y. Sugimoto, "Structural Sources of Popular Revolts and the Tōbaku Movement at the Time of the Meiji Restoration," *Journal of Asian Studies* 34, no. 4 (1975): 875–90; G. McCormack and Y. Sugimoto (eds.), *The Japanese Trajectory: Modernization and Beyond* (Cambridge: Cambridge University Press, 1988); R. W. Bowen, *Rebellion and Democracy in Meiji Japan* (Berkeley: University of California Press, 1980); Michio Umegaki, *After the Restoration: The Beginning of Japan's Modern State* (New York: New York University Press, 1988); M. W. Steele, "Against the Restoration: Katsu Kaishū's Attempt to Reinstate the Tokugawa Family," *Monumenta Nipponica* 36, no. 3 (1981): 299–316.

7. Jansen, *Cambridge History of Japan,* vol. 5; B. S. Silberman, "Elite Transformation in the Meiji Restoration: The Upper Civil Service, 1868–1873," in B. S. Silberman and H. D. Harootunian (eds.), *Modern Japanese Leadership* (Tucson, Ariz.: University of Arizona Press, 1966), 233–60; *idem, Cages of Reason* (Chicago: University of Chicago Press, 1993); B. S. Silberman and H. D. Harootunian (eds.), *Japan in Crisis: Essays on Taishō Democracy* (Princeton: Princeton University Press, 1974); R. F. Hackett, "Nishi Amane: A Tokugawa-Meiji Bureaucrat," *Journal of Asian Studies* 18, no. 2 (1959): 213–26; H. Wray and H. Conroy (eds.), "The Meiji Government and Its Critics: What Is Best for the Nation?," in their *Japan Examined: Perspectives on Modern Japanese History* (Honolulu: University of Hawaii Press, 1983), 79–120.

8. E. H. Norman, *Soldier and Peasant in Japan: The Origins of Conscription* (New York: Institute of Pacific Relations, 1943); Jansen and Rozman, *Japan in Transition;* P. Duus, *The Rise of Modern Japan* (Boston: Houghton Mifflin, 1976).

9. I. Scheiner, "Christian Samurai and Samurai Values," in Silberman and Harootunian, *Modern Japanese Leadership,* 171–94; R. J. Smith, "Japanese Re-

ligious Attitudes from the Standpoint of the Comparative Study," in T. Umesao, H. Befu, and J. Kreiner (eds.), *Japanese Civilization in the Modern World*, 5 vols. (Osaka: National Museum of Ethology, 1984–1992); R. S. Schwantes, "The Teacher as Carrier of Culture: Japan, the Meiji Era," paper presented at International Symposium on History of Eastern and Western Contacts, 28 October– 5 November, Tokyo and Kyoto, 121–27; R. Rubinger, "Continuity and Change in Mid-Nineteenth Century Japanese Education," in J. J. Shields (ed.), *Japanese Schooling* (University Park: Pennsylvania State University Press, 1990), 224–33; E. P. Tsurumi, "Meiji Primary School Language and Ethics Textbook: Old Values for a New Society," *Modern Asian Studies* 8, pt. 2 (April 1974): 247–62; R. H. Mitchell, *Censorship in Imperial Japan* (Princeton: Princeton University Press, 1983); J. L. Huffman, "The Meiji Roots and Contemporary Practices of the Japanese Press," *Japan Interpreter* 11, no. 4 (spring 1972): 448–66.

10. H. Befu, *Japan: An Anthropological Introduction* (San Francisco: Chandler, 1971).

11. See H. Rosovsky, *Capital Formation in Japan 1868–1940* (New York: Free Press, 1961).

12. W. G. Runciman, *A Treatise on Social Theory* (Cambridge: Cambridge University Press, 1988), 415; E. Norbeck, "Continuities in Japanese Social Stratification," in L. Plotninov and A. Tuden (eds.), *Essays in Comparative Social Stratification* (Pittsburgh: University of Pittsburgh Press, 1970), 173–95. See also Hirota Teruyuki, *Marriage, Education and Social Mobility in a Former Samurai Society after the Meiji Restoration*, Nissan Occasional Papers no. 19 (Oxford, 1994).

13. Norbeck, "Continuities in Japanese Social Stratification."

14. The quote continues: "There was no longer a hereditary nobility [except for the new hereditary peerage established in the 1880s, which was however much more restricted than the former samurai estate, and was not necessarily based on lands]; a few peasants could and did become landlords; a few peasant sons could and did make careers in industry and commerce; a few of the peasant recruits into the army could and did achieve promotion to higher rank within it; and even a few burakumin could (since physically indistinguishable from other Japanese) successfully 'pass' as born outside their ghettoes. The ambitious minority could, therefore, succeed at the level of individual competition, while the majority's collective systactic location remained what it had been." Runciman, *Treatise on Social Theory*, 417–21.

15. H. Sonoda, "The Decline of the Japanese Warrior Class, 1840–1880," *Nichibunken Japan Review* 1 (1990): 73–113.

16. P. Duus, "Bounded Democracy: Tradition and Politics in Modern Japan," unpublished article.

17. P. Duus, Introduction (1–55) and P. Duus and I. Scheiner, "Socialism, Liberalism and Marxism" (654–711), in Duus, *Cambridge History of Japan*, vol. 6; R. A. Scalapino, *The Early Japanese Labor Movement: Labor and Politics in a Developing Society* (Berkeley: University of California Press, 1984); *idem, Democracy and the Party Movement in Prewar Japan* (Berkeley: University of California Press, 1953).

18. S. Okamoto, "A Phase of Meiji Japan's Attitude toward China: The

Case of Kamura Juntarō," *Journal of Asian Studies* 13, no. 3 (1979): 431–57; B. A. Shillony, "The Meiji Restoration: Japan's Attempt to Inherit China," in I. Neary (ed.), *War, Revolution and Japan* (Sandgete, Kent: Japan Library, 1993), 20–32; H. D. Harootunian, "The Functions of China in Tokugawa Thought," in A. Iriye (ed.), *The Chinese and the Japanese* (Princeton: Princeton University Press, 1980), 9–36.

19. R. H. Meyers and M. R. Peattie (eds.), *The Japanese Colonial Empire 1895–1945* (Princeton: Princeton University Press, 1984); Shillony, "Meiji Restoration"; Duus, *Cambridge History of Japan*, vol. 6; Silberman and Harootunian, *Japan in Crisis*; H. Wray and H. Conroy, "Meiji Imperialism: Planned or Unplanned" (121–48) and "The Russo-Japanese War: Turning Point in Japanese History?" (149–70), in their *Japan Examined*.

20. T. J. Pempel, *Patterns of Japanese Policy-Making* (Boulder, Colo.: Westview Press, 1978); *idem, Policy and Politics in Japan: Creative Conservatism* (Philadelphia: Temple University Press, 1982); Silberman and Harootunian, *Japan in Crisis*; M. Silverberg, *Changing Song: The Marxist Manifestos of Nakano Shigeharu* (Princeton: Princeton University Press, 1990).

21. Silberman and Harootunian, *Japan in Crisis*; Silverberg, *Changing Song*; G. L. Bernstein (ed.), *Recreating Japanese Women, 1600–1945* (Berkeley: University of California Press, 1990).

22. Irokawa Daikichi, "The Emperor System as a Spiritual Structure in Meiji," *Colloquium 8*, Center for Japanese and Korean Studies (Berkeley: University of California Press, 1971); Takeda Kiyoko, "Emperor Hirohito and the Turbulent Shōwa Era," *Japan Foundation Newsletter* 16, nos. 5–6 (June 1989): 1–5. And, for more general discussion, Duus, *Rise of Modern Japan*; B. Silberman, *The Cages of Reason* (Chicago: University of Chicago Press, 1993).

23. Takeda Kiyoko, "Emperor Hirohito"; *idem, The Dual Image of the Japanese Emperor* (New York: New York University Press, 1988).

24. Duus, "Bounded Democracy." Duus indicates that in arguing against a direct importation of foreign political institutions, Ōkubo Toshimichi stated in 1873 that the *seitai* of Russia was not suited to become the *seitai* of England; neither was the *seitai* of England suited to become that of America, nor that of any of them to become the *seitai* of Japan: "Our *seitai* must be erected in accordance with the land, customs, popular sentiment, and trends in our own country."

25. W. Davis, "The Civil Theology of Inoue Tetsujirō," *Japanese Journal of Religious Studies* 3, no. 1 (1976): 25–36.

26. E. Weber, *Peasants into Frenchmen* (Stanford: Stanford University Press, 1976).

27. See Karine Marandjian, "Some Aspects of the Tokugawa Outer World View," in Neary, *War, Revolution and Japan*, 10–19.

28. E. Ohnuki-Tierney, "The Emperor in Japan as Deity (Kami): An Anthropology of the Imperial System in Historical Perspective," *Ethnology* 30, no. 3 (July 1991): 20–22, 31–32; C. Gluck, *Japan's Modern Myths: Ideology in the Late Meiji Period* (Princeton: Princeton University Press, 1985); G. Hoston, *Marxism and the Crisis of Development in Prewar Japan* (Princeton: Princeton University Press, 1986); Nakamura Masanori, *The Japanese Monarchy: Ambassador Joseph Grew and the Making of the "Symbol Emperor System," 1931–1991* (Armonk,

N.Y.: M. E. Sharpe, 1992); T. Fujitani, "Investing, Forgetting, Remembering: Toward a Historical Ethnography of the Nation-State," in H. Befu (ed.), *Cultural Nationalism in East Asia: Representation and Identity* (Berkeley: University of California Press, 1993); *idem*, "Crowds and Imperial Pageantry in Modern Japan: Some Thoughts on Visual Domination," presented at the 42nd annual meeting of the Association for Asian Studies, Chicago, 5–8 April 1990. See also Sato Kazuhiko, "'Des gens étranges à l'allure insolite': Contestation et valeurs nouvelles dans le Japon médiéval"; Katsumata Shizuo, "Ikki, Ligues, conjurations et révoltes dans la société médiévale japonaise"; and Fujiki Hisashi, "Le village et son seigneur (14e–16e siècles): Domination sur le terroir, autodéfense et justice"— all in *Annales* 50, no. 2 (March–April 1995): 307–40, 373–94, and 395–420.

See also, for later development, T. Fujitani, "Electronic Pageantry and Japan's 'Symbolic Emperor,'" *Journal of Asian Studies* 51, no. 4 (November 1992): 824–50; A. C. Mayer, "Recent Succession Ceremonies of the Emperor of Japan," *Nichibunken Japan Review* (1991), 35–62; Sakamoto Yoshikazu (ed.), *The Emperor System as a Japan Problem: The Case of Meiji Gakuin University*, International Peace Research Institute, Meigaku (Prime), occasional papers, no. 5 (Yokohama: Meiji Gakuin University, 1989); Amino Yoshihiko, "Emperor, Rice and Commoners," presented at Stirrup, Sail and Plough conference, Canberra, September 1993; Gluck, *Japan's Modern Myths;* Silberman, *Cages of Reason;* A. Hirai, "Ancestor Worship in Yatsuka Hozumi's State and Constitutional Theory," in Edmund Skrzypczak (ed.), *Japan's Modern Century,* a special issue of *Monumenta Nipponica* prepared in celebration of the centennial of the Meiji restoration (Tokyo: E. Tuttle, in cooperation with Sophia University, 1968), 40–50; A. E. Barshay, "The Problem of the Emperor System in Japanese Social Science," presented at CJS regional seminar "Reflections on Tennōsei: Culture, Politics and Japan's Emperor," 18 November 1989.

29. S. Tanaka, *Japan's Orient: Rendering Pasts into History* (Berkeley: University of California Press, 1993).

30. Ohnuki-Tierney, "Emperor in Japan."

31. Gluck, *Japan's Modern Myths;* see also Hirai, "Ancestor Worship"; Irokawa Daikichi, "Japanese Identity as Seen from 'Ancestor Rites'", presented at ANU Stirrup, Sail and Plough conference, Canberra, September 1993; M. Weiner, *Race and Migration in Imperial Japan* (London: Routledge, 1994).

32. B. S. Silberman, "Japan and Social Theory: Modernism and Modernisation in Japanese Politics," presented at the International Conference on Japanese Studies, Kyoto, November 1994.

33. See John Caiger, "The Aims and Content of School Courses in Japanese History, 1872–1945," in Skrzypczak, *Japan's Modern Century,* 51–83; Schwantes, "Teacher as Carrier of Culture."

34. Gluck, *Japan's Modern Myths,* 110–12.

35. Hoston, *Marxism and the Crisis of Development,* 28.

36. Silberman and Harootunian, *Japan in Crisis.*

37. Silberman, *Cages of Reason;* K. B. Pyle, *The New Generation in Meiji Japan: Problems of Cultural Identity, 1885–1895* (Stanford: Stanford University Press, 1969). See also S. H. Yamashita, "Confucianism and the Modern Japanese State, 1904–1945," in Tu Weiming (ed.), *Confucian Traditions in East Asian Mo-*

dernity (Cambridge, Mass.: Harvard University Press, forthcoming). For the political implication of this term see D. Williams, *Japan: Beyond the End of Theory* (London: Routledge, 1994), chap. 9.

38. Silberman and Harootunian, *Japan in Crisis.*

39. Ibid., 115–17.

40. See A. E. Barshay, *State and Intellectual in Imperial Japan: The Public Man in Crisis* (Berkeley: University of California Press, 1988), 887, and the review of this book by G. A. Hoston, "State and Intellectual in Imperial Japan: The Public Man," *Monumenta Nipponica* 45, no. 1 (spring 1990), 112–15. See also Ian Inkster, "The Other Side of Meiji: Conflict and Conflict Management," in McCormack and Sugimoto, *Japanese Trajectory,* 107–29; M. Nagai, "The Development of Intellectuals in the Meiji and Taishō Periods," *Journal of Social and Political Ideas in Japan* 2, no. 1 (1964), 28–32, as well as the rest of the articles in this volume; Maruyama Masao, *Denken in Japan* (Frankfurt: Suhrkamp, 1992).

41. Barshay, *State and Intellectual,* 246. See also Inkster, "Other Side of Meiji."

42. See S. Garon, "Women's Groups and the Japanese State: Contending Approaches to Political Integration, 1890–1945," *Journal of Japanese Studies* 19, no. 1 (Winter 1993), 5–43.

43. Silberman, *Cages of Reason,* 221.

44. For a detailed account of these developments, see J. E. Ketelaar, *Of Heretics and Martyrs in Meiji Japan: Buddhism and Its Persecution* (Princeton: Princeton University Press, 1990); K. M. Staggs, "Defend the Nation and Love the Truth: Inoue Enryō and the Revival of Meiji Buddhism," *Monumenta Nipponica* 38, no. 3 (1983): 251–81; S. M. Garon, "State and Religion in Imperial Japan, 1912–1945," *Journal of Japanese Studies* 12, no. 2 (1986): 273–302; J. Herbert, *Shinto: Another Fountain-Head of Japan* (New York, Stein and Day, 1967); D. C. Holtom, *Modern Japan and Shinto Nationalism: A Study of Present-Day Trends in Japanese Religions* (Chicago: University of Chicago Press, 1943); Genichi Kato, *A Historical Study of the Religious Development of Shinto,* trans. Shoyu Hanayama (Tokyo: Japan Society for the Promotion of Science, 1973).

45. Hardacre, *Shinto and the State, 1868–1988* (Princeton: Princeton University Press, 1989), 131. See also W. M. Fridell, *Japanese Shrine Mergers 1906–12: State Shinto Moves to the Grassroots* (Tokyo: Sophia University, Kawata Press, 1973); E. Lokowandt, "Die rechtliche Entwicklung des Staats-Shinto in der ersten Hälfte der Meiji-Zeit (1868–1890)," in W. Heissing and H. J. Klimkeit (eds.), *Studies in Oriental Religions,* vol. 3 (Wiesbaden: Otto Harrassowitz, 1978).

46. Hardacre, *Shinto and the State,* 131; Garon, "State and Religion in Imperial Japan"; D. C. Holtom, "The Political Philosophy of Modern Shinto: A Study of the State Religion in Japan," dissertation submitted to the Faculty of Graduate Divinity School, distributed by the University of Chicago Libraries, 1922; Fridell, *Japanese Shrine Mergers;* Lokowandt, "Die Rechtliche Entwicklung des Staadts-Shinto."

47. Hardacre, *Shinto and the State,* 131. A. Nakano, "Death and History: An Emperor's Funeral," *Public Culture* 2, no. 2 (spring 1990): 33–40; Fujitani, "Electronic Pageantry"; Fridell, *Japanese Shrine Mergers.*

48. Nakano, "Death and History."

49. P. Nosco, editor's introduction to special issue on the emperor system and religion in Japan, *Japanese Journal of Religious Studies* 17, nos. 2–3 (1990): 99. In this issue see especially the articles by Sasaki Kōkan, "Priest, Shaman, King" (105–28); J. M. Kitagawa, "Some Reflections on Japanese Religion and Its Relationship to the Imperial System" (129–78); and Miyazaki Fumiko, "The Formation of Emperor Worship in the New Religions: The Case of Fujidō" (281–314).

50. F. G. Bock, "The Great Feast of the Enthronement, *Monumenta Nipponica* 45, no. 1 (spring 1990): 27–39. For detailed descriptions of earlier enthronement ceremonies, see D. C. Holtom, *Japanese Enthronement Ceremonies: With an Account of the Imperial Regalia* (Tokyo: Sophia University, 1972); and R. Ellwood, *The Feast of Kingship* (Tokyo: Sophia University, 1973).

The following newspaper excerpt about the then-forthcoming enthronement or coronation of Emperor Akihito is also very illustrative.

The new emperor is coming to the Grand Shrine of Ise, where he is still worshiped as a god. The carpenters, sons and grandsons of Ise shrine carpenters before them, are building a bridge so that the emperor can cross where no one has crossed before.

Next fall, important people from around the world will visit Tokyo to witness the pomp and splendor of Emperor Akihito's official enthronement, the first such ceremony in 62 years, and pay tribute to Japan's status as economic superpower. But to understand Japan, they would do well to come here—like the emperor, who will repair to Ise after his coronation to report to his ancestors and spend two nights in a simple thatched-roof house. . . .

Here the river runs clear, even after storms. Here a lone horse, retired from service to the emperor or crown prince, sometimes stands guard. The horse, too, is seen as a god, which stable hands must exercise by running alongside, and never atop.

Here the sun goddess, from whom the emperor is supposedly descended, is nourished with the four essential foods: rice, salt, water and abalone.

And here six million people—one in twenty Japanese—annually come as pilgrims or tourists, more than a million during the first three days of each year. They come even though they cannot see the central shrine, the sun goddess's home, which stands inside four fences, accessible only to the emperor and empress and high priests. Emperor Akihito, 56, who became emperor last year when his father, Hirohito, died, will approach the central shrine for the first time when he pays his call in autumn.

This is the center of Shinto, Japan's nature-worshiping and tribal religion that predates Buddhism, Confucianism and Christianity. Here in concrete form are the contradictions that often baffle outsiders: permanence in renewal, renewal in destruction, sacredness in the ordinary.

Even here, the Japanese do not take their religion too seriously. Some elderly tourists dip their hands into the sacred Isuzu River, gazing at hills of dark pines feathered with young green maples. Then, patting their hands dry with handkerchiefs, they laugh as their tour guide, a young woman holding the inevitable tour banner, cracks a joke she clearly has cracked a hundred times before.

A priest, Masayuki Nakanishi, 45, walked along the pebbled path. In his suit and tie, he looks like a typical Mitsubishi employee, and he says he sees himself that way: a typical Japanese with a job at the shrine, a schoolteacher wife, four children. Shinto, unlike some sects of Buddhism, has no moral code and demands no ascetic living; it wants to be part of everyday life, to be everyday life.

"We'd like you to think that these hills themselves are gods," Mr. Nakanishi said. "The Japanese image of god is not one built into a house. It's one that is diffused into nature itself."

Just off the path leading to Shinto's highest shrine, Mr. Nakanishi pointed out one of its lowliest: one rock, on a pile of other rocks, surrounded by a string decorated with strips of white paper.

"This is the god of turbulent water," he said. "Just one stone is enough to be a shrine."

It is the singular feature of Ise that the central shrine is destroyed and rebuilt every twenty years, along with 2,400 treasures inside it—everything the sun goddess, Amaterasu, needs for daily life, from combs and kimonos to looms and rice bowls. The wooden fences of the existing shrine are weathered, and what can be seen of its thatched roof is covered with moss; the shrine is due for rebuilding on an adjacent field of stones in 1993.

For 1,300 years, it is said, the Ise shrine has been built and rebuilt on these two adjacent sites. The carpenters beginning to stir now will use much the same tools, the same woods, the same methods as their ancestors a millennium ago. Each shrine is new, and yet ancient—gleaming, and yet identical to one that has stood there since Charlemagne ruled France.

In the same way, Mr. Nakanishi says, the emperor is an individual who nonetheless embodies a divinity passed down from generation to generation.

"By becoming emperor, he carries the divinity of Amaterasu," he said. "Each emperor has his own character, but the divinity of Amaterasu is conveyed as one."

Such talk rings alarm bells for some. Before World War II, the government pumped up Shinto into a national religion justifying military conquest. Ise was the center of this cult. Emperor Hirohito came here to report the beginning of the war to his ancestors, and to tell them of Japan's surrender, too.

Since that defeat 45 years ago, much has changed. Tax money no longer supports the shrine, and attendance has yet to return to its prewar high of eight million a year. Emperor Hirohito renounced his divinity under U.S. surrender orders, and so Emperor Akihito is the first emperor never to have been officially a god.

And yet, at Ise, much is quite obviously unchanged. "Some people will say that only before the war did people think the emperor was a god," Mr. Nakanishi said. "That is not so."

Before Emperor Akihito visits Ise next fall he will commune with Amaterasu in a mysterious nighttime ritual that will leave him, by Shinto belief, a god. After a group of Christian college presidents recently complained that the government should not finance such a religious ceremony, one of the educators narrowly missed death when someone fired two bullets through his bedroom window. The assailant is believed to have been one of Japan's right-wing extremists who consider themselves protectors of the imperial faith.

So the question of emperor worship remains serious business for some Japanese, and to some it is worrisome. And yet, on a beautiful spring afternoon, chatting with an amiable Shinto employee, it is difficult to be alarmed. The hills are gods, the rice is a god, even the horse is a god, so why not the emperor?" (S. R. Weisman, "An Ancient Shrine Is Testing a New Emperor," *New York Times Magazine*, 3 October 1988)

See also Kurita Wataru, "Enthroning a New Emperor," *Japan Quarterly*, January–March 1991, 42–49.

51. Kitagawa, "Some Reflections on Japanese Religion."

52. W. Davis, "Japan Theory and Civil Religion," in *idem, Japanese Religion*

and Society: Paradigms of Structure and Change (Albany: State University of New York Press, 1992), 253–71.

53. Gluck, *Japan's Modern Myths.*

54. See T. Najita, *Japan: The Intellectual Foundations of Modern Japanese Politics* (Chicago: University of Chicago Press, 1974), 101; Gluck, *Japan's Modern Myths.*

55. See McCormack and Sugimoto, *Japanese Trajectory;* Huffman, "Meiji Roots."

56. G. A. Hoston, "A 'Theology' of Liberation? Socialist Revolution and Spiritual Regeneration in Chinese and Japanese Marxism," in P. Cohen and M. Goldman (eds.), *Ideas across Cultures* (Cambridge, Mass.: Council on East Asian Studies, Harvard University, 1990), 165–98; G. L. Bernstein, *Japanese Marxist: A Portrait of Kawakami Hajime 1879–1946* (Cambridge, Mass.: Harvard University Press, 1976).

57. Hoston, "A 'Theology' of Liberation?"

58. Najita, *Japan,* 101; B. A. Shillony, *Politics and Culture in Wartime Japan* (New York: Clarendon Press, 1981); Gluck, *Japan's Modern Myths.*

59. Silberman and Harootunian, *Japan in Crisis.*

60. Silberman and Harootunian, *Japan in Crisis.*

61. B. Silberman, "Taishō Japan and the Crisis of Secularism," in Silberman and Harootunian, *Japan in Crisis,* 442 ff.

62. Ketelaar, *Of Heretics and Martyrs,* 213.

63. C. Fawcett, "The Practice of Archeology in Japan and Japanese Identity," presented at the Stirrup, Sail and Plough Conference, Canberra, September 1993.

64. W. Davis, "Civil Religion in Modern Japan," dissertation, University of Chicago, Divinity School, 1973; *idem,* "Pilgrimage and the World Renewal: A Study of Religion and Social Values in Tokugawa Japan," part 1, *History of Religions* 23, no. 2 (1983): 97–116; R. N. Bellah, "The Japanese and American Cases," in *Varieties of Civil Religion* (San Francisco: Harper & Row, 1980), 27–40.

65. N. L. Waters, "The Second Transition: Early to Mid-Meiji in Kanagawa Prefecture," *Journal of Asian Studies* 49, no. 2 (May 1990). See also McCormack and Sugimoto, *Japanese Trajectory.*

66. Kojin Karatani, *Origins of Modern Japanese Literature* (Durham: Duke University Press, 1993).

67. H. D. Harootunian, "Disciplinizing Native Knowledge and Producing Place: Yanagita Kunio, Origuchi Shinobu, Takata Yasuma," in Rimer (ed.), *Culture and Identity* (Princeton: Princeton University Press, 1990), 125–27.

68. Ibid., 98–129.

69. J. V. Koschmann, "Folklore Studies and the Conservative Anti-Establishment in Modern Japan," in J. V. Koschmann et al., *International Perspectives on Yanagita Kunio and Japanese Folklore Studies* (Ithaca: China-Japan Program, Cornell University, 1985), 131–64.

70. Ibid.

71. See for instance: D. Shively (ed.), *Tradition and Modernization in Japanese Culture* (Princeton: Princeton University Press, 1971); R. E. Ward and D. A. Rustow (eds.), *Political Modernization in Japan and Turkey* (Princeton: Princeton University Press, 1964).

72. E. H. Norman, *Japan's Emergence as a Modern State* (New York: International Secretariat, Institute of Pacific Relations, 1940); P. Anderson, *Lineages of the Absolutist State* (London: New Left Books, 1974); J. P. Arnason, "Paths to Modernity: The Peculiarities of Japanese Feudalism," in McCormack and Sugimoto, *Japanese Trajectory*, 235–63.

73. Gluck, *Japan's Modern Myths*. For a broader analysis of the Meiji regime in the framework of the modern revolutions see S. N. Eisenstadt, "Framework of the Great Revolutions: Culture, Social Structure, History and Human Agency," *International Social Science Journal* 33 (August 1992): 385–401.

74. Davis, "Civil Religion in Modern Japan." See also Bellah, "Japanese and American Cases," 27–40.

75. Gluck, *Japan's Modern Myths*, 127. Davis, "Civil Theology."

76. M. Ozouf, *Festivals and the French Revolution* (Cambridge, Mass.: Harvard University Press, 1988); L. Hunt, *Politics, Culture and Class in the French Revolution* (Berkeley: University of California Press, 1984).

77. Hunt, *Politics, Culture and Class*; L. Hunt, "The Sacred and the French Revolution," in J. C. Alexander (ed.), *Durkheimian Sociology: Cultural Studies* (Cambridge: Cambridge University Press, 1988), 25–43; M. Ozouf, *Festivals and the French Revolution*.

78. See, for instance, Thomas R. Havens, *Farm and Nation in Modern Japan: Agrarian Nationalism 1870–1940* (Princeton: Princeton University Press, 1974). Also the review of G. M. Wilson in *Japan Interpreter* 11, no. 1 (1976): 109–16; Davis, "Civil Theology."

CHAPTER THREE

1. R. E. Ward, *Democratizing Japan: The Allied Occupation* (Honolulu: University of Hawaii Press, 1987); Kataoka Tetsuya (ed.), *Creating Single-Party Democracy: Japan's Postwar Political System* (Stanford: Hoover Institution Press, Stanford University, 1992); R. J. Hrebenar, *The Japanese Party System: From One Party Rule to Coalition Government* (Boulder, Colo.: Westview Press, 1986).

2. Ikuo Kabashima, "Supportive Participation with Economic Growth: The Case of Japan," *World Politics* 36, no. 3 (April 1984): 309–38.

3. A. Gordon, *The Evolution of Labor Relations in Japan* (Cambridge, Mass.: Council on East Asia Studies, Harvard University, 1985). See also the following essays on the Japanese employment system in *Journal of Japanese Studies* 4, no. 2 (Summer 1978): S. Crawcour, "The Japanese Employment System," 225–46; R. Cole, "The Late-Developer Hypothesis: An Evaluation of Its Relevance for Japanese Employment Patterns," 247–66; W. M. Fruin, "The Japanese Company Controversy: Ideology and Organization in a Historical Perspective," 267–500.

4. J. O. Haley, "Consensual Governance: A Study of Law, Culture and the Political Economy of Post-War Japan," in S. Kumon and H. Rosovsky (eds.), *Cultural and Social Dynamics*, vol. 3 of Y. Murakami and H. T. Patrick (eds.), *The Political Economy of Japan* (Stanford: Stanford University Press, 1992), 32–62; K. Haitani, *The Japanese Economic System: An Institutional Overview* (Lexing-

ton: Lexington Books D.C., 1976); C. Johnson, *MITI and the Japanese Miracle: The Growth of Industrial Policy 1925–1975* (Stanford: Stanford University Press, 1982); *idem*, "The Japanese Economy: A Different Kind of Capitalism," in S. N. Eisenstadt and E. Ben-Ari (eds.), *Japanese Models of Conflict Resolution* (London: Kegan Paul International, 1990); H. Patrick and H. Rosovsky, *Asia's New Giant: How the Japanese Economy Works* (Washington, D.C.: Brookings Institution, 1976); T. Ishida, "The Development of Interest Groups and the Pattern of Modernization in Japan," *Papers in Modern Japan* (Canberra: Australian National University, 1965), 1–17; W. W. Lockwood (ed.), *The Economic Development of Japan: Growth and Structural Change* (Princeton: Princeton University Press, 1968).

5. H. Rosovsky, quoted in "Political Culture and Economic Ethics," in Tu Weiming, M. Hejtmanek, and A. Wachman (eds.), *The Confucian World Observed: A Contemporary Discussion of Confucian Humanism in East Asia* (Honolulu: Institute of Culture and Communication, East-West Center, 1992); C. Gluck, *Japan's Modern Myths: Ideology in the Late Meiji Period* (Princeton: Princeton University Press, 1985).

6. I. Inukai and A. R. Tussing, "Kogyo Iken: Japan's Ten Year Plan, 1884," *Economic Development and Cultural Growth* 16, no. 1 (1967): 51.

7. H. Rosovsky, quoted in Weiming, Hejmanek, and Wachman, *Confucian World Observed*, 79. See also Inukai and Tussing, "Kōgyō Iken," 51–71; Bai Gao, "Jissen-ha Economics and Japanese Economic Reasoning," paper presented at the International Conference on Japanese Studies, Kyoto, November 1994.

8. Johnson, *MITI and the Japanese Miracle; idem*, "The People Who Invented the Mechanical Nightingale," *Daedalus* 119, no. 3 (1990): 71–90; *idem, Japan: Who Governs? The Rise of the Developmental State* (New York: Norton, 1995). See also W. Leontielf, "Mysterious Japan: A Diary," *New York Review of Books*, 4 June 1970, 23–29.

9. S. Garon, *The State and Labor in Modern Japan* (Berkeley: University of California Press, 1987); Gordon, *Evolution of Labor Relations in Japan*.

10. K. E. Calder, "Linking Welfare and the Development State: Postal Savings in Japan," *Journal of Japanese Studies* 15 (winter 1990): 51–61; S. J. Anderson, "The Political Economy of Japanese Saving: How Postal Savings and Public Pensions Support High Rates of Household Saving in Japan," *Journal of Japanese Studies* 16, no. 1 (winter 1990): 61–92. See also H. Rosovsky, "Japan's Transition to Modern Economic Growth 1868–1885," in H. Rosovsky (ed.), *Industrialization in Two Systems: Essays in Honor of Alexander Gerscheron* (New York: J. Wiley and Sons, 1966). 91–139.

11. For an interesting discussion of the concrete working of such reforms, see J. Sterngold, "A Japanese-Style 'Old Boy' Network," *New York Times*, 7 June 1991, C1–C6:

> When Japan's banks and securities houses began battling several years ago to break into each other's business, policy makers at the formidable Finance Ministry were deadlocked over what to do. It finally took an even greater power to break the stalemate: the "Old Boys."
>
> Occasionally an issue arises in this seemingly harmonious society that lifts the facade of orderliness and illuminates both the intensity of the business rivalries and

the real lines of power for resolving disputes. The five-year tug-of-war over financial deregulation has done just that.

It is particularly interesting to observe this process at the Finance Ministry, which is widely seen as the most powerful arm of the Government. The ministry combines what in the United States would be all the bank regulatory agencies, the Securities and Exchange Commission, the Internal Revenue Service, the Office of Management and Budget and a few lesser agencies.

The Old Boys, who are widely referred to, even by themselves, by this English phrase and often in shorthand as "O.B.s," are dozens of retired senior Finance Ministry officials. At the top of the heap are the former vice ministers, the highest career post. They might hold the job for only a year or two before moving on to lucrative jobs in industry and O.B. status, from which they continue to hold sway over policy and personnel moves at the ministry. The finance minister's post is a political appointment and thus former ministers do not continue to have as much say over financial policy.

The momentous battle between the banks and securities houses over eliminating the barriers in Japan's version of the Glass-Steagall Act, the United States law that separates commercial banking from investment banking, is no ordinary struggle. Put simply, commercial banks want to get into the highly protected securities business, and the securities brokers want to keep them out.

The banks, which enjoy a decidedly higher status in Japan as the partners of industry, had prevailed initially by offering to build "firewalls" between their banking and securities operations to protect against conflicts of interest and other abuses.

At the ministry, the securities and banking bureaus usually reflect the thinking of the industries they regulate. The bureaus thus found themselves at odds over how to lower the barriers separating the businesses, so a small group of O.B.'s quietly decided how to break the impasse. There were no weekend hunting trips, no intensive lobbying efforts.

Instead, the Old Boys merely passed the word to the bureaucrats through advisory panels on which they sat that the securities industry should give up only a little to Japan's huge banking institutions. The result: Perhaps in 1993, banks will get modest powers to engage in the securities business. Through separate subsidiaries they will be allowed to do bond underwriting and brokerage operations, however. They will be able to deal in some new kinds of securities and private placements, but they will have very limited ability to trade securities.

In return, securities houses will be permitted to trade foreign currencies and to engage in some kinds of trust banking.

"The banks were too optimistic; they thought it would go too easily," said Hiroshi Tanimura, 75 years old, a pleasant man who as an O.B. occupies a large corner office at the Finance Ministry.

"They thought they could build the firewalls rather easily," he added in an interview, breaking into one of his broad smiles. "But I thought that would be rather difficult."

Although he insisted in an interview that he had been essentially neutral, Mr. Tanimura did hint that it had been sort of fun taking the banks down a few pegs.

"The banks were in a sort of go-go mood," he explained. "They don't need a strong cheerleader. So the Old Boys' voices are not so strong on their side." Coming from such an influential person, the importance of such hints is not lost on Japan's policy makers.

Besides Mr. Tanimura, the ruling O.B.s in this case were Minoru Nagaoka, 67, and Michio Takeuchi, 70, collectively known as "N.T.T." (Mr. Takeuchi and Mr. Nagaoka declined to be interviewed.)

"Really, those three are not known just as O.B.s, but as Godfathers," explained Yukio Noguchi, a former bureaucrat who is now a professor at Hitotsubashi University and an expert on financial policy. "We call them 'Don.' It's very difficult to explain this process, though, because it's all informal."

He added: "They are all former vice ministers, but not all vice ministers can be Godfathers. It is hard to explain how they obtain this."

The affiliations of these three give some indication of where their interests lie. Mr. Nagaoka is currently president of the Tokyo Stock Exchange, a friend to the securities industry. Mr. Takeuchi and Mr. Tanimura are former presidents of the exchange and currently head Government-affiliated research centers connected to the securities markets. They deny favoring either side, of course, but their innate conservatism has worked to the unmistakable advantage of the securities houses, whose aim is to preserve much of the status quo and stanch competition from the banks.

Perhaps the surest sign of the power of these three Old Boys is the fact that they deny having any. If a Japanese official is asked to explain how the Old Boys do it, the answer is usually a shrug of the shoulders. But that informality lends the Old Boys even more influence, because they are not constrained by any transparent process that could be examined and criticized.

The Old Boys "have to be seen as independent of the political world, as politically neutral," Mr. Noguchi explained. "There is a real fear within the ministry that personnel decisions will be influenced by politicians. And the bureaucrats respect the Old Boys' judgment as intelligent and objective."

In fact, that is what most acknowledge in their candid moments to be the real source of the power of the O.B.'s—their ability to influence personnel decisions. The process of determining promotions and work assignments is one of the most opaque and secretive at the Finance Ministry. Those decisions cannot be questioned and affect a bureaucrat's entire career.

Privately, several bureaucrats acknowledged that some of the more powerful Old Boys had been consulted on these assignments. Thus, no bureaucrat is willing to ignore the Old Boys' advice and risk angering them.

The issue now is that changes in Article 65, as the law separating banking and the securities businesses is known, will have a bigger impact on the international realm than most of the matters on which the Old Boys are usually consulted. Permitting Japan's banks into the securities markets could make them more competitive in garnering the business of Japan's largest industrial corporations; the securities houses could shrink their profits and make it tougher for them to build their businesses globally.

The clash over Article 65 has raged in the dim hallways of the rundown Finance Ministry building here for nearly six years. Advisory panels of outside experts, including many of the O.B.s, have met to hammer out compromises. But in the end, according to many of those involved in the process, the Old Boys were able to tip the balance slightly in favor of less change.

"Yes, I would have to say that behind the scenes the Old Boys have influenced this to some degree," said Shoichi Toyama, an economics professor at Osaka University and chairman of a Finance Ministry advisory panel making recommendations on financial deregulation. The current bureaucrats always pay their respects to the Old Boys, although that does not mean the Old Boys dominate them."

The Old Boys are consulted on a range of policy questions, of which the battle over Article 65 is just the most visible. For instance, Mr. Noguchi said that in the recent battle over raising taxes on land holdings, several Old Boys had weighed in by trying to shift the power to collect property taxes to the central Government rather than local governments.

The single greatest threat to the Old Boys and the Bureaucrats in the Finance Ministry are the politicians. The politicians are the only independent force that can influence bureaucratic debates, an enormous threat to the Finance Ministry. The bureaucrats both sneer at and fear the politicians.

That concern was evident recently when Tetsuo Kondo, a former bureaucrat and now a senior member of the ruling Liberal Democratic Party, publicly suggested that the consumer was being forgotten in the debate on financial deregulation. Finance Ministry officials did little to hide their resentment of this intrusion into their field, all but ignoring the substance of Mr. Kondo's remarks.

But Mr. Tanimura made it clear that, as powerful as Mr. Kondo might be, there was still a higher power to be reckoned with in Japan.

"Yes, he's an Old Boy," Mr. Tanimura said, "but not as much an Old Boy as me!"

See also Rosovsky, "Japan's Transition to Modern Economic Growth," 91–139.

12. E. Lincoln, "Economic Experience in Shōwa: The Japan of Hirohito," in *Shōwa, the Japan of Hirohito*, special issue of *Daedalus* 119, no. 3 (summer 1990): 201; see also Shigeto Tsuru, *Japan's Capitalism: Creative Defeat and Beyond* (Cambridge: Cambridge University Press, 1993).

13. Lincoln, "Economic Experience in Shōwa," 204.

14. K. E. Calder, *Strategic Capitalism: Private Business and Public Purpose in Japan* (Princeton: Princeton University Press, 1993).

15. M. Gerlach, *Alliance Capitalism: The Social Organization of Japanese Business* (Berkeley: University of California Press, 1992), 5. See also M. Y. Yoshino and Thomas B. Lifson, *The Invisible Link: Japan's Sogo Sosha and the Organization of Trade* (Cambridge, Mass.: MIT Press, 1986); Ishida Hideto, "Anticompetitive Practices in the Distribution of Goods and Services in Japan: The Problem of Distribution *Keiretsu*," John O. Haley (trans.), *Journal of Japanese Studies* 9, no. 2 (1983): 319–34. For a broader institutional background see R. Whitley, *Business Systems in East Asia: Firms, Markets and Societies* (London: Sage Publications, 1992); W. Mark Fruin, *The Japanese Enterprise System: Competitive Strategies and Cooperative Structures* (Oxford: Clarendon Press, 1992).

16. R. Dore, *Taking Japan Seriously: A Confucian Perspective on Leading Economic Issues* (Stanford: Stanford University Press, 1987), 173–75. See also *idem, Flexible Rigidities* (Stanford: Stanford University Press, 1986); *idem, British Factory—Japanese Factory: The Origins of National Diversity in Industrial Relations* (Berkeley: University of California Press, 1973). See for illustration of this pattern John W. Bennett, *Paternalism in the Japanese Economy: Anthropological Studies of Oyabun-Kobun Patterns* (Minneapolis: University of Minnesota Press, 1963).

17. G. G. Hamilton and R. C. Feenstra, "Varieties of Traditions and Hierarchies, An Introduction," *Industrial and Corporative Change* 4, no. 1 (1995, forthcoming).

18. B. M. Richardson and T. Ueda (eds.), *Business and Society in Japan: Fundamentals for Businessmen* (Columbus, Ohio: East Asian Studies Program, Ohio State University, Praeger, 1972).

19. See N. J. Chalmers, *Industrial Relations in Japan: The Peripheral Workforce* (London: Routledge, 1989), esp. chap. 6, 173–97; Iwata Ryūshi, "The Japan

Enterprise as a Unified Body of Employees: Origins and Development," in Kumon and Rosovsky, *Cultural and Social Dynamics*, 170–97; H. Shimada, "Japan's Industrial Culture and Labor-Management Relations," in Murakami, *Political Economy of Japan*, 267–91.

20. K. Okochi, B. Karsh, and S. B. Levine (eds.), *Workers and Employers in Japan: The Japanese Employment Relations System* (Princeton: Princeton University Press, 1974), esp. chap. 13, "The Japanese Industrial Relations Systems: A Summary," 485–512; Shigeyoshi Tokunaga, "Die Beziehungen zwischen Lohnarbeit und Kapital im japanischen Grobunternehmen," and J. Bergman, "Die Fragmentierung der Lohnarbeiterklasse in Japan: Bemerkungen zu dem Aufsatz von Tokunaga," both in *Westdeutscher Verlag* (Opladen, 1984).

21. E. Harari, "Resolving and Managing Policy Conflict: Advisory Bodies," in Eisenstadt and Ben Ari, *Japanese Models of Conflict Resolution*, 138–61; H. Hazama and J. Kaminski, "Japanese Labor-Management Relations and Uno Riemon," *Journal of Japanese Studies* 5, no. 1 (1979): 71–106; Karel O. Cool, "Second Thoughts on the Transferability of the Japanese Management System," paper no. 815, Krannert Graduate School of Management, West Lafayette, Ind., 1983.

22. T. J. Pempel, "Japan and Sweden: Polarities of 'Responsible Capitalism,'" in D. A. Rustow and K. P. Erickson (eds.), *Comparative Political Dynamics: Global Research Perspectives* (New York: Harper Collins, 1991), 408–34; *idem, Policy and Politics in Japan: Creative Conservatism*, (Philadelphia: Temple University Press, 1982); A. L. Kalleberg and J. R. Lincoln, "The Structure of Earnings Inequality in the United States and Japan," *American Journal of Sociology* 94 (1988): 121–153; T. K. McCraw, *America versus Japan: A Comparative Study of Business Government Relations Conducted at the Harvard Business School* (Boston: Harvard Business School Press, 1986).

23. See A. Gordon, "Contests for the Workplace," in A. Gordon (ed.), *Postwar Japan as History* (Berkeley: University of California Press, 1993), 373–95. See also R. Dore, "International Markets and National Traditions: Japanese Capitalism in the 21st Century," occasional paper no. 5, Department of Sociology, University of Hong Kong, 1992.

24. G. McCormack and Y. Sugimoto (eds.), *The Japanese Trajectory: Modernization and Beyond* (Cambridge: Cambridge University Press, 1988).

25. Kumon and Rosovsky, *Cultural and Social Dynamics*; D. I. Okimoto and T. P. Rohlen (eds.), *Inside the Japanese System: Readings on Contemporary Society and Political Economy* (Stanford: Stanford University Press, 1988); "Symposium: Japan in the 1970s" (articles by T. P. Rohlen, G. R. Saxonhouse, J. C. Campbell, and Moriyama Takeshi), *Journal of Japanese Studies* 5, no. 2 (summer 1979): 235–385.

26. M. Gerlach, "Business Alliances and the Strategy in the Japanese Firm," *California Management Review*, reprint series 30, no. 1 (1987); see also *idem, Alliance Capitalism*; Imai Ken-Ichi, "Japan's Corporate Networks," in Kumon and Rosovsky, *Cultural and Social Dynamics*, 198–230.

27. M. Aoki and N. Rosenberg, "The Japanese Firm as an Innovating Institution," in T. Shiraishi and S. Tsuru (eds.), *Economic Institutions in a Dynamic Society: Search for a New Frontier* (New York: St. Martin's Press, 1989), 137–54;

M. Aoki, *Economic Analysis of the Japanese Firm* (Amsterdam: North Holland, 1984); *idem, Information, Incentives and Bargaining in the Japanese Economy* (Cambridge: Cambridge University Press, 1988); *idem,* "Toward an Economic Model of the Japanese Firm," *Journal of Economic Literature* 28 (March 1990): 1–27; *idem,* "The Japanese Firm as a System of Attributes: A Survey and Research Agenda," paper presented at the conference "Japan in a Global Economy: A European Perspective," Stockholm School of Economics, September 1991; D. I. Okimoto and T. P. Rohlen (eds.), *Inside the Japanese System: Readings on Contemporary Society and Political Economy* (Stanford: Stanford University Press, 1988), esp. Sakakibara Eisuke and Noguchi Yukio, "Organization for Economic Reconstruction," 43–53; R. Clark, *The Japanese Company* (New Haven: Yale University Press, 1979). See also Theo Parker, "Die real nicht existierende japanische Schreibmaschine, oder: Wie funktioniert das japanische Büro ohne Maschinenschrift?," *Leviathan* 14, no. 3 (1986): 328–60.

28. The differences between these two models are spelled out in Aoki and Rosenberg, *Japanese Firm as an Innovating Institution,* as follows:

1. In greater detail: *Reliance upon on-site information:* At the operating level, much less emphasis is placed on economies of specialization in the Japanese organization than is the case in its Western counterpart. Problem solving is integrated with, rather than separated from, the operating task. [For example, the work team on the shop floor is delegated a wide range of responsibility for coping with local emergencies, such as breakdown of machinery, absenteeism, and defective outputs, without much reliance upon outside experts such as engineers, relief men, and inspectors.] Informationally, this aspect of the Japanese organization may be interpreted as aiming at the better use of on-site information made possible through learning by doing at the operational level, as contrasted to the more intensive use of specialized skills acquired from formal training. Within the government bureaucracy, a similar characteristic appears as a tendency toward jurisdictional autonomy (the so-called 'bottom-up' decision-making process).

2. *Semi-horizontal communications:* When problem solving must be dealt with co-jointly by multiple functional units, direct communication among the relevant units, without the clear direction of a common super-ordinate, is typical (for example, the 'kanban' system in the manufacturing process, the 'ringi' system in administrative organization, etc.).

Even when a superordinate does mediate, his role is more of an arbitrative than of a controlling nature. Politically the Japanese organization may appear as a coalition of semiautonomous component units rather than a coherent whole directed by the visible authority of the central office. According to Rosenberg and Aoki, such a mode of internal organization seems especially suitable to an "intermediate" type of environment:

In both these two contrasting cases [highly unstable or highly volatile environments], the H-mode may be superior in achieving the organizational goal. In the intermediate situation, however, where external environments are continually changing but not too drastically, the J-mode is superior. In this case, the information value created by learning and horizontal coordination at the operational level may more than compensate for the loss of efficiency due to the sacrifice of operational specialization.

3. *Ranking hierarchy:* If functional units are entrusted with semi-autonomous problem solving and semi-horizontal co-ordination responsibilities without clear

hierarchical direction, each of them may develop its own unit-specific interest and pursue that interest in ways that are inefficient from the point of view of the goals of the organization. As a safeguard against the emergence of such localized interests, and as an incentive for learning to enhance semi-autonomous problem-solving capabilities, the Japanese organization utilizes a ranking hierarchy. In both manufacturing and bureaucratic organizations, personnel (workers and bureaucrats) are ranked according to seniority and merit. . . . Personnel are evaluated by their contributions to collective, semi-autonomous problem solving, learning achievements, and ability to communicate with one another, rather than by some more abstract measure of their individual skills. Promotion often takes the form of transfer to other departments.

Aoki and Rosenberg call the mode of organization they attribute to Japanese firms the "J-mode"; its main features are (1) the horizontal coordination among operating units based on (2) the sharing of results learned on-site. That is, prior planning sets only the indicative framework of an operation. As new information becomes available to operating units during implementation (e.g., customers' orders at dealers, defects that become apparent at a workshop, engineering problems in a new product that become evident only at the plant site), prior plans may be modified. But in order for on-site information to be utilized in a way that is consistent with the organizational goal, adaptation must be coordinated among interrelated operating units.

In the J-mode, on-site information may be better utilized for the realization of organizational goals (more formally, one may say that the J-mode can generate information value by the use of *ex post* information). Such a gain, of course, is not without cost; economies of specialization of operational activities are sacrificed, as time and effort is expended in acquiring new information (i.e., learning) as well as in communicating and bargaining with other units. Such costs may be reduced by the development of information technology—hardware, software, and humanware. Therefore, the comparative advantages of the H-mode and the J-mode depend on such factors as the learning ability of personnel, the ease of communication among operating units, and the degree of economies of specialization with regard to the variety and volatility of market demand.

For one interesting difference between these two modes of internal organization with regard to their impact on industrial research, see D. E. Janfer, "When the Corporate Lab Goes to Japan: Companies Are Learning the Wisdom of Doing R & D in Japan," *New York Times,* 28 April 1991, sect. 3, pp. 1, 6:

> Sadaaki Nanai says it took him a while to realize that research and development work in Rochester, N.Y., where Eastman Kodak Company has its headquarters, is very different from research and development in Yokohama, the Japanese industrial center where he opened Kodak's new research laboratory two years ago.
>
> In Rochester, Kodak's top researchers rely heavily on technicians to perform much of the laboratory work, freeing scientists and engineers to think about the results. When the basic research is done, the work is turned over to a development team responsible for translating it into new Kodak products. Except in rare cases, Kodak's American researchers do not visit customers. "Rochester is discovery-driven," said Mr. Nanai, a veteran of the Citizen Watch Company and several other Japanese enterprises, of Kodak's American ways. "Visiting customers doesn't help you make discoveries."
>
> So the first thing Mr. Nanai and Tom Kelly, a veteran Kodak executive who is

head of research for the company's Japan operation, do when Japanese researchers come back from orientation trips to Rochester is to sit them down, ask them how they liked America and tell them to forget much of what they saw.

"They all come back wanting technicians, and we tell them, 'Absolutely not.'" The essence of research in Japan is to put your best people in the laboratory, where they can see the unexpected firsthand. We want them visiting customers all the time, so they can see what the market needs."

Mr. Nanai is trying an experiment in Yokahama that is still rare among American companies: to conduct serious research in Japan, Japanese-style, and then transfer the method back to the United States.

Among others trying the same experiment are large companies like International Business Machines, Hewlett-Packard and Texas Instruments, and smaller ones like the Dow Corning Corporation and Applied Materials Inc. It is a path fraught with friction—mostly between the established laboratories in the United States and the upstarts here—and frustration over high expenses and competition for talent, which often is gobbled up by Japanese competitors.

But the converts contend that in many technologies the center of gravity has moved across the Pacific, that not being here is a near-certain formula for being blindsided by new technologies and, soon after, the products that contain them.

Until just a few years ago, what most American companies called "research" in Japan was often the tailoring of existing products to fit the Japanese market—replacing a 120-volt transformer with a 100-volt one, moving a steering wheel or packaging products with instructions in Japanese. That is still the approach of most American companies, although it is one that increasingly looks shortsighted. "It presumes that the best technology is in the United States," says Nabuo Mii, a senior executive of I.B.M. Japan. "Often-times, that is not the case."

This year, Mr. Mii must prove his point. I.B.M. is moving much of its research and development for smaller systems, especially laptop computers and their components, to Japan. The move has provoked resentment in the company's laboratories in the United States, where the laptop machines, including a series of models introduced a month ago, were developed. But so many of the components come from Japan that I.B.M. decided the research should be based here, as well. The first product, a notebook computer that weighs five and a half pounds, came out last month.

See also Keitaro Hasegawa, *Japanese-Style Management: An Insider's Analysis* (Tokyo: Kodansha International, 1986); M. A. Cusumano, *The Japanese Automobile Industry: Technology and Management at Nissan and Toyota* (Cambridge, Mass.: Council on East Asian Studies, Harvard University Press, 1985); Iwata Ryushi, *Japanese-Style Management: Its Foundations and Prospects* (Tokyo: Asian Productivity Organization, 1982).

29. This description of the stages of Japanese economic development in the post–Second World War era follows D. Williams, *Japan: Beyond the End of History* (London: Routledge, 1994), 136.

30. Masumi Junnosuke, "The 1955 System: Origin and Transformation," in Kataoka, *Creating Single-Party Democracy*, 34–54.

31. T. J. Pempel, *Policy and Politics in Japan: Creative Conservatism* (Philadelphia: Temple University Press, 1982); see Aoki and Rosenberg, "The Japanese Firm as an Innovating Institution."

32. Aoki and Rosenberg, "The Japanese Firm as an Innovating Institution."

33. *OECD 1991–92 Economic Surveys, Japan* (Paris: Organization for

Economic Cooperation and Development, 1992), 106–10, 112–13. See also E. J. Lincoln, *Japan: Facing Economic Maturity* (Washington, D.C.: Brookings Institution, 1988).

34. R. Rubinger, "Continuity and Change in Mid-Nineteenth Century Japanese Education," in J. J. Shields (ed.), *Japanese Schooling* (University Park: Pennsylvania State University Press, 1990), 224–33, cited in Shields, introduction to part 3 of the same volume, 217. See also W. K. Cummings, *Education and Equality in Japan* (Princeton: Princeton University Press, 1980); H. Passin, *Japanese Education* (New York: Teachers College Press, 1970); idem, *Society and Education in Japan* (Los Angeles: Teachers College Press, 1967); Lauren J. Kotloff, "The Airplane Project: Fostering Individuality and Cooperative Group Norms in a Progressive Japanese Pre-School," paper presented at the ninth annual University of Pennsylvania Ethnography in Education Research conference; R. Lynn, *Educational Achievement in Japan: Lessons for the West* (London: Macmillan, 1988); Nagai Michio, *Higher Education in Japan: Its Take-Off and Crash,* J. Duseubury (trans.) (Tokyo: University of Tokyo Press, 1971).

For a positive assessment of Japanese education see Mery White, *The Japanese Educational Challenge: A Commitment to Children* (New York: Free Press, 1987); for the darker view, see K. Schoolland, *Shogun's Ghost: The Dark Side of Japanese Education* (New York: Bergin & Garvey, 1990).

35. J. J. Shields, Introduction to part 2, "Discontinuities in Moral Education and Educational Quality," in *idem, Japanese Schooling*, 99.

36. T. P. Rohlen, "Education and the Japanese Political Economy," in Kumon and Rosovsky, *Cultural and Social Dynamics.*

37. Rohlen, "Education and the Japanese Political Economy"; see also M. J. Bowman, *Educational Choice and Labor Markets in Japan* (Chicago: University of Chicago Press, 1981).

38. J. E. Rosenbaum and Kariya Takeaki, "From High School to Work: Market and Institutional Mechanism in Japan," *American Journal of Sociology* 94, no. 6 (May 1988): 1334–65; J. E. Thomas, *Making Japan Work: Origins, Education, and Training of the Japanese Salarymen* (Tokyo: Japanese Library, 1993).

39. Rohlen, "Education and the Japanese Political Economy."

40. J. J. Shields, Introduction, in *idem, Japanese Schooling*, 103–5.

41. For one report of such bullying to death of a schoolboy in Japan, see David E. Sanger, "Student's Killing Displays Dark Side of Japanese Schools," *New York Times*, 3 April 1993, 1.

42. K. Tominaga and D. J. Treiman, "Social Stratification Research in Japan and the United States," in *idem, More Alike Than Different: Social Stratification in Japan and the United States*, unpublished manuscript, February 1990; E. F. Vogel, *Japan's New Middle Class: The Salary Man and His Family in a Tokyo Suburb* (Berkeley: University of California Press, 1963); Kusaka Kimindo, "What Is the Japanese Middle Class?," 40–46, and Ozawa Masako, "Consumption in the Age of Stratification," 54–59, both in *Japan Echo* 12, no. 3 (autumn 1985); Taira Kōji, "The Middle Class in Japan and the United States," *Japan Echo* 6, no. 2 (1979): 18–28. See also Amano Ikuo, "The Bright and Dark Sides of Japanese Education," *Japan Foundation Newsletter* 19, nos. 5–6 (May 1992): 1–8; Schoolland, *Shogun's Ghost.*

43. Hiroshi Ishida, *Social Mobility in Contemporary Japan* (Stanford: Stanford University Press, 1993).
44. Ibid., 127–28.
45. Ibid., 236–37.
46. Ibid., 159–60.
47. Ibid., 237.
48. According to Hiroshi Ishida:

An important difference between the Japanese and American educational systems that is somewhat less equivocal is the fact that Japanese universities are more clearly organized into a national status hierarchy than are American universities. Access to promising careers in the national government, established corporations, the legal profession, the academic world, etc., is highly dependent on graduation from one of a handful of leading universities. For example, one quarter of the 24,500 section chiefs in the firms listed on the eight Japanese stock exchanges in 1976 were graduates of three of the several hundred Japanese universities—Waseda, Tokyo, and Keio; and another quarter were graduates of just seven institutions: Chuō, Kyoto, Nippon, Meiji, Tohoku, Osaka, and Kyushu. Consequently, competition to gain entrance to these universities and a small number of others that are nearly as prestigious is intense [even if this tendency has been weakened since the war]. . . .

. . . While there is certainly a status hierarchy among American universities, it is not nearly so unitary and hence competition is not so intense as in Japan. . . .

[Koike and Watanabe] note that the Japanese university system has been lately operating by creation of numerous provincial national universities, weakening, as [they] note, the propensity to draw the Japanese elite from a small number of universities which declined rapidly among cohorts entering elementary school after the war.

Yet it is doubtful whether these openings have changed the strong elitist orientation and tendency to creation of multiple status sets in Japan, although they have certainly created many new, more flexible such sets—as for instance those of the local elite who graduated from the local universities.

49. Tominaga and Treiman, "Social Stratification Research."
50. T. Bestor, *Neighborhood Tokyo* (Stanford: Stanford University Press, 1989); M. M. Hamabata, *The Crested Kimono: Power and Love in the Japanese Business Family* (Ithaca: Cornell University Press, 1990); D. Kondo, *Crafting Selves: Power, Gender, and Discourses of Identity in a Japanese Workplace* (Chicago: University of Chicago Press, 1990); I. Scheiner, "The Japanese Village Imagined, Real, Contested," unpublished manuscript.

51. Of some interest from this point of view is the analysis of what Regine Mattias Paueser called "reading for culture" in her essay "Reading for Culture and the Dawn of Mass Produced Literature in Germany and Japan in the Twentieth Century," in Tadao Umesao, Catherine C. Lewis, and Yasuyuki Kurita (eds.), *Japanese Civilization in the Modern World*, vol. 5, *Culturedness*, Senri Ethnological Studies no. 28 (Osaka: National Museum of Ethnology, 1990), 111–27. Paueser shows that while such reading was seen in Germany—following early Stände traditions—as part of distinct status, this was not the case in Japan. The more technocratic orientation of the Japanese educational system did not generate strong class relations between general mass reading and specific avenues of occupational advancement.

52. W. W. Kelly, "Directions in the Anthropology of Contemporary Japan," *Annual Review of Anthropology* 20 (1991): 395–431; W. W. Kelly, "Rationalization and Nostalgia: Cultural Dynamics of New Middle Class Japan," *American Ethnologist* 13, no. 4 (1986): 603–18; idem, "Japanese No-Noh: The Crosstalk of Public Culture in a Rural Festivity," *Public Culture* 2 (1990): 65–81; idem, "Regional Japan: The Price of Prosperity and the Benefits of Dependency," in *Shōwa, The Japan of Hirohito*, special issue of *Daedalus*, no. 119 (1990): 209–27; idem, "Finding a Place in Metropolitan Japan: Transpositions of Everyday Life," in A. Gordon (ed.), *Postwar Japan as History* (Berkeley: University of California Press, 1993); Hamabata, *The Crested Kimono*; Kondo, *Crafting Selves*; J. E. Robertson, "Japanese Farm Manuals: A Literature of Discovery," *Peasant Studies* 11, no. 3 (1984): 169–92; idem, "A Dialectic of Native and Newcomer: The Kodaira Citizen's Festival in Suburban Tokyo," *Anthropological Quarterly* 60, no. 3 (1987): 124–36; Bestor, *Neighborhood Tokyo*; E. Ben-Ari, *Changing Japanese Suburbia* (London: Kegan Paul International, 1993).

53. Bestor, *Neighborhood Tokyo*; Kelly, "Japanese No-Noh"; Robertson, "Japanese Farm Manuals"; idem, "Dialectic of Native and Newcomer."

54. Miyoshi Masao and H. D. Harootunian (eds.), "Postmodernism and Japan," special issue of *South Atlantic Quarterly* 87, no. 3 (Summer 1988).

55. T. Fujitake, *The Japanese Social Structure: Its Evolution in the Modern Century* (Tokyo: University of Tokyo Press, 1982); S. B. Hanley, "Symposium on Japanese Society," *Journal of Japanese Studies* 8, no. 1 (1982): 1–19; S. De-Roy, "How Others See Us, a One Class Society?" *Japan Quarterly* 26 (1979): 204–11; R. Steven, *Classes in Contemporary Japan* (New York: Cambridge University Press, 1983); review article by D. Plath, *Journal of Japanese Studies* 12, no. 1 (1986).

56. H. Kato, "Japanese Popular Culture Reconsidered," in R. G. Power and H. Kato (eds.), *Handbook of Japanese Popular Culture* (New York: Greenwood Press, 1989). See also B. Christopher, *The Japanese Mind* (Tokyo: Charles E. Turtle, 1983).

57. Ishida, *Social Mobility in Contemporary Japan*; see also Margaret A. McKean, "Equality," in T. Ishida and E. S. Krauss (eds.), *Democracy in Japan* (Pittsburgh: University of Pittsburgh Press, 1989). 220–25.

58. Kato, "Japanese Popular Culture Reconsidered," 314–15.

59. T. Sonoda, "The Decline of the Japanese Warrior Class, 1840–1880," *Nichibunken Japan Review* 1 (1990): 73–112; Bestor, *Neighborhood Tokyo*; Kelly, "Japanese No-Noh"; J. E. Robertson, *Native and Newcomer: Making and Remaking a Japanese City* (Berkeley: University of California Press, 1991). See also Kelly, "Regional Japan," 209–20.

60. A. Gordon, *Labor and Imperial Democracy in Prewar Japan* (Berkeley: University of California Press, 1991).

61. P. Herzog, *Japan's Pseudo-Democracy* (New York: New York University Press, 1993); see also the critical article by Ellis S. Krauss, *Journal of Japanese Studies* 20, no. 2 (1994): 578–82.

62. Harumi Befu and Manabe Kazufumi, "An Empirical Study of Nihonjinron: How Real Is the Myth?," *Kwansei Gakuin University Annual Studies* 36 (1981): 97–111; idem, "Nihonjinron: The Discussion and Confrontation of Cul-

tural Nationalism," *Kwansei Gakuin University Annual Studies* 40 (1991). See also Kosaku Yoshino, *Cultural Nationalism in Contemporary Japan* (London: Routledge, 1992).

63. T. Najita, "Presidential Address: Personal Reflections on Modernity and Modernization," *Journal of Asian Studies* 52, no. 4 (1993): 845–53.

64. M. Silverberg, "Constructing a New Cultural History of Prewar Japan," in M. Miyoshi and H. D. Harootunian (eds.), *Japan in the World* (Durham: Duke University Press, 1993), 115–43; see also J. Y. Tobin, "Introduction: Domesticating the West," in J. Y. Tobin (ed.), *Re-Made in Japan* (New Haven: Yale University Press, 1992), 1–42.

65. Kelly, "Japanese No-Noh"; Bestor, *Neighborhood Tokyo*; Robertson, "Dialectic of Native and Newcomer"; E. Ben-Ari, "Multiple Images of Japanese Society: Emerging Models and A Counter Modelism in Social Sciences," third meeting of the Japan Anthropology Workshop, Jerusalem, 1987; *idem, Changing Japanese Suburbia*; E. Ben-Ari, B. Moeran, and J. Valentine (eds.), *Unwrapping Japan: Society and Culture in Anthropological Perspectives* (Manchester: Manchester University Press, 1990), 221–34.

66. See Tobin, *Re-Made in Japan*.

67. S. Garon, "Rethinking Modernization and Modernity in Japanese History: A Focus on State-Society Relations," *Journal of Asian Studies* 53, no. 2 (May 1994), 346–66.

68. See H. Neill McFarland, *The Rush Hour of the Gods: A Study of New Religious Movements in Japan* (New York: Macmillan, 1967); Shigeyoshi Murakami, *Japanese Religion in the Modern Century* trans. H. Byron Earhart (Tokyo: University of Tokyo Press, 1983).

69. C. Blacker, "Millenarian Aspects of the New Religions in Japan," in D. Shively (ed.), *Tradition and Modernization in Japanese Culture* (Princeton: Princeton University Press, 1971), 597–98. For a general survey see *Japanese Religion: A Survey by the Agency for Cultural Affairs* (Tokyo: Kodansha International, 1972), esp. chaps. 5, 7, 8. See also James White, *The Sokagakkai and Mass Society* (Stanford: Stanford University Press, 1970); H. Hardacre, "Creating State Shinto: The Great Promulgation Campaign and the New Religions," *Journal of Japanese Studies* 12, no. 1 (winter 1986): 29–64.

70. H. Hardacre, *Kurozumikyō and the New Religions of Japan* (Princeton: Princeton University Press, 1986), 14; also *idem*, "The Impact of Fundamentalism on Women, the Family and Interpersonal Relations" (129–50) and "The New Religions, Family and Society in Japan" (294–312), in M. Marty and Scott P. Appleby (eds.), *Fundamentalism and Society* (Chicago: University of Chicago Press, 1983). See also Emily Groszos Ooms, "Women and Millenarian Protest in Meiji Japan: Deguchi Nao and Ōmotokyō," *East Asia Series* no. 61 (Ithaca: Cornell University, 1993); Brian McVeigh, "The Vitalistic Conception of Salvation as Expressed in Sūkyō Mahikari," *Japanese Journal of Religious Studies* 19, no. 1 (March 1992): 41–69.

71. Murakami, *Japanese Religion*.

72. W. Davis, *Dojo: Magic and Exorcism in Modern Japan* (Stanford: Stanford University Press, 1980). See also David Lewis, "Practical Religion in Japan: A Study of Two Urban Neighborhoods," doctoral thesis, University of

Manchester, Department of Social Anthropology, 1984, 851–52; Richard Fox Young, "Magic and Morality in Modern Japanese Exorcistic Technologies: A Study of Mahikari," *Japanese Journal of Religious Studies* 17, no. 1 (March 1990): 29–51; Shimazono Susumu, "Conversion Stories and Their Popularization in Japan's New Religions," *Japanese Journal of Religious Studies* 13, nos. 2–3 (1983): 157–76.

73. Ian Reader, "The Rise of a Japanese 'New New Religion': Themes in the Development of Agonshū," *Japanese Journal of Religious Studies* 15, no. 4 (December 1988): 235–63. See also Ashida Tetsurō, "The Festival and Religion Boom: Irony of the 'Age of the Heart,'" in *Nihonbunka-Kenkyūshō-Kiyō* (Tokyo: Institute for Japanese Culture and Classics, Kokugakuin University, March 1993), 1–30; Inoue Nobutaka (ed.), *New Religions: Contemporary Papers in Japanese Religion* (Tokyo: Institute for Japanese Culture and Classics, Kokugakuin University, 1991), especially Inoue Nobutaka, "Recent Trends in the Study of Japanese New Religions" (4–25) and Tsushima Michihito, "Emperor and World Renewal in the New Religions: The Case of Shinsei Ryujinkai" (58–93). See also T. M. Ludwig, "'New' Religions and Japanese Worldview," *History of Religions* 28, no. 4 (May 1989): 359–61; Komuro Naoki, "Japanese Buddhism and the Sōka Gakkai," *Japan Echo* 8, no. 2 (1981): 109–21.

74. See, for instance, K. van Wolferen, *The Enigma of Japanese Power* (New York: Knopf, 1989).

CHAPTER FOUR

1. For greater detail on the multiple patterns of modernity, see S. N. Eisenstadt (ed.), *Patterns of Modernity* (New York: New York University Press, 1987); *idem, A Dinâmica des Civilizaçoẽs: Tradição e Modernidade* (Lisbon: Ediçoẽs Cosmos, 1991).

2. A similar view is presented by Y. Sugimoto, "A Post-Modern Japan?," *Arena* 91 (1990): 48–59.

3. A. Gordon, *Labor and Imperial Democracy in Prewar Japan* (Berkeley: University of California Press, 1991); G. Totten, *The Social Democratic Movement in Prewar Japan* (New Haven: Yale University Press, 1966); J. Crump, *The Origins of Socialist Thought in Japan* (London: Croom Helm, 1983); R. W. Bowen, *Rebellion and Democracy in Meiji Japan* (Berkeley: University of California Press, 1980) B. S. Silberman and H. D. Harootunian (eds.), *Japan in Crisis: Essays on Taishō Democracy* (Princeton: Princeton University Press, 1974).

4. P. Duus, Introduction, in P. Duus (ed.), *The Cambridge History of Japan*, vol. 6 (Cambridge: Cambridge University Press, 1988), 36.

5. Taichirō Mitani, "The Establishment of Party Cabinets 1878–1932," in Duus, *Cambridge History of Japan*, 6:96.

6. R. Smethurst, *A Social Basis for Prewar Japanese Militarism* (Berkeley: University of California Press, 1974).

7. H. Wray and H. Conroy (eds.), *Japan Examined: Perspectives on Modern Japanese History* (Honolulu: University of Hawaii Press, 1983).

8. H. Smith, "The Non-Liberal Roots of Taishō Democracy," in Wray and Conroy, *Japan Examined*, 192.

9. P. Duus, *Party Rivalry and Political Change in Taishō Japan* (Cambridge, Mass.: Harvard University Press, 1968).

10. A. Barshay, "Imagining Democracy in Postwar Japan: Reflections on Maruyama Masao and Modernism," *Journal of Japanese Studies* 18, no. 2 (1992): 365–406.

11. P. Duus, "Liberal Intellectuals and Social Conflict in Taishō Japan," in T. Najita and J. V. Koschmann (eds.), *Conflict in Modern Japanese History: The Neglected Tradition* (Princeton: Princeton University Press, 1982), 412–40. See also J. Pierson, *Tokotomi Sohō, 1863–1957: A Journalist for Modern Japan* (Princeton: Princeton University Press, 1980); Atsuko Hirai, "Self Realization and Common Good: T. H. Green in Meiji Ethical Thought," *Journal of Japanese Studies* 5, no. 1 (1979): 107–36; T. Ishida, "The Introduction of Western Political Concepts into Japan: Non-Western Societies' Response to the Impact of the West," in *Wissenschaftskolleg Berlin Jahrbuch 1985–1986*, 1986.

12. G. Hoston, "The State, Modernity and the Fate of Liberalism in Prewar Japan," *Journal of Asian Studies* 51, no. 2 (1992): 309–10; idem, *Marxism and the Crisis of Development in Prewar Japan* (Princeton: Princeton University Press, 1986). See also S. Nolte, *Liberalism in Modern Japan* (Berkeley: University of California Press, 1987).

13. Duus, "Liberal Intellectuals and Social Conflict in Taishō Japan," 418.

14. For a picture of a more radical leftist intellectual, see P. Duus, "Ōyama Ikuo and the Search for Democracy," in J. Morley (ed.), *Dilemmas of Growth in Prewar Japan* (Princeton: Princeton University Press, 1971), 423–60; on a rightist nationalist see T. Najita, "Nakano Seigō and the Spirit of the Meiji Restoration in Twentieth-Century Japan," in the same volume, 375–423.

15. For the background of the period see Kozo Yamamura, "Then Came the Great Depression: Japan's Interwar Years," in H. van der Wee, *The Great Depression Revisited: Essays in the Economy of the Thirties* (The Hague: Nijhoff, 1979), 182–211.

16. For fuller details and a summary see Gordon, *Labor and Imperial Democracy.*

17. See Morley, *Dilemmas of Growth.*

18. G. McCormack, "1930s Japan: Fascist?," in R. Mouer and Y. Sugimoto (eds.), *Social Analysis*, nos. 5–6 (1980): 125–43; Nishikawa Masao and Miyachi Masato (eds.), *Japan zwischen den Kriegen: Eine Auswahl japanischer Forschungen zu Faschismus und Ultranationalismus* (Hamburg: Moag, 1990); S. Minichiello, *Retreat from Reform: Patterns of Political Behavior in Interwar Japan* (Honolulu: University of Hawaii Press, 1984).

19. McCormack, "1930s Japan."

20. G. Wilson (ed.), *Crisis Politics in Prewar Japan: Institutional and Ideological Problems of the 1930s* (Tokyo: Sophia University, 1970).

21. G. Berger, *Parties Out of Power in Japan: 1931–1941* (Princeton: Princeton University Press, 1977).

22. P. Duus and D. Okimoto, "Fascism and the History of Pre-War Japan: The Failure of the Concept," *Journal of Asian Studies* 39, no. 1 (1979): 65–76.

23. E. Tipton, "The Civil Police in the Suppression of the Prewar Japanese

Left," dissertation, University of Indiana, 1977; *idem, The Japanese Police State: The Tokkō in Interwar Japan* (Honolulu: University of Hawaii Press, 1990).

24. B. Shillony, "Traditional Constraint on Totalitarianism in Japan," in *Totalitarian Democracy,* an international colloquium, Jerusalem, 21–24 June 1982, Israel Academy of Sciences and Humanities (Jerusalem: Magnes Press, Hebrew University of Jerusalem, 1984), 158, 167.

25. H. Bix, "Rethinking 'Emperor-System Fascism': Ruptures and Continuities in Modern Japanese History," *Bulletin of Concerned Asian Scholars* 14, no. 2 (1988), 2–19; Kojima Noboru, "Militarism and the Emperor System," *Japan Interpreter* 8, no. 2 (1973), 219–27.

26. To quote Gordon

One scholar who has done an excellent job of defining fascism with such a strategy and using the concept in a comparative analysis of Italy, Germany, and Japan is Yamaguchi Yasushi. His 1979 book *Fascism* distinguishes fascist ideologies (*shisō*), movements (*undō*) and ruling systems (*taisei*), a term that encompasses both regime and program. He begins with movements and, of course, recognizes the differences between the two processes by which fascist systems have emerged. In Germany and Italy fascist party movements took power and created single-party regimes; in Japan radical reformers in the bureaucratic and military elites took political control, stimulated by the violent outbursts "from below" of the civilian and military right. Maruyama Masao has called this process "fascism from above," and Gregory Kasza has recently described it as an "administrative revolution."

Maruyama's classic argument, echoed by Yamaguchi, remains suggestive. He recognizes the importance of "the unprecedented advance of the labor movement" in Japan in the late 1920's and the "crisis in rural tenancy disputes," and he asserts that Marxism had a broad impact on Japanese society, beyond the "lecture platforms and journals" of the intellectuals. He then contends that the popular social movements of the left, of workers or farmers, in Japan, when contrasted to the tremendous force of the German communists and socialists or the Italian socialists, were relatively weak. This *relative* difference explains the variance between Japan's "fascism from above" and European "fascism from below": "the power of the mass-movement in Germany and even Italy . . . is the reason that popular bases had to be preserved to some extent in the fascist organization." Another way of putting this is to echo a point made in the introduction to this book: Japanese elites historically have had a comparatively low threshold for social crisis. This phenomenon deserves further study; it gives the trajectory traced here a particularly "Japanese" quality, but should not rule out comparative analysis. (Gordon, *Labor and Imperial Democracy in Prewar Japan,* 338–39.)

27. Ibid.

28. See also Takeshi Ishida, *Japanese Political Culture: Change and Continuity* (New Brunswick, N.J.: Transaction Books, 1983).

29. For a fuller presentation of her argument see P. Steinhoff, *Tenkō: Ideology and Societal Integration in Prewar Japan* (New York: Garland Publishing, 1991).

30. G. Hoston, "A 'Theology' of Liberation? Socialist Revolution and Spiritual Regeneration in Chinese and Japanese Marxism," in P. Cohen and M. Goldman (eds.), *Ideas across Cultures: Essays on Chinese Thought in Honor of Benjamin J. Schwartz* (Cambridge, Mass.: Council on East Asian Studies, Harvard University

Press, 1990). See also, for instance, F. Notehelfer, "On Idealism and Realism in the Thought of Okakura Tenshin," *Journal of Japanese Studies* 16, no. 2 (1990): 309–56; T. Najita, "Nakano Seigō and the Spirit of the Meiji Restoration in Twentieth-Century Japan"; J. Crowley, "Intellectuals as Visionaries of the New Asian Order," in Morley, *Dilemmas of Growth in Prewar Japan*, 319–75.

31. See, for instance, the discussion in Suzuki Takao, "Eine verschtsmene Sprache: Die Welt des Japanische," *Berliner Beiträge* (München: Iudicium Verlag, 1990), esp. the introduction by Irmela Hijiyan-Kirschenret, 9–29; "Sprache und Nation: Zur Aktueller Diskussion um der Sozialer Funktioner das japanischen," in *idem, Das Ende der Exotik: Zur Japanischen Kultur und Gesellschaft der Gegenwart* (Frankfurt: Suhrkamp, 1988), 62–98; R. Miller, *Japan's Modern Myth: The Language and Beyond* (New York: Weatherhill, 1982).

32. L. H. Gann, "Reflections on the Japanese and German Empires of World War II," Working paper in International Studies, Hoover Institution (Stanford: Stanford University, 1992).

33. Ibid.

34. J. Thomas, *Learning Democracy in Japan* (London: Sage Publications, 1985).

35. R. Ward and Sakamoto Yoshikazu (eds.), *Democratizing Japan* (Honolulu: University of Hawaii Press, 1987). But see also E. Tsurumi, Introduction, in her *The Other Japan: Postwar Realities* (New York: M. E. Sharpe, 1988); R. Finn, *Winners in Peace* (Berkeley: University of California Press, 1993).

36. Kyoko Inoue, *MacArthur's Japanese Constitution: A Linguistic and Cultural Study of Its Making* (Chicago: University of Chicago Press, 1991), 220.

37. R. Duus, "Bounded Democracy: Tradition and Politics in Modern Japan," unpublished article; Seizaburo Sato, "Institutionalization and Democracy in Japan," in S. Sato, R. Scalapino, and J. Wanadi (eds.), *Asian Political Institutionalization* (Berkeley: Institute of East Asian Studies, University of California, 1986), 95–115.

38. T. Havens, *Artist and Patron in Postwar Japan* (Princeton: Princeton University Press, 1982). See also R. Whiting, *The Chrysanthemum and the Bat* (Tokyo: Permanent Press, 1977).

39. H. Wakefield, *New Paths for Japan* (London: Royal Institute of International Affairs, 1948).

40. See Ikuo Kabashima, "Supportive Participation with Economic Growth: The Case of Japan," *World Politics* 36, no. 3 (1984): 309–38.

41. R. A. Scalapino, *The Early Japanese Labor Movement: Labor and Politics in a Developing Society* (Berkeley: Institute of East Asian Studies, University of California Press, 1983).

42. J. Livingston, J. Moore, and F. Oldfather (eds.), *Postwar Japan: 1945 to the Present* (New York: Random House, 1973).

43. W. Sombart, *Why Is There No Socialism in the United States?* (London: MacMillan, 1912; 1976).

44. H. Passin, *Encounter With Japan* (Tokyo: Kodansha International, 1982).

45. See Sakamoto Yoshikazu, *The Emperor System as a Japan Problem: The Case of Meiji Gakuin University*, International Peace Research Institute, Meigake (Prime), occasional papers, no. 5 (Yokohama: Meiji Gakuin University, 1989).

46. J. Koschmann, "Intellectuals and Politics," in A. Gordon (ed.), *Postwar Japan as History* (Berkeley: University of California Press, 1993), 395–423.

47. E. Krauss, *Japanese Radicals Revisited: Student Protest in Postwar Japan* (Berkeley: University of California Press, 1974); E. Krauss, K. Steiner, and S. Flanagan (eds.), *Political Opposition and Local Politics in Japan* (Princeton: Princeton University Press, 1980).

48. See in G. L. Bernstein (ed.), *Recreating Japanese Women, 1600–1945* (Berkeley: University of California Press, 1990), especially the following articles: L. Dasplica Rodd, "Yosano Akiko and the Taishō Debate over the 'New Women,'" 175–98; B. Molony, "Activism among Women in the Taishō Cotton Textile Industry," 217–38; M. Silverberg, "The Modern Girl as Militant," 239–60. See also G. Kasza, "The State and the Organization of Women in Prewar Japan," *Japan Foundation Newsletter* 18, no. 2 (1990): 9–13; V. Burkolter-Trachsel, *Different Modes of Articulation of Social Protest: Social Movements in Japan* (Kyoto: Kyoto International Student House, 1984).

49. For an overall survey see P. Steinhoff, "Protest and Democracy," in T. Ishida and E. S. Krauss (eds.), *Democracy in Japan* (Pittsburgh: University of Pittsburgh Press, 1989), 171–200.

50. T. Ishida, "Conflict and Its Accommodation: Omote-Ura and Uchi-Soto Relations," in E. Krauss, T. Rohlen, and P. Steinhoff (eds.), *Conflict in Japan* (Honolulu: University of Hawaii Press, 1984), 16–38.

51. B. Szajkowski (ed.), *Marxist Local Governments in Western Europe and Japan* (London: France Pinter, 1986); J. A. A. Stockwin, *Dynamic and Immobilist Politics in Japan* (Honolulu: University of Hawaii Press, 1989); *idem, The Japanese Socialist Party and Neutralism: A Study of a Political Party and Its Foreign Policy* (London: Melbourne University Press, 1968).

52. Kubota Akira, *Higher Civil Servants in Postwar Japan* (Princeton: Princeton University Press, 1969).

53. Gordon, *Labor and Imperial Democracy in Prewar Japan*.

54. W. Davis, "The Hollow Onion: The Secularization of Japanese Civil Religion," in Hiroshi Mannari and Harumi Befu (eds.), *The Challenge of Japan's Internationalization: Organization and Culture* (Tokyo: Kodansha International, 1984), 201–11; C. Gluck, *Japan's Modern Myths: Ideology in the Late Meiji Period* (Princeton: Princeton University Press, 1985).

CHAPTER FIVE

1. Iga Mamoru, *The Thorn in the Chrysanthemum: Suicide and Economic Success in Modern Japan* (Berkeley: University of California Press, 1986).

2. J. Pelzel, "Japanese Personality in Culture," *Culture, Medicine and Psychiatry* 1, no. 3 (1977), 299–315.

3. For a seemingly trivial but interesting case, see P. Noguchi, "Law, Custom and Morality in Japan: The Culture of Cheating on the Japanese National Railways," *Anthropological Quarterly* 52, no. 3 (1979), 165–77.

4. R. Thornton and K. Endo, *Preventing Crime in America and Japan* (Armonk, N.Y.: M. E. Sharpe, 1992).

5. R. Smith, Kumasaka Yorihiko, and Aiba Hitoshi, "Crimes in New York and

Tokyo: Sociocultural Perspectives," *Community Mental Health Journal* 11, no. 1 (1975), 19–26; S. Kinko, *Why Is There Less Crime in Japan?*, Orientation Seminars on Japan, no. 15 (Tokyo: Japan Foundation, Office of Japanese Studies, 1984).

6. P. Katzenstein and Y. Tsujinaka, *Defending the Japanese State* (Ithaca: Cornell University East Asia Program, 1991), 7–8.

7. D. Bayley, "Police, Crime and the Community in Japan," in G. De Vos (ed.), *Institutions for Change in Japanese Society* (Berkeley: University of California Press, 1984), 182.

8. W. Ames, *Police and Community in Japan* (Berkeley: University of California Press, 1981), 1.

9. D. Stark, "The Yakuza: Japanese Crime Incorporated," doctoral dissertation, Department of Anthropology, University of Michigan, 1981.

10. M. Pinguet, *Voluntary Death in Japan* (Cambridge: Basil Blackwell, 1993).

11. Y. Sugimoto and R. Mouer, *Images of Japanese Society* (London: Kegan Paul International, 1986).

12. E. Krauss, T. Rohlen, and P. Steinhoff (eds.), *Conflict in Japan* (Honolulu: University of Hawaii Press, 1984); V. Koschmann (ed.), *Authority and the Individual in Japan* (Tokyo: University of Tokyo, 1978); T. Najita and J. V. Koschmann (eds.), *Conflict in Modern Japanese History: The Neglected Tradition* (Princeton: Princeton University Press, 1982).

13. See Krauss, Rohlen, and Steinhoff, *Conflict in Japan;* Najita and Koschman, *Conflict in Modern Japanese History.*

14. Irokawa Daikichi, "Popular Movements in Modern Japanese History," in G. McCormack and Y. Sugimoto, *The Japanese Trajectory: Modernization and Beyond* (Cambridge: Cambridge University Press, 1988), 69–86.

15. Muramatsu Michio, "The Impact of Economic Growth Policies on Local Politics in Japan," *Asian Survey* 15, no. 9 (1975): 799–816.

16. J. Moore, *Japanese Workers and the Struggle for Power 1945–1947* (London: University of Wisconsin Press, 1983).

17. Katzenstein and Tsujinaka, *Defending the Japanese State.*

18. D. Pollack, *Reading against Culture* (Ithaca, N.Y.: Cornell University Press, 1993).

19. Pelzel, *Japanese Personality in Culture.*

20. G. De Vos, with contributions by Hiroshi Wagatsuma, William Caudill, and Keiichi Mizushima, *Socialization for Achievement: Essays on the Cultural Psychology of the Japanese* (Berkeley: University of California Press, 1973), esp. chaps. 1 and 5 and pt. 3. Doi T. has attempted to build on his earlier analysis of Japanese personality—especially the emphasis on dependence and the ability to move between *omote* and *ura* (inside and outside; see, for greater detail, chap. 13)—a general approach to the causes and symptomatology of personality disorders. For two critical evaluations, and to some extent extensions, of Doi's analysis of *amae,* see J. Pelzel, "Japanese Personality and Culture," *Culture, Medicine and Psychiatry* 1 (1977): 299–315; Hisa A. Kumagai, "A Dissection of Intimacy: A Study of 'Bipolar Posturing' in Japanese Social Interaction, Amaeru and Amayakasu, Indulgence and Deference," *Culture, Medicine and Psychiatry* 5 (1981): 249–72.

21. See D. Plath (ed.), *Adult Episodes in Japan* (London: E. J. Brill, 1975).

22. Teigo Yoshida, "Spirit Possession and Village Conflict," in Kraus, Rohlen, and Steinhoff, *Conflict in Japan*, 85–104.

23. J. Ramseyer, "Legal Rules in Repeated Deals: Banking in the Shadow of Defection in Japan," *Journal of Legal Studies* 20, no. 1 (1991): 91–117.

24. P. Steinhoff, "Hijackers, Bombers and Bank Robbers: Managerial Style in the Japanese Red Army," *Journal of Asian Studies* 48, no. 4 (1989): 738.

25. Stark, "The Yakuza."

26. See G. De Vos and Keiichi Mizushima, "Organization and Social Function of Japanese Gangs—Historical Developments and Modern Parallels," in R. P. Dore (ed.), *Aspects of Social Change in Modern Japan* (Princeton: Princeton University Press, 1967), 289–326.

27. Stark, "The Yakuza."

28. Thornton and Endo, *Preventing Crime in America and Japan.*

29. Stark, "The Yakuza."

30. I owe this observation to Ben-Ami Shillony (personal communication).

31. It is interesting to note that a new tax law pertaining to Yakuza members, while it greatly affects the gang system, at the same time attempts to incorporate and legitimize at least the Yakuza's money. (I owe this remark to Elizabeth McSweeney.) On the Yakuza's filling of artist's mediatory roles, see J. Raz, "Self-presentation and Performance in the *Yakuza* Way of Life: Fieldwork with a Japanese Underworld Group," in R. Goodman and K. Refsing (eds.), *Ideology and Practice in Modern Japan* (New York: Routledge, 1992), 210–34.

32. V. Burkolter-Trachsel, *Different Modes of Articulation of Social Protest: Social Movements in Japan* (Kyoto: Kyoto International Student House, 1984).

33. D. Apter and N. Sawa, *Against the State: Politics and Social Protest in Japan* (Cambridge, Mass.: Harvard University Press, 1984), 5.

34. Ibid., 237.

35. Ibid.

36. For a study of a different relatively broad—but basically apolitical—movement, see S. Large, "For Self and Society: Seno'o Giro and Buddhist in Post-War Japanese Peace," in McCormack and Sugimoto, *Japanese Trajectory*, 87–105; see also Oda Makoto, "The Ethics of Peace," in Koschmann, *Authority and the Individual in Japan*, 154–70.

37. *Japan Interpreter* 8, no. 3 (1973): 279–95.

38. J. White, "Protest and Change in Contemporary Japan: An Overview," in De Vos, *Institutions for Change in Japanese Society*, 53–82; F. Upham, "Litigation and Moral Consciousness in Japan: An Interpretative Analysis of Four Japanese Pollution Suits," *Law and Society Review* 10, no. 4 (1976): 579–620.

39. See, for instance, C. Turner, "Breaking the Silence: Consciousness, Commitment and Action in Japanese Unions," dissertation, Department of Anthropology, Stanford University, 1987.

40. Tani Satomi, "Japan Socialist Party before the Mid-1960s: An Analysis of Its Stagnation," Okayama University. Draft paper presented to the Conference on the 1955 System, Hoover Institution, March 1988; R. Boyd, "The Japanese Communist Party in Local Government," in B. Szajkowski (ed.), *Marxist Local Gov-*

ernments in Western Europe and Japan (London: France Printer, 1986), 173–97; Large, "For Self and Society"; J. Crump, *The Origins of Socialist Thought in Japan* (London: Croom Helm, 1983); G. Hoston, *Marxism and the Crisis of Development in Prewar Japan* (Princeton: Princeton University Press, 1986).

41. J. Broadbent and J. Kabashima, "Referent Pluralism: Mass Media and Politics in Japan," *Journal of Japanese Studies* 12, no. 2 (1986): 329–62; Szajkowski, *Marxist Local Governments in Western Europe and Japan*, 1–20.

42. T. Smith, "The Right to Benevolence," in *idem, Native Sources of Japanese Industrialization, 1750–1920* (Berkeley: University of California Press, 1988), 236–70.

43. W. Davis, *Japanese Religion and Society: Paradigms of Structure and Change* (Albany: State University of New York Press, 1992), 45–80.

44. Ibid. See also E. Krauss, *Japanese Radicals Revisited: Student Protest in Postwar Japan* (Berkeley: University of California Press, 1974).

45. Matsumoto Sannosuke notes in his essay "The Roots of Political Disillusionment: 'Public' and 'Private' in Japan," in Koschmann, *Authority and the Individual in Japan*, 36–37: "Post-war democracy was set in motion by Japan's externally imposed defeat in World War II, and the primary impetus for democratization was provided by the occupation policy of the Allied Powers. The actual process of democratization also bears the stamp of 'externality' and 'faith in institutions': legal and institutional reforms inevitably *preceded* the reform of values, social relationships, and political attitudes which logically should be primary. In other words, democratic systems were not allowed to originate in the democratic spirit of life of each individual and then be tested in the crucible of praxis."

46. E. Krauss, review of J. Koschmann, *Authority and the Individual in Japan, Journal of Japanese Studies* 7, no. 1 (1981): 167.

47. Maruyama Masao, *Studies in the Intellectual History of Tokugawa Japan* (Princeton: Princeton University Press, 1974); *idem, Thought and Behavior in Modern Japanese Politics* (London: Oxford University Press, 1963).

48. See Sonoda Hidehiro, "The Decline of Japanese Warrior Class, 1840–1880," *Japan Review* 1 (1990): 73–112.

49. Hoston, *Marxism and the Crisis of Development; idem,* "Ikkoku Shakaishugi: Sano Manabu and the Limits of Marxism as Cultural Criticism," in T. Rimer (ed.), *Culture and Identity* (Princeton: Princeton University Press, 1990).

50. See Pollack, *Reading against Culture;* J. A. Fujii, *Complicit Fictions: The Subject in the Modern Japanese Prose Narrative* (Berkeley: University of California Press, 1993).

51. M. Silverberg, *Changing Song: The Marxist Manifestos of Nakano Shigeharu* (Princeton: Princeton University Press, 1990).

52. H. Harootunian, "Disciplinizing Native Knowledge and Producing Place: Yanagita Kunio, Origuchi Shinobu, Takata Yasuma," in Rimer, *Culture and Identity;* Silverberg, *Changing Song;* A. Barshay, review of M. Silverberg, *Changing Song: The Marxist Manifestos of Nakano Shigeharu, Journal of Japanese Studies* 17, no. 2 (summer 1991): 475–81.

53. Rimer, *Culture and Identity.*

54. R. Matthew, *Japanese Science Fiction: A View of a Changing Society* (London: Oxford University Press, 1989).

55. For the explanation of this term, see chapter 13.

56. One of the most vivid descriptions of these tendencies has been given by Ian Buruma, possibly in an exaggerated way:

> The question is how does this soft, meek stereotype (like most stereotypes it has some truth in it) tally with the extreme violence that is such a predominant feature of popular culture? . . .
>
> Photographs of nude women trussed up in ropes appear regularly in mass circulation newspapers; torture scenes are common on television, even in children's programmes; glossy, poster-sized pictures of naked pre-pubescent girls are on display in the main shopping streets; sado-masochistic pornography is perused quite openly by a large number of men on their way to work on the subway.
>
> This is not to say that what is to be seen on the streets of Tokyo is any more *outre* than available merchandise in Times Square or Amsterdam; in fact it is less so, but what there is, is more openly accepted, more a part of the main-stream of life. There is no furtive huddling in dank little shops with darkened windows. People feel no need to pretend that sex and violence cater only to a sinful minority, because these fantasies are neither thought to be sinful, nor, quite evidently, are they confined to a minority. Otherwise, what would they be doing on national television and in weekly magazines? . . .
>
> So, although the Japanese can privately disagree, conflict is hidden behind a bland veil of politeness. When serious differences do come to the fore, they often lead to emotional crises ending in a complete rupture with the group. Harmony can at times be violently disturbed by bitterness and fisticuffs after simply bypassing the intermediate stage of rational debate. In short, consensus may often be a public facade, but then facade counts for a great deal in Japanese life. . . .
>
> Respect for human life, dignity, the female body, and all those other matters we are taught to take so seriously in the West, are taken seriously in Japan too, but not on the level of play. For, once again, it is not the overriding principle people adhere to, but the proper rules of conduct governing human relations. One has no relationship with an actress playing a part, or a character in a comic-book so why ever should one feel any compassion for them?
>
> If there were a universal moral principle, everything, in fantasy and reality, would have to be judged morally. Hence in the West a cartoon in a national newspaper of a woman tied up in ropes would be considered by many to be morally offensive. In Japan, even the most horrifying violence, as long as it is not real, can be judged purely aesthetically. This is even true when the violence depicted is based on a real event. . . .
>
> Encouraging people to act out their violent impulses in fantasy, while suppressing them in real life, is an effective way of preserving order. Vicarious crime is after all one of the functions of theater. As long as the *tatemae* of hierarchy, etiquette and propriety is upheld, the frustrated company man can look at pictures of tied-up women as much as he likes. . . .
>
> Popular fantasies of sex and violence are usually hysterical, too. They remind one of children screaming because they have no other way of expressing their needs. A scream, though, is normally a spontaneous action. Ritual screaming, naturally, is not. The bizarre excesses of Japanese popular culture are as bound by stylistic conventions as the tea ceremony, flower arranging and other aesthetic pastimes. Even play conforms to strict patterns. (Buruma, *Behind the Mask: On Sexual Demons,*

Sacred Mothers, Transvestites, Gangsters, and Other Japanese Cultural Heroes [New York: New American Library, 1984], 219–25.)

57. See M. Silverberg, "Constructing A New Cultural History of Prewar Japan," in M. Miyoshi and H. D. Harootunian (eds.), *Japan in the World* (Durham: Duke University Press, 1993): 115–43. See also M. Silverberg, "Constructing the Japanese Ethnography of Modernity," *Journal of Asian Studies* 51, no. 1 (1992): 30–54.

58. I. Morris, *The Nobility of Failure: The Tragic Heroes in the History of Japan* (New York: Holt, Rinehart and Winston, 1975).

59. G. De Vos, "Dimensions of the Self in Japanese Culture," in A. Marsella, G. De Vos, and F. Hsu (eds.), *Culture and Self: Asian and Western Perspectives* (New York: Tavistock, 1985), 141–84.

60. W. Kelly, "Directions in the Anthropology of Contemporary Japan," *Annual Review of Anthropology* 20 (1991): 395–431; E. Ohnuki-Tierney, *Illness and Culture in Contemporary Japan* (Cambridge: Cambridge University Press, 1984); E. Norbeck and M. Lock (eds.), *Health, Illness and Medical Care in Japan: Cultural and Social Dimensions* (Honolulu: University of Hawaii Press, 1987).

61. Pelzel, "Japanese Personality in Culture."

62. Kelly, "Directions in the Anthropology of Contemporary Japan," 420.

63. T. Lebra, "Self in Japanese Culture," in N. Rosenberg (ed.), *Japanese Sense of Self* (Cambridge: Cambridge University Press, 1992), 116.

64. M. Miura and H. Usa, "A Psychotherapy of Neurosis Morita Therapy," *Psychologia* 13, no. 1 (1970): 18–55.

65. Ibid.

66. For a more recent Japanese view of the Western cultural foundations of psychoanalysis, see Doi T., "The Cultural Assumption of Psychoanalysis," in J. Stigler, R. A. Schweder, and G. Herdt (eds.), *Cultural Psychology: Essays on Comparative Human Development* (Cambridge: Cambridge University Press, 1990), 446–53.

67. Takemoto Yasuniko, "Cultural Adaptation to Psychoanalysis in Japan 1912–1952," *Social Research* 57, no. 4 (winter 1990): 951–93.

68. D. Plath (ed.), *Work and Lifecourse in Japan* (Albany: State University of New York Press, 1983).

69. See also, for greater detail, T. Lebra, "Self-Reconstruction in Japanese Religious Psychotherapy," in A. Marsella and G. White (eds.), *Cultural Conceptions of Mental Health and Therapy* (Dordrecht: D. Reidel, 1984), 269–83.

70. Kelly, "Directions in the Anthropology of Contemporary Japan," 420.

71. J. Ramseyer, "Reluctant Litigant Revisited: Rationality and Disputes in Japan"; Thornton and Endo, *Preventing Crime in America and Japan;* see also Abe Haruo, "The Accused and Society: Therapeutic and Preventive Aspects of Criminal Justice in Japan," in A. T. Von Mehren (ed.), *Law in Japan: The Legal Order in a Changing Society* (Cambridge, Mass.: Harvard University Press, 1963), 324–63.

72. See, for instance, Nishi Toshio, *Unconditional Democracy: Education and Politics in Occupied Japan 1945–1952* (Stanford: Hoover Institute Press, Stanford University, 1982).

73. R. Mitchell, *Janus-Faced Justice: Political Criminals in Imperial Japan* (Honolulu: University of Hawaii Press, 1992).

74. Katzenstein and Tsujinaka, *Defending the Japanese State*, 133–34.

75. L. Parker Jr., *The Japanese Police System Today: An American Perspective* (Tokyo: Kodansha International, 1984).

76. Thornton and Endo, *Preventing Crime in America and Japan.*

77. Ibid.; Setsuo Miyazawa, *Policing in Japan: A Study in Making Crime* (Albany: State University of New York Press, 1992).

78. W. Clifford, *Crime Control in Japan* (Lexington, Mass.: D. C. Heath, 1976); *idem*, "The Development of Comparative Criminal Justice in the Asian Region," in B. J. George Jr. (ed.), *Criminal Justice in Asia: The Quest for an Integrated Approach* (Tokyo: United Nations Asia and Far East Institute for the Prevention of Crime and the Treatment of Offenders, 1982), 72–90; see also R. Smith, *Japanese Society: Tradition, Self, and the Social Order* (Cambridge: Cambridge University Press, 1983).

79. J. Braithwaite, *Crime, Shame and Reintegration* (Cambridge: Cambridge University Press, 1989). See also Nicholas D. Kristof, "Japanese Say No Crime: Tough Methods, at a Price," *New York Times* 14 May 1995, 1, 4.

80. J. Haley, "The Politics of Informal Justice: The Japanese Experience, 1922–1942," in R. Abel (ed.), *The Politics of Informal Justice* (New York: Academic Press, 1982), 2:125–47; Smith, *Japanese Society*, chap. 2; E. Krauss, T. Rohlen, and P. Steinhoff, "Introduction: Conflict—An Approach to the Study of Japan," in Krauss, Rohlen, and Steinhoff, *Conflict in Japan*, 10–11.

81. Ramseyer, "Reluctant Litigant Revisited."

82. E. Krauss, T. Rohlen, and P. Steinhoff, "Conflict and Its Resolution in Post-War Japan," in Krauss, Rohlen, and Steinhoff, *Conflict in Japan*, 390.

83. See T. Ishida, "Conflict and Its Accommodation: Omote-Ura and Uchi-Soto Relations," in Krauss, Rohlen, and Steinhoff, *Conflict in Japan*, 16–38.

84. S. Pharr, *Losing Face: Status Politics in Japan* (Berkeley: University of California Press, 1990), 35–37; quoted text italicized in original.

85. Ibid.

86. See B. Silberman, review of S. Pharr, *Losing Face*, *American Political Science Review* 85, no. 2 (June 1991): 599.

87. J. Haley, *Authority without Power: Law and the Japanese Paradox* (New York: Oxford University Press, 1991).

88. Ramseyer, "Reluctant Litigant Revisited"; Wada Hideo, "The Administrative Court under the Meiji Constitution," *Law in Japan* 10 (1977): 1–64; Yamanoguchi Kazuo, "Administrative Guidance and the Rule of Law," *Law in Japan* 7 (1974): 22–33; Sanekata Kenji, "Administrative Guidance and the Antimonopoly Law: Another View of the Oil Cartel Criminal Decisions," *Law in Japan* 15 (1982): 95–98.

89. R. Minear, "Nishi Amane and the Reception of Western Law in Japan," *Monumenta Nipponica* 28, no. 2 (1973): 151–75; C. Steenstrup, "German Reception of Roman Law and Japanese Reception of German Law," *Intercultural Communication Studies* 1, no. 1 (1991): 273–93; Von Mehren, *Law in Japan.*

90. Haley, *Authority without Power.*

91. Ibid.; Von Mehren, *Law in Japan*; Ito Masami, "The Rule of Law: Con-

stitutional Development," in Von Mehren, *Law in Japan*, 205–38; Sato Isao, "Debate on Constitutional Amendment: Origins and Status," *Law in Japan* 12 (1979): 1–22.

92. Haley, *Authority without Power*.

93. For an earlier exposition see R. Rabinowitz, "The Historical Development of the Japanese Bar," *Harvard Law Review* 70 (1956–57): 61–81.

94. F. Upham, *Law and Social Change in Postwar Japan* (Cambridge, Mass.: Harvard University Press, 1987); J. Haley, "Sheathing the Sword of Justice in Japan: An Essay on Law without Sanctions," *Journal of Japanese Studies* 8, no. 2 (1982): 265–82.

95. Upham, *Law and Social Change in Postwar Japan*, 207–8.

96. L. Hamilton and J. Sanders, *Everyday Justice: Responsibility and the Individual in Japan and the United States* (New Haven: Yale University Press, 1992), 134.

97. D. F. Henderson, *Conciliation and Japanese Law: Tokugawa and Modern*, 2 vols. (Seattle: University of Washington Press, 1965).

98. Takeyoshi Kawashima, "Dispute Resolution in Contemporary Japan," in Von Mehren, *Law in Japan*, 41–72.

99. Ramseyer, "Reluctant Litigant Revisited."

100. See, for instance, T. Bryant, "Marital Dissolution in Japan: Legal Obstacles and Their Impact," *Law in Japan* 17 (1984): 73–97. See also T. Bryant, "'Responsible' Husbands, 'Recalcitrant' Wives, Retributive Judges: Judicial Management of Contested Divorce in Japan," *Journal of Japanese Studies* 18, no. 2 (summer 1992): 407–44; Yoshikawa Seiichi, "The Judge's Power to Propose Terms for Settlement: The S.M.O.N. Case," *Law in Japan* 11 (1978): 76–90.

101. Hirano Ryuichi, "The Accused and Society: Some Aspects of Japanese Criminal Law," in Von Mehren, *Law in Japan*, 274–98; see also, in the same volume, Nagashima Atsushi, "The Accused and Society: The Administration of Criminal Justice in Japan," 297–323.

102. H. Wagatsuma and A. Rosset, "The Implications of Apology: Law and Culture in Japan and the United States," *Law and Society Review* 20, no. 4 (1986): 461–98.

103. Von Mehren, *Law in Japan*.

104. Hashimoto Kiminobu, "The Rule of Law: Some Aspects of Judicial Review of Administrative Action," in Von Mehren, *Law in Japan*; Fujikura Koichiro, "A Comparative View of Legal Culture in Japan and the United States," *Law in Japan* 16 (1983): 129–34.

105. Itoh Hiroshi and L. Beer, *The Constitutional Case Law of Japan: Selected Supreme Court Decisions, 1961–1970* (Seattle: University of Washington Press, 1978); Shuzo Hayashi, "Supreme Court Rulings on Constitutional Issues," *Japan Echo* 5, no. 3 (1978): 17–30; J. Maki, *Court and Constitution in Japan: Selected Supreme Court Decisions 1948–1960* (Seattle: University of Washington Press, 1964).

106. Bryant, "'Responsible' Husbands, 'Recalcitrant' Wives, Retributive Judges." See also Hashimoto "Rule of Law."

107. Takeyoshi Kawashima, "Dispute Resolution in Contempary Japan," 41–72.

108. J. Haley, "Comment: The Implications of Apology," *Law and Society Review* 20, no. 4 (1986): 499–508.

109. Minear, "Nishi Amane and the Reception of Western Law in Japan."

110. Wagatsuma and Rosset, "Implications of Apology," 492–95. John C. Haley in his comments on this article extends the argument of Wagatsuma and Rosset to a comparison with China: "There is a pervasive emphasis on confession throughout East Asia. . . . In contemporary China, as in Japan, it is used to correct behavior. But Chinese procurators visiting Japan share the surprise of their American and European counterparts in finding that in Japan confession elicits suspended prosecution or sentences, not simply a lighter penalty. The [Japanese] pattern of confession, repentance, and absolution thus appears to be as alien to Chinese criminal justice as it is in the West" (J. Haley, "Comment: The Implications of Apology," *Law and Society Review* 20, no. 4 [1986]: 501–2).

Similarly, J. Mark Ramseyer has analyzed the limited scope of antitrust enforcement in Japan.

111. Pharr, *Losing Face*.

112. Maruyama Masao, *Chūsei to hangyaku: tenkeiki Nihon no seishinshiteki iso* (Loyalty and Revolt: An Intellectual History of Japan's Modern Transformation) (Tokyo: Chikuma Shobo, 1992). See the review on the latest collection of Maruyama's essays in Japanese by Matsumoto Reiji, *Japan Foundation Newsletter* 21, no. 4 (1993): 16–19.

113. Thus, if the tendency toward different modes of deviant behavior is attributed to overwhelming pressures of the outer-oriented, disciplined *Ki* energy, the regulation of such behavior may entail the creation of outlets for the more inner-oriented, spontaneous expressions of *Ki* energy. But at the same time the movement between the different spaces that serve as outlets for the different types of *Ki* energy is structured within broader contextual frameworks, which encompass all of these arenas without granting any of them distinct, separate autonomy.

114. E. Ben-Ari, "Ritual Strikes, Ceremonial Slowdowns: Some Thoughts on the Management of Conflict in Large Japanese Enterprises," in S. N. Eisenstadt and E. Ben-Ari (eds.), *Japanese Models of Conflict Resolution* (London: Kegan Paul International, 1990), 95–123; E. Ben Ari, "Wrapping Up: Some General Implications," in E. Ben Ari, B. Moeran, and J. Valentine (eds.), *Unwrapping Japan: Society and Culture in Anthropological Perspectives* (Manchester: Manchester University Press, 1990), 221–34; E. Ben Ari, "At the Interstices: Drinking, Management, and Temporary Groups in a Local Japanese Organization," *Social Analysis*, no. 26 (December 1989), 46–69.

115. E. Hamaguchi (ed.), *Japanese Systems: An Alternative Civilization?*, Research Project Team for Japanese Systems, Masuda Foundation (Yokohama: Sekotac, 1992); Pharr, *Losing Face*.

116. H. Befu, private communication.

117. R. Wargo, "Japanese Ethic: Beyond Good and Evil," *Philosophy East and West* 40, no. 4 (1990): 499–511. See also K. Pyle, "Introduction: Japan Faces Her Future," 347–50, F. Notehelfer, "Japan's First Pollution Incident," 351–84, and A. Stone, "The Japanese Muckrakers," 385–408, all in "Symposium: The Ashio Copper Mine Pollution Incident," *Journal of Japanese Studies* 1, no. 2 (1975).

118. Setsuo Miyazawa, "Taking Kagashima Seriously: A Review of Japanese Research on Japanese Legal Consciousness and Disputing Behavior," *Law and Society Review* 21, no. 2 (1987): 219–42.

119. Ito Masami, "Rule of Law."

120. M. Hechter and Satoshi Kanazawa, "Group Solidarity and Social Order in Japan," *Journal of Theoretical Politics* 4 (1993): 455–93.

121. G. De Vos and Wagatsuma Hiroshi, *Japan's Invisible Race: Caste in Culture and Personality* (Berkeley: University of California Press, 1966).

122. See, for instance, "A Modest Proposal for a New Japan," editorial in *Wall Street Journal Europe*, 8 November 1933:

> We've written here recently about the problem of finding national leaders up to the task of governing in a world in which revolutions in telecommunications and trade simultaneously cause benefits and strains on political systems. One of the largest strains clearly is the clash of nationality groups as peoples, for all sorts of reasons, cross borders. Japan, an island, has an especially troubled history.
>
> Consider the following: An applicant who looks and speaks Japanese and whose family has lived in Japan for generations—let's call him Mr. Kono—applies for a job at a Tokyo blue-chip company. Things are going swimmingly, until the interviewer asks for his family registration. He can't produce one. The interview ends abruptly.
>
> Dejected, Mr. Kono walks home to his new flat, where a fine awaits because he has failed to inform the police that he has moved. Then his fiancee calls, and her family insists their engagement be broken because a private detective has discovered the awful truth behind his troubles: Mr. Kono is of Korean descent.
>
> Also, Mr. Kono cannot vote or join the civil service. He has to reapply for entry every time he leaves Japan; if he decides to become a Japanese citizen, there is no assurance he will be allowed to. The screening is ferocious, and everything from his taxes to his relations with his neighbors will be scrutinized.
>
> There are some 700,000 residents in Japan of Korean ethnicity, most of whom are descendants of laborers shipped over from then-colonized Korea to fill dirty jobs for the Japanese before and during World War II. They probably would have gone home if the Korean War had not quickly ensued, killing hundreds of thousands, cutting off the North and destroying the economy. So they stayed, but neither they nor their children, and now grandchildren, have ever been accepted as full members of Japanese society.
>
> To be sure, things have improved, marginally. As of this year, they no longer have to be fingerprinted, a particularly galling practice. (Like all non-Japanese permanent residents, who comprise just 1% of the population, they must still carry an alien Registration Card at all times.) Nor are they required any longer to assume a Japanese-sounding name when taking Japanese citizenship.
>
> Most fundamentally here, many Asians suspect Japan of suffering a deep-rooted superiority complex, a not very different mentality than the one that wrought Japanese imperialism earlier this century. We think that assessment is overblown, but acknowledge the bitter experience from which it is drawn. As a free, prosperous and vibrant society, Japan has much to be proud of. But there are dark shadows to Japan's success story, and its continued mistreatment of ethnic Koreans is the darkest of these.

123. Upham provides the following summary:

> Since the war, the annual rate of litigation has remained virtually stable at between 140 and 180 formal trials per 100,000 persons. To give this statistic some perspective, the number of trials commenced in all of Japan with 113 million inhabitants in 1970 was approximately 175,000; the number commenced in the American state of Ohio

with 10.6 million was 138,653 in 1970 (not including juvenile and probate cases). Nor is the contrast limited to the United States. Some sources indicate that the Danes sue approximately four times as often as the Japanese, the British three times, and the West Germans almost twice as often. . . .

. . . But such statistics can be exceedingly unreliable and deceiving. Definition problems abound, and many Westerners, especially Americans, must use courts for many matters such as divorces that are rarely handled legally in Japan. The situation is perhaps more effectively presented by the two studies of personal injury litigation in Japan in the 1940's. One investigated railroad accidents and discovered that of 145 accidents causing physical injury in which the given railroad was involved, not one case was brought to litigation and attorneys were involved in only two. Similarly a study of Tokyo taxicab companies showed that out of a total of 2,567 accidents causing either physical injury or property damage, only two cases were filed. (F. Upham, "Law in Japan," chap. 6 in B. Richardson and Taizo Ueda [eds.], *Business and Society in Japan* [Columbus, Ohio: East Asian Studies Program, Ohio State University, Praeger, 1972], 149–50.) See also Haley, *Authority Without Power.*

124. These numbers are to some extent deceptive, as the country has about "125,000 suppliers of legal services dealing with particular aspects of law, and in home corporate legal departments filled with law graduates who never bother to pass the bar exam" ("The Legal Profession," survey, *Economist*, 18 July 1992, 12); see also Hamilton and Sanders, *Everyday Justice*, 23. But the very fact that these suppliers of legal services are not deemed to be full lawyers attests to the distinctive structure of legal activities in Japan. See also Upham, *Law and Social Change in Postwar Japan*, 151.

125. J. Mark Ramseyer and Minoru Nakazato, "The Rational Litigant: Settlement Amounts and Verdict Rates in Japan," *Journal of Legal Studies* 18 (June 1989): 263–90.

126. J. Ramseyer and F. Rosenbluth, *Japan's Political Marketplace* (Cambridge, Mass.: Harvard University Press, 1993).

127. For trends in the occupational and educational status of women in Japan, see M. Brinton, "Gender Stratification in Contemporary Urban Japan," *American Sociological Review* 54 (1989): 549–64. For a more detailed analysis of women and the labor force, see chap. 6.

128. Matsuzawa Tessei, "Street Labor Markets, Day Laborers and the Structure of Oppression," in McCormack and Sugimoto, *Japanese Trajectory*, 147–65.

129. M. A. Cusumano, *The Japanese Automobile Industry: Technology and Management at Nissan and Toyota* (Cambridge, Mass.: Council on East Asian Studies, Harvard University Press, 1985), chap. 3; Andrew Gordon, *The Evolution of Labor Relations in Japan* (Cambridge, Mass.: Council on East Asian Studies, Harvard University Press, 1985), chap. 9.

CHAPTER SIX

1. J. White, "Protest and Change in Contemporary Japan: An Overview," 53–82, and E. Krauss, "Protest and Social Change: A Commentary," 166–73, both in G. De Vos (ed.), *Institutions for Change in Japanese Society* (Berkeley: University of California Press, 1984); Sugimoto Yoshio, *Popular Disturbance in Postwar Japan* (Hong Kong: Asian Research Service, 1981).

2. F. Upham, *Law and Social Change in Postwar Japan* (Cambridge, Mass.: Harvard University Press, 1987), 216.

3. S. Pharr, *Losing Face: Status Politics in Japan* (Berkeley: University of California Press, 1990).

4. White, "Protest and Change in Contemporary Japan: An Overview."

5. M. Reich, "Crisis and Routine: Pollution Reporting by the Japanese Press," in De Vos, *Institutions for Change in Japanese Society*, 148–65; M. McKean, *Environmental Protest and Citizen Politics in Japan* (Berkeley: University of California Press, 1981); G. Jost, "Some Reconsiderations Concerning the Political Function of Anti-Pollution Movements in Japan," in I. Nish and C. Dunn (eds.), *European Studies on Japan* (Kent: Paul Norbury Publications, 1979), 45–50.

6. S. Nolte, *Liberalism in Modern Japan* (Berkeley: University of California Press, 1987).

7. T. Rimer (ed.), *Culture and Identity* (Princeton: Princeton University Press, 1990); M. Nagai, "The Development of Intellectuals in the Meiji and Taishō Periods," *Journal of Social and Political Ideas in Japan* 2, no. 1 (1964): 28–32; L. Olson, "Intellectuals and 'The People': On Yoshimoto Takaaki," *Journal of Japanese Studies* 4, no. 2 (1978): 327–58; H. Passin, "Modernization and the Japanese Intellectual: Some Comparative Observations," in M. Jansen (ed.), *Changing Japanese Attitudes toward Modernization* (Princeton: Princeton University Press, 1965), chap. 12.

8. A. Gordon, *Labor and Imperial Democracy in Prewar Japan* (Berkeley: University of California Press, 1991).

9. Kusatsu Osamu and D. W. Collingwood, "Japanese Rastafarians: Non-Conformity in Modern Japan," unpublished paper, University of Chicago, Department of Sociology, 1991.

10. R. Goodman, *Japan's "International Youth": The Emergence of a New Class of Schoolchildren* (Oxford: Clarendon Press, 1990).

11. S. Linhart, "Some Observations on the Development of 'Typical' Japanese Attitudes towards Working Hours and Leisure," in J. Hendry (ed.), *Europe Interprets Japan* (Kent: Paul Norbury Publications, 1984), 207–14; idem, "From Industrial to Postindustrial Society: Changing in Japanese Leisure-Related Values and Behavior," *Journal of Japanese Studies* 14, no. 2 (1988): 271–308. See also G. McCormack, "The Price of Affluence: The Political Economy of Japanese Leisure," *New Left Review* 88 (1991): 121–34; E. Ben-Ari, "A Sports Day in Suburban Japan: Leisure, Artificial Communities and the Creation of Local Sentiments," 211–25, in J. Hendry and J. Webber (eds.), *Interpreting Japanese Society*, JASO Occasional Papers no. 5, (Oxford, 1986).

12. M. Brinton, *Women and the Economic Miracle: Gender and Work in Postwar Japan* (Berkeley: University of California Press, 1993); A. Lam, *Women and Japanese Management: Discrimination and Reform* (London: Routledge, 1992); J. Hunter (ed.), *Japanese Women Working* (London: Routledge, 1993). Additional material on the situations of women in Japan can be found in Michiko Naoi, "Women and Stratification: Framework and Ideas," *International Journal of Japanese Sociology*, no. 1 (1992): 47–60; M. Berger, "Japanese Women: Old Images and New Realities," *Japan Interpreter* 11, no. 1 (1976): 56–67; Ruth Linhart and Fleur Woss (eds.), *Nippon Neue Frauen* (Frankfurt: Rowohlt, 1990); idem,

Japan's Frauen Heute: Vom Stereotyp zur Wirklichkeit (Vienna: Literas Universitatsverlag, 1988); M. Brinton, "Christmas Cakes and Wedding Cakes: The Social Organization of Japanese Women's Life Course," in T. S. Lebra (ed.), *Japanese Social Organization* (Honolulu: University of Hawaii Press, 1992), 79–108; T. S. Lebra, "Autonomy through Interdependence: The Housewives' Labor Bank," *Japan Interpreter* 13, no. 1 (1980): 133–42; *idem*, "Japanese Women in Male Dominated Careers: Cultural Barriers and Accommodations for Sex-Role Transcendence," *Ethnology* 20, no. 4 (1981): 291–306; *idem*, "Japanese Women and Marital Strain," *Ethos* 6, no. 1 (1978): 22–41; *idem*, "Sex Equality for Japanese Women," *Japan Interpreter* 10, nos. 3–4 (1976): 284–95; J. Condon, *A Half Step Behind: Japanese Women of the '80s* (New York: Dodd Mead and Company, 1985).

13. Iwao Sumiko, "The Quiet Revolution: Japanese Women Today," *Japan Foundation Newsletter* 19, no. 3 (December 1991): 1–9; *idem*, *The Japanese Woman: Traditional Image and Changing Reality* (Cambridge, Mass.: Harvard University Press, 1993).

14. J. Lo, *Office Ladies, Factory Women: Life and Work at a Japanese Company* (London: East Gate Book, 1990).

15. Brinton, "Christmas Cakes and Wedding Cakes"; Iwao Sumiko, "The Quiet Revolution."

16. M. Hamabata, "Ethnographic Boundaries: Culture, Class and Sexuality in Tokyo," *Qualitative Sociology* 9, no. 4 (1986): 354–71; R. Smith, "Gender Inequality in Contemporary Japan," *Journal of Japanese Studies* 13, no. 1 (1987): 1–26.

17. Cited in *Nihon Keizai Shimbun*, 10 February 1993 (Heisei 5), 15. (I owe this reference to Elizabeth McSweeney.)

18. For an insightful analysis of the problem facing Japanese women, published in connection with the wedding of the crown prince to Owada Masako, a young diplomatic career woman, see David E. Sanger, "The Career and the Kimono," *New York Times Magazine*, 30 May 1993, 18 ff.

19. Kuniko Miyanaga, *Creative Edge*.

20. K. Calder, *Crisis and Compensation: Public Policy and Political Stability in Japan, 1949–1986* (Princeton: Princeton University Press, 1988); T. Pempel, "The Dilemma of Parliamentary Opposition in Japan," *Polity* 8, no. 1 (1975): 63–79; G. Allinson, "Citizenship, Fragmentation, and the Negotiated Polity," in G. Allinson and Yasunori Sone (eds.), *Political Dynamics in Contemporary Japan* (Ithaca: Cornell University Press, 1993), 17–49; D. Patterson, "Electoral Influence and Economic Policy: Political Origins of Financial Aid to Small Business in Japan," *Comparative Political Studies* 27, no. 3 (1994): 425–47.

21. Odawara Atsushi, "The Union of the LDP and the Bureaucracy," 68–75, and Michisada Hiroshi, "Pressure Groups in Japanese Politics," 61–67, both in *Japan Echo* 11, no. 4 (1984); M. Muramatsu and E. Krauss, "Bureaucrats and Politicians in Policymaking: The Case of Japan," *American Political Science Review* 78, no. 1 (1984): 126–46; Komiya Ryutaro, Okuno Masahiro, and Suzumura Kotaro (eds.), *Industrial Policy of Japan* (Tokyo: Academic Press, 1988).

22. Sasaki Takeshi, "Postwar Japanese Politics at a Turning Point," *Japan Foundation Newsletter* 18, nos. 5–6 (1991): 1–8.

23. Yasusuke Murakami and T. P. Rohlen, "Social-Exchange Aspects of the Japanese Political Economy: Culture, Efficiency, and Change," in S. Kumon and H. Rosovsky (eds.), *Cultural and Social Dynamics*, vol. 3 of Y. Murakami and H. T. Patrick (eds.), *The Political Economy of Japan* (Stanford: Stanford University Press, 1992), 63–108.

24. Allinson, "Citizenship, Fragmentation and the Negotiated Polity" (17–49), M. Muramatsu, "Patterned Pluralism under Challenge: the Policies of the 1980s" (50–71), and M. McKean, "State Strength and the Public Interest" (72–104), in Allinson and Sone, *Political Dynamics in Contemporary Japan*.

25. See Frank Schwartz, "Of Fairy Cloaks and Familiar Talks: The Politics of Consultation," in Allinson and Sone, *Political Dynamics in Contemporary Japan*, 217–42; T. Ishida, "Emerging or Eclipsing Citizenship? A Study of Changes in Political Attitudes in Postwar Japan," in Miyohei Shinohara (ed.), *Japan Developing Economies* (Tokyo: Institute of Asian Economic Affairs, 1967).

26. M. Peck, R. Levin, and Akira Goto, "Picking Losers: Public Policy toward Declining Industries in Japan," *Journal of Japanese Studies* 13, no. 1 (1987): 79–124; R. Cole, "Changing Labor Force Characteristics and Their Impact on Japanese Industrial Relations," in L. Austin (ed.), *Japan: The Paradox of Progress* (New Haven: Yale University Press, 1976), 165–214; S. Garon, *The State and Labor in Modern Japan* (Berkeley: University of California Press, 1987). On the processes leading to the development of distributive policies in the educational area, see E. James and G. Benjamin, *Public Policy and Private Education in Japan* (London: MacMillan, 1987), 146–49, 162–64, 166–79.

27. Allinson, "Citizenship, Fragmentation and the Negotiated Polity." See also Kabashima Ikuo and Jeffrey Broadbent, "Referent Pluralism: Mass Media and Politics in Japan," *Journal of Japanese Studies* 12, no. 2 (1986): 329–45.

28. For a very good analysis of such accommodative policies, see M. Mochizuki, *Managing and Influencing the Japanese Legislative Process: The Role of Parties and the National Diet*, doctoral thesis, Harvard University, 1982; E. Harari, *The Politics of Labor Legislation in Japan* (Berkeley: University of California Press, 1973); F. Valeo and C. Morrison (eds.), *The Japanese Diet and the U.S. Congress* (Boulder, Colo.: Westview Press, 1983).

29. Pempel elaborates on this process in the following way:

The alternative to such compromise however is direct confrontation. When a conservative proposal raises an ideological challenge, the most frequent reaction in the Diet is the introduction of a counterproposal or a nullifying amendment. The statistics above show that the chance of formal success for such action are almost nil; however their prime function is to become the focal point of a campaign to block passage of the government bill, or to make its passage as politically costly to the government as possible. Inside the Diet, the Opposition's aim is to reveal, through intensive (and rarely polite) questioning of government officials, any unsavory aspects of the government proposal with the intention of turning media and public opinion against the proposed action. Critical to this strategy is a continual campaign designed to manifest the "genuineness" of the Opposition's antagonism to the proposal; in effect it makes a public declaration that "We feel these actions would be so detrimental to the well-being of Japan, that we are willing to go even to these extreme lengths to alert everyone to their dangers and to prevent their passage." Even if the measure passes, such tactics make the government's "success" extremely costly in terms of the political resources it must muster to assure passage and of the other governmental proposals that must be delayed.

Such adamant opposition has frequently forced the withdrawal of government proposals. The Police Duties Bill of 1958, the Anti-Violence Bill of 1961, and the proposed electoral changes of 1956 are all good examples. . . .

. . . In less dramatic ways, the Opposition's uncompromising approach has also brought results. Protest has secured increased time for debate on many issues, giving the Opposition more opportunity to make its case to the public. Resignations have been forced, such as that of Nishimura Naomi, former Director-General of the Self-defense Forces, who complained publicly that the United Nations was a "rural credit association" and that its system of one vote per nation was unwise. At other times, the Opposition has delayed all policy-making activities with the result that even though the proposals under attack eventually passed unchanged, other less controversial legislation was postponed, thereby hindering overall governmental operations. . . .

. . . The Symbolic rewards of uncompromising opposition must also be recognized. Often procedural changes are made to placate Opposition forces. These often lack substantive implications, but reported as a "leftist" victory in the media, they gain exaggerated significance giving a *post hoc* justification to Opposition tactics; its public credibility is therefore enhanced. . . .

. . . Finally such tactics have long been recognized as quite effective in sustaining internal unity among the Japanese opposition parties; at times there is nothing like a rousing struggle to bring formerly lax members back to the fold. Therefore on numerous counts it is a mistake to suggest that the tactics of total opposition are futile. They do not always insure success, and often only a partial victory results, but they have succeeded sufficiently frequently in the past so as to convince many of their desirability for the future.

Either strategy, compromise or confrontation, gives the Opposition important influence on decision-making in Japan despite its limitations in the formal policy-making arenas.

Yet each approach also has disadvantages. Behind-the-scenes compromise is desirable only on non-ideological issues and rarely results in any public political acknowledgement for the influencer; indeed it frequently redounds to the political credit of the government. But resort to direct confrontation continually reinforces current images of the opposition parties as practitioners of opposition for its own sake. Although such tactics may appeal to ideological purists, they hardly attract the sympathies of the less committed; rather they reinforce the widespread impression of the Japanese left as unconcerned with "genuine" political problems. Confrontation used too frequently destroys the Opposition's credibility and thus can be extremely costly. Depending on the issue, Japan's Opposition parties have usually found themselves impaled on one or the other horn of this dilemma. (Pempel, "Dilemma of Parliamentary Opposition in Japan," 76–79.)

30. See Takako Kishima, *Political Life in Japan: Democracy in a Reversible World* (Princeton: Princeton University Press, 1991).

31. S. Flanagan, Shinsaku Kohei, Ichiro Miyake, B. Richardson, and Joji Watanuki (eds.), *The Japanese Voter* (New Haven: Yale University Press, 1991).

32. See J. White, "The Dynamics of Political Opposition," in A. Gordon (ed.), *Postwar Japan as History* (Berkeley: University of California Press, 1991), 424–48. See also Muramatsu M., "Center-Local Political Relations in Japan: A Lateral Competition Model," *Journal of Japanese Studies* 12, no. 2 (1986): 303–28. T. MacDougall, "Japanese Urban Local Politics: Toward a Viable Progressive Political

Opposition," in Austin, *Japan*, 31–56; M. Kimitada, "Toward a Rediscovery of Localism," *Japan Quarterly* 23, no. 1 (1976): 44–52; K. Steiner, E. Krauss, and S. Flanagan (eds.), *Political Opposition and Local Politics in Japan* (Princeton: Princeton University Press, 1980).

33. N. Field, *In the Realm of a Dying Emperor: A Portrait of Japan at Century's End* (New York: Pantheon, 1991).

34. S. Kumon, "Some Principles Governing the Thought and Behavior of Japanists (Contextualists)," *Journal of Japanese Studies* 8, no. 1 (1982): 5–28; J. Bachnik, "Time, Space and Person in Japanese Relationship," in Hendry and Webber, *Interpreting Japanese Society*, 49–57; J. Bachnik, "Kejime: Defining a Shifting Sense of Self in Multiple Organizational Modes," in Rosenberger, *Japanese Sense of Self* (Cambridge: Cambridge University Press, 1992), 152–72; J. Bachnik and C. Quinn Jr. (eds.), *Situated Meaning: Inside and Outside in Japanese Self, Society and Language* (Princeton: Princeton University Press, 1993). See also E. Hamaguchi, *Japanese Systems: An Alternative Civilization?*, Research Project Team for Japanese Systems, Masuda Foundation (Yokohama: Sekotac, 1992).

35. T. J. Pempel, "Japan and Sweden: Polarities of 'Responsible Capitalism,'" in D. A. Rustow and K. P. Erickson (eds.), *Comparative Political Dynamics: Global Research Perspectives* (New York: Harper Collins, 1991).

36. S. Garon, "Women's Groups and the Japanese State: Contending Approaches to Political Integration, 1890–1945," *Journal of Japanese Studies* 19, no. 1 (winter 1993): 5–43.

37. Pharr, *Losing Face*.

38. P. Steinhoff, "Protest and Democracy," in Ishida and Krauss, *Democracy in Japan*.

39. Some aspects of this success have been treated in, for instance, Hirose Michisada, "The Ingredients of LDP Success," *Japan Echo* 10, no. 2 (1983): 54–61; Satō Seizaburō, "Can Single Party Rule Endure?" *Japan Echo* 10, no. 4 (1983): 9–14; G. Curtis, *The Japanese Way of Politics* (New York: Columbia University Press, 1988); Ōtake Hideo, "Postwar Politics: Liberalism Versus Social Democracy," *Japan Echo* 10, no. 2 (1983): 43–54; Murakami Yasusuke, "The Age of New Middle Mass Politics: The Case of Japan," *Journal of Japanese Studies* 8, no. 1 (1982): 29–72.

40. E. Krauss and J. Pierre, "The Decline of Dominant Parties: Parliamentary Politics in Sweden and Japan in the 1970s," in T. Pempel (ed.), *Uncommon Democracies: The One-Party Dominant Regimes* (Ithaca, N.Y.: Cornell University Press, 1990).

41. T. Pempel, Conclusion, in Pempel, *Uncommon Democracies*, 351. See also G. Allinson, "Politics in Contemporary Japan: Pluralist Scholarship in the Conservative Era—A Review Article," *Journal of Asian Studies* 48, no. 2 (1989): 324–32; L. McSweeney: The Nature of Political Opposition in Japan," unpublished paper, University of Chicago, Department of Sociology, 1995.

42. See also K. Hayao, *The Japanese Prime Minister and Public Policy* (Pittsburgh: University of Pittsburgh Press, 1993).

43. K. van Wolferen, "Japan's Non-Revolution," *Foreign Affairs* 72, no. 4 (1993): 54–66.

44. J. A. A. Stockwin, *Dynamic and Immobilist Politics in Japan* (Honolulu: University of Hawaii Press, 1988). See also S. Reed, "Is Japanese Government Really Centralized?" *Journal of Japanese Studies* 8, no. 1 (1982): 133–64. See also C. Johnson, *Japan: Who Governs? The Rise of the Developmental State* (New York: Norton, 1985).

45. T. Ishida and E. S. Krauss (eds.), *Democracy in Japan* (Pittsburgh: University of Pittsburgh Press, 1989); T. Pempel, *Japanese Democracy: A Comparative Perspective* (Washington, D.C.: Woodrow Wilson Center Asia Program, no. 46, 1994).

46. See W. Kelly, "Directions in the Anthropology of Contemporary Japan," *Annual Review of Anthropology* 20 (1991): 395–431, for a list of some such "underdevelopments."

47. P. J. Herzog, *Japan's Pseudo-Democracy* (New York: New York University Press, 1993).

48. See, for instance, R. Steven, "Hybrid Constitutionalism in Prewar Japan," *Journal of Japanese Studies* 3, no. 1 (1977): 99–134.

49. Kelly, "Directions in the Anthropology of Contemporary Japan," 421–22.

50. See, for discussion of these aspects of the structuration of modernity in Japan, S. Garon, "Rethinking Modernization and Modernity in Japanese History: A Focus on State-Society Relations," *Journal of Asian Studies* 53, no. 2 (May 1994): 346–66. See also Marilyn Ivy, *Discourses of the Vanishing: Modernity, Phantasm, Japan* (Chicago: University of Chicago Press, 1995).

51. T. Havens, "Beyond Modernization: Society, Culture and the Underside of Japanese History," in H. Wray and H. Conroy (eds.), *Japan Examined: Perspectives on Modern Japanese History* (Honolulu: University of Hawaii Press, 1983), 45–47.

52. W. Kelly, "Rationalization and Nostalgia: Cultural Dynamics of New Middle Class Japan," *American Ethnologist* 13, no. 4 (1986): 603–18.

CHAPTER SEVEN

1. R. Coulborn (ed.), *Feudalism in History* (Princeton: Princeton University Press, 1956); O. Hintze, *Wesen und Verbreitung: Des Feudalismus, Sitzungsberichte der Preussischsen* (Berlin: Akademie der Wissenschaften Phil-Hist Klasse, 1929), 321–47; N. Keije, "Reflections on Recent Trends in Japan Historiography," *Journal of Japanese Studies* 10, no. 1 (1984): 167–83.

2. See A. Lewis, *Knights and Samurai: Feudalism in Northern France and Japan* (London: Temple Smith, 1974), passim. Those are the dates in Japan—others would apply in Europe. As we shall see in greater detail later on, an interesting controversy—which sheds light on some distinctive aspects of Japanese institutional history—developed among scholars with respect to whether the last, Tokugawa stage of Japanese premodern society was a feudal or an absolutist era. See Ishii Ryōsuke, "Japanese Feudalism," *Acta Asiatica* 35 (1978): 1–29; P. Duus, *Feudalism in Japan* (New York: Knopf, 1976), 71–73; K. A. Grossberg, "From Feudal Chieftain to Secular Monarchy," *Monumenta Nipponica* 31, no. 1 (1976): 29–49.

Some recent works have challenged the view that Japanese feudalism had begun already in the eleventh or twelfth century—that the courtiers competed with the warriors until the twelfth century. See Karl F. Friday, *Hired Swords: The Rise of Private Warrior Power in Early Japan* (Stanford: Stanford University Press, 1992). See also G. Cameron Hurst III, "The Structure of the Heian Court: Some Thoughts on the Nature of the Familial Authority in Heian Japan," in J. W. Hall and J. P. Mass (eds.), *Medieval Japan: Essays in Institutional History* (New Haven: Yale University Press, 1974), 39–59.

3. J. R. Stayer, "The Tokugawa Period and Japanese Feudalism," 3–14, and J. W. Hall, "Feudalism in Japan as Reassessment," 15–55, in J. W. Hall and M. B. Jansen (eds.), *Studies in the Institutional History of Early Modern Japan* (Princeton: Princeton University Press, 1968), 3–14; Duus, *Feudalism in Japan*: Hitomi Tonomura, *Community and Commerce in Late Medieval Japan: The Corporate Village of Tokuchin-ho* (Stanford: Stanford University Press, 1992).

4. M. Bloch, *La société féodale* (Paris: A. Michel, 1939). (*Feudal Society*, trans. L. A. Manyon [Chicago: University of Chicago Press, 1961].)

5. Hintze, *Wesen und Verbreitung*.

6. F. Jouon Des Longrais, *L'Est et l'Ouest: Institutions du Japon et de l'Occident comparées* (Paris: Maison Franco-Japonaise, 1958); Lewis, *Knights and Samurai*.

7. Coulborn, *Feudalism in History*; Duus, *Feudalism in Japan*.

8. J. Baechler, *The Origins of Capitalism* (Oxford: Blackwell, 1975).

9. Johann P. Arnason, "Paths to Modernity: The Peculiarities of Japanese Feudalism," in G. McCormack and Yoshio Sugimoto (eds.), *The Japanese Trajectory: Modernization and Beyond* (Cambridge: Cambridge University Press, 1988), 235–63.

10. Lewis, *Knights and Samurai*. See also J. P. Mass, *Antiquity and Anachronism in Japanese History* (Stanford: Stanford University Press, 1992).

11. Akio Yoshio, "The Kamakura Bakufu as a Legitimate Public Authority," *Acta Asiatica* 49 (1985): 15–33; J. P. Mass, *The Development of Kamakura Rule, 1180–1250* (Stanford: Stanford University Press, 1979); idem, *The Kamakura Bakufu: A Study in Documents* (Stanford: Stanford University Press, 1979), 127–56; J. P. Mass (ed.), *Court and Bakufu in Japan: Essays in Kamakura History* (New Haven: Yale University Press, 1974), especially the article by C. J. Kiley, "Imperial Court as an Authority in Kamakura Age," 29–44; J. P. Mass, *Lordship and Inheritance in Early Medieval Japan: A Study in the Kamakura Soryō System* (Stanford: Stanford University Press, 1989).

12. Bloch, *Feudal Society*; Nagahara Keiji, "The Lord-Vassal System and Public Authority (Kogi): The Case of Sengoku Daimyō," *Acta Asiatica* 49 (1985): 34–45; S. Gay, "The Kawashima: Warrior-Peasants of Medieval Japan," *Harvard Journal of Asiatic Studies* 46 (1986): 81–119; H. Iwasaki, "Portrait of a Daimyō: Comical Fiction by Matsudaira Sadanobu," *Monumenta Nipponica* 38, no. 1 (spring 1983): 1–148.

13. Duus, *Feudalism in Japan*, 71–73.

14. J. R. Stayer, Introduction in Hall and Jansen, *Studies in the Institutional History of Early Modern Japan*, 8; J. W. Hall, *Government and Local Power in Japan, 500–1700* (1966; Princeton: Princeton University Press, 1980); Hall and Mass, *Medieval Japan* (reviewed by Nagahara Keiji, *Journal of Japanese Studies*

1, no. 2 [1975]: 437–44); R. J. Miller, *Ancient Japanese Nobility* (Berkeley: University of California Press, 1971).

15. E. O. Reischauer, "Japanese Feudalism," in Coulborn, *Feudalism in History*, 26–48.

16. Duus, *Feudalism in Japan*.

17. C. J. Kiley, "Estate and Property in the Late Heian Period," in Hall and Mass, *Medieval Japan*, 109–26.

18. Bloch, *Feudal Society*, 552.

19. Stayer, "Tokugawa Period and Japanese Feudalism."

20. Stayer, Introduction, 5–7.

21. Hall, *Government and Local Power*, 41.

22. Mass, *Kamakura Bakufu*.

23. Akio, "Kamakura Bakufu"; Mass, *Kamakura Bakufu;* J. W. Hall and Toyoda Takashi (eds.), *Japan in the Muromachi Age* (Berkeley: University of California Press, 1977); K. A. Grossberg, *Japan's Renaissance: The Politics of the Muromachi Bakufu* (Cambridge, Mass.: Harvard University, East Asian Monographs, 1981); *idem*, "From Feudal Chieftain to Secular Monarchy"; *idem*, "Bakufu Buyōnin: The Size of the Lower Bureaucracy in Muromachi Japan," *Journal of Asian Studies* 35, no. 4 (1976): 651–54; P. B. Winterstein Jr., "The Early Muromachi Bakufu in Kyoto," in Hall and Mass, *Medieval Japan*, 201–9.

24. One of the best historical analyses of the *bakufu* in different periods of Japanese history is to be found in J. P. Mass and William B. Hauser (eds.), *The Bakufu in Japanese History* (Stanford: Stanford University Press, 1985).

25. Lewis, *Knights and Samurai*, 38.

26. K. Wildman Nakai, *Shogunal Politics* (Cambridge, Mass.: Council of East Asian Studies, Harvard University Press, 1988).

27. See George Elison, "Hideyoshi, the Bountiful Minister," in G. Elison and B. C. Smith (eds.), *Warlords, Artists and Commoners: Japan in the Sixteenth Century* (Honolulu: University of Hawaii Press, 1981), 223–44. See also the analysis in chap. 4.

28. Matthew V. Lamberti, "Tokugawa Nariaki and the Japanese Imperial Institution," *Harvard Journal of Asiatic Studies* 32 (1972): 97–123.

29. W. G. Runciman, *A Treatise on Social Theory* (Cambridge: Cambridge University Press, 1989), 2:374–79.

30. J. P. Arnason, "The Modern Constellation and the Japanese Enigma," *Thesis Eleven*, no. 17 (1987): 4–40.

31. Lewis, *Knights and Samurai*.

32. Coulborn, *Feudalism in History*.

33. Hall, *Government and Local Power*, 99–128.

34. J. P. Arnason, "Comparing Japan and the West: Prolegomena to a Research Programme," in L. Gule and O. Storebo (eds.), *Development and Modernity: Perspectives on Western Theories of Modernisation* (Bergen: Ariadne, 1993), 182.

35. J. W. Hall, "Rule by Status in Tokugawa Japan," *Journal of Japanese Studies* 1, no. 1 (autumn 1974): 39–50.

36. Hurst, "Structure of the Heian Court"; W. H. McCullough, "Japanese Marriage Institutions in the Heian Period," *Harvard Journal of Asiatic Studies* 27 (1967): 103–67.

37. Mass, *Development of Kamakura Rule.*

38. See also J. P. Mass's recent work, which shows it was in the Kamakura period that the system of primogeniture characteristic of the *ie* type of kinship was instituted. See Mass, *Lordship and Inheritance.*

39. Murakami Y., "'Ie Society as a Pattern of Civilization," *Journal of Japanese Studies* 10, no. 2 (1984): 279–363; J. W. Hall, "Reflections on Murakami Yasusuke's 'Ie Society as a Pattern of Civilization,'" *Journal of Japanese Studies* 11, no. 1 (1985): 47–56. For discussions of the "*ie* society thesis," see R. J. Smith, "A Pattern of Japanese Society: Ie Society or Acknowledgment of Interdependence," *Journal of Japanese Studies* 11, no. 1 (1985): 29–45. On the *ie* see also J. M. Bachnik, "Inside and Outside the Japanese Household (Ie): A Contextual Approach to Japanese Social Organization," doctoral thesis, Harvard University, Department of Anthropology, 1978; S. Kumon, Y. Murakami, and S. Sato, "Japan Viewed as Ie Society: Analysis of Japan's Modernisation Process," *Japan Echo* 3, no. 1 (1976): 16–36.

40. K. Asakawa, *The Early Institutional Life of Japan: A Study in the Reform of 645* A.D. (New York: Paragon, 1963).

CHAPTER EIGHT

1. J. Baechler, *The Origins of Capitalism* (Oxford: Blackwell, 1975); J. Baechler, J. A. Hall, and M. Mann (eds.), *Europe and the Rise of Capitalism* (Oxford: Basil Blackwell, 1988); Ishii Ryōsuke, "Japanese Feudalism," *Acta Asiatica* 35 (1978): 1–29. The exposition here is to a large extent based on S. N. Eisenstadt and A. Schachar, *Society, Culture and Urbanisation* (Newbury Park: Sage Publications, 1987), chap. 10, 241–77.

2. N. Gutschow, *Die Japanische Burgstadt* (Paderborn: Shoningh, 1976); Wakita H., "Cities in Medieval Japan," *Acta Asiatica* 44 (1983): 28–52.

3. P. Wheatley and T. See, *From Court to Capital: A Tentative Interpretation of the Origins of the Japanese Urban Tradition* (Chicago: University of Chicago Press, 1978); T. Yazaki, *Social Change and the City in Japan* (Tokyo: Japan Publications, 1968); T. Yazaki, *The Japanese City* (Tokyo: Japan Publishing Trading Co., 1963).

4. Wheatley and See, *From Court to Capital;* J. W. Hall, *Government and Local Power in Japan, 500–1700* (1966; Princeton: Princeton University Press, 1980); Wakita, "Cities in Medieval Japan."

5. J. W. Hall, *Japan: From Prehistory to Modern Times* (London: Weidenfeld & Nicolson, 1970), 132. See also H. Wakita and S. B. Hanley, "Dimensions of Development: Cities in Fifteenth and Sixteenth Century Japan," in J. W. Hall, K. Nagahara, and K. Yamamura (eds.), *Japan Before Tokugawa* (Princeton: Princeton University Press, 1981); J. McClain, *Kanazawa: A Seventeenth-Century Japanese Castle Town* (New Haven: Yale University Press, 1982); idem, "Castle Towns and Daimyō Authority: Kanazawa in the Years 1583–1630," *Journal of Japanese Studies* 6, no. 2 (1980): 267.

6. G. Rozman, *Urban Networks in Ch'ing China and Tokugawa Japan* (Princeton: Princeton University Press, 1973), 46; McClain, "Castle Towns"; *idem, Kanazawa;* J. W. Hall, "The Castle Town and Japan's Modern Urbaniza-

tion," *Far Eastern Quarterly* 15, no. 1 (1955): 37–56; R. J. Smith, "Pre-Industrial Urbanism in Japan: A Consideration of Multiple Traditions in Feudal Society," *Economic Development and Cultural Change* 9, no. 1 (1960): 241–57.

7. Hall, *Japan*, 132; McClain, "Castle Towns"; *idem, Kanazawa*, 267; Wakita and Hanley, "Dimensions of Development."

8. McClain, "Castle Towns"; *idem, Kanazawa*; Rozman, *Urban Networks*; Hall, "Castle Town"; A. Naito, "Planning and Development of Early Edo," *Japan Echo* 14 (1987): 30–38; W. Hauser, *Economic Institutional Change in Tokugawa Japan* (Cambridge: Cambridge University Press, 1974).

9. Rozman, *Urban Networks*; J. W. Hall, *Tanuma Okitsugu, 1719–1788: Forerunner of Modern Japan* (Cambridge, Mass.: Harvard University Press, 1955); *idem,* "Castle Town"; Hauser, *Economic Institutional Change*; McClain, *Kanazawa*; Smith, "Pre-Industrial Urbanism."

10. Rozman, *Urban Networks*.

11. E. O. Reischauer, *Japan*, 3d ed. (New York: Knopf, 1981), 97; Rozman, *Urban Networks*; Hall, "Castle Town"; E. Seidensticker, *Low City, High City: Tokyo from Edo to the Earthquake* (New York: Charles E. Tuttle, 1983).

12. Reischauer, *Japan*, 72; *idem, Japan, the Story of a Nation* (Tokyo: Tuttle, 1981), 72; D. V. Morris, "The City of Sakai and Urban Economy," in G. Elison and B. K. Smith (eds.), *Warlords, Artists and Commoners: Japan in the Sixteenth Century* (Honolulu: University of Hawaii Press, 1981).

13. Gutschow, *Die Japanische Burgstadt;* Hall, *Japan*, 123–24; McClain, "Castle Towns"; Rozman, *Urban Networks*, 39.

14. Hall, *Japan*, 123–24; Morris, "City of Sakai"; Rozman, *Urban Networks*, 39; Reischauer, *Japan, the Story of a Nation*, 72; Smith, "Pre-Industrial Urbanism."

15. P. F. Henderson, "The Evolution of the Tokugawa State," in J. W. Hall and M. B. Jansen (eds.), *Studies in the Institutional History of Early Modern Japan* (Princeton: Princeton University Press, 1968), 205; H. Befu, "Village Autonomy and Articulation with the State," in Hall and Jansen, *Studies in the Institutional History of Early Modern Japan*, 301–16; T. Yazaki, *Japanese City*; R. C. Smith (ed.), "City and Village in Japan," *Economic Development and Cultural Change* 9, no. 1, pt. 2 (October 1960); Miura Keiichi, "Village and Train in Medieval Japan," *Acta Asiatica* 44 (1983): 53–76.

16. Reischauer, *Japan*, 96; D. H. Shively, "Bakufu vs. Kabuki," in Hall and Jansen, *Studies in the Institutional History of Early Modern Japan*, 237, 180–81; Hall, *Japan*; R. J. Smith, "Small Families, Small Households and Residential Instability: Town and City in Pre-Modern Japan," in P. Laslett (ed.), *Household and Family in Past Time: Comparative Studies in the Size and Structure of the Domestic Bourgeois Time* (Cambridge: Cambridge University Press, 1972), 429–71; R. J. Smith, "The Domestic Cycle in Selected Commoner Families in Urban Japan, 1757–1858," *Journal of Family History* 3, no. 3 (1978) 219–35; Rozman, *Urban Networks*, 96.

17. Hall and Jansen, *Studies in the Institutional History of Early Modern Japan*, 180–81; Rozman, *Urban Networks*.

18. See R. Sieffert, "Bourgeois et Chōnin," in T. Umesao, H. A. Smith, Moriya Takeshi (eds.), *Japanese Civilization in the Modern World*, vol. 7, *Cities*

and Urbanization, Senri Ethnological Studies, no. 19 (Osaka: National Museum of Ethnology, 1986), 21–28; Hall and Jansen, *Studies in the Institutional History of Early Modern Japan,* 204; H. Webb, *The Japanese Imperial Institution in the Tokugawa Period* (New York: Columbia University Press, 1968).

19. Hall and Jansen, *Studies in the Institutional History of Early Modern Japan,* 205; D. F. Henderson, *Conciliation and Japanese Law: Tokugawa and Modern,* 2 vols., (Seattle: University of Washington Press, 1965).

20. C. Sheldon, "'Pre-Modern' Merchants and Modernization in Japan," *Modern Asian Studies* 5 (1971): 193–206; Reischauer, *Japan, the Story of a Nation,* 96; T. C. Smith, *The Agrarian Origins of Modern Japan* (Stanford: Stanford University Press, 1959); *idem, Native Sources of Japanese Industrialization, 1750–1920* (Berkeley: University of California Press, 1988).

21. Reischauer, *Japan,* 96; Hall, *Japan,* 237; H. D. Harootunian, "Late Tokugawa Culture and Thought", in M. Jansen (ed.), *The Cambridge History of Japan,* vol. 5, *The Nineteenth Century* (Cambridge: Cambridge University Press, 1989), 168–259.

22. T. Najita, *Visions of Virtue in Tokugawa Japan* (Chicago: University of Chicago Press, 1987); Smith, "Pre-Industrial Urbanism."

23. Sieffert, "Bourgeois et Chōnin."

CHAPTER NINE

1. A very forceful argument against the designation of the Tokugawa state as a feudal one (see note 3 below) is presented by Ishii Shiro—who observes that, being divorced from land, the aristocrats did not have the material means to oppose the shogun. Ishii Shiro, "Recht und Verfassung in Japan Während der Tokugawa-Zeit," in H. Helbig, *Beitrage Zur Wirtschafts und Sozialgeschichte des Mittelalters,* herausgegeben von K. Schultz (Cologne and Vienna: Bohlau Verlag, 1976), 322–38.

2. E. H. Norman, *Japan's Emergence as a Modern State* (New York: International Secretariat, Institute of Pacific Relations, 1940).

3. R. Reischauer, *Early Japanese History* (Gloucester: P. Smith, 1967); R. Coulborn (ed.), *Feudalism in History* (Princeton: Princeton University Press, 1956); E. Norman, "Andō Shōeki and the Anatomy of Japanese Feudalism," *Transactions of the Asiatic Society of Japan,* 3d ser., 2 (1949); Wakita Osamu, "The Emergence of the State in Sixteenth Century Japan: From Oda to Tokugawa," *Journal of Japanese Studies* 8, no. 2 (1982): 343–67.

4. P. Duus, *Feudalism in Japan* (New York: Knopf, 1976).

5. P. Anderson, *Lineages of the Absolutist State* (London: New Left Books, 1974).

6. For this line of argument see also G. Sansom, *A History of Japan, 1615–1867* (Stanford: Stanford University Press, 1958).

7. Umesao Tadao, "Leçons données au Collège de France, du 9 Mai 1984 au 16 Mai 1984," draft in print, courtesy of Mr. Umesao, lesson 3, "L'époque d'Edo: Une Monarchie absolue, Pax Tokugawana."

8. M. Birt and K. Yamamura, "Introduction to a Symposium on the Tran-

sition from Medieval to Early Modern Japan," *Journal of Japanese Studies* 12, no. 2 (1986): 233–36. For general surveys of the preceding periods see Kozo Yamamura (ed.), *The Cambridge History of Japan*, vol. 3, *Medieval Japan* (Cambridge: Cambridge University Press, 1990), and the very important view by C. Steenstrup, "The Middle Ages Survey'd," *Monumenta Nipponica* 46, no. 2 (1991): 237–52.

9. J. Hall, "Hideyoshi's Domestic Policies," 194–223, and J. Hall, K. Nagahara, and K. Yamamura, Introduction, 7–26, in J. W. Hall, Nagahara Keiji, and K. Yamamura (eds.), *Japan before Tokugawa* (Princeton: Princeton University Press, 1981).

10. Birt and Yamamura, "Introduction"; M. Birt, "Samurai in Passage: The Transformation of the Sixteenth Century Kantō," *Journal of Japanese Studies* 11, no. 2 (1985): 369–99.

11. Kozo Yamamura, "From Coins to Rice: Hypothesis on the Kandaka and Kokudaka Systems," *Journal of Japanese Studies* 14, no. 2 (1988): 341–67.

12. For detailed studies of the periods before the crystallization of the Tokugawa regime and the processes leading to unification, see Hall, Nagahara, and Yamamura, *Japan Before Tokugawa*; K. A. Grossberg, *Japan's Renaissance: The Politics of the Muromachi Bakufu* (Cambridge, Mass.: Harvard University Press, 1981); and G. Elison and B. C. Smith, *Warlords, Artists and Commoners: Japan in the Sixteenth Century* (Honolulu: University of Hawaii Press, 1981); M. Berry, *Hideyoshi* (Cambridge, Mass.: Harvard University Press, 1992); Sansom, *History of Japan*.

13. See H. Pauly, *Ikko-Ikki: Die Ikko Aufstände und ihre Entwickelung aus den Aufständen der bündischen Bauer und Provinzialen des Japanischen Mittelalters*, dissertation, University of Bonn, 1985; Katsumata Shizuo, "Ikki, Ligues, conjurations et révoltes dans la société médiévale japonaise, *Annales* 50, no. 2 (March–April 1995): 373–94.

14. M. Berry, "Public Peace and Public Attachment: The Goals and Conduct of Power in Early Modern Japan," *Journal of Japanese Studies* 12, no. 2 (1986): 237–39; C. Totman, *Politics in the Tokugawa Bakufu 1600–1843* (Cambridge, Mass.: Harvard University Press, 1967); R. Toby, *State and Diplomacy in Early Modern Japan: Asia in the Development of the Tokugawa Bakufu* (Princeton: Princeton University Press, 1984).

15. G. Elison, *Deus Destroyed: The Image of Christianity in Early Modern Japan* (Cambridge, Mass.: Harvard University Press, 1973); Hayao Kawai, "The Transformation of Biblical Myths in Japan," *Diogenes* 42/1, no. 165 (1994): 49–66.

16. G. Rozman, "Edo's Importance in Changing Tokugawa Society," *Journal of Japanese Studies* 1, no. 1 (1974): 91–112; D. Howell, "Ainu Ethnicity and the Boundaries of the Early Modern Japanese State," *Past and Present*, no. 142 (1994): 69–93; M. B. Jansen, *Japan and Its World* (Princeton: Princeton University Press, 1980). See also Amino Yoshihiko, "Les Japonais et la mer"; and Tanaka Yuko, "Le monde comme représentation symbolique: Le Japon de l'époque d'Edo et l'univers du mitate"—both in *Annales* 50, no. 2 (March–April 1995): 235–58 and 259–82.

17. J. White's description of the political system of Tokugawa brings out these combined characteristics very successfully; J. White, "State Building and Modernization: The Meiji Restoration," in G. Almond, S. Flanagan, and R. Mundt, *Crisis, Choice and Change: Historical Studies of Political Development* (Boston: Little, Brown, 1973), 503–5:

> Politically, Tokugawa Japan was subject to a centralized variation of feudalism known as the bakuhan system. Under the nominal authority of the Shogunate, the central Tokugawa government, were several hundred internally autonomous han, or fiefs. At the apex of the bakuhan system was the Shogun, or Barbarian-Subduing Generalissimo. Although nominally appointed by the emperor, the Shogun in fact controlled him; the emperor himself was kept secluded in Kyoto, away from the political arenas. At the heads of their respective fiefs were feudal lords (daimyō) in four broad classes: the related houses (shimpan) were branches of the Tokugawa family; the liege vassals (hatamoto and gokenin), who constituted most of the officials of the bakufu; the vassal lords (fudai); and the outside lords (tozama). . . .
>
> . . . With the internal autonomy of the fiefs and the attitudes of the related and outside lords toward the Shogunate, the centrifugal potential in the Tokugawa system was considerable. Moreover, the Shogunate could no longer depend on coercive power to hold the disintegrative and conflictual tendencies within the system in check. It had never penetrated Japanese society to any real depth nor controlled an economic base upon which a commanding coercive force might be founded. Shogunal military power depended upon a standing army of some 12,000 men (which could in theory be increased to 35,000 before levies upon the fiefs became necessary), but the effect of 250 years of unbroken peace upon this force may be imagined. In any case, the distribution of Japan's arable land between the Tokugawa family, its retainers, and the lords suggests that the economic foundation of the Shogunate could be overshadowed by any number of coalitions of lords, especially if divisions should arise in the ranks of the vassal lords.
>
> . . . Another regulatory agency, the metsuke or Inspectorate, spied intermittently upon the internal affairs of the fiefs, but never approximated a regular police force.
>
> . . . Although the Shogunate could not hope to survive through military means, four important stabilizing factors compensated for its weak coercive potential: the legitimacy of Tokugawa hegemony, the institutionalized regulation of the lords, ad hoc extractions from the fiefs, and the isolation of the fiefs from each other and the international environment. The Tokugawa enjoyed a legitimacy "of immense proportions"; they had ended decades of political chaos; they were appointed by the emperor; they had rewarded their allies after victory with lands and offices; and in a militarist culture they endeavored to protect the samurai social and political primacy. Legitimacy grew with time. Every peaceful generation strengthened the Tokugawa claim, and in the early nineteenth century, despite some intellectual schools that focused upon the throne, most political actors had no notions of any feasible or desirable alternative to the feudal system.
>
> Numerous institutional regulations and ad hoc extractions kept the lords in a weak military and economic position. The lords were forbidden to build fortifications or intermarry without Shogunal consent. They were required to spend alternate years in residence in Edo (the capital) and, when absent, to leave their families in Edo as hostages. The expenses incurred by the grandiose processions to and from Edo were a significant indirect extraction from the fiefs, keeping their finances below the point at which heavy military expenditures were feasible. In addition, although no regular levies were ever made, the fiefs were subject to extraordinary claims for services (such as disaster relief) or money (e.g., for reconstruction after fires), which

considerably strained tight fief finances. These measures were initially imposed under the shadow of Tokugawa armed force. Once in effect and buttressed by other factors, they continued in force for over two hundred years even though Shogunal military power declined.

Also, the Shogunal stability was ensured by the isolation of the fiefs. They were denied access to the emperor (the only alternative source of legitimate political power in Japan) by law and by a net of Shogunal officials in Kyoto. Contacts between the fiefs were also minimized. All roads led to Edo, which hampered interfief communication. Well into the nineteenth century Japan was composed of over two hundred domains, often geographically separated from one another by the fragmented Tokugawa lands and integrated only at the supra-fief level by the nominal Tokugawa overlord.

For a detailed exposition of the Tokugawa administration, see C. Totman, *Politics in the Tokugawa Bakufu*, 2d ed. (Berkeley: University of California Press, 1988).

18. J. Morris, "Hatamoto Rule: A Study of the Tokugawa Polity as a Seigneurial Rule," *Papers on Eastern Theory*, Australian National University, vol. 41, 1990.

19. See, for instance, M. Berry, "Public Official or Feudal Lord?" *Monumenta Nipponica* 36, no. 2 (1981): 187–95.

20. J. Hall, "Feudalism in Japan: A Reassessment," in J. W. Hall and M. B. Jansen, *Studies in the Institutional History of Early Modern Japan* (Princeton: Princeton University Press, 1968), 15–57.

21. H. Bolitho, *Treasures among Men: The Fudai Daimyō in Tokugawa Japan* (New Haven: Yale University Press, 1974).

22. See Berry, "Public Peace and Public Attachment"; J. White, "State Growth and Popular Protest in Tokugawa Japan," *Journal of Japanese Studies* 14 (1988): 1.

23. See M. Collcutt, "Bushido," *Kodansha Encyclopedia of Japan* (Tokyo: Kodansha International, 1983), 1:221–23.

24. Eiko Ikegami, *The Taming of the Samurai: Honorific Individualism and the Making of Modern Japan* (Cambridge, Mass.: Harvard University Press, 1995).

25. See Berry, "Public Peace and Public Attachment." See also Philip C. Brown's recent presentation of the theory that the Tokugawa regime was much less effective as a centralized power—even within the limits presented above—and that it might have exhibited some of the characteristics of the Geertzian "theater state"; Brown, *The Shogun's New Clothes: Image, "Reality" and the Political Authority of the Tokugawa Bakufu*, paper presented at the Washington and Southeast Region Japan Seminar, American University, 24 April 1992.

26. J. Haley, *Authority without Power: Law and the Japanese Paradox* (New York: Oxford University Press, 1991), chaps. 2 and 3; see also C. Steenstrup, *A History of Law in Japan until 1868* (Leiden: Brill, 1991), esp. chap. 4.

27. D. F. Henderson, "Evolution of Tokugawa Law", in Hall and Jansen, *Studies in the Institutional History of Early Modern Japan*, 210–11. See also Oishi Shinzaburō, "Pax Tokugawa," *Japanese Foundation Newsletter* 9, no. 1 (1981): 1–5; Hiramatsu Yoshiro, "Tokugawa Law," D. F. Henderson (trans.), *Law in Japan* 14 (1981): 1–48. Noda indicates in his discussion of Japanese law the relation of this concept of law to the basic characteristics of the feudal relations in Japan.

See Yoshiyuki Noda, *Introduction to Japanese Law* (Tokyo: University of Tokyo Press, 1976); idem, *Conciliation and Japanese Law in Tokugawa and Modern Japan* (Seattle: University of Washington Press, 1965); idem, *Village Contracts in Tokugawa Japan.*

28. Henderson, "Evolution of Tokugawa Law."

29. Ibid.

30. W. Coaldrake, "Edo Architecture and Tokugawa Law," *Monumenta Nipponica* 36, no. 3 (1981): 235–83; D. Shively, "Sumptuary Regulation and Status in Early Tokugawa Japan," *Journal of Asian Studies* 25 (1964–65): 123–64.

According to A. Walthall: "Fukaya Katsumi has defined the four central criteria of the status system: (1) It relied on an inherited social division of labor based on the concept of service (*yaku*) to the state; (2) it established vertical relationships within each status as well as between statuses, relationships marked by the opposing attitudes of respect and scorn; (3) it was used in an effort to perfect a thoroughgoing control over the personality of the ruled; (4) it provided the ruling class with an extra-economic means of coercion" (Walthall, *Peasant Uprisings in Japan* [Chicago: University of Chicago Press, 1991], 233). See also D. Howell, "Ainu Ethnicity." For an overall view, see J. W. Hall, "Rule by Status in Tokugawa Japan," *Journal of Japanese Studies* 1, no. 1 (autumn 1974): 39–50.

31. H. Bolitho, "Concrete Discourse, Manifest Metaphor, and the Tokugawa Intellectual Paradigm," *Monumenta Nipponica* 35, no. 1 (1980): 89–98.

32. Hall, Nagahara, and Yamamura, *Japan before Tokugawa.*

33. Katsumata Shizuo and M. Collcutt, "The Development of Sengoku Law," in Hall, Nagahara, and Yamamura, *Japan before Tokugawa*, 101–24.

34. Ibid., 119–23. See also Nagahara Keiji, "The Lord-Vassal System and Public Authority (Kōgi): The Case of the Sengoku Daimyō," *Acta Asiatica* 49 (1985): 34–45; Fujiki Hisashi and G. Elison, "The Political Posture of Oda Nobunaga," in Hall, Nagahara, and Yamamura, *Japan before Tokugawa*, 149–93.

35. Berry, "Public Peace and Public Attachment."

36. H. Ooms, "Neo-Confucianism and the Formation of Early Tokugawa Ideology: Contours of a Problem," in P. Nosco (ed.), *Confucianism and Tokugawa Culture* (Princeton: Princeton University Press, 1984), 27–61. See also Bolitho, "Concrete Discourse."

37. P. Nosco, "Introduction: Neo-Confucianism and Tokugawan Discourse— An Idea," in Nosco, *Confucianism and Tokugawa Culture*, 3–20; idem, *Remembering Paradise: Nativism and Nostalgia in Eighteenth-Century Japan* (Cambridge, Mass.: Council on East Asian Studies, Harvard University Press, 1990).

38. H. Bolitho, "The Tempō Crisis," in M. Jansen (ed.), *The Cambridge History of Japan*, vol. 5, *The Nineteenth Century* (Cambridge: Cambridge University Press, 1989), 116–67.

39. K. Wildman Nakai, "The Naturalization of Confucianism in Tokugawa Japan: The Problem of Sinocentrism," *Harvard Journal of Asiatic Studies* 40 (1980): 157–99; H. D. Harootunian, "The Functions of China in Tokugawa Thought," in A. Iriye (ed.), *The Chinese and the Japanese* (Princeton: Princeton University Press, 1980), 9–37.

40. H. Ooms, *Tokugawa Ideology: Early Constructs, 1570–1680* (Princeton: Princeton University Press, 1985). See also *idem, Charismatic Bureaucrat: A Political Biography of Matsudaira Sadanobu, 1758–1829* (Chicago: University of Chicago Press, 1975).

41. Ooms, "Neo-Confucianism."

42. See, for instance, J. Spae, *Shinto Man* (Tokyo: Oriens Institute for Religious Research, 1972); Nakai, "Naturalization of Confucianism."

43. D. Earl, *Emperor and Nation in Japan: Political Thinkers of the Tokugawa Period* (Seattle: University of Washington Press, 1964).

44. T. Fujitani, "Electronic Pageantry and Japan's 'Symbolic Emperor,'" *Journal of Asian Studies* 51, no. 4 (November 1992): 824–50.

45. See Chikamatsu Monzaemon, *The Battles of Coxinga,* trans. D. Keene (London: Taylor's Foreign Press, 1951).

46. See, for greater detail, Yamaguchi Masao, "La structure mythico-théatrale de la Royauté japonaise," *Esprit,* 1973, 337–39.

47. G. Elison, "Hideyoshi, The Bountiful Minister," in Elison and Smith, *Warlords, Artists and Commoners,* 223–44.

48. Michele Marra, *Representations of Power: The Literary Politics of Medieval Japan* (Honolulu: University of Hawaii Press, 1993), esp. chap. 3. See also Kitabatake Chikafusa, *Jinno Shōtōki,* trans. P. Varley as *Chronicle of Gods and Sovereigns* (New York: Columbia University Press, 1980).

49. The story of the "deification" is well presented in A. Sadler, *The Maker of Modern Japan: The Life of Shogun Tokugawa Ieyasu* (Rutland, Vt.: Charles Tuttle & Co., 1978). For a critical discussion, see W. Boot, "The Deification of Tokugawa Ieyasu," *Japan Foundation Newsletter* 11, no. 5 (1987): 10–13; Boot says that Ieyasu's deification was a traditional, if extreme "attempt to harness the divine powers of a divine ancestor to the protection of the fortunes of the lineage."

50. See Asao Naohiro with M. Jansen, "Shogun and Tennō," in Hall, Nagahara, and Yamamura, *Japan before Tokugawa,* 248–71; Katsumata and Collcutt, "Development of Sengoku Law," 101–25.

51. B. Wakabayashi, "In Name Only: Imperial Sovereignty in Early Modern Japan," *Journal of Japanese Studies* 17, no. 1 (1991): 39.

52. K. Wildman Nakai, *Shogunal Politics* (Cambridge, Mass.: Council on East Asian Studies, Harvard University, 1988), 338.

53. See Ooms, *Tokugawa Ideology,* and the review by K. Wildman Nakai, *Journal of Japanese Studies* 13, no. 1 (1987): 200–7, which disagrees with Ooms's view of this ideology as very tight and homogeneous and compares it with Watanabe's book on the reception of Sung concepts in Japan. See also Nosco, *Confucianism and Tokugawa Culture.*

54. See N. Elias, *The Civilizing Process* (New York: Horizon Books, 1982). For developments in the daimyō courts, see M. Collcutt, "Daimyō and Daimyō Culture," 1–46, and Shimizu Yoshiaki, "Daimyō Art," 47–52, in Shimizu Yoshiaki (ed.), *Japan: The Shaping of Daimyō Culture* (Washington, D.C.: National Gallery of Art, 1988); Collcutt, "Bushido." See also Ikegami, *Taming of the Samurai.*

55. See Collcutt, "Bushido."

56. J. P. Arnason, "Paths to Modernity: The Peculiarities of Japanese Feudalism," in G. McCormack and Y. Sugimoto (eds.), *The Japanese Trajectory: Modernization and Beyond* (Cambridge: Cambridge University Press, 1988).

57. For social and economic processes in the Tokugawa period, see S. Hanley and K. Yamamura, *Economic and Demographic Change in Pre-Industrial Japan 1600–1868* (Princeton: Princeton University Press, 1977); Sonoda Hidehiro, "The Decline of Japanese Warrior Class, 1840–1880," *Japan Review* 1 (1990): 73–112; R. Moore, "Samurai Discontent and Social Mobility in the Late Tokugawa Period," *Monumenta Nipponica* 24, nos. 1–2 (1979): 79–91; J. W. White, "Cycles and Repertoires of Popular Contention in Early Modern Japan," in M. Traugott (ed.), *Repertoires and Cycles of Collective Action* (Durham: Duke University Press, 1995).

58. Moore describes the situation as follows:

In sum, much of the samurai discontent in the nineteenth century can be traced directly to the failure of the system of hereditary status to provide security for the two large groups in the class. The middle ranks of *shi*, from which most of the chief administrators were drawn and which had formed the basis of the daimyō's power since the seventeenth century, feared the gradual erosion of their privileged positions. . . . The lower ranks enjoyed greater opportunity for promotion than did the middle *shi*. In a society which valued and rewarded individual ability and performance they might have been satisfied with their relatively frequent promotions, new responsibilities and stipends. But Tokugawa Japan was not such a society. . . . Income and position were still determined by birth, and hereditary membership in the elite samurai class was still the highest honor which the society could offer. (Moore, "Samurai Discontent," 79–91).

59. Torao Haraguchi, R. Sakai, Mitsugu Sakihara, Kazuko Yamada, and Masato Matsui (trans.), *The Status System and Social Organization of Satsuma: A Translation of the Shumon tefuda aratame jōmoku* (Honolulu: University of Hawaii Press, 1975).

60. R. Rubinger, *Private Academies of Tokugawa Japan* (Princeton: Princeton University Press, 1982). On education in the Tokugawa era, see R. Dore, *Education in Tokugawa Japan* (London: Routledge and Kegan Paul, 1964); T. Najita, *Visions of Virtue in Tokugawa Japan* (Chicago: University of Chicago Press, 1987); R. Backus, "The Relationship of Confucianism to the Tokugawa Bakufu as Revealed in the Kansei Educational Reform," *Harvard Journal of Asiatic Studies* 34 (1974): 97–162.

61. See J. White, "State Growth and Popular Protest in Tokugawa Japan," *Journal of Japanese Studies* 14, no. 1 (1988): 1–26.

62. J. V. Koschmann, *The Mito Ideology: Discourse, Reform and Insurrection in Late Tokugawa Japan, 1790–1864* (Berkeley: University of California Press, 1987); H. Harootunian, "Late Tokugawa Culture and Thought," in Jansen, *Cambridge History of Japan*, 5:168–259.

63. Rubinger, *Private Academies*; Najita, *Visions of Virtue*.

64. Harootunian, "Late Tokugawa Culture and Thought"; J. V. Koschmann, "Parts and Wholes," in J. Koschmann and T. Najita (eds.), *Conflict in Modern Japanese History* (Princeton: Princeton University Press, 1982), 441–48.

65. Koschmann, "Parts and Wholes," 446.

66. E. H. Norman, *Soldier and Peasant in Japan* (Westport: Greenwood Press,

1943); H. Borton, "Peasants' Uprising in Japan of the Tokugawa Period," *Transactions of the Asiatic Society of Japan*, 2d ser., 16, no. 1 (1938). For a somewhat later period, see Y. Sugimoto, "Structural Sources of Popular Revolts and the Tobaku Movement at the Time of the Meiji Restoration," *Journal of Asian Studies* 34, no. 4 (1975): 875–90.

67. T. Smith, *The Agrarian Origins of Modern Japan* (Stanford: Stanford University Press, 1959); *idem, Native Sources of Japanese Industrialization, 1750–1920* (Berkeley: University of California Press, 1988).

68. I. Scheiner, "Benevolent Lords and Honorable Peasants: Rebellion and Peasant Consciousness in Tokugawa Japan," in T. Najita and I. Scheiner (eds.), *Japanese Thought in the Tokugawa Period, 1600–1868, Methods and Metaphors* (Chicago: University of Chicago Press, 1978), 39–63.

69. H. Bix, *Peasant Protest in Japan 1590–1884* (New Haven: Yale University Press, 1986); W. Kelly, *Deference and Defiance in Nineteenth-Century Japan* (Princeton: Princeton University Press, 1985); S. Vlastos, *Peasant Protests and Uprisings in Tokugawa Japan* (Berkeley: University of California Press, 1986); Walthall, *Social Protest and Popular Culture in Eighteenth Century Japan;* S. Tozeran, "Takaino Village and the Nokano Uprising of 1871," doctoral thesis, Columbia University, 1987. See also Hashimoto Mitsuru, "The Social Background of Peasant Uprisings in Tokugawa Japan," in Najita and Koschmann, *Conflict in Modern Japanese History*, 145–63.

For a somewhat later period, see S. Vlastos, "Opposition Movements in Early Meiji, 1868–1885," in Jansen, *Cambridge History of Japan*, 5:369–431; A. Walthall, "Narratives of Peasant Uprisings in Japan," *Journal of Asian Studies* 42, no. 3 (1983): 571–87; R. Varner, "The Organized Peasant: The *Wakamonogumi* in the Edo Period," *Monumenta Nipponica* 32, no. 4 (1977): 459–83.

For more detailed analysis, see White, "State Growth and Popular Protest"; P. Sippel, "Popular Protest in Early Modern Japan: The Bushū Outburst," *Harvard Journal of Asiatic Studies* 37, no. 2 (1977): 273–322; Walthall, *Social Protest and Popular Culture in Eighteenth Century Japan*.

70. White, *State Growth and Popular Protest*.

71. Scheiner, "Benevolent Lords and Honorable Peasants."

72. T. Keirstead, "The Theater of Protest, Petitions, Oaths, and Rebellions in the Shōen," *Journal of Japanese Studies* 16, no. 2 (1990): 388; D. Davis, "Ikki in Late Medieval Japan," in J. W. Hall and J. P. Mass (eds.), *Medieval Japan: Essays in Institutional History* (New Haven: Yale University Press, 1974), 220–47. See also Sato Kazuhiko, " 'Des gens étranges a l'allure insolite': Contestation et valeurs nouvelles dans le Japon médiéval"; Yoshimi Shun'ya, "Les rituels politiques du Japon moderne: Tournées impériales et stratégies du regard dans le Japon de Meiji"; Katsumata Shizuo, "Ikki, Ligues, conjurations et révoltes dans la société médiévale japonaise"; and Fujiki Hisashi, "Le village et son seigneur (14e–16e siècles): Domination sur le terroir, autodéfense et justice"—all in *Annales* 50, no. 2 (March–April 1995): 307–40, 341–72, 373–94, and 395–420.

73. Scheiner, "Benevolent Lords and Honorable Peasants," 59.

74. Walthall, *Social Protest and Popular Culture in Eighteenth Century Japan; idem*, "Narratives of Peasant Uprisings in Japan"; *idem*, "Peripheries: Rural Culture in Tokugawa Japan," *Monumenta Nipponica* 39, no. 4 (1984): 371–92.

75. Bix, *Peasant Protest in Japan*.

76. Ibid.

77. J. White, "Scholarly Discourse and Peasant Discontent: Four Studies of Popular Contention in the Tokugawa Period," *Journal of Japanese Studies* 15, no. 1 (1989): 159–75.

78. J. White, *Ikki: Social Conflict and Political Protest in Early Modern Japan* (Ithaca: Cornell University Press, 1995).

79. Walthall, *Social Protest and Popular Culture in Eighteenth Century Japan; idem*, "Narratives of Peasant Uprisings in Japan"; *idem*, "Peripheries."

80. I. Morris, *The Nobility of Failure: Tragic Heroes in the History of Japan* (New York: Holt, Rinehart and Winston, 1975).

81. Harootunian, "Late Tokugawa Culture and Thought."

82. See, for greater detail, H. Harootunian, "Late Tokugawa Culture and Thought." See also Najita, *Visions of Virtue*.

83. K. Wildman Nakai, review of J. V. Koschmann, "The Mito Ideology: Discourse, Reform and Insurrection in Late Tokugawa Japan, 1790–1864," *Journal of Japanese Studies* 14, no. 2 (1988): 526–27; H. Webb, *The Japanese Imperial Institution in the Tokugawa Period* (New York: Columbia University Press, 1968). See also L. Antoni, "Kokuton, Das Nationalwesen als Japanische Utopia," *Saeculum* 38, no. 1 (1987): 266–83.

84. G. Wilson, "Pursuing the Millennium in the Meiji Restoration," in Koschmann and Najita, *Conflict in Modern Japanese History*, 176–96.

85. Koschmann, *Mito Ideology*, 9.

86. Ibid.

87. Najita, *Visions of Virtue; idem*, "Japan's Industrial Revolution: Historical Perspective," in M. Miyoshi and H. Harootunian (eds.), *Japan in the World* (Durham: Duke University Press, 1993), 13–30. See also C. Sheldon, "Merchants and Society in Tokugawa Japan," *Modern Asian Studies* 17, no. 3 (1983): 477–88.

88. Najita, "Japan's Industrial Revolution."

89. Harootunian, "Late Tokugawa Culture and Thought."

90. H. Harootunian, "Ideology as Conflict," in Najita and Koschmann, *Conflict in Modern Japanese History*, 25–61.

91. Nakai, review of Koschmann.

92. W. G. Beasley, "Politics and the Samurai Class Structure in Satsuma, 1858–1868," *Modern Asian Studies* 1, no. 1 (1967): 47–57. See also Al Craig's classical study *Choshū in the Meiji Restoration* (Cambridge, Mass.: Harvard University Press, 1961); Haraguchi et al., *Status System and Social Organization of Satsuma*.

93. J. Ramseyer, "Thrift and Diligence: House Codes of Tokugawa Merchant Families," *Monumenta Nipponica* 34, no. 2 (1979): 209–30; S. Crawcour, "Some Observations on Merchants, a Translation of Mitsui Takafusa's Chōnin Koken Roku," *Transactions of the Asiatic Society of Japan*, 3d ser., vol. 8 (Tokyo: Kenkyusha Printing Company, 1962): 1–139; Najita, *Visions of Virtue*.

94. B. Wakabayashi, *Anti-Foreignism and Western Learning in Early Modern Japan: The New Theses of 1825* (Cambridge, Mass.: Harvard University Press, 1991).

95. See T. Smith, "'Merit' as Ideology," in *idem, Native Sources of Japanese Industrialization* (Berkeley: University of California Press, 1988), 136–72; Sonoda Hidehiro, "Decline of Japanese Warrior Class"; Beasley, "Politics and the Samurai Class Structure."

96. On the liminal characteristics of the Mito movement, see also Koschmann and Najita, *Conflict in Modern Japanese History*, 441–48.

97. O. Statler, *Japanese Pilgrimage* (Tokyo: Charles Tuttle, 1983).

98. W. Davis, "Ittoen: The Myths and Rituals of Liminality," pts. 1–3, *History of Religions* 14, no. 4 (1975): 282–321. See also Koschmann, *Mito Ideology.*

99. Sonoda Hidehiro, "Decline of Japanese Warrior Class"; Moore, "Samurai Discontent and Social Mobility"; C. Totman, "Fudai Daimyō and the Collapse of the Tokugawa Bakufu," *Journal of Asian Studies* 34, no. 3 (1975): 581–92.

100. Earl, *Emperor and Nation in Japan;* T. Smith, *Political Change and Industrial Development in Japan: Government Enterprise 1868–1880* (Stanford: Stanford University Press, 1955).

101. Smith, *Native Sources of Japanese Industrialization.* See also C. Sheldon, "'Pre-Modern' Merchants and Modernization in Japan," *Modern Asian Studies* 5 (1971): 193–206; S. Crawcour, "The Tokugawa Period and Japan's Preparation for Modern Economic Growth," *Journal of Japanese Studies* 1, no. 1 (1974): 113–26.

102. Smith, *Native Sources of Japanese Industrialization;* Sheldon, "'Pre-Modern' Merchants and Modernization in Japan"; D. Henderson, "Contracts in Tokugawa Villages," *Journal of Japanese Studies* 1, no. 1 (1974): 51–90; W. Hauser, *Economic Institutional Change in Tokugawa Japan* (Cambridge: Cambridge University Press, 1974); Ramseyer, "Thrift and Diligence"; Crawcour, "Some Observations on Merchants"; *idem, Tokugawa Period.*

103. A. Gerschenkron, *Economic Backwardness in Historical Perspective* (Cambridge, Mass.: Harvard University Press, 1962), chap. 1.

CHAPTER TEN

1. H. Bechert and R. Gombrich (eds.), *The World of Buddhism: Buddhist Monks and Nuns in Society and Culture* (London: Thames and Hudson, 1991); M. Eder, "Geschichte der Japanischen Religion," *Asian Folklore Studies Monographs* 7, nos. 1–2 (1978); D. Matsunaga and A. Matsunaga, *Foundations of Japanese Buddhism*, vol. 1, *The Aristocratic Age* (Tokyo: Buddhist Books International, 1974); *idem, Foundations of Japanese Buddhism*, vol. 2, *The Mass Movements, Kamakura and Muromachi Periods* (Tokyo: Buddhist Books International, 1976); E. Saunders, *Buddhism in Japan with an Outline of Its Origins in India* (Philadelphia: University of Pennsylvania Press, 1964); Tamaru Noriyoshi, "Buddhism in Japan," in M. Eliade (ed.), *The Encyclopedia of Religion* (New York: McMillan, 1987), 2:426–35.

2. P. Nosco (ed.), *Confucianism and Tokugawa Culture* (Princeton: Princeton University Press, 1984); R. Backus, "The Motivation of Confucian Orthodoxy in Tokugawa Japan," *Harvard Journal of Asiatic Studies* 39, no. 2 (1979): 275–338; T. de Bary and I. Bloom (eds.), *Principle and Practicality: Essays in Neo-Confucianism and Practical Learning* (New York: Columbia University Press,

1979); T. Najita, "Intellectual Change in Early Eighteenth Century Tokugawa Confucianism," *Journal of Asian Studies* 34, no. 4 (1975): 931–44; R. Smith, "Japanese Religious Attitudes from the Standpoint of the Comparative Study of Civilization," in T. Umesao, H. Befu, and J. Kreiner (eds.), *Japanese Civilization in the Modern World* (Osaka: National Museum of Ethnology, 1984), 99–104.

3. See, for greater detail, S. N. Eisenstadt, "The Expansion of Religion: Some Comparative Observations on Different Modes," *Comparative Social Research* 13 (1991): 45–73.

4. One of the best recent analyses of Confucianism in China, Korea, and Japan is to be found in G. Rozman (ed.), *The East Asian Region: Confucian Heritage and Its Modern Adaptation* (Princeton: Princeton University Press, 1991). See also Watanabe Hiroshi, "Jusha, Literati and Yangban: Confucianists in Japan, China and Korea," *Senri Ethnological Studies* 28 (1990): 13–30; Abe Yoshio, "Development of Neo Confucianism in Japan, Korea and China: A Comparative Study," *Acta Asiatica* 19 (1970): 16–39. On Vietnam, see the sources cited in note 6 below.

5. J. Haboush, "The Confucianization of Korean Society," in Rozman, *East Asian Region*, 84–110. See also M. Deuchler, *The Confucian Transformation of Korea: A Study of Society and Ideology* (Cambridge, Mass.: Harvard University Press, 1992).

6. A. Woodside, "History, Structure and Revolution in Vietnam," *International Political Science Review* 10, no. 2 (1989): 143–59; Hyes Nguen, and Tu Van Tai, *The Le Code: Law in Traditional Vietnam* (Athens, Ohio: Ohio University Press, 1982).

7. A. Miller, "Ritsuryō Japan: The State as Liturgical Community," *History of Religions* 11, no. 1 (1971): 98–124.

8. Robert J. Smith, "The Japanese (Confucian) Family: The Tradition from Bottom Up," in Tu Wei-ming (ed.), *Confucian Traditions in East Asian Modernity: Exploring Moral Education and Economic Culture in Japan and the Four Mini-Dragons* (Cambridge, Mass.: Harvard University Press, 1995); E. Patricia Tsurumi, "Meiji Primary School Language and Their Textbooks: Old Values for a New Society?" *Modern Asian Studies* 8, no. 2 (1974): 247–61.

9. Asaki Michio, "The Schools of Japanese Buddhism," in *The Encyclopedia of Buddhism*. See also Ōsumi Kazuo, "Buddhism in the Kamakura Period," in M. Jansen (ed.), *The Cambridge History of Japan*, vol. 3, *Medieval Japan* (Cambridge: Cambridge University Press, 1989), 544–82. For a good recent overall analysis of the Confucianism of Japan, see M. Collcutt, "The Legacy of Confucianism in Japan," in G. Rozman (ed.), *The East Asian Region: Confucian Heritage and Its Modern Adaptation* (Princeton: Princeton University Press, 1991), 111–56; Tamura Enchō, "Japan and the Eastward Permeation of Buddhism," *Acta Asiatica* 47 (1985): 1–30; Kanaji Isamu, "Three Stages in Shōtoku Taishi's Acceptance of Buddhism," *Acta Asiatica* 47 (1985): 31–47; T. Hoover, *Zen Culture* (New York: Random House, 1977).

10. J. Kitagawa, *On Understanding Japanese Religion* (Princeton: Princeton University Press, 1987), esp. pt. 4.

11. R. Heineman, "This World and the Other Power: Contrasting Paths to Deliverance in Japan," in Bechert and Gombrich, *World of Buddhism*, 218;

P. Groner, *Saichō: The Establishment of the Japanese Tendai School* (Berkeley: Buddhist Studies Series, 1984).

12. C. Bielefeldt, "The One Vehicle and the Three Jewels: On Japanese Sectarianism and Some Ecumenical Alternatives," *Buddhist Christian Studies* 10 (1990): 5–16. See also M. Collcutt, *Five Mountains: The Rinzai Zen Monastic Institution in Medieval Japan* (Cambridge, Mass.: Council on East Asian Studies, Harvard University, 1981); J. Foard, "In Search of a Lost Reformation: A Reconsideration of Kamakura Buddhism," *Japanese Journal of Religious Studies* 7, no. 4 (1980): 260–91; Takasaki Jikidō, "Kōbō Daishi (Kūkai) and Tatāgatagarbha thought," *Acta Asiatica* 47 (1985): 109–29. And in general, see also Kitagawa, *On Understanding Japanese Religion*.

13. Okonogi Keigo, "Nichiren and Shinran: Two Faces of Buddhism," *Japan Echo* 10, no. 4 (1983): 67–70.

14. F. Reynolds and C. Hallisey, "Buddhism, an Overview," in Eliade, *Encyclopedia of Religion*, 335–51.

15. Ibid.

16. W. Davis, *Japanese Religion and Society: Paradigms of Structure and Change* (Albany: State University of New York Press, 1992), chap. 1.

17. Ibid., chap. 3.

18. Ōsumi, "Buddhism in the Kamakura Period."

19. E. Ohnuki-Tierney, *Rice as Self* (Princeton: Princeton University Press, 1993), 78.

20. C. Bielefeldt, "Religion in Japan," lecture at Stanford Summer College, 1988; Shinohara Koichi, "Religion and Political Order in Nichiren's Buddhism," *Japanese Journal of Religious Studies* 8, nos. 3–4 (1981): 225–35. See also P. Harvey, *An Introduction to Buddhism* (New Delhi: Munshiram Manoharlal Publishers, 1990), 89–111.

21. Bechert and Gombrich, *World of Buddhism*.

22. J. Kitagawa, *On Understanding Japanese Religion*, 190 ff. Miller, "Ritsuryō Japan."

23. T. Kasulis, "Kūkai: Philosophizing in the Archaic," in F. Reynolds and D. Tracy (eds.), *Myth and Philosophy* (New York: State University of New York Press, 1990), 131–50.

24. M. MacWilliams, "*Kannon Engi*: Strategies of Indigenization in Kannon Temple Myths of the *Saikoku Sanjūsansho Kannon Reijōki* and the *Sanjūsansho Bandō Kannon Reijōki*," doctoral dissertation, University of Chicago, Divinity School, 1990.

25. Kitagawa, *On Understanding Japanese Religion*, pt. 4. See also L. Gomez, "Shinran's Face and the Sacred Name of Amida," in P. Gregory (ed.), *Sudden and Gradual: Approaches to Enlightenment in Chinese Thought* (Honolulu: University of Hawaii Press, 1987), 67–167; Matsunaga and Matsunaga, *Foundations of Japanese Buddhism*, vol. 2.

26. Kitagawa, *On Understanding Japanese Religion*. See also L. Kawamura (ed.), *The Bodhisattva Doctrine in Buddhism* (Waterloo, Ont.: Wilfrid Laurier University Press, 1981), esp. the articles by Hisao Inagaki, "The Bodhisattva Doctrine as Conceived and Developed by the Founders of the New Sects in the Heian and Kamakura Periods," Minoru Kiyota, "Japan's New Religions (1945–

65): Secularization or Spiritualization?," L. Kawamura, "The Myōkōnin: Japan's Representation of the Bodhisattva," 1965–82.

27. See T. Kasulis, "Action Performs Man: The Meaning of the Person in Japanese Zen Buddhism," doctoral dissertation, Yale University, 1975, esp. 211–38; *idem, Zen Action, Zen Person* (Honolulu: University of Hawaii Press, 1987), esp. chaps. 7, 9. See also M. Collcutt, "Zen and the *Gozan*," 583–653, and H. Varley, "Cultural Life in Medieval Japan," 342–500, in Jansen, *Cambridge History of Japan*, vol. 3.

28. See C. Bielefeldt, "No-mind and Sudden Awakening: Thoughts on the Soteriology of a Kamakura Zen Text," in R. Buswell and R. Gimello (eds.), *Paths to Liberation: The Marga and Its Transformations in Buddhist Thought*, Studies in East Asian Buddhism, no. 7 (Honolulu: University of Hawaii Press, 1992), 475–505.

> In one sense, then, the emphasis on these three elements—faith, and the abandonment and commitment that flow from it—can be seen as a reflex of the particular purposes of the apologetic genre itself: as the goal of the genre was to turn the faith of its reader from the old religion and establish him in the new, so the goal of the new religion was to be found precisely in this turning. In this sense, the model of sudden awakening that I have proposed here might be styled a soteriology of conversion of a sort we could look for in Zen (and perhaps elsewhere) especially in those contexts of religious reformation where the new is pitted against the old. At this implicit level, the *Zazen ron's* critique of the bodhisattva path, despite (or rather, precisely because of) its assertion of the radical immediacy of Buddhahood, may amount to much the same result: whether the end of the path is too far away to see or too close at hand to miss, the way is open all the way to the horizon and the wayfarer is free to linger along it where he will.

29. C. Bielefeldt, *Dōgen's Manuals of Zen Meditation* (Berkeley: University of California Press, 1988), 170. The difference in emphasis that developed between Buddhism and Zen also had its analogue within Zen; cf. the proverb "Sōtō for the farmer, Rinzai for the Samurai."

30. P. Gregory, Introduction, in Gregory, *Sudden and Gradual*, 1–12; W. La Fleur, "Saigyō and the Buddhist Value of Nature," *History of Religions* (2 pts.) 13, no. 2 (November 1973): 93–128, 13, no. 3 (February 1974): 227–46.

31. See Gregory, *Sudden and Gradual;* in this volume, see especially, for the general problematics and scope of this discussion, L. Gomez, "Purifying Gold: The Metaphor of Effort and Intuition in Buddhist Thought and Practice," 67–69, and John R. McRae, "Shen-hui and the Teaching of Sudden Enlightenment in Early Ch'an Buddhism," 227–79, and, for the more "populist" tendencies, R. Busswell Jr., "The Short Cut Approach of K'anhua Meditation: The Evolution of a Practical Subitism in Chinese Ch'an Buddhism," 321–81.

See also Shotaro Lide, *Facets of Buddhism* (Delhi: Motilal Banarsiduss, 1991), esp. chaps. 5 and 6. The great popularity and growing "this-worldliness" in Japan of a major Buddhist sect with origins in China, the Jizō Cult, is discussed by Yoshiko Kurata Dykstra, "Jizō, the Most Merciful," *Monumenta Nipponica* 33 (1978): 185–200. See also B. Faure, *The Rhetoric of Immediacy: A Cultural Critique of Chan/Zen Buddhism* (Princeton: Princeton University Press, 1992).

32. A. Grappard, "The Textualized Mountain, Enmountained Text: The *Lotus*

Sutra in Kunisaki," in S. J. Tanabe and W. J. Tanabe (eds.), *The Lotus Sutra in Japanese Culture* (Honolulu: University of Hawaii Press, 1984). See also M. Collcutt, "Mt. Fuji as the Realm of Miroku: The Transformation of Maitreya in the Cult of Mt. Fuji in Early Modern Japan," in A. Sponberg and H. Hardacre (eds.), *Maitreya: The Future Buddha* (Cambridge: Cambridge University Press, 1988), 248–69.

33. La Fleur, "Saigyō and the Buddhist Value of Nature," 245–46.

34. See John Stevens, *Lust for Enlightenment* (Boston: Shambala Publications, 1990), esp. 95 ff.

35. "Thus in Japan we see not only a considerable variety of Maitreyan motifs but their combination with indigenous traditions in many different ways. The power of indigenous traditions to shape and transform Maitreya is remarkable and distinctive" (Helen Hardacre, Introduction, in Sponberg and Hardacre, *Maitreya*, 174).

36. For the characteristics of this synthesis, mainly from the point of view of religious practices, see Robert K. Heineman:

> Firstly, the new religion did not come to Japan on a popular level, but was first accepted by the imperial court and then disseminated in the country from the top. In Japanese history the Buddhist faith is often connected with absolute devotion to a leader: veneration for the founders of the various sects is emphasized, and the majority of the sects stand in close relation to the central governmental authority of their times. This may account for the fact that Japanese Buddhism has less local color than Indian or Chinese Buddhism.
>
> Secondly, Buddhism was (and still is) often associated with magic powers and was used by the court as a means of preventing or curing disease, of preserving the peace, of bringing rainfall and abundant crops, etc. In a later, more developed state of Buddhism this aspect was referred to by the expression *chingo-kokka*, "pacifying and protecting the state."
>
> Thirdly, the newly introduced religion did not replace the indigenous *kami*, but always recognized their existence and power. This led to numerous varieties of Shinto-Buddhist amalgamation: in some cases functions and responsibilities were distributed among both the members of the Buddhist pantheon and the *kami* of the native religion, but most frequently the *kami* were considered manifestations (avatars) of the Buddhas or—in later reactions (from the 14th century onwards) to this form of syncretism—it was sometimes the Buddhas who were relegated to the status of avatars of the *kami*. [Here again, with respect to the attitude both to the state and to the indigenous spirits, we find some very interesting parallels with developments in India.]
>
> The "Way of the *kami*," i.e. Shinto (the word was coined after the introduction of Buddhism, by analogy with the "Way of the Buddha," *Butsudō* in Japanese), came later to be moulded into a unified system (we find it in the 8th-century chronicles such as the one cited above) with a complex genealogy of the *kami* and everything they created: the Japanese archipelago, its natural phenomena and the nation. In this system, absolute superiority was given to the imperial lineage and their *kami* ancestors—headed by the sun goddess Amaterasu-Ōmikami—to justify the supreme position of the imperial line and the evolution of the ruling aristocracy. But even this more elaborate form of Shinto still lacked a universally valid principle, a theoretical framework strong enough to resist foreign influence. Thus Shinto proved to be open to other religions and philosophies—Buddhism, Taoism, Confucianism,

in modern times even Christianity—and throughout history was disposed to borrow such elements from them as would compensate for its own structural insufficiencies in the fields of dogma or ritual. . . .

. . . A further bridge to the people was provided by the connection between Buddhism and Shinto. Buddhism taught that the native divinities were dependent on it: the *kami* were said to long for Buddhist redemption. So little Buddhist temples, the "kami-shrine-temples" (*jingu-ji*), were erected for them in their shrines and sutra readings were held there for their salvation. Conversely, certain *kami* were raised to the rank of protective divinities (*chinju*) of Buddhist temples and worshipped in temple shrines dedicated to them inside the temple precincts. There are already signs in the Nara period that the process of the harmonization of *kami* with Buddhas had begun. When, according to legend the sun goddess Amaterasu was asked if she was opposed to the erection of the "Great Buddha" Vairocana in Nara, her reply was that she herself was nothing other than a manifestation of this Buddha." (Heineman, "This World and the Other Power," 213–14, 218.)

37. See J. Kitagawa, *Dimensions of the East Asian Religious Universe;* W. La Fleur, *The Karma of Words: Buddhism and the Literary Arts in Medieval Japan* (Berkeley: University of California Press, 1983). For an interesting case of such Shinto-Buddhist syncretism, with the strong emphasis on the attainment of salvation or enlightenment, see R. Morrell, "Mujō Ichien's Shinto-Buddhist Syncretism: Shasekishū, Book I," *Monumenta Nipponica* 28, no. 4 (1973): 447–87.

38. R. Werblowsky, "Polytheism," in *Encyclopaedia Britannica* (1983), 14: 435–39.

39. See, for instance, E. Cohen, "Christianity and Buddhism in Thailand: The Battle of the Axes and the Contest of Power," *Social Compass* 38, no. 2 (1991): 115–40.

40. J. Sanford, W. La Fleur, and Masatoshi Nagatomi (eds.), *Flowing Traces: Buddhism in the Literary and Visual Arts of Japan* (Princeton: Princeton University Press, 1992).

41. Ibid., Introduction, 11.

42. Ibid., 12–13.

43. On these developments, see M. Marra, *Representations of Power: The Literary Politics of Medieval Japan* (Honolulu: University of Hawaii Press, 1993). On the presence of potentially subversive themes in many works of art, see M. Marra, *The Aesthetics of Discontent: Politics and Reclusion in Medieval Japanese Literature* (Honolulu: University of Hawaii Press, 1991).

44. It might be interesting to note that similar, often even stronger, tendencies to this-worldly immanentism can be found in the transformation of Taoism in Japan. True enough, Taoism did not play such a central role in Japan as Buddhism or Confucianism, although it did have more influence than was usually envisaged. To follow H. B. Earhart:

As Japan borrowed Buddhism and Confucianism from China, it also borrowed religious Taoism. In Japan religious Taoism is known technically as Dōkyō, which is the Japanese pronunciation for the Chinese term Tao-chiao. This phrase means literally the "teaching of the Tao or Way," indicating the "Way" of the universe. But in Japanese religious history the term "religious Taoism" is usually understood in the broader sense of including Onmyō-dō (the way of *yin-yang*), as well as many popular practices. . . . Religious Taoism made its way into Japan via several channels.

The books of religious Taoism were brought to Japan at an early date. The practices of religious Taoism were adopted at the court, and in the Taiho Code of 702 a bureau of religious Taoism (Onmyō-ryō) was organized. The officials of this bureau studied the books and performed the divinations, astronomical and astrological, and other practices prescribed therein. One of their chief tasks was the regulation of the calendar. In addition, many of the popular divinities and cults of religious Taoism were accepted in early Japan. In a more elusive fashion the lover of nature in religious Taoism influenced Japanese arts, especially landscape painting. We cannot trace the complicated histories of these various elements, but a look at some important features of religious Taoism will indicate its significance for understanding Japanese religious history. . . .

During the Heian period religious Taoism entered Shinto and Buddhism in the guise of formulas, charms, and cosmological theories. Eventually the various divinities of religious Taoism became accepted within both Shinto and Buddhism, almost losing their original Taoistic identity. . . .

. . . The influence of religious Taoism is difficult to assess because it became so thoroughly Japanized. Taoistic festivals, legends, and cults became woven right into the fabric of Japanese life. For example, the Taoist mountain wizards of China (*hsien* in Chinese, *sen* or *sennin* in Japanese) were thought to dwell also in the Japanese mountains. Another example of Taoistic influence is the cult and belief called Koshin. This cult is typical of Japanese village associations organized for worship of specific divinities at regular intervals. In fact, it is so typical, so blended with Shinto and Buddhist elements, that its Taoist origin was completely forgotten by the cult members. (H. B. Earhart, *Japanese Religions* [Belmont, Mass.: Dickenson Publishing Company, 1969], 29–31.)

On the divinational role of Taoism, see E. D. Saunders, "Kōshin: An Example of Taoist Ideas in Japan" (Tokyo: Maruzen, 1960), sec. 3, 423–32. *Proceedings of the IXth International Congress for the History of Religions, Tokyo and Kyoto, 1958.*

45. La Fleur, *Karma of Words.*

46. R. Bellah, "Values and Social Change in Japan," in *idem, Beyond Belief* (New York: Harper & Row, 1970), 114–46.

47. Ama Toshimaro, "Japanese Religiosity and Kamakura Buddhism," *Japan Foundation Newsletter* 18, no. 3 (1990); 8–13. See also M. Collcutt, "Religion in the Formation of the Kamakura Bakufu: As Seen through the Azuma Kagami," *Nichibunken (Japan Review)* 5 (1994): 55–86.

48. Yamada Shozen, "Japanese Esoteric Buddhism and the Moon," in I. Nish and C. Dunn (eds.), *European Studies on Japan* (Kent: Paul Norbury Publications, 1979), 77–83.

49. For a recent analysis of the Shintoization of Japanese Buddhism and its consequent development in a this-worldly and particularistic direction, see Umehara Takeshi, "The Japanese View of the 'Other World': Japanese Religion in World Perspective," *Nichibunken Newsletter,* no. 2 (1991): 161–91. Although this paper does not pay enough attention to the "bracketing out" of the transcendental orientations of Buddhism in specific institutional settings, or to the creation by Buddhism of new levels of public discourse and consciousness, within its own framework it provides a very useful and forceful analysis of the process of Shintoization.

50. Foard, "In Search of a Lost Reformation."

51. Nakamura Hajime, *Ansaetze Modernen Denkens in den Religionen Japans* (Leiden: E. J. Brill, 1982).

52. See, for greater detail, Marra, *Aesthetics of Discontent.*

53. Ibid.

54. Kasulis, "Kūkai."

55. P. Nosco, "Introduction: Neo Confucianism and Tokugawa Discourse," in Nosco, *Confucianism and Tokugawa Culture*, 3–26.

56. Nakamura Hajime, *Ways of Thinking of Eastern People* (Honolulu: East-West Center Press, 1964).

57. B. Faure, "Space and Place in Chinese Religious Traditions," *History of Religions* 26, no. 4 (1987): 337–56, esp. 355–56.

58. J. Berling, "Bringing the Buddha Down to Earth: Notes on the Emergence of Yu-lu as a Buddhist Genre," *History of Religions* 27, no. 1 (1987): 83–84.

59. La Fleur, "Saigyō and the Buddhist Value of Nature."

60. See P. Nosco, *Remembering Paradise: Nativism and Nostalgia in Eighteenth Century Japan* (Cambridge, Mass.: Harvard University Press, 1990).

61. See H. D. Harootunian, "The Functions of China in Tokugawa Thought," in A. Iriye (ed.), *The Chinese and the Japanese* (Princeton: Princeton University Press, 1980), 9–36; K. Wildman Nakai, "The Naturalization of Confucianism in Tokugawa Japan: The Problem of Sinocentrism," *Harvard Journal of Asiatic Studies* 40 (1980): 157–99.

62. See Kasulis, "Kūkai"; *idem*, "Philosophising in Plato's, and Kūkai's Shōjin, Philosophy East and West," in Kasulis, *Zen Action, Zen Person*, 774–835; Yoshito Hakeda, *Kūkai: Major Works* (New York: Columbia University Press, 1972).

63. Kasulis, *Zen Action, Zen Person.* See also Bellah, "Values and Social Change."

64. See Nosco, *Remembering Paradise.*

65. Ibid.

66. J. Spae, *Shinto Man* (Tokyo: Oriens Institute for Religious Research, 1972).

67. See Nosco, *Remembering Paradise;* T. Najita, "Presidential Address: Personal Reflections on Modernity and Modernization," *Journal of Asian Studies* 52, no. 4 (1993): 845–53.

68. Nosco, *Remembering Paradise.*

69. H. Watanabe, "The Transformation of Neo-Confucianism in Early Tokugawa Japan," in Wei Ming, *Confucian Traditions in East Asian Modernity;* W. Boot, "Hayashi Razan as a Confucian Philosopher," in Nish and Dunn, *European Studies on Japan*, 89–94. See also Hiraishi Naoki and I. Nish, *Borrowing and Adaptation: Studies in Tokugawa, Meiji and Taishō Japan* (London: London School of Economics, 1988).

70. See Najita, "Intellectual Change," 934–938. See also the recent work of Kurozumi Makoto, "The Nature of Early Tokugawa Confucianism," *Journal of Japanese Studies* 20, no. 2 (1994): 331–76.

71. M. Tucker, *Moral and Spiritual Cultivation in Japanese Neo-Confucianism: The Life and Thought of Kaibara Ekken 1630–1740* (New York: State University of New York Press, 1989). See also Najita, "Presidential Address."

72. Tucker, *Moral and Spiritual Cultivation.*

73. Park Choong-seok, "Neo Confucianism in Yi Dynasty Korea and Toku-

gawa Japan: Why and How Their Reactions to Western Influence Differed," *Japan Foundation Newsletter* 14, no. 6 (May 1987): 8–11. See also a very interesting analysis by a Chinese scholar of the differences between Chinese and Japanese neo-Confucianism: Li Suping, "The Philosophical Concept of *Li* in Chinese and Japanese Neo-Confucianism: A Comparative Study," *Japan Foundation Newsletter* 23, no. 4 (January 1996): 12–15.

74. Toshinobu Yasunaga, *Andō Shōeki: Social and Ecological Philosopher in Eighteenth-Century Japan* (New York: Weatherhill, 1993).

75. Najita, "Presidential Address." Najita elaborates as follows:

> The idea of authority or *ken*, here, is closer to its Tokugawa reading as independent power or authority than as a constitutional "right." In Shōeki the idea of oneself doing, or oneself feeling in work refers to the autonomous physical or sensate body which contains within itself the "authority" and the "limitation" of action. With the acknowledgement of the natural basis of action, "community" becomes possible not as a judgmental or legalistic system, but as the interactivity or "interaffectivity" of equals.
>
> The idea of oneself doing and working—hitori suru; hitori hataraku—may therefore be a statement of "freedom" from the interventions of artificial authority; and it is also a definition of the independence of the "power" that is inherent in every concrete physical entity. It is about the power of every organism whose extension is warranted only by nature, and whose limit is similarly determined only by nature. Freedom, in this sense, is not abstract and unlimited. It is not "free will"; nor is it comparable to the political idea of "independent agency." It is not a "right" that can be given away, alienated, to a nation state. As an outside authority, the nation state cannot make a discrete natural entity into something other than what it is naturally. . . .
>
> . . . For Shōeki the idea of "heaven" as the trans-natural source of political mandate to create kings was a total falsehood, whether it was said of Ancient China or of Ancient Japan. For Shōeki the only source of power was nature as it endowed each particular "individual" with the capacity to realize its "natural mean."

76. Najita, "Intellectual Change"; *idem*, "Political Economism in the Thought of Dazai Shundai (1680–1747)," *Journal of Asian Studies* 31 (1972): 821–39. See also Najita, "Presidential Address."

77. Maruyama Masao, *Studies in the Intellectual History of Tokugawa Japan* (Princeton: Princeton University Press, 1974). For critical discussion, see T. Najita, "Reconsidering Maruyama Masao's Studies," *Japan Interpreter* 11 (spring 1976).

78. Yui Kiyomitsu, "Theories on Modernization of Japan Today," *International Journal of Japanese Studies*, no. 3 (1994), 45–59.

One of the most incisive analyses is presented by Naoki Sakai in his analysis of several key aspects of philosophical discourse in eighteenth-century Japan, especially those focusing on the nature of language:

> The primary trait he ascribes to sage-kinship is the ability to create and install institutions thanks to which the people are able to imagine themselves to be together, to communicate with one other transparently and reciprocally, and to know the subjective position of each in relation to the whole. Thus, in a sense, Ogyū probed into the political use of nostalgia by assessing the relationship of institutions and the interior. Consequently, the benevolent act of the sage-kings simultaneously ensures the identification of each member with the whole of the community and the identification of

each subjective position within the whole: it generates the sense of belonging to the whole and the sense of being recognized by the whole. In this respect, I think, Ogyū installed at the center of his politics a conception of desire similar to Hegel's, namely, that the desire to be recognized constitutes one's identity. . . .

. . . According to Ogyū, the essence of political power consists in the ability not to prevent something from happening but to let someone desire: it is not prohibitive but positive and creative. Insofar as both the ruler and the ruled belong to the interior and are programmed to desire according to the system of institutions, there can be no basic difference between the ruler and the ruled. What decisively distinguishes the ruler from the ruled must be found in the domain of knowledge. The ruler knows, and the ruled do not. Or rather, the ruler should know, but the ruled must not. ("Yorashimu beshi, shirashimu bekarazu.")

The ruler concerns himself with the task of creating institutions. Ogyū located the true business of the ruler in the creation of institutions; he claimed that in the business appropriate for the ruler he could be authentically and properly benevolent and impartial. This is to say that the ruler and the ruled are basically social roles, so that the same person could be the ruler on some occasions and the ruled on others.

Here we face a series of propositions that form a tautological circuit:

1. The ruler is the one who creates *seido*, or institutions.
2. The ruled desire and act according to the institutions.
3. The ruler is benevolent because he represents the totality.

(Naoki Sakai, *Voices of the Past* [Ithaca, N.Y.: Cornell University Press, 1991], 287–89)

79. Toshinobu Yasunaga, *Andō Shōeki*. See also Najita, "Presidential Address."

80. Kitagawa, *On Understanding Japanese Religion;* see also Miller, "Ritsuryō Japan."

81. Grappard, "Textualized Mountain." See also G. Tanabe Jr., "Tanaka Chikagu: the *Lotus Sutra* and the Body Politic," 191–209, and H. Harlowe, "The Lotus Sutra in Modern Japan," 209–224, both in Tanabe and Tanabe, *Lotus Sutra in Japanese Culture.*

82. See R. Toby, "The Mountain That Needs No Interpreter: Mount Fuji and the Subjection of the Foreign," paper presented at Symposium Montreal on State and Civil Society in Asia, 23–25 October 1992; P. Swanson, "Shugendō and the Yoshimo-Kumano Pilgrimage: An Example of Mountain Pilgrimage," *Monumenta Nipponica* 36, no. 1 (1981): 55–84.

83. J. R. Werblowski, *Beyond Tradition and Modernity* (London: Athlone Press, 1976).

84. M. Carrithers, "They Will Be Lords upon the Islands: Buddhism in Sri Lanka," in Bechert and Gombrich, *World of Buddhism,* 11. See also B. Kapferer, *Legends of People, Myths of State: Violence, Intolerance and Political Culture in Sri Lanka and Australia* (Washington, D.C.: Smithsonian Institute, 1984), esp. pt. 1; W. Vande Walle, "Japan: From Petty Kingdom to Buddha Land," *Nichibunken (Japan Review)* (1994), 87–102.

85. H. Webb, *The Japanese Imperial Institution in the Tokugawa Period* (New York: Columbia University Press, 1968).

86. S. Tanaka, *Japan's Orient: Rendering Past into History* (Los Angeles: University of California Press, 1993), 151. See also Vande Walle, "Japan: From Petty Kingdom to Buddha Land."

87. P. Nosco, Introduction, in Nosco, *Confucianism and Tokugawa Culture*, 9–10.

88. I. McMullen, "Non-Agnatic Adoption: A Confucian Controversy in Seventeenth- and Eighteenth-Century Japan," *Harvard Journal of Asiatic Studies* 35 (1975): 133–89; Collcutt, "Legacy of Confucianism"; Watanabe, "Transformation of Neo-Confucianism"; F. Hsu, *Iemoto: The Heart of Japan* (New York: John Wiley, 1975). See also T. Bryant, "Sons and Lovers: Adoption in Japan," *American Journal of Comparative Law* 38 (1990): 299–336. See also B. Wakabayashi, *Japanese Loyalism Reconsidered: Yamagata Daini's Ryushi Shinron of 1759* (Honolulu: University of Hawaii Press, 1995).

For an interesting comparative case see K. Ch'en, "Filial Piety in Chinese Buddhism," *Harvard Journal of Asiatic Studies* 28 (1968): 81–97. See also P. Ebrey, "The Chinese Family and the Spread of Confucian Values," in Rozman, *East Asian Region*, 45–83; Collcutt, "Legacy of Confucianism"; H. Watanabe, "Tokugawa Thought and Family Structure," unpublished manuscript.

89. Ebrey, "Chinese Family."

90. Watanabe makes similar observations:

We can see the rationalistic, normative character of Zhu Xi's image of the lord-vassal relationship here. The contrast with samurai's relationship and his lord is really remarkable. And yet the Japanese Confucianists thought of samurai's relationship when they read Neo-Confucian teachings on the scholar-official's relationships. They must have been embarrassed sometimes. They used the same terms and wrote in classical Chinese, but we have to understand that what they were talking about was quite different from what Chinese philosophers had talked about.

. . . So here too was a big task for Japanese Confucianists. It seems to me that most of them accepted or compromised with the samurai version of the loyalty relationship.

. . . Unlike in China, in Japan a vassal's duty to his lord often came to be regarded as prior to his duty to his father, as many scholars have pointed out. And Confucianists almost unanimously applauded the deed of Akō masterless samurai, the heroes of the famous play Chūshingura, though there were a few conspicuous exceptions. (Watanabe, "Transformation of Neo-Confucianism")

See also Watabayashi, *Japanese Loyalism Reconsidered*.

91. Webb, *Japanese Imperial Institution*, 218–19.

92. Ibid. See also R. N. Bellah, *Tokugawa Religion: The Values of Pre-Industrial Japan* (Glencoe, Ill.: Free Press, 1957).

93. J. V. Koschmann, *The Mito Ideology: Discourse and Insurrection in Late Tokugawa Japan 1790–1864* (Berkeley: University of California Press, 1987).

94. See M. Tucker, *Confucian Education in Seventeenth-Century Japan: The Case of the Shizutani Gakko in Okayama Prefecture*, (Lewisburg, Pa.: Bucknell University, n.d.). See also B. Bodart-Bailey, "The Confucian Scholar in Early Tokugawa Japan," paper presented at Symposium Montreal, 23–25 October 1992; B. M. Bodart-Bailey, "Tokugawa's Tsunyoshi (1646–1709): A Weberian Analysis," *Asiatische Studien / Etudes Asiatiques* 43, no. 1 (1989): 5–27.

95. Watanabe, "Transformation of Neo-Confucianism," 17.

96. Kamikawa Michio, "Accession Rituals and Buddhism in Medieval Japan," *Japanese Journal of Religious Studies* 17, nos. 2–3 (1990): 269.

97. See Davis, *Japanese Religion and Society*; Bechert and Gombrich, *World of Buddhism*.

98. See Marra, *Representations of Power.*

99. See Watanabe, "Transformation of Neo-Confucianism."

100. J. Dobbins, *Jōdō Shinshū: Shin Buddhism in Medieval Japan* (Bloomington: Indiana University Press, 1989).

101. See Mochizuki Masato, "Miolen Nichiren Buddhism and Japan's Political Tradition"; and, for greater detail, Tanaka Chigaku, *What Is Nippon Kokutai?* (Tokyo: Shishio Bunko, 1936).

102. See H. McFarland, *The Rush Hour of the Gods* (New York: Harper & Row, 1967); J. White, *The Sōkagakkai and Mass Society* (Stanford: Stanford University Press, 1970).

103. On Japanese reflexivity see also E. Ohnuki-Tierney, *Illness and Culture in Contemporary Japan* (Cambridge: Cambridge University Press, 1984).

104. On the process of selection of Confucian themes in different periods of Japanese history and different sectors of Japanese society, see Collcutt, "Legacy of Confucianism." On such selective appropriation of Confucian themes by the Meiji elites, see G. Rozman, "Comparisons of Modern Confucian Values in China and Japan," in Rozman, *East Asian Region*, 157–204; Smith, "The Japanese (Confucian) Family."

105. H. Befu, "Religion in Japanese Civilization (Concluding Remarks)," in Umesao Tadao, Helen Hardacre, and Nakami Hirochika (eds.), *Japanese Civilizations in the Modern World*, vol. 5, *Religion*, (Osaka: National Museum of Ethnology, 1990), 137–49.

106. W. T. de Bary, *East Asian Civilizations* (Cambridge, Mass.: Harvard University Press, 1988).

107. Marra, *Aesthetics of Discontent.*

108. Rozman, "Comparisons of Modern Confucian Values"; S. H. Yamashita, "Confucianism and the Modern Japanese State, 1904–1945," prepared for the Conference on the Role of Confucian Institution, The Rise of East Asia: The Challenge of the Post-Confucian States; American Academy of Arts and Sciences (Cambridge, Mass., May 15–18, 1991).

CHAPTER ELEVEN

1. For the most recent presentation on the process of the Restoration, see M. B. Jansen (ed.), "The Meiji Restoration," in J. W. Hall et al. (eds.), *The Cambridge History of Japan*, vol. 5 (Cambridge: Cambridge University Press, 1989), 308–67; C. Totman, H. Bolitho, and T. M. Huber, "The Meiji Restoration: Product of Gradual Decay, Abrupt Crisis or Creative Will?" in H. Wray and H. Conroy (eds.), *Japan Examined: Perspectives on Modern Japanese History*, part 3 (Honolulu: University of Hawaii Press, 1983), 55–78; W. G. Beasley, *The Meiji Restoration* (Stanford: Stanford University Press, 1972); K. Trimberger, *Revolution from Above* (New Brunswick: Transactions Publishers, 1978).

2. For an early analysis, see Itani Zenichi, "The Economic Causes of the Meiji Restoration," *Transactions of the Asiatic Society of Japan*, 2d ser., 5, no. 17 (1938), 191–208.

3. H. P. Bix, *Peasant Protest in Japan 1590–1884* (New Haven: Yale University Press, 1986).

4. A. M. Craig, *Choshū in the Meiji Restoration* (Cambridge, Mass.: Harvard University Press, 1961); W. G. Beasley, "Politics and the Samurai Class Structure in Satsuma, 1858–1868," *Modern Asian Studies* 1, no. 1 (1967): 47–57.

5. H. D. Harootunian, *Toward Restoration* (Berkeley: University of California Press, 1970).

6. H. D. Harootunian, "Ideology and Conflict," in Tetsuo Najita and J. V. Koschmann (eds.), *Conflict in Modern Japanese History: The Neglected Tradition* (Princeton: Princeton University Press, 1982), 60.

7. M. B. Jansen and G. Rozman (eds.), *Japan in Transition: From Tokugawa to Meiji* (Princeton: Princeton University Press, 1986); Hall et al., *Cambridge History of Japan*, chap. 5.

8. Jansen and Rozman, *Japan in Transition;* Hall et al., *Cambridge History of Japan.*

9. See G. M. Wilson, *Patriots and Redeemers in Japan: Motives in the Meiji Restoration* (Chicago: University of Chicago Press, 1992), chap. 2; Tetsuo Najita, "Conceptual Consciousness in the Meiji Ishin," in Nagai Michio and M. Urrutia (eds.), *Meiji Ishin: Restoration and Revolution* (Tokyo: United Nations University Press, 1985), 83–88. On the modernity of this programme, see B. Silberman, "Japan and Social Theory: Modernism and Modernization in Japanese Politics," paper presented at the International Conference on Japanese Studies, Kyoto, November 1994.

10. T. M. Huber, *The Revolutionary Origins of Modern Japan,* (Stanford: Stanford University Press, 1981).

11. See S. Vlastos, "The Revolutionary Origins of Modern Japan," *Journal of Asian Studies* 42, no. 4 (1983): 959–68. See also the review by A. M. Craig, *Journal of Japanese Studies* 1 (1983): 139–49, and the reply by Huber, *Journal of Japanese Studies* 2 (1983): 440–60.

12. Wilson, *Patriots and Redeemers,* esp. chaps. 6, 7.

13. See the discussion and notes in chapter 10.

14. Y. Sugimoto, "Structural Sources of Popular Revolts and Tobaku Movement at the Time of Meiji Restoration," *Journal of Asian Studies* 34, no. 4 (1975): 875–90; Harootunian, *Toward Restoration.* See the discussion in chapter 10, as well as references in notes 1 and 2 of this chapter.

15. Harootunian, *Toward Restoration.*

16. H. D. Harootunian, "Late Tokugawa Culture and Thought," in Hall et al., *Cambridge History of Japan*, vol. 5.

17. On the Puritans, see M. Walzer, *The Revolution of the Saints* (Cambridge, Mass.: Harvard University Press, 1966). On the intellectuals in the French Revolution, see A. Cochin, *La revolution et la libre pensee* (Paris: Plon-Nourrit, 1924); idem, *L'esprit du Jacobinisme* (Paris: Presses Universitaires de France, 1979); F. Furet, *French Revolution* (New York: Macmillan, 1970); idem, *Interpreting the French Revolution* (Cambridge: Cambridge University Press, 1981). On the Russian intelligentsia, see V. C. Nahirny, *The Russian Intelligentsia: From Torment to Silence* (Rutgers, N.J.: Transaction Publications, 1983).

18. Najita, "Conceptual Consciousness"; Harootunian, "Religions of Relief." For a comparative analysis, see S. N. Eisenstadt, "Framework of the Great Revolutions: Culture, Social Structure, History and Human Agency," *International Social Science Journal* 33 (August 1992): 385–401.

19. M. B. Jansen, *Sakamoto Ryōma and the Meiji Restoration* (Princeton: Princeton University Press, 1961); J. Morris, *The Nobility of Failure: Tragic Heroes in the History of Japan* (New York: Holt, Rinehart and Winston, 1975); N. L. Waters, *Japan's Local Pragmatists: The Transition from Bakumatsu to Meiji in the Kawasaki Region* (Cambridge, Mass.: Harvard University, Council on East Asian Studies, 1983).

20. Wilson, *Patriots and Redeemers.*

21. Najita, "Conceptual Consciousness," 83–88; idem, *Japan: The Intellectual Foundations of Modern Japanese Politics* (Chicago: University of Chicago Press, 1974).

22. T. Najita and I. Scheiner (eds.), *Japanese Thought in the Tokugawa Period 1600–1868* (Chicago: University of Chicago Press, 1978); Hall et al., *Cambridge History of Japan,* vol. 5; B. S. Silberman, *Cages of Reason* (Chicago: University of Chicago Press, 1993), 159–91.

23. M. B. Jansen, "The Meiji Restoration," in Jansen, *Cambridge History of Japan,* vol. 5; Harootunian, *Toward Restoration;* Tetsuo Najita, "Conceptual Consciousness"; W. Davis, "The Civil Theology of Inoue Tetsujirō," *Japanese Journal of Religious Studies* 3, no. 1 (1976): 5–40.

24. H. Webb, *The Imperial Institution in the Tokugawa Period* (New York: Columbia University Press, 1968).

25. Many of the reformers viewed the *bakufu* as a traditional despotic ruler and the emperor as a new one, but this view was necessarily couched in "traditional," that is, restorative, terms. See Webb, *Imperial Institution;* H. Sonoda, "The Decline of the Japanese Warrior Class, 1840–1880," *Nichibunken (Japan Review),* no. 1 (1990), 73–111. See also Silberman, "Japan and Social Theory."

26. P. Duus, R. Myers, and M. R. Peattie (eds.), *The Japanese Informal Empire in China, 1895–1937* (Princeton: Princeton University Press, 1989). See also L. H. Gann, "Reflections on the Japanese and German Empires of WWII," Working paper in International Studies, Hoover Institution (Stanford University, 1992).

27. Sonoda, "Decline of the Japanese Warrior Class."

28. Ibid., 101.

29. P. Duus, "Bounded Democracy: Tradition and Politics in Modern Japan," unpublished article; Gann, "Reflections on the Japanese and German Empires of WWII."

30. T. Smith, "Japan's Aristocratic Revolution," in *idem, Native Sources of Japanese Industrialization 1750–1920* (Berkeley: University of California Press, 1988), 133–48. See also Silberman, "Japan and Social Theory."

31. Sonoda, "Decline of the Japanese Warrior Class."

32. Jansen and Rozman, *Japan in Transition,* 12.

33. H. D. Harootunian, "Ideology as Conflict," in T. Najita and J. V. Koschmann (eds.), *Conflict in Modern Japanese History* (Princeton: Princeton University Press, 1982), 25–61; Tetsuo Najita, *Japan: The Intellectual Foundations of*

Modern Japanese Politics (Chicago: University of Chicago Press, 1974); Sonoda, "Decline of the Japanese Warrior Class."

34. Ibid.

35. See, for instance, Trimberger, *Revolution from Above*.

36. See R. Bendix, "Preconditions of Development: A Comparison of Japan and Germany," in *idem, Nation Building and Citizenship* (New York: John Wiley, 1964), 177–214; Arima Tatsuo, *The Failure of Freedom: A Portrait of Modern Japanese Intellectuals* (Cambridge, Mass.: Harvard University Press, 1969).

CHAPTER TWELVE

1. J. M. Kitagawa, "Some Remarks on Shinto," *History of Religion* 27, no. 3 (February 1988): 227–45; A. G. Grappard, "Institution, Ritual and Ideology: The Twenty-Two Shrine-Temple Multiplexes of Heian Japan," *History of Religions* 27, no. 3 (February 1988): 245–69; Hirai Naofusa, "Studies on Shinto in Pre- and Post-War Japan," *Acta Asiatica* 51 (1987): 96–118.

2. C. Blacker, "The Shinza or God-seat in the Daijōsai: Throne, Bed, or Incubation Couch," *Japanese Journal of Religious Studies* 17, nos. 2–3 (June–September 1990): 179–98. See also C. Blacker, "Two Shinto Myths: The Golden Age and the Chosen People," in S. Kenny and J. P. Lehmann (eds.), *Themes and Theories in Modern Japanese History* (London: Athlone Press, 1988), 64–78.

3. J. R. Werblowski, *Beyond Tradition and Modernity* (London: Athlone Press, 1976); Blacker, "Two Shinto Myths."

4. See, for instance, S. Tanaka, *Japan's Orient: Rendering Past into History* (Berkeley: University of California Press, 1993).

5. G. A. Hoston, "A 'Theology' of Liberation? Socialist Revolution and Spiritual Regeneration in Chinese and Japanese Marxism," in P. A. Cohen and M. Goldman (eds.), *Ideas across Cultures: Essays on Chinese Thought in Honor of Benjamin J. Schwartz* (Cambridge, Mass.: Council on East Asian Studies, Harvard University Press, 1990), 165–94.

6. K. Pyle, "The Future of Japanese Nationality: An Essay in Contemporary Study," *Journal of Japanese Studies* 8, no. 2 (1982): 223–65; Kosaku Yoshino, *Cultural Nationalism in Contemporary Japan* (London: Routledge, 1992); H. Befu and Manabe Kazufumi, "An Empirical Study of Nihonjinron: How Real Is the Myth?" *Kwansai Gakuin University Annual Studies* 36 (1987): 97–111. On some very important dimensions of Japanese collective self in historical times, see E. Ohnuki-Tierney, *Rice as Self* (Princeton: Princeton University Press, 1993).

7. Befu and Manabe Kazufumi, *Empirical Study of Nihonjinron*; Kosaku Yoshino, *Cultural Nationalism*.

8. D. L. Howell, "Ainu Ethnicity and the Boundaries of the Early Modern Japanese State," *Past and Present*, no. 142 (February 1994), 69–93; Amino Yoshihiko, "Les Japonais et la mer," *Annales* 50, no. 2 (March–April 1995): 235–58.

9. Significant in this context are the ways in which modern Japanese historians, following the tenets of modern Western historiography, attempted to place

Japan within the context of world history. As Stefan Tanaka has shown in his incisive analysis, most of these historians, who naturally refused to accept the Western characterization of the "Orient," first redefined it as autonomous, equal to the West. Yet faced with the problem of their own relation to China and its disintegration, most of them ended by taking Japan out of the "Orient," making its history distinct, separate, and unique, often portraying Japan as the bearer of the pristine values that other civilizations—Western or Chinese—claimed as their own. See Tanaka, *Japan's Orient.* See also W. Vande Walle, "Japan: From Petty Kingdom to Buddha Land," *Nichibunken (Japan Review)* 5 (1994): 87–102.

10. Kosaku Yoshino, *Cultural Nationalism;* Befu and Manabe Kazufumi, *Empirical Study of Nihonjinron.*

11. T. Rohlen, "Order in Japanese Society: Attachment, Authority and Routine," *Journal of Japanese Studies* 15, no. 1 (1989): 17.

12. Rohlen, "Order in Japanese Society," 17.

13. I. J. MacMullan, "Rulers or Fathers? A Casuistical Problem in Early Modern Japanese Thought," *Past and Present,* no. 116 (August 1987), 56–98; F. L. K. Hsu, "Filial Piety in Japan and China: Borrowing Some Variations and Significance," *Journal of Comparative Family Studies,* spring 1971, 57–74; *idem, Iemoto: The Heart of Japan* (New York: J. Wiley, 1973). See, for instance, G. Cameron Hurst III, "Death, Honor and Loyalty: The Buddhist Ideal," *Philosophy East and West* 40, no. 4 (October 1990): 511–29.

14. R. Benedict, *The Chrysanthemum and the Sword* (London: Secker and Warburg, 1947).

15. Befu and Manabe Kazufumi, *Empirical Study of Nihonjinron;* Kosaku Yoshino, *Cultural Nationalism.*

16. Maruyama Masao, "The Structure of Matsurigoto: The Basso Ostinato of Japanese Political Life," in Kenny and Lehmann, *Themes and Theories,* 27–49.

17. Maruyama, "Structure of Matsurigoto," 38–43. This constitutes also the major thesis of John Haley, *Authority without Power: Law and the Japanese Paradox* (New York: Oxford University Press, 1991). This mode of exercise of authority is also closely related to what Kawai Hayao, the noted Jungian psychologist and folklorist, describes as a major characteristic of Japanese decision making—the structure of the empty middle or center; see Kawai Hayao, "Die Krise Japans als Krise der Struktur der leeren Mitte," in Jens Heise (ed.), *Die kühle Seele* (Frankfurt: Fischer Taschenbuch Verlag, 1990), 121–37.

18. J. P. Arnason, "Comparing Japan and the West: Prolegomena to a Research Programme," in L. Gule and O. Storebo (eds.), *Development and Modernity: Perspectives on Western Theories of Modernisation* (Bergen: Ariadne, 1993), 167–95.

19. Murakami Y., "Ie Society as a Pattern of Civilization," *Journal of Japanese Studies* 10, no. 2 (1984): 279–363.

20. D. Okimoto, *Power in Japan: The Societal State* (Stanford: Stanford University Press, 1989); Haley, *Authority without Power.*

21. Okimoto, *Power in Japan.*

22. J. V. Koschmann (ed.), *Authority and the Individual in Japan: Citizen Protest in Historical Perspective* (Tokyo: University of Tokyo Press, 1978).

23. R. K. Hall (ed.), *Kokutai No Hongi: Cardinal Principles of the National*

Entity of Japan (Cambridge, Mass.: Harvard University Press, 1949); J. M. Kitagawa, "The Japanese Kokutai (National Community): History and Myth," *History of Religions* 13, no. 3 (1974): 209–226.

24. See, for instance, Robert J. Wargo, "Japanese Ethics: Beyond Good and Evil," *Philosophy East and West* 40, no. 4 (October 1990): 499–511.

25. Koschmann, *Authority and the Individual.*

26. Significantly, Koschmann relates this pattern of "soft rule"—and by implication the weakness of civil society in the European sense—to some of the basic conceptions of ontological reality that have developed in Japan. As Ellis Krauss, reviewing Koschmann's argument, put it:

> Koschmann presents the view that Japan's early socio-political development and escape from foreign invasion provided no alternative examples of political authority such as Europe experienced, and resulted in authority being perceived as "given," and "as an inalienable part of the natural order" (pp. 6–7). Thus, no philosophy of transcendence and negation developed as in the West, and little differentiation between the sacred and the profane. The sacred and the profane were seen rather as imminent in group life and the heads of groups acquired the role of intermediaries between their group and the gods. "Public" (ōyake or kō) elements of social life acquired a positive meaning and the "private" (watakushi or shi) aspects a negative connotation. The givenness of authority and its association with higher, sacred ideals therefore made individuality and opposition in the name of a transcendent principle exceedingly difficult.
>
> (Krauss, review of Koschmann, *Authority and the Individual in Japan, Journal of Japanese Studies* 7 (1981): 165–80.

27. C. Gluck, *Japan's Modern Myths: Ideology in the Late Meiji Period* (Princeton: Princeton University Press, 1985). For numerous illustrations of this mode of political activities, presumably rooted in the agrarian as against the equestrian society, see Shōichi Watanabe, *The Peasant Soul of Japan* (New York: St. Martin's Press, 1989). See also R. Smith, *Japanese Society, Tradition, Self and the Social Order* (Cambridge: Cambridge University Press, 1981).

28. See, for instance, Tessa Morris-Surkian, *A History of Japanese Economic Thought* (London: Routledge Kegan, 1989), chap. 1; Sugiyama Chūji and Mizuta Hiroshi (eds.), *Enlightenment and Beyond: Political Economy Comes to Japan* (Tokyo: Tokyo University Press, 1987); Bai Gao, "Jissen Economics and Japanese Economic Reasoning," paper presented at the International Conference on Japanese Studies, Kyoto, November 1994.

29. David Williams, *Japan beyond the End of History* (London: Routledge, 1994); Bai Gao, "Jissen Economics."

30. R. P. Dore (ed.), *Aspects of Social Change in Modern Japan* (Princeton: Princeton University Press, 1967); E. Pauer, "Japanischer Geist—westliche Technik: Zur Rezeption westlicher Technologie in Japan," *Saeculum* 38 (1987): 19–51.

31. J. J. Sullivan, *Visions of Work in America and Japan: A Universal Theory of Work Motivation* (Seattle: University of Washington Press, forthcoming).

32. F. L. K. Hsu, *Iemoto: The Heart of Japan* (New York: John Wiley & Son, 1973). T. S. Lebra, *Above the Clouds: Status Culture of the Modern Japanese Nobility* (Berkeley: University of California Press, 1993).

33. W. W. Kelly, "Directions in the Anthropology of Contemporary Japan," *Annual Review of Anthropology* 20 (1991): esp. 410–13; Hsu, *Iemoto.*

34. See also H. Sonoda, "The Decline of the Japanese Warrior Class, 1840–1880," *Japan Review* 7 (1990): 73–112. One Japanese scholar has presented a very interesting hypothesis that it was also the self-imposed isolation of the Tokugawa in contrast to the West that gave rise to the deflection of resources from external expansion to internal change; Katō Hidetoshi, "The Significance of the Period of National Seclusion Reconsidered," *Journal of Japanese Studies* 7, no. 1 (October 1987): 85–111.

35. E. H. Kinmoth, *The Self-Made Man in Meiji Japanese Thought* (Berkeley: University of California Press, 1981).

36. See Lebra, *Above the Clouds; idem,* "The Socialization of Aristocratic Children by Commoners: Recalled Experiences of Hereditary Elite in Modern Japan," *Cultural Anthropology* 5, no. 1 (February 1990): 77–100; *idem,* "The Cultural Significance of Silence in Japanese Communication," *Multilingua: Journal of Cross-Cultural and Interlanguage Communication* 6, no. 4 (1987): 343–57. See also Kelly, "Directions in the Anthropology of Contemporary Japan"; *idem,* "Rationalization and Nostalgia: Cultural Dynamics of New Middle Class Japan," *American Ethnologist* 13, no. 4 (1986): 603–18; *idem,* "Japanese No-Noh: The Crosstalk of Public Culture in a Rural Festivity," *Public Culture* 2 (1990): 65–81; *idem,* "Finding a Place in Metropolitan Japan: Transpositions of Everyday Life," in A. Gordon (ed.), *Postwar Japan as History* (Berkeley: University of California Press, 1993); T. C. Bestor, *Neighborhood Tokyo* (Stanford: Stanford University Press, 1989).

37. J. W. Hall, "Rule by Status in Tokugawa Japan," *Journal of Japanese Studies* 1, no. 1 (autumn 1974): 39–50.

38. E. Vogel (ed.), *Modern Japanese Organization and Decision Making* (Berkeley: University of California Press, 1985).

39. Hall, *Kokutai No Hongi.*

40. M. Hechter and Satoshi Kanazawa, "Group Solidarity and Social Order in Japan," *Journal of Theoretical Politics* 5, no. 4 (1993): 455–93.

41. E. Hamaguchi (ed.), *Japanese Systems: An Alternative Civilization?,* Research Project Team for Japanese Systems, Masuda Foundation (Yokohama: Sekotac, 1992); C. Deutschmann, "The Japanese Type of Organisation as a Challenge to the Sociological Theory of Modernization," *Thesis Eleven,* no. 17 (1987), 40–58.

42. See the following articles in Kumon Shumpei and H. Rosovsky (eds.), *The Political Economy of Japan,* vol. 3, *Cultural and Social Dynamics* (Stanford: Stanford University Press, 1993): Murakami Yasusuke and T. P. Rohlen, "Social-Exchange Aspects of the Japanese Political Economy: Culture, Efficiency and Change," 63–108, Kumon Shumpei, "Japan as a Network Society," 109–41, and Imai Ken-Ichi, "Japan's Corporate Networks," 198–230. See also A. G. Grappard, "Flying Mountains and Walkers of Emptiness: Toward a Definition of Sacred Space in Japanese Religions," *History of Religions* 20, no. 3 (February 1982): 195–221; B. Faure, "Space and Place in Chinese Religious Traditions," *History of Religions* 26, no. 4 (May 1987): 337–56.

43. M. S. Aoki, *Information, Incentives and Bargaining in the Japanese Economy* (Cambridge: Cambridge University Press, 1988), 298–315; Deutschmann, "Japanese Type of Organization."

44. S. N. Eisenstadt and E. Ben-Ari (eds.), *Japanese Models of Conflict Resolution* (London: Kegan Paul International, 1990); J. V. Koschmann and T. Najita (eds.), *Conflict in Japanese Culture: The Neglected Tradition* (Princeton: Princeton University Press, 1982); T. P. Rohlen, P. S. Steinhoff, and E. S. Krauss (eds.), *Conflict in Japan* (Honolulu: University of Hawaii Press, 1984).

45. See, for instance, John S. Brownlee, *Political Thought in Japanese Historical Writing, From Kojiki (712) to Tokushi Yōron (1712)* (Waterloo, Ont.: Wilfred Laurier University Press, 1992). See also the bibliographic notes in chapter 15.

46. Tanaka Atsushi, "Yōga: Malerei in Westlichen Stil 1868–1912," 178–89, and Iwasaki Yoshikura, "Nihonga: Malerei in Japanische Stil," 189–204, both in Doris Croissant and Lothar Ledderose (eds.), *Japan und Europa 1543–1929* (Berlin: Berliner Festspiele, Argon, 1993).

47. R. Goodman, *Japan's "International Youth": The Emergence of a New Class of Schoolchildren* (Oxford: Clarendon Press, 1990).

48. Y. Murakami, "Two Types of Civilization: Transcendental and Hermeneutic," *Nichibuken (Japan Review)* 1 (1990): 1–34.

49. E. Ohnuki-Tierney, *Rice as Self: Japanese Identities through Time* (Princeton: Princeton University Press, 1992), esp. 39, 82, 183–84; idem, *The Monkey as Mirror: Symbolic Transformations in Japanese History and Ritual* (Princeton: Princeton University Press, 1987); idem, "Monkey as Metaphor? Transformations of a Polytropic Symbol in Japanese Culture," *Man* 25 (1990): 399–416.

50. Ikuya Sato, *Kamikaze Biker: Parody and Anomy in Affluent Japan* (Chicago: University of Chicago Press, 1991).

51. Goodman, *Japan's "International Youth"*.

52. Endō Shūsaku, *Silence* (New York: Tarlinger Publishing, 1969).

53. R. N. Bellah, "Values and Social Change in Modern Japan," in idem, *Beyond Belief* (New York: Harper & Row, 1970), 114–46. See also Kawai, "Die Krise Japans"; idem, "The Transformation of Biblical Myth in Japan," *Diogenes* 42 (1994): 49–66.

54. See. R. Whiting, *The Chrysanthemum and the Bat: The Game Japanese Play* (Tokyo: Permanent Press, 1977); M. Kiyota and H. Kinoshita (eds.), *Japanese Martial Arts and American Sports: Cross Cultural Perspectives on Means to Personal Growth* (Tokyo: Nihon University, 1990), 173–87; Dean W. Collingwood and Osamu Kusatsu, "Japanese Rastafarians: Non-Conformity in Modern Japan," unpublished paper, University of Chicago.

55. On Japanese reflexivity, see also E. Ohnuki-Tierney, "The Monkey as Self in Japanese Culture," in E. Ohnuki-Tierney (ed.), *Culture through Time* (Stanford: Stanford University Press, 1990), 128–54; idem, "The Ambivalent Self of the Contemporary Japanese," *Cultural Anthropology* 5, no. 2 (May, 1990): 197–216. D. Pollack, *The Fracture of Meaning: Japan's Synthesis of China from the Eighth through the Eighteenth Century* (Princeton: Princeton University Press, 1986).

56. See T. Najita, "Remembering Forgotten Texts: Andō Shōeki and the Predicament of Modernity," paper presented at Hachinote Aomori symposium "Andō Shōeki Today," Hachinote Aomori Symposium published in Japanese in

Gendai nogyo 4 (1992): 34–54. Irokawa Daikichi (ed.), *The Culture of the Meiji Period,* Marius B. Jansen (trans.) (Princeton: Princeton University Press, 1985).

57. H. Passin, "Modernization and the Japanese Intellectual: Some Comparative Observations," in M. B. Jansen (ed.), *Changing Japanese Attitudes toward Modernization* (Princeton: Princeton University Press, 1965); H. Passin, "The Stratigraphy of Protest in Japan," in M. Kaplan (ed.), *The Revolution in World Politics* (New York: John Wiley & Sons, 1962), 92–101.

58. See Sakamoto Yoshiharu, "The Emperor System as a Japanese Problem: The Case of Meiji Gakuin University," *Prime Occasional Papers,* ser. no. 5.

59. See J. A. Fujii, *Complicit Fictions: The Subject in the Modern Japanese Prose Narrative* (Berkeley: University of California Press, 1993).

60. See also D. W. Plath, "The Fate of Utopia: Adaptive Tactics in Four Japanese Groups," *American Anthropologist* 68 (1966): 1152–62.

61. See Carl Steenstrup, "Did Political Rationalism Develop along Parallel Lines in Premodern Japan and in the Premodern West? Prolegomenon to a Comparative Study," *Journal of Intercultural Studies,* no. 3 (1970), 1–12. See also endnotes 67–69 in chapter 10.

62. Schwartz, "The Age of Transcendance," in *Daedalus,* Special Issue, *Wisdom, Revelation and Doubt: Perspectives on the First Millennium B.C.,* 104, no. 2 (spring, 1975): 1–7. See also Arnason, "Japan and the West."

63. See Nakamura Hajime, *Ways of Thinking of Eastern People* (Honolulu: East-West Center Press, 1964), 345–530.

64. Maruyama Masao, *Chūsei to hangyaku: tenkeiki Nihon no seishinshiteki iso* (Loyalty and Revolt: An Intellectual History of Japan's Modern Transformation (Tokyo: Chikuma Shobo, 1992).

65. See, for a very interesting discussion of such discourse in the Taishō and early Shōwa period, D. Rimer, *In Search of Identity* (Princeton: Princeton University Press, 1990).

66. The distinction between hegemonic premises and ideology income has been elaborated by Jean Comaroff and John L. Comaroff, *Of Religion and Revolution: Christianity, Colonialism and Consequences in South Africa* (Chicago: University of Chicago Press, 1991). See Ohnuki-Tierney, *Rice as Self.*

67. F. Maraini, *Meeting with Japan* (New York: Viking Press, 1960); *idem,* "Japan the Essential Modernizer," in Kenny and Lehmann, *Themes and Theories in Modern Japanese History,* 44–63; P. Veyne, *Did the Greeks Believe in Their Myths?* (Chicago: University of Chicago Press, 1988).

68. Walter Edwards, *Modern Japan through Its Weddings, Gender, Person, and Society in Ritual Portrayal* (Stanford: Stanford University Press, 1989), 144–45. See also Whiting, *Chrysanthemum and the Bat;* Kiyota and Kinoshita, *Japanese Martial Arts and American Sports.*

69. R. Cole, "The Late-Developer Hypothesis: An Evaluation of Its Relevance for Japanese Employment Patterns," *Journal of Japanese Studies* 4, no. 2 (summer 1978): 262.

70. Kelly, "Directions in the Anthropology of Contemporary Japan"; *idem,* "Japanese No-Noh"; Bestor, *Neighborhood Tokyo;* J. Robertson, "A Dialectic of Native and Newcomer: The Kodaira Citizens' Festival in Suburban Tokyo," *Anthropological Quarterly* 60, no. 2 (1987): 124–136; E. Ben-Ari, "At the Inter-

stices: Drinking, Management, and the Temporary Groups in a Local Japanese Organization," *Social Analysis*, no. 26 (December 1989), 46–69; Kohara Yukinari, "Folk without Festivals," *Japan Interpreter* 8, no. 1 (winter 1973): 55–62.

71. M. Marra, *Representations of Power: The Literary Politics of Medieval Japan* (Honolulu: University of Hawaii Press, 1993).

72. N. Field, *In the Realm of a Dying Emperor: A Portrait of Japan at Century's End* (New York: Pantheon, 1991).

73. Maraini, "Japan, the Essential Modernizer."

CHAPTER THIRTEEN

1. Introduction to J. Pelzel, "Human Nature in the Japanese Myths," in W. P. Lebra and T. Sugiyama Lebra (eds.), *Japanese Culture and Behavior* (Honolulu: University of Hawaii Press, 1986), 3–4. See also Hitomi Tonomura, "Positioning Amaterasu: A Reading of the Kojiki," *Japan Foundation Newsletter* 22, no. 2 (1994): 12–16.

2. I. Munakata, "Struktur und Wandel der kulturellen Identität in modernem Japan: Ein vergleichender hermeneutischer Ansatz," in C. von Barloewen and K. Werhahn-Mees (eds.), *Japan und der Westen*, vol. 1 (Frankfurt: Fischer Taschenbuch Verlag, 1986), 38–56.

3. A. Berque, "Das Verhältnis der Ekonomie zu Raum und Zeit in der japanische Kultur," in von Barloewen and Werhahn-Mees, *Japan und der Westen*, 21–38; *idem*, "Some Traits of Japanese Fudōsei," *Japan Foundation Newsletter* 14, no. 5 (February 1987): 1–7; Sokyo Ono (in collaboration with W. P. Woodard), *Shinto, The Kami Way* (Rutland, Vt.: Charles E. Tuttle, 1962).

4. For several detailed discussions of the development of Shinto, see "Shinto as Religion and as Ideology: Perspectives from the History of Religions," a special issue of *History of Religions* 27, no. 3 (February 1988).

5. F. Maraini, "Japan the Essential Modernizer," in S. Kenny and J. Lehman (eds.), *Themes and Theories in Modern Japanese History* (London: Athlone Press, 1988), 53. See also F. Maraini, *Meeting with Japan* (New York: Viking Press, 1960).

Ian Buruma presents a similar picture of this Japanese "Shintoistic" worldview in Buruma, *Behind the Mask: On Sexual Demons, Sacred Mothers, Transvestites, Gangsters, and Other Japanese Cultural Heroes* (New York: New American Library, 1984), 3–10:

Culture of any kind is always influenced by many fads and fashions. Japanese culture has been worked on by history, both native and foreign, by Buddhism, Confucianism, and even at times by Christianity. But underneath the changing surface it has never quite let go of its oldest native roots which are connected to the Shinto cult. By this I do not mean the nationalistic State Shinto concocted by politicians in the late nineteenth century when they were pushing for a strong national identity, but the whole range of sensual nature worship, folk beliefs, ancient deities and rituals. It is the creed of a nation of born farmers, which Japan in many ways still is.

. . . The word Shinto was first coined in the seventh century to distinguish it from Buddhism, called Butsudo. It means Way of the Gods, but it can hardly be called a religion, for there is almost no trace in it of abstract speculation, neither is there much awareness of, or even interest in, another world outside our own. Heaven in the midst of the ancient Japanese was a cozy sort of place full of industrious villagers tending rice-fields. There is no evidence of a system of ethics or statecraft, such as we see in China. The earliest myths are, in fact, typically Japanese dramas revolving around human relationships, liberally spiced with sex. Shinto has many rituals, but no dogma. A person is Shinto in the same way that he is born Japanese. It is a collection of myths and ceremonies that give form to a way of life. It is a celebration, not a belief. There is no such thing as a Shintoist, for there is no Shintoism. . . .

. . . Worship of nature obviously includes sex. Like most Japanese, the gods felt no guilt about sex as such. Once the wagtail showed the way Izanami and Izanagi could not stop. Sex is an essential, indeed central part of nature. There is no question of sin. The brother and sister gods were not the only ones in the Japanese pantheon to so enjoy themselves. The Master of the Land (Okuninushi) had numerous lovers in the world he pacified and the only time he ran into trouble was when he refused to go to bed with his lover's ugly sister. For this breach of good manners, the Japanese emperors—his descendants—were doomed to be mortal. . . .

. . . Izanagi and Izanami were not directly punished for anything they did. They were certainly not removed from the Garden of Eden. Their crisis came when Izanami was seen by her husband in a state of pollution. The disaster concerned her shame rather than anything she consciously did. Although the gods enjoyed sex with impunity, they were terrified of pollution, especially the pollution of death. Izanagi, seeing the putrid body of his sister, barely escaped death himself. One could perhaps say that pollution is the Japanese version of original sin. One must add that women in Shinto, as in many religions, are considered to be more polluted than men, because blood is a form of pollution. In some parts of Japan women used to be segregated in special huts during menstruation. . . .

. . . Jealousy in particular is one such force the Japanese fear. This explains their deeply ambivalent attitude to women. They worship them, especially as mothers, but also fear them as corrupters of purity. Izanami is the creator of life as well as the personification of death and pollution. Her jealousy further prompted her to vow to strangle a thousand people a day. She had no reason to be jealous of another woman, however, for, as far as we know, there was not one in Izanagi's life. But she hated losing her marital status. And social status, however hard it may be to be bullied by possessive mothers-in-law or neglected by unfaithful husbands, is something most Japanese women cannot do without. Any threat to take it away from them can unleash jealousy of the most violent kind and there is sufficient evidence that men live in morbid fear of it. It is still customary for brides to wear a white hood at their wedding. It looks like a loosely wrapped turban made out of a bed-sheet and it is called tsunakakushi, a "concealer of horns," the horns namely of jealousy.

. . . The fascination in religious ceremonies, myths and the popular arts for the sexual organs (the grotesque stylization of male and female genitals in erotic woodblock prints, for example) is as much a celebration of life and fertility as a form of exorcism. It is as if one can ward off the dangers inherent in the mysteries of nature by laughter or stylization, by turning raw nature into man-made symbols. In various parts of Japan there are literally "laughing festivals," where people laugh at local shrines to please the gods. Inside these shrines one often finds images of female and male sexual organs. . . .

. . . Though absolute Evil seems to be absent from Japanese thought, every form of pollution, including wounds, sores, blood, death and even simple uncleanliness is to be feared. The traditional antidote to the polluting forces of nature is purification. Izanagi's ablutions in the Tachibana river after his return from the Underworld are a typical example. Naturally, purification in one form or another exists in religious ceremonies everywhere, but in few cultures is it taken as seriously and is it as much a part of daily life. . . .

. . . One finds evidence of it in the most disparate places: in the wrestling ring, for example, which sumo-wrestlers sprinkle with purifying salt before every bout. Little heaps of salt can also be seen in front of homes, on the doorsteps of bars, massage parlors and any other place where pleasure is bought and sold. The Japanese feeling for purity manifests itself in other, less obvious ways: the ubiquitous habit of wearing white gloves by people performing public functions, for instance. Politicians making speeches wear them, taxi drivers are never without them, policemen and even elevator operators in department stores wear them; everywhere one goes in Japan, one sees this ceremonial white on people's hands. . . .

. . . Bathing is a cult. Keeping clean is so universal a preoccupation that all one smells in packed commuter trains during rush hours in Tokyo is a faint whiff of soap. Most Shinto festivals involve ritual bathing. The first bathhouses, still a social institution in cities, were part of Buddhist temples, dating from the seventh century. But, like many religious habits in Japan—drinking sake is another—bathing soon became a sensual experience enjoyed for its own sake.

6. Y. Saito, "The Japanese Appreciation of Nature," *British Journal of Aesthetics* 25, no. 3 (summer 1985): 239–57. See also H. Tellenbach and K. Bin, "The Japanese Concept of Nature," D. E. Shaner, "The Japanese Experience of Nature," and W. R. La Fleur, "Saigyō and the Buddhist Value of Nature," all in J. B. Callicott and R. T. Ames (eds.), *Nature and Asian Traditions of Thought: Essays in Environmental Philosophy* (Albany: State University of New York Press, 1989); A. Kalland, "Culture in Japanese Nature," in O. Brum and A. Kalland (eds.), *Asian Perceptions of Nature, Nordic Proceedings in Asian Studies* (Copenhagen: NIAS, 1994), 218–33; F. H. Meyer, "Fauna and Flora in Japanese Folklore," *Asian Folklore Studies* 40, no. 1 (1981): 23–34.

7. E. Ohnuki-Tierney, *The Monkey as Mirror: Symbolic Transformations in Japanese History and Ritual* (Princeton: Princeton University Press, 1987), 130.

8. See E. Ohnuki-Tierney, *Rice as Self* (Princeton: Princeton University Press, 1993), 56, which follows the interpretation offered by Sakurai Tokutaro.

9. Emiko Ohnuki-Tierney, comment on E. Namihira, "Pollution in the Folk Belief System," *Current Anthropology* 28, no. 4 (August–October 1987), supplement s72.

10. Ohnuki-Tierney, comment on Namihira, "Pollution in the Folk Belief System," s71. Ohnuki-Tierney observes, "Thus the concept of pollution, having undergone a number of twists, becomes a rationale for discrimination. The concept of pollution is linked to the logic of the inversion of values and order. This is apparent, for example, as Katsumata points out, in the adoption of the attire of *hinin* (the outcasts once called 'non-humans') and the strategic use of temples for sanctuary by those involved in the insurrections of the late medieval period. The background to the use of this attire as a symbol of the inversion of order is the structure of religious and social discrimination to which the concept of pollution had been appended" (s70–s71).

11. Namihira, "Pollution in the Folk Belief System," with comment by Emiko Ohnuki-Tierney, s65–s74. See also Yoshie Akio, "Eviter la souillure: Le processus de civilisation dans le Japon ancien"; and Sato Kazuhiko, " 'Des gens étranges

a l'allure insolite': Contestation et valeurs nouvelles dans le Japon médiéval"—
both in *Annales* 50, no. 2 (March–April 1995): 283–306 and 307–40.

12. Yoshida Teigo, "The Stranger as God: The Place of the Outsider in Japanese Folk Religion," *Ethnology* 20, no. 2 (April 1981): 87–99.

13. See Ohnuki-Tierney, *Monkey as Mirror; idem,* "The Monkey as Self in Japanese Culture," in *idem* (ed.), *Culture through Time: Anthropological Approaches* (Stanford: Stanford University Press, 1990), 128–54.

14. J. Raz, "Self-presentation and Performance in the *Yakuza* Way of Life: Fieldwork with a Japanese Underworld Group," in R. Goodman and K. Refsing (eds.), *Ideology and Practice in Modern Japan* (London: Routledge, 1992), 210–35.

15. "On peut dire qu'en perdant le pouvoir politique, la royauté a rétabli, dans un certain sens, sa forme originelle de gardienne de la parole non-quotidienne. De roi en roi, la tradition de la poésie devait se maintenir, d'où une grande intimité entre les rois et les groupes de saltimbanques itinerants qui étaient les seuls à pouvoir entrer librement à la cour du roi. . . . Dans le repertoire du théâtre Kabuki, on rencontre sans cesse des rois. Dans l'ensemble de ces pièces, à travers l'image du roi et celle du clan royal, s'expriment des themes constants: la naissance d'un prince grotesque, sa violence, le parricide, l'inceste, la redemption, la folie. Ainsi le thème mythique de la royauté du Japon archaïque se voit renaître sur la scène même du théâtre Kabuki et sur celle du théâtre des marionnettes. Ainsi le théâtre Kabuki continua d'être le lieu privilégié où se montre la cassure entre culture et nature et cela au dela même du temps et de l'espace bien ordonnés. Il en resulte que la royauté était encore le plus puissant signe de l'intrusion de l'étrangeté dans la vie banale et quotidienne. . . . Nous venons d'examiner comment la royauté persiste comme un modèle immergé à tous les niveaux culturels de la civilisation japonaise à travers le mythe, la sensation du temps, l'esthétique, l'intensité de l'expérience. Aujourd'hui, ces divers niveaux ont trouvé leurs équivalents dans l'âge du changement technologique. Ainsi la royauté en tant que modèle idéal du centre politique continue d'exister, de même que, pour la réalisation de la scène mythique et pour celle de la situation en marge, la royauté sert également de modèle répétitif" Yamaguchi Masao, "La Structure mythico-théâtrale de la royauté japonaise", *Esprit,* n.s. 44 (1973): 337–39. See also Amino Yoshihiko, "Les Japonais et la mer"; and Tanaka Yuko, "Le monde comme représentation symbolique: Le Japon de l'époque d'Edo et l'univers du mitate"—both in *Annales* 50, no. 2 (March–April 1995): 235–58 and 259–82.

16. Yamaguchi Masao, "The Dual Structure of Japanese Emperorship," with comment by Brian Moeran, *Current Anthropology* 28, no. 4 (1987), supplement: *An Anthropological Profile of Japan,* 8–20. See also Miyata Noboru, "Theater Watching and Emperorship," also in *Current Anthropology* 28, no. 4 (1987), supplement; Yamaguchi Masao, "Kingship, Theatricity and Marginal Reality in Japan," in R. Jain (ed.), *Text and Context* (Philadelphia: Institute for the Study of Human Issues, 1977), 159–79; *idem,* "Le Prototype des Exclus dans l'Histoire Japonaise," *Stanford French Review* 7 (summer 1983): 193–206; see also E. Ohnuki-Tierney, "The Emperor of Japan as Deity (Kami)," *Ethnology* 30, no. 3 (1991): 199–215; Matsubara Ryūichirō, "Reflections on Sumo and the Imperial Household," *Japan Echo* 20, no. 2 (1993): 86–90.

For a detailed discussion of many such marginal "defiled" persons—murderers, courtesans, slaves—and their purifying ritual powers as they developed around Buddhist temples in medieval Japan but building on earlier "Shinto" or "native" traditions, see Michele Marra, *Representations of Power: The Literary Politics of Medieval Japan* (Honolulu: University of Hawaii Press, 1933), esp. chap. 2, 55–115.

17. E. Ohnuki-Tierney, *The Emperor of Japan as Kami.* See also Matsubara Ryuichiro, "Reflections on Sumo."

18. For a very insightful analysis of the Japanese attitude toward nature, see Edward Seidensticker, "The Japanese and Nature, with Special Reference to the Tale of Genji," in *idem, This Country* (Tokyo: Kodansha International, 1989). See also D. Richie, *A Lateral View: Essays on Culture and Style in Contemporary Japan* (Berkeley, Calif.: Stone Bridge Press, 1992), esp. chaps. 1–3. See also the discussion by J. Pelzel, "Japanese Personality and Culture," *Culture, Medicine and Psychiatry* 1 (1977): 299–315; Nakamura Hajime, "The Acceptance ofMan's Natural Dispositions," *Japan Foundation Newsletter* 7, no. 2 (June–July 1979); W. Kuitert, *Themes, Scenes and Taste in the History of Japanese Garden Art* (Amsterdam: Gieben, 1988); I. Schaarrschmidt-Richtner, *Der Japanische Garten: Ein Kunstwerk* (Wurzburg: Auflage, 1980). See also the bibliography in note 6.

19. Editors' comments on P. J. Asquith, "The Monkey Memorial Service of Japanese Primatologists," in Lebra and Lebra, *Japanese Culture and Behavior,* 29–33.

20. R. J. Zwi Werblowski, "Mizuko Kuyō, Notulae on the Most Important 'New Religion' of Japan," *Japanese Journal of Religious Studies* 8, no. 4 (1991): 295–354; W. R. La Fleur, *Liquid Life: Abortion and Buddhism in Japan* (Princeton: Princeton University Press, 1993).

21. M. Pinguet, *La mort volontaire au Japon* (Paris: Gallimard, 1984); in English, *Voluntary Death in Japan* (Cambridge: Polity Press, 1983).

22. See LaFleur, *Liquid Life.*

23. R. J. Smith, *Ancestor Worship in Contemporary Japan* (Stanford: Stanford University Press, 1974); *idem,* "Who Are the 'Ancestors' in Japan? A 1963 Census of Memorial Tablets," in W. H. Newell (ed.), *Ancestors* (Hague: Mouton Publishers, 1976), 33–60; Hirano Toshimasa, "Aruga Kizaemon: The Household, the Ancestors and the Tutelary Deities," *Japanese Journal of Religious Studies* 7, nos. 2–3 (June–September 1980): 144–66.

24. Mayer, "Fauna and Flora in Japanese Folktales."

25. Yoshiharu Iijima, "Folk Culture and the Liminality of Children" and Kazuhiko Komatsu, "The Dragon Palace Child: An Anthropological and Sociohistorical Approach," *Current Anthropology* 28, no. 4 (August–October 1987), supplement. For various works on Japanese folklore, see R. M. Dorson, *Studies in Japanese Folklore* (Bloomington: Indiana University Press, 1963).

26. Leo Loveday and Satouni Cyba, "Partaking with the Divine and Symbolizing the Societal: The Semiotics of Japanese Food and Drink," *Semiotika* 56, no. 2 (1985): 115–31; N. Ben-Ari Roessler, *Comparative Reading in Chinese and Japanese "Fo(l)xtales,"* seminar paper, Jerusalem, Hebrew University, 1987.

27. J. Hendry, *Wrapping Culture: Politeness, Presentation and Power in Japan*

and Other Societies (Oxford: Clarendon Press, 1993). See also *idem*, "Humidity, Hygiene or Ritual Care: Some Thought on Wrapping as a Social Phenomenon," 18–13, Teigo Yoshida, "The Feminine in Japanese Folk Religion: Polluted or Divine?," 38–77, and E. Ben-Ari, "Wrapping Up: Some General Implications," 221–34, all in E. Ben-Ari, B. Moeran, and J. Valentine (eds.), *Unwrapping Japan: Society and Culture in Anthropological Perspectives* (Manchester: Manchester University Press, 1990).

28. J. Heise (ed.), *Die Kuehle Seele: Selbstinterpretationen der Japanischen Kultur* (Frankfurt: Fischer Taschenbuch Verlag, 1990); H. A. Shapiro, "The Japanese Sense of Nature," *Japan Quarterly* 32, no. 1 (January–March 1985): 73–76; G. Wienold, "Natur oder Naturdarstellug? Ein Blick im Japanische Garten," *Semiotic* 13, nos. 1–2 (1991): 123–43.

29. E. Ohnuki-Tierney, *Illness and Culture in Contemporary Japan* (Cambridge: Cambridge University Press, 1987).

30. Robert J. Wargo, "Japanese Ethics: Beyond Good and Evil," *Philosophy East and West* 40, no. 5 (October 1990): 499–511.

31. Maraini, *Meeting with Japan; idem,* Japan: "The Essential Modernizer."

32. Maraini, "Japan, the Essential Modernizer."

33. J. Bachnik, "Time, Space and Person in Japanese Relationship," in J. Hendry and J. Webber (eds.), *Interpreting Japanese Society*, JASO Occasional Papers no. 5 (Oxford: 1986), 49–57.

34. G. M. Wilson, "Time and History in Japan," *American Historical Review* 85 (1990): 557–71.

35. H. Bolitho, "Concrete Discourse, Manifest Metaphor, and the Tokugawa Intellectual Paradigm," *Monumenta Nipponica* 35, no. 1 (1980): 89–98. See the discussion and bibliography in chapter 12.

36. T. P. Kasulis, "Kūkai, Philosophizing in Plato's and Kūkai's Shojin, Philosophy East and West," in *idem, Zen Action, Zen Person* (Honolulu: University of Hawaii Press, 1981), 774–835; M. Nakamura, *Ways of Thinking of Eastern People* (Honolulu: East-West Center Press, 1964).

37. J. Pelzel makes a similar point when he says, "Principles are properly the servants of reality rather than the reverse" (Pelzel, "Japanese Personality and Culture," *Culture, Medicine and Psychiatry* 1 (1977): 299–315).

38. A. Berque, "The Sense of Nature and Its Relation to Space in Japan," in Hendry and Webber, *Interpreting Japanese Society*, 101–2; Manabu Waida, "Symbolism of the Moon and the Waters of Immortality," *History of Religions* 16 (1977): 207–423; J. H. Foard, "The Boundaries of Comparison: Buddhism and National Tradition in Japanese Pilgrimage," *Journal of Asian Studies* 41, no. 2 (1982): 232–51; A. G. Grappard, "Flying Mountains and Walkers of Emptiness: Toward a Definition of Sacred Space in Japanese Religions," *History of Religions* 20, no. 3 (February 1982): 195–221; B. Faure, "Space and Place in Chinese Religious Traditions," *History of Religions* 26, no. 4 (1987): 337–56; Kuiter, *Themes, Scenes and Taste in the History of Japanese Garden Art;* Schaarschmidt-Richer, *Der japanische Garten;* idem., "Gartenkunst," in H. Hammitzsch (ed.), *Japan Handbuch* (Wiesbaden: 2d ed., 1984), 768–76.

39. Berque defines this topological metaphor in the following way:

The existing subject can be topologically related to a spontaneous environment instead of actively ordering it around itself; culture may be put on even terms with nature.

This metaphorical process works, of course, at the heart of any culture; but a sense of place (bashosei) is particularly pronounced in cultures which, as in the Japanese case, do not enhance the subject's pre-eminence to the degree European culture has done. This culture less easily assimilates itself to nature because, fundamentally, the subject's spontaneous self-definition, or particularity, acts in opposition to the spontaneous definition, or naturalness, of its environment. . . .

It must be stressed that, between the realm of man and that of the gods, nature conspicuously intervenes; the Japanese way of organizing space systematically provides such points of transition.

Liminality is linked to nature in other ways too. Japanese notions of space dislike general coordinates and perspectives. They refer rather to local, concrete landmarks. (Berque, "Sense of Nature," 102–3)

40. A. Berque, "Some Traits of Japanese Fudōsei," *Japan Foundation Newsletter* 14, no. 5 (1987): 5; *idem, Le sauvage et l'artifice* (Paris: Gallimard, 1986); *idem, Du geste a la cité: Formes urbaines et lien social au Japon* (Paris: Gallimard, 1993).

41. Lebra and Lebra, *Japanese Culture and Behavior;* T. Sugiyama Lebra, "The Tri-Dimensional Space of Hierarchy: The Japanese Nobility," paper presented for the panel "The Ascribed Hierarchy Revisited: Subtle Dimensions," American Anthropological Association annual meeting, Washington D.C., 15–19 November 1989; *idem,* Introduction and "The Special Layout of Hierarchy: Residential Style of the Modern Japanese Nobility," in *idem* (ed.), *Japanese Social Organization* (Honolulu: University of Hawaii Press, 1992), 1–22, 49–78. See also M. Jeremy and M. E. Robinson (eds.), *Ceremony and Symbolism in the Japanese Home* (Manchester: Manchester University Press, 1989), esp. chaps. 3, 5; Terunobu Fujimori, "Traditional Houses and the Japanese View of Life," *Japan Foundation Newsletter* 23, no. 1 (August 1990): 10–15; W. Muntschick, *Das Traditionelle Japanische Bauernhaus* (Hamburg: Mitteilungen der Gessellschaft fur Natur- und Volkerkunde Ostasiens e.V., 1985).

42. On the conception of space prevalent in Japan, see also Ian Nish and Charles Dunn (eds.), "Space and Travel: An Interpretation of the Travel Poems of the Man'yōshū," *Contemporary European Writing on Japan* (Tendere: Paul Norbury, 1988), 269–83.

43. J. M. Bachnik, "Time, Space and Person in Japanese Relationships," in Hendry and Webber, *Interpreting Japanese Society,* 56–58; Bachnik, "Native Perspectives of Distance and Anthropological Perspectives of Culture," *Anthropological Quarterly* 60, no. 1 (January 1987): 25–34; Shingo Shimada, "Überlegungen zur Genesis Wirtschaftliche Regelung in Japan," J. Matthes (ed.), *Zwischen Kulturen, Soziale Welt,* Sonderband N.8, Verlag Otto Schwartz Co., Gottemberg, 1992, 375–93.

44. See also J. Bachnik, "Kejime: Defining a Shifting Self in Multiple Organizational Modes," in N. Rosenberger (ed.), *Japanese Sense of Self* (Cambridge: Cambridge University Press, 1992), 152–72; Ohnuki-Tierney, *Rice as Self,* 53 ff.

45. Berque, *Le sauvage et l'artifice;* Murakami Yasusuke, "Two Types of Civi-

lization: Transcendental and Hermeneutical," *Nichibuken (Japan Review)* 1 (1980): 1–38.

46. K. Singer, *Mirror, Sword and Jewel* (Tokyo: Kodansha International, 1987).

47. Ohnuki-Tierney, comment on Namihara, "Pollution in the Folk Belief System."

48. Nakamura Hajime, *Ways of Thinking of Eastern People* (Honolulu: East-West Center Press, 1964), xx. For greater detail, see the detailed table of contents of his chapter on Japan:

> The Acceptance of Phenomenalism and the Tendency To Emphasize A Limited Social Nexus and Non-Rationalistic Tendencies
>
> The Acceptance of Phenomenalism as Manifest in Phenomenal World as Absolute-This-Worldliness—The Acceptance of Man's Natural Dispositions—Emphasis on the Love of Human Beings—The Spirit of Tolerance—Cultural Multiplicity (Consisting of Several Still Preserved) and Weakness of the Spirit of Criticism
>
> The Tendency to Emphasize a Limited Social Nexus—Overstressing of Social Relations—Social Relationships Take Precedence over the Individual-Unconditional Belief in a Limited Social Nexus—Observance of Family Morals—Emphasis on Rank and Social Position—Problems of Ultra Nationalism—Absolute Devotion to Specific Individual Symbolic of the Social Nexus—Emperor Worship—Sectarian and Factional Closedness—Defense of Human Nexus by Force—Emphasis upon Human Activities—Acuteness of Moral Self-Reflection—Weak Awareness of Religious Values
>
> Non-Rationalistic Tendencies are Manifest
>
> Indifference to Logical Rules—Lack of Interest in Formal Consistency—Slow Development of Exact Logic in Japan—Hopes for Development of Exact Logical Thinking in Japan—Intuitive and Emotional Tendencies—Tendency to Avoid Complex Ideas—Fondness for Simple Symbolic Expressions—The Lack of Knowledge Concerning the Objective Order.

49. For a very incisive analysis of the difference between Japanese and American conceptions of personality, see Alisdair MacIntyre, "Individual and Social Morality in Japan and the United States: Rival Conceptions of the Self," *Philosophy East and West* 11, no. 4 (October 1990): 489–99. See also J. C. Condon and Mitsuko Saito (eds.), *Intercultural Encounters with Japan* (Tokyo: Simul Press, 1974).

50. Nakane Chie, *Japanese Society* (London: Weidenfeld and Nicholson, 1971); *idem, Human Relations in Japan* (Tokyo: Ministry of Foreign Affairs, 1972).

51. Lebra and Lebra, editorial note to part 2 of *Japanese Culture and Behavior,* 107. See also S. T. Lebra, *Japanese Patterns of Behavior* (Honolulu: University of Hawaii Press, 1976).

52. Kasulis, *Zen Action, Zen Person,* 7–9. For a more general analysis of contextual frameworks, see E. Hamaguchi, "A Context Model of the Japanese: Toward a Methodological Innovation in Japan Studies," *Journal of Japanese Studies* 11, no. 2 (1985), 289–322.

53. H. Mosbach, "Major Psychological Factors Influencing Japanese Personal Relations," in N. Warren (ed.), *Studies in Cross Cultural Psychology* (London: Academic Press, 1980), 314–44; Bachnik, "Kejime, Defining a Shifting Self."

54. Tani Yutaka, "Status, Role and Self Identity in Japanese Social Relations,"

in G. Fodella (ed.), *Social Structures and Economic Dynamics in Japan Up to 1980*, vol. 1 (Milan: Luigi Bocconi University, 1975), 79–90; F. L. K. Hsu, *Iemoto: The Heart of Japan* (New York: J. Wiley and Sons, 1975); Nakanishi Susumu, "Renunciation: One Aspect of the Nature of Japanese Thought," *Japan Foundation Newsletter* 15, no. 2 (October 1987): 1–8.

55. S. Y. Kuroda, "Where Epistemology, Style and Grammar Meet," in S. Anderson and P. Kiparsky (eds.), *A Festschrift for Morris Halle* (New York: Holt Rinehart and Winston, 1973), 377–91; B. Saint-Jacques, "Language Attitudes in Contemporary Japan," *Japan Foundation Newsletter* 11, nos. 1–2 (1983): 7–15; Tsunoda Tadanobu, "The Left Cerebral Hemisphere of the Brain and the Japanese Language," *Japan Foundation Newsletter* 6, no. 1 (April–May 1987): 7–10; J. M. Bachnik, *Deixis and Self/Other Reference in Japanese Discourse*, Working Papers in Sociolinguistics, no. 99 (Austin: Southwestern Educational Development Laboratory, 1982); Suzuki Takao, *Japanese and the Japanese* (Tokyo: Kodansha, 1987); H. Passin, "Intra-Familial Linguistic Usage in Japan," *Monumenta Nipponica* 21 (1966): 97–113; H. Befu and E. Norbeck, "Japanese Usage of Terms of Relationships," *Southwestern Journal of Anthropology* 14 (1958): 66–87; D. C. Barnlund, *Communicative Styles of Two Cultures: Public and Private Self in Japan and the United States.* (Tokyo: Simul Press, 1975); S. E. Martin, *The Japanese Language through Time* (New Haven: Yale University Press, 1987).

More detailed analyses of Japanese language from the point of view discussed here have been presented in Masayoshi Shibatani (ed.), *Syntax and Semantics*, vol. 5, *Japanese Generative Grammar* (New York: Academic Press, 1976), esp. S. Y. Kuroda, "Subject," 1–10, Kuno Susumu, "Subject Raising," 17–51, and S. I. Harada, "Honorifics," 499–562. For more general linguistic discussions of these problems, see Joseph H. Greenberg, (ed.), *Universals of Human Language*, vol. 3, *Word Structure* (Stanford: Stanford University Press, 1978), esp. David Ingram, "Typology and Universals of Personal Pronouns," 213–49, and Elizabeth Closs Traugott, "On the Expression of Spatio-Temporal Relations in Language," 369–401; For a general survey of Japanese language, see Robert J. Smith and Richard K. Beardsley (eds.), *Japanese Culture: Its Development and Characteristics* (Chicago: Aldine Publishing Company, 1962), esp. Susumu Ono, "The Japanese Language: Its Origin and Its Sources." See also Fred C. C. Peng (ed.), *Language in Japanese Society* (Tokyo: University of Tokyo Press, 1975), esp. Fred C. C. Peng, "Sociolinguistic Patterns of Japanese Kinship Behavior," 91–129, John Hinds, "Third Person Pronouns in Japanese," 129–159, and Nobuyuki Honna, "A Note on Social Structure and Linguistic Behavior: A Case Study of a Japanese Community, 193–215.

56. R. J. Smith, *Japanese Society, Tradition, Self, and the Social Order* (Cambridge: Cambridge University Press, 1984), 77. For a detailed explanation of these numerous personal referents and their embeddednes in different situations or contexts based on field observations, see Dorinne K. Kondo, *Crafting Selves: Power, Gender and Discourses of Identity in a Japanese Workplace* (Chicago: University of Chicago Press, 1990), 28–35.

57. Smith, *Japanese Society, Tradition, Self, and the Social Order.*

58. Recently Isamu Kamada has reformulated in an interesting way the relation between the linguistic images and conceptions of self in Japan:

The so-called Japanese lack of individuality is primarily ascribed to the language's peculiar syntactical rules which permit the omission of pronouns while at the same time encouraging the use of a variety of personal pronouns. However, Wittgenstein's linguistic analysis of the "I" of experiential predicates denies this view. Rather, it can be said that Japanese omission of pronouns and multiplicity of pronouns for "I" and "you" negate the metaphysics of "I" (which considers "I" to be a substantial entity inside man) by showing that "I" is a relational term specifying the speaker.

It is not relevant to the understanding of "self" to analyze the language which is presupposed to consist of fixed meanings; what is necessary is to study social relations and the social system in which individuals are treated. Nonetheless, if language is understood as consisting in social interaction with its meanings residing in interaction, then linguistic analyses can be productive for understanding what is called "self."

The individuality of a person should not be sought in speculatively posited rationality or self-consciousness but in the particularity of action which is embedded in a specific context and which can be observed. When social scientists stop constraining action within the social and mental structures posited by them, it becomes clear that action is situated in the socio-historical, interactive context and is open to the new situation as potentiality. (Isamu Kamada, " 'I' and Self-Consciousness in the Japanese Language and in Society," *International Journal of Japanese Sociology*, no. 2 (October 1993), 47–65.

59. Albert M. Craig, "Introspective: Perspectives on Personality in Japanese History," in A. M. Craig and D. H. Shively (eds.), *Personality in Japanese History* (Berkeley: University of California Press, 1970), 17–29; I. Morris, *The Nobility of Failure: Tragic Heroes in the History of Japan* (New York: Holt Rinehart and Winston, 1975).

60. D. K. Kondo, "Work, Family and the Self: A Cultural Analysis of Japanese Family Enterprise," doctoral dissertation, Harvard University, May 1982, 192–97. See also *idem, Crafting Selves*. See also D. W. Plath, *Long Engagements: Maturity in Modern Japan* (Stanford: Stanford University Press, 1980), 218. Kondo also offers the following, more detailed expression in "Work, Family and the Self":

Here, more than in the family, "work" is self-validating in the sense of affirming one's personal achievement and maturity, and in validating one's belonging and participation in a social group. When the frame of reference is internal to the group, the members of the company define themselves vis-à-vis each other in a hierarchy of positions, but when they step outside the company boundaries, they do so first as employees of their company, defined in contrast to all others. As in the family one's sense of self is intimately bound up with belonging to the group.

What is crucial in both cases is precisely this relationship of the self to others. One learns the meaning of human relationships, of the critical links to other people, through these contexts, in a complex and finely tuned dialectic mediated by the paradigmatic set of oppositions centered around inner/outer, feeling/form. Both family and company are so structured, and consequently, each can act as a template for the other.

What the self is taught through these differences and similarities is, precisely, the importance of these distinctions as mediating his/her identity. This finely tuned dialectic reinforces the conviction, the "social fact," that it is *people who matter.* . . .

. . . This logic defines not only the anatomy of the self, the family, and the company, but it is a dialectic lived out as a social process; that is, its meaning and power is only realized in action. For it is by moving outside, say, the household, that the meaning of household is defined, in such concrete details as putting on different clothes, slipping into shoes, adjusting one's language and posture appropriately, and having to "ki o tsukau," or be attentive, to details of status and etiquette. These distinctions of inside/outside, feeling/form, are an inescapable social reality, molding Japanese experience from the concrete details of language and behavior to the definition of identity and selfhood. All the oppositions partake of a similar structure, yet they can be set against and played off one another in different contexts. For example, the household is to the company as uchi is to soto, as inside is to outside. But within each domain, there are both inside and outside elements when the frame of reference is narrowed, and so on. These oppositions, then, are variations on a theme, repeated over and over in everyday life, in which both similarities and differences are meaningful.

61. Nancy Rosenberger, "Dialectic Balance in the Polar Mode of Self: The Japan Case," *Ethos* 17 (1989): 88–113, 94–99. The concept of *ki* has also been analyzed by T. P. Rohlen, "The Promise of Adulthood in the Japanese Spiritualism," *Daedalus*," special issue: "Adulthood," spring 1976, 125–143. Rosenberger analyses the details of these movements in the following way:

The personal accomplishment mode is disciplined, but inner-oriented; the person is task-oriented, but not necessarily in terms of the group consensus. The goal could be individual progress (as for promotion in a company) or self-development (as in judo or tea ceremony). Both creativity and competition emerge here. Because competition and creativity are increasingly important to effective functioning in Japanese society, an intriguing interface exists between this mode and the group production mode, which is presently the accepted mode for accomplishing society's main tasks.

The mode of harmony or affection is outer-oriented and spontaneous, but in a culturally patterned form of spontaneity. The self is consciously directed to express the warmth of the "pure heart." This arena of life is represented in after-hour parties of the work group, and at home in bathing and sleeping together and in general affection. Vertical hierarchy is played down in this mode but still defines the relationship.

. . . The pure impulse or gratification mode is spontaneous in form and content, and oriented toward the inner self. In the ideal, there are no holds barred in exchange of inner-motivated opinion, feeling and action in this model. Honest relationships between old friends, passionate relationships between lovers, and bitter relationships between rivals obtain here. This mode can impinge on the harmony mode and the personal accomplishment mode, particularly in the area of competition. . . .

. . . The inner-oriented but directed mode of self is presented in an ego-centered work group; the inner-oriented, spontaneous mode of self is manifested in an ego-centered group for relaxation. The outer-oriented, directed mode of self would be expressed in a structured work group, while the outer-directed but spontaneous mode of self would be called for in a structured relaxation group. The modes cannot be labeled as individual or group modes because all modes are developed and expressed through different kinds of groups, although inner-directed modes can be expressed by the isolated person. (Rosenberger, "Dialectic Balance," 98–100)

62. Rosenberger, "Dialectic Balance."

63. T. Ishida, "Conflict and Its Accommodation: Omote-Ura and Uchi-Soto Relations," in E. S. Krauss, T. P. Rohlen, and P. G. Steinhoff (eds.), *Conflict in Japan* (Honolulu: University of Hawaii Press, 1976), 17–18.

64. Ibid.

65. Pelzel provides the following observations:

The pedigree of the individual as a sentient being is thus as well known as is the view of him as a social drone. However these seemingly irreconcilable approaches originated, they have in fact co-existed so steadily it seems to me impossible to deny either. It also seems impossible to deny that both have been built into the behavior sets of individuals. Perhaps the most striking impression Japanese behavior *in toto* makes on the tyro foreigner from a logically-homogenizing tradition like our own is the radical reversal of behaviors of which most Japanese seem routinely capable. In one situation conformist to the role and the rules, compulsive in task performance and ritualistic in procedure, seemingly unaware of human weakness and uncomprehending of any need for privacy; at another moment they become not only capable of, but addicted to, behavior more *sui pien* ("willful") than that most Chinese would consider appropriate in this supposedly Chinese posture, compelled to parade failures, weaknesses, and even perversions that would seem utterly to disqualify them for their sober roles, delighted to extend an almost preternaturally sensitive appreciation and tolerance to the sensibilities and idiosyncrasies of others, and in a word pure humanists, unchecked by either the chilly canons of an equal-but-separate humanitarianism or the disciplines of social duty.

I am quite content to see these separate traditions, and these "logically incompatible" behaviors—as I believe Ruth Benedict saw them—as expressions of a logic of situations rather than of principle, of an understanding that reality varies from case to case and that principles are properly the servants of reality rather than the reverse (which is also one sense in which I accept Reynolds' characterization of the Japanese world view as "naturalistic"). (Pelzel, "Japanese Personality and Culture")

See also Hisa A. Kumagai, "A Dissection of Intimacy: A Study of 'Bipolar' Positions in Japanese Social Interaction, Amaeru and Amayakasu, Indulgence and Deference," *Culture, Medicine and Psychiatry* 5, no. 3 (1981): 249–72.

66. Bachnik, "Kejime," 154 ff. See also Tobin, "Japanese Preschools," 21–39: "I suggest that the Japanese preschools help children develop and integrate this twofold selfhood not by offering a world completely unlike the world of mother and home, but instead by offering a world that is simultaneously home (uchi) and not-home (soto), front (omote) and rear (ura), a world of both spontaneous human feeling (honne) and prescribed, formal pretense (tatemae). If preschools were purely a world of omote and home purely a world of ura, Japanese children might never learn to integrate the two sides of the self. Without an opportunity to integrate the omote and the ura dimensions of the self, Japanese children might grow up to be the caricatured human being of this paper's preface, spoiled and impulsive at heart, externally controlled."

67. See Wargo, "Japanese Ethics." See, for greater detail, chapter 14, specifically the section on processes of socialization. See also Yutaka Yamamoto, "A Morality Based on Trust: Some Reflections on Japanese Morality," *Philosophy East and West* 40, no. 4 (October 1990): 451–71; T. Kasulis, "Intimacy: A General Orientation in Japanese Religious Values," *Philosophy East and West*, 90, no. 4 (1990): 433–49.

68. Fred Rothbaum, John R. Wisz, and Samuel S. Snyder, "Changing the World and Changing the Self: A Two-Process Model of Perceived Control," *Journal of Personality and Social Psychology* 42, no. 1 (January 1982): M5–M38.

69. J. Pelzel, "Human Nature in the Japanese Myths," in Lebra and Lebra, *Japanese Culture and Behavior*, 7–28; idem, "Japanese Personality in Culture," in *Culture, Medicine and Psychiatry* 1 (1977): 299–315.

70. See Mosbach, "Major Psychological Factors," 331–33. See also Reiko Atsumi, "Friend in a Cross-Cultural Perspective," paper presented at the International Colloquium on the Comparative Study of Japan, Noosa Heads, Australia, 29 January–6 February 1982. See also H. Befu, *Self and Society in Japan,* the fourth teaching module in the series "Japanese Society through Film," Japanese Society, 1992.

71. For a somewhat popular explanation of the meaning of silence in Japanese language, see Matsumoto Michihiro, *The Unspoken Way: Haragei: Silence in Japanese Business and Society* (Tokyo: Kodansha International, 1988). See also S. Takie Lebra, "The Cultural Significance of Silence in Japanese Communication, *Multilingua: Journal of Cross-Cultural and Interlanguage Communication* 6, no. 4 (1987): 343–57.

72. R. N. Bellah, *Tokugawa Religion: The Values of Pre-Industrial Japan* (Glencoe, Ill.: Free Press, 1957); J. J. Sullivan, "Visions of Work in America and Japan: A Universal Theory of Work Motivation," (Seattle: University of Washington Press, forthcoming).

73. The specific characteristics of the achievement orientation to be found in Japan have been succinctly analyzed by George De Vos who, in a series of researches spanning more than twenty-five years, has elaborated the importance of a strong achievement orientation in large sectors of Japanese society—an orientation most clearly manifested in the modern era in the "educational" arena:

> In this chapter I have reversed somewhat the priority of the order of consideration of interpersonal patterns from some of my previous writings on achievement motivation. In the present instance, I have emphasized more strongly the expressive aspects of Japanese concerns rather than commencing my discussion with the instrumental patterns which have been the primary concern in my writings on Japanese role behavior. The essence of instrumental behavior is that it is goal-oriented—that it has objectives to be realized regardless of the affective components found in the necessary behavior. What I have again emphasized is how the Japanese sense of duty and obligation is very central to understanding instrumental motivations. This sense of responsibility, I have contended, is highly internalized. Social constraints so very evident in external patterns of social control in Japanese society are also internalized, albeit with some costs in terms of personal tension for most Japanese; and additional costs, in terms of suppression of personal needs, for Japanese women. Behavior, if not thought, remains in harmony with the external reinforcements of social control in Japanese society. Japanese socialization tends to legitimize authority rather than raise issues about autonomy. There is a positive assessment of subordinate compliance rather than the characteristic ambivalence about being or remaining subordinate found prevailing in American society, for example. The Japanese concept of instrumental behavior de-emphasizes autonomy as an acceptable mode of instrumental interaction with others.
>
> Single stars who overemphasize their individual prowess may be disruptive to group spirit and, at least overtly, they must contain themselves within the group purpose in order to continue to function as part of the group. Conversely, unethical behavior is sometimes tolerated toward the outside since there is no feeling of necessary identification with one's competitors; and it is in some forms of unethical behavior that one can perceive most clearly the Japanese lack of identification with others that are not part of their own group. And as mentioned already, it is very difficult to bring outsiders in as part of one's cooperative team since the underlying expressive considerations may be considered lacking. One cannot therefore separate

out Japanese cooperative behavior as a form of strictly instrumental juxtaposition of individual needs. There is in the cooperative behavior itself a continual expression of a sense of belonging. The rituals exercised in Japanese companies in the morning might seem slightly ridiculous to the Western observer. To the Japanese, however, such behavior symbolizes the collectivity and the sense of belonging, which are positively experienced, as well as focusing on the instrumental purposes of the organization. (De Vos, "Dimensions of the Self in Japanese Culture," in A. Marsella, G. De Vos, and F. Hsu (eds.), *Culture and Self: Asian and Western Perspectives* [New York: Tavistock, 1985], 177–79.

See also Mosbach, "Major Psychological Factors."

74. P. Reasoner, "Sincerity and Japanese Values," *Philosophy East and West* 40, no. 4 (October 1990): 483–85.

75. Maraini, "Japan, the Essential Modernizer."

76. B. Moeran, "Individual, Group and Seishin in Japan's Internal Debate," *Man*, n.s. 19, no. 2 (June 1989): 252–61. See also Lebra and Lebra, editorial note to part 1 of *Japanese Culture and Behavior*, 6; MacIntyre, "Individual and Social Morality in Japan and the United States"; H. Mosbach, "An Attempt to Identify the Major Theoretical Issues Related to Comparing the Japanese Concept of Individual Cross-Culturality," paper presented at the International Colloquium on the Comparative Study of Japan, Noosa Heads, Australia, 29 January–6 February 1982.

77. R. Benedict, *The Chrysanthemum and the Sword* (London: Secker and Warburg, 1947). The discussion of Japan as a shame society is relevant here: S. T. Lebra, "Shame and Guilt: A Psychocultural View of the Japanese Self," *Ethos* 11, no. 3 (fall 1983): 129–209; *idem*, "Nonconfrontational Strategies for Management of Interpersonal Conflicts," in E. Krauss, T. Rohlen, and P. Steinhoff (eds.), *Conflict in Japan* (Honolulu: University of Hawaii Press, 1984); Lebra, *Japanese Patterns of Behavior; idem*, "An Alternative Approach to Reciprocity: American Self in Japanese Culture," paper presented at Symposium of Cultural Meaning and Self-Representation, Chicago, 1987.

78. See Lebra, *Japanese Patterns of Behavior.*

79. Befu, *Self and Society in Japan*, 608. See also Hsu, *Iemoto.*

80. R. Goodman and K. Refsing (eds.), *Ideology and Practice in Modern Japan* (London: Routledge, 1972).

81. Mosbach, "Major Psychological Aspects," 327–28.

82. B. Moeran, *Language and Popular Culture in Japan* (Manchester: Manchester University Press, 1989).

83. J. Bachnik and C. J. Quinn Jr. (eds.), *Situated Meaning: Inside and Outside in Japanese Self, Society and Language* (Princeton: Princeton University Press, 1993).

CHAPTER FOURTEEN

1. F. Maraini, "Japan, the Essential Modernizer," in S. Kenny and J. Lehman, *Themes and Theories in Modern Japanese History* (London: Athlone Press, 1988), 44–63; A. M. Craig, *Personality in Japanese History* (Berkeley: University of California Press, 1990).

2. T. P. Rohlen, "Order in Japanese Society: Attachment, Authority and Routine," *Journal of Japanese Studies* 15, no. 1 (1989): 18–19.

3. E. Ohnuki-Tierney, "The Ambivalent Self of the Contemporary Japanese," *Cultural Anthropology* 5 (1990): 196–215. See also Maraini, "Japan, the Essential Modernizer."

4. N. P. Rosenberger (ed.), *Japanese Sense of Self* (Cambridge: Cambridge University Press, 1992); *idem*, "Dialectic Balance in the Polar Model of Self," *Ethos* 17 (1988): 88–113; T. S. Lebra (ed.), *Japanese Social Organization* (Honolulu: University of Hawaii Press, 1992).

5. Joseph J. Tobin, David Y. H. Wu, and Dana H. Davidson (eds.), *Preschool in Three Cultures: Japan, China and the United States* (New Haven: Yale University Press, 1989), 70–71; M. White, *The Japanese Educational Challenge: A Commitment to Children* (New York: Free Press, 1987); L. J. Kotloff, "The Airplane Project: Fostering Individuality in a Progressive Japanese Preschool," paper presented at the ninth annual University of Pennsylvania Conference on ethnography in education research; C. C. Lewis, "From Indulgence to Internalization: Social Control in the Early School Years," *Journal of Japanese Studies* 15, no. 1 (1989): 139–57; N. Kobayashi and T. Berry Brazelton (eds.), *The Growing Child in the Family and Society* (Tokyo: University of Tokyo Press, 1984).

6. Tobin, Wu, and Davidson, *Preschool in Three Cultures*, 192. See the articles in the symposium "Social Control and Early Socialization," *Journal of Japanese Studies* 15, no. 1 (1989): 1–158, esp. Lewis, "From Indulgence to Internalization."

7. Paraphrasing C. C. Lewis, "From Indulgence to Internalization," 142–52.

8. D. K. Kondo, *Crafting Selves: Power, Gender, and Discourses of Identity in a Japanese Workplace* (Chicago: University of Chicago Press, 1990), esp. chap. 3. See also C. L. Turner, "Breaking the Silence: Consciousness, Commitment and Action in Japanese Unions," dissertation, Department of Anthropology, Stanford University, September 1987.

9. Rohlen, "Order in Japanese Society," 9–35. See also J. Heise (ed.), *Die Kuhle Seele: Selbstinterpretationen der Japanischen Kultur* (Frankfurt: Fischer Taschenbuch Verlag, 1990).

10. On the centrality of trust, see also Yamamoto Yutaka, "A Morality Based on Trust: Some Reflections on Japanese Morality," *Philosophy East and West* 40, no. 4 (October 1990): 451–71.

11. R. N. Bellah, *Tokugawa Religion: The Values of Pre-Industrial Japan* (Glencoe, Ill.: Free Press, 1957); H. Webb, *The Japanese Imperial Institution in the Tokugawa Period* (New York: Columbia University Press, 1968). See also Yamamota Yutaka, "Morality Based on Trust." Some psychological dimensions of trust are analyzed in Toshio Yamagishi and Midori Yamagishi, "Trust and Commitment in the United States and Japan," *Motivations and Emotions* 18, no. 2 (1994): 129 ff.

12. P. Steinhoff, "Tenkō and Thought Control," in G. L. Bernstein and H. Fukui (eds.), *Japan and the World: Essays of Japanese History and Politics in Honor of Ishida Takeshi* (London: MacMillan, 1988), 78, 81, 88; D. Pollack, *The Fracture of Meaning: Japan's Synthesis of China from the Eighth through the Eighteenth Centuries* (Princeton: Princeton University Press, 1986).

13. R. J. Smith, *Ancestor Worship in Contemporary Japan* (Stanford: Stan-

ford University Press, 1974); *idem, Japanese Society, Tradition, Self and the Social Order* (Cambridge: Cambridge University Press, 1984); F. Maraini, *Meeting with Japan* (New York: Viking, 1960). J. P. Arnason, "Comparing Japan and the West: Prolegomena to a Research Programme," in L. Gule and O. Storebo (eds.), *Development and Modernity: Perspectives on Western Theories of Modernisation* (Bergen: Ariadne, 1993), 167–95.

14. Kondo, *Crafting Selves,* 122. See also J. M. Bachnik, *Family, Self and Society in Contemporary Japan* (Berkeley: University of California Press, forthcoming); *idem,* "The Two 'Faces' of Self and Society in Japan," *Ethos* 20, no. 1 (1992): 3–32; *idem,* "Native Perspectives of Distance and Anthropological Perspective of Culture," *Anthropological Quarterly* 60, no. 1 (January 1987): 25–34; *idem,* "Kejime: Defining a Shifting Self in Multiple Organizational Modes," in Rosenberger, *Japanese Sense of Self;* Bachnik in J. M. Bachnik and C. J. Quinn Jr. (eds.), *Situated Meaning: Inside and Outside in Japanese Self, Society and Language* (Princeton: Princeton University Press, 1993).

15. F. L. K. Hsu, *Iemoto: The Heart of Japan* (New York: John Wiley & Sons, 1975).

16. On the historical structure of urban merchant families, see E. Crawcour (ed.), "Some Observations on Merchants, a Translation of Mitsui Takafusa's Chōnin Koken Roku," *Transactions of the Asiatic Society of Japan,* 3d ser., vol. 8 (Tokyo: Kenkyusha Printing Company, 1962). On contemporary urban mercantile and industrial science, see Kondo, *Crafting Selves;* M. Hamabata, *The Crested Kimono: Power and Love in the Japanese Business Family* (Ithaca: Cornell University Press, 1990).

See also K. Tominaga, "Max Weber and the Modernization of China and Japan," in Melvin L. Kohn, *Cross-National Research in Sociology* (Newbury Park: Sage Publications, 1989), 125–48, in which the "looseness" of the Japanese family kinship structure, in contrast to that of China, is emphasized as one factor which facilitated the modernization of Japan. See also Bachnik, *Family, Self and Society.*

17. See Bachnik, *Family, Self and Society.*

18. I. McMullin, "Non-Agnatic Adoption: A Confucian Controversy in Seventeenth and Eighteenth Century Japan," *Harvard Journal of Asiatic Studies* 15 (1975): 133–89; Hsu, *Iemoto.* On adoptions in modern and contemporary Japan, see T. L. Bryant, "Sons and Lovers: Adoption in Japan," *American Journal of Comparative Law* 38 (1990): 299–336. See also Durkheim's combined review of Kojiro Twasaky, *Das japanische Eherecht* (Japanese matrimonial law, 1904) and Saburo Sakamoto, *Das Ehescheidungsrecht Japans* (Divorce in Japan, 1903), in *Année Sociologique* 8 (1904–5).

19. P. Hall, Epilogue, in J. P. Mass, *Court and Bakufu in Japan: Essays in Kamakura History* (New Haven: Yale University Press, 1974).

20. Y. Murakami, "Ie Society as a Pattern of Civilization," *Journal of Japanese Studies* 10, no. 2 (1984): 279–363; Hsu, *Iemoto;* J. M. Bachnik, "Recruitment Strategies for Household Succession: Rethinking Japanese Household Organization," *Man* 18 (1983): 160–82; K. Brown, "The Content of Dozoku Relations in Japan," *Ethnology* 7 (1968): 113–38.

21. S. Matsumoto, *Motoori Norinaga, 1730–1801,* Harvard East Asian Series, no. 44 (Cambridge, Mass.: Harvard University Press, 1970).

22. R. N. Bellah, "The Japanese Emperor as a Mother Figure: Some Preliminary Notes," paper presented at the Colloquium of the Center for Japanese Studies and Korean Studies, 11 October 1967. See also D. Robins-Mowry, *The Hidden Sun: Women of Modern Japan* (Boulder, Colo.: Westview Press, 1983). See also Matsumoto, *Motoori Norinaga*.

23. E. Ohnuki-Tierney, *Rice as Self* (Princeton: Princeton University Press, 1993).

24. C. Lévi-Strauss, "L'organization sociale des Kwakiutl," in his *La Voie des Masques* (Paris: Plon, 1979), 164–92.

25. Ohnuki-Tierney, *Rice as Self*.

26. Hamabata, *Crested Kimono*; H. Befu, "Four Models of Japanese Society and Their Relevance to Conflict," in S. N. Eisenstadt and E. Ben-Ari (eds.), *Japanese Models of Conflict Resolution* (London: Kegan Paul International, 1990), 213–38; Y. Murakami and T. P. Rohlen, "Social Exchange Aspects of the Japanese Political Economy: Culture, Efficiency, and Change," in S. Kumon and H. Rosovsky (eds.), *The Political Economy of Japan*, vol. 3 (Stanford: Stanford University Press, 1993), 63–108.

27. R. P. Dore, *Flexible Rigidities* (Stanford: Stanford University Press, 1986); idem, *Taking Japan Seriously: A Confucian Perspective on Leading Economic Issues* (Stanford: Stanford University Press, 1987); M. E. Berry, "Public Peace and Public Attachment: The Goals and Conduct of Power in Early Modern Japan," *Journal of Japanese Studies* 12, no. 2 (1986): 237–72.

28. Murakami and Rohlen, "Social Exchange Aspects of the Japanese Economy."

29. S. N. Eisenstadt and L. Roniger, *Patrons, Clients and Friends: Interpersonal Relations and the Structure of Trust in Society* (Cambridge: Cambridge University Press, 1984), 174–75.

30. Befu, "Four Models of Japanese Society."

31. E. Hamaguchi (ed.), *Japanese Systems: An Alternative Civilization?*, Research Project Team for Japanese Systems, Masuda Foundation (Yokohama: Sekotac, 1992). See James R. Lincoln and Arne L. Kelleberg (eds.), *Culture, Control, and Commitment: A Study of Work Organization and Work Attitudes in the United States and Japan* (Cambridge: Cambridge University Press, 1990), 217; C. Deutschmann, "The Japanese Type of Organization as a Challenge to the Sociological Theory of Modernization," *Thesis Eleven*, no. 17 (1987), 40–58; Theo Parker, "Die real nicht existierende japanische Schreibmaschine, oder: Wie funktioniert das Japanische Büro ohne Maschinenschrift?" *Leviathan* 14, no. 3 (1986): 328–60.

32. See Lincoln and Kelleberg, *Culture, Control, and Commitment*; Deutschmann, "Japanese Type of Organization."

33. S. Garon, *The State and Labor in Modern Japan* (Berkeley: University of California Press, 1987).

34. Kent E. Calder, *Crisis and Compensation: Public Policy and Political Stability in Japan, 1949–1986* (Princeton: Princeton University Press, 1988), esp. chaps. 4, 11.

35. Hamaguchi, *Japanese Systems*; Murakami and Rohlen, "Social-Exchange Aspects of the Japanese Political Economy."

36. Murakami, "Ie Society"; K. Shumpei, "Some Principles Governing the Thought and Behaviour of Japanist Contextualist," *Journal of Japanese Studies* 8, no. 1 (1982): 5–28.

37. See Hamaguchi, *Japanese Systems;* Bachnik, *Family, Self and Society.*

38. See Maruyama Masao, "Die Japanische Intellektuellen," in *idem, Denken in Japan* (Frankfurt: Suhrkamp, 1988), 89–132; H. Sonoda, "The Religious Situation in Japan in Relation to Shinto," *Acta Asiatica* 51 (1987): 1–21; C. Steenstrup, "Hōjō Shigetoki: A Buddhist Philosopher-Statesman of Thirteenth-Century Japan," in I. Nish and C. Dunn (eds.), *European Studies on Japan* (Tenterden, Kent: Paul Norbury Publications, 1979), 95–101. See also C. Steenstrup, "Did Political Rationalism Develop along Parallel Lines in Premodern Japan and in Premodern West? Prolegomena to a Comparative Study," *Journal of Intercultural Studies*, no. 3 (1976), 1–11.

39. See, for instance, C. Blacker, *The Japanese Enlightenment* (Cambridge: Cambridge University Press, 1964); Maruyama, *Denken in Japan.*

40. Murakami Yasusuke, "Two Types of Civilization: Transcendental and Hermeneutic," *Nichibunken (Japan Review)* 1 (1990): 1–34.

41. See K. Singer, *Mirror, Sword and Jewel* (Tokyo: Kodansha International, 1987). It is interesting to note in this context that one of the major chronicles of medieval Japan was termed *Ōkagami* (Great Mirror); see H. McCullough (trans.), *Ōkagami, The Great Mirror*, (Princeton: Princeton University Press, 1980). See also M. Marra, *Representations of Power: The Literary Politics of Medieval Japan* (Honolulu: University of Hawaii Press, 1993). Emiko Ohnuki-Tierney has underlined the centrality of the metaphor of the mirror in Japanese culture:

> In the *Kojiki* and the *Nihonshoki* a mirror plays a significant role. In the episode in which Amaterasu Ōmikami (Sun Goddess, or "the heaven illuminating god"), ancestress of the Japanese in the creation myth, emerged from seclusion because of a mirror, that is, was reborn, and the Japanese universe was reborn with her light, she mistook her own image as that of a deity superior to her. The mirror represents, I think, her transcendental self. In other words, the rebirth of the Sun Goddess and the Japanese universe was facilitated by a mirror, which, in turn, symbolizes a self perceived at a higher level. The *Nihonshoki* also contains many passages that symbolically equate a mirror with a deity. For example, two deities are described as being born from white-copper mirrors.
> Other ethnographic data describe mirrors or reflections in water as the embodiment of deities. The belief that supernatural power can be harnessed by a mirror is illustrated by the figures found in ancient tombs who hold mirrors on their chests. These figurines, called *haniwa*, are considered to represent ancient shamans. Even today mirrors are installed in many shrines as the embodiment (*goshintai*) of the deity enshrined there. Throughout Japan, a number of valleys, ponds, mountains, hills, and rocks bear the word *kagami* (mirror) in their names; these are sacred places where supernatural powers are thought to reside. (Ohnuki-Tierney, *Rice as Self*, 54–55)

42. See Robert J. Wargo, "Japanese Ethics: Beyond Good and Evil," *Philosophy East and West* 40, no. 4 (October 1990): 499–510.

43. E. Ben-Ari, "At the Interstices: Drinking, Management, and Temporary Groups in a Local Japanese Organization," *Social Analysis*, no. 26 (Decem-

ber 1989), 46–69; *idem,* "Wrapping Up: Some Implications," in E. Ben-Ari, B. Moeran, and J. Valentine (eds.), *Unwrapping Japan: Society and Culture in Anthropological Perspectives* (Manchester: Manchester University Press, 1990), 221–34. See also P. G. O'Neil (ed.), *Tradition and Modern Japan* (Tenterden, Kent: Paul Norbury Publications, 1981); Kohara Yukinari, "Folk without Festivals," *Japan Interpreter* 8, no. 1 (winter 1983): 55–62; J. Robertson, "A Dialectic of Native and Newcomer: The Kodaira Citizens' Festival in Suburban Tokyo," *Anthropological Quarterly* 60, no. 3 (1987): 124–36; Nishinaga Yoshinari, "Violent Humans, Human Violence: Fukazawa Shichirō's 'The Oak Mountain Song,'" *Japan Quarterly* 30 (1983): 367–72.

44. Kondo, *Crafting Selves.*

45. E. Ben-Ari, "Ritual Strikes, Ceremonial Slowdowns: Some Thoughts on the Management of Conflict in Large Japanese Enterprises," in Eisenstadt and Ben-Ari, *Japanese Models of Conflict Resolution,* 95–123; Ben-Ari, "At the Interstices"; *idem,* "Posing, Posturing and Photographic Presences: A Rite of Passage in a Japanese Commuter Village," *Man* 26 (1991): 87–104; *idem,* "Wrapping Up." See also Eshun Hamaguchi, *Japanese Systems.*

46. M. Gluckman, "Rituals of Rebellion in South Africa," in *idem, Order and Rebellion in African Tribal Society* (London: Cohen & West, 1963).

47. B. Moeran, *Language and Popular Culture in Japan* (Manchester: University of Manchester Press, 1989). See also D. P. Martinez, "Tourism and the Ama: The Search for a Real Japan," in Ben-Ari, Moeran, and Valentine, *Unwrapping Japan,* 97–116; Bachnik and Quinn, *Situated Meaning.*

For early developments, see M. Marra, *The Aesthetics of Discontent and Reclusion in Medieval Japanese Literature* (Honolulu: University of Hawaii Press, 1991).

48. S. J. Pharr, *Losing Face: Status Politics in Japan* (Berkeley: University of California Press, 1990).

49. Murakami and Rohlen, "Social Exchange Aspects of the Japanese Economy"; Hamaguchi, *Japanese Systems.*

50. Rob Steven, *Classes in Contemporary Japan* (Cambridge: Cambridge University Press, 1983).

51. T. Najita, "Japan's Industrial Revolution in Historical Perspective," in M. Miyoshi and H. Harootunian (eds.), *Japan in the World* (Durham: Duke University Press, 1993), 13–30.

52. Arnason summarizing Pollack: Arnason, "Comparing Japan and the West," 167–96.

53. Arnason, "Comparing Japan and the West." See also Ohnuki-Tierney, *Rice as Self,* esp. chaps. 6, 7; G. Sansom, *A History of Japan* (Stanford: Stanford University Press, 1958); K. Asakawa, *The Early Institutional Life of Japan: A Study in the Reform of 645 A.D.* (New York: Paragon, 1963).

54. Arnason, "Comparing Japan and the West," citing Asakawa, *Early Institutional Life of Japan.*

55. This is also the claim made by Bai Gao in his review of Ramseyer and Frances, *Japan's Political Marketplace,* in *Journal of Asian Studies* 53, no. 2 (1994): 570–72.

CHAPTER FIFTEEN

1. S. Kato, *History of Japanese Literature*, 3 vols. (London: MacMillan Press, 1979–1990).

2. See Kato, *History of Japanese Literature*. See also W. F. Sibley, "Naturalism in Japanese Literature," *Harvard Journal of Asiatic Studies* 28 (1968): 157–69.

3. A. Berque, "Das Verhältnis der Ökonomie zu Raum und Zeit in der japanische Kulture," in C. von Barloewen and K. Werhahn Mees (eds.), *Japan und der Westen* (Frankfurt: Fischer Verlag, 1986), 1:21–38.

4. A. Berque, "Some Traits of Japanese Fudōsei," *Japan Foundation Newsletter* 14, no. 5 (1987): 5. Berque also states (p. 4): "I am not saying here that the Japanese language is illogical, nor that it is less suited to scientific reasoning than, say, English (as, among many others, a Japanese Nobel Prize winner professed some time ago). It can, just as any other language on Earth, translate the European type of inference as a technical paradigm for modern science and technology. But this does not alter the fact that its own intrinsic logic is not that of Greek or French or German. As compared to these languages, its logic is, as I said above, a little closer to sensible experience, which is definitely not the same as conceptualization." See also *idem, Du geste a la cité: Formes urbaines et lien social au Japon* (Paris: Gallimard, 1993).

5. N. Burch, *To the Distant Observer: Form and Meaning in the Japanese Cinema* (Los Angeles: University of California Press, 1979), 53.

6. See T. Kasulis, "Philosophising in Plato, and Kukai's Shojin," in *idem, Zen Action, Zen Person* (Honolulu: University of Hawaii Press, 1987); *idem*, "Kukai: Philosophizing in the Archaic," in F. Reynolds and D. Tracy (eds.), *Myth and Philosophy* (New York: State University of New York Press, 1990), 131–50. See also C. R. Moore (ed.), *The Japanese Mind: Essentials of Japanese Philosophy and Culture* (Honolulu: East-West Center Press, University of Hawaii Press, 1967).

7. Tzvetana Kristeva, "The Pattern of Signification in the *Taketori Monogatari*: The 'Ancestor' of all *Monogatari*," *Japan Forum* 2, no. 2 (November 1990): 253–60. See also Fukui Teisuke, "On Ise monogatari," in Ian Nish and Charles Dunn (eds.), *Contemporary European Writing on Japan* (Tenterden, Kent: Paul Norbury Publications, 1988), 264–68.

8. Ishiguru Hidé, "Access to the Shining Prince," *London Review of Books*, 21 May–3 June 1981, 11–13.

9. Masao Miyoshi, "Against the Native Grain: The Japanese Novel and the 'Postmodern' West," in "Postmodernism and Japan," special issue of the *South Atlantic Quarterly* 87, no. 3 (1988): 543–44. A parallel and highly elaborate analysis of the *shishōsetsu* has been provided by Irmela Hijiya-Kirschnereit, in "The Stubborn Persistence of a Much Abused Genre: On the Popularity of *Shishōsetsu* in Contemporary Japanese Literature," in G. Daniels (ed.), *Europe Interprets Japan* (Tenterden, Kent: Paul Norbury Publications, 1984), 173–80. For greater detail, see I. Hijiya Kirschnereit, *Was heisst: Japanische Literatur verstehen* (Frankfurt: Suhrkamp, 1990), esp. chaps. 7, 8; *idem, Das Ende der Exotik* (Frankfurt: Suhrkamp, 1988), esp. "Qualen des Lebens—Quellen der Kunst: Zur gesellschaftlichen Funktion eines zentralen literarischen Genres der Gegenwart," 119–38.

See also Katō Shūichi, review of I. Hijiya-Kirschnereit, "Selbsstentblössun-grituale," *Journal of Japanese Studies* 10, no. 1 (winter 1984): 196–204; Oscar Benz, "Naturalism in Japanese Literature: The Realism of the Meiji Period till the Beginning of Naturalism," *Monumenta Nipponica* 9 (1953): 1–33; Noguchi Takehiko, "Love and Death in the Early Modern Novel: America and Japan," in A. M. Craig (ed.), *Japan: A Comparative View* (Princeton: Princeton University Press, 1979), 160–81; Jacob Raz, *Audience and Actors: A Study of Their Interaction in the Japanese Traditional Theater* (Leiden: E. J. Brill, 1983); Saeki Shōichi, "Autobiographical Literature in Japan," *Japan Echo* 10, no. 3 (autumn 1983): 69–75.

10. Miyoshi, "Against the Native Grain."

11. A similar illustration of such tendencies in the development of Japanese literature is offered by Kristeva in her comparative analysis of Japanese and Western diaries and memoirs, in Daniels, *Europe Interprets Japan*, 157–60:

> These words give the clue to a fundamental difference between European autobiographical literature and the Japanese lyrical diaries. Whereas in Europe the genre centers round "some theoretical and intellectual interest in religion, politics, or art," the Japanese diary grows from an interest in the psychological development of the human being, in one's individual feeling and emotions. ('This is a structural peculiarity which has little to do with the idiosyncratic preferences of individual readers.) Thus, for example, Oscar Wilde has one of his characters in *The Artist as Critic* say with regard to Newman's *Apologia pro Vita Sua:*
>
> "The mode of thought that Cardinal Newman represented . . . may not, cannot, I think, survive. But the world will never weary of watching that troubled soul in its progress from darkness to darkness. The lonely church at Littlemore, where 'the breath of the morning is damp, and worshippers are few,' will always be dear to it . . ."
>
> (Note that the speaker pinpoints precisely the same dichotomy of thought and emotion.)
>
> It has become commonplace to cite the *Hotaru* Chapter of *Genji* in connection with the origin of the Japanese dairies: (Waley translation.)
>
> ". . . the storyteller's own experience of men and things, whether for good or ill—not only that he has passed through himself, but even events that he has only witnessed or been told of—has moved him to an emotion so passionate that he can no longer keep it shut up in his heart. Again and again something in his own life or in that around him will seem to the writer so important that he cannot bear to let it pass into oblivion."
>
> Feeling and emotion, then, constitute the mainspring of the Japanese lyrical diary, whereas in Europe the chief impulse comes from thought and ideas. . . .
>
> The historical origin of the autobiographical tradition is somewhat similar in Europe and Japan; Augustine belongs to the transition period from late antiquity to the early Middle Ages, whereas Kino Tsurayuki is related to the early Japanese Middle Ages. Thus, from their very dawn the two traditions took two different ways of development because they depended on and expressed two different kinds of religious consciousness. This in itself is a very complicated problem which calls for the joint efforts of scholars from several areas. Hence we will confine ourselves to certain basic and evident distinctions.
>
> The nature of autobiographic writing as the story of one's own life is determined by the anthropological views prevalent in a specific society. Thus, the outlook of the medieval Japanese was defined by Buddhism with its insistence on the idea of the

karma which contains a twofold causal relation: former life–present life and present life–future life. The crucial thing about the *karma* is that it is individual. Hence, one's present life is pre-determined; it is contained in one's own individual former life. Herein probably lies the reason for the extraordinary interest which medieval Japanese took in the past: the further we go back into the past, the closer we come to the code of our own former life. And it is no accident that the Japanese say *kako-ni sakanoboru,* that is, "to *ascend* into the past." On the other hand, the idea of the *karma* means that one can secure a more comfortable incarnation in one's future life by means of righteous deeds. This reinforces the value of one's individual life and indirectly bolsters up self-assertion. In this sense, the writers of lyrical diaries can be said to "ascend into the past" in order to *endorse* it.

Christian anthropology, on the other hand, is a metaphysical super-structure of an entirely different order. Its transpersonal teleology tends to deny the *here-and-now* in favour of eternity; hence, a retrospective examination of one's life is of worth in so far as it reveals to what extent one may have succeeded in atoning for the consequences of original sin. Furthermore, once the here-and-now is subordinated to what Auerbach calls the figural mode or allegory, there is no place for an intrinsic interest in personality; it tends to stand for something else. Thus, unlike the Japanese diarists, early European confession-writers go back or *down* to the past in order to *denounce* it. Underlying the Japanese lyrical diary is a strong personalism that reminds one rather of the memoir, whereas the confession presupposes some external point of reference in accordance with Christian teleology. Furthermore, it is noteworthy that the European Middle Ages produced practically no autobiography. Augustine himself is rather a transitional figure and his *Confessions* still bear evidence of the personalism of classical antiquity.

An interesting illustration of such "anthropologies" can be found in aspects of the transmission of tales from the Icelandic sagas in contemporary Japanese cartoons. See Halldór Stefánsson, "Foreign Myths and Sagas in Japan: The Academics and the Cartoonists", in Gìsli Pálsson (ed.), *Beyond Boundaries: Understanding, Translation and Anthropological Discourse* (Oxford: Berg, 1992), 25–100.

12. E. Fowler, *The Rhetoric of Confession: Shishōsetsu in Early Twentieth-Century Japanese Fiction* (Berkeley: University of California Press, 1988), xxiii.

13. Masao Miyoshi, *Accomplices of Silence: The Modern Japanese Novel* (Berkeley: University of California Press, 1979), xv (preface).

14. "Yet while individualism in the west suggests a dynamic (as opposed to regulated or tradition-bound) relationship between the self and the other, it came in Japan, because of the traditional equation of spiritual autonomy with aloofness from society, to imply just the opposite: a withdrawal into the world of nature and private experience. This notion of individualism as a form of isolated self-contemplation may have been the only avenue to spiritual independence in a society that placed severe constraints on interpersonal relations. The typical Japanese writer, moreover, aware of the limits of his intellectual and social liberties, may have seen in his private life the only area he could exploit with confidence. In a society generally hostile to nonconformist behavior, he discovered in confession a literary form that matched his conception of self, something fulfilled by unilateral and almost instinctive expression rather than by integration in a matrix of human relationships. He saw confession, moreover, as an embodiment of his uniqueness, insofar as it could be authored only by one person, namely, himself.

The shishōsetsu was eminently suited to this view of individualism." (Fowler, *Rhetoric of Confession*, 15).

15. A. Wolfe, *Suicidal Narrative in Modern Japan: The Case of Dazai Osamu* (Princeton: Princeton University Press, 1990), chaps. 1, 2, 9, epilogue.

16. N. Field, *In the Realm of a Dying Emperor: A Portrait of Japan at Century's End* (New York: Pantheon, 1991); D. Pollack, *Reading against Culture: Ideology and Narrative in the Japanese Novel* (Ithaca: Cornell University Press, 1992); J. A. Fujii, *Complicit Fictions: The Subject in the Modern Japanese Narrative* (Berkeley: University of California Press, 1993).

17. Berque, "Some Traits of Japanese Fudōsei." On the conception of space, see also Ian Nish and Charles Dunn (eds.), "Space and Travel: An Interpretation of the Travel Poems of the Man'yōshū," *European Studies of Japan* (Tenterden, Kent: Paul Norbury, 1988), 269–83; Yasuyuki Kurita, "Urban Life Seen Through Household Possessions," *Japan Echo* 5 (1978): 114 ff.; Maki Fumihiko, "The City and Inner Space," *Japan Echo* 6 (1979): 91–103. See also Yoshinobu Ashihara, *The Hidden Order: Tokyo through the Twentieth Century* (Tokyo: Kodansha, 1991). For an interesting parallel literary development, see Eduard Klopfenstein, "Exclusive Conformism: The Best-Seller 'Nantonaku Kuristaru,' 1981," in Daniels, *Europe Interprets Japan*, 180–87.

18. Berque, "Some Traits of Japanese Fudōsei"; *idem, Du geste a la cité*, 5.

19. D. Kondo, "The Way of Tea: A Symbolic Analysis," *Man* 20, no. 2 (1985): 302. For a historical analysis of the tea ceremony, see P. Varley and Kumakura Isao, *Tea in Japan: Essays on the History of Chanoyu* (Honolulu: University of Hawaii Press, 1989); J. L. Anderson, "Japanese Tea Ritual: Religion in Practice," *Man* 22 (1989): 475–98; T. M. Ludwig, "Before Rikyu: Religions and Aesthetic Influences in the Early History of the Tea Ceremony," *Monumenta Nipponica* 36, no. 4 (1981): 367–390.

20. Katō Shūichi, *Form, Style, Tradition: Reflections on Japanese Art and Society* (Tokyo: Kodansha International, 1979), 159.

21. D. Pollack, *The Fracture of Meaning: Japan's Synthesis of China from the Eighth through the Eighteenth Centuries* (Princeton: Princeton University Press, 1986). See also B. A. Shillony, "Friend or Foe: The Ambivalent Images of the U.S. and China in Wartime Japan," in J. W. White, Michio Umegaki, and T. H. Havens (eds.), *The Ambivalence of Nationalism: Modern Japan between East and West* (New York: University Press of America, 1990), 187–211.

22. J. S. Baker, *Japanese Art* (London: Thames and Hudson, 1981).

23. As Booth has aptly analyzed,

All cultures lavish care and attention on the design of objects that possess special significance for them, but in Japan you regularly find the same criteria of taste applied to the most commonplace objects, particularly those that have remained in use since feudal times. Furoshiki (wrapping cloths for parcels or boxed lunches), tenugui (cotton towels sometimes worn as headscarves) and noren (cloth shop signs that are hung out when a shop is open and taken in when it closes) usually cost very little, but the same canons of taste are often applied to their design as would apply to a lavishly designed kimono. If calligraphy is used on them, the curves and strokes of the letters will invariably be dictated more by a concern for balance and elegance of form than with legibility and, even when printed or stitched, these letters will generally mimic the handwritten effects of brush and ink. (A. Booth, *Holland Herald.*)

24. To quote Kuroda Toshio:

This historical consciousness corresponds to the notion expressed in Jien's *Gukanshō* and other medieval texts according to which both chronicles (past history) and prophecies (history to come) were apprehended at the same time. This phenomenon is to be associated with the concept of the "sacred nation," based on religious notions concerning the past and the future of the nation and the state.

This means that within the aforementioned framework of the historical consciousness of the chroniclers, history was a matter to be extolled according to the fundamental principles of "essence" and "hypostasis," that is, of what is prior and what necessarily follows. This historical consciousness of the chroniclers was representative of a medieval consciousness which, it must be said, did have a tremendous impact in Japan, all the way from the intellectuals to the common people." (Kuroda Toshio, "Historical Consciousness and Hon-Jaku Philosophy in the Medieval Period on Mount Hiei," in G. T. Tanabe [ed.], *The Lotus Sutra in Japanese Culture* [Honolulu: University of Hawaii Press, 1989], 152–53)

For an even earlier historical exposition, see Delmer M. Brown and Ichiro Ishida, *The Future and the Past: A Translation and Study of the Gukanshō, an Interpretative History of Japan Written in 1219* (Berkeley: University of California Press, 1988), esp. part 3.

25. G. M. Wilson, *Patriots and Redeemers in Japan: Motives in the Meiji Restoration* (Chicago: University of Chicago Press, 1992), 23–24. The book's initial phrases, referring to the *Gukanshō*, capture the point: "Japan is the divine land, the land of the *kami*. The original heavenly ancestor [Ninigi] laid the foundation, and the Sun Goddess will forever transmit the succession. Only in our country does this situation exist. In other dynasties its like is not to be found. That is why we call it the divine land." George Sansom brands *Jinnō shōtōki* "a polemic treatise rather than a history [even though its] general attitude reveals influence of the *Gukanshō*. But this chronicle again reaffirms the orthodox succession as the characteristic trait of Japanese political history. From the clouds of myth to the fourteenth century this principle was reiterated, and it permeates Japanese thought in the subsequent Tokugawa period right to the Meiji Restoration" (ibid., 24).

26. G. Barrett, *Archetypes in the Japanese Film: The Sociopolitical and Religious Significance as the Principle of Heros and Heroines* (London: Associated University Press, 1989). See also T. Sato, *Currents in Japanese Cinema*, trans. G. Barrett (Tokyo: Kodansha International, 1982); J. Mellen, *The Waves at Genji's Door: Japan through Its Cinema* (New York: Pantheon, 1976).

27. See Robert Rolf and John Gillespie (eds.), *Alternative Japanese Drama* (Honolulu: University of Hawaii Press, 1992); Noguchi Takehiko, "Mishima Yukio and Kita Ikki: The Aesthetics and Politics of Ultranationalism in Japan," trans. Teruko Craig, *Journal of Japanese Studies* 10, no. 2 (summer 1984):437–54; R. Matthew, *Japanese Science Fiction: A View of a Changing Society* (London: Routledge; Nissan Institute of Japanese Studies, Oxford University, 1989).

28. Pollack, *Reading against Culture*; Fujii, *Compliant Visions*; J. Robertson, "Mon Japan: The Revue Theater and Stating the State in Interwar Japan, 1931–

45," paper presented at the symposium "Civil Society in East Asian Countries (II)," Montreal, 23–25 November 1992. See also B. Moeran, "Confucian Confusion: The Good, the Bad and the Noodle Western," in D. Parkin (ed.), *The Anthropology of Evil* (New York: Basil Blackwell, 1985); Ōe Kenzaburō, "Post-War Japanese Literature and the Contemporary Impasse: Account of a Participant Observer," *Japan Foundation Newsletter* 14, no. 3 (October 1986): 1–16; B. Mito Reed, "Chikamatsu Shukō: An Inquiry into Narrative Modes in Modern Japanese Fiction," *Journal of Japanese Studies* 14, no. 1 (winter 1988): 59–76; D. Pollack, "Action as Fitting Match to Knowledge: Language and Symbol in Mishima's Kinkakuji," *Monumenta Nipponica* 40, no. 4 (1985), 387–98; S. Heine, "Tragedy and Salvation in the Floating World: Chikamatsu's Double Suicide Drama as Millenarian Discourse," *Journal of Asian Studies* 53, no. 2 (May 1994): 367–93.

29. B. Moeran, *Language and Popular Culture in Japan* (Manchester: Manchester University Press, 1989).

30. See, for instance, the collection, A. Birnbaum (ed.), *Monkey Brain Sushi: New Tastes in Japanese Fiction* (Tokyo: Kodansha International, 1991).

CHAPTER SIXTEEN

1. J. P. Arnason, "Comparing Japan and the West: Prolegomena to a Research Program," in L. Gule and O. Storebo (eds.), *Development and Modernity: Perspectives on Western Theories of Modernisation* (Bergen: Ariadne, 1993), 167–95; Ishida Eiichirō, *Japanese Culture: A Study of Origins and Characteristics*, trans. Tekuko Kachi (Tokyo: University of Tokyo Press, 1974).

2. On Europe, see S. N. Eisenstadt, *European Civilization in a Comparative Perspective* (Oslo: Norwegian University Press, 1987); F. Heer, *The Intellectual History of Europe*, vol. 1, *From the Beginnings of Western Thought to Luther* (Garden City: Doubleday Anchor, 1968); J. K. O'Dea, T. F. O'Dea, and C. Adams, *Religion and Man: Judaism, Christianity and Islam* (New York: Harper and Row, 1972), 111. See also the various articles on "Christentum" in *Die Religion in Geschichte und Gegenwart* (Tubingen: J. C. B. Mohr, 1961), 1:1685–721; A. Von Harnack, *The Mission and Expansion of Christianity in the First Three Centuries* (New York: Putnam, 1908); E. Troeltsch, *The Social Teaching of the Christian Churches* (New York: MacMillan, 1931).

3. S. N. Eisenstadt, "Heterodoxies and the Dynamics of Civilizations," *Proceedings of the American Philosophical Society* 128, no. 2 (June 1984): 104–13; idem, *Revolution and the Transformation of Societies* (New York: Free Press, 1978).

4. Eisenstadt, *European Civilization*.

5. S. N. Eisenstadt, "Some Observations on the Dynamics of Traditions," *Comparative Studies on Society and Culture History*, 11 (1969): 451–75; idem, *Tradition, Change and Modernity* (New York: John Wiley, 1973).

6. Eisenstadt, *European Civilization; idem*, "Socialism and Tradition," in S. N. Eisenstadt and Y. Azmon (eds.), *Socialism and Tradition* (Jerusalem: Van Leer Jerusalem Institute, 1971), 1–20.

7. Eisenstadt, "Some Observations on the Dynamics of Traditions."

8. On the basic tenets of Hinduism, see M. Biardeau, *Clefs pour la pensée hindoue* (Paris: Seghers, 1972); J. B. Carman and F. A. Margolin, *Purity and Auspiciousness in Indian Society* (Leiden: E. J. Brill, 1985); M. Weber, *The Religion in India: The Sociology of Hinduism and Buddhism,* trans. H. M. Gerth and D. Martindale (New York: Free Press, 1958); W. T. De Bary et al., (comp.), *Sources of Indian Tradition* (New York: Columbia University Press, 1958); C. de Bougle, *Essais sur le regime des castes* (Paris: Presses Universitaires de France, 1969); L. Dumont and D. Potock, *Contributions to Indian Sociology* (Paris: Mounton, 1957–66), vol. 1.

9. See, for one of the most elaborate analyses of these dimensions of the Indian cosmology, John C. Heesterman, *The Broken World of Sacrifice: An Essay in Ancient Indian Ritual* (Chicago: University of Chicago Press, 1993).

10. L. Dumont, *Religion, Politics and History in India,* Collected Papers in Indian Sociology (Paris: Mounton, 1970). For a general discussion, see S. N. Eisenstadt, "The Paradox of the Construction of Other-Worldly Civilizations: Some Observations on the Characteristics and Dynamics of Hindu and Buddhist Civilizations," in Y. K. Malik (ed.), *Boeing and Bullock-Carts: Studies in Change and Continuity in Indian Civilization* (Delhi: Chanakya Publications, 1990), 21–56.

11. J. C. Heesterman, *The Inner Conflict of Tradition: Essays in Indian Ritual, Kinship and Society* (Chicago: University of Chicago Press, 1985), esp. the chapter "Brahmin, Ritual and Renouncer," 26–44; idem, *The Ancient Indian Royal Consecration* (The Hague: Montondie, 1957); idem, *Broken World of Sacrifice.* In T. N. Madan (ed.), *Way of Life: King Householders and Renouncer* (Delhi, Vikas Publishing House, 1982), see 251–72; R. Thapar, "Householders and Renouncers in the Brahmanical and Buddhist Traditions," 273–98; and S. T. Tambiah, "The Renouncer: His Individuality and His Community," 299–308. See also N. B. Dirks, "Political Authority and Structural Change in Early South Indian History," *Indian Economic and Social History Review* 13, no. 2 (April–June 1976): 125–57.

12. A. Beteille, *Caste, Class and Power: Changing Patterns of Stratification in a Tanjore Village* (Berkeley: University of California Press, 1965); K. Ishwaran (ed.), *Change and Continuity in India's Villages* (New York: Columbia University Press, 1970); D. G. Mandelbaum, *Society in India,* 2 vols. (Berkeley: University of California Press, 1970).

13. L. Dumont, *Homo Hierarchicus: The Caste System and Its Implications* (Chicago: University of Chicago Press, 1980); idem, *Religion, Politics and History in India;* J. C. Heesterman, "The Conundrum of the King's Authority," in idem, *Inner Conflict of Tradition,* 108–27.

14. G. Goodwin-Raheja, "Caste Kingships and Dominance Reconsidered," *Annual Review of Anthropology* 17 (1988): 517.

15. P. Price, *Competition and Conflict in Hindu Polity, 1550–1750* (Cambridge: Cambridge University Press, forthcoming).

16. A. Wink, *Land and Sovereignty in India* (Cambridge: Cambridge University Press, 1986); J. C. Heesterman, "Tradition, Empire and Modern State," Leiden University, draft paper, 1988; H. Kulke, *Kings and Cults: State Formation*

and Legitimation in India and Southeast Asia (New Delhi: Manohar, 1993);
S. Rudolph, "Presidential Address: State Formation in Asia—Prolegomena to
a Comparative Study," *Journal of Asian Studies* 46, no. 4 (November 1987):
731–46.

17. Sheldon Pollock, "Rāmāyama and Political Imagination in India," *Journal
of Asian Studies* 52, no. 2 (May 1993): 261–97.

18. On Jainism, see C. Gaillat, "Jainism," in M. Eliade (ed.), *The Encyclopaedia of Religion* (New York: MacMillan, 1987), 7:507–14; A. L. Basham, "Jainism
and Buddhism," pt. 2 of De Bary et al., *Sources of Indian Tradition*, 37–93; S.
Jain, "The Pure and the Auspicious in the Jaina Tradition," in J. B. Carman and
F. A. Marglin (eds.), *Purity and Auspiciousness in Indian Society* (Leiden: E. J.
Brill, 1985). See also Marie-Claude Mahias, *Deliverance et convivialite: Le
systeme culinaire des Jaina* (Paris: Editions de la Maison des Sciences de
l'Homme, 1985); R. J. Zydenbos, *Moksa in Jainism, According to Umasuati*
(Wiesbaden: Franz Steiner Verlag, 1983). On Bhakti, see J. B. Carman, "Bhakti,"
in *Encyclopaedia of Religion*, 2:130–34; J. Lele (ed.), *Tradition and Modernity in
Bhakti Movements* (Leiden: E. J. Brill, 1981); F. Hardy, *Viraya Bhakti: The Early
Development of Krisna Devotion in South India* (Oxford: Oxford University
Press, 1981).

19. R. Inden, *Imagining India* (Oxford: Blackwell, 1990), 220 ff.

20. W. Doniger, "Pluralism and Intolerance in Hinduism," in W. G. Lea-
nard and J. L. Rike (eds.), *Radical Pluralism and Truth: David Tracy and the Her-
meneutics of Religion* (New York: Crossroad, 1991), 45–233. For the philosophical roots of such tolerance, especially in the idea that all knowledge is present in
the individualization and dehistoricization of cultural practices, see S. Pollock,
"The Theory of Practice and the Practice of Theory in Indian Intellectual History," *Journal of the American Oriental Society* 10, no. 3 (1985): 499–519. See
also W. Halbfass, *Tradition and Reflection: Explorations in Indian Thought*, (Albany: State University of New York Press, 1991).

21. S. Pollock, "Mimansa and the Problem of History in Traditional India,"
Journal of the American Oriental Society 1988. This follows V. Narayana Rao
and D. Shulman, "History, Biography and Poetry at the Tanjavur Nayaka Court,"
Social Analysis (1991): 115.

22. Rao and Shulman, "History, Biography and Poetry." For some pertinent
aspects of Indian historiography, see H. Kulke, "Geschichtsschreibung und Ges-
chichtsbild in Hinduistischen Mittelalter," *Saeculum* 30 (1978): 100–12.

23. V. S. Naipaul, *India: A Wounded Civilization* (New York: Village Books,
1976).

24. On Chinese civilization, see E. O. Reischauer and J. K. Fairbank, *A History
of East Asian Civilization*, vol. 1, *East Asia: The Great Tradition* (Boston: Houghton Mifflin, 1960); M. Weber, *The Religion of China: Confucianism and Taoism*,
trans. H. Gerth (New York: Free Press, 1964); C. K. Yang, "The Functional Relationship between Confucian Thought and Chinese Religion," in J. K. Fairbank
(ed.), *Chinese Thought and Institutions* (Chicago: University of Chicago Press,
1957), 269–91; A. F. Wright, *The Confucian Persuasion* (Stanford: Stanford University Press, 1960); D. S. Nivison and A. F. Wright (eds.), *Confucianism in Action* (Stanford: Stanford University Press, 1959); A. F. Wright et al. (eds.), *Studies*

in Chinese Thought (Chicago: University of Chicago Press, 1953). In S. R. Schram (ed.), *Foundations and Limits of State Power in China* (London: University of London, School of Oriental and African Studies, 1987), see J. Gernet, Introduction, xv–xxxvii; D. McMullen, "View of the State in Du You and Liu Zonngyuan," 59–86; B. L. Schwartz, "The Primacy of the Political Order in East Asian Societies: Some Preliminary Generalizations," 1–10; A. Hulsewe, "Law as One of the Foundations of State Power in Early Imperial China," 11–32; M. Loewe, "Imperial Sovereignty: Dong Zhongshu's Contribution and His Predecessors," 33–58; and H. Franke, "The Role of the State as a Structural Element in Polyethnic Societies," 87–112.

25. See Fairbank, *Chinese Thought and Institutions*; F. Mote, *Intellectual Foundations of China* (New York: Knopf, 1971); Nivison and Wright, *Confucianism in Action*; B. Schwartz, "Transcendence in Ancient China," in "Wisdom Revelation and Doubt," special issue of *Daedalus*, spring 1975, 57–63; *idem, The World of Thought in Ancient China* (Cambridge, Mass.: Harvard University Press, 1985); Wright, *Confucian Persuasion*. See also D. Bodde, *Essays in Chinese Civilization* (Princeton: Princeton University Press, 1981), esp. chaps. 6–17.

26. For greater detail, see S. N. Eisenstadt, "This Worldly Transcendentalism and the Structuring of the World: Weber's 'Religion of China' and the Format of Chinese History and Civilization", in A. E. Buss (ed.), *Max Weber in Asian Studies*, Internal Studies in Sociology and Social Anthropology (Leiden: E. J. Brill, 1985), 46–64.

27. Schwartz, "Transcendence in Ancient China," 64.

28. H. Fingarette, "Human Community as Holy Rite: an Interpretation of Confucius's Analects," *Harvard Theological Review* 59, no. 1 (1968): 53–67; *idem, Confucius, the Secular as Sacred* (New York: Harper & Row, 1972).

29. Eisenstadt, "This Worldly Transcendentalism."

30. The patterns of rebellion, warlordship, and state reconstruction in China are discussed in S. N. Eisenstadt, *The Political Systems of Empires* (New York: Free Press, 1963), chaps. 10, 11; F. Wakeman, "Rebellion and Revolution: The Study of Popular Movements in Chinese History," *Journal of Asian Studies* 36, no. 2 (1977): 201–38; J. B. Parsons, "The Culmination of a Chinese Peasant Rebellion," *Journal of Asian Studies* 16, no. 3 (1975): 387–401; E. Pullyblank, *The Background of the Rebellion of An Lu-shan* (New York: Oxford University Press, 1955), chaps. 3, 5; A. Feuerwerker, *Rebellion in Nineteenth-Century China* (Ann Arbor: University of Michigan, Center for Chinese Studies, 1975).

31. On the impact of Buddhism and Taoism on Chinese society, see Reischauer and Fairbank, *A History of East Asian Civilization*; M. Kaltenmark, *Lao Tzu and Taoism* (Stanford: Stanford University Press, 1969); C. Y. Chiu, "The Church-State Conflict in the T'ang Dynasty," in E. Z. Sun and J. de Francis (eds.), *Chinese Social History* (Washington, D.C.: American Council of Learned Societies, 1956), 197–207. For a more general discussion, see A. F. Wolf (ed.), *Religion and Ritual in Chinese Society* (Stanford: Stanford University Press, 1974); H. Welch and A. Seidel (eds.), *Facets of Taoism* (New Haven: Yale University Press, 1979).

32. On the political structure and dynamism of the Chinese empire, see Reischauer and Fairbank, *A History of East Asian Civilization;* C. O. Hucker (ed.), *Chinese Government in Ming Times: Seven Studies* (New York: Columbia University Press, 1969); J. T. C. Liu, "An Administration Cycle in Chinese History," in J. A. Harrison (ed.), *China: Enduring Scholarship* (Tucson: University of Arizona Press, 1972), 1:75–90; Eisenstadt, *Political Systems of Empires,* esp. chaps. 10, 11; *idem,* "Innerweltliche Transzenden und die Strukturierung der Welt: Max Weber Studie ueber China und die Gestalt der chinesischen Zivilisation," in W. Schluchter (ed.), *Max Webers Studie ueber Confuzianismus und Taoismus: Interpretation und Kritik* (Frankfurt: Suhrkamp, 1983); A. E. Wright and D. Twitchett (eds.), *Perspectives on the T'ang* (New Haven: Yale University Press, 1973); J. A. Langlois Jr. (ed.), *China under Mongol Rule* (Princeton: Princeton University Press, 1981); J. D. Spence and J. E. Wills (eds.), *From Ming to Ch'ing* (New Haven: Yale University Press, 1979); F. Wakeman Jr., *The Great Enterprise: The Manchu Reconstruction of the Imperial Order in Seventeenth-Century China* (Berkeley: University of California Press, 1986); Schram, *Scope of State Power in China.*

33. See the bibliography in notes 26–28 of this chapter.

34. N. Field, *In the Realm of a Dying Emperor: A Portrait of Japan at the Century's End* (New York: Pantheon, 1991).

CHAPTER SEVENTEEN

1. M. Jansen and G. Rozman (eds.), *Japan in Transition: From Tokugawa to Meiji* (Princeton: Princeton University Press, 1986).

2. See, for instance, on Russia, A. von Schelting, *Russland und Europa in Russichen Geschichtichten Denken* (Bern: Franke, 1948).

3. T. Najita and H. Harootunian, "Japanese Revolt against the West: Political and Cultural Criticism in the Twentieth Century," in P. Duus (ed.), *The Cambridge History of Japan,* vol. 6 (Cambridge: Cambridge University Press, 1988), 711–13. See also M. Ivy, *Discourses of the Vanishing: Modernity, Phantasms, Japan* (Chicago: University of Chicago Press, 1995).

4. See, for instance, Kano Masanao, "The Changing Concept of Modernization," *Japan Quarterly* 23, no. 1 (January–March 1976): 28–36. See also G. McCormack and Y. Sugimoto (eds.), *The Japanese Trajectory* (Cambridge: Cambridge University Press, 1988); Najita and Harootunian, "Japanese Revolt." See, for a general discussion of the predicament of modernity in Japan, Tetsuo Najita, "Presidential Address: Personal Reflections on Modernity and Modernization," *Journal of Asian Studies* 52, no. 4 (1993): 845–53. See also M. B. Jansen, *Japan and Its World,* Kyoto Conference on Japanese Studies, 1994. See also Ivy, *Discourses of the Vanishing.*

5. Maruyama Masao, *Studies in the Intellectual History of Tokugawa Japan* (Tokyo: University of Tokyo Press, 1974).

6. Maruyama Masao, "Die Japanische Intellektuellen," in *idem, Denken in Japan* (Frankfurt: Suhrkamp, 1988), 89–132. *Idem, Chūsei to hangyaku: tenkeiki Nihon no Seishinshiteki iso* (Loyalty and Revolt: An Intellectual History of Ja-

pan's Modern Transformation) (Tokyo: Chikuma Shobo, 1992). See the review by Matsumoto Reiji of this latest collection of Maruyama's essays in Japanese, in *Japan Foundation Newsletter* 21, no. 4. See also R. Kersten, *Diverging Discourses: Shimizu Ikutarō, Maruyama Masao and Postwar Tenkō*, Nissan Occasional Paper series no. 20 (Oxford, 1994), and the following articles from *Journal of Social and Political Ideas in Japan*, special issue on Japanese intellectuals, vol. 11, no. 1 (1964): M. Nakamura, "The Intellectual Class," 17–20; T. Fukuda, "The Intellectual Class of Japan," 21–23; C. Nakane, "Characteristics of Japanese Intellectuals," 24–27.

7. S. Tanaka, *Japan's Orient: Rendering Past into History* (Los Angeles: University of California Press, 1993). See, for greater detail, David Williams, *Japan Beyond the End of History* (London: Routledge, 1994).

8. See, for instance, N. Sakai, "Return to the West/Return to the East: Watsuji Tetsuo's Anthropology and Discussions of Authenticy," 237–70, and K. Karatani, "The Discursive Space of Modern Japan," 288–315, both in M. Miyoshi and H. D. Harootunian (eds.), *Japan in the World* (Durham: Duke University Press, 1993). See also Lawrence Olson, *Ambivalent Moderns: Portraits of Japanese Cultural Identity* (London: Rowman & Littlefield, 1992); Najita, "Presidential Address"; Ivy, *Discourses of the Vanishing*.

9. Befu Harumi and Manabe Kazufumi, "An Empirical Study of Nihonjinron: How Real is the Myth?" *Kwansei Gakuin University Annual Studies* 36 (1981): 97–111. See also *idem*, "Nihonjinron: The Discursive Manifestation of Cultural Nationalism," *Kwansei Gakuin University Annual Studies* 40 (1991): 101–15; Kosaku Yoshino, *Cultural Nationalism in Contemporary Japan* (London: Routledge, 1992).

10. Najita, "Presidential Address."

11. See, for instance, Nishizawa Jun'ichi, "Science and Technology and Japanese Culture," *Japan Foundation Newsletter* 21, no. 6 (1994): 1–7.

12. W. Kelly, "Rationalization and Nostalgia: Cultural Dynamics of New Middle Class Japan," *American Ethnologist* 13, no. 4 (1986): 603–18; T. Bestor, *Neighborhood Tokyo* (Stanford: Stanford University Press, 1989); J. E. Robertson, "A Dialectic of Native and Newcomer: The Kodaira Citizen's Festival in Suburban Tokyo," *Anthropological Quarterly* 60, no. 3 (1987): 124–36; E. Ben-Ari, *Changing Japanese Suburbia* (London: Kegan Paul International, 1993).

13. See, in addition to the items in note 12, J. Tobin (ed.), *Re-made in Japan: Everyday Life and Consumer Taste in a Changing Society* (New Haven: Yale University Press, 1992); and also M. Ivy, *Discourses of the Vanishing*.

14. See S. Garon, "Rethinking Modernization and Modernity in Japanese History: A Focus on State-Society Relations," *Journal of Asian Studies* 53, no. 2 (May 1994): 346–66.

15. Tobin, *Re-made in Japan*; M. Ivy, *Discourses of the Vanishing*.

16. A. Kojeve, *Introduction to the Reading of Hegel* (Ithaca, N.Y.: Cornell University Press, 1980), 159–61. For a discussion of Kojeve on Japan, see also S. B. Drury, *Alexandre Kojeve: The Roots of Postmodern Politics* (New York: St. Martin's Press, 1994), 53–56.

17. M. Ivy, "Critical Texts, Mass Artifacts: The Consumption of Knowledge

in Postmodern Japan," *South Atlantic Quarterly* 87, no. 3 (1988): 419–44; *idem, Discourses of the Vanishing.*

18. D. Williams, *Japan beyond the End of History.* See also C. Gluck's review, "The Triumph of the East," *Times Literary Supplement,* 28 October 1994, 10.

19. See, for instance, Jean-Marc Gutenno, "Asia Offers a New Model of Politics," *International Herald Tribune,* 16 May 1994, 4.

20. K. Pyle, "The Future of Japanese Nationality: An Essay in Contemporary History," *Journal of Japanese Studies* 8, no. 2 (1982): 223–65. See, for instance, Akira Iriye, *China and Japan in the Global Setting* (Cambridge, Mass.: Harvard University Press, 1993).

21. See B. Edstrom (ed.), *Internationalization of Japan: Japanization of the World,* Occasional Paper no. 21, Center for Pacific Asia Studies at Stockholm University (1994); B. Pospelov, *An Analysis of Contemporary Japanese International Positions,* Occasional Papers nos. 22, 23, 24, Center for Pacific Asia Studies at Stockholm University (1994). See also Yoichi Funabashi (ed.), *Japan's International Agenda* (New York: New York University Press, 1994). For the view from Asian countries, see Chi Myong Kwan, "Japan's 'Mob Nationalism' at Stake," *Korea Focus* 3, no. 2 (March–April 1995): 24–33. For a historical survey of modern Japan's view of the world, see "Japan's View of the World," a special issue of *Japan Echo,* vol. 22 (1995).

22. G. McCormack, "Kokusaika: Impediments in Japan's Deep Structure," paper presented at ANU Stirrup, Sail and Plough conference, Canberra, September 1993. See also T. Morris-Suzuki, "The Frontier of Japanese Identity," paper presented at NIAS Conference on Comparative Approaches to National Identity in Asia, Copenhagen, 26–28 May 1994; Irokawa Daikichi, "Japanese Identity as Seen from 'Ancestor Rites,'" paper presented at ANU Stirrup, Sail and Plough conference, Canberra, September 1993.

23. See "Postwar Japanese Social Change since the Early 1970s," a special issue of the *International Journal of Japanese Sociology,* no. 1 (October 1992). See also the special issue of *Japan Echo* 15, no. 1 (1988).

24. See, from among the endless reports on these processes, for instance, "Japan Encourages Its Young," *Economist,* 10 August 1991; A. Fisher, "The End of a Tradition," *Financial Times,* 20 July 1994; R. Dale, "Now the Foreign Tide Laps at Japan," *International Herald Tribune,* 25 October 1994, 13; "The Ambush Awaiting Japan," *Economist,* 6 July 1991, 63–64. See also "The Giants That Refused to Die," *Economist,* 1 June 1991, 68–69.

25. G. Curtis, *Japan's Political Transfiguration: Interpretation and Implications,* Woodrow Wilson Center Asia Program, Occasional Paper (1993); S. Sato, "Japan's New Domestic Politics and Its Foreign Policy Implications," preliminary paper (Tokyo, 1994); Kohyama Kenichi, "The Limits of the Postwar Political System," *Japan Echo* 19, no. 3 (1992): 8–13; W. Dawkins, "'Mr. Clean' Foresees New Power Bloc," *Financial Times,* 2 September 1994, 4; Shōichi Oikawa, "Political Machinations Exacerbate Fruitless Confrontations in the Diet," *Daily Yomiuri,* 18 October 1994, 7; "How for Someone a Little Principled?" *Economist,* 12 December 1991, 69–70.

26. See the data reported at the Japanese/American National Character Con-

ference, Hoover Institution, Stanford University, and Tokyo, Institute of Statistical Mathematics, 1991, esp. 49–107. See also "Postwar Japanese Social Change since the Early 1970s," *International Journal of Japanese Sociology.*

27. W. Davis, "Japan Theory and Civil Religion," in *idem, Japanese Religion and Society: Paradigms of Structure and Change* (Albany: State University of New York Press, 1992), chap. 8, pp. 253–70.

28. See, for instance, Brendon R. Schlender, "Japan Is It Changing for Good?" *Fortune* 13 June 1994, 20–25.

29. "Forming Personal Networks Becoming Popular," *Yomiuri Shimbun,* 18 October 1994, 9.

30. Fischer, "The End of a Tradition"; Dale, "Now the Foreign Tide Laps at Japan." See also, for instance, "Tokyo Sings the Blues," *Economist,* 24 November 1990, 59–60; "Watch Out for Devil Head," *Economist,* 5 October 1991, 71. See also the section on Japan in *Time,* 7 February 1994; "Postwar Japanese Social Change since the Early 1970s," *International Journal of Japanese Sociology;* "Japan's Intellectual Revolution," *Economist,* 30 April 1994.

31. James Sterngold, "Japan's Inscrutability Is Starting to Fray," *International Herald Tribune,* 16 May 1994, 1.

32. *International Herald Tribune,* 21–22 May 1994, 8.

33. *International Herald Tribune,* 7 July 1994, 2. See also "Japanese Leader Honors Singapore's War Victims," *International Herald Tribune,* 29 August 1994, 6. On the declaration about Japanese conduct in the Second World War, see, for instance, *New York Times,* Sunday, 4 June 1995, 4; *Financial Times,* 7 June 1995, 4; *International Herald Tribune,* 10–11 June 1995, 7; *Economist,* 3 June 1995, 59.

34. Yayama Tarō, "Japan Besieged: The Textbook Controversy," introduction by K. Pyle, "The Newspapers Conduct a Mad Rhapsody over the Textbook Issue," *Journal of Japanese Studies* 9, no. 2 (1993): 297–316; Hasegawa Michiko, "A Postwar View of Greater East Asia War," *Japan Echo* 11 (1984): 29–37; P. Duus, *Remembering the Empire: Postwar Interpretations of the Greater East Asia Co-prosperity Sphere,* Woodrow Wilson Center Asia Program (Washington, D.C., 1993). For a more general survey, see I. Buruma, *The Wages of Guilt: Memories of War in Germany and Japan* (London: Jonathan Cape, 1994).

35. Ritsuko Nakamura, "In Loving Memory of 'Sempo' Sugihara," *Japan Times,* 20 October 1994, 16.

36. Williams, *Japan Beyond the End of History.* See also Akio Moritz, "Toward a New Economic Order," *Atlantic* 271, no. 6 (June 1993): 88–99. For the way in which the Japanese big concerns, the *keiretsu,* cope with the new economic situation, see William Dawkins, "Loosening of the Corporate Web," *Financial Times,* 30 November 1994, 13.

37. See, for instance, "Japan's Nakauchi Just Says No (to Coke)," *Wall Street Journal Europe,* 20 July 1994; Maya Maruko, "MITI Sees Victory in Holding Out," and Ako Washio, "Trade Talks Are 'Too Political'," both in *Japan Times,* 15 October 1994, 3. "Japan's New Nice Nationalism," *Economist,* 14 January 1995, 11, 16–17. See also "Japan's Nationalisms," *Economist,* 12–18 August 1995, 55–57.

38. See Ian Buruma, "A New Japanese Nationalism," *New York Times Magazine*, 12 April 1987, 23–19, 38, and the subsequent exchange (in Japanese) between Umehara Takeshi and Buruma in *Chūō Kōron*, August and October 1987. For recent discussion, see Peter Dale, "Tendenzen der Japanischen Kulturpolitik" (Nichibunken and Japan's International Cultural Policy), conference of German social scientists on Japan, "Die Internationalisierung Japans im Spannungsfeld zwischen oekonomischer und sozialer Dynamik," Loccum, Germany, (paper courtesy Sugimoto Yoshio) 7 November 1992; "Japan's New Nice Nationalism," *Economist*.

39. Sachiko Hirao, "Ōe Links Japanese, World Literature," *Japan Times*, 19 October 1994, 2; "Ōe Awarded Nobel Prize," *Japan Times*, 15 October 1994, 1. For the reaction to his refusal to accept the Order of Culture, see J. Sterngold, "Japan Asks Why a Prophet Bothers," *New York Times*, 6 November 1994.

40. See the Associated Press report, *Jerusalem Post*, 22 November 1994, 5. See also "Bewildered in Japan," *Economist*, 26 November 1994, 69–70.

41. See S. M. Lipset, "Pacific Divide: American Exceptionalism and Japanese Uniqueness," *International Journal of Public Opinion Research* 5, no. 2 (1993): 121–66.

42. Wonho Yang, memos and working paper, Department of Sociology, University of Chicago, 1995.

43. Ōe Kenzaburō, "Speaking on Japanese Culture before a Scandinavian audience," *Stockholm Journal of East Asian Studies* 4 (1993): 15–16. See also *idem*, *Japan, the Ambiguous and Myself: The Nobel Prize Speech and Other Lectures* (Tokyo: Kodansha International, 1994).

44. H. D. Harootunian, "The Tail of the Headless Emperor: Symbol without Referent," paper presented at CJS regional seminar, "Reflections on Tennōsei," University of California, Berkeley, 18 November 1989; published as "An Emperor System and Every Blade of Grass," *Shisō* (Tokyo), no. 11 (1990). For the impact of the emperor's declaration of surrender at the end of the Second World War, see also Ōe Kenzaburō, "The Day the Emperor Spoke in a Human Voice," *New York Times Magazine*, 7 May 1995, 103–5. See also N. Field, *In the Realm of a Dying Emperor: A Portrait of Japan at Century's End* (New York: Pantheon, 1991). Schūichi Katō, the noted philosopher and historian of Japanese literature, points out another aspect of such continuity, as it relates to conceptions of the accountability of rulers. S. Katō, "Niemand kritisiert den König" ("Nobody criticizes the king"), *Die Zeit*, no. 32, 5 August 1994.

45. C. Gluck, *Japan's Modern Myths: Ideology in the Late Meiji Period* (Princeton: Princeton University Press, 1985). See also, for instance, "Policy Speech by Prime Minister Tomiichi Murayama to the 130th Session of the Diet (July 18, 1994)," Foreign Press Center, Japan.

46. McCormack, "Kokusaika."

47. See S. Jameson, "Miyazawa Discusses Change in Japan," *Daily Yomiuri*, 19 October 1994, 3. See also, for a later discussion, William Dawkins, "Market Test for Japan Wage Round," *Financial Times*, 6 February 1996, 6.

48. K. van Wolferen, "Japan's Non-Revolution," *Foreign Affairs* 72, no. 4 (September–October 1993): 54–66.

49. See, for instance, "Why Japan Is Jittery," *Economist*, 22–28 April, 1995, 11–14.

50. For a report on van Wolferen's new book, see Nicholas D. Kristoff, "Dutchman Strikes Chord in a Less Confident Japan," *New York Times*, 4 June 1995, 4.

51. Sugahara Mariko, "Five Fatal Symptoms of the Japanese Disease," *Japan Echo* 21, no. 2 (summer 1994): 68–75, and the critical comment by Iwao Sumiko.

INDEX

Abé Kōbō, 109
Abortion, 325
Accountability of rulers, 252–53, 289–91
Achievement orientation, 8, 68, 327, 339,
    349, 541n.73
  coalitions, 367
  educational track system, 65–66, 71
  Meiji era, 27–28, 42
  principled individualism and, 117
  samurai, 214
Administrative guidance, 54–57, 156
Administrative reform, 155–56, 213
Adoption, 253, 353, 355
Aesthetics, 339 (*see also* Cultural
    creativity)
Agonshū, 81
Ainu, 136, 284, 421, 422, 440
Akihito, Emperor, 459
Allinson, G., 149, 150
Alternative Japanese drama, 395
Amaterasu-Ōmikami, 356–57, 513n.36,
    546n.41
American Federation of Labor, 139
Amino Yoshihiko, 302
Ancestor worship, 325, 357
Anderson, Perry, 46, 184
Andō Shōeki, 77, 246–47, 307, 390, 432,
    517n.75
Animal souls, 324
Apology, 130, 285, 290, 439, 487n.110
Apter, D., 112

Arai Hakuseki, 169, 198
Architecture, 391, 393
Arnason, Johann, 46, 164, 170, 171, 173,
    304, 307, 315, 376–77
Art
  Buddhist influences, 236, 239
  disharmony in, 119–20
  foreign influences, 299
  See also Cultural creativity
Artisans, 178–81
Artists, 323
Asakawa Kanichi, 3, 173, 377
Asquith, P., 324
Assimilation, of minorities, 284
Atrocities, 439–40
Authenticity, 76–78, 432, 433
Authority, 286–91, 517n.75
  bakufu, 191
  Buddhist ideology, 256–57
  Confucian implications, 252
  contexts defined in sacral, natural, or pri-
    mordial terms, 286–87, 295–97
  feudal system, 167
  Indian conceptions, 406–8
  Japanese organizational characteristics,
    468–70n.28
  soft rule, 288, 525n.26
  structuration of social hierarchies, 293–
    97 (*see also* Social order;
    Status)
  See also Legitimation; Social control

563